EXCEPTIONAL CHILDREN

EXCEPTIONAL CHILDREN

An Introductory Survey of Special Education

THIRD EDITION

William L. Heward
Michael D. Orlansky

The Ohio State University

Merrill Publishing Company
A Bell & Howell Information Company
Columbus   Toronto   London   Melbourne

Cover Photo: David Brownell

Published by Merrill Publishing Company
A Bell & Howell Information Company
Columbus, Ohio 43216

This book was set in Quorum.

Administrative Editor: Vicki Knight
Developmental Editor: Amy Macionis
Production Coordinator: Jeffrey Putnam
Art Coordinator: Patrick Welch
Cover Designer: Cathy Watterson
Text Designer: Cynthia Brunk
Copy Editor: Mary Benis

Library of Congress Catalog Card Number: 87-61583
International Standard Book Number: 0-675-20890-4
Printed in the United States of America
4 5 6 7 8 9—93 92 91 90

Photo credits: Merrill Publishing/photographs by Kevin
Fitzsimons, 110, 181, 219, 240, 253, 397, 517, 539, 545,
555, 562; Lloyd Lemmerman, 33, 81, 86, 95, 250, 371, 376;
Tom Hubbard, 17, 79, 323, 352, 461; Andy Brunk, 23, 60,
106, 126, 130, 139, 142, 149, 315, 382, 443, 569; Bruce
Johnson, 45, 51, 90, 171, 184, 188, 203, 281, 286, 448,
521, 525; Tom Hutchinson, 13, 288, 307, 580, 581; Richard
DeMott, 309; Rich Bucurel, 409; Mary Hagler, 294; Larry
Hamill, 30; Jean Greenwald, 404; Michael Davis/Franklin
County Board of M.R. and D.D., 2, 119, 212, 552, 583.

William Heward and Michael Orlansky, 47, 158, 278, 283,
284, 421; Harvey R. Phillips/Phillips Photo Illustrators, 64,
311, 428; Ed Heston, 111; Marie Skandera, 100; Mark
Freado, 176, 205; Jan Smyth, 225, 282; Susan Bolton, 242,
243; Charles J. Quinlan, 297; David S. Strickler/Strix Pix, 332,
342, 416, 431, 474, 487, 491; Tom Tondee, 339; Luanna
Voeltz, 468; Joanne Kash, 564; Martin Wiig, 161; Gale
Zucker, 168, 330, 368, 440; Randall Williams, 514; The
Lighthouse, The New York Association for the Blind, 302;
Research Library, Perkins School for the Blind, Watertown,
MA, 320; Faculty for Exceptional Children, Ohio State
University, 424; Jill C. Dardig, 602; Mike Penney, 439.

PREFACE

Special education is the story of *people*. It is the story of the parents and teachers who work together to meet the needs of a preschool child with multiple handicaps. It is the story of the sixth-grader with cerebral palsy who encounters both "regular" and "special" teachers in her public school. It is the story of the gifted child who brings new insights to old problems, the blind high school student who is learning English as his second language, and the woman who has recently moved into a group home, after spending many years in a large institution. Special education is their story.

Our field is comparatively young and is evolving rapidly; we have never found special education to be dry, dull, or pendantic. In writing the first edition of *Exceptional Children* more than eight years ago, we sought to convey the diversity and excitement of special education, and to tell the story of the many people who participate in it. This objective remains unchanged. We hope, in this book, to present a comprehensive, current, and up-to-date survey of professional research, practice, and trends in the education of people with special needs. We believe that this can be done without sacrificing a "human" perspective, and have thus again incorporated into each chapter several special features, our "Focus" inserts. These inserts present firsthand stories of exceptional individuals, parents, or teachers, or focus on attitudes, practical strategies, or innovative programs. We think you will find that they add a useful and inviting dimension to the study of special education.

The book consists of fifteen chapters, organized into three sections. Part I, *Introduction*, presents an overview of terminology, and a discussion of laws, policies, and practices that are consistent with the exceptional child's right to receive an education in the least restrictive and most appropriate environment. Part II, *Exceptional Children*, offers a survey of nine specific categories of exceptionality, introducing the reader to definitions, prevalence, causes, historical background, approaches to assessment, education and treatment, and current and future trends. And Part III, *Cultural, Family, and Life-Span Issues in Special Education*, considers several topics of general importance to special educators, namely cultural and linguistic differences, parent and family involvement, early intervention, and adulthood. Thus the book maintains a largely "categorical" approach, which in our experience is most favored by students and instructors in introductory special education courses, yet also treats many issues in a generic or cross-categorical manner.

Special education does not stand still for long. Since the appearance of the previous edition, the field has seen many new research studies, theoretical contributions, significant laws and judicial cases, and approaches to education and training. Technology has been increasingly utilized in virtually all areas of special education, as it holds much promise for enhancing the learning, development, and independence of children and adults with special needs. More than a decade after the implementation of Public Law 94-142, the Education For All Handicapped Children Act, there is much discussion of the ways in which special education and "regular" education can interact with each other most effectively. And a new law, Public Law 99-457, has focused a great deal of attention on the importance of identifying and serving infants and pre-school children who may have disabilities. All of these and many other recent developments are incorporated into this third edition.

Attitudes are at least as important as laws and theories, and we believe that language can influence the ways in which exceptional individuals are viewed. To the extent possible in a text of this kind, we have endeavored to use terminology that is consistent with respect for the individuality and dignity of persons with special needs. Impersonal terms such as "the handicapped," "the mentally retarded," and "the cerebral palsied" create the impression of a group that is somehow very different from "normal" people, and mistakenly imply that all persons within a given category are alike. Rather than use such terms extensively, we have emphasized more human words, referring to "children," "adults," "students," or "people," as the case may be.

We hope that you will find the third edition of *Exceptional Children* to be an informative, readable, and a challenging introduction to special education. Whether you are a beginner or a person with years of experience, we hope that you will continue your study and involvement with children and adults who have special needs. For you, too, can make a worthwhile contribution to the still-unfinished story of special education.

ACKNOWLEDGMENTS

We are grateful to all of the people who contributed ideas, suggestions, insights, and constructive criticism during the preparation of *Exceptional Children*. The third edition has been enhanced by the combined efforts of a talented team of professional editors at Merrill Publishing Company, without whom the book would not have become a reality. Vicki Knight, Administrative Editor, exemplified the highest standards of professionalism in coordinating every phase of the production, review, and revision process, and Amy Macionis, Developmental Editor, was diligent in her commitment to bringing about many notable improvements in the content and appearance of this revision. We also thank our skillful copy editor, Mary Benis, and our production editor, Jeff Putnam, for their substantial contributions.

The following professors—all of whom have served as instructors of introductory special education courses at other colleges and universities—provided timely and helpful reviews of the manuscript: Marsha H. Lupi, Hunter College; Gabriel Nardi, West Virginia University; Elizabeth Reis, Baruch College; Leonila Rivera, Southwest Missouri State University; John Umbreit, University of Arizona; James Van Tassel, Ball State University; Paul B. Woods, Winston-Salem State University; Donald Zemanek, University of Cincinnati; Rebecca MacDonald, Wheelock College; and Bruce A. Ostertag, California State University-Sacramento. Their perspectives and experiences were of much value to us.

We thank our colleague, Raymond H. Swassing, for his contribution of Chapter 11, "Gifted and Talented Children." Ray has been a leader in the development of innovative programs for gifted students in Ohio and the nation. Wayne Secord offered many useful resources during the preparation of Chapter 6, "Communication Disorders," and Tim Heron gave valuable input to Chapter 4, "Learning Disabilities." We continue to be grateful to Tom Hutchinson, who introduced us to each other and was the moving force behind the first edition, and to Francie Margolin, who worked closely with us on the previous two editions. Fran Courson assumed primary responsibility for preparing the revised Instructor's Manual and authored more than 1500 questions for the Test Bank that accompany this edition. Julie Edwards, Chris Mayhall, Janani Narayan, and Sean Reardon, able and dedicated graduate students at Ohio State, provided practical assistance by helping out at various stages of the book's development.

Special education is of interest to people the world over, and both of us have been enriched by the opportunity to serve as visiting Fulbright lecturers in other nations. For their insights, cooperation, and hospitality, Bill would like to thank Professor Rui Abrunhosa and colleagues in Portugal, and Mike extends his gratitude to Professor Borka Teodorovic, Gojko Zovko, and colleagues at the University of Zagreb, Yugoslavia. We also appreciate the support of the Council for International Exchange of Scholars and Ohio State University in making these international exchanges possible.

Our thanks go to all of the people who shared their experiences, strategies, and accomplishments with us in the many "inserts" and photographs in this edition. In particular, we acknowledge Michael Giangreco of Ithaca, New York, Ronni Hochman of Upper Arlington, Ohio, Kevin Lessard of Watertown, Massachusetts, Dave Test of the University of North Carolina at Charlotte, and Barbara Ward of Westerville, Ohio for their valuable contributions to the text.

A book may justly be regarded as a family affair, and we owe a great debt of thanks to our families for putting up with us (or frequently putting up *without* us!). Thanks, Jill, Jan, Lee, Lynn, Tamar, and Robin for your patience and support. We also owe a special thanks to Evelyn and Ben Dardig for their tireless work on the reference list.

Perhaps most of all, we owe a great debt to our students. Over the years they have taught us a great deal about our field, and this book reflects their contributions.

CONTENTS

PART ONE
INTRODUCTION

1

KEYS TO SPECIAL EDUCATION

Educating children with special needs or abilities presents a difficult challenge. Special educators, those teachers and related professionals who have accepted that challenge, are engaged in an exciting and rapidly changing field. In this introductory text we have tried to capture for you some of the action and excitement that characterize this important and dynamic field. Throughout the book we will present specific information about exceptional children, describe both proven and promising instructional techniques, share some of the accomplishments that can be attained when professionals and parents work together, and examine areas that present continuing difficulty and concern for the future. To begin, we need to present some background information, concepts, and perspectives that are basic to an understanding of exceptional children and special education.

WHO ARE EXCEPTIONAL CHILDREN?

We will begin our study of special education by defining four terms: *exceptional children, disability, handicap,* and *at risk.* All children exhibit differences from one another in terms of their physical attributes (some are shorter, some are stronger) and learning abilities (some learn quickly and generalize what they have learned to new situations, others need repeated practice and have difficulty remembering what they have been taught). The differences among most children are relatively small, enabling them to benefit from the general education program. However, the physical attributes and/ or learning abilities of some children, those we call **exceptional children,** differ from the norm—either below or above—to such an extent that an individualized program of special education is required to meet their needs. The term *exceptional children* includes both children who experience difficulties in learning and children whose performance is so superior that special education is necessary if they are to fulfill their potential. Thus, *exceptional children* is an inclusive term that refers to children with physical disabilities and children with learning and/or behavior problems, as well as children who are intellectually gifted.

Terms in **boldface** are defined in the glossary.

Disability refers to the reduced function or loss of a particular body part or organ; the term **impairment** is often used synonymously with disability. A disability limits a person's ability to perform certain tasks (e.g., seeing, hearing, walking) in the same manner in which most nondisabled persons do. A disabled person is not handicapped, however, unless the physical disability leads to educational, personal, social, vocational, or other problems. For example, if a child who has lost a leg can, after learning to use an artificial limb, function in and out of school without problems, she is not handicapped.

Handicap refers to the problems a person with a disability or impairment encounters when interacting with the environment. A disability may pose a handicap in one environment but not in another. For example, the child with an artificial limb may be handicapped when competing against nondisabled peers on the basketball court but experience no handicap in the classroom. The term *handicapped children* is more restrictive than *exceptional children* and does not include gifted and talented children.

At risk refers to children who are not currently identified as handicapped or disabled but are considered to have a greater-than-usual chance of developing a handicap. The term is most often used with infants and preschoolers who, because of conditions surrounding their birth or the home environment, may be expected to experience developmental problems at a later time. The term is also being used to refer to students who are experiencing learning problems in the regular classroom and are therefore "at risk" of being identified as handicapped.

The nine chapters that comprise part two of this book examine the defining characteristics and educational implications of each of the following so-called categories of exceptional children:

1. Mental retardation
2. Learning disabilities
3. Behavior disorders (emotional disturbance)
4. Communication (speech and language) disorders
5. Hearing impairments
6. Visual impairments
7. Physical and other health impairments
8. Severe handicaps
9. Gifted and talented

Physicians also use the terms *at risk* or *high risk* to identify pregnancies with a greater-than-normal probability of producing babies with handicaps. For example, a pregnancy may be considered high risk if the pregnant woman is above or below normal child-bearing age, if she is a heavy user of alcohol, or if she is drug-dependent.

Handicapism refers to the negative stereotyping and unequal and unjust treatment of people with disabilities. See page 5 for suggestions on reducing the incidence of handicapism in children's books.

However, it is a mistake to think that there are two distinct kinds of children—that is, those who are special and those who are regular. As already stated, all children differ from one another in individual characteristics along a continuum; exceptional children are those whose differences from the norm are large enough to require a specially designed instructional program if they are to benefit fully from education. *Exceptional children are more like other children than they are different.* All children are unique individuals who require individual attention, nurturing, and caring.

THE ABLE DISABLED

Handicapism is "attitudes and practices that lead to unequal and unjust treatment of people with disabilities." The word handicap, *in fact, is thought to come from a time when disabled people had to beg in the streets, with cap in hand ("Avoiding Handicapist Stereotypes," 1977, p. 1). Today, an increasing number of disabled and non-disabled people are trying to overcome handicapism—to change presentations of disabled people as strange, odd, fearsome, helpless, or otherwise stereotyped. These images of disabled people are frequently found in books and TV shows for children. Does every character in the story have a name except "the blind man"? Have you ever seen a villain portrayed as hunchbacked, one-eyed, and limping? What about a dim-witted cartoon animal who constantly stutters? Some people feel that realistic presentations of disabled people are especially important, because they can encourage children to interact with exceptional people on a more "human" basis—rather than mock them, pity them, or be scared. Several organizations interested in the realistic portrayal of disabled people in children's books prepared these guidelines.*

AVOIDING HANDICAPIST STEREOTYPES

☐ Shun one-dimensional characterizations of disabled persons. Portray people with disabilities as having individual and complex personalities and capable of a full range of emotions.

☐ Avoid depicting disabled persons only in the role of receiving; show disabled people *interacting* as equals and giving as well as receiving. Too often the handicapped person is presented solely as the recipient of pity.

☐ Avoid presenting physical characteristics of any kind as determining factors of personality. Be especially cautious about implying a correlation between disability and evil.

☐ Refrain from depicting persons with disabilities as objects of curiosity. It is entirely appropriate to show disabled people as members of an average population or cast of characters. Most disabled people are able to participate in all facets of life and should be shown in many situations.

☐ A person's disability should not be ridiculed or made the butt of a joke. (Blind people do not mistake fire hydrants for people or bump into every object in their path.)

☐ Avoid the sensational in depicting disabled people. Be wary of the stereotype of disabled persons as either the victims or perpetrators of violence.

☐ Refrain from endowing disabled characters with superhuman attributes. To do so is to imply that a disabled person must overcompensate and become superhuman to win acceptance.

☐ Avoid a Pollyanna-ish plot that implies a disabled person need only have the "will" and the "right attitude" to succeed. Young readers need insights into the societal barriers that keep disabled people from living full lives—discrimination in employment, education, and housing; inaccessible transportation and buildings; and exorbitant expense for necessities.

☐ Avoid showing disabled people as nonsexual. Show disabled people in loving relationships and expressing the same sexual needs and desires as nondisabled people.

Source: From *Interracial Books for Children Bulletin,* 1977, *8* (6,7), p. 1. Published by Council on Interracial Books for Children, 1841 Broadway, New York, NY 10023. Reprinted by permission.

HOW MANY EXCEPTIONAL CHILDREN ARE
THERE AND WHERE ARE THEY SERVED?

Each year the U.S. Department of Education, Office of Special Education and Rehabilitation Services (OSERS) reports to Congress on the education of handicapped children in the United States. At the time this book went to press, the most recent data available pertained to the 1984–85 school year (*Eighth Annual Report to Congress*, 1986).

Let's take a quick look at some of the numerical facts about special education in the United States.

We will define the terms used in these statements as they become relevant; right now we simply want to get a broad look at the current picture.

☐ Over 4.3 million handicapped children, aged 3 to 21, received special education services during the 1984–85 school year.

☐ Handicapped children in special education represent approximately 11% of the entire school-age population.

☐ About twice as many males as females receive special education.

☐ The vast majority—approximately 90%—of school-age children receiving special education are "mildly handicapped" (Hagerty & Abramson, 1987).

☐ The three largest categories of children with handicaps are learning disabilities, speech and language impairment, and mental retardation. These three handicapping conditions accounted for 42%, 26%, and 16%, respectively, of all handicapped children who received special education in 1984–85.

☐ From 1976–77 to 1984–85 the number of handicapped preschoolers aged 3 to 5 receiving special education services rose 32%, to 259,483. This total represented about 2.8% of all 3-to-5-year-old children in the United States.

☐ From 1978–79 to 1984–85 the number of secondary handicapped students aged 18 to 21 receiving special education services rose 88%, to 192,438. This total represented about 1.2% of the 18-to-21-year-old population.

What factors do you think might be responsible for the huge increase from 1976–77 to 1984–85 in the number of children identified as learning disabled? Compare your ideas with what you learn later in chapter 4.

Figure 1.1 shows the number of children served in special education in 1984–85 according to the categories of handicapping conditions recognized by the federal government. These numbers reflect the child-count data that states are required to include in their yearly reports to the federal government. The figure also shows the number of children receiving special education for each of the handicapping conditions during the 1976–77 school year, allowing comparison of changes within and among categories.

During fiscal year 1981 it was reported that 909,437 children were served in programs for gifted and talented students (Mitchell, 1981). This number would rank as the third largest group of exceptional children receiving special education services in 1984–85. However, special education for gifted and talented children is not mandated by federal law as it is for children with handicaps. Following the estimate that gifted and talented children comprise 3% to 5% of the school-age population, between 1.45 and 2.42 million gifted children may require special education. This discrepancy between service and need may make gifted and talented children the most underserved group of exceptional children.

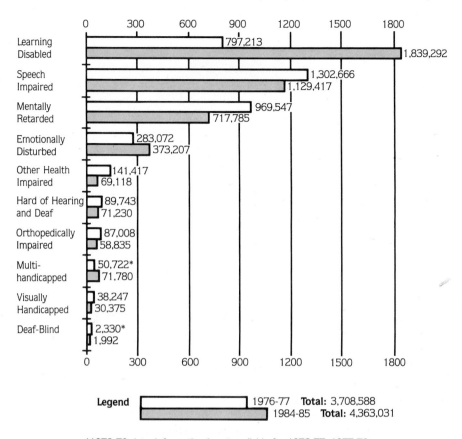

FIGURE 1.1

Number of children aged 3 to 21 years, identified by handicapping condition, who received special education in the United States during the 1976–77 and 1984–85 school years.

Source: From *Eighth Annual Report to Congress on the Implementation of the Education of the Handicapped Act* (p. 4), 1986, U.S. Department of Education.

Stating precisely how many exceptional children live in the United States is virtually impossible for many reasons: the different criteria used by states and local school systems to identify exceptional children, the relative ability of a school system to provide effective instructional support to the regular classroom teacher so that an at-risk student does not become a special education student, the imprecise nature of assessment, the large part played by subjective judgment in the interpretation of assessment data, and the fact that a child may be diagnosed as handicapped at one time in his school career and not handicapped (or included in a different handicapping condition) at another time.

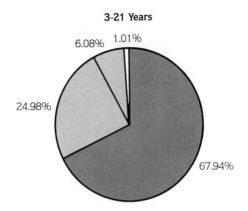

3-21 Years

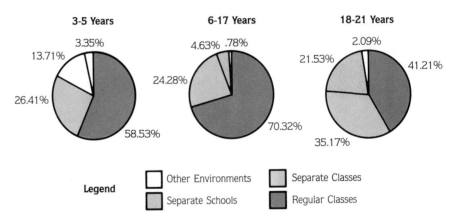

3-5 Years	**6-17 Years**	**18-21 Years**

Legend

☐ Other Environments   ▨ Separate Classes

▨ Separate Schools   ▨ Regular Classes

FIGURE 1.2

Percentages of all handicapped children, identified by age range, served in four educational environments during the 1983–84 school year.

Source: From *Eighth Annual Report to Congress on the Implementation of the Education of the Handicapped Act* (p. 59), 1986, U.S. Department of Education.

What factors do you think have contributed to the higher percentages of children in the 3-to-5- and 18-to-21-year-old groups who are educated in separate classes and separate schools?

Two-thirds of all children with handicaps received at least part of their educational instruction in regular classrooms with nonhandicapped children during the 1983–84 school year (see Figure 1.2). Many of these children spend part of each school day in a special setting, called a resource room, in which they receive individualized instruction from a special educator. Approximately 1 in 4 handicapped children is educated in separate classrooms within a regular school. Slightly more than 1 in 20 school-age handicapped students, usually the student with the most severe handicaps, is educated in special schools. About 1% of all handicapped children are educated at home or in nonschool environments such as hospitals.

The vast majority of children in the two largest groups of students with handicaps spend most of the school day in regular classrooms: 77% of children with learning disabilities and 93% of children with speech or language impairments (see Figure 1.3). In contrast, only 13% of deaf/blind children and 14% of multihandicapped children were educated in regular classrooms during the 1983–84 school year, although these figures represent increases over those of previous years.

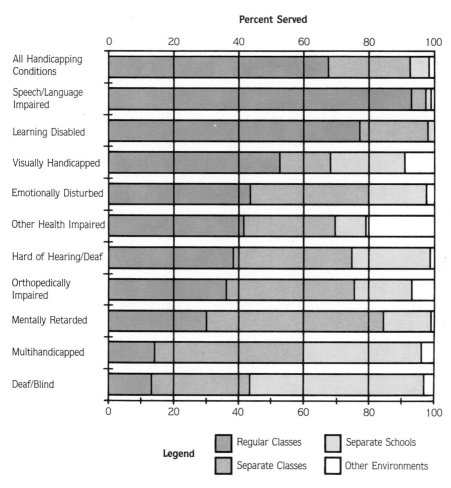

FIGURE 1.3

Percentages of handicapped children (aged 3 to 21) identified by handicapping condition, served in four educational environments during the 1983–84 school year.

Source: From *Eighth Annual Report to Congress on Implementation of the Education of the Handicapped Act* (p. 60), 1986, U.S. Department of Education.

Many programs are designed to meet the special needs of preschool children with handicaps.

PROBLEMS OF LABELING AND CLASSIFYING EXCEPTIONAL CHILDREN

Centuries ago, labeling and classifying people was of little importance. Survival was the main concern. Those whose handicaps prevented their full participation in the activities necessary for survival were left on their own to perish or, in some instances, were even exterminated. In later years derogatory labels like "dunce," "imbecile," and "fool" were applied to mentally retarded and emotionally disturbed people. Other demeaning words were often used to refer to persons with other disabilities or physical deformities. In each instance, however, the purpose of classification was the same—to *exclude* the person with handicaps from the activities, privileges, and facilities of normal society.

Some educators argue that even today the classification of exceptional children functions to exclude people from normal society. Others argue that a workable system of classifying exceptional children (or their exceptional learning needs) is a prerequisite to providing the special educational programs that those children require if they are to be integrated into normal society. No other aspect of special education has been more widely debated during the past two decades than the classification and labeling of exceptional children. The classification of children is a complex issue, involving emotional, political, and humane considerations, in addition to scientific and educational interests. Research results shed little light on the problem; those studies that have been conducted to assess the effects of labeling have produced inconclusive, often contradictory, evidence and have generally been marked by methodological weakness (MacMillan, 1982).

As with most complex, important questions, there are valid arguments on both sides. Here are some of the reasons that have been given for and against the classification and labeling of exceptional children.

Possible Benefits of Labeling

1. Categories can relate diagnosis to specific treatment.
2. Labeling may lead to a "protective" response in which nonlabeled children accept certain behaviors of their handicapped peers more fully than they would accept those same behaviors in "normal" children (MacMillan, 1982).
3. Labeling helps professionals to communicate with one another and to classify and assess research findings.
4. Funding of special education programs is often based on specific categories of exceptionality.
5. Labels allow special interest groups to promote specific programs and spur legislative action.
6. Labeling helps make the special needs of exceptional children more visible in the public eye.

A protective response by a nonhandicapped child toward a handicapped peer could be a disadvantage if it decreased the labeled child's chances to develop independence and learn appropriate social skills.

Possible Disadvantages of Labeling

1. Labels usually focus on negative aspects of the child, causing others to think about the child only in terms of inadequacies or defects.
2. Labels may cause others to react to and hold low expectations for a child based on the label, resulting in a self-fulfilling prophecy.
3. Labels that describe a child's performance deficit often mistakenly acquire the role of explanatory constructs (e.g., "Sherry acts that way *because* she is emotionally disturbed").
4. Labels used to classify children in special education emphasize that learning problems are primarily the result of something wrong within the child, thereby reducing the likelihood of examining instructional variables as the cause of performance deficits.
5. A labeled child may develop a poor self-concept.
6. Labels may lead peers to reject or ridicule the labeled child.
7. Special education labels have a certain permanence about them. Once labeled as "retarded" or "learning disabled," a child has difficulty ever again achieving the status of being "just like all the other kids."
8. Labels often provide a basis for keeping children out of the regular classroom.
9. A disproportionate number of children from minority culture groups have been inaccurately labeled "handicapped," especially as educably mentally retarded.
10. The classification of exceptional children requires the expenditure of a great amount of professional and student time that could better be spent in planning and delivering instruction.

Not all of the labels used to classify children with handicaps are viewed as equally negative or stigmatizing. It is believed that one factor contributing to the large increase in the number of children identified as learning disabled is that many parents view learning disabilities as a socially acceptable classification (Algozzine & Korinek, 1985; Lieberman, 1985).

For more on culturally diverse children, see chapter 12.

Clearly, there are strong reasons both for and against the classification and labeling of exceptional children. In the early 1970s the U.S. government ordered a comprehensive study of the classification of exceptional children. This two-year project involved 93 psychologists, educators, lawyers, and parents working on 31 different task forces. The results of this extensive and carefully done project can be found in *Issues in the Classification of Children* (volumes 1 and 2), edited by the project's director, Nicholas Hobbs (Hobbs, 1976a, 1976b). A third book, *The Futures of Children* (Hobbs, 1975), summarizes the findings and recommendations of the project. These important works are available for anyone who wants to understand fully all the perspectives surrounding this complex issue. Other sensitive and well-documented reviews of labeling and classification of exceptional children can be found in MacMillan (1982) and Smith, Neisworth, and Hunt (1983). None of these discussions has produced conclusive arguments that could lead to the total acceptance or absolute rejection of the practice of labeling.

On one level the various labels that are given to children with special learning needs can be viewed as a means of organizing the funding and administration of special education services in the schools. In order to receive special education services, a child must be labeled as handicapped and, with few exceptions, be further classified into one of that state's categories, such as mental retardation or learning disabilities (Stainback & Stainback, 1984; Wang & Reynolds, 1985). In practice, therefore, a student becomes eligible for various kinds of special education and related services because of membership in a given category. However, many special educators believe that the classification of exceptional children by category of handicapping condition may actually interfere with assessment and instructional planning that is directed toward the real learning needs of each student. Stainback and Stainback (1984) argue that

> these categories often do not reflect the specific educational needs and interests of students in relation to such services. For example, some students categorized as visually handicapped may not need large print books, while others who are not labeled visually impaired and thus are ineligible for large print books could benefit from their use. Similarly, not all students labeled behaviorally disordered may need self-control training, while some students not so labeled may need self-control training as a part of their educational experience. Such categories . . . actually interfere with providing some students with the services they require to progress toward their individual educational goals. Eligibility for educational and related services . . . should be based on the abilities, interests, and needs of each student as they relate to instructional options and services, rather than on the student's inclusion in a categorical group. (p. 105)

What we *can* say about the possible benefits of classifying exceptional children is that most of those benefits are experienced not by individual children, but rather by groups of children, parents, and professionals who are associated with a certain category. On the other hand, the negative aspects of labeling all affect the individual child who has been labeled. Of the possible advantages of labeling listed earlier, only the

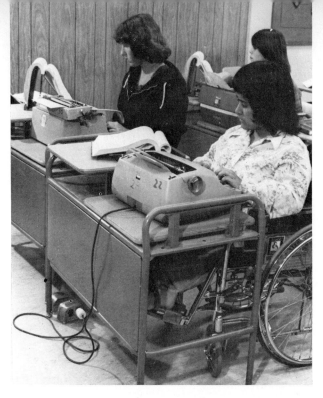

Most students with disabilities now participate in regular classes alongside their nonhandicapped peers.

first two could be said to benefit an individual child. And the argument that labels associate diagnosis with proper treatment is tenuous at best, particularly when you consider the kinds of labels used in special education today.

See pages 24–25 for a thought-provoking response to the question "What should we call them?"

> The children are given various labels including deaf, blind, orthopedically handicapped, trainable mentally retarded, educable mentally retarded, autistic, socially maladjusted, perceptually handicapped, brain-injured, emotionally disturbed, disadvantaged, and those with learning disabilities. For the most part the labels are not important. They rarely tell the teacher who can be taught in what way. One could put five or six labels on the same child and still not know what to teach him or how. (Becker, Engelmann, & Thomas, 1971, pp. 435–436)

A number of special educators have proposed alternative approaches to classifying exceptional children that focus on educationally relevant variables (e.g., Iscoe & Payne, 1972; Lovitt, 1982; Quay, 1968; Sontag, Smith, & Sailor, 1977). Lovitt (1982) has suggested that exceptional children be classified according to the skills they need to learn. College students are effectively classified according to their major area of study: John is an English literature major, and Manuela is a premed student. Perhaps children with special learning needs should be identified in a similar manner: Carol is learning self-help skills, and Michael is studying orientation and mobility. In a system such as this, students would be assessed and classified relative to the degree to which they are learning specific curriculum content. This approach is called **curriculum-based assessment** (Howell & Morehead, 1987; Tucker, 1985).

See the November 1985 issue of *Exceptional Children* for a series of articles on curriculum-based assessment in special education.

The fundamental question asked in curriculum-based assessment is "How is the student progressing in the curriculum of the local school?" (Tucker, 1985). Educators who employ curriculum-based assessment believe it is much more important to assess (and thereby classify) students in terms of their acquisition of the skills and knowledge included in their school's curriculum, rather than the degree to which they differ from the normative score of all children in some general physical attribute or learning characteristic.

Even though curriculum-based assessment is being used with increased frequency in special education, use of the traditional labels and categories of exceptional children is likely to continue for some time. However, the continued development and use of educationally relevant classification systems will increase the likelihood that diagnosis and assessment will lead to meaningful instructional programs for children, promote more educationally meaningful communication and research by professionals, and perhaps decrease some of the negative aspects of the current practice of labeling children.

LEGISLATION AFFECTING EXCEPTIONAL CHILDREN

The 14th Amendment to the United States Constitution guarantees equal protection under the law for all citizens. Yet a long series of court cases and federal legislation has been required to make equal protection with respect to education a reality for children with handicaps in this country. Closely related to the civil rights movement of the 1950s and 1960s, a civil rights movement for persons with handicaps has resulted in legislation guaranteeing that exceptional children can no longer be denied appropriate educational services.

A discussion of the many court cases and laws pertaining to exceptional children is far beyond the scope and intent of this book. (LaVor, 1976, reports that 36 federal bills that affected handicapped and gifted individuals were passed by Congress in 1974 alone. See Table 2.1, page 35, for an outline of some of the major court cases and legislation that have affected the education of exceptional children.) Instead, we will focus our attention on Public Law 94–142, the Education for All Handicapped Children Act, which became law in 1975. P.L. 94–142 has been called landmark legislation. It is the culmination of the efforts of a great many educators, parents, and legislators to bring together in one comprehensive bill this country's laws regarding the education of handicapped children. The law reflects society's current concern for treating people with handicaps as full citizens, with the same rights and privileges that all other citizens enjoy.

We will discuss each of these features of P.L. 94–142 in chapter 2.

A basic understanding of P.L. 94–142 is central to understanding many of the practices and trends in special education today. The major features of the law are that (1) a free, appropriate public education must be provided for all handicapped children; (2) school systems must provide safeguards to protect the rights of handicapped children and their parents; (3) handicapped children must be educated with nonhandicapped children to the maximum extent possible; (4) an individualized education program (IEP) must be developed and implemented for each handicapped child; and (5) parents of handicapped children are to play an active role in the process used to make any educational decision about their handicapped children. States meeting the requirements of P.L. 94–142 receive federal tax dollars to help offset the additional costs incurred in providing special education services.

We will look at the relationship between educators and parents in depth in chapter 13.

Gifted children are not mentioned in P.L. 94–142, which deals only with the education of children with handicaps. Special education for children who are gifted and talented is not mandated by federal law, although the federal government "encourages" states to develop gifted programs. Federal monies that might be used for the development and support of programs for gifted and talented children are included as part of a block grant that each state receives to fund a wide range of elementary and secondary education programs. Mitchell (1982) reports that 48 states have programs of some sort for gifted and talented students. However, the amount of funding available at either the federal or the state level for support of gifted programs is only a tiny fraction of the dollars expended for the education of children with handicaps.

Since P.L. 94–142 became law in 1975, Congress has amended it twice, once in 1983 and again in 1986. However, the basic features and requirements of the law have remained unchanged. We will examine special education legislation more fully in chapter 2.

WHAT IS SPECIAL EDUCATION?

Special education can be defined from many different perspectives. For example, one might view special education as a legislatively governed enterprise. From such a viewpoint one would be concerned about the legal implications of informing parents of handicapped students about their rights in participating in the planning of their children's individualized education programs. From a purely administrative point of view, special education might be seen as that part of a school system's operation that requires certain teacher-pupil ratios in the classroom and has special formulas for determining levels of funding according to the category of exceptional children served. Or special education might be thought of as an outgrowth of the civil rights movement, a demonstration of society's changing attitudes about people with disabilities in general. Each of these perspectives holds some validity, and each continues to play a role in defining what special education is and how it is practiced.

Ultimately, teaching is what special education is most about—but that is true of all of education. What then is *special* about special education? One way to try to answer that question is by looking at special education in terms of the who, what, how, and where of its teaching. We have already identified the most important *who* in special education, the exceptional children whose special needs or abilities necessitate an individualized program of education. In addition, exceptional children receive some or all of their instruction from teachers who have completed specialized teacher training programs in preparation for their work with students with special needs. Working with special educators and regular classroom teachers are many other professionals—including school psychologists, speech and language therapists, physical therapists, and medical specialists to name only a few—who work together to provide all of the educational and related services needed by exceptional children. Together, this **interdisciplinary team** of professionals bears the primary responsibility for helping exceptional children learn in spite of their differences and special needs.

In the 1983–84 school year there were 247,791 special education teachers employed in the United States, with a reported 17,103 more needed (U.S. Department of Education, 1986). During the same year there were 226,505 special education personnel other than teachers employed, with a reported shortage of 17,504. In a 1986 national survey of special education personnel, all 50 states reported shortages in one or more areas (McLaughlin, Smith-Davis, & Burke, 1986).

Special education can sometimes be differentiated from regular education by its curriculum, that is, by *what* is taught. Some exceptional children need intensive, systematic instruction in order to learn skills that normally developing children acquire naturally. For example, self-help skills such as dressing, eating, and toileting would not be found in the regular education curriculum, yet these skills comprise an important part of the curriculum for many students with severe handicaps. Also, some exceptional children are taught certain skills designed to compensate for or reduce the handicapping effects of a disability. For example, a child who is blind may receive special training in reading and writing braille, whereas the seeing child would not need these skills. It can be said that in regular education the school system dictates the curriculum, but in special education the individual needs of the child dictate the curriculum (Lieberman, 1985).

How special educators teach can, at times, be differentiated from the methods used by regular education teachers. One special educator may use sign language to communicate with his students. Another special educator may use a carefully structured procedure for gradually withdrawing visual prompts in helping a student learn to discriminate her own name from others. But for the most part, effective special teachers employ the same set of fundamental teaching skills that all good teachers use. There are not two distinct sets of instructional methods—one for use with special students, the other for regular students. Nor is there a certain set of teaching methods appropriate for students within a given category that differs significantly from the teaching methods that are effective with students in another category. Morsink, Thomas, and Davis (in press) reviewed the literature and found no evidence that specific teaching methods are differentially effective with students labeled as learning disabled, mildly mentally retarded, and emotionally disturbed. Instead, all special educators should be skilled in the procedures needed to systematically design, implement, and evaluate instruction.

Special education can sometimes be identified by *where* it takes place. We noted earlier that about two-thirds of all children with handicaps receive most of their education in regular classrooms. But one-third are someplace else—mostly in separate classrooms and separate residential and day schools. And many of those who are in a regular classroom leave it to spend a portion of each school day in a resource room where they receive individualized instruction. Special educators also teach in many environments not usually thought of as "school." An early childhood special educator may spend much of his time teaching parents how to work with their handicapped toddler at home. Teachers of students with severe handicaps are spending increasing amounts of instructional time in community and employment settings, helping their students learn important daily living and job skills.

Braille is a system of representing letters, numbers, words, and other symbols with a series of raised dots (see chapter 8). A blind person reads braille by touching the raised dots with her finger.

The April 1986 issue of *Exceptional Children* describes a variety of teaching strategies and methods that have proven effective with hard-to-teach students (Algozzine & Maheady, 1986). See Howell (1983) for an interesting account of what special educators do and how they view their work.

Special Education as Intervention

See chapter 14, which focuses on these and other early intervention efforts.

Intervention is a general name for all of the efforts made on behalf of handicapped people. The overall goal of intervention is to eliminate, or at least reduce, the obstacles that keep a handicapped person from full and active participation in society.

There are three basic kinds of intervention efforts: preventive (keeping possible problems from becoming serious handicaps), remedial (overcoming handicaps through training or education), and compensatory (giving the handicapped person new ways of dealing with her disability).

Preventive efforts are most promising when they begin early in life—even before birth in many cases. In later chapters we will explore some of the exciting new methods available for preventing handicaps—methods such as genetic counseling, amniocentesis, and screening early in infancy for metabolic disorders and other conditions that produce disabilities. We will explore, too, the efforts being made in social and educational programs to stimulate infants and very young children to acquire skills that most children learn normally, without special help.

Ultimately, teaching is what special education is most about.

Unfortunately, prevention programs have only just begun to affect the number and severity of handicaps in this country. And some researchers estimate that we will move well into the 21st century before we are able to reduce handicaps by even a small percentage (Hayden & Pious, 1979). In the meantime we must count on remedial and compensatory efforts to help handicapped people achieve fuller and more independent lives.

Remedial programs are supported largely by educational institutions and social agencies. In fact, the word **remediation** is primarily an educational term; the word **rehabilitation** is used more often by social service agencies. Both have a common purpose—to teach the handicapped person basic skills needed for independence. In school those skills may be academic (reading, writing, speaking, computing), social (getting along with other children; following instructions, schedules, and other daily routines), or even personal (feeding, dressing, using the toilet without assistance). More and more, schools are also teaching career and job skills, to prepare exceptional youngsters for jobs as adults in the community. In so doing, schools are sharing more of the responsibilities that social service agencies have historically accepted. Vocational training, or **vocational rehabilitation,** includes preparation to develop work habits and work attitudes, as well as specific training in a particular skill like auto mechanics, carpentry, or assembly-line work (Flexer & Martin, 1978).

The underlying assumption of both remedial and habilitative programs is that handicapped people need special help if they are to succeed in the normal world. Whenever possible, this special help is designed to teach handicapped people the same skills that nonhandicapped people have, but through different or more intensive methods than nonhandicapped people use.

Still another approach is to compensate for a handicapped person's loss or disability by giving him a kind of substitute skill or device on which to rely. An example of this kind of compensatory effort can be seen with physically disabled children. A child with cerebral palsy can be trained to make maximum use of her hands, but the use of a headstick and a template placed over a regular typewriter may effectively compensate for lack of muscle control by letting her type instead of writing lessons by hand. (Of course, the device itself requires training—she will have to learn to type with the headstick). The point here is that compensatory efforts aim to give the handicapped person some kind of asset that normal individuals do not need, whether it be a device like a headstick or special training like mobility instruction for a blind child.

What then is special education? In one sense it is a profession, with its own tools, techniques, and research efforts all focused on improving instructional arrangements and procedures for evaluating and meeting the learning needs of exceptional children and adults. At a more practical level, special education is the individually planned and systematically monitored arrangement of physical settings, special equipment and materials, teaching procedures, and other interventions designed to help exceptional children achieve the greatest possible personal self-sufficiency and academic success.

SPECIAL EDUCATION: SOME CURRENT CHALLENGES
AND SOME PREDICTIONS ABOUT THE FUTURE

Special education has accomplished a great deal during the past two decades, and there is legitimate reason for those in the field to feel good about the progress that has been made. Much has been accomplished in terms of making a free, appropriate education available to many handicapped children who were previously denied access to an education. Much has been learned about how to effectively teach children with severe handicaps, children who many had thought were not capable of learning. Special educators and parents have learned to work together on behalf of exceptional children. Technological advances have helped many students overcome physical disabilities or communication handicaps. Throughout the remaining chapters of this text we will describe many of these advances, but attempting to reveal the state of the art in a fast-changing discipline like special education is difficult at best.

Although the beginnings of special education can be traced back several centuries, in many respects the field is in its infancy. There is much to learn about teaching exceptional children and much to be done in order for special education to be most useful to those who need it most. Here are four areas considered as critical issues by many in the field today.

1. *Least restrictive environment.* We must increase the movement of handicapped students, particularly those with severe handicaps, into educational settings that are as normalized as possible. Even though two out of three handicapped students do spend part of each day in a regular classroom, for many children with handicaps a special education means a separate education. In chapter 2 we will examine the concept of educating exceptional children in the least restrictive environment.

2. *Early intervention.* We must increase the availability of special education and related services for handicapped and at-risk infants and toddlers. It is likely that the number of preschool children who receive special education will increase significantly during the coming years. The most recent federal law amending the Education for All Handicapped Children Act (P.L. 99–457, which was signed into law in 1986) requires that by 1991 all handicapped preschoolers aged 3 to 5 receive special education, and it increases the level of federal support to states for providing early intervention programs to handicapped and at-risk infants and toddlers. Chapter 14 is devoted to early intervention.

3. *School-to-adult-life transition.* We must improve the ability of young adults leaving secondary special education programs to live and work independently in their communities. Chapter 15 is devoted to the special needs of adults with disabilities and to efforts to help them make a successful transition from school to community life.

4. *Special-regular education relationship.* It has been estimated that in addition to the children with handicaps who are receiving special education, another 10% to 20% of the student population has mild to moderate learning problems that interfere with their ability to progress and succeed in the regular education program (Will,

1986). Both special and regular educators must develop strategies for working together and sharing their skills and resources in order to prevent these millions of at-risk students from becoming failures of our educational system. Some special educators have recommended that a major restructuring of the relationship between special education and regular education is needed to form a single educational system responsive to the individual needs of *all* students (Reynolds, Wang, & Walberg, 1987; Stainback & Stainback, 1984).

These four areas are not the only important issues in special education today. We could easily identify other challenges that many in the field would argue are equally or even more important. For example,

☐ increasing the availability and quality of special education programs for gifted and talented students
☐ developing teaching strategies that enable severely handicapped students to generalize newly learned skills to other settings
☐ applying advances in high technology to greatly reduce or eliminate the handicapping effects of physical and sensory disabilities
☐ improving the behavior of nonhandicapped people toward those with disabilities
☐ opening up more opportunities for individuals with handicaps to participate in the full range of residential, employment, and recreational options available to nondisabled persons

We do not know how successful special education will be in its efforts to meet these challenges. However, we can report some of the results Putnam and Bruininks (1986) discovered in an interesting study designed to forecast the future of special education. They asked 33 persons in a variety of leadership positions in special education around the country to identify the desirability of certain outcomes and to predict the probability that those outcomes would occur at a future date. Following are 20 of the 31 outcomes the respondents as a group identified as both desirable and likely to occur.

Philosophical, Conceptual, and Legal Trends

1. Our terminology (professional and layman), as it relates to different types of handicaps, will become functional (e.g., moderatey handicapped) rather than specific to particular handicaps (e.g., autistic, educable mentally retarded). (By the year 2000)
2. Institutional settings for persons who represent no physical threat to others will be viewed as a totally unacceptable strategy to provide for persons who are not fully independent. (By 1991)
3. Regulation of service will shift from monitoring processes to monitoring outcomes, giving programs greater flexibility and greater responsibility in meeting targets. (By 1996)
4. Special educators and human service providers will take the position that programming in the least restrictive environment is ultimately a fundamental civil right. (By 1996)

Residential, Educational, and Community Services

5. Educational services for mildly handicapped learners will be moved from special education into regular education along with other remedial programs. (By 2000)

6. Assuming that IEPs will still be required, about 85% of all students for whom IEPs are written will spend some of their school day in regular education classrooms (compared with about 70% in 1985). (By 1991)

7. Employment options for handicapped persons will increase by at least one-third as a result of advances in micro-technology. (By 2000)

Service System Perspectives

8. Service delivery patterns will be oriented to child needs and not disciplinary interests and traditions. (By 2000)

9. Increased stress on life-long learning and employment will force greater integration of services between schools and human service agencies, especially for people between 18 and 25 years. (By 1996)

10. When multiple agencies/programs are involved with a single client, a single habilitation plan will be developed with input from each of the major agencies/programs providing service to the client. (By 1996)

Intervention Strategies

11. Instruction of handicapped persons will increasingly occur in natural environments and situations, using natural cues and correction procedures. (By 1996)

12. Identification of instructional priorities—critical skills or "key stone" behaviors, related to multiple improvements/goals will be a research priority. (By 1991)

13. Technological advances will enable the design of learning and living environments that substantially eliminate functional limitations resulting from sensory and physical disabilities. (By 1996)

14. There will be significant growth in research that focuses on the cost effectiveness and efficiency of various instructional strategies (e.g., one-to-one instruction versus group instruction) in educating handicapped persons. (By 1996)

15. There will be greater emphasis on training that enhances functioning in extra-school settings rather than sequential developmental learning sequences. (By 1996)

Attitudes

16. Shaping the attitudes of the next generation (today's school children) will be a major focus of those who advocate the integration and acceptance of handicapped people into society. (By 1991)

17. Nonhandicapped children who attend school and socially associate with severely handicapped peers will become an adult generation better capable of facilitating the social integration of handicapped persons into all community environments. (By 1991)

18. The cultural revolution that has increased the "valuing" of persons with handicaps will continue. (By 1996)
19. There will be increased understanding and acceptance of differences by nonhandicapped persons who grow up alongside handicapped persons in regular school classes. (By 1991)
20. Great societal willingness to support habilitative programs for handicapped people will come with increased face-to-face interactions between persons with handicaps and nonhandicapped people. (By 2000) (Putnam & Bruininks, 1986, pp. 58–61)

Do these predictions represent the reality to come or merely a wish list of hoped-for outcomes? Only time will tell. But we do know there are many people who are working hard to make these predictions reality in the not-too-distant future—people with and without handicaps, people within and outside special education. Whether or not you pursue a career in special education, we hope your introductory study of the field will help you decide to work with those people.

OUR PERSONAL VIEW OF SPECIAL EDUCATION

We have tried throughout this chapter to give a clear and objective explanation of some of the basic concepts that combine to make up special education. We recognize, of course, that our own views of the field and of exceptional children are surely implicit in our words—between the lines, as they say. But we believe we owe you an even clearer statement of what we have already implied. And we want you to know that our views affect both the substance and the tone of the remaining chapters. The seven statements that follow summarize our personal view of special education.

1. We believe that people with handicaps have a fundamental right to live and participate in settings and programs—in school, at home, in the workplace, and in the community—that are as normalized as possible. That is, the settings and programs in which children and adults with handicaps learn, live, work, and recreate should be, to the greatest extent possible, in the same location, of the same type and style, and for the same purpose as the settings and programs in which people without handicaps participate. We believe a defining feature of normalized settings and programs is the integration of handicapped and nonhandicapped participants.

2. We believe that individuals with handicaps have the right to as much independence as we can help them achieve. The ultimate effectiveness of special education should be evaluated in terms of its success in assisting students with handicaps in maximizing their level of independent functioning in normalized environments.

3. We believe that special education must continue to expand and improve its efforts to recognize and respond appropriately to all learners with special needs and attributes—the gifted and talented child, the preschooler with a handicap or at risk for

a future learning problem, the exceptional child from a different cultural back-ground, and the adult with disabilities. In support of this belief, we have included a chapter on each of these important areas of special education.

4. We believe that professionals have for too long ignored the needs of parents and families of exceptional children, treating them many times as patients, clients, or even adversaries, instead of realizing that they are partners with the same goals. We believe that special educators have too often given the impression (and, worse, have too often believed it to be true) that parents are there to serve professionals, when in fact the opposite is more correct. We believe that we have long neglected to recognize parents as a child's first—and in many ways best—teachers. We believe that learning to work effectively with parents is one of the most important skills the special educator can acquire. We have devoted a chapter to the impor-tance of the parent-professional partnership.

5. We believe that the efforts of special educators are most effective when they in-corporate the input and services of all of the disciplines in the helping professions. We see our primary responsibility as educators to be the design and implementa-tion of effective instruction for personal, social, vocational, and academic skills. But we consider it foolish to argue over territorial rights when we can accomplish more

Peter's program emphasizes the skills he will need in order to live in the community.

WHAT SHOULD WE CALL THEM?

In this article Tom Lovitt, a professor of special education at the University of Washington, offers his views about how to refer to the exceptional children who will be entering regular classes because of new federal and state laws.

"What should we call the special children who are sent to our classes?" This question might be asked by regular education teachers who are about to have special education children mainstreamed in their classes. Should they carefully study the dossiers of the children to figure out what others have called them? Should a regular teacher, for instance, try to remember that Roy, who will soon be sent to his regular class, was called *emotionally disturbed* by two school psychologists, a social worker, and a reading teacher (even though he was referred to as *learning disabled* by another school psychologist)? Should he hang onto the fact that Amy was called *mentally retarded* by most of the people who wrote reports for her folder? Likewise, should he make every effort to recall that Tim was most often referred to as *learning disabled?*

No. Those labels do not help teachers design effective programs for the special children they will teach. They won't help teachers decide where to seat the children; they certainly won't help them to design educational and management strategies.

But if regular teachers shouldn't call them mentally retarded, etc., why did the special teachers and others do so? Good question. I'm not certain how the labeling business as we know it today got started, but even special education teachers will admit (most of them at least) that the labels have not helped them to teach children to read, write, or cipher, or to behave more appropriately.

But if we shouldn't refer to these special children by using those old labels, then how should we refer to them? What should we call them? For openers, call them Roy, Amy, and Tim. Beyond that,

refer to them on the basis of what you're trying to teach them. For example, if a teacher wants to teach Roy to compute, read, and comprehend, he might call him a student of computation, reading, and comprehension. We do this all the time with older students. Sam, who attends Juilliard, is referred to as "the trumpet student"; Jane, who attends Harvard, is called "the law student."

But categories can be useful to regular teachers with special children; we shouldn't do away with all categories simply because the current system doesn't help. It seems to me that most of these children fall into one of five categories or have characteristics of more than one of the categories. Many children share doses of several of the various types, but there are some "purees." Let me elaborate a bit.

WHAT TO CALL THEM?

Slow Academically

A great majority of the first wave of children to be sent back into the mainstream are having problems in the basic skills, more often than not in reading. Many of them are good citizens and highly motivated, but for some reason or other they can't read, spell, or write as well as some people think they should.

Poorly Motivated

These are the children who could do certain things but they don't want to. On one day a child of this type can finish his arithmetic assignment, but he won't do it the next. He's the one who never gets a thrill out of learning, the one who moans and groans each time he is asked to do something. Not that they don't have enough of these children already, but with the advent of mainstreaming, regular teachers will receive dozens of these youngsters.

Naughty Behaviors

Perhaps the main reason for evicting youngsters from regular classes in the past was because of their naughty behaviors—professionally referred to as "inappropriate behaviors." Hundreds of children were sent from regular to special classes because they talked out of turn too often or popped out of their chairs more times than they should. Other children, of course, were dismissed from regular classes because of more irksome behaviors: they hit, lied, stole, threatened, or defiled.

Poor Endurance

Some children who could perform many academic tasks, were good citizens, and were reasonably well motivated were still sent to special classes. They are the youngsters who can't sit still and don't finish their tasks. They shift from one activity to another very rapidly. Although they might do well on their arithmetic or spelling assignments as long as they work, they seem to be distracted by almost any object and sound. If someone comes into the room or simply passes by outside, they drop everything and focus on the visitor. Or if they hear a paper or pencil rustle to the floor, they attend to the noise.

Special Equipment

Many children have been sent to special classes because they need special equipment or a special type of instruction. In fact, the first children who were sent from regular classes were dismissed for these reasons. They were the youngsters classified as deaf, blind, and orthopedically handicapped.

CONCLUSION

Regular teachers cannot take their responsibilities lightly now that many special children will be returning to their classes. And I'm certain they won't. Neither should they be overly concerned about their new pupils, for in the past many regular teachers have dealt with pupils a lot like the ones they will receive. The difference is that now those pupils are returning with labels like *mentally retarded* and *emotionally disturbed* and *learning disabled*. When they left, they were referred to as *naughty* and *slow*.

Teachers must forget about these labels and go about the business of designing individualized programs. To do so, they should continue using the practices that have been successful in the past and be prepared to add to their repertoires when they need to.

Source: What Should We Call Them? by T. Lovitt, 1979, *Exceptional Teacher*, 1(1), pp. 5–7. Reprinted by permission of Special Press.

for exceptional children by working together within an interdisciplinary team that includes our colleagues in psychology, medicine, social services, and vocational rehabilitation.

6. We believe that teachers must demand effectiveness from their instructional approaches. The belief that special educators require unending patience is a disservice to exceptional children and to the teachers whose job it is to help them learn. The special educator should not wait patiently for the exceptional child to learn, attributing his lack of progress to retardation, a learning disability, or some other label. Instead, the special educator should modify the instructional program in an effort to improve its effectiveness, using the information obtained from direct observations of the child's performance of the skills being taught. Although we make no pretense that you will know how to teach exceptional children after reading this introductory text, we do hope you will gain an understanding of the kinds of teaching skills the special educator should possess.

7. Finally, we are essentially optimistic about the futures of exceptional children. That is to say, we have enough confidence in their potentials to affirm that they can succeed in building fuller and more independent lives in the community. We believe that we have only begun to discover the ways to improve teaching, to increase learning, to prevent handicapping conditions, to encourage acceptance, and to develop technology to compensate for disabilities. And although we make no predictions for the future, we are certain that we have not come as far as we can in helping exceptional individuals to help themselves.

SUMMARY

1. *Exceptional children* are those whose physical attributes and/or learning abilities differ from the norm, either above or below, to such an extent that an individualized program of special education is indicated. *Disability* refers to the reduced function or loss of a particular body part or organ. *Handicap* refers to the problems a person with a disability or impairment encounters when interacting with the environment. A child who is at risk is not currently identified as handicapped or disabled but is considered to have a greater-than-usual chance of developing a handicap.

2. Handicapped children in special education represent approximately 11% of the school-age population. The three biggest categories of handicapped children receiving special education are learning disabilities, speech and language impairments, and mental retardation. As a group, children participating in programs for the gifted and talented make up the third largest category of special education.

3. Two-thirds of children with handicaps receive at least part of their education in regular classrooms.

4. The labeling and classification of exceptional children is a controversial issue.
   a. Current labeling practices may have administrative and political benefits but seem to

have a negative effect on the individual child who is labeled.

   b. Classification systems are generally based on deviation from "normal" or on supposed "causes" of handicapping conditions.

   c. New proposed classification systems are based on educational characteristics of individual children.

5. P.L. 94–142, the Education for All Handicapped Children Act, reflects today's concern for treating handicapped persons as full citizens, with all the rights of other citizens. Gifted and talented children are not included in P.L. 94–142; federal legislation does not mandate special education programs for gifted children.

6. There are three kinds of intervention efforts: preventive, remedial, and compensatory.

   a. Most educational programs are either remedial (to teach basic necessary skills that everyone needs) or compensatory (to teach a substitute skill needed to overcome a specific disability).

   b. Effective intervention requires the cooperation of many different professionals, including educators, medical professionals, social workers, and vocational rehabilitation professionals.

7. Special education is a profession focused on improving instructional arrangements and procedures for teaching exceptional children and adults.

8. Some of the major challenges faced by special education today are (a) educating children with handicaps in the least restrictive environment; (b) making early intervention programs more widely available to infants and toddlers who are handicapped or at risk; (c) improving the ability of young adults with disabilities to make a successful transition from school to community life; and (d) improving the relationship with regular education in order to better serve the many students who have not been identified as handicapped but who are not progressing in the general education program.

FOR MORE INFORMATION

Journals

Exceptional Children. The flagship journal of special education, published six times a year by the Council for Exceptional Children (see address below). Designed to assist all professionals who work with exceptional children.

Journal of Special Education. A quarterly journal that publishes articles from all disciplines; deals with research, theory, opinion, and reviews of the literature in special education.

Remedial and Special Education. Published six times per year by Pro-Ed, Austin, TX 78735. Devoted to discussion of issues involving the education of persons for whom typical instruction is not effective. Emphasizes interpretation of research literature and recommendations for the practice of remedial and special education.

Teaching Exceptional Children. Published quarterly by the Council for Exceptional Children. Presents articles suggesting classroom teaching strategies, reports of materials, a teacher idea exchange, and other information designed to assist the teacher of exceptional children.

Books

Howell, K. (1983). *Inside special education.* Columbus, OH: Merrill.

Morris, R. J., & Blatt, B. (Eds.). (1986). *Special education: Reasearch and trends.* Elmsford, NY: Pergamon Press.

Orlansky, M. D., & Heward, W. L. (1981). *Voices: Interviews with handicapped people.* Columbus, OH: Merrill.

Payne, J. S., Patton, J.R., Kauffman, J. M., Brown, G. B., & Payne, R. A. (1987). *Exceptional children in focus,* (4th ed.). Columbus, OH: Merrill.

Ysseldyke, J. E., & Algozzine, B. (1982). *Critical issues in special and remedial eduation.* Boston: Houghton–Mifflin.

Organizations

Council for Exceptional Children, 1920 Association Drive, Reston, VA 22091. Includes over 50,000 teachers, teacher educators, administrators, researchers, and other professionals involved in education exceptional children and adults.

2

THE PROMISE AND THE CHALLENGE: SPECIAL EDUCATION IN THE SCHOOLS

A society can be judged, it is said, by the way it treats those who are different. By this criterion, as Fiske (1976) has noted, our educational system has seldom distinguished itself. Often children who are different because of race, culture, language, gender, or exceptionality have not had full and fair access to educational opportunities.

For many years the field of special education simply did not exist. Of course, exceptional children—those who are handicapped and those who are gifted—have always been with us. But attention has not always been paid to their special needs. The integration of exceptional children into regular schools and classes is a relatively recent phenomenon.

In the past, many children with handicaps were entirely excluded from any publicly supported program of education. Some children were totally neglected and hidden away; others were abused, exploited, or even put to death (Morgan, 1987). In many communities there were no facilities or services whatsoever to help exceptional children and their families. However, past practices should not be viewed as entirely negative. Some children with special needs were educated by devoted parents or teachers before there was any legal requirement to do so.

The full extension of educational services to exceptional children has involved immense changes—for special educators, regular educators, parents, and many other people. Earlier in this century, when local public schools began to accept a measure of responsibility for the education of certain exceptional students, a philosophy of segregation usually prevailed, a philosophy that continued unchanged until recently. Children received labels—such as mentally retarded, crippled, or emotionally disturbed—and were mainly confined to isolated special classrooms. One special education teacher describes the sense of isolation she felt and the crude facilities in which her special class operated.

> In the 1960s I accepted my first teaching position, a special education class in a basement room next door to the furnace. Of the 15 "educable mentally retarded"

children assigned to work with me, most were simply nonreaders from poor families. One child had been banished to my room because she posed a behavior problem to her fourth-grade teacher.

My class and I were assigned a recess spot on the opposite side of the play yard, far away from the "normal" children. I was the only teacher who did not have a lunch break. I was required to eat with my "retarded" children while other teachers were permitted to leave their students. . . . Isolated from my colleagues, I closed my door and did my thing, oblivious to the larger educational circles in which I was immersed. Although it was the basement room, with all the negative perceptions that arrangement implies, I was secure in the knowledge that despite the ignominy of it all I did good things for children who were previously unloved and untaught. (Aiello, 1976)

Over the past 100 years or so, there has been a "painfully slow process of integration and participation" for children with handicaps and for their families (Cremins, 1983, p. 3). In the past, parents were often viewed as the source of their child's disability and, later, as the passive recipients of professionals' judgments and decisions (Turnbull & Turnbull, 1986). Children with mild learning and behavior disorders were usually given no special treatment and were kept in the regular classroom. There they were often labeled "disciplinary problems" and suspended from school; or they were termed "slow learners," "failures," or "ineducable" if they did not make satisfactory academic progress. Children with more severe disabilities—including many with visual, hearing, other physical, and health impairments—were generally placed in segregated schools or institutions or kept at home. Children who were gifted and talented seldom received special attention in schools. They could make it on their own, it was felt, without help.

Prior to the 1970s, as Johnson (1986) has pointed out, many state laws permitted public schools to exclude handicapped children from their educational programs. Local school officials had no legal obligation to grant them the same educational access that nonhandicapped students enjoyed. One state law, for example, allowed schools to refuse to serve "children physically or mentally incapacitated for school work"; another state had a law stipulating that children with "bodily or mental conditions rendering attendance inadvisable" could be turned away. And the nation's courts generally supported such exclusion. In a 1919 case, for example, a 13-year-old student with physical handicaps (but normal intellectual ability) was excluded from his local school because he "produces a depressing and nauseating effect upon the teachers and school children . . . he takes up an undue portion of the teacher's time and attention, distracts attention of other pupils, and interferes generally with the discipline and progress of the school" (Johnson, 1986, p. 2).

Society's response to exceptional children has come a long way in a comparatively short time. As our concepts of equality, freedom, and justice have expanded, exceptional children and their families have moved from isolation to participation. No longer may a child who is different from the norm or "unable to appropriately benefit from typical instruction" be turned away from school.

Through the efforts of special educators, parents, exceptional persons, legislators, and other advocates, continual improvement has taken place in the range of stu-

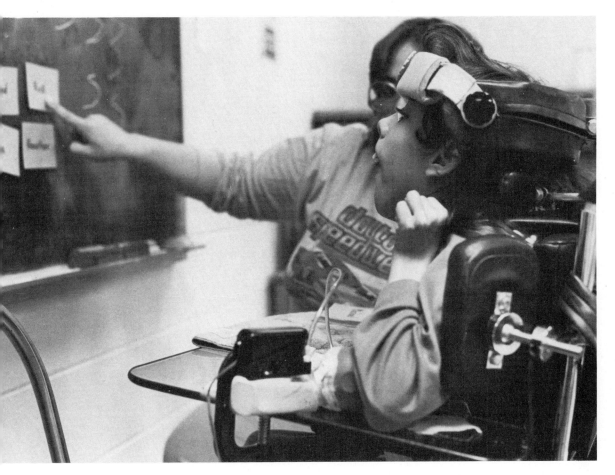

Today, children with severe and multiple handicaps, like Tony, are benefiting from systematic instruction.

dents being served; the quality of the personnel providing special education and related services; and the methodology, curriculum, and technology for educating exceptional children. For most exceptional students of school age, special educational opportunity is now a right, and progress continues in guaranteeing this most fundamental right for all students who need it. (Weintraub, 1986, p. 1)

We can no longer regard exceptional children as beyond the responsibility of their local public schools. Recent legislation and court decisions have confirmed that the exceptional child, no less than any other citizen, has the right to a *free, appropriate program of public education in the least restrictive learning environment possible.* This means that most handicapped students will spend at least part of the school day in regular classrooms, alongside their nonhandicapped peers. Other students will receive

We will be looking at these concepts in depth later in this chapter.

an appropriate education in special classes within regular public schools and will have some contact with nonhandicapped students. Still other students, who may not be able to attend regular public schools, will receive a specially designed program of education within a special school, institution, hospital, or perhaps at home.

As Biklen (1985) observes, special education is now at a crossroads. A decade ago the primary issue for exceptional children was one of access. Would they receive an education at all? Could they be served in their local community? Some problems of access persist (for children who live in poverty or in institutions or in extremely isolated areas, for example), but today "the primary issue of contention in special education is whether students will receive a quality education *in regular public schools*" (Biklen, 1985, p. 174). For those who might think this goal has already been achieved, Biklen cites several commonly heard statements that reflect negative attitudes toward special education and people with disabilities.

"Can these people really benefit from an education?"
"How much can society afford to spend on this; we don't have unlimited resources, you know."
"Isn't it terribly frustrating work when you don't see progress?"
"Isn't it mainly babysitting?"
"I like working with bright kids, but I'd get depressed if I had to work with the handicapped." (p. 182)

How can special education and regular education work together most effectively for the benefit of all students? This is a critical and frequently articulated issue today. Every handicapped child, regardless of the service setting, must have an **individualized education program (IEP)** developed especially to suit individual abilities and needs. Thus, special educators, regular educators, and parents should no longer be in an us-versus-them relationship. Instead, they can work together to individualize instruction, manage behavior, and plan cooperatively to meet students' immediate and long-range needs. Attempting to meet the individual needs of all students with handicaps has had enormous consequences for schools. We will examine several of these in this chapter.

LEGAL BACKGROUND: SPECIAL EDUCATION AS CIVIL RIGHTS

The recent provision of equal educational opportunities to exceptional children in the public schools did not come about by chance. Many laws and court cases, reflecting the issues and concepts of our times, have had important effects on the education of children with special needs and on public education in general. And the process of change is never finished. As Prasse (1986) notes, legal influences on special education are not fixed or static, but rather fluid and dynamic. Table 2.1 presents a summary of several laws and judicial cases that have had significant impact on special education.

The concept of educating handicapped children in regular public schools can be considered an outgrowth of the civil rights movement. It was strongly influenced by social developments and court decisions in the 1950s and 1960s, especially by the landmark case of *Brown v. Board of Education of Topeka* (1954). This case challenged

TABLE 2.1
Court cases and legislation affecting education of exceptional children.

Court cases

1954	*Brown* v. *Board of Education of Topeka* (Kansas) → ~~Race Case~~

Established the right of all children to an equal opportunity to an education.

1967   *Hobson* v. *Hansen* (Washington, DC)
Declared the track system, which used standardized tests as a basis for special education placement, unconstitutional because it discriminated against black and poor children.

1970   *Diana* v. *State Board of Education* (California)
Declared that children cannot be placed in special education on the basis of culturally biased tests or tests given in other than the child's native language.

1972   *Mills* v. *Board of Education of the District of Columbia*
Established the right of every child to an equal opportunity for education; declared that lack of funds was not an acceptable excuse for lack of educational opportunity.

1972   *Pennsylvania Association for Retarded Citizens* v. *the Commonwealth of Pennsylvania*
Class action suit to establish the right to free public education for all retarded children.

(handwritten: Parents were key individual programs for kids.)

1972   *Wyatt* v. *Stickney* (Alabama)
Declared that individuals in state institutions have the right to appropriate treatment within those institutions.

1979   *Central York District* v. *Commonwealth of Pennsylvania Department of Education*
Ruled that school districts must provide services for gifted and talented children whether or not advance guarantee of reimbursement from the state has been received.

1979   *Larry P.* v. *Riles* (California)
First brought to court in 1972; ruled that IQ tests cannot be used as the sole basis for placing children in special classes.

1979   *Armstrong* v. *Kline* (Pennsylvania)
Established right of some severely handicapped children to an extension of the 180-day public school year.

(handwritten: Regression over the summer)

1982   *Rowley* v. *Hendrik Hudson School District* (New York)
First case based on P.L. 94–142 to reach the U.S. Supreme Court; while denying plaintiff's specific request, upheld each handicapped child's right to a personalized program of instruction and necessary supportive services.

1983   *Abrahamson* v. *Hershman* (Massachusetts)
Ruled that residential placement in a private school was necessary for a child with multiple handicaps who needed around-the-clock training; required the school district to pay for the private placement.

1984   *Department of Education* v. *Katherine D.* (Hawaii)
Ruled that a homebound instructional program for a child with multiple health impairments did not meet the least-restrictive-environment standard; called for the child to be placed in a class with nonhandicapped children and provided with related medical services.

1984   *Irving Independent School District* v. *Tatro* (Texas)
Ruled that catheterization was necessary for a physically handicapped child to remain in school and that it could be performed by a nonphysician, thus obligating the school district to provide that service.

1984   *Smith* v. *Robinson* (Rhode Island)
Ordered the state to pay a severely handicapped child's placement in a residential

TABLE 2.1
continued

program and ordered the school district to reimburse the parents' attorney fees. U.S. Supreme Court later ruled that P.L. 94–142 did not entitle parents to recover such fees, but Congress subsequently passed an "Attorney's Fees" bill, leading to the enactment of P.L. 99–372.

1985   *Cleburne* v. *Cleburne Living Center* (Texas)

U.S. Supreme Court ruled unanimously that communities cannot use a discriminatory zoning ordinance to prevent the establishment of group homes for persons with mental retardation.

1986   *Doe* v. *Maher* (California)

Ruled that handicapped children could not be excluded from school for any misbehavior that is "handicap-related" (in this case "aggressive behavior against other students" on the part of two "emotionally handicapped" students) but that educational services could be stopped if the misbehavior is not related to the handicap.

Legislation

1958   P.L. 85–926 National Defense Education Act
        Provided funds for training professionals to train teachers of mentally retarded children.

1961   P.L. 87–276 Special Education Act
        Provided funds for training professionals to train teachers of deaf children.

1963   P.L. 88–164 Mental Retardation Facility and Community Center Construction Act
        Extended support given in P.L. 85–926 to training teachers of other handicapped children, as well as mentally retarded children.

1965   P.L. 89–10 Elementary and Secondary Education Act
        Provided money to states and local districts for developing programs for economically disadvantaged and handicapped children.

1966   P.L. 89–313 Amendment to Title I of the Elementary and Secondary Education Act
        Provided funding for state-supported programs in institutions and other settings for handicapped children.

1966   P.L. 89–750 Amendments to the Elementary and Secondary Education Act
        Created the Bureau of Education for the Handicapped.

1969   P.L. 91–230 Elementary, Secondary, and Other Educational Amendments. Defined learning disabilities; provided funds for state-level programs for children with learning disabilities.

1973   P.L. 93–112, Section 504 of the Rehabilitation Act
        Actually adopted in 1977, declared that handicapped people cannot be excluded on the basis of the handicap alone from any program or activity receiving federal funds.

1974   P.L. 93–380 Education Amendments
        Extended previous legislation; provided money to state and local districts for programs for gifted and talented students for the first time. Also protected rights of handicapped children and parents in placement decisions.

1975   P.L. 94–103 Developmental Disabilities Assistance and Bill of Rights Act
        Affirmed rights of mentally retarded citizens and cited areas where services must be provided for retarded and other developmentally disabled people.

TABLE 2.1
continued

1975	P.L. 94–142 Education for All Handicapped Children Act *Ages 3-21* Mandated free, appropriate public education for all handicapped children regardless of degree of severity of handicap; protected rights of handicapped children and parents in educational decision making; required that an individualized education program (IEP) be developed for each handicapped child; and that handicapped students receive educational services in the least restrictive environment.
1978	P.L. 95–561 Gifted and Talented Children's Education Act Provided financial incentives for states and local education agencies to identify and educate gifted and talented students, for in-service training, and for research.
1983	P.L. 98–199 Amendments to the Education of the Handicapped Act Required states to collect data on the number of handicapped youth exiting their systems and to address their anticipated service needs. Also gave incentives to states to provide services to handicapped infants and preschool children.
1986	P.L. 99–372 Handicapped Children's Protection Act Provided authority for the reimbursement of attorney's fees to parents who must go to court to secure an appropriate education for their child. Parents who prevail in a hearing or court case may recover the costs incurred for lawyers to represent them, retroactive to July 4, 1984.
1986	P.L. 99–457 Education of the Handicapped Amendments of 1986 Encouraged states to develop comprehensive interdisciplinary services for handicapped infants and toddlers (birth through age 2) and to expand services for preschool children (aged 3 through 5). By the 1990–91 school year states must provide free, appropriate education to all handicapped 3-to-5-year-olds in order to apply for federal preschool funding.

the then-existing practice of segregating schools according to the race of the children. The U.S. Supreme Court declared that education must be made available to *all* children on equal terms.

> Today, education is perhaps the most important function of state and local governments. Compulsory school attendance laws and the great expenditure for education both demonstrate our recognition of the importance of education to our democratic society. It is required in the performance of our most basic responsibilities. . . . *In these days, it is doubtful that any child may reasonably be expected to succeed in life if he is denied the opportunity of an education* [italics added].

The *Brown* decision, and the ensuing extension of public school education to black and white children on equal terms, began a period of intense concern and questioning among parents of handicapped children. Did not the same principles of equal access to education apply to their children as well? Many cases brought by parents and other advocates expressed a growing dissatisfaction with school procedures that resulted in the segregation of handicapped students or the denial of educational programs to them. Generally, the parents based their arguments on the 14th Amendment to the Constitution, which provides that no state shall deny any person within its jurisdiction the **equal protection** of the law and that no state shall deprive any person of life, liberty, or property without **due process** of law. The concepts of equal protection and due process are of such fundamental importance in special education today that it is worthwhile to examine them in some detail.

Equal Protection

In the past, children with disabilities usually received differential treatment. That is, they were excluded from certain educational programs or were given special education in segregated settings. Basically, the courts have examined whether such treatment is *rational* and whether it is *necessary* (Williams, 1977). One of the most important cases to examine these questions in regard to handicapped children was the case of the *Pennsylvania Association for Retarded Children* v. *Commonwealth of Pennsylvania* (1972). The association (PARC) challenged a state law that denied public school education to certain children who were then considered "unable to profit from public school attendance."

The lawyers and parents supporting PARC argued that, though the children had intellectual disabilities, it was neither rational nor necessary to assume that they were ineducable and untrainable. And the state was not able to prove that the children were, in fact, ineducable and untrainable or to demonstrate a rational basis for excluding them from public school programs. The court decided that the children were entitled to receive a free, public education. In addition, the court maintained that the children's parents had the right to be notified before any change was made in the children's educational program. These and other rights are guaranteed under the equal protection clause of the 14th Amendment, which holds that people may not be deprived of their equality or liberty because of any classification (such as race, nationality, or religion). As Thomas (1985) observes, courts have often regarded handicapped people as belonging to a minority group that has a history of discrimination, political powerlessness, and unequal treatment. Thus, equal protection and certain procedures known as due process of law must be provided to ensure that handicapped children and their families are fully informed of their rights and that they are treated fairly and reasonably as citizens.

The wording of the PARC decision is particularly interesting, not only for its influence on subsequent federal legislation, but also for its recognition of the particular learning needs of exceptional children.

> It is the Commonwealth's obligation to place each mentally retarded child in a free, public program of education and training appropriate to the child's capacity. . . . [P]lacement in a regular public school class is preferable to placement in a special public school class and placement in a special public school is preferable to placement in any other type of program of education and training. An assignment to homebound instruction shall be re-evaluated not less than every 3 months, and notice of the evaluation and an opportunity for a hearing thereon shall be accorded to the parent or guardian.

Due Process

In the past, handicapped students (and some nonhandicapped students as well) were not always considered "people" in the eyes of the law. Several recent laws and court decisions, however, have clearly established that students are, indeed, people, entitled to exercise such rights as privacy, freedom of travel, the practice of religion, and personal rights, such as choosing their own clothing and hair styles. Although school officials may enforce reasonable regulations, they may *not* operate unfairly or arbitrarily, and they do not have absolute authority over their students.

The extension of due process of law to exceptional students is a broad concept that cannot be reduced to a simple step-by-step procedure. It is constantly changing as the values and priorities of our society change. An important element of due process is the acknowledgment of a student as a person, with important rights and responsibilities. Some people have questioned why highly specific legal safeguards are necessary to protect the rights of handicapped children—aren't they protected by the same laws and due process procedures that apply to all citizens? But a review of how handicapped children were treated by schools (and by society in general) in the past shows that our laws and legal procedures were often not equally applied to handicapped people. Meyen (1978) cites five reasons that specific legal safeguards for handicapped children are necessary.

1. Once placed in a special education program, many handicapped children remained there for the rest of their educational careers. Such a system permanently excluded many children from regular classrooms once they were placed elsewhere.
2. Decisions to place students in special education programs were often made primarily on the basis of teacher recommendation or the results of a single test.
3. Severely and profoundly handicapped children were routinely excluded from public school programs. If they received any education at all, their parents usually had to pay for it.
4. A disproportionate number of children from minority cultural groups were placed in special education programs.
5. The level of educational services provided to residents of institutions was often very low or even nonexistent.

These circumstances led to increased activism by parents of exceptional children and by lawyers, educators, and other advocates who were concerned that these children were not being treated fairly. Many legislators and judges agreed. The concept of due process for handicapped students is now embodied in our legal and educational systems. Several elements of this concept, as Williams (1977) points out, have particularly important implications for special education in the schools today.

1. *Notice.* The person (or parents) must be told about a decision or change in educational program that is about to take place. This gives the affected persons the information necessary to respond to issues or charges. Notice of providing or removing services must be given because the child's status may be substantially altered by decisions regarding her educational program.

2. *A hearing before an impartial party.* Parents and students have the right to challenge or examine the decision before an impartial party. *Impartial* is generally interpreted to mean not employed by the school district that has made the decision
affecting the child.

3. *The right to present a defense.* This includes the right to present evidence, answer
charges, and in general "give your best effort at convincing that decision maker in
the way that you want to convince him." The school must give parents or students
adequate time and information to prepare a defense and must allow them to be
represented by lawyers or other advocates if they so desire.

4. *Written decision.* Following any hearing, parents, students, and the school district
must have a written statement that specifies the facts that were considered and
the conclusions that were drawn.

5. *Right to appeal.* If the parents, students, or school district is not satisfied with the
results of the impartial hearing, the decision may be appealed to the state department of education and to the courts.

Turnbull and Turnbull, who are special educators and parents of an exceptional
child, describe due process as "the legal technique that seeks to assure fairness among
professionals, service systems, families, and students." Due process, they further note,
is "a way of changing the balance of power between professionals, who have traditionally wielded power, and families, who have felt they could not affect their children's education" (1986, p. 254).

Further guidelines on due process, written especially for parents of exceptional
children, are provided in Figure 2.1. Teachers, administrators, and other service providers should also be familiar with these guidelines.

Other Court Cases

In addition to the PARC case, several other judicial decisions have had far-reaching
effects on special education. The findings of some cases have been incorporated into
subsequent legislation, most notably P.L. 94–142, the Education for All Handicapped
Children Act. We will briefly discuss some of the most important of these cases.

Hobson v. Hansen (1967)

Standardized intelligence
tests are examined in
more detail on pages
85–91.

In this case a court ruled against the so-called tracking system, in which children were
placed into either regular or special classes according to their scores on intelligence
tests. Most of these tests had been standardized on a population of white middle-class
children. This case involved black working-class children, who comprise most of the
student population of public schools in Washington, DC. These children, it was decided,
were not being classified according to their ability to learn, but rather according to
environmental and social factors that were irrelevant to their learning ability and potential.

FIGURE 2.1
Guidelines on due process for parents.

IN A NUTSHELL

Here's a quick review to keep in mind the main steps involved in due process. Each of these steps reinforces your right to stay on top of decisions about your child.

1. You must receive notice in writing before the school system takes (or recommends) any action that may change your child's school program. Notice in writing is also required if a school refuses to take action to change your child's program.

2. You have the right to give—or withhold—permission for your child to be tested to determine whether or not he requires special education services (identification); evaluated by specialists to determine what his educational needs are (evaluation); placed in a specific school program to meet his needs (placement).

3. You have the right to see and examine all school records related to the identification, evaluation and placement of your child. If you find that certain records are inaccurate or misleading, you have the right to ask that they be removed from your child's file. Once removed, they may *not* be used in planning for your child's placement.

4. If you do not agree with the school's course of action at *any* point along the way, you have the right to request an impartial due process hearing. This means that you can initiate a hearing to protest any decision related to identification, evaluation or placement of your child.

5. If you fail to win your case, you have the right to appeal the results of the due process hearing to the State Department of Education; you can appeal to the courts if you lose your case at the state level.

Calling for a due process hearing is your right, but remember that it can be an exhausting process. Before going this route, be sure you have tried to settle differences through every other means—by being as persuasive as possible in meetings with teachers, the principal, special education administrators. If you know that you're up against a brick wall, and you're sure that a due process hearing must be held to resolve conflicting points of view, then you must prepare your case as thoroughly as possible. Be sure to get help from an advocacy group or a lawyer who is familiar with education law and procedures in your state, or an experienced parent. (According to law, the school system must tell you about sources of free legal aid. Ask for this information.)

Know your rights at a hearing:

☐ The hearing officer must be impartial, may not be employed by the school district or involved in the education of your child.

☐ You have the right to legal counsel (which includes the advice and support of any advocate, not necessarily a lawyer); to examine witnesses; present evidence; ask questions of school spokespeople; obtain a record of the hearing and all of its findings.

NOTE: Write directly to the superintendent of schools in your district to request a hearing. Hearings must be held not later than 45 days after requested. State Departments of Education must review appeals within 30 days.

Source: From *Closer Look*, Fall 1977, p. 4, Washington, DC: Department of Health, Education, and Welfare.

Diana v. State Board of Education (1970)

A Spanish-speaking student in California had been placed in a special class for mentally retarded children on the basis of intelligence tests that were given in English. The court ruled that this placement was inappropriate and that the child must be given another evaluation in her native language.

Mills v. Board of Education (1972)

Seven children had been excluded from the public schools in Washington, DC, because of learning and behavior problems. The school district contended that it did not have enough money to provide special education programs for them. The court held that lack of funds is no excuse for failing to educate the children and ordered the schools to readmit and serve them appropriately. Even if funds are limited (as is often the case today), handicapped children must not be denied access to public schools. Financial problems cannot be allowed to impact more heavily on exceptional children than on nonhandicapped students.

Larry P. v. Riles (1979)

This case found the placement of black children in special classes inappropriate because of unfair testing. The IQ tests that were used, said the court, failed to recognize the children's cultural background and the learning that took place in their homes and communities. When different tests were used, it was found that the children were not mentally retarded. The court ordered that IQ tests not be used as the *sole* basis for placing children into special classes.

These important decisions and many others helped establish the schools' responsibility to provide education for handicapped children and to treat them fairly. Exceptional children, who suffered from exclusion and segregation in the past, are today moving toward greater inclusion and integration in the schools. Gilhool (1976), an attorney who was instrumental in the PARC case, aptly summarizes recent judicial and social developments: "Integration is a central constitutional value. Not integration that *denies* differences, but rather integration that *accommodates* difference."

LEGISLATION: P.L. 94–142

Federal legislation is identified by a numerical system. P.L. 94–142, for example, was the 142nd bill passed by the 94th U.S. Congress.

The trend toward inclusion and integration of handicapped children culminated in P.L. 94–142, the Education for All Handicapped Children Act. This law was passed by the U.S. Congress in 1975 but was not fully implemented until 1980. It has been described as "blockbuster legislation" (Goodman, 1976) and hailed as the law that "will probably become known as having the greatest impact on education in history" (Stowell & Terry, 1977). In our view the law has clearly had a great deal of impact, but its long-range effects on special education and regular education have yet to be determined.

In this section we will present and discuss the major features of P.L. 94–142 that indicate important current trends in the field of special education. These trends have affected virtually every school in the country and have changed the roles of regular and special educators, school administrators, and many others who are involved in the educational process.

What Does the Law Say?

P.L. 94–142 states that all handicapped children between the ages of 3 and 21, regardless of the type or severity of their disability, shall receive a "free, appropriate public education which emphasizes special education and related services designed to meet their unique needs." This education must be provided at public expense—that is, without cost to the child's parents.

Note that P.L. 94–142 does not refer to gifted and talented children.

Education of exceptional students is expensive. The law was designed to back up its mandate for free, appropriate public education by providing federal funds to help state education departments and local school districts meet the additional costs of educating handicapped children (many of whom had not previously been served by public schools). States and local school districts are required to pay at least the amount of money that is spent to educate a nonhandicapped child, and Congress intended that approximately 40% of the total cost of educating each handicapped child would be covered by federal funds. Many state and local educational administrators, however, contend that the federal financial assistance for the education of handicapped students has not been sufficient and that their schools are hard-pressed to meet the costs of educating exceptional children. This problem is particularly serious today, when many school districts are experiencing severe financial difficulties.

P.L. 94–142 is directed primarily at the states, which are responsible for providing education to their citizens. To receive financial assistance from the federal government to aid in educating handicapped students, each state must ensure that its local school districts comply with the law and

☐ locate and identify all children who have handicaps, evaluate their educational needs, and determine whether those needs are being met

☐ develop an individualized education program (IEP) for every handicapped child in the state

☐ submit to the federal government a state plan for the education of handicapped children and revise the state plan yearly

☐ describe the means by which handicapped children will be identified and referred for diagnosis

☐ avoid using racially or culturally discriminatory testing and evaluation procedures in placing handicapped children; administer tests in the child's native language

☐ protect the rights of handicapped children and their parents by ensuring due process, confidentiality of records, and parental involvement in educational planning and placement decisions

☐ provide a comprehensive system for personnel development, including in-service training programs for regular education teachers, special education teachers, school administrators, and other support personnel

☐ educate handicapped and nonhandicapped children together to the maximum extent that is appropriate. Handicapped children are to be placed in special classes or separate schools only when education cannot be achieved satisfactorily in the regular classroom, even with special aids and services.

The Least Restrictive Environment

P.L. 94–142 supports each handicapped child's right to be educated in the **least restrictive environment** (LRE). It stipulates that

> to the maximum extent appropriate, handicapped children, including children in public or private institutions or other care facilities, are educated with children who are not handicapped, and that special classes, separate schooling, or other removal of handicapped children from the regular educational environment occurs only when the nature or severity of the handicap is such that education in regular classes with the use of supplementary aids and services cannot be achieved satisfactorily. . . . (Section 612(5)B of P.L. 94–142)

As Bliton and Schroeder (1986) explain, if we expect students to live and work in a heterogeneous society, we must prepare them by first integrating them in schools—each school, in a sense, becomes a microcosm of the community. Thus, the least restrictive environment is considered to be the setting that most closely parallels a regular school program and also meets the child's special educational needs. Conversely, the most restrictive environment is the setting that is farthest removed from a regular public school program. A child educated at home or in a hospital, for example, would have little or no opportunity to interact with nonhandicapped children.

The least restrictive environment is a relative concept, of course. The LRE for one child might be inappropriate for another. Since the passage of P.L. 94–142, there have been many differences of opinion over which type of setting is least restrictive and most appropriate for handicapped students. Even though a few educators, parents, and lawyers consider *any* decision to place a handicapped child in a special class or school to be overly restrictive, most recognize that a regular class placement can be restrictive and inappropriate if the child's instructional and social needs are not adequately met. It is also generally accepted that there are wide individual differences among children and that there can be more than one "best" way of providing appropriate educational services to an exceptional child. As Taylor, Biklen, and Searl (1986) observe, decisions concerning a child's educational program are based on a consideration of that child's needs. Not all children with the same disability should be placed in the same setting; the goal, instead, is to find an appropriate LRE for each child.

Current interpretation of the least restrictive environment, based on recent court cases, is that a child should be removed from the regular school program only to the extent that there is clear evidence that this removal is necessary for that child to receive appropriate educational services. The child's parents must be properly informed if removal from the regular classroom is being considered so that they can either consent or object to the removal and can present additional information if they wish. No removal from the regular school program should be regarded as permanent; there should be a plan for returning the child to as normal a setting as possible, as

Successful integration of students with handicaps into the academic and social life of the regular classroom can be accomplished in a variety of ways. One proven and increasingly popular method is peer tutoring. See pages 47–48 for a description of a classwide peer tutoring system in which handicapped and nonhandicapped students help teach one another.

To meet the educational needs of exceptional children, school districts must develop a wide range of placement and service options. Together these alternatives are often referred to as a "continuum of services," a concept presented later in this chapter.

The least restrictive environment for Sebine is the regular classroom, supplemented by individualized instruction in a resource room.

soon as certain needs or conditions are met. Each handicapped child, thus, must have access to educational experiences appropriate to that child's special needs and as similar as possible to those that a nonhandicapped child would have.

Other Provisions of P.L. 94–142

Two priorities are set forth in P.L. 94–142 for the expenditure of funds to educate handicapped children. The first priority is given to those handicapped children currently unserved by an educational program of any kind. The second priority is given to those children who are currently inadequately served. Many previously unserved and inadequately served children are those with severe and multiple handicaps; many have been kept at home or in institutions. An especially high priority is given to unserved and inadequately served children with severe disabilities.

P.L. 94–142 also stipulates that, in cases where appropriate education cannot be provided in the public schools, handicapped children may be placed in private school programs at no cost to their parents. This has proven to be a particularly controversial aspect of the law. Parents and school officials have frequently disagreed over whether private school placement, at public expense, is the most appropriate way of meeting the needs of an exceptional child.

Handicapped children are sometimes prevented from attending regular schools by circumstances other than their educational performance. A child who uses a wheelchair, for example, may require a specially equipped school bus. A child with special health problems may need to be given medication several times a day. The law calls for schools to provide any *related services*—such as special transportation, counseling, physical therapy, and other supportive assistance—that a handicapped child may need in order to benefit from special education. This provision has also been highly controversial, with much disagreement over what kind of related services are necessary and reasonable for the schools to provide and what services should be the responsibility of the child's parents.

What Effects Has the Law Had?

P.L. 94–142 was enacted more than a decade ago. Since then there has been a steady increase in the number of exceptional children identified and served in public educational programs. As noted in chapter 1, the U.S. Department of Education (1986) reports that more than 4 million handicapped students are currently receiving special education services, that two-thirds of them are at least partially integrated into regular classes, and that only about 7% of the children with handicaps now receive their education outside regular school buildings. There has been an especially rapid increase in the number of adolescents and young adults with disabilities who have recently been provided special education services.

As Turnbull and Turnbull (1986) observe, P.L. 94–142 has had far-reaching effects: "The student is no longer required to fit the school, but the school is required to fit the student" (p. 183). Schools today provide far more than academic training. In effect, they have become diversified agencies offering such services as medical support, physical therapy, vocational training, parent counseling, recreation, special transportation, and in-service education for staff members. In place of the once-prevalent practice of excluding children with handicaps from programs, schools now seek the most appropriate ways of including them. The schools' commitment to provide wide-ranging services to children from different backgrounds and with different characteristics is a highly complex and ambitious one. Jellinek (1986) calls for citizens to support schools in this effort by allocating the necessary funds so that schools may "implement that commitment by carefully weaving a fabric of services that have a demonstrable benefit for children with special needs" (p. xvii).

Legal Challenges Based on P.L. 94–142

Although P.L. 94–142 has resulted in dramatic increases in the numbers of students receiving special education services and in an increased recognition of the legal rights of exceptional children and their families, it has also brought about an ever-increasing number of disputes concerning the education of handicapped students. Thousands of due process hearings and numerous court cases have been brought about by parents and other advocates; as Gluckman (1986) puts it, there has been "a constant parade of cases marching through the federal district courts to the U.S. Courts of Appeal, and even to the U.S. Supreme Court" (p. v). According to another observer, "Most of these cases involve merely factual disputes over whether the public school is capable of providing a free appropriate education" (Murphy, 1986, p. 86). Due process hearings and court cases often place parents and schools in confrontations, one against the other; and they are typically expensive and time-consuming for all parties involved.

Few generalities can be made regarding the ways that judges and courts have resolved the various legal challenges based on P.L. 94–142. There have been many different interpretations of such terms as *free, appropriate education* and *least restrictive environment.* In the view of many parents, educators, judges, and attorneys, the law uses these terms repeatedly but does not define them with sufficient clarity. Thus, the questions of what is appropriate and least restrictive for a particular handicapped child and whether a public school district should be compelled to provide a certain

CLASSWIDE PEER TUTORING: INTEGRATING HANDICAPPED CHILDREN INTO THE REGULAR CLASSROOM

Including a handicapped child in classwide academic activities can present a difficult challenge. The regular classroom teacher is expected to deliver individualized instruction to the handicapped student, maintain effective programming for the rest of the class, and help the mainstreamed child become socially integrated into the classroom. One method that has been used successfully to individualize instruction for handicapped students without requiring them to leave the regular classroom is in-class tutoring. Certified tutors, classroom aides, parent and grandparent volunteers, and older students have all served as effective in-class tutors for handicapped children. However, obtaining extra adult help or out-of-class students as tutors on a regular basis is frequently a problem.

An often-untapped and always-available source of tutoring help exists in every classroom—the students themselves. Although the idea of peer tutoring (same-age classmates teaching one another) is not new (Lancaster, 1806), it has recently become the focus of renewed interest and research. As peer tutoring is typically implemented, a few high-achieving students are assigned to tutor students who have not mastered a particular skill, and the handicapped or low-achieving student is singled out for special help. By contrast, a *classwide* peer tutoring system allows the handicapped student to become a full participant in an ongoing whole-class activity. Direct, individualized instruction is provided to *every* student in the class, and social interactions between handicapped and non-handicapped classmates are encouraged. One classwide peer tutoring program that has been developed for teaching basic reading and math skills in the primary grades is described here.

Every student in the class has a tutoring folder containing 10 flash cards in a "GO" pocket (see page 48). Each card has one word (sound or math fact) to be taught to the child's partner. Thus, children serve as both tutor and student each day. When in the role of student, each child practices words from an individualized list of new words determined by a teacher-given pretest.

TUTOR HUDDLE

The daily peer tutoring session begins with the students getting their folders and participating in a 5-minute tutor huddle with two or three other tutors. (See the photo below.) The children take turns presenting and orally reading the sight words they will shortly be responsible for teaching to their partners. (Meanwhile, their partners are in other tutor huddles working on the words they will soon be teaching.) Fellow tutors confirm correct responses by saying "Yes" and try to help identify words a tutor doesn't know. The teacher circulates around the room, helping tutor huddles that cannot identify or agree upon a given word.

PRACTICE

After the tutor huddles, partners join one another to practice their words. One child begins in the role of tutor and presents the word cards as many

Tutor huddle.

times as possible during the 5-minute practice period. Tutors are trained to praise their students from time to time for correct responses. When a student makes an error, the tutor says, "Try again." If the student still does not read the word correctly, the tutor says, "The word is *tree;* say *tree.*" A timer signals the end of the first practice period, and the partners switch roles.

TESTING

After the second practice period, roles are again reversed, and the first tutor tests her partner by presenting each sight word once, providing no prompts or cues. Words the student reads correctly are placed in one pile, and words missed in another. Roles are then switched again, and the first tutor is now tested on the words she practiced. The peer tutoring session ends with the tutors marking on the animal chart the number of words said correctly by their partners during the test and praising one another for their good work. When a child correctly reads a word on the test for three consecutive sessions, that word is considered learned and is moved to the folder's STOP pocket. When all 10 words have been learned, a new set of words is placed in the GO pocket.

RESULTS

This peer tutoring system was originally developed and evaluated over a 5-month period in a first-grade classroom of 28 children. The class included one learning disabled boy and one mentally re-

tarded girl, both of whom attended a special education resource room for part of the school day. Results showed that all children in the classroom learned sight words at a rapid, consistent pace (Heward, Heron, & Cooke, 1982). The children also retained the words they had taught one another. The class average on 10-word review tests given 1 week after each set of words was learned was 8.9 words correct. Of particular interest was the performance of the two handicapped children in the class. The learning disabled boy functioned successfully both as a student and as a tutor. Although the mentally retarded child did not serve as a tutor, she participated as a student, learning at the rate of almost one new word each day. Her sight word vocabulary increased from a pretest score of 4 to a total of 51 words by the end of the study (Cooke, Heron, Heward, & Test, 1982). She, too, remembered the words she had learned, averaging 8.7 words correct out of a possible 10 on the 1-week review tests. And both she and her tutor enjoyed the daily sessions. When the long program ended, her tutor wrote, "I like peer tutoring. I liked my student vary [sic] much." The positive social interactions of a classwide peer tutoring program such as this one may, in the long run, prove to be of equal or even greater benefit to the children involved than the actual learning gains themselves.

This classwide peer tutoring system has been replicated with both sight words and math facts in many primary classrooms. Interested readers may obtain a detailed description of the peer tutoring system by writing William L. Heward, College of Education, Ohio State University, Columbus, OH 43210.

service are often decided by judges and courts, based on their consideration of the evidence presented to them.

Some cases have resulted from parents' protesting the suspension or expulsion of their handicapped child. The case of *Stuart v. Nappi* (1978), for example, concerned a high school student who spent much of her time wandering in the halls, even though she was assigned to special classes. The school sought to have the student expelled on disciplinary grounds because her conduct was considered detrimental to order in the school. The court agreed with the student's mother that expulsion would deny the student a free, appropriate public education, as called for in P.L. 94–142. In other cases, however, the expulsion or suspension of handicapped students has been upheld if the school could show that the grounds for expulsion were not related to the student's disability.

Most public school programs operate for approximately 180 school days each year. Parents and educators have argued that for some handicapped children, particularly those with severe and multiple disabilities, a 180-day school year is not sufficient to meet their needs. In the case of *Armstrong v. Kline* (1979), the parents of five severely handicapped students claimed that their children tended to regress during the usual breaks in the school year and called on the schools to provide a period of instruction longer than 180 days. The court agreed and ordered the schools to extend the school year for these students. Several states and local districts now provide year-round educational programs for some handicapped students, but there are no clear and universally accepted guidelines regarding which students are entitled to free public education for a longer-than-usual school year.

The first case based on P.L. 94–142 to reach the U.S. Supreme Court was *Rowley* v. *Hendrick Hudson School District* (1982). The parents of a fourth-grade deaf student who attended regular classes requested that the school provide a sign-language interpreter to accompany the child in all of her classes. The school had provided several special services for this student but contended that she did not require a full-time interpreter. They felt, in fact, that an interpreter might hinder the child's interactions with her teacher and peers. It was also noted that this service would cost the school district as much as $25,000 per year. The Supreme Court ruled that the child, who was doing well in school without an interpreter, was receiving an adequate education and that the school district could not be compelled to hire a full-time interpreter.

The *Rowley* case marked the first time a deaf attorney had ever argued a case before the U.S. Supreme Court.

The second P.L. 94–142 case to reach the Supreme Court was *Irving Independent School District v. Tatro* (1984). In this case the Court decided that a school district was obligated to provide catheterization and other related medical services to enable a young child with physical impairments to attend school (see chapter 9 for further discussion of this case).

No clear direction has emerged from these and other recent court cases based on P.L. 94–142. Challenges to existing services and differing views on whether a particular program is appropriate or least restrictive are certain to continue. The high costs of providing special education and related services, although clearly not a valid basis for excluding handicapped students, will likely be increasingly taken into consideration by judges and courts as they determine what schools may reasonably be expected to do. In Kauffman's (1985) words, "One of the problems we are going to have to resolve in the next decade or so is what the limits of special education are, where it stops" (p. 14). Some observers predict a lack of further expansion of related services for handicapped children, but others are more optimistic. H. R. Turnbull (1986a), for example, notes that although the Supreme Court decided against the provision of related services in the *Rowley* case and in favor of them in the *Tatro* case, the decisions are consistent: the Court recognized the need for integration of handicapped children with nonhandicapped children in both cases and kept the student's individualized education program as "the focal point of appropriateness" (p. 351). Although some requests will be granted by the courts in the future and others denied, it is now a well-established principle that each handicapped student is entitled to a personalized program of instruction and supportive services that will enable him to benefit from an education in as integrated a setting as possible.

1986 Amendments to P.L. 94–142

Like other comprehensive federal laws, P.L. 94–142 periodically undergoes reauthorization and amendment in response to changing circumstances. It is important to note that Congress allocates funds to each state on a yearly basis, to assist it in implementing the law's goals and policies. Each state then directs much of the money it receives from the federal government to local school districts for providing services to handicapped students. Obviously, laws and regulations calling for special education would be of limited value if the schools lacked the necessary financial resources.

Services to Handicapped Infants and Toddlers

A significant series of changes to P.L. 94–142 occurred in 1986 with the passage of Public Law 99–457, officially known as the Education of the Handicapped Act Amendments of 1986. P.L. 99–457 emphasizes the provision of special education services to handicapped infants and toddlers; that is, children from birth through age 2 who need early intervention services because they are experiencing developmental delays or because they have a diagnosed physical or mental impairment with a high probability of resulting in developmental delays. The law states that Congress has found "an urgent and substantial need" to

(1) enhance the development of handicapped infants and toddlers and to minimize their potential for developmental delay,
(2) reduce the educational costs to our society, including our Nation's schools, by minimizing the need for special education and related services after handicapped infants and toddlers reach school age,
(3) iminimize the likelihood of institutionalization of handicapped individuals and maximize their potential for independent living in society, and
(4) enhance the capacity of families to meet the special needs of their infants and toddlers with handicaps. (P.L. 99–457, Sec. 1471)

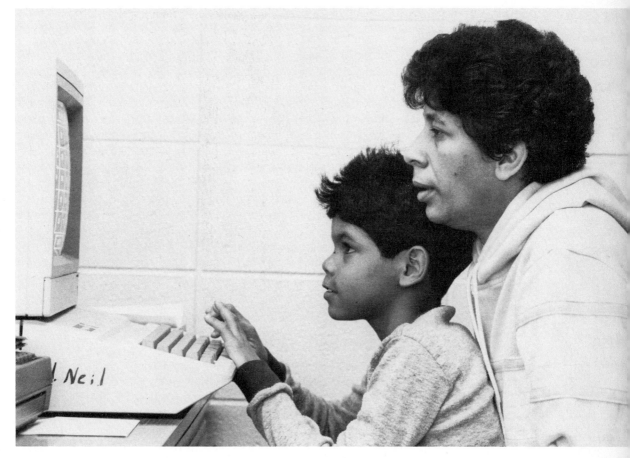

An appropriate education for Manuel, who is deaf, requires specially trained teachers and related services.

Rather than mandating special services for this population, P.L. 99–457 encourages each state to "develop and implement a statewide, comprehensive, coordinated, multidisciplinary, interagency program of early intervention services for handicapped infants and toddlers and their families." The encouragement is in the form of a gradually increasing amount of federal money to be awarded to states that agree to identify and serve all handicapped infants and toddlers. By the 1990–91 school year only those states that have developed a comprehensive service delivery system for handicapped children from birth through age 2 will be eligible to receive federal grants for handicapped infants and toddlers. Various agencies will be required to work together in providing such services as medical and educational assessment, physical therapy, speech and language intervention, and parent counseling and training. Early intervention services will need to be coordinated, and an **individualized family services plan** is to be written by a multidisciplinary team that includes the child's parents.

Services to Handicapped Preschool Children

Noting that more than 20% of handicapped preschool children (aged 3 through 5) were still not receiving appropriate services and that more than 30 states and territories still did not require preschool services for all of their handicapped preschoolers, Congress also included provisions in P.L. 99–457 to expand services for this segment of the population. By the 1990–91 school year a state must serve all handicapped preschool children fully—that is, with the same services and protections available to school-age children—or lose all future federal funds for preschoolers with handicaps. A formula for awarding money to each state, based on the number of handicapped preschool children identified and served, is included in P.L. 99–457.

In light of these important amendments to P.L. 94–142, it seems certain that there will be a continuing expansion of services to infants, toddlers, and preschool children with special needs. By the time most handicapped children reach the traditional school age of 5 or 6, they and their families may well have already received needed services. More and more schools will find it necessary to work with parents and other agencies in helping these children make a successful transition into elementary school.

RELATED LEGISLATION

Section 504

Another important law that extends civil rights to people with disabilities is Section 504 of the Rehabilitation Act of 1973 (actually adopted in 1977). This regulation states, in part, that "no otherwise qualified handicapped individual shall, solely by reason of his handicap, be excluded from the participation in, be denied the benefits of, or be subjected to discrimination in any program or activity receiving federal financial assistance." This law, worded in language almost identical to that of the Civil Rights Act of 1964 (which prohibited discrimination based on race, color, or national origin), promises to expand opportunities to handicapped children and adults in education, employment, and various other settings. It calls for the provision of "auxiliary aids for students with impaired sensory, manual, or speaking skills"—for example, readers for blind students, interpreters for deaf students, and people to assist physically disabled students in moving from place to place. This requirement does not mean that schools, colleges, and employers must have *all* such aids available at *all* times; it simply demands that no handicapped person may be excluded from a program because of the lack of an appropriate aid. Section 504 is also expected to increase the number of handicapped people employed as teachers in public schools.

Section 504 is not a federal grant program; unlike P.L. 94–142 and P.L. 99–457, it does not provide any federal money to assist people with handicaps. Rather, as Johnson (1986) points out, it "imposes a duty on every recipient of federal funds not to discriminate against handicapped persons" (p. 8). This, of course, includes public school districts, for virtually all of them receive federal support. Most colleges and universities are also affected; even in a private institution many students receive federal financial aid. The Office of Civil Rights conducts periodic compliance reviews and acts on complaints when parents, disabled individuals, or others contend that a school district is violating Section 504. Johnson notes that the Office of Civil Rights has recently been especially interested in ensuring that local public schools are not discriminating against disabled persons in their employment practices, plans for new construction, and accessibility to school buildings and facilities.

Can you identify any Section 504 related activities that have taken place at your college or university?

Architectural accessibility for students, teachers, and others with physical and sensory impairments is, of course, an important feature of Section 504. However, this law does not call for a completely barrier-free environment. The emphasis is placed on accessibility to programs, not on the physical modification of all existing structures. If a chemistry class, for example, is required for a premedical program of study, a college might make this program accessible to a physically disabled student by reassigning the class to an accessible location or by providing assistance to the student in traveling to an otherwise inaccessible location. All sections of all courses need not be made accessible, but a college should not segregate handicapped students by assigning them all to a particular section, regardless of disability. Like P.L. 94–142, Section 504 calls for nondiscriminatory placement in the "most integrated setting appropriate" and has served as the basis for many court cases over alleged discrimination against disabled individuals, particularly in their right to employment.

Gifted and Talented Children

Although P.L. 94–142 and Section 504 do not specifically apply to gifted and talented children, the specialized needs of this population have also been addressed in federal legislation. Public Law 95–561, the Gifted and Talented Children's Education Act of 1978, provides financial incentives for state and local education agencies to develop programs for their gifted and talented students. P.L. 95–561 provides for the identification of gifted and talented children and includes special procedures for identifying and educating those from disadvantaged backgrounds. The law makes funding available for in-service training programs, research, and other projects meeting the needs of gifted and talented students.

In 1982 the Education Consolidation Act phased out the federal Office of Gifted and Talented and merged gifted education with 29 other programs. Federal dollars to support these 30 different and wide-ranging education programs (K–12) are sent to the states in the form of block grants. Each state has the responsibility to determine what portion, if any, of the block grant funds will be used to support programs and services for students who are gifted and talented. There is no federal legislation that requires states to provide special education programs for gifted students. Nevertheless, Sisk (1984) found in a national survey that 47 states had appointed a state consultant or director of gifted programs. This is significant when compared to Marland's (1972) earlier report that only 10 state departments of education had a consultant for the gifted on their staff.

SPECIAL EDUCATION IN THE SCHOOLS
TODAY: BEYOND COMPLIANCE

Maynard Reynolds (1978), an experienced and articulate special educator, offers the following observation on the implementation of P.L. 94–142:

> Without even trying, I have been shown at least six sets of transparencies, listened to endless audio cassettes on the requirements of Public Law 94–142, and I have been guided through several versions of "sure-fire" forms to satisfy all of the new regulations.
>
> What I see and hear seems well designed to keep teachers out of jail—to comply with the law, that is—but usually I sense little vision of how people might come together creatively to design environments for better learning and living by handicapped students. (p. 60)

Indeed, the creation of effective learning environments for exceptional students and their peers must involve far more than filling out forms and staying out of jail. Regular educators and special educators now find themselves confronted with countless new challenges and responsibilities; in effect, they are defining a new relationship with each other and with their students. Where children were formerly given a label and removed from the regular classroom, it is now increasingly recognized that exceptional children have special needs and the services are moving to the children.

Another well-known special educator, M. Stephen Lilly (1986), describes the current state of special education programs as "cumbersome and complex." Lilly contends that the barriers between general and special education are gradually being broken down and that, although supportive services are needed by many students who have difficulty in learning and behaving, "we need not and should not offer these services through special education. . . . A single coordinated system of service delivery is preferable to the array of special programs currently offered in the schools" (p. 10).

See Heron and Harris (1987) for descriptions of consultation procedures that special educators can use in helping regular educators deliver needed services to students with handicaps.

Special education services are often provided in the form of consultation, continuing education, and support for the regular teacher. In the schools today special education may rightly be viewed as a *system* for the delivery of services to children with special needs, rather than a separate, specialized content area apart from regular education (Reynolds & Birch, 1982; Weintraub, 1986). The regular teacher who works with Sharon in her classroom; the physical therapist who consults with Sharon's teacher twice each week; and the resource room teacher who works directly with Sharon and communicates with the regular teacher—all are participating in the system that delivers special education services to Sharon.

Mainstreaming

The word **mainstreaming** has been popularly used to describe the process of integrating exceptional children into regular schools and classes. Much discussion and controversy and many misconceptions have arisen regarding whether all handicapped children must now attend regular classes—the so-called mainstream of our public school system. Some people view mainstreaming as placing all exceptional children into regular classrooms with no additional supportive services, whereas others have the idea that mainstreaming can mean completely segregated placement of handicapped children, as long as they interact with nonhandicapped peers in a few activities (perhaps at lunch or on the playground). Many parents have strongly supported the placement of their exceptional children in regular classes; others have resisted it just as strongly, feeling that the regular classroom does not offer the intense, individualized education that their children need.

Interestingly, P.L. 94–142, which has generated most of the discussion and debate, does not even mention the word *mainstreaming*. What the law does call for is the education of the handicapped child in the least restrictive appropriate educational setting, removed no further than necessary from the regular public school program. As Turnbull and Turnbull (1986) note, the least restrictive environment principle prevents the unwarranted segregation of students with disabilities from their nondisabled peers. Heron and Skinner (1981) describe the least restrictive environment as

> that educational setting which maximizes the . . . student's opportunity to respond and achieve, permits the regular education teacher to interact proportionally with all the students in the classroom, and fosters acceptable social relations between non-handicapped and [handicapped] students. (p. 116)

P.L. 94–142 does not advocate the placement of all handicapped children in regular classes, call for handicapped children to remain in regular classes without the supportive services they need, or suggest that regular teachers should educate handicapped students without help from special educators and other specialists. It does, however, specifically call for regular and special educators to cooperate in providing an equal educational opportunity to exceptional students.

As Gresham (1982) points out, simply placing a handicapped child in a regular classroom does not mean that the child will learn and behave appropriately or that she will be socially accepted by nonhandicapped children. It is important for special educators to teach appropriate social skills and behavior to the handicapped child and to educate nonhandicapped children about the differences in their handicapped classmates. But these challenges should not mean that handicapped children are denied the right to participate in a regular classroom for all or part of the school day. Becky's main educational handicap, for example, is that she has very limited vision. It would be overly restrictive to send Becky to a residential school 200 miles from her home, where she could interact only with other visually impaired children (though this would probably have been done not too long ago). Her needs may well be met in the regular public school, if the school can provide special materials and tutoring for Becky and consultation for her regular teacher.

Sapon-Shevin (1978) suggests that mainstreaming not be interpreted to mean "changing the special child so that he will fit back into the unchanged regular classroom, but rather as changing the nature of the regular classroom so that it is more accommodating to all children" (p. 120). As Biklen (1985) observes, there is a deeper concept embedded in the least restrictive environment principle.

> The question of whether or not to promote mainstreaming is not essentially a question for science. It is a moral question. It is a goal, indeed a value, we decide to pursue or reject on the basis of what we want our society to look like. (p. 3)

Page 58 offers a checklist of important factors that the special educator should consider in preparing a handicapped student, the regular class teacher, and others for the student's return to a regular classroom placement.

Heron (1978) offers a decision-making model for analyzing problems and adapting the regular classroom environment to allow handicapped children to participate. This model could be used when a problem involving an exceptional child develops within the regular classroom in which he has been placed. Figure 2.2 shows the sequence of alternatives. The first step is to define the problem. For example, is the student having difficulty in academic or social skills? Is he having difficulty with his normal peers? Is the classroom teacher having problems interacting with the exceptional student?

Given that the problem can be reasonably determined, the second step is to decide whether the primary focus of intervention should be directed toward child behavior or teacher behavior. If the focus is to be the child's behavior, then the strategies listed under "exceptional child" should be used. If an intervention is needed with the nonhandicapped children in the classroom, then those options listed under "normal child" should be considered. The same procedure would apply if the focus of the intervention was to be directed toward teacher behavior.

The alternatives recommended under each category are arranged in a hierarchy. That is, those options requiring the least amount of teacher time or effort are listed first, and those requiring more teacher time or effort follow. The alternatives are based on three criteria: (1) their demonstrated effectiveness in previous studies, (2) their applicability to a wide range of behaviors, and (3) the likelihood that their effects will endure over time.

These strategies are already familiar to many regular education teachers, supervisors, and principals, so the implementation of this model should not require extensive retraining. Implementation of Heron's model would enable school personnel at all levels to use their current teaching and management skills more efficiently and systematically.

A Continuum of Services

A wide variety of special assistance may be needed from time to time by exceptional children, their teachers, and their families. Today, most schools make a sincere effort to provide a *continuum of services*—that is, a range of different placement and service options that can be offered to meet students' needs. The continuum is often symbolically depicted as a pyramid, with placements ranging from least restrictive (regular classroom placement) at the bottom to most restrictive (special schools or institutions for handicapped children) at the top. The fact that the pyramid is widest at the bottom indicates that the greatest number of exceptional children can be accommodated in regular classrooms, and the number of children who require more restrictive, intensive, and specialized placements gets smaller as we move up. As we have already noted, most children who are considered handicapped have mild or moderate disabilities. The number of mildly mentally retarded children, for example, is far greater than those who are severely retarded. Likewise, children with mild or moderate behavior disorders greatly outnumber those with severe behavior disorders. As the severity of problems increases, the need for more specialized services also increases, but the number of students involved decreases.

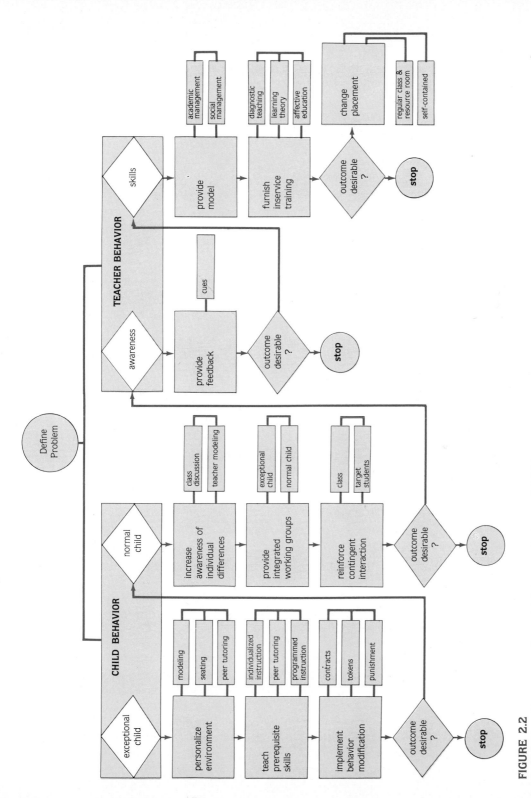

FIGURE 2.2

A decision-making process for maintaining a mainstreamed child in the regular classroom.

Source: From ''Maintaining the Mainstreamed Child in the Regular Classroom: The Decision-Making Process'' by T. E. Heron, 1978, *Journal of Learning Disabilities, 11*(4), p. 213. Copyright 1978 by Professional Press, Inc. Reprinted by special permission of Professional Press, Inc.

PREPARING FOR MAINSTREAMING: A SPECIAL TEACHER'S CHECKLIST

Teachers and parents must be committed to carrying out the least restrictive alternative concept for handicapped children. If handicapped individuals are ever to be fully accepted in our society, this integration should occur as early and widely as possible. Educators should be willing to put forth their best efforts to make a regular class experience rewarding and enriching for handicapped students. Special class teachers can do much to make these mainstreaming successes happen.

The key to a successful mainstreaming experience is preparation. The checklist that follows can serve as a guide for the special class teacher in preparing not only the handicapped student, but also the other people who must support the mainstreaming effort. Before placing a handicapped student in a mainstreamed setting, the teacher should examine and work on each element of the checklist until most, if not all, of the "yes" boxes can be checked. For more information on each item in the checklist see Dardig (1981) cited in the source note that follows.

1. Handicapped student:
Yes No
- ☐ ☐ Is familiar with rules and routine of the regular classroom?
- ☐ ☐ Follows verbal and written directions used in the regular classroom?
- ☐ ☐ Remains on-task for adequate time periods?
- ☐ ☐ Has expressed a desire to participate in the regular class setting?
- ☐ ☐ Reacts appropriately to teasing, questions, criticism, etc.?
- ☐ ☐ Student's IEP objectives match instructional objectives in regular class?

2. Regular class teacher:
Yes No
- ☐ ☐ Has been given rationale for mainstreaming activities and asked to cooperate?
- ☐ ☐ Has information about handicapped student's needs, present skills, and current learning objectives?
- ☐ ☐ Has been provided with special materials and/or support services as needed?
- ☐ ☐ Has prepared class for mainstreaming?
- ☐ ☐ Has acquired special helping skills if necessary?
- ☐ ☐ Will be monitored regularly to identify any problems that arise?

3. Nonhandicapped peers:
Yes No
- ☐ ☐ Have been informed about handicapped student's participation and about handicapping condition (if appropriate) with the opportunity to ask questions?
- ☐ ☐ Have been asked for their cooperation and friendship toward handicapped student?
- ☐ ☐ Have learned helping skills and praising behaviors?

4. Handicapped student's parents:
Yes No
- ☐ ☐ Have received verbal or written information about mainstreaming situation?
- ☐ ☐ Have been asked to praise and encourage child's progress in regular and special class?

5. Nonhandicapped students' parents:
Yes No
- ☐ ☐ Have been informed about mainstreaming activities at PTA meeting, conferences, or through other vehicle, and asked for their cooperation?

6. School administrator:
Yes No
- ☐ ☐ Has been informed about specifics of mainstreaming activities?
- ☐ ☐ Has indicated specific steps she or he will take to encourage and support these activities?

Source: Adapted from "Helping Teachers Integrate Handicapped Students into the Regular Classroom" by J. C. Dardig, 1981, *Educational Horizons, 59*, pp. 124–130. Reprinted by permission.

It is worth noting that, of the seven levels of service depicted in Figure 2.3, the first five are generally available in regular public school buildings. Children at Levels 1 through 4 attend regular classes with their nonhandicapped peers; supportive help is given by special teachers who provide consultation to the children's regular teachers or in special resource rooms. A **resource room** usually has a specially trained teacher who provides instruction to exceptional students for part of the school day, either individually or in small groups. Children at Level 5, who require full-time placement in a special **self-contained class,** are with other exceptional children for all or most of the school day. But they may still have the opportunity to interact with nonhandicapped children at certain times, such as during recess or on the bus to school. Although this alternative provides less integration than the regular classroom, it provides much more opportunity for interaction than placement in a residential institution or a special school for handicapped children. Self-contained classes in regular school buildings are gaining acceptance as an appropriate placement for many children with severe and multiple disabilities.

Again, recall that each child must be placed in the least restrictive environment in which he or she can succeed.

Pages 73–74 describe three placement options along the continuum of services, as they are experienced by three different exceptional students.

Level 7: Specialized facilities—Nonpublic school
Pupil needs more protective or more intensive education setting than can be provided in public schools.
(Day or residential program)

Level 6: Special school
Pupil receives prescribed program under the direction of a specially trained staff in a specially designed facility within the public school system. (Day program)

Level 5: Full-time special class
Pupil receives prescribed program under the direction of a special class teacher.

Level 4: Regular classroom and resource room
Pupil receives prescribed program under the direction of the regular classroom teacher; in addition he or she spends part time in a specially staffed and equipped resource room.

Level 3: Regular classroom with supplementary instruction and services
Pupil receives prescribed program under the direction of the regular classroom teacher; in addition he or she receives supplementary instruction or service from an itinerant or school-based specialist.

Level 2: Regular classroom with consultation to teacher
Pupil receives prescribed program under the direction of regular classroom teacher who is supported by on-going consultation from specialists.

Level 1: Regular classroom
Pupil receives prescribed programs under the direction of the regular classroom teacher.

most · *least* · *severity of problems* · *number of pupils* · *least* · *most*

FIGURE 2.3
Continuum of educational services.
Source: From Montgomery County Public Schools, Rockville, MD. Reprinted by permission.

Reading instruction for these students with learning disabilities often involves small-group activities in the resource room.

The placement of an exceptional child at any level on the continuum of services should not be regarded as permanent. The child's specific goals and objectives should be periodically reviewed by teachers, parents, and administrators. New placement decisions can be made; in fact, the continuum concept is intended to be flexible, with children moving from one placement to another as dictated by their current educational needs. A child may be placed in a less integrated setting for a limited time; then, when a performance review shows that certain goals have been achieved, the child should return to a more normalized setting as soon as possible. The continuum concept requires that several options be available to handicapped children in order to meet their current needs.

The Team Approach

Many students need services from several different disciplines. One survey of handicapped preschool children in a noncategorical public school program found that, of the 81 children receiving services, 56 were served by four or more professionals, 16 were served by three professionals, and 9 were served by two professionals. No child was served by only one professional (Northcott & Erickson, 1977). In view of the recent expansion of services to handicapped infants, toddlers, and preschool children under P.L. 99–457 and the ongoing concern for planning transitional services for young adults after they leave programs of special education, the practice of involving professional and paraprofessional personnel as a team to assess students and plan cooperatively to meet their diverse needs is sure to gain even wider acceptance. Henderson (1986) describes the functioning of a "building planning and placement team," a group of full-time and part-time professionals assigned to a given school building to diagnose special needs, deliver services, and review children's placements.

Although there are many variations of the team approach in terms of size and structure, each member of a team generally assumes certain clearly assigned responsibilities and recognizes the importance of learning from, contributing to, and interacting with the other members of the team. Many believe that the consensus and group decisions arising from a team's involvement provide a form of insurance against erroneous or arbitrary conclusions in the complex issues that face educators of exceptional students.

One study by Pfeiffer (1982) concluded that team decision making was generally consistent, effective, and superior to individual decision making in the placement of exceptional children. "A cooperative work group brings to bear on a complex task differing values as well as unique professional perspectives. This enhances the problem-solving effectiveness that is required" (p. 69) when determining the most appropriate educational program for an exceptional child.

Other potential advantages of the team approach have been summarized by Williamson (1978).

☐ The child need no longer be "splintered" into segments along disciplinary lines. An old saying described the handicapped child as giving "his hands to the occupational therapist, his legs to the physical therapist, and his brain to the teacher."
☐ There is opportunity for increased communication among team members.
☐ The child is encouraged to develop a trusting relationship with the professionals on the team. Usually, the child sees the same specialists over an extended period of time.
☐ The team approach is thought to be more cost-effective, because professionals can share their expertise with each other and serve a greater number of children through consultation.

An effective interdisciplinary team, with all members sharing their information and skills, can do much to provide an appropriate and consistent educational program for exceptional children and to increase the individual effectiveness of each of its members. Of course, not all of these advantages are realized in all cases. It is sometimes difficult for members of an interdisciplinary team to agree on what learning objectives are most important for the child. In response to this problem Dardig and Heward (1981b) have developed a six-step procedure that can be used by an IEP planning team to help set priorities for a child's learning goals while giving equal consideration to each member's input. Team members must learn to put aside professional rivalries and work for the benefit of each handicapped child.

Assessment and Educational Planning

For many years handicapped students were tested largely to exclude them from public school programs. Charles may have been denied entrance into his local school, for example, if he obtained a score below 50 on an IQ test, or if he was unable to follow verbal directions, or if he required assistance in using the toilet. Assessment was typically done in a special testing room, often by an examiner who was unfamiliar with the child and who had had little or no contact with the child's parents or teachers. The examiner than interpreted the results of the tests, applied a label to the child, and ruled the child eligible or ineligible to remain in the public school program.

Today, assessment is a process of including a person on the basis of what she can do, rather than excluding a person because of what she cannot do. As Hammer (1978) observes, we must not limit assessment to the defining of disability (we probably already know that the child has some difficulty before assessment even begins) but should focus instead on finding ability. What can the child do? How and in what situation does he learn most effectively? What are some materials and techniques that appear to be appropriate? The answers to these and other questions can be of great value in planning a child's educational program. Assessment is virtually useless unless it leads to action, in the form of specific instruction, treatment, or other intervention given to the child.

Chapter 4 discusses specific types of instruments often used to assess children's learning problems.

Assessment is thus coming to be seen not as an isolated discipline, but as an inseparable part of the child's ongoing educational program. Today, assessment is often accomplished in natural settings, such as the child's regular classroom or home. There is generally less reliance on standardized tests that give numerical scores and predictions of children's potential, and more reliance on precise, structured observations of children's behavior. A teacher might, for example, count how many times Greg is out of his seat during a 10-minute period. A parent might observe that Jill is able to pick up small pieces of meat with a spoon but has difficulty using a fork. Observations like these, made over a period of time by people who are familiar with the child, can readily be translated into educational goals and objectives.

P.L. 94–142 reflects current concern for fair, appropriate, multifaceted assessment. The law specifically calls for certain safeguards, including

☐ evaluation that assesses the child's specific areas of educational need, not merely providing a single general intelligence quotient
☐ assessment to be made by a multidisciplinary team or group of persons
☐ assessment of all areas in which disability may be suspected (including vision, hearing, motor abilities, health, communication, and other appropriate areas)
☐ tests to be administered by trained personnel
☐ evaluation that does not discriminate against the child because of racial or cultural background or because the child speaks a language other than English
☐ a wide range of evaluation procedures, *never* using a single assessment as the sole criterion for determining the child's placement

Strichart and Lazarus (1986) observe that school psychologists, who have traditionally performed the majority of assessments in school settings, are now finding it necessary to broaden their skills to enable them to assess children with various special needs, including such disabilities as blindness, deafness, and severe behavior handicaps. The problems in finding appropriate ways of measuring children's abilities are complex, because relatively few reliable instruments exist for students with such disabilities. If specially designed tests cannot be found, psychologists frequently adapt existing test procedures to enable the child to respond appropriately. They may also find it useful to rely on the observations of teachers, parents, and others who regularly interact with the child in a variety of environments. The assessment of an exceptional child should never be limited to the psychologist's office or testing room.

Parents have the right to obtain an independent evaluation of their child by examiners of their choice from outside the school system. The results of any such independent evaluations must be considered along with the school's assessment in determining the child's program and placement. The outcome of any evaluation process should be to obtain information that will be useful to the student, the teachers, and the parents in planning activities that will enhance the child's learning and future development.

The Individualized Education Program (IEP)

Perhaps the most significant component of P.L. 94–142 (and certainly one of the most controversial) is the requirement that an individualized education program (IEP) be developed and maintained for every handicapped child. The law is specific in stating what an IEP must include and who is to take part in its formulation. Each IEP must be the product of the joint efforts of the members of a child study team, which must include at least (1) the child's teacher(s), (2) a representative of the local school district other than the child's teacher, (3) the child's parents or guardian, and (4) whenever appropriate, the child herself. Support staff such as physical educators or speech-language pathologists may also be involved in the IEP conference.

Although the formats used by different school districts vary, most IEPs include

1. a statement of the child's present levels of educational performance, including academic achievement, social adaptation, prevocational and vocational skills, psychomotor skills, and self-help skills
2. a statement of annual goals that describes the educational performance to be achieved by the end of the school year under the child's program
3. a statement of short-term instructional objectives presented in measurable, intermediate steps between the present level of educational performance and the annual goals
4. a statement of specific educational services needed by the child (determined without regard to the availability of services), including a description of
   a. all special education and related services needed to meet the unique needs of the child, including the physical education program
   b. any special instructional media and materials that are needed
5. the date when those services will begin and the length of time the services will be given
6. a description of the extent to which the child will participate in regular education programs

An IEP planning meeting.

7. objective criteria, evaluation procedures, and schedules of determining, at least annually, whether the short-term instructional objectives are being achieved
8. a justification for the type of educational placement the child will have
9. a list of the individuals who are responsible for implementing the individualized
   education program

   Ideally, the child's IEP is a system for spelling out where the child is, where he
should be going, how he will get there, how long it will take, and how to tell when
he has arrived (Bierly, 1978). The legal requirement of an IEP is new, but the principles of sound planning and systematic teaching are not. For many years regular and
special education teachers have been using assessment, short-range objectives leading
to long-range goals, and evaluation procedures in working with their students. "In
reality," state Hayden and Edgar (1978), "almost everything required for the IEP is
currently being done by competent teachers" (p. 67). Other special educators are more
critical, however. Of all the requirements of P.L. 94–142, contends Gallagher (1984),
the IEP is "probably the single most unpopular aspect of the law, not only because it

requires a great deal of work, but because the essence of the plan itself seems to have been lost in the mountains of paperwork" (p. 228).

Figure 2.4 shows one format for IEPs, but the format varies according to the needs of each child and the services provided. Some school districts now use computerized systems to keep track of a child's performance, goals, and evaluations (Brown, 1982). Although written forms are required, the IEP is not a legally binding contract.

FIGURE 2.4

Portions of a completed IEP (continued on page 66).

INDIVIDUAL EDUCATION PROGRAM

Date 11-25-87

(1) Student	(2) Committee	
		Initial
Name: Joe S.	Mr. Havlichek Principal	CH
School: Adams	Mrs. Snow Regular Teacher	GS
Grade: 5	Mr. Bigelow Counselor	CB
Current Placement: Regular Class Resource Room	Mr. Sheets Resource Teacher	RS
	Mrs. S. Parent	AS
Date of Birth: 10-1-76 Age: 11-1	IEP from 12-1-87 to 12-1-88	

(3) Present Level of Educational Functioning	(4) Annual Goal Statements	(5) Instructional Objectives	(6) Objective Criteria and Evaluation
<u>MATH</u> Strengths 1. Can successfully compute addition and subtraction problems to two places with regrouping and zeros. 2. Knows 100 basic multiplication facts. Weaknesses 1. Frequently makes computational errors on problems with which he has had experience. 2. Does not complete seatwork. Key Math total score of 2.1 Grade Equivalent	Joe will appy knowledge of regrouping in addition and renaming in subtraction to four-digit numbers.	1. When presented with addition problems of 3-digit numbers requiring two renamings, the student will compute the answer at a rate of one problem per minute and an accuracy of 90%. 2. When presented with subtraction problems of 3-digit numbers requiring two renamings, the student will compute the answer at a rate of one problem per minute with 90% accuracy. 3. When presented with addition problems of 4-digit numbers requiring three renamings, the student will compute the answer at a rate of one problem per minute and an accuracy of 90%. 4. When presented with subtraction problems of 4-digit numbers requiring three renamings, the student will compute the answer at a rate of one problem per minute with 90% accuracy.	Key Math (after 4 mos.) Teacher-made tests (weekly) Key Math (after 4 mos.) Teacher-made tests (weekly) 1 Key Math (after 4 mos.) Teacher-made tests (weekly)

FIGURE 2.4 *continued*

READING

Woodcock Reading Mastery Tests

	Grade Equivalent
Letter identification	3.0
Word identification	1.8
Word attack	2.0
Word comprehension	4.3

Joe's oral reading rate for reading material at his comfortable reading level will increase from 30 words per minute to 60 words per minute.

1. When presented with a list of 250 basic sight vocabulary words listed in order of difficulty and/or commonly taught, the student will correctly pronounce 200 of them by the end of the year.

2. When presented with a list of 37 direction words listed in order of difficulty and/or commonly taught, the student will correctly pronounce 24 of them.

3. When presented with a list of 40 words and phrases frequently seen on signs and listed in order of difficulty, the student will correctly pronounce 30 of them.

Brigance Diagnostic Inventory of Basic Skill (after 4 and 9 mos.) Teacher observation (daily)

Brigance Diagnostic Inventory of Basic Skill (after 4 and 9 mos.) Teacher observation (daily)

Brigance Diagnostic Inventory of Basic Skill (after 4 and 9 mos.) Teacher observation (daily)

SOCIAL EMOTIONAL

Strengths
1. Cooperates in group activities.

2. Attentive and cooperative in class.

Weaknesses
1. Reluctant participant on playground.

2. Makes derogatory comments about himself frequently during the school day.

3. Has few friends, is ignored by peers.

Joe will speak about himself in a positive manner.

Joe will participate with peers in small groups on the playground and in class.

1. In a one-to-one situation with the teacher Joe will talk about his strengths as a person for 5 min. a day.

2. In a one-to-one situation with the teacher Joe will state 5 strengths he possesses for 3 days in a row.

3. After a small group activity (3-4 students). Joe will tell the teacher 3 things he did well in the group.

4. After a small group activity Joe will tell the teacher 6 things he did well in the group.

5. In a small group activity Joe will ask a peer for help instead of asking an adult:
   a) With verbal reminders from an adult 70% of the time
   b) With nonverbal reminders 60% of the time
   c) With no signals 60% of the time

6. In a small group activity Joe will offer assistance to a peer.
   a) With verbal reminders from an adult 60% of the time
   b) With nonverbal reminders 50% of the time
   c) With no signals 50% of the time

Teacher observation (daily) for 15 days Anecdotal records (daily)

Anecdotal records (daily) 3 consecutive days

Anecdotal records (daily) 5 consecutive days

Anecdotal records (daily) 5 consecutive days

Teacher observation Data collected 30 min. a day, 3 days a week

Teacher observation Data collected 30 min. a day, 3 days a week

FIGURE 2.4 *continued*

(7) Educational Services to Be Provided

Services Required	Date Initiated	Duration of Service	Individual Responsible for the Service
Regular reading—adapted	12-1-87	12-1-88	Mrs. Jones
Resource room	12-1-87	12-1-88	Mrs. Green
Counselor consultant	12-1-87	12-1-88	Mr. Baskin
Monitoring diet and general health	12-1-87	12-1-88	Health Dept.—Mrs. Winger/ School Nurse—Ms. Allen
Dental examination	1-10-88	1-17-88	Health Dept.—Mrs. Winger
Counseling family	12-1-87	6-1-88	Mental Health Center—Mr. Sanford

Extent of time in the regular education program: 60% increasing to 80%
Justification of the educational placement:
It is felt that the structure of the resource room can best meet the goals stated for Joe, especially when coordinated with the regular classroom.

It is also felt that Joe could profit enormously from talking with a counselor. He needs someone with whom to talk and with whom he can share his feelings.

(8) I have had the opportunity to participate in the development of the Individual Education Program.
I agree with the Individual Education Program (✔)
I disagree with the Individual Education Program ( )

_____*Mrs. S.*_____

Parent's Signature

Source: From *Developing and Implementing Individualized Education Programs* by A. P. Turnbull, B. B. Strickland, and J. C. Brantley, (pp. 195, 198, 200, 203) 1982, Columbus, OH: Merrill. Reprinted by permission.

That is, a child's teacher and school cannot be prosecuted in the courts if the child does not achieve all the goals set forth in the IEP. Nevertheless, the teacher should be able to document that a conscientious and systematic effort was made to achieve those goals.

Each child's IEP must be reviewed, and revised if necessary, at least once each year. The child's parent or guardian must consent to the IEP and must receive a copy of the document. Figure 2.5 illustrates a format that one school district uses for its annual review of exceptional children's IEPs.

Some observers have asked, "If handicapped children must have IEPs, then why not extend this requirement to all children in the public schools?" Indeed, some states and local school districts now use individual educational planning with both handicapped and nonhandicapped students. Utah, for example, has adopted the requirement that an "individual education plan for the projected education program to be pursued by each student during membership in the school" be developed cooperatively by teachers, parents, and the student herself. It has reportedly led to increased conferences, improved career planning, and greater parental involvement (Robinson, 1982). Although some teachers view IEPs as an added burden of paperwork and some parents do not wish to become involved in the planning process, the IEP seems to be gaining acceptance. All children can benefit from the accurate specification of individual

For a detailed explanation of the development and implementation of IEPs, see Turnbull, Strickland, and Brantley (1982).

FIGURE 2.5

Sample of a form used for the annual review of a child's IEP.

ANNUAL REVIEW OF IEP AND PLACEMENT

Student _____Birth Date _____Date of Review _____

Description of student's current educational placement:

Annual Goals Met:	Annual Goals Not Met:

Recommendations of Review Team:

   A. Related Services Currently Provided

      Services to be continued: _____

      Services to be discontinued: _____

   B. New Related Services to be Implemented: _____

      _____

   C. Placement

      Continue in same placement next year, without modification

      Continue in same placement next year, with the following modifications: _____

      Change to different special education placement, as follows: _____

      Discontinue special education services

      Other placement recommendations (specify): _____

Additional comments and recommendations:

Members of Review Team _____

               _____

               _____

               _____

               _____

Parent or Guardian   _____

goals, periodic evaluation, parent involvement, and contributions from various disciplines that the IEP offers to exceptional children.

The IEP is an inescapable measure of accountability for teachers and schools. Whether a particular school or educational program is effective will be judged, to some extent, by how well it is able to help children meet the goals and objectives set forth in their IEPs. Like other professionals, teachers are being called on increasingly to demonstrate competent performance, and the IEP provides one way for them to do so. However, the IEP is much more than an accountability device. Its real benefits are improved planning (including planning for the student's needs after leaving school), consistency, regular evaluation, and clearer communication between parents, teachers, and others involved in providing services to the student.

Regular and Special Education: A New Relationship?

Although not all exceptional children attend regular classes, it is generally true that regular teachers are being expected to deal with a much wider variety of learning, behavioral, sensory, and physical differences among their students than was the case just a few years ago. Thus, the provision of **in-service training** for regular educators is an important (and sometimes overlooked) requirement of P.L. 94–142. Regular educators are understandably wary of having exceptional children placed in their classes when little or no training or support is provided. The role of regular teachers is already a demanding one; they do not want their classrooms to become any larger, especially if they perceive exceptional children as unmanageable. Regular classroom teachers are entitled to be involved in decisions about children who are placed in their classes and to be offered continuous consultation and other supportive services from special educators.

Today, special educators are often called on to provide training in the specialized techniques and materials that are to be used with exceptional children. Many school districts have set up cooperative relationships with universities, special education schools, and other facilities so that their regular teachers can become more familiar with the needs of exceptional students. Some states now require all regular elementary or secondary teachers to take certain courses in special education before they can be certified.

As Rauth (1980) points out in a report to the American Federation of Teachers, the most typical attitude of regular teachers is "a cautious acceptance of mainstreaming across the country." Most teachers want to see each exceptional child educated in the most suitable, least restrictive environment. But regular teachers tend to justifiably resent administrators who view mainstreaming as a way to cut costs and ultimately increase problems of class size, paperwork, and discipline by placing exceptional students in regular classes without adequate support.

The relationship between special education and regular education has been the subject of a good deal of recent debate and discussion. Stainback and Stainback (1984) have called for a merger of special and regular education, contending that the current dual system is inefficient and outdated: "It is time to stop developing criteria for who does or does not belong in the mainstream and instead turn the spotlight to increasing the capabilities of the regular school environment, the mainstream, to meet the needs of *all* students" (p. 110). Reynolds, Wang, and Walberg (1987) call for "the joining of demonstrably effective practices from special, compensatory, and general education to establish a general education system that is more inclusive and better serves all students, particularly those who require greater-than-usual educational support" (p. 394).

The idea of merging general and special education is by no means a universally popular one. Mesinger (1985) describes Stainback and Stainback as holding "a distinctly minority viewpoint" and explains, "I am reluctant to abandon special education as a system until I see *evidence* of a drastic improvement in regular educational teacher training and professional practice in the public schools" (p. 512). Similarly, Lieberman (1985) calls for special education to maintain its separate identity because, among other reasons, "in regular education, the system dictates the curriculum; in special education, the child dictates the curriculum" (p. 514). Even though special educators may advocate changes in categories and practices, it appears that relatively few of them would seek to be totally absorbed by the regular educational system.

Administrators of general education programs—school principals and superintendents—are often the most influential people in establishing the climate for including exceptional students in their schools. Some administrators set a positive climate for mainstreaming, whereas others are neutral or even negative in tone. The administrator is clearly in a position to make important decisions about the quality of education offered to handicapped children in the regular school. Joiner and Sabatino (1981) found that general education administrators demonstrated a relatively low level of "consciousness" toward important provisions of P.L. 94–142, such as due process, parent involvement, and student assessment. Special educators should devote increased attention to making general education administrators more aware of the key principles involved in providing an appropriate education to exceptional students in the least restrictive environment.

PROMISE, PROGRESS, AND PROBLEMS

The promise of a free, appropriate public education for all handicapped children was indeed an ambitious one. The process of bringing this goal about has been described in such lofty terms as a "revolution" and a "new Bill of Rights" for exceptional persons (Goodman, 1976). Today, most observers would acknowledge that substantial progress has been made toward the fulfillment of that promise.

Many citizens—both within and outside the field of education—have welcomed the recognition of disabled children's rights in their schools and communities. Additionally, the increased involvement of parents and families in the educational process and the emphasis on team planning to meet individual needs throughout the life span are widely regarded as positive developments. Reports from teachers and students, as well as a growing number of data-based studies, indicate that many handicapped children are being successfully educated in regular schools and that, for the most part, they are well accepted by their nonhandicapped schoolmates. Examples of effective mainstreaming programs can be found at age levels ranging from preschool (Esposito & Reed, 1986; Jenkins, Speltz, & Odom, 1985) to high school (Warger, Aldinger, & Okun, 1983), and include exceptional children whose disabilities range from mild (Algozzine & Korinek, 1985; Thomas & Jackson, 1986) to severe (Brinker, 1985; Condon, York, Heal, & Fortschneider, 1986).

H. R. Turnbull III (1986b), a leading advocate of right-to-education legislation for disabled students and their families, has defined three general subtypes or patterns of service delivery that are now in use to bring about equal educational opportunity.

1. It is possible to obtain equal educational opportunities for some disabled students by treating them exactly like nondisabled students. Educating an orthopedically impaired student in the same academic classes as nondisabled students is an example of "pure equal treatment" (assuming the school is barrier-free).
2. It is possible to obtain equal educational opportunities for other disabled students by treating them substantially like nondisabled students but also by making simultaneous accommodations to them. For example, educating a deaf child in the same classroom as children who do not have a hearing deficiency may require only a few adaptations by the teacher or school system.
3. It is possible to obtain equal educational opportunities for still other students by treating them very differently, but not less effectively, than nondisabled students. For example, educating severely disabled students in separate classes, using a different curriculum and different methods of instruction, may provide those students with educational opportunities that, for them, are comparable to the opportunities provided to nondisabled students who are educated in their own classes with a different curriculum and different methods of instruction. (p. 257)

In spite of this ample evidence of progress toward providing equal educational opportunity, it is equally true that many people—both within and outside the field of education—have detected significant problems in the implementation of P.L. 94–142 and other laws and policies that have gradually extended services to handicapped students in the public schools. Many school administrators maintain that the federal government has never provided sufficient financial resources to the states and local school districts to assist them in providing special services, which are often very costly. Special education teachers have frequently expressed dissatisfaction over excessive paperwork, unclear guidelines, and inappropriate grouping of exceptional students. Regular class teachers often contend that they receive little or no training or support when exceptional children are placed in their classes. Some parents of handicapped and nonhandicapped children have voiced opposition to the integration of exceptional children in regular classes. Some observers have found that the schedules and procedures used in mainstreaming programs actually allow for relatively little integration (Sansone & Zigmond, 1986). There are many other problems, real and perceived; and no "quick fix" or easy solution can be offered.

Recently, Simpkins (1987) conducted a survey of special education teachers who were working with handicapped children in regular schools. The comments of these teachers (in this case teachers of visually impaired students) give a good indication of some current positives and negatives in our field today.

- ☐ Children have benefited from being in the real world.
- ☐ More students, less time per student, more travel time to be with students.
- ☐ Funds seem to have dried up . . . there is less money for equipment and our caseloads are much larger.
- ☐ Most classroom teachers are willing and cooperative. However, if the administrators in the school aren't supportive, the staff usually isn't either.
- ☐ I serve a three county area; each county's views are affecting each situation differently. This is an end result of differing interpretations of P.L. 94–142's meaning and county idiosyncrasies.
- ☐ More and more time is spent in busy paperwork, while less and less is spent in preparation or teaching.
- ☐ I have found actual instruction has a very positive effect on classroom performance. In my experience I have found schools to be most cooperative in allowing for the time I recommend, which varies greatly from student to student. Actually, I feel a bit of one-on-one instruction with *any* student (special education or not) is bound to influence the quality of education.
- ☐ Parents feel they have more of a voice in their children's education. Schools have an alternative when faced with an uncooperative parent.
- ☐ Regular educators at the Junior High level are least receptive to working with my visually handicapped students. Other level teacher relationships have been enhanced due to working closely with them.
- ☐ Many regular education teachers *do not want* visually impaired students.
- ☐ It's a great program. Regular teachers have much less fear of visual impairment. They find students to be independent and have a sense of humor. I can help them to exist better in the sighted world and handle day-to-day problems immediately. (pp. 18–22)

As the teachers' comments imply, special education is continually evolving and is in the process of defining its relationship with regular education. The challenge of special education in the schools today is great, and the future will hold many additional problems. A significantly greater proportion of tomorrow's children and youth will be "educationally at risk because they will have grown up in poverty and will be racially, ethnically, and linguistically diverse" (Weintraub, 1986, p. 1). Many new technologies are becoming available, but whether they can be used effectively to enhance the quality of instruction remains to be seen. There is much room for improvement in the quality of vocational training and employment opportunities available to people with disabilities, and attitudinal barriers still prohibit full acceptance of these individuals in schools, neighborhoods, and workplaces. We do not know what the long-range outcome of our current efforts will be.

Can the promise of a free, appropriate public education for all exceptional students be fulfilled? The answer will depend largely on the readiness of professionals to work together, to assume new roles, to communicate with each other, and to involve parents, families, and exceptional individuals themselves. Caution, at times, seems well

THREE STUDENTS—THREE TEACHERS—THREE SCHOOLS

A RESOURCE ROOM

Vincent is 9 years old. He attends a regular elementary school near his home in San Jose, California. Although Vincent performs well in some academic areas, his teachers became concerned over his slow progress in reading. He was not able to keep up with his classmates last year and frequently displayed behavior problems in the regular third grade classroom, apparently because of frustration with his reading difficulties.

Vincent now goes to a resource room for two hours each day. During this time Ms. Roberts, the resource room teacher, provides individual and small-group instruction for Vincent and five other children who have similar reading and language problems. The resource room has tables at which students can work independently and some quiet, screened-off areas for individual tutoring and testing. There are many instructional and audiovisual aids, including tape recorders, overhead projectors, a Language Master (which reads words and sentences aloud), and a personal computer on which students follow individualized programs.

"Some people think I function simply as a tutor," Ms. Roberts explains, "but there's a lot more to a good resource room program than that. I look for ways of finding out how children learn. I work with the child's regular teacher in providing instruction that is appropriate to that child's special needs."

So far, the resource room placement appears to have helped Vincent. The flexible schedule enables him to be with his peers in the regular classroom for most of the school day. His behavior seems to have improved as a result of the additional instruction he now receives in reading and language arts. Ms. Roberts also feels that Vincent is benefiting from extra attention and encouragement. At the end of this school year Vincent's progress will be reviewed by his teachers and parents. He may be assigned to a resource room again next year, or he may spend virtually all of his time in the regular classroom, with a special education teacher providing consultation to his regular teacher.

A SELF-CONTAINED SPECIAL CLASS

Teresa, 15, is considered to have moderate to severe mental retardation as a result of Down syndrome. She previously lived in a large residential institution in another state, where little education or training was provided. Recently, Teresa left the institution and was placed in a foster home in Houston, Texas. She now attends a self-contained special class located in a regular high school building.

Teresa spends most of the day in her special classroom with nine other students who have moderate, severe, and multiple disabilities. A teacher, Mr. Simmons, and two para-professional aides are assigned to the class. Teresa interacts with nonhandicapped students on the school bus, at recess, and in the cafeteria. In addition, a peer tutoring program brings students from the regular high school classes into Teresa's room to provide individual help under the teacher's supervision. Mr. Simmons seeks to provide a mixture of group and individualized instruction, emphasizing practical tasks for living and working in the community. He frequently teaches outside the school building. For example, Teresa has learned how to ride a city bus from her home to a shopping center.

"At first I didn't know how well we'd be accepted in a regular high school," reports Mr. Simmons. "We've had a bit of a problem with kids calling our students 'retards' or 'dummies' and imitating some of their less desirable behaviors. But most of the high school students are friendly and helpful, and Teresa has made some new friends. Our principal is supportive; she considers our class a part of this school in every way. We have our pictures in the yearbook, and we go to dances and basketball games just like everyone else."

Teresa will probably remain in a self-contained special class next year, with additional attention being given to exploring vocational placements and independent living opportunities in the community. Her foster parents have visited the class several times and are pleased with Teresa's progress.

A SPECIAL SCHOOL

Nadine, who is 11 years old, has severe spastic cerebral palsy. She usually uses a wheelchair for mobility, although she is learning to use a walker for short periods. She has occasional seizures and has considerable difficulty articulating clearly. Nadine requires a special diet, regular medication, and assistance in dressing and toileting.

Nadine lives in a large suburban school district on Long Island, New York. She attends Bayview School, a public special school exclusively for children who have physical, orthopedic, neurological, and health-related disabilities. Nadine's parents had the option of sending her to a public school closer to home but preferred that she attend Bayview. They feel that Nadine benefits from the smaller class size and greater concentration of teachers and therapists that Bayview offers. They also have become involved in the school's parent-teacher organization and have assisted with numerous field trips and recreational outings.

Bayview looks much like any other public school except that most of the children use adaptive devices such as wheelchairs, walkers, protective helmets, and communication boards. The school is completely barrier-free. There are no stairs; all doorways and restroom stalls are wider than usual. Nadine enjoys swimming in the school's pool. In the cafeteria, staff members bring food to those children who cannot go through the serving line and also help them learn to eat if necessary. Nadine rides to school on a specially equipped bus, with a driver and aide who have received training in positioning, seizure management, communication, and other procedures.

The students at Bayview range in age from 5 to 21. "We have 10 children in our class this year," says Ms. Hamner, Nadine's teacher, "and most of them are functioning pretty close to grade level. We basically follow an academic program with extra instruction and therapy to meet each student's needs. We have a hard-working staff that cares. I think it's good for the kids to be exposed to other youngsters with disabilities."

Nadine's placement will be reviewed at the end of each school year. In the future she may attend a regular public school for all or part of the day, if it is considered appropriate by her parents and teachers—and by Nadine herself.

advised; as Hechinger (1976) suggests, we may need to "slow down the bandwagon of instant change" and avoid confusing civil rights and the "right kind of education for every child." Yet efforts to fulfill the promise continue. As Weintraub and Abeson (1974) wrote some years ago in support of the Education for All Handicapped Children Act," "At the minimum, it will make educational opportunities a reality for all handicapped children. At the maximum, it will make our schools healthier learning environments for *all* our children" (p. 529).

SUMMARY

1. Public school programs for exceptional children are a relatively recent development in American education.
   a. For many years special education simply did not exist.
   b. Early special education programs were segregated from the rest of the educational world in separate buildings or classrooms.
   c. Today, most handicapped children spend at least part of the school day in regular classrooms with nonhandicapped peers. Others attend special classes in regular schools, and a few others are educated in other special settings.
2. The current movement to extend educational opportunities to handicapped children is an outgrowth of the civil rights movement.
   a. All children are now recognized to have the right to equal protection under the law, which has been interpreted to mean the right to a free public education in the least restrictive, appropriate setting.
   b. All children and their parents also have the right to due process under the law, which includes the rights to be notified of any decision affecting the child's educational placement, to have a hearing and present a defense, to see a written decision, and to appeal any decision.
   c. Court cases have also established the rights of handicapped children to fair assessment in their native language and to education at public expense, regardless of the school district's financial constraints.
3. Recent legislation has extended and clarified the legal rights of exceptional children.
   a. P.L. 94–142 made many already-occurring trends in special education part of federal law. It extends public education to all handicapped children between the ages of 3 and 21, with special priority for those currently unserved and underserved.
   b. P.L. 94–142 requires that handicapped students be educated in the least restrictive environment (LRE). LRE is a relative concept (i.e., it is not the regular classroom for every handicapped student) stipulating that to the maximum extent possible handicapped students are to be educated with nonhandicapped peers in regular educational environments. The law also sets out requirements for diagnosis, nondiscriminatory assessment, individualization of programming, and personnel development.
   c. A number of court cases have challenged the way particular school districts implement specific provisions of P.L. 94–142. No trend has yet emerged from these cases. Rulings from the various court cases have established the principle that each handicapped student is entitled to a personalized program of instruction and suppor-

tive services that will enable him to benefit from an education in as integrated a setting as possible.

    d. P.L. 99–457 (Education of the Handicapped Act Amendments of 1986) requires states to provide special education services to all handicapped preschoolers aged 3 to 5 by 1991 or lose all future federal funds for preschoolers with handicaps. This law also makes available federal money to encourage states to develop early intervention programs for handicapped and at-risk infants and toddlers, from birth to age 2. Early intervention services must be coordinated by an individualized family services plan.

    e. Section 504 of the Rehabilitation Act forbids discrimination in all federally funded programs—including educational and vocational programs—on the basis of handicap alone.

4. Special education today is a system of delivering services to exceptional students.

    a. The concept of mainstreaming remains controversial. It does not mean the movement of all handicapped children into regular classrooms. Rather, each student should be placed in the most integrated setting in which she can succeed.

    b. There should be a continuum of service options available to all exceptional students so that each student can receive the necessary help for as long as it is indicated and can then move to a less restrictive setting as soon as possible. The less integrated the setting, the fewer students it should serve.

    c. A team approach in which teachers, other professionals, and paraprofessionals share information and skills can help make each student's education as effective and consistent as possible.

    d. Assessment is now seen as an ongoing part of a child's program, through which a teacher (or other member of the team) finds out what the child currently can do in a specific situation.

    e. The individualized education program (IEP), which many teachers have been using in one form or another for years, is simply a way of ensuring that each child is assessed, that long-range goals and short-term objectives are set, and that the child's progress is evaluated regularly.

    f. Currently, there is no specific federal legislation governing programs for students who are gifted and talented. Individual states have the responsibility to determine what portion, if any, of their federal education block-grant money will be used to support programs and services for gifted and talented students.

    g. Many professionals today believe that special and regular educators must work together in a cooperative, unified manner in order for an appropriate education to become a reality for all children.

5. Although the new laws and court decisions promise many welcome advances in special education, they also present a tremendous challenge to the field. There is still much to be done to reach the day when all students with handicaps are receiving a quality education in our nation's schools.

FOR MORE INFORMATION

Books

Biklen, D. (1985). *Achieving the complete school: Strategies for effective mainstreaming.* New York: Teachers College Press.

Heron, T. E., & Harris, K. C. (1987). *The educational consultant: Helping professionals, parents and mainstreamed students* (2nd ed.). Austin, TX: Pro-Ed.

Lewis, R. B., & Doorlag, D. H. (1987). *Teaching special students in the mainstream* (2nd ed.). Columbus, OH: Merrill.

Turnbull, A. P., Strickland, B. B., & Brantley, J. (1982). *Developing and implementing individualized education programs.* Columbus, OH: Merrill.

Turnbull, H. R. (1986). *Free appropriate public education: The law and children with disabilities.* Denver: Love.

Weintraub, F. J. (1986). *Goals for the future of special education.* Reston, VA: Council for Exceptional Children.

Wood, J. W. (1984). *Adapting instruction for the mainstream.* Columbus, OH: Merrill.

PART TWO
EXCEPTIONAL CHILDREN

3

MENTAL RETARDATION

Most people have some ideas of what mental retardation is and what people with mental retardation are like. When they hear the words "special education," they think of mental retardation. The first public school special education classes, in 1896, were indeed held for mentally retarded children. Of course, things have changed since then. The past 25 years especially have witnessed significant improvements in the education, care, and treatment of children and adults with retarded development. Persons with mental retardation have experienced increased opportunities to participate in some of the benefits and responsibilities of mainstream society. Unfortunately, although there is more public awareness concerning mental retardation, much of that awareness still consists of superstition, half-truths, and oversimplifications. This chapter presents some key factors in understanding that very complex concept called mental retardation. It will also look at some contemporary educational practices that have helped improve the outlook for mentally retarded children—one of the largest categories of exceptionality.

HISTORY OF TREATMENT AND SERVICES FOR INDIVIDUALS WITH MENTAL RETARDATION

The history of mental retardation is long. In all probability some people have been slower to learn than others as long as people have populated the earth. The Greeks in 1552 B.C. and the Romans in 449 B.C. were among the first to recognize people officially as mentally retarded. There are also passages in the Bible referring to slow learners (Barr, 1913; Lindman & McIntyre, 1961).

Several special educators and historians have written detailed and interesting accounts of the changing philosophies and beliefs toward and treatment of mentally retarded people over the years. For example, Hewett and Forness (1977) describe the role and importance of survival, superstition, science, and service in the treatment of mentally retarded people during different historical periods. Kolstoe and Frey (1965) describe five chronological eras of treatment: extermination, ridicule, asylum, education, and occupational adequacy. Gearheart and Litton (1975) characterize the early history of mental retardation (prior to the 1800s) as consisting primarily of superstition and extermination; the 19th century as the era that produced institutions for mentally retarded persons; the 20th century as the era of public school classes; the 1950s and 1960s as the era of legislation and national support; and the 1970s as the era of normalization, child advocacy, and litigation. Here we can only briefly describe some of the changing attitudes and significant events that have affected the manner in which persons with mental retardation have been treated over the years.

Readers wishing to examine the history of mental retardation in more detail might begin by reading Blatt (1987), MacMillan (1982), Patton (1986), and/or Scheerenberger (1983).

The primary goal of human beings in primitive societies was survival. The sick, physically handicapped, and elderly were often abandoned or even killed to increase the chance of survival by others. The Greeks and Romans often sent mentally and physically defective children to places far away from the community, where they would perish on their own. Later, as survival became less of a 24-hour concern and society separated into levels, ridicule of mentally retarded people was common. Superstitions and myths developed. Words like *idiot, imbecile,* and *dunce* were used, and some kings and queens and other wealthy people kept "fools" or imbeciles as clowns or court jesters.

During the Middle Ages, as religion became a dominant force, a more humanitarian view was taken. Asylums and monasteries were erected to care for mentally retarded people. However, no one thought their behavior could be altered.

Around the beginning of the 19th century, the first attempt to educate a retarded person was recorded. In 1798 three hunters found and captured an 11- or 12-year-old boy in the woods of Aveyron, France. The boy—later called Victor, the Wild Boy of Aveyron (Itard, 1894/1962)—was completely unsocialized and had no language. He was pronounced an "uncurable idiot." Jean Marc Gaspard Itard, a physician working at an institution for the deaf, refused to believe that Victor was uneducable. Itard began an intensive training program with Victor. After almost 5 years he concluded his work, deeming it a miserable failure because he did not reach his original goals for Victor. However, the changes that did occur with Victor were significant: he was much more socialized and could read and write a few words. "The French Academy of Science encouraged Itard to publish his memoirs of his work with Victor. Itard did, which not only made Itard very famous, but may have been the single most important event in the creation of what is now viewed as a genuine field" (Blatt, 1987, p. 34).

Edouard Seguin worked briefly with Itard prior to Itard's death in 1838 and was inspired by the work with Victor. Seguin immigrated to the United States in 1848 and had tremendous influence on the creation of facilities and educational programs for mentally retarded persons in this country. He helped to establish the Pennsylvania Training School, an early educational facility.

The first person to advocate educational programs for mentally retarded children in the United States was Samuel Gridley Howe, who had already devoted much of his life to the education of blind, deaf, and other disadvantaged children. In 1848, thanks to his powerful letter arguing for the rights of mentally retarded people in a democratic society, the Massachusetts legislature overrode the governor's veto and provided Howe with $2,500 for the first institution for mentally retarded persons in this country. During the remainder of the 19th century, large state institutions for individuals who were mentally retarded or mentally ill (they were often viewed as the same) became the primary means of service delivery. As the institutions became overcrowded and understaffed, the optimism sparked by the educational gains produced by Itard, Seguin, and Howe began to wane. State institutions came to be viewed as custodial rather than educational, a view that has taken years of effort to change, extending even to the present.

The first public school class for mentally retarded children was formed in 1896 in Providence, Rhode Island. Thus began the special class movement, which saw 87,030 children enrolled in special classes in 1948; 703,800 in 1969; and 1,305,000 in 1974. The great increases in the number of children being served by the public schools paralleled increases in federal aid to education, particularly to special education, in the 1950s and 1960s.

In the education and care of mentally retarded children today, we are witnessing a move away from total reliance on the large state institution and the self-contained special class. The trend is toward more normalized, community-based facilities and education in the least retrictive environment, which includes the regular classroom for a significant number of mentally retarded children.

DEFINING MENTAL RETARDATION

Mental retardation is, above all, a label; it is a term used to identify an observed performance deficit—failure to demonstrate age-appropriate intellectual and social behavior. Definitions of mental retardation have been proposed, debated, revised, and counterproposed over many years. And still the debate goes on.

> Mental retardation describes performance; it is not a "thing" children are born with inside their heads.

Since mental retardation is a concept that affects and is affected by people in many different disciplines, it has been defined from many different perspectives. A definition offered by a professional within a given discipline may be functional only from that particular perspective. For example, a definition of mental retardation based solely on biological or medical criteria, although useful to doctors and nurses, would not be functional for a teacher or a psychologist.

But, as MacMillan (1982) points out, disagreements among professionals over what constitutes mental retardation are "not merely academic exercises in semantics." A subtle difference between two definitions can determine whether or not the label of mental retardation will be affixed to a particular child. The critical importance of definition was noted as early as 1924 by Kuhlman, who recognized that definitions of mental deficiency can be used to "decide the fate of thousands every year."

You might reasonably ask why classification as mentally retarded or not mentally retarded is so important. There are some children and adults so clearly deficient in academic and social skills that it is obvious to anyone who interacts with them that they require special services and educational programming. How mental retardation is defined is not much of an issue for these individuals; they are severely retarded in all areas of development. But this group comprises only a small segment of the total population of persons identified as mentally retarded. The largest segment of that population consists of school-age children who are mildly retarded. Thus, the way that mental retardation is defined determines what special educational services thousands of children may be eligible to receive.

In early times only the severely retarded were identified; the term *idiocy* was used (derived from a Greek word meaning "people who did not hold public office" [MacMillan, 1982]). In the 19th century the label *imbecile* (derived from the Latin word for "weak and feeble") was applied to not-so-severely retarded people. The term *simpleton* was eventually added to identify those cases less severe than imbeciles (Clausen, 1967). As defined by Ireland in 1900,

> Idiocy is mental deficiency, or extreme stupidity, depending upon malnutrition or disease of the nervous centers, occurring either before birth or before the evolution of mental faculties in childhood. The word *imbecility* is generally used to denote a less decided degree of mental incapacity. (p. 1)

Because physicians were the first professional groups to work with people with mental retardation, it is not surprising that early definitions emphasized biological or medical aspects of mental retardation. The two definitions most widely used during the first half of this century were written by Tredgold and Doll. Tredgold's (1937) reads,

> A state of incomplete mental development of such a kind and degree that the individual is incapable of adapting himself to the normal environment of his fellows in such a way to maintain existence independently of supervision, control, or external support. (p. 4)

In 1941 Doll wrote that six criteria were essential to the definition and concept of mental retardation.

> These are (1) social incompetence, (2) due to mental subnormality, (3) which has been developmentally arrested, (4) which obtains at maturity, (5) is of constitutional origin, and (6) is essentially incurable. (p. 215)

The AAMD Definitions

AAMD is a national organization comprised of professionals—in education, medicine, psychology, social work, speech pathology, etc.—as well as students, parents, and others concerned about the study, treatment, and prevention of mental retardation.

In 1959 the American Association on Mental Deficiency (AAMD) published a manual of terminology and classification of mental retardation that included a definition. That definition was revised in 1961 to read,

> Mental retardation refers to subaverage general intellectual functioning which originates during the developmental period and is associated with impairment in adaptive behavior. (Heber, 1961, p. 3)

Twelve years later the AAMD definition was revised to read,

> Mental retardation refers to significantly subaverage general intellectual functioning existing concurrently with deficits in adaptive behavior, and manifested during the developmental period. (Grossman, 1973, p. 5)

- based upon *heridity* or a *biological*

At first glance the two definitions seem almost the same: they use the same terminology and similar word order. However, there are important differences between the two. First, according to the 1961 definition, mental retardation is equated with "subaverage general intellectual functioning," *associated with* adaptive behavior impairments. According to the revised definition, however, an individual must be well below average in *both* intellectual functioning *and* adaptive behavior. That is, intellectual functioning is no longer the sole defining criterion. A second important change is the degree of subaverage intellectual functioning that must be demonstrated before a person is considered mentally retarded. The word *significantly* in the 1973 definition refers to a score of two or more standard deviations below the mean on a standardized intelligence test (we will explain this in the next section); the 1961 definition requires a score of only one standard deviation below the mean. Furthermore, this change eliminates the category of borderline mental retardation. A third change, although not as important as the first two, is also included in the revised definition. The developmental period is extended from 16 years to 18 years, to coincide with the usual period of public schooling. The definition specifies that the deficits in intellectual functioning and adaptive behavior occur during the developmental period in order to help distinguish mental retardation from other disorders (for instance, sudden impairment resulting from severe physical injury to an adult).

Measuring Intellectual Functioning

Intellectual functioning, as used in special education, is most often measured by a score on a standardized intelligence (IQ) test. An IQ test consists of a series of questions and problem-solving tasks that are assumed to require certain amounts of intelligence to answer or solve correctly. Thus, an IQ test samples a small portion of the full range of an individual's skills and abilities. That observed performance sample is used to derive a score that is taken to represent the test taker's overall intelligence.

The test taker's age is considered when computing an IQ. To obtain a score of 100, a 5-year-old child must respond correctly to those questions and tasks most 5-year-olds get right. A 16-year-old who responds correctly to only those test items the average 5-year-old gets right would receive a score much lower than 100.

When we say that an IQ test is standardized, we mean that the same questions and tasks are to be presented in a certain, specified way and that the same procedures are to be used to score each test taker's responses each time the test is administered. A standardized test has also been normed; that is, it has been administered to a large sample of people, selected at random from the population for whom the test is intended. The test scores of the people in the random sample are then used as norms, or averages of how people perform on the test. On the two most widely used intelligence tests, the Stanford-Binet (Terman & Merrill, 1973) and the revised Wechsler Intelligence Scale for Children (WISC-R) (Wechsler, 1974), the norm or average score is 100.

Standard deviation is a mathematical concept. It refers to the amount by which a particular score on a given test varies from the mean, or average score, of all the scores in the norm sample. (See Figure 3.1 on page 87 for further information about standard deviation.) One standard deviation on the Stanford-Binet is 16 points; on the WISC-R, 15 points. (The difference stems from the difference in the distribution of scores obtained from the samples of children used to derive the norms for the two tests.) Thus, according to the 1961 AAMD definition of mental retardation, a child

Not too long ago, most children whose IQ scores were as low as Kathy's would have been prohibited from receiving a public education.

could be labeled mentally retarded on the basis of an IQ score as high as 84 or 85, depending on the test used. The 1973 AAMD definition of mental retardation requires an IQ score two standard deviations below the mean, which would be 68 or 70 on the two tests.

As you might guess, this change in the definition of mental retardation affected many children. In California a state law was passed saying that a child must fall two full standard deviations or more below the mean on both the verbal and performance subtests of the WISC-R in order to be classified as mentally retarded. Virtually overnight 20,000 school children who had been considered mentally retarded no longer were. Of course, even though the category of "borderline" mental retardation was eliminated by the revised definition, some of those children may still need special education services in order to succeed in school.

There are a number of reasons that educators and other professionals in mental retardation advocated the 1973 AAMD definition, which is much more conservative than the early definition in terms of who is to be called mentally retarded. Four of those reasons are summarized here.

1. *Labeling a child mentally retarded can have negative effects.* Some educators feel that when a child is officially labeled mentally retarded, the damage done by the label itself outweighs any positive effects of special education and treatment that result from the label (Kugel & Wolfensberger, 1969; Smith & Neisworth, 1975).

2. *Intelligence tests can be culturally biased.* Both the Binet and Wechsler IQ tests have been heavily criticized for being culturally biased. That is, the tests tend to favor children from the population on which they were normed—primarily white, middle-class children. Some of the questions on an IQ test may tap learning that only a middle-class child is likely to have experienced. The tests, which are highly verbal, are especially inappropriate for children for whom English is a second language. Mercer (1973a) points out that when an IQ test is used to identify children for special class placement, many more black, Mexican-American, and poor children are labeled mentally retarded than are white, middle-class children.

One of the possible negative outcomes experienced by a child who is labeled mentally retarded is that peers may be more likely to avoid or ridicule the child. See pages 89–90 for the report of what one young researcher did to improve children's attitudes about people with mental retardation.

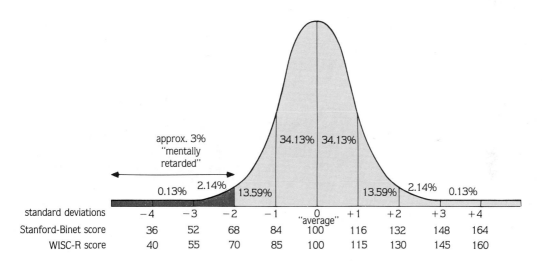

FIGURE 3.1

IQ scores seem to be distributed throughout the population according to a phenomenon called the **normal curve,** shown here. To describe how one particular score varies from the mean (average score), the population is broken into units called *standard deviations.* Each standard deviation includes a fixed portion of the population. For example, we know that 34.13% of the population will fall within one standard deviation above the mean, and another 34.13% will be within one standard deviation below "normal." By applying an algebraic formula to the scores achieved by the norm sample on a test, we can tell what value equals one standard deviation for that test. We can then take a person's IQ test score and describe it in terms of how many standard deviations above or below the mean it is. In this graph we can see that just under 3% of the population falls two or more standard deviations below the mean, which the AAMD calls "significantly subaverage." That means that if we used IQ scores as the sole criterion, about 3% of the population would be considered mentally retarded.

3. *IQ scores can change significantly.* Several studies have shown that IQ scores can change, particularly in the range that used to constitute borderline retardation (MacMillan, 1982). And because mental retardation tends to become a permanent label for a child even though it is supposed to describe only present performance, educators were concerned that many children were being identified as mentally retarded on the basis of a test score that might be increased by as many as 15 to 20 points after a period of effective instruction (Bruening & Davis, 1981).

4. *Intelligence testing is not an exact science.* Even though the major intelligence tests are among the most carefully developed and standardized psychological tests, they are still far from perfect. Among the variables that can affect a child's final score on an IQ test are motivation, the time and location of the test, and bias on the test giver's part in the scoring of responses that are not precisely covered by the test manual. Even the choice of which test to use can be critical. For example, Wechsler (1974) reports that the WISC-R and the revised Stanford-Binet correlate with each other at about the .70 level. This means that it is possible for a child to be identified as mentally retarded by one test but not by the other.

Robinson and Robinson (1976), in their excellent discussion of intelligence testing, summarize some potential values and pitfalls of IQ tests.

> The development and popular utilization of the IQ as a single, simple, objective index of the rate of intellectual growth has been a mixed blessing. When properly understood and carefully used, an IQ test can be valuable in assessing a child's rate of progress, but it refers to only those aspects of mental ability tapped by a particular test. Its measurement is subject to error from a number of sources, some of them capable of drastically affecting scores. There is little doubt that IQs have been seriously misused because of persistent and erroneous notions about their supposed permanence or their magical power to predict future performance. Such a simple index of present behavior as the IQ cannot possibly reflect all the many aspects of the complex developmental phenomenon known as intelligence.
>
> Nowhere has the IQ proved to be a more mixed blessing than in matters concerning the welfare of mentally retarded children. To be sure, the development of intelligence tests provided a means for more objective assessment. Tests have been very useful in helping to identify children who need special training and in establishing more orderly methods for admissions procedures in institutions. Many retarded children have been helped to lead more productive lives because of the early identification of their problems. Other children whose school failures were not due to overall intellectual deficits have also been identified and treated accordingly.
>
> On the other hand, the apparent simplicity of the IQ led to an enthusiastic but largely misguided movement to label or classify children primarily on the basis of their scores on intelligence tests. Accurate classification of intellectual deficit was thought to be all that was required to achieve understanding of retarded children, individual characteristics being grossly underestimated. Furthermore, undue belief in IQ constancy led to a diminution in research and treatment. Professional interest in many complex problems declined over a long period, not to be rejuvenated until the mid-1960s. Fortunately, a more realistic view now prevails. (p. 343)

CHANGING SECOND GRADERS' ATTITUDES TOWARD PEOPLE WITH MENTAL RETARDATION: USING KID POWER

The following is excerpted from a research study conducted by 10-year-old Amy Turnbull, a student at Hillcrest Elementary School in Lawrence, Kansas. Her study, conducted as a school science project, was later presented at the national meeting of AAMD and published in the journal Mental Retardation *(Turnbull & Bronicki, 1986). The second author served as design and statistical consultant. All other aspects of the project were performed by the first author.*

Many young kids have poor attitudes about people who are mentally retarded. The reason I wanted to solve this problem is because I have a brother who is mentally retarded. I want kids to have positive attitudes about him and everyone else, too. My hypothesis was: Teaching second graders about mental retardation *will* improve their attitudes about people with mental retardation.

METHOD

I decided to do my science project with second graders. I selected two second-grade classes: an experimental group and a control group. I pretested both groups on February 26, 1985. The test I used was the Student Attitude and Perspective Scale (Rude, 1982).

I taught the experimental group about mental retardation. I read a book about a boy who is mentally retarded, and I showed them a film about the Special Olympics. I also showed them my brother's Special Olympic medals. I asked the class questions and they asked me questions.

I told them that people who are mentally retarded learn slower than us. But they can still learn. I also said that brains are like a record player, be-

cause they work on different speeds. They learned that music is played on both slow and fast speeds. I told them that the brains of kids with mental retardation work slowly and our brains work fast, but *all of us can learn and have happy lives.* I taught this lesson on February 27, 1985. The lesson lasted about 50 minutes.

I posttested the experimental and control groups on February 29, 1985. I scored the pretests and the posttests of each group.

RESULTS AND DISCUSSION

I compared pretest and posttest scores for each group using the Wilcoxen Sign Test for related samples. There were no significant differences between the control group's pre- and posttest scores. I found a significant difference between the experimental group's pre- and posttest scores, $p < .01$. The posttest scores of the kids in this group very clearly changed in a positive direction following my lesson about mental retardation.

Teaching second graders about mental retardation *did* improve their attitudes about people with mental retardation. My hypothesis was correct.

I think important research questions for the future are: (a) Do attitudes improve more when adults or kids teach? (b) Will teaching kindergartners about mental retardation improve their attitudes about people with mental retardation? (c) Do positive attitudes mean that the kids are really nicer to people who are mentally retarded?

I was the only one who did a science project on mental retardation in my school. There were special awards given by different groups and clubs, like the United States Army, Kansas University Engineering Club, and Dental Society, for projects important to these groups. I think that if state and local AAMR groups sponsored awards at different science fairs, maybe more children would be interested and would do projects about mental retardation. This way more children might learn about mental retardation. I do not think it would cost much—a certificate in a frame and a handshake could get a lot more children interested in an important area. Please, think about it.

REFERENCE

Rude, H. A. (1982). *The Student attitude and perspective scale.* Greeley, CO: University of Northern Colorado.

Source: From Changing Second Graders' Attitudes Toward People with Mental Retardation: Using Kid Power" by A. Turnbull and G. J. Bronicki, 1986. *Mental Retardation, 24,* pp. 44–45. Reprinted by permission.

A recent alternative to traditional tests of intelligence is the Kaufman Assessment Battery for Children (K-ABC) (Kaufman & Kaufman, 1983). The K-ABC is based on the theory that intelligence is composed of two different information-processing abilities: sequential processing and simultaneous processing. "Sequential processing places a premium on the serial or temporal order of stimuli when solving problems; in contrast, simultaneous processing demands a gestalt-like, frequently spatial, integration of stimuli to solve problems with maximum efficiency" (*K-ABC Interpretive Manual*, p. 2). The K-ABC is viewed by some as a significant advancement in the understanding and measurement of children's intelligence. Numerous school psychologists are now using the test as part of their battery of assessment instruments to determine eligibility for and placement in special education programs. However, several authorities on special education assessment suggest that complete acceptance of the new approach be deferred until a significant body of research demonstrates the validity of the K-ABC's constructs and the remedial approach it recommends (McLoughlin & Lewis, 1986; Salvia & Ysseldyke, 1985).

See the Fall 1984 issue of the *Journal of Special Education* for a series of articles on the K-ABC.

Clearly, intelligence tests have both advantages and disadvantages. Here are several more important considerations to keep in mind.

☐ The concept of intelligence is a hypothetical construct. No one has ever seen a thing called intelligence; it is not a precise entity, but rather something that we infer from observed performance. We assume that it takes more intelligence to learn to perform certain tasks.

☐ There is nothing mysterious or powerful about an IQ test. An IQ test is simply a series of questions and problem-solving tasks.

☐ An IQ test measures only how a child performs at one point in time on the items included in one test. We infer from that performance how a child might perform in other situations.

☐ IQ tests have proven to be the best single predictor of school achievement. Because IQ tests are composed largely of verbal and academic tasks—the same things that a child must master in order to succeed in school—they correlate with school achievement more highly than any other single testing device.

☐ In the hands of a competent school psychologist, IQ tests can provide useful information, particularly in objectively identifying an overall performance deficit.

☐ Results from an IQ test are generally not useful in planning individualized educational objectives and teaching strategies for a child. Direct, teacher-administered, criterion-referenced assessment of a child's performance on the specific skills he needs to learn is more useful for planning instruction.

For example, a criterion-referenced test for single-digit addition might give the child 10 such problems. Rather than judging the child's performance by comparing it to other children's (as in norm-referenced testing), the child's performance is compared to a standard criterion. If the child gets 9 or 10 correct, instruction will not be necessary on that skill; if she gets fewer than 9 correct, a teaching program for single-digit addition problems will be implemented.

☐ Results from an IQ test should never be used as the only criterion to label, classify, or place a child in a special program.

Measuring Adaptive Behavior

To be classified as mentally retarded, a person must be *clearly* subnormal in adaptive behavior. It would be pointless to identify and classify as mentally retarded a person who faces no unusual problems or whose needs are met without profes-

TABLE 3.1
Areas covered by the AAMR Adaptive Behavior Scale.

Part One	Part Two

I. Independent Functioning
  A. Eating
  B. Toilet Use
  C. Cleanliness
  D. Appearance
  E. Care of Clothing
  F. Dressing and Undressing
  G. Travel
  H. General Independent Functioning
	I. Violent and Destructive Behavior

II. Physical Development
  A. Sensory Development
  B. Motor Development
	II. Antisocial Behavior
	III. Rebellious Behavior
	IV. Untrustworthy Behavior
	V. Withdrawal
	VI. Stereotyped Behavior and Odd Mannerisms

III. Economic Activity
  A. Money Handling and Budgeting
  B. Shopping Skills
	VII. Inappropriate Interpersonal Manners
	VIII. Unacceptable Vocal Habits
	IX. Unacceptable or Eccentric Habits
	X. Self-Abusive Behavior

IV. Language Development
  A. Expression
  B. Comprehension
  C. Social Language Development
	XI. Hyperactive Tendencies
	XII. Sexually Aberrant Behavior
	XIII. Psychological Disturbances
	XIV. Use of Medications

V. Numbers and Time	

VI. Domestic Activity
  A. Cleaning
  B. Kitchen Duties
  C. Other Domestic Activities	

VII. Vocational Activity	

VIII. Self-Direction
  A. Initiative
  B. Perseverance
  C. Leisure Time	

IX. Responsibility	
X. Socialization	

Source: From *AAMR Adaptive Behavior Scale* (pp. 6–7), by K. Nihira, R. Foster, M. Shellhaas, and H. Leland, 1975. Washington, DC: American Association on Mental Retardation. Reprinted by permission.

sional attention. Some people with an IQ below 70 do well in school and society. Such people are not mentally retarded, and should not be labeled as such. (MacMillan, 1982, p. 42)

Many children who used to be called retarded were anything but retarded outside school; they coped very well indeed with the requirements of their homes, their neighborhoods, and their friends. In 1969 the President's Committee on Mental Retardation described the "6-hour retarded child," referring to the fact that many children are considered mentally retarded only during the 6 hours of each day spent in school; during the other 18 hours of the day they function normally and are not considered retarded by the people they interact with. In this sense the demands of school could be said to "cause" mental retardation. To counteract this problem and other criticisms of the use of an IQ test as the sole criterion for mental retardation, the definition was revised to require that a child show deficits in adaptive behavior as well as intellectual functioning.

Grossman (1973) defined adaptive behavior as "the effectiveness or degree with which the individual meets the standards of personal independence and social responsibility expected of his age and social group." AAMD further defines the areas where deficits in adaptive behavior can be found within different age groups.

During infancy and early childhood:
1. Sensory-motor skills
2. Communication skills (speech and language)
3. Self-help skills
4. Socialization skills (interacting and getting along with others)

During childhood and early adolescence:
5. Application of basic academic skills in daily life activities
6. Application of appropriate reasoning and judgment in mastery of the environment
7. Social skills (participation in group activities and interpersonal relationships)

During late adolescence and adulthood:
8. Vocational and social responsibility and performance (Grossman, 1973, p. 11–12)

The most frequently used instrument for assessing adaptive behavior is the AAMD Adaptive Behavior Scale (ABS) (Nihira, Foster, Shellhaas, & Leland, 1974). The ABS consists of two parts. Part 1 consists of 10 domains related to independent functioning and daily living skills. It is further broken down into 21 subdomains. Part 2 of the ABS assesses the individual's level of maladaptive (inappropriate) behavior. Table 3.1 lists the parts of the ABS, and Figure 3.2 shows one page of Part 1. Another version of the ABS has been developed for use in public schools to measure the adaptive behavior of children with suspected mild retardation (Lambert, Windmiller, Cole, & Figueroa, 1975). However, this scale is quite long: it has 95 items with 3 to 12 subparts per item. A shorter (75 total items) and easier-to-score adaptation of the scale, called the Classroom Adaptive Behavior Checklist, has been developed by Hunsucker, Nelson, and Clark (1986).

The ABS can be administered in several ways. Sometimes it is completed by someone familiar with the person being assessed, such as a direct care worker, teacher, or parent; sometimes an examiner completes the ABS by interviewing a direct care worker or parent; and sometimes direct observation is conducted.

The Vineland Social Maturity Scale (Doll, 1965) is another widely used method for assessing adaptive behavior. The Vineland has recently undergone substantial revi-

Measurement of adaptive behavior is important for reasons other than identifying who will be called mentally retarded. The severity of maladaptive behavior emitted by persons with mental retardation is one of the most critical factors in determining their placement and acceptance in many school, work, and residential settings (Campbell, Smith, & Wool, 1982). Because part 2 of the ABS focuses primarily on the frequency rather than the severity of maladaptive behavior, MacDonald and Barton (1986) have developed a revision that enables a more accurate assessment of the severity of a person's maladaptive behavior.

PART ONE
I. INDEPENDENT FUNCTIONING

A. Eating

(1) Use of Table Utensils (Circle only ONE)

Uses knife and fork correctly and neatly	6
Uses table knife for cutting or spreading	5
Feeds self with spoon and fork—neatly	4
Feeds self with spoon and fork—considerable spilling	3
Feeds self with spoon—neatly	2
Feeds self with spoon—considerable spilling	1
Feeds self with fingers or must be fed	0

(2) Eating in Public (Circle only ONE)

Orders complete meals in restaurants	3
Orders simple meals like hamburgers or hot dogs	2
Orders soft drinks at soda fountain or canteen	1
Does not order at public eating places	0

(3) Drinking (Circle only ONE)

Drinks without spilling, holding glass in one hand	3
Drinks from cup or glass unassisted—neatly	2
Drinks from cup or glass unassisted considerable spilling	1
Does not drink from cup or glass unassisted	0

(4) Table Manners (Check ALL statements which apply)

Swallows food without chewing	_____ 8-number
Chews food with mouth open	_____ checked =
Drops food on table or floor	_____
Uses napkin incorrectly or not at all	_____
Talks with mouth full	_____
Takes food off others' plates	_____
Eats too fast or too slow	_____
Plays in food with fingers	_____
None of the above _____	
Does not apply, e.g., because he or she is _____ bedfast, and/or has liquid food only. (If checked, enter "0" in the circle to the right.)	

A. Eating ———————→ **ADD 1-4**

B. Toilet Use

(5) Toilet Training (Circle only ONE)

Never has toilet accidents	4
Never has toilet accidents during the day	3
Occasionally has toilet accidents during the day	2
Frequently has toilet accidents during the day	1
Is not toilet trained at all	0

(6) Self-Care at Toilet (Check ALL statements which apply)

Lowers pants at the toilet without help	_____
Sits on toilet seat without help	_____
Uses toilet tissue appropriately	_____
Flushes toilet after use	_____
Puts on clothes without help	_____
Washes hands, without help	_____
None of the above _____	

B. Toilet Use ———————→ **ADD 5-6**

C. Cleanliness

(7) Washing Hands and Face (Check ALL statements which apply)

Washes hands with soap	_____
Washes face with soap	_____
Washes hands and face with water	_____
Dries hands and face	_____
None of the above _____	

(8) Bathing (Circle only ONE)

Prepares and completes bathing unaided	6
Washes and dries self completely without prompting or helping	5
Washes and dries self reasonably well with prompting	4
Washes and dries self with help	3
Attempts to soap and wash self	2
Cooperates when being washed and dried by others	1
Makes no attempt to wash or dry self	0

(9) Personal Hygiene (Check ALL statements which apply)

Has strong underarm odor	_____ 4-number
Does not change underwear regularly by self	_____ checked =
Skin is often dirty if not assisted	_____
Does not keep nails clean by self	_____
None of the above _____	
Does not apply, e.g., because he or she is completely dependent on others. (If checked enter "0" in the circle to the right.)	

(10) Tooth Brushing (Circle only ONE)

Applies toothpaste and brushes teeth with up and down motion	5
Applies toothpaste and brushes teeth	4
Brushes teeth without help but cannot apply toothpaste	3
Brushes teeth with supervision	2
Cooperates in having teeth brushed	1
Makes no attempt to brush teeth	0

FIGURE 3.2
AAMR Adaptive Behavior Scale.

Source: From *AAMR Adaptive Behavior Scale* (p. 3) by K. Nihira, R. Foster, M. Shellhaas, and H. Leland, 1975, Washington, DC: American Association on Mental Retardation. Reprinted by permission.

sion and is now available in three different versions under the name Vineland Adaptive Behavior Scales (Sparrow, Balla, & Cicchetti, 1984). Two of the versions, the Interview Editions in Survey Form or Expanded Form, are administered to an individual, such as a teacher or direct caregiver, who knows well the person being assessed. The Classroom Edition is designed to be completed by a teacher. Numerous other adaptive behavior scales, checklists, and observation procedures have also been developed.

Measurement of adaptive behavior has proven difficult, in large part because of the relative nature of social adjustment and competence—what is considered appropriate in one situation or by one group may not be in or by another. Nowhere is there

Direct observation of the child's performance in the natural environment is the best method of assessing adaptive behavior.

a list that everyone would agree describes exactly those adaptive behaviors that all of us should exhibit. And as with IQ tests, cultural bias can be a problem in adaptive behavior scales. For instance, one item on some scales requires a child to tie a laced shoe, but some children have never had a shoe with laces. Research being conducted today on the measurement of adaptive behavior may help resolve these problems.

Some professionals have argued against inclusion of adaptive behavior in the definition of mental retardation (e.g., Clausen, 1972). Zigler, Balla, and Hodapp (1984) contend that mental retardation should be determined only by a score of less than 70 on a standardized IQ test. In a rebuttal that probably reflects the position of most professionals in the field, Barnett (1986) attacks the proposal of Zigler et al. (1984) by explaining the necessity of retaining adaptive behavior in the definition of mental retardation if the concept is to remain socially valid.

Coulter and Morrow (1978) provide an excellent discussion of the many issues that surround the concept and measurement of adaptive behavior.

However, despite the fact that most professionals view adaptive behavior as an important component of mental retardation, a child's IQ score remains the primary variable in determining whether she is identified as mentally retarded. A summary by Payne, Patton, and Patton (1986) of the results of two surveys of state departments of education (Huberty, Koller, & Brink, 1980; Patrick & Reschly, 1982) reveals that 25 states do not require an assessment of adaptive behavior in the identification of a mentally retarded child. By contrast, these surveys found that only 6 states allow a child to be identified as mentally retarded without the use of an IQ test.

The Still-Unresolved Issue of Definition

The 1973 AAMD definition was incorporated into P.L. 94–142 as the federal definition of mental retardation and is the definition most frequently cited in the special education literature. Since 1973 the AAMD definition has been slightly revised two times (Grossman, 1977, 1983) in efforts to clarify the importance of clinical judgment in the diagnosis of mental retardation. When the 1973 AAMD definition reduced the upper IQ limit from 85 to 70, the largest group of children previously considered mentally retarded could no longer be classified as such and, in some cases, were denied needed special education services. Kidd (1979) contended that many children who desperately needed the specialized instruction offered in programs for the mildly retarded were "being drowned in the mainstream" (p. 75). The newest AAMD manual (Grossman, 1983) emphasizes that the IQ cutoff score of 70 is intended only as a guideline and should not be interpreted as a hard and fast requirement. A higher IQ score of 75 or more may be associated with mental retardation if, according to a clinician's judgment, the child exhibits deficits in adaptive behavior thought to be caused by impaired intellectual functioning.

Even though the AAMD definition of mental retardation dominates the field, not everyone is happy with it. Sidney Bijou (1966) prefers a strictly behavioral definition that states that "a retarded individual is one who has a limited repertoire of behavior shaped by events that constitute his history" (p. 2). Bijou and Dunitz-Johnson (1981) have described an "interbehavior analysis" view of mental retardation that attributes a limited (retarded) behavioral repertoire to the hampering effects of biomedical impairment, handicapping sociocultural conditions, or both. Biomedical impairment can retard an individual's development through injury to the response equipment or to the internal or external sources of stimulation. Handicapping sociocultural conditions may include an impoverished home environment, limited educational opportunities, and negative parental practices such as indifference or abuse. This view maintains that if the environment was properly arranged, the individual might no longer act retarded. And, in fact, research is beginning to show that much of the retarded behavior of many persons with mental retardation can be replaced with more normal behavior.

Jane Mercer, a sociologist, believes that the concept of mental retardation is a sociological phenomenon and that the label *mentally retarded* is "an achieved social status in a social system" (Mercer, 1973a, p. 3). Mercer's research (1973a, 1973b) shows that many children identified as mildly retarded by the school system, especially children from cultural minorities, are labeled mentally retarded because their behavior does not meet the norms of the white, middle-class social system. She has developed a system for diagnosing mental retardation in children from minority groups. Called SOMPA (System of Multicultural Pluralistic Assessment), it is designed to eliminate cultural bias in intelligence testing. Using SOMPA, the examiner converts the WISC-R IQ scores into what is called an estimated learning potential (ELP) score. The ELP score is affected by such variables as ethnic group membership and family size and structure. Although many school districts have begun using SOMPA, its validity and ultimate usefulness must await further research. Oakland (1980) found that WISC-R IQ scores correlated more highly with achievement than did ELP scores. As MacMillan (1982) points out, it is yet to be determined precisely how SOMPA can be used in education.

> At present, the SOMPA system might reduce the number of minority children eligible for EMR [educable mentally retarded] programs, but whether this is in their best interest remains to be seen; it will probably depend on the availability of alternative programs to meet their learning needs when they are no longer eligible for EMR-related services. (p. 234)

Another alternative definition of mental retardation was proposed by Marc Gold (1980a). According to Gold, mental retardation should be viewed as failure by society to provide sufficient training and education, rather than as a deficit within the individual.

> Mental retardation refers to a level of functioning which requires from society significantly above average training procedures and superior assets in adaptive behavior, manifested throughout life. The mentally retarded person is characterized by the level of power needed in the training process for [the person] to learn, and not by limitations on what [the person] can learn. The height of a retarded person's level of functioning is determined by the availability of training technology and the amount of resources society is willing to allocate and not by significant limitations in biological potential. (p. 148)

Gold's "social responsibility" perspective is a highly optimistic one in its claim that the ultimate level of functioning of a mentally retarded person is determined by the technology available for training and the amount of resources devoted to the task.

Response equipment refers to parts of the body that produce movement or responses. It includes the brain, the eyes, the speech organs, and so forth.

For more on special education students from culturally diverse subgroups, see chapter 12.

The alternate definitions of mental retardation offered by Bijou, Mercer, and Gold are important ones. All three emphasize the fundamental notion that mental retardation represents a current level of performance; it is not something a person *has* in the same way you have the measles or red hair. Furthermore, performance can often be altered significantly by manipulating certain aspects of the environment (teaching nonretarded behavior or, in Mercer's view, altering one's own culturally biased perspective of what constitutes retarded behavior). All of these approaches agree that mental retardation is a relative phenomenon and need not be a permanent condition.

The debate over the definition of mental retardation is likely to continue. In the meantime all of the major professional organizations that work with mentally retarded children and adults use the AAMD definition and advocate its continued use because it promotes universal standards and communication to a greater degree than do other definitions.

Perhaps it is best to end this discussion of definition with the words of Burton Blatt—one of the field's most prolific, influential, and controversial figures—who argues that when all is said and done, mental retardation is best viewed as an administrative category. In his final book, *The Conquest of Mental Retardation* (1987), Blatt writes, "Simply stated, someone is mentally retarded when he or she is 'officially' identified as such" (p. 72).

[handwritten margin note:] ① mental R is not a general phon. the person can learn + how to be a self-sufficient person.

CLASSIFICATION OF MENTAL RETARDATION

See page 100 for the story of Daniel, an 11-year-old with Down syndrome.

Many systems have been proposed for the classification of mentally retarded persons. In 1963 Gelof reported that 23 different classification systems were in use in English-speaking countries. As we discussed in chapter 1, classification of exceptional children is a difficult but necessary task. Various systems have been developed that classify mental retardation according to **etiology** (cause) or clinical type (for example, **Down syndrome**). Although these classification systems are useful to physicians, they have little utility for educators. For example, two children might be classified correctly as having Down syndrome, but one might be able to function well in a regular second grade classroom for part of the day, whereas the other is unable to perform even the most basic self-help tasks. The AAMD classifies mental retardation by degree or level of severity, as measured by an IQ test. Table 3.2 lists the levels of mental retardation according to the most recent AAMD manual (Grossman, 1983). The range of scores representing the high and low end of each level indicates an awareness of the inexactness of intelligence testing and the importance of clinical judgment in determining the level of severity.

The AAMD classification system is the most widely used by diagnosticians. But because the skills and abilities of mentally retarded children vary so widely, particular care must be devoted to classification. Classifying a child as severely retarded solely on the basis of IQ score could limit that child's access to potentially useful programming designated for higher-functioning children. Because of this limitation, a system of classification that parallels the AAMD system has been developed in education

TABLE 3.2
Levels of mental retardation.

Level	Intelligence Test Score
Mild	50–55 to approx. 70 ($+/-5$)
Moderate	35–40 to 50–55
Severe	20–25 to 35–40
Profound	Below 20–25

(Smith, 1971). Even though IQ scores play an important role in educational classification, the specific skill levels and educational needs of a given child are the primary determinants of his placement.

Mild Retardation

Children with mild retardation have traditionally been educated in self-contained classrooms in the public schools. Today, many mildly retarded elementary school children are being educated in regular classrooms, with a special educator helping the classroom teacher with individualized instruction for the child and providing extra tutoring in a resource room as needed. Most mildly retarded children are not identified as retarded until they enter school and sometimes not until the second or third grade, when more difficult academic work is required.

Educators sometimes refer to mildly retarded children as educable mentally retarded (EMR).

School programs for mildly retarded students usually stress the basic academic subjects—reading, writing, and arithmetic—during the elementary years. The emphasis shifts to vocational training and work-study programs in junior high and high school. Most mildly retarded children master academic skills up to about the sixth grade level and are likely to be able to handle semiskilled jobs well enough to support themselves independently or semi-independently. Mildly retarded adults usually develop social and communication skills similar to those of their nonretarded peers; many are not recognized as retarded outside school or after they finish school.

A self-contained classroom is a class made up of only handicapped children. It may have only EMR children, or it may include children wih physical handicaps or sensory impairments.

Moderate Retardation

Unlike mildly retarded children, who are usually not identified as needing special education until they reach school, most children with moderate retardation show significant delays in development during their preschool years. As they grow older, discrepancies generally grow wider between moderately retarded children and their nonhandicapped age-mates in overall intellectual, social, and motor development. Of those persons classified as moderately retarded, approximately 30% are children with Down syndrome, and about 50% have some form of brain damage (Neisworth & Smith, 1978). Additional handicapping conditions and physical abnormalities are more common in moderately retarded people than in the mildly retarded population.

Until recently, educators referred to moderately retarded children as trainable mentally retarded (TMR). The word *trainable* was used because of the belief that most moderately retarded children would not benefit from a traditional school curriculum featuring academics and needed a specialized training program concentrating on self-care, communication, and social skills.

During their school years moderately retarded children are usually taught in self-contained classrooms with highly structured instructional programs designed to teach

DANIEL

"Hey, hey, hey, Fact Track!" The 11-year-old speaker chose one of his favorite programs from the table next to the computer in his parents' dining room. He inserted the floppy disc, booted the system, and waited for the program to load.

"What is your name?" appeared on the monitor.

"Daniel Skandera," he typed. A menu scrolled up listing the program's possibilities. Daniel chose multiplication facts, Level 1.

"How many problems do you want to do?" the computer asked,

"20."

"Do you want to set a goal for yourself, Daniel?"

"Yes, 80 sec."

"Get ready!"

Daniel Skandera, Jr., was born with Down syndrome, a chromosomal abnormality that usually causes moderate to severe mental retardation. "A psychologist tested Daniel at 12 months and told us he was three standard deviations below normal, untestable. That assessment was the basis for Daniel's being denied enrollment in an infant stimulation program. We knew the tests were invalid and accepted the challenge of teaching Daniel ourselves," explained Daniel's father, himself a clinical neuropsychologist at a children's mental health center. "Between Marie and me, we had spent about 10,000 hours working with Daniel by the time he was 5. It's paid off a million times over. He's an inspiration and joy."

"We believed that we had learned enough about how Daniel learns to work with him confidently," says his mother, Marie, a former IBM systems instructor. "If something doesn't work, if he becomes frustrated, we are challenged to try another approach. Daniel is an only child, and we were older when he was born. When we're gone, we want him to be able to take care of himself, to be a taxpayer instead of a tax burden."

Randomly generated multiplication facts flashed on the screen: "4 × 6," "2 × 9," "3 × 3," "7 × 6." Daniel responded, deftly punching in his answers on the computer's numeric key-pad. Twice he recognized errors and corrected them before inputting his answers.

Daniel attends a regular fourth grade classroom at Robinwood Elementary School in Whitehall, Ohio. Academically he performs at grade level except for two subjects. For math and spelling, his best subjects ("Hooray, I love spellin'! "), he leaves the fourth grade classroom each day—and moves to the fifth grade. Daniel is not a special education student; he has no IEP. His extracurricular activities are those of his classmates and neighborhood friends—riding his bicycle, working out on his regulation-size trampoline, playing along with tape recorded rock 'n' roll on his professional six-piece drum set, rough-housing, spending the night at a buddy's.

"Positive expectations are the key words," agreed Daniel's parents. "With Daniel it might take a little longer, but we get there."

The computer tallied the results. "You completed 20 problems in 66 seconds. You beat your goal. Problems correct = 20. Congratulations Daniel!" And with that the 11-year-old retreated hastily to the TV room. The Lakers and 76ers were about to tip off for an NBA championship game, and Daniel wanted to see the first half before bedtime.

Daniel brought his computer to school for a demonstration.

daily living skills. Academics are usually limited to development of a basic sight-word vocabulary (e.g., "survival" words such as *exit, don't walk, stop*), perhaps some functional reading skills (such as simple recipes), and some basic number concepts. Some moderately retarded adults hold unskilled jobs in the community, but most who work do so in sheltered workshops. In the past many moderately retarded persons were removed from society and placed in institutions, where they had little opportunity to develop and learn how to get along in the world. Even though it is likely that moderately retarded people will require some supervision throughout their lives, small, community-based residences and neighborhood group homes are proving to be a workable alternative to large institutions.

See chapter 15 for more information on how adults with mental retardation live and work.

Severe and Profound Retardation

Individuals with severe and profound retardation are almost always identified at birth or shortly afterwards. Most of these infants have significant central nervous system damage, and many have other handicapping conditions. Although the AAMD distinguishes between severe and profound retardation on the basis of IQ scores, the difference is primarily one of functional impairment. Training for individuals with severe retardation typically focuses on self-care skills—toileting, dressing, and eating and drinking—and language development. A person with profound retardation may not be able to care for personal needs, may be confined to a bed or wheelchair, and may require 24-hour nursing care. However, recent developments in instructional technology are showing that many severely and profoundly retarded persons can learn skills previously thought beyond their capability—even to the point of becoming semi-independent adults able to live and work in the community.

Until very recently, children with severe/profound mental retardation were virtually ignored by the American educational system. Fortunately, this situation is changing. Litigation and legislation assuring the rights of handicapped children, regardless of the type or degree of handicap, and advances in educational methods (see Snell, 1987) have contributed to this change. P.L. 94–142 mandates that all children must receive an appropriate education and furthermore that the first priority for use of federal special education monies is to be those children currently not receiving educational services. The unserved are mostly severely and profoundly retarded children. The outlook for these individuals is improving. A growing organization of researchers, teachers, parents, and other interested individuals—The Association for Persons with Severe Handicaps (TASH)—is working to help that future.

Chapter 10 is devoted to the special characteristics, programming, and educational issues related to students with severe and profound handicaps.

Problems in Classifying Individuals with Mental Retardation

As with the definition of mental retardation, there have been numerous suggestions and schemes for the classification of people with mental retardation. And also as with the definitions, most classification schemes have been designed to meet the needs of their developers. Unfortunately, educators have not yet developed a functional classification system for those children whose development is retarded. Salvia (1978) describes the situation like this:

Education has borrowed definitions and classificatons from biology, psychology, and sociology; unfortunately, these definitions have only limited utility in the education of children. In the past, the label of mental retardation could be used to exclude individuals from the public schools. Today, according to various state and federal laws (e.g., P.L. 94–142), all handicapped children are entitled to a free and appropriate education at public expense—as are all other children. The classification of mental retardation, as well as its many subclassifications, has less, really, to do with the task of educating people than alternative classifications which denote a child's level of achievement and anticipated progress under various educational plans. Knowing that a person reads at the second-grade level and has the social maturity of an adolescent has more to do with planning and implementing an educational program than the fact he or she earns a score of 70 on the Stanford-Binet. The schools must teach individuals, regardless of whether they are retarded. Now, perhaps educators will develop a functional classification system that is related to educational treatment. (p. 46)

PREVALENCE

Changing definitions of mental retardation, the lack of a nationwide systematic reporting system, and the relatively uncertain status of mildly retarded school children (are they still retarded after they have left school?) contribute to the difficulty of estimating the number of mentally retarded people. When prevalence figures are based on IQ scores alone, approximately 3% of the population theoretically scores in the retarded range—two standard deviations below the mean (see Figure 3.1). This 3% prevalence figure is still widely quoted.

However, basing prevalence estimates only on IQ scores ignores the other necessary criterion for mental retardation—deficits in adaptive behavior. Because there are, as of yet, no universally accepted measures of adaptive behavior, no major prevalence studies have assessed it. Some professionals believe that if adaptive behavior was included with intellectual ability when estimating prevalence, the figure would drop to about 1% (Baroff, 1982; Mercer, 1973b; Tarjan, Wright, Eyman, & Keeran, 1973). The percentage of all U.S. school children being served in programs for the mentally retarded was approximately 1.8% in the 1984–85 school year.

MacMillan (1982) and Neisworth and Smith (1978) suggest that the 3% figure probably more accurately reflects **incidence**—the percentage of people who, at some time in their lives, are diagnosed as mentally retarded—and that the number of retarded persons at any one time, or the **prevalence,** is probably closer to 1%. Two factors causing the discrepancy between incidence and prevalence are the high mortality rate of severely and profoundly retarded infants and the fact that many mildly retarded school children are independent and self-sufficient as adults (Edgerton & Bercovici, 1976; Richardson, 1978), and so are no longer counted as mentally retarded.

Baroff (1982) has developed a formula for estimating the number of persons needing services for the mentally retarded. He suggests that there are 4 people per 1,000 population in the moderate-severe-profound ranges and 5 people per 1,000 with mild retardation. This .9% is about one-third the traditional 3% estimate. Using IQ score only as a basis for classification, Haywood (1979) estimates that on a population base of 222 million persons (which the United States Bureau of the Census estimates will be our population in 1980) we shall have 110,000 persons with IQs less than 20, and 444,000 with IQs between 20 and 50, but we shall have 6,693,940 individuals with IQs between 50 and 70. Thus in 1980 there will be more than 12 times as many mentally retarded persons in the IQ 50 to 70 range as there will be with IQs less than 50. (pp. 430–31)

CAUSES OF MENTAL RETARDATION

Mildly retarded individuals make up 80% to 85% of the people identified as mentally retarded, and in the vast majority of those cases the etiology (cause) is unknown. The individuals have no demonstrable organic pathology—no brain damage or other physical problem. In general, when no actual organic damage can be found, we say the cause of the retardation is **cultural-familial.** The term suggests that the combination of a poor social and cultural environment early in the child's life has led to retarded development. Although there is no direct proof that social and familial interactions cause mental retardation, it is generally believed that these influences cause most mild cases of retardation.

The 1973 AAMD manual introduced the term **psychosocial disadvantage** as a suggested replacement for the term *cultural-familial retardation.* Although there are slight differences in the meaning of the two terms, they are both used today to refer to mental retardation caused by environmental influences.

Even though over 250 known causes of mental retardation have been identified, the actual cause is determined in only about 10% to 20% of all cases—usually in the less prevalent ranges—the moderate, severe, and profound cases (Dunn, 1973; Kolstoe, 1972). All of the known causes of retardation are biological or medical. They are referred to as *clinical* or *pathological* (brain damage) retardation. These causes have been categorized by the AAMD.

1. Infections and intoxications (e.g., **rubella,** syphilis, encephalitis, meningitis, exposure to drugs or poisons, blood group incompatibility)
2. Trauma and physical agent (e.g., accidents before, during, and after birth; **anoxia**)
3. Metabolism and nutrition (e.g., **phenylketonuria,** or PKU)
4. Gross brain disease (such as tumors)
5. Unknown prenatal influence (e.g., **hydrocephalus, microcephalus**)
6. Chromosomal abnormality (e.g., **Cri-du-chat syndrome,** Down syndrome, **Turner syndrome**)
7. Gestational disorders (e.g., prematurity, low birth weight)

EDUCATIONAL PLACEMENT AND METHODOLOGY

Regular Public Schools

The regular public schools, which are now responsible for the education of all handicapped children, are changing their ways of providing services to students with mental retardation. Traditionally, the mildly retarded (EMR) student was educated in a self-contained classroom with 12 to 18 other EMR students. Children whose retardation was more severe were usually placed in special schools or institutions. Today, P.L. 94–142 mandates that handicapped children are to be educated with their nonhandi-

See Polloway (1984) for a comprehensive review of the history and current status of research concerning the most effective classroom placement for mildly retarded students.

capped peers to the greatest extent possible. Thus, many EMR students are now spending all or part of the school day in the regular classroom, with supplemental instruction provided by a resource teacher. In addition, some school districts that, in the past, offered no educational programming for moderately retarded children are now beginning to provide classrooms and teachers for these learners.

But, as we saw in chapter 2, simply putting a handicapped child in a regular classroom does not necessarily mean that he will be accepted socially or receive the instructional programming most needed (Gottlieb, 1981). Research shows that many regular classroom teachers still hold a generally negative attitude toward main-streamed EMR students (Childs, 1981). Nevertheless, many special and regular educators are developing programs and methods for integrating the instruction of mentally retarded students with that of their nonhandicapped peers. Systematically planning for the integration of retarded students into the classroom through team games and group investigation projects and directly training handicapped and nonhandicapped students in specific skills for interacting with one another are just some of the methods for increasing the chances of a successful regular class placement (Gottlieb & Leyser, 1981; Stainback, Stainback, Raschke, & Anderson, 1981; Strain, Guralnick, & Walker, 1986). Peer tutoring programs have also proven effective in promoting the instructional and social integration of mentally retarded children into regular classrooms (Delquadri, Greenwood, Whorton, Carta, & Hall, 1986; Osguthorpe & Scruggs, 1986). Cooke, Heron, Heward, and Test (1982) describe a classwide peer tutoring system implemented in a first grade classroom in which a student with Down syndrome participated. Over the course of this 5-month study, the child not only interacted directly and positively with her peer tutor but was taught more than 40 sight words by her nonhandicapped classmate.

See pages 47–48 for a description of this peer tutoring program.

Special Schools

Many states, counties, and large school districts operate special schools for students who are mentally retarded. These special schools offer an education and training curriculum specially designed for their students, usually moderately and severely mentally retarded children. These children usually live at home with their families. Although in the past many of these programs were completely administered by state departments of mental health and mental retardation, P.L. 94–142 requires that state departments of education be responsible now for the education of all children. Sometimes a number of small neighboring school districts pool their resources to offer a special school program for moderately and severely mentally retarded students in their area.

Educational Methodology

Research in specific educational techniques for mentally retarded children began when Itard started his work with Victor, the Wild Boy of Aveyron. But not until the last 2 decades has the scientific method been employed systematically in an attempt to discover effective and reliable teaching methods for retarded students. Although this research is far from finished—indeed, we must continually search for better teaching methods—one instructional approach has produced the most consistent educational improvements in students with mental retardation. This method is the behavioral approach, or **applied behavior analysis.**

Applied behavior analysis can be defined as systematically arranging environmental events to produce desired changes in behavior. Behavior analysts verify the effects of their instruction by directly measuring student performance (Cooper, 1981). Behavior analysis is not a single technique, but an entire approach to education based on scientifically proven principles that describe how the environment affects learning.

For a detailed description of applied behavior analysis see Cooper, Heron, and Heward (1987).

Applied behavior analysis has not only been used effectively with mentally retarded learners (Snell, 1987) but has also been successfully applied with students with other handicapping conditions (Nelson & Polsgrove, 1984). One indication of the role of applied behavior analysis as an instructional approach in special education is the April 1986 issue of *Exceptional Children,* which was devoted to effective instructional practices. The issue consisted largely of articles describing behavioral teaching strategies (Anderson-Inman, 1986; Delquadri et al., 1986; Fowler, 1986; Strain & Odom, 1986; White, 1986).

The first step in the behavioral approach to instruction is to specify exactly what skills, or behaviors, the learner is to acquire. Task analysis, a method in which large skills are broken down and sequenced into a series of subskills, lets a teacher break a task into small, easy-to-teach subtasks. These subtasks are then sequenced from easiest to most difficult or in the natural order in which they must be performed. Assessing a child's performance on a sequence of task-analyzed subskills helps pinpoint exactly where instruction should begin.

Excellent descriptions of how to perform and validate a task analysis can be found in Bellamy, Horner, and Inman (1979), Bailey and Wolery (1984), Gold (1976), Moyer and Dardig (1978), and Snell (1987).

Another hallmark of the behavioral approach is direct and continuous measurement. Academic achievement tests have traditionally been the major source of data used in evaluating educational programs. Although these data have some use, they are not useful for daily instructional planning. Achievement tests are usually given only once or twice a year, and the information they provide is too general. Systematic instruction requires direct and continuous measurement.

> When the purpose of measurement is to facilitate daily instructional planning, measurement tactics that are both direct and continuous must be selected. Measurement must be direct by providing data on student responses to materials used during the instructional process. Measurement must be continuous by providing frequent samples of performance throughout the instructional process. (Cooper & Johnson, 1979, p. 10)

Only through diligent direct and continuous measurement of student performance are teachers able to provide the individualized instruction so vital to the growth and progress of mentally retarded children.

In addition, most behaviorally based teaching techniques hold the following in common:

1. They can be replicated by people other than the originator.
2. They require the student to perform the target behavior repeatedly during each session.

The curriculum for secondary students with mental retardation must focus on acquiring skills that will lead to competence in the adult community.

3. Immediate feedback, usually in the form of **positive reinforcement,** is provided to the student.
4. Cues and prompts that help the student respond correctly from the very beginning of the lesson are systematically withdrawn.
5. Efforts are included to help the student generalize the newly learned skill to different, nontraining environments.

Teaching Mentally Retarded Students to Eat in Fast-Food Restaurants

An instructional program that was developed to teach mentally retarded secondary students to eat in fast-food restaurants (van den Pol et al., 1981) is an excellent example of how applied behavior analysis can be used to design and evaluate educational programs. Although successful programs have been developed to teach basic survival skills, such as money handling (Cuvo, Veitch, Trace, & Konke, 1978) and telephone use (Leff, 1975), to mentally retarded students, it is not clear whether these skills will continue to be used unless they are part of more complex, functional activities (such as going to the store and purchasing a needed item).

Van den Pol and his colleagues designed and evaluated a program to teach restaurant skills to three mentally retarded students. The students, all males, were 17 to 22 years of age, and their handicaps included mental retardation (IQ scores 46 to 75) and at least one other disability, including emotional impairment, epilepsy, and deafness. The students' math and reading abilities had been assessed at the first to second grade level. All three students had previously eaten in restaurants but could not order or pay for a meal without assistance. The first step in developing the teaching program was to construct a task analysis of the skills needed to order and eat at a fast-food restaurant. The experimenters accomplished this by eating at several fast-food restaurants and recording each step of the process. Four major components were identified: locating, ordering, paying, and eating and exiting. Table 3.3 shows the list of steps generated and descriptions of appropriate and inappropriate responses at each step.

The students were trained in each of the four components, in sequence, in the classroom. Instruction consisted of students role-playing with the teacher the various

TABLE 3.3
Task analysis of skills required to eat in a fast-food restaurant.

Skill	Appropriate Response	Inappropriate Response
1.1	Does not initiate social interaction. Does not self-stimulate.	Talks/makes manual sign to customer or trainer. Engages in motor/vocal self-stimulation so that customers differentially attend to him.
1.2	Enters double door within 2 min of start.	Uses wrong door. Does not enter within 2 min.
1.3	Goes directly to counter. Does not leave line except to get into shorter line.	Not in line or at counter within 30 sec. Gets out of line.
2.1	Makes ordering response within 10 sec of cue. If written, finishes within 2 min.	Does not respond within 10 sec. Responds before cue. Makes inappropriate (i.e., nonordering-related) verbalization. Not finished writing within 2 min.
2.2	Says "How much for . . .? when giving order.	Does not inquire "How much for . . .?"
2.3	Orders food that he can afford, appropriate item combination (i.e., minimum order—sandwich & drink; maximum—sandwich, drink, side order, & any other item).	Orders more food than he can pay for. Uses inappropriate item combination.
2.4	Says "Eat here" when asked.	Does not say order is to dine in. Says "To go."
3.1	Begins to get money within 10 sec of cue. Does not let go of money on counter before cashier cue.	Does not get money within 10 sec. Releases money before cue.
3.2	Hands cashier appropriate combination of bills.	Does not give enough money. Gives too much money so that same bill is returned.

TABLE 3.3 *continued*

Skill	Appropriate Response	Inappropriate Response
3.3	Displays fingers on at least one hand.	Does not display fingers.
3.4	Inquires "Mistake?" if short billed.	Does not inquire if short billed. Inquires "Mistake?" when change is accurate.
3.5	Puts money in pocket.	Does not take change. Puts money on tray instead of pocket.
3.6	Requests salt, pepper, or catsup.	Does not request any condiments.
3.7	Takes a napkin from dispenser.	Does not take napkin from dispenser.
3.8	Says "Thank you."	Does not say "Thank you."
4.1	Sits at unoccupied, trashfree table within 1 min of availability.	Sits with other customer. Sits at a table with trash present. Does not sit down within 1 min.
4.2	Eats food placed only on paper.	Eats food off tray, table, etc.
4.3	Puts napkin in lap *and* wipes mouth or hands.	Does not put napkin in lap. Does not wipe hands or mouth on it.
4.4	Does not spill food or drink.	Drops food off tray or spills drink.
4.5	If spills occur, picks up every one, does not eat any spilled item.	Does not pick up or blot. Eats spilled food.
4.6	Puts trash in container, tray on top, within 2 min of finishing eating.	Does not put trash in container within 2 min. Uses inappropriate container. Throws tray in container.
4.7	Exits within 1 min of trash or 3 min of finishing eating.	Does not exit within time limits.

Source: From "Teaching the Handicapped to Eat in Public Places: Acquisition, Generalization, and Maintenance of Restaurant Skills" by R. A. van den Pol, B. A. Iwata, M. T. Ivancic, T. J. Page, N. A. Neef, and F. P. Whitley, 1981, *Journal of Applied Behavior Analysis, 14,* p. 63. Copyright by the Society for the Experimental Analysis of Behavior, Inc. Reprinted by permission.

steps in simulated customer-cashier interactions and responding to questions about slides showing customers at a fast-food restaurant performing various steps in the sequence. Correct student responses during instruction were followed by social reinforcement (e.g., "Good job! You remembered to ask for your change.") Incorrect responses were followed by feedback describing why the response was incorrect and a remedial trial. If the student response on a remedial trial was incorrect, the teacher modeled the correct response and gave another remedial trial. This sequence was followed until a correct response was made. Each training session consisted of 10 trials, not counting remedial trials. Only one component skill was taught during each session. The next skill was not taught until the student performed at 100% accuracy on the previous skill for two consecutive sessions. When a student mastered the final skill of a component, a review was conducted, consisting of 10 trials covering all previously learned skills.

The program's effects were evaluated by giving each student a randomly determined amount of money between $2.00 and $5.00 and instructing him to go to lunch. These restaurant "probes" were conducted before training, during the instructional

program, and after training. Observers inside the restaurant recorded the students'
performance of the various steps but offered no assistance.

Figure 3.3 shows the results of the program. Before instruction the three students correctly performed an average of 48%, 30%, and 39% of the 22 steps. Their
scores on the final training probe were 86%, 80%, and 95%. Follow-up data collected

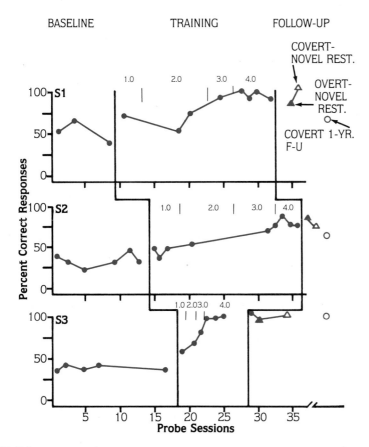

FIGURE 3.3
Percent correct responses during restaurant probes for Students 1, 2, and 3 across experimental conditions. During follow-up, closed triangles represent probes conducted at a
Burger King restaurant, using typical observation procedures; open triangles represent
Burger King probes during which students did not know that their performances were
being observed; and open circles represent covert probes conducted in a McDonald's (different from the one in which previous probe sessions had been conducted) 1 year after
the termination of training.

Source: From "Teaching the Handicapped to Eat in Public Places: Acquisition, Generalization, and Maintenance of Restaurant Skills," by R. A. van den Pol, B. A. Iwata, M. T. Ivancic, T. J. Page, N. A. Neef,
and F. P. Whitley, 1981, *Journal of Applied Behavior Analysis, 14*, p. 66. Copyright by the Society for
the Experimental Analysis of Behavior, Inc. Reprinted by permission.

in a different restaurant showed that the students were able to generalize skills to another fast-food restaurant. One-year follow-up observations showed a drop in performance for two of the students, but all three followed the restaurant sequence more accurately than a sample of 10 randomly chosen regular customers observed as a normative sample. Discussing their study, the authors wrote,

> Results indicate that following approximately 10 hours of classroom instruction, students' restaurant skills generalized to several different natural environment settings, and that their posttraining performance was not dependent upon either the assistance or even the presence of known trainers/observers in the restaurant. Additional probe data collected one year following the termination of training suggested that restaurant skills maintained at high levels or were at least comparable to those exhibited by a nonretarded sample of persons. (van den Pol et al., 1981, p. 68)

This instructional program offers an excellent example of how applied behavior analysis is advancing an effective technology of teaching mentally retarded students.

The following journals contain numerous other examples of applied behavior analysis teaching programs for mentally retarded and other handicapped learners: *Analysis and Intervention of Developmental Disabilities, Behavior Modification, Education & Treatment of Children, Journal of Applied Behavior Analysis, Journal of the Association for Persons with Severe Handicaps.*

RESIDENTIAL ALTERNATIVES FOR INDIVIDUALS WITH MENTAL RETARDATION

Institutions

A 50-state survey conducted in 1983 discovered that 111,311 persons were living in 247 large state-operated facilities for individuals with mental retardation (Epple, Jacobson, & Janicki, 1985). This same survey found that 79% of these residents were persons with severe and profound retardation. Most of our nation's public institutions were set up in the 19th or early 20th century, when it was generally believed that people with mental retardation could not be educated or trained. Large custodial institutions have helped keep mentally retarded people segregated from the rest of society; they were never designed to train people to live in normal society. Institutions have come under severe criticism in recent years for their general inability to provide individualized services in a comfortable, humane, and normalized environment. The complaints are not leveled against the concept of residential facilities; there will always be persons with severe and profound handicaps who need the 24-hour care and supervision that only residential facilities can offer. The problem lies with the level of humane treatment large institutions can offer and with the concept of **normalization.**

In recent years much effort has been expended to improve the quality of life and services provided by institutions for mentally retarded children and adults. The United States Department of Health, Education and Welfare (1974) and the Joint Commission on the Accreditation of Hospitals (JCAH, 1971) have both developed extensive and almost identical standards for residential facilities for individuals with mental retardation. These standards cover a wide range of topics, from building construction to staffing to habilitative and educational programming. Residential units meeting the government or JCAH standards are called licensed facilities. Licensed units are usually eligible for additional funding not available to units that do not meet the accreditation standards.

See, for example, Blatt, (1976); Blatt and Kaplan, (1966); Kugel and Wolfensberger, (1969); Wolfensberger, (1969).

We will return to the concept of normalization later in the chapter

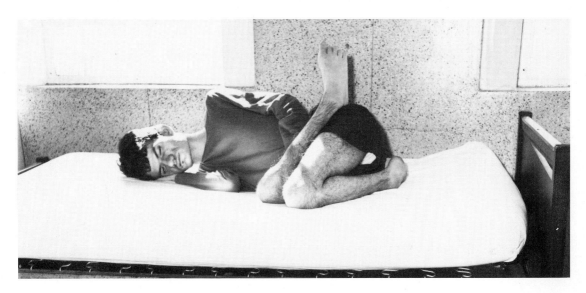

In spite of legislation, court cases, and improved educational methodology, some of our citizens with severe and profound mental retardation experience long periods of inactivity in large institutional facilities. We still have a long way to go.

Repp and Barton (1980) compared the interactions (verbal instruction, custodial guidance, no interaction, and so on) between residents and staff and the behaviors of residents (on-task, no programming, self-stimulatory, and so on) that took place in two licensed and six unlicensed cottages at a large state institution. Each of the eight cottages had from 12 to 40 severely and profoundly mentally retarded residents, some with additional handicaps (hearing or visual impairments physical handicaps). The licensed cottages had resident-to-staff ratios of 4 to 1, whereas in the unlicensed cottages the resident-to-staff ratios ranged from 4 to 1 to 10 to 1. Thus, the licensed units had an advantage of more staff available to provide programming. For 16 days four observers each recorded staff and resident behavior for more than 4 hours per day, yielding almost 160,000 individual 6-second observations.

Figures 3.4 and 3.5 display the study's results. The most striking finding is the overwhelming number of observations in which no interactions between residents and staff (Figure 3.4) and no programming (Figure 3.5) occurred. Whether licensed or not, there were few instances of praise or encouragement (see social behavior in Figure 3.4) directed by staff toward the residents. Figure 3.5 shows that, on the average, every resident, whether in a licensed or unlicensed cottage, spent more time engaging in self-stimulatory behaviors than in programming. In discussing the results of their study, Repp and Barton (1980) wrote,

> These data, quite objective and reliable, show that despite all the excitement over the Education for All Handicapped Children Act, 1975, that despite all the promises of court cases . . . , we still do not provide sufficient educational opportunities for many retarded citizens, even in our licensed facilities. These data cannot be interpreted too strongly, for they were recorded with the complete awareness of the

FIGURE 3.4

The mean percentage of 6-second observations in which each type of staff interaction with residents occurred. Cottages A and B were licensed, but none of the other cottages were.

Source: From "Naturalistic Observation of Institutionalized Retarded Persons: A Comparison of Licensure Decisions and Behavioral Observations" by A. C. Repp and L. E. Barton, 1980, *Journal of Applied Behavior Analysis, 13,* p. 337. Copyright by the Society for the Experimental Analysis of Behavior, Inc. Reprinted by permission.

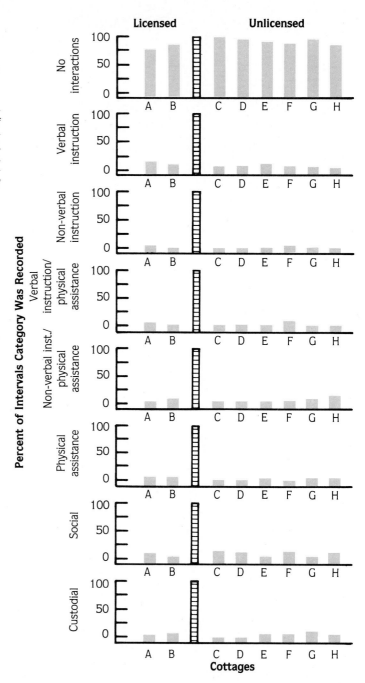

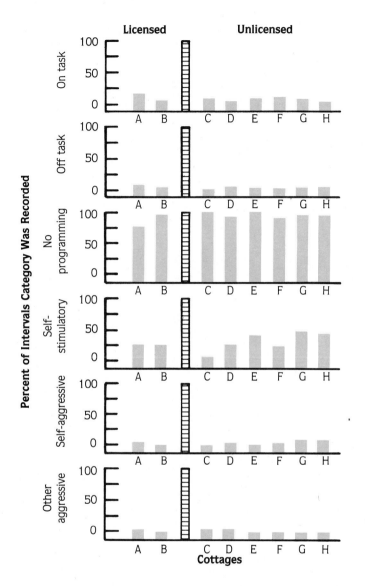

FIGURE 3.5

The mean percentage of 6-second observations in which each type of resident activity was recorded. After each observation no programming, on task, or off task was recorded. If self-stimulation, self-aggressive, or other aggressive behavior occurred, it was marked during the same interval. Cottages A and B were licensed, whereas none of the other cottages were. Source: From "Naturalistic Observation of Institutionalized Retarded Persons: A Comparison of Licensure Decisions and Behavioral Observations" by A. C. Repp and L. E. Barton, 1980, *Journal of Applied Behavior Analysis, 13,* p. 338. Copyright by the Society for the Experimental Analysis of Behavior, Inc. Reprinted by permission.

administration and of the staff being observed, and they were recorded during the hours one would expect most of the educational opportunities in a resident's life to be made available. If they are biased, they are biased in a direction *favorable* to the facility. . . .

In summary, these results are extremely discouraging. They indicate that (1) facilities can be licensed and still not provide habilitation for their clients; (2) despite the technology we have developed for teaching adaptive and reducing maladaptive behaviors, many people remain unaffected; and (3) we still do not provide habilitative opportunities for all retarded citizens, despite all that the recent judicial decisions and governmental regulations seem to promise. (pp. 339–41)

Fortunately, no new large state institutions for persons with mental retardation are presently on the drawing boards, and a variety of alternative residential placements are coming into reality. We will briefly describe some of these in the sections that follow. Before moving on, however, it is important to make one point. There are many caring and competent professionals working in institutions who have dedicated their careers to providing the best possible education and living conditions for the people who reside there. Many of these professionals themselves do not think large institutions are the best way to care for our severely and profoundly retarded citizens. Yet they are trying to do the best job possible under the prevailing conditions. Happily, the movement toward deinstitutionalization has decreased the population of some institutions to a more manageable number so that some programs are now able to provide more appropriate services for their residents.

Chapter 15 provides more information on deinstitutionalization.

Regional Facilities

Regional facilities offer total-care, 24-hour residential programs like those of the large state institutions but on a much smaller basis, serving only those persons in a given geographical area within a state. The reduced distance to family and community allows for more normalized and individualized treatment programs. Hemming, Lavender, and Pill (1981) compared the quality of life of 51 retarded adults who were transferred from a large institution to smaller living units and a matched control group of 50 adults who remained in the large institution. Residents who had been transferred to the smaller units showed significant improvement in adaptive behavior (as measured by the Adaptive Behavior Scale) and increased participation in culturally normative activities.

Group Homes

More information on group homes and other community-based residential alternatives for handicapped persons is presented in chapter 15.

A group home usually consists of between four and eight mentally retarded adolescents or adults living in a family-type dwelling in a residential neighborhood. Professional staff are responsible for supervision and overall programming for the residents, who often work at sheltered workshops and participate in social and recreational activities in the community.

In recent years we have witnessed tremendous growth in the establishment of group homes and other community-based residential alternatives for mentally retarded persons. A 1982 survey found 7,669 community-based residential facilities operating throughout the country, a significant increase over the 4,290 community-based residences operating in 1977 (Center for Residential and Community Services, 1983; Conroy, 1977).

Apartment Living

A variety of residential alternatives involve apartment living for adults with mental retardation. Alternatives include independent apartments with minimal supervision, apartment clusters, and coresidence arrangements (a retarded resident and a nonretarded roommate). A follow-up study of 69 mentally retarded adults 5 years after they had been placed in independent living arrangements found 80% of the group still in their original independent housing placement (Schalock, Harper, & Carver, 1981). These adults reported that they were proud of their apartments and that they felt good about "doing their own thing."

CURRENT ISSUES/FUTURE TRENDS

In 1961 the first President's Committee on Mental Retardation was created by John F. Kennedy. The committee was charged with conducting an intensive study of mental retardation and making recommendations for national policy. A year later, results of the many task forces, public hearings, visits to facilities for retarded people, and extensive interviews with professionals, parents, and mentally retarded persons were compiled into the committee's report, *A Proposed Program for National Action to Combat Mental Retardation* (Mayo, 1962). The report contained specific recommendations related to human and legal rights, prevention, research, education, and medical and other services for individuals with mental retardation. Many of the committee's recommendations set the stage for much of what took place in the 1960s and early 1970s, particularly in the areas of research and legislation confirming the rights of retarded citizens.

Subsequent presidents have reconvened the Committee on Mental Retardation in order to track the accomplishment of earlier goals and to attempt to predict the future needs of retarded citizens. In their 1976 report to the president entitled *Mental Retardation: A Century of Decision*, the committee outlined the country's major objectives in the field of mental retardation through the year 2000. Seven major goals were stated.

1. Attainment of citizenship status in law and in fact for all mentally retarded individuals in the United States, exercised to the fullest degree possible under the conditions of disability.
2. Reduction of the incidence of mental retardation from biomedical causes by at least 50% by the year 2000.
3. Reduction of the incidence and prevalence of mental retardation associated with social disadvantage to the lowest level possible by the end of this century.
4. Adequate and humane service systems for all retarded persons in need of them.
5. Attainment of a high and stable level of international relations in the cooperative resolution of the universal human problems of preventing and ameliorating mental retardation.
6. Achievement of a firm and deep public acceptance of mentally retarded persons as members in common of the social community and as citizens in their own right.
7. Equitable, coordinated, efficient, and effective use of public resources in all mental retardation programs.

The Committee went on to list specific objectives by which they thought the major goals could be obtained. Although a great deal remains to be done if these goals are to be realized, some accomplishments have been made in each of the seven areas.

We will briefly describe some recent accomplishments and current activities in three related areas: human and legal rights, prevention, and normalization.

Rights of Mentally Retarded Citizens

See Bogdan (1986) for a historical documentation of the exhibition of mentally retarded people for amusement and profit, from 1850–1940.

We have come a long way since the time when mentally retarded people were exterminated, ridiculed, or employed as court jesters—but we still have a long way to go. Of all the goals of the first President's Committee on Mental Retardation, we have the most concrete evidence of accomplishment of the goal of legal rights for persons with mental retardation.

Friedman (1976, 1977) has detailed the history of the legal rights movement on behalf of mentally retarded people. Numerous court cases in recent years have advanced the position that a mentally retarded person has and should be able to exercise, with assistance from society if necessary, the same rights and freedoms as a nonhandicapped citizen. Following are the rights of mentally retarded persons as advocated by the AAMD.

Mentally retarded citizens are entitled to enjoy and to exercise the same rights as are available to nonretarded citizens, to the limits of their ability to do so. As handicapped citizens, they are also entitled to specific extensions of, and additions to, these basic rights, in order to allow their free exercise and enjoyment. When an individual retarded citizen is unable to enjoy and exercise his or her rights, it is the obligation of the society to intervene so as to safeguard these rights, and to act humanely and conscientiously on that person's behalf.

Basic Rights

I. The basic rights that a retarded person shares with his or her nonretarded peers include, but are not limited to, those implied in "life, liberty, and the pursuit of happiness," and those specified in detail in the various documents that provide the basis for governing democratic nations. Specific rights of mentally retarded persons include, but are not limited to:

  A. The right to freedom of choice within the individual's capacity to make decisions and within the limitations imposed on all persons.

  B. The right to live in the least restrictive individually appropriate environment.

  C. The right to gainful employment, and to a fair day's pay for a fair day's labor.

  D. The right to be part of a family.

  E. The right to marry and have a family of his or her own.

  F. The right to freedom of movement, hence not to be interned without just cause and due process of law, including the right not to be permanently deprived of liberty by institutionalization in lieu of imprisonment.

  G. The rights to speak openly and fully without fear of undue punishment, to privacy, to the practice of a religion (or the practice of no religion), and to interaction with peers.

Specific Extensions

II. Specific extensions of, and additions to, these basic rights, which are due mentally handicapped persons because of their special needs, include, but are not limited to:

A. The right to a publicly supported and administered comprehensive and integrated set of rehabilitative programs and services designed to minimize handicap or handicaps.

B. The right to a publicly supported and administered program of training and education including, but not restricted to, basic academic and interpersonal skills.

C. The right, beyond those implicit in the right to education described above, to a publicly administered and supported program of training toward the goal of maximum gainful employment, insofar as the individual is capable.

D. The right to protection against exploitation, demeaning treatment, or abuse.

E. The right, when participating in research, to be safeguarded from violations of human dignity and to be protected from physical and psychological harm.

F. The right, for a retarded individual who may not be able to act effectively in his or her own behalf, to have a responsible impartial guardian or advocate appointed by the society to protect and effect the exercise and enjoyment of these foregoing rights, insofar as this guardian, in accordance with responsible professional opinion, determines that the retarded citizen is able to enjoy and exercise these rights.*

Many states have organized citizen advocacy programs for the mentally retarded. An **advocate** is a volunteer committed to becoming personally involved with the welfare of a mentally retarded person and to becoming knowledgeable about the services that are available for that person. In a sense an advocate is an informed friend who can legally take a stand to see that her client's rights are not abused and that the necessary educational and other services are in fact delivered. Being an advocate can be an excellent way to serve a citizen with mental retardation and learn much about the field in the process.

Prevention of Mental Retardation

Each week in this country about 2,100 babies are born who are either mentally retarded or will, at some point, become retarded. As scientific research—both medical and psychological—has generated new knowledge about the causes of mental retardation, procedures and programs designed to prevent its occurrence have increased.

Probably the biggest single preventive strike against mental retardation (and many other handicapping conditions, including blindness and deafness) was the development of an effective rubella vaccine in 1962. When rubella (German measles) is contracted by mothers during the first three months of pregnancy, it causes severe damage in 10% to 40% of the unborn children (Krim, 1969). Fortunately, this cause

---

*From *Rights of Mentally Retarded Persons: An Official Policy Statement of the American Association on Mental Deficiency,* 1973.

of mental retardation can be eliminated if women are vaccinated for rubella before becoming pregnant.

Phenylketonuria (PKU) is a genetically inherited condition in which a child is born without an important enzyme needed to break down the amino acid phenylalanine, which is found in many common foods. Failure to break down this amino acid causes brain damage that results in severe mental retardation. By analyzing the concentration of phenylalanine in a newborn's blood plasma, doctors can diagnose PKU, and it can be treated with a special diet. Most PKU children who receive a phenylalanine-restricted diet early enough have normal intellectual development (Berman & Ford, 1970).

Advances in medical science have enabled doctors to identify certain genetic influences strongly associated with mental retardation. One approach to prevention that is being offered by many health service organizations is **genetic counselling,** a discussion between a specially trained medical counselor and prospective parents about the possibilities that they may give birth to a handicapped child, based on the parents' genetic backgrounds.

Amniocentesis is a procedure in which a sample of fluid is withdrawn from the amniotic sac surrounding the fetus during the second trimester of pregnancy. A chromosomal analysis of the amniotic fluid allows doctors to identify the presence of about 80 specific genetic disorders prior to birth. Many of these disorders, such as Down syndrome (O'Brien, 1971), are associated with mental retardation.

Medical advances such as these have noticeably reduced the incidence of mental retardation caused by some of the known biological factors, but huge advancements in research are needed if the goal of reducing the incidence of biomedical retardation by 50% by the year 2000 is to be reached.

As we saw earlier, the great majority of those children labeled mentally retarded fall in the mild range and have no clear-cut etiology. These are the children whose developmental delays are thought to be primarily the result of a poor environment during their early years. The poor environment may be a result of parental neglect, poverty, disease, poor diet, and other factors—many of which are completely out of the hands of the child's parents. During the last 10 years or so, the number of research projects aimed at serving high-risk preschoolers and their parents has increased. Although measuring the effects of a preventive program is much more difficult than measuring the decreased number of children suffering from a disease like PKU, the preliminary results of these projects are encouraging.

See chapter 13 for more on intervention programs for young handicapped children.

Normalization

The principle of normalization refers to the use of progressively more normal settings and procedures "to establish and/or maintain personal behaviors which are as culturally normal as possible" (Wolfensberger, 1972, p. 28). Normalization is not a single technique or set of procedures that is done to people, but rather an overriding philosophy. That philosophy says that persons with mental retardation should be both phys-

"COACHES" HELP WITH SCHOOL-TO-WORK TRANSITION

Recent follow-up studies of handicapped high school graduates have generated serious concern over the ability of public school special education programs to prepare handicapped learners for competitive employment and community integration (e.g., Bellamy, 1985; Hasazi, Gordon, & Roe, 1985). As a result of these findings the development of programs to improve the handicapped student's transition from school to work has become a national priority. One such program is called Competitive Employment Through Vocational Experience (CETVE), a joint project between the University of North Carolina at Charlotte and the Charlotte-Mecklenberg Public Schools. Special education and vocational teachers, vocational rehabilitation counselors, CETVE staff, the students, and their parents all work together to ease the transition from school to work. CETVE services include supervised

volunteer and competitive vocational experiences, job coaching, and written transition plans. One student's experience with the program is described here.

When the CETVE project found work for 18-year-old Faye as a janitor with a cleaning service company, it was the first time that this high school senior with mild mental retardation had ever worked. Faye's responsibility was to clean one side of each floor of a 21-story office tower—to empty all of the ashtrays and trashcans, dust and clean the furniture, and vacuum the carpet. She was to complete all of this work within 3 hours each weekday evening and was to receive minimum wages with no fringe benefits.

After locating the potential placement, Faye's job coach, Teresa, assisted Faye with the application and interview process, coordinated transportation,

Faye has learned to perform her new job with competence.

and ensured family support. Then Teresa's role as an on-the-job coach really began. During the first week Teresa oriented Faye to the building and grounds, the work environment, and the work routine. Because Faye could not complete all three cleaning tasks independently, she began with emptying trash and dusting and cleaning the furniture. Teresa did all the vacuuming during the first 2 weeks. After 2 weeks Faye was doing each of her tasks accurately, but her rate was too slow to allow enough time to complete the vacuuming by herself. At this point a performance feedback system (Van Houten, 1980) was begun to encourage and motivate Faye to decrease the amount of time she spent emptying trash and dusting and cleaning. As she became more proficient at these aspects of the job, Faye did more and more of the vacuuming. By the end of the fourth week, Faye was independently completing all of the required tasks within the 3-hour time limit. Faye continued to work at this job for 5 months. Her employers described her performance as excellent.

Following graduation from high school, Faye was hired as a full-time packager for a plumbing supplies company. Her starting salary was $4 per hour with full company benefits to begin after 3 months of employment. Once again, Teresa was on the job as Faye's coach, gradually reducing the amount of assistance provided and the time spent with Faye as she learned to perform the job accurately and proficiently. Training Faye to do her second job was much easier. According to Faye, she had learned many important skills on her first job: "to be on time, to call in if you are sick, and to listen to your supervisor."

Faye has come a long way during the past year. She now has a full-time job and is a contributing member of society. And what does she do with her paycheck? As Faye explains, "I put some in my savings account, but I spend most of it on clothes!"

For further information about Project CETVE, write to David W. Test or Patricia K. Keul, Department of Curriculum and Instruction, University of North Carolina at Charlotte, Charlotte, NC 28223.

ically and socially integrated into the mainstream of society to the greatest extent possible, regardless of the degree or type of disability. Madle (1978) states that

> such integration is maximized when all people live in a culturally normative setting in ordinary community housing, can move and communicate in age-appropriate ways and are able to use typical community services such as schools, stores, churches, and physicians. (p. 469)

Menolascino (1977) makes the following recommendations for normalizing the delivery of educational, residential, and community services to people with mental retardation.

1. Programs and facilities for mentally retarded persons should be physically and socially integrated into the community.
2. No more mentally retarded people should be congregated in one service facility than the surrounding neighborhood can readily integrate into its resources, community social life, and so on.
3. Integration—and, therefore, normalization—can best be attained if the location of services follows population density and distribution patterns.
4. Services and facilities for retarded persons, if they are to be normalizing in their intent, must meet the same standards as other comparable services and facilities for nonretarded people; they should not be stricter or more lenient.
5. Staff personnel working with retarded persons must meet at least the same standards as those required of persons working with comparable nonretarded individuals.
6. In order to accomplish maximum normalization, mentally retarded persons must have maximum exposure to the nonretarded population in the community.
7. Daily routines should be comparable to those of nonretarded persons of the same age.
8. Services for children and adults should be physically separated, both because the probability that children will imitate the deviant behavior of their elders will be less and because services to adults and children tend to be separated in the mainstream of our society.
9. Mentally retarded individuals should be taught to dress and groom themselves like other persons their age; they should be taught a normal gait, normal movements, and normal expressive behavior patterns; their diet should be adjusted to assure normal weight.
10. As much as possible, the mentally retarded adult, even if severely handicapped, should be provided the opportunity to engage in work that is culturally normal in type, quantity, and setting. (Adapted from Menolascino, 1977, pp. 79–83)

See pages 119–20 for the story of how one special education project helps high school students make the transition from school to the world of work.

As belief in normalization grows among both professionals and the public, the time draws nearer when all mentally retarded people can have humane and effective treatment and education.

SUMMARY

1. Society's attitude toward people with mental retardation has gone through many stages.
   a. Primitive people left retarded and other handicapped people to die. Later, superstitions about people with mental retardation became common; they were often ridiculed.
   b. In the Middle Ages a more humanitarian view led to the development of asylums.
   c. The first attempts to educate mentally retarded children came during the early 19th century, beginning in Europe and spreading to the United States. Later in that century, however, large state institutions—which came to be seen as custodial rather than educational—became the primary means of service.
   d. Around the turn of the century, separate public school classes for mentally retarded students began to be popular.
   e. The movement today is away from institutions and segregation and toward normalized education in the least restrictive environment.

2. Mental retardation is a complex concept that is difficult to define and measure.
   a. The current AAMD definition, used in P.L. 94–142, states that mental retardation involves both "significantly subaverage general intellectual functioning" *and* "deficits in adaptive behavior," manifested between birth and 18 years of age.
   b. Intellectual functioning is usually measured by a score on a normed, standardized intelligence test.
   c. An observation scale is usually used in evaluating adaptive behavior.
   d. Both intelligence tests and adaptive behavior scales can be culturally biased and scored subjectively. However, IQ tests are the best single predictor of school achievement.
   e. Important alternate definitions stress that mental retardation denotes a level of performance that can be altered.
   f. The trend today is toward using a more conservative approach to labeling children mentally retarded because of the negative effects of labeling and the limitations of the tests.

3. Mental retardation is classified by degree of severity, as measured by IQ scores.
   a. Children who are mildly retarded may be retarded only in school. Their social and communication skills may be normal or nearly so. They are likely to become independent or semi-independent adults.
   b. Many mildly retarded children are educated in regular classrooms with extra help provided as needed. They can generally master standard academic skills up to about a sixth grade level.
   c. Moderately retarded children usually show significant early delays before they reach school age, and most will require some degree of lifelong supervision.
   d. In school, moderately retarded students are usually taught communication, self-help and daily living skills, and vocational skills, along with limited academics. Most moderately retarded children are educated in self-contained classrooms.
   e. Most severely and profoundly retarded persons are identified in infancy. Many have physical damage and multiple handicaps. Although some severely and profoundly

retarded adults can be semi-independent in the community, others need 24-hour care throughout their lives.

f. In spite of their severe handicaps, people with severe and profound retardation can learn. Curricula stress communication and self-help skills.

4. It is difficult to estimate the number of people with mental retardation. Theoretically, 3% of the population would score in the retarded range on IQ tests, but this does not account for adaptive behavior, the other criterion. Many experts now cite an incidence figure of approximately 1% of the total population.

5. It is difficult to determine the cause of most cases of retardation.

a. About 80% to 85% of all retarded people are mildly retarded. In most of these cases, there is no known cause, and the terms *cultural-familial retardation* and/or *psychosocial disadvantage* are used when referring to etiology.

b. The cause is known in 10% to 20% of the cases, usually in the moderate, severe, and profound ranges. All the known causes are biological.

6. Today there are many different options available for residential and educational placement of mentally retarded children and adults.

a. Institutions are seen as necessary for fewer and fewer people, and thus, some are able to provide more humane and more appropriate services for their residents.

b. Small regional residential programs help mentally retarded people live more normal lives within their own communities.

c. Some mentally retarded adults live in supervised apartments, some with nonretarded roommates; others live in group homes with houseparents.

d. Although some mentally retarded children attend special public schools, more and more are being educated in their neighborhood schools—either in special classes or in regular classes where they receive special help or attend a resource room for part of the day.

7. Applied behavior analysis is widely used in teaching mentally retarded students. Effective techniques include

a. task analysis

b. repeated opportunities to respond

c. positive reinforcement

d. direct and continuous measurement

8. Recent laws, including P.L. 94–103 and P.L. 94–142, have extended and affirmed the rights of mentally retarded persons as citizens. Advocates can help protect the rights of individual retarded people.

9. Recent scientific advances—including genetic counseling, amniocentesis, virus vaccines, and early screening tests—are helping reduce the incidence of clinical retardation. However, there is still no widely used technique to decrease the incidence of cultural-familial retardation, although early identification and intensive services to high-risk infants show promise.

10. Our current goal is to make the lives of people with mental retardation—at home, in school, and at work—as normal as possible. With this in mind, institutions are necessarily inappropriate. Thus, we must develop normalized and effective training and transition programs and community services for retarded individuals and work to change public attitudes.

FOR MORE INFORMATION

Journals

American Journal of Mental Retardation. Published bimonthly by the American Association on Mental Retardation. Publishes studies and discussions of original material dealing with the behavioral and biological aspects of retardation, as well as theoretical articles.

Analysis and Intervention of Developmental Disabilities. Published quarterly by Pergamon Press, Elmsford, New York. Publishes original behavioral research and theory on severe and pervasive developmental disabilities.

Applied Research in Mental Retardation. Published quarterly by Pergamon Press, Elmsford, New York. Publishes descriptions of effective methods of treatment and assessment as well as coverage of the legal and ethical aspects of applying treatment procedures to mentally retarded children and adults.

Education and Training of the Mentally Retarded. Published four times per school year by the Division on Mental Retardation of the Council for Exceptional Children. Publishes experimental studies and discussion articles dealing with the education of mentally retarded persons.

Mental Retardation. Published bimonthly by the American Association on Mental Deficiency. Concerned with new approaches to methodology, critical summaries, essays, program descriptions, and research studies dealing with mental retardation.

Books

Blatt, B. (1987). *The conquest of mental retardation.* Austin, TX: Pro-Ed.

Drew, C. J., Logan, D. R., & Hardman, M. L. (1984). *Mental retardation: A life cycle approach* (3rd ed.). St. Louis: Mosby.

Ehlers, W. H., Prothero, J. C., & Langone, J. (1982). *Mental retardation and other developmental disabilities: A programmed introduction* (3rd ed.). Columbus, OH: Merrill.

MacMillan, D. L., (1982). *Mental retardation in school and society* (2d ed.). Boston: Little, Brown.

Matson, J. L., & Breuning, S. E. (Eds.). (1983). *Assessing the mentally retarded.* New York: Grune & Stratton.

Neisworth, J. T., & Smith, R. M. (1978). *Retardation: Issues, assessment, and intervention.* New York: McGraw-Hill.

Patton, J. R., Payne, J. S., & Beirne-Smith, M. (1986). *Mental retardation* (2nd ed.). Columbus, OH: Merrill.

Polloway, E. A., Payne, J. S., Patton, J. R., & Payne, R. A. (1985). *Strategies for teaching retarded and special needs learners* (3rd ed.). Columbus, OH: Merrill.

Robinson, N. M., & Robinson, H. B. (1976). *The mentally retarded child* (2nd ed.). New York: McGraw-Hill.

Organizations

American Association on Mental Retardation, 5201 Connecticut Avenue, NW, Washington, DC 20015. Primarily includes researchers, teacher educators, and psychologists interested in mental retardation.

Association for Retarded Citizens, 2709 Avenue E East, Arlington, TX 76011. An advocacy organization including parents and professionals, with active local chapters in most states.

Division on Mental Retardation, Council for Exceptional Children. 1920 Association Drive, Reston, VA 22091. Includes teachers, teacher educators, researchers, and other members of CEC working with mentally retarded persons from preschool on.

4
LEARNING DISABILITIES

No field of special education—or probably all of education, for that matter—has experienced as much rapid growth, extreme interest, and frantic activity as learning disabilities. We used that same sentence to begin the learning disabilities chapter in the first edition of this text. And it is as true today as it was in 1980. The number of children identified as learning disabled has increased greatly in recent years, and the category is now the largest in special education. This increase has helped to fuel an ongoing debate among professionals over the very nature of the learning disability concept. Some believe the increase in the number of children identified as learning disabled indicates the true extent of the handicapping condition. Others contend that too many low achievers—nonhandicapped children who are simply doing poorly in school—have been improperly identified as learning disabled, placing a severe strain on the limited resources available to serve the truly learning disabled student.

Learning disabilities have also been the focus of much public attention and interest, as demonstrated by the countless newspaper stories, magazine articles, and television documentaries with titles like "Does Your Child Have a Learning Disability?" and "New Vitamin and Diet Regimen Halts Learning Disabilities!" It has become a breeding ground for fads and miracle cures. Learning disabilities, more than any other field of special education, seems to create misunderstanding and controversy. There is considerable confusion and disagreement not just on the part of the general public, but among professionals and parents as well, on such basic questions as, What is a learning disability? and How should students with learning disabilities be taught? Yet teachers and researchers in the field of learning disabilities have developed methods of assessment and systematic instruction that have influenced and benefited all of education.

HISTORY OF THE FIELD OF LEARNING DISABILITIES

By the 1950s most public schools had established special education programs (or at least offered some type of special service) for mentally retarded, blind, deaf, physically

Our discussion of the history of learning disabilities is very limited. Although the term *learning disabilities* itself and the rapid growth of the field were phenomena of the 1960s, the field is closely related to research conducted with mentally retarded and brain-injured children in the 1940s and 1950s by Werner, Strauss, Lehtinen, and Kephart. For more detail on the development of the field, see Kauffman and Hallahan (1976), Mercer (1987), Myers and Hammill (1982), and Wiederholt (1974a).

See Sleeter (1986) for an interesting perspective on the history of learning disabilities that is quite different from that provided by most textbooks. She contends that the category of learning disabilities was originally created to explain the failures of white middle-class children when American school achievement standards were raised following the Soviet Union's launching of Sputnik.

In 1982 the membership of DCLD left CEC to form an independent organization, the Council for Learning Disabilities (CLD). In that same year a new Division for Learning Disabilities (DLD) was created within CEC. Many learning disabilities professionals maintain membership in both CLD and DLD.

handicapped, and emotionally disturbed students. But there remained a group of children who were having serious learning problems at school yet did not fit into any of the existing categories of exceptionality. They did not "appear" to be handicapped. That is, the children seemed physically intact; yet they were unable to learn certain basic skills and subjects at school. In searching for help in identifying the source of their children's problems and finding someone who could help them (remember, the public schools had no programs for these children), parents turned to other professionals—most notably doctors, psychologists, and speech and language specialists. Understandably, these professionals viewed the children from the vantage points of their respective disciplines. As a result, terms such as *brain damage,* **minimal brain dysfunction, neurological impairment, perceptual handicap, dyslexia,** and **aphasia** were often used to describe or account for the various problems of the children. Many of these terms are still used today, as a variety of disciplines have been and continue to be influential in the field of learning disabilities.

Most historians of special education place the official beginning of the learning disabilities movement in 1963, when Dr. Samuel Kirk delivered an address to a group of parents. The children of these parents were experiencing serious difficulties in learning to read, they were **hyperactive,** or they could not solve math problems. These parents did not consider their children's learning problems to be the result of mental retardation or emotional disturbance, nor did they like the labels that were often applied to their children. Kirk said, "Recently, I have used the term 'learning disabilities' to describe a group of children who have disorders in development in language, speech, reading, and associated communication skills" (Kirk, 1963). The parents liked the term and that very evening voted to form the Association for Children with Learning Disabilities (ACLD). Today, the organization's name is the Association for Children and Adults with Learning Disabilities (ACALD), and it is a powerful advocacy group dedicated to the support of services and programs for persons with learning disabilities. Most ACALD members are parents, though many teachers and other professionals are also members.

In 1968 three more milestones were reached. First, the National Advisory Committee on Handicapped Children drafted and presented to Congress a definition of learning disabilities, one that still stands as the basic definition used to govern dispersal of federal funds for support of services to learning disabled children. Second, the Council for Exceptional Children (CEC), the largest organization of educators and other professionals serving exceptional children, established the Division for Children with Learning Disabilities (DCLD). Third, 1968 was the year in which Dunn published his article "Special Education for the Mildly Retarded—Is Much of It Justifiable?" (Dunn, 1968). Dunn argued that the proliferation of self-contained classrooms at that time was not supported by efficacy studies and that the evaluation and placement procedures typically used were questionable on many grounds. This article led many special educators to a much closer self-examination of all their practices, including those involving learning disabilities.

Largely because of the efforts of the ACALD and DCLD, legislators were made aware of learning disabled children, who were not covered under any previous legislation providing educational support for handicapped students. As a result of intense lobbying (particularly by the ACALD), the Children with Learning Disabilities Act (part of P.L. 91–230) was passed by Congress in 1969. This legislation authorized a 5-year program of federal funds for teacher training and the establishment of model demonstration programs for learning disabled students. In 1977 five federally funded research institutes were begun at universities to develop empirical data on a wide range of issues related to the education of students with learning disabilities. Today, learning disabilities is one of the handicapping conditions included in P.L. 94–142 as being eligible for federal special education funds.

See pages 139–40 for more on the learning disabilities research institutes.

DEFINING LEARNING DISABILITIES

A major controversy in the field of learning disabilities has centered on definition. Of the many definitions of learning disabilities that have been proposed during the field's relatively short history, none has been universally accepted. However, the definition most widely used today was first written in 1968. In that year the National Advisory Committee on Handicapped Children of the U.S. Office of Education drafted a definition of learning disabilities that was eventually included, with only minor changes in wording, in P.L. 94–142, the Education for All Handicapped Children Act of 1975. It reads:

> "Specific learning disability" means a disorder in one or more of the basic psychological processes involved in understanding or in using language, spoken or written, which may manifest itself in an imperfect ability to listen, think, speak, read, write, spell, or to do mathematical calculations. The term includes such conditions as perceptual handicaps, brain injury, minimal brain dysfunction, dyslexia, and developmental aphasia. The term does not include children who have learning problems which are primarily the result of visual, hearing or motor handicaps, of mental retardation, or of environmental, cultural, or economic disadvantages (Section 5(b)(4) of P.L. 94–142).

When operationalizing the definition of learning disabilities, most states and school districts require that three criteria be met. These three criteria are: (1) a discrepancy between the child's potential and actual achievement, (2) an exclusion criterion, and (3) the need for special education services. Each of these three factors is stated or implied in most definitions of learning disabilities.

Discrepancy

The term *learning disability* is not meant to be used for children who are having minor or temporary difficulties in learning. The term is meant to identify children with a severe discrepancy between ability and achievement. Even though this is a fairly well agreed-upon criterion, there is considerable disagreement and confusion over what constitutes a severe discrepancy. Johnson and Myklebust (1967) found 1 or 2 years below the expected level of achievement to be the most commonly used measure of discrepancy. But they pointed out a serious problem with that practice because "one year below expectancy at eight years of age is not comparable to one year below

As many as 40 different definitions have been proposed for learning disability (Bennett & Ragosta, 1984). However, in a survey of all 50 states and the District of Columbia, Mercer, Hughes, and Mercer (1985) found that 72% of the states were using a definition of learning disabilities based on the federal definition.

Reading is the most common area in which students with learning disabilities experience a discrepancy between ability and achievement.

expectancy at sixteen years of age or, for that matter, at three or four years of age." (p. 18)

McLoughlin and Netick (1983) point out that "efforts to develop a formula by which to establish the existence of a learning disability have occupied many individuals since the early days of the field." Various mathematical formulas have been proposed for determining whether a severe discrepancy exists between a student's ability and achievement. One formula offered by federal agencies involves the child's chronological age (CA), IQ, and several predetermined constants. The result of calculating the formula is supposed to be the academic achievement (grade) level at or below which the child must be functioning in order for a severe discrepancy to exist. The formula was rejected for two main reasons. First, it did not take into account preschool children. Second, the decision as to whether a child is eligible for special educational services should not be based only on general measures like IQ and grade level that would not be responsive to the individual needs of the child.

Still, lack of a specific definition of a severe discrepancy in the criteria published by the federal government for identifying learning disabled students (see *Federal Register,* Thursday, December 29, 1977, p. 65083) has forced state and local educators to find some means of objectively identifying those children who are to receive special services. For example, the Ohio Department of Education has issued the following rules for determining whether the severe discrepancy criterion is met.

The proposed federal formula was [CA(IQ/300 + 0.17) − 2.5 = Severe Discrepancy Level.] Clearly, it implied more meaningful precision in measurement of the variables included than is practical or realistic.

Each child shall have a severe discrepancy between achievement and ability which adversely affects his or her educational performance to such a degree that special education and related services are required. The basis for making the determination shall be:

(i) Evidence of a discrepancy score of two or greater than two between intellectual ability and achievement in one or more of the following seven areas:
   (a) Oral expression,
   (b) Listening comprehension,
   (c) Written expression,
   (d) Basic reading skills,
   (e) Reading comprehension,
   (f) Mathematics calculation, or
   (g) Mathematics reasoning.
(ii) The following formula shall be used in computing the discrepancy score:
   (a) From:
      (i) The score obtained for the measure of intellectual ability,
      (ii) Minus the mean of the measure of intellectual ability,
      (iii) Divided by the standard deviation of the measure of intellectual ability.
   (b) Subtract:
      (i) Score obtained for the measure of achievement,
      (ii) Minus the mean of the measure of achievement,
      (iii) Divided by the standard deviation of the measure of achievement.
   (c) The result of this computation equals the discrepancy score. If the discrepancy score is two or greater than two, a severe discrepancy exists. (Rules for the Education of Handicapped Children, effective July 1, 1982, p. 69)

The Council for Learning Disabilities published a position statement opposing the use of discrepancy formulas and cited eight reasons for that opposition.

1. Discrepancy formulas tend to focus on a single aspect of learning disabilities (usually reading or mathematics) to the exclusion of other types of learning disabilities.
2. Technically adequate and age-appropriate assessment tests are not available for all areas of performance, especially for preschool children and adults.
3. Discrepancy formulas may contribute to inaccurate conclusions when based on assessment instruments that lack adequate reliability or validity.
4. Some learning disabled individuals may be denied access to, or may be removed from, needed special education services because their intelligence test scores are

sufficiently depressed to result in a discrepancy not large enough between intelligence and achievement test scores.

5. Many underachieving students obtain significant discrepancies between intelligence and achievement test scores for reasons other than the presence of a learning disability.

6. The statistical nature of discrepancy formulas creates a false sense of objectivity and precision among diagnosticians.

7. Discrepancy formulas are often used as the sole or primary criterion for determining legal eligibility for learning disability services.

8. Although promoted as a procedure for increasing accuracy in decision making, discrepancy formulas often represent a relatively simplistic attempt to reduce the incidence of learning disabilities. (Adapted from the Summer 1986 issue of *Learning Disability Quarterly*, p. 245.)

The CLD position statement also includes these recommendations: (1) that discrepancy formulas be phased out as required procedure for identifying individuals with learning disabilities, (2) that when discrepancy formulas must be used, they should be used with extreme caution, and (3) the results of discrepancy formulas should never be used to dictate whether individuals have a learning disability. In the place of discrepancy formulas, CLD recommends improved comprehensive multidisciplinary assessment of all areas of learning disabilities identified by federal rules and regulations (i.e., oral expression, listening comprehension, and writing expression in addition to reading and mathematics). Although the concept of discrepancy seems to be logically valid, it remains to be seen whether any given practice will be widely accepted as an objective and reliable means to identify and measure it.

Exclusion

The concept of learning disabilities is meant to identify children with significant learning problems that cannot be explained by mental retardation, sensory impairment, emotional disturbance, or lack of opportunity to learn. Kirk (1978b) uses the term *specific learning disabilities* to differentiate truly learning disabled students from the larger group of children with various learning problems.

Several noted special educators have criticized the exclusion clause in the federal definition of learning disabilities because it says that children with other handicapping conditions cannot be considered learning disabled as well. For example, some children whose primary diagnosis is mental retardation do not achieve up to their expected potential (Wallace & McLoughlin, 1979). Hammill (1976) challenges the notion that only children with IQ scores in the normal range can be identified as learning disabled. He rests his criticism on two arguments. First, most IQ tests are made up of items that measure past learning. If a child with a learning disability has not learned enough of the information included on the IQ test, he will score in the retarded range. Second, there are too many sources of measurement error involved in intelligence testing to make clear-cut differential diagnosis statements such as "This child is mildly retarded, and this one is learning disabled."

Special Education

A learning disabled student needs special education that "should involve practices that are unique, uncommon, of unusual quality and that, in particular, supplement the organizational and instructional procedures used with the majority of children" (Ames, 1977). This criterion is meant to keep children who have not had the opportunity to learn from being identified as learning disabled. Those children should progress normally as soon as they are placed in a developmentally appropriate regular education program. Learning disabled children are those who show specific and severe learning problems in spite of normal educational efforts. Therefore, special educational services are needed to help remediate their achievement deficiencies.

The NJCLD-Proposed Definition

The National Joint Committee for Learning Disabilities (NJCLD) is a group comprised of official representatives from eight professional organizations involved with learning disabled students. The NJCLD believed that the federal definition of learning disabilities had served the educational community reasonably well but had several inherent weaknesses (Hammill, Leigh, McNutt, & Larsen, 1981). Myers and Hammill (1982) identify those elements of the P.L. 94–142 definition with which the NJCLD was not satisfied.

1. *Exclusion of adults.* Major interest in understanding the special needs of and developing programs for learning disabled adolescents and adults has emerged recently (Alley & Deschler, 1979; Marsh, Gearheart, & Gearheart, 1978). In keeping with this trend, the ACLD recently changed its official name to the Association for Children and Adults with Learning Disabilities. Because it deals with public school education, the P.L. 94–142 definition refers only to school-age children, thereby eliminating adults from consideration.
2. *Reference to basic psychological processes.* Members of the NJCLD maintain that use of the phrase "basic psychological processes" has allowed much debate over how to teach learning disabled students but that how-to-teach is a curricular issue, not a definitional one. The NJCLD believes the intent of the original phrase was only to show that a learning disability is intrinsic to the person affected.
3. *Inclusion of spelling as a learning disability.* Because spelling can be integrated with other areas of functioning, namely written expression, it is redundant and should be eliminated from the definition.
4. *Inclusion of obsolete terms.* The NJCLD believes that inclusion of terms such as *dyslexia, minimal brain dysfunction, perceptual handicaps,* and *developmental aphasia,* which historically have proven difficult to define, only adds confusion to the definition of learning disability.
5. *The exclusion clause.* The wording of the final clause in the P.L. 94–142 definition has led to the belief that learning disabilities cannot occur along with other handicapping conditions. A more accurate statement, according to the NJCLD, is that a person may have a learning disability *along with* another handicap but not *because of* another handicap. In other words a learning disability is to be considered a handicap in its own right.

The NJCLD consists of representatives from the American Speech-Language-Hearing Association (ASHA), the Association for Children and Adults with Learning Disabilities (ACALD), the Council for Learning Disabilities (CLD), the Division for Children with Communication Disorders (DCCD), the Division for Learning Disabilities (DLD), the International Reading Association (IRA), the National Association of School Psychologists (NASP), and the Orton-Dyslexia Society (ODS).

See the "Educational Approaches" section of this chapter.

In response to these problems with the federal definition, the NJCLD has proposed the following definition of learning disabilities:

> Learning disabilities is a generic term that refers to a heterogeneous group of disorders manifested by significant difficulties in the acquisition and use of listening, speaking, reading, writing, reasoning, or mathematical abilities. These disorders are intrinsic to the individual and presumed to be due to central nervous system dysfunction. Even though a learning disability may occur concomitantly with other handicapping conditions (e.g., sensory impairment, mental retardation, social and emotional disturbance) or environmental influences (e.g., cultural differences, insufficient/inappropriate instruction, psychogenic factors), it is not the direct result of those conditions or influences. (Hammill, Leigh, McNutt, & Larsen, 1981, p. 336)

For further rationale and detailed exploration of the NJCLD definition, see Hammill et al. (1981) and Myers and Hammill (1982).

McLoughlin and Netick (1983) have discussed some of the practical implications the proposed definition may hold for assessment and identification of learning disabled students. Commenting on the newly proposed definition, NJCLD members Hammill, Leigh, McNutt, and Larsen (1981) write,

> The NJCLD members are the first to acknowledge that the proposed definition is not perfect. Yet, they are convinced that the definition is a substantial improvement over existing ones. They never intended to write the ultimate definition, only a better one; and, doubtlessly, in the years to come, their effort will also be discarded in favor of a newer, improved version. Until then, the Committee believes that the proposed definition is the best one available and recommends that it be considered as a theoretical statement about the nature of learning disabilities. (p. 341)

It is too early to tell what impact the NJCLD definition will have on the field. On one level the NJCLD definition can be seen as an effort to limit the term *learning disabilities* to the "hard-core" or truly handicapped (Myers & Hammill, 1982) with its statement that the disorder is "intrinsic to the individual and presumed to be due to central nervous system dysfunction."

Other special educators have proposed broader defintions of learning disabilities that do not involve causal explanations. Hallahan and Kauffman (1976, 1977) suggest that a learning disabled child is simply one who is not achieving up to potential. The child may be at any intelligence level, and his learning difficulties may be caused by any number of factors. Many more children—perhaps up to half the population of some school districts—might be considered learning disabled with this broad definition.

We believe the most important issue, from the educator's standpoint, is not whether or not a student *has* a learning disability, but *how* to assess and remediate the specific skill deficiencies in each child's repertoire.

CHARACTERISTICS OF LEARNING DISABLED CHILDREN

In describing the various categories of exceptionality, it is often useful to list the physical and psychological characteristics commonly found in the children who make up that group. The inherent danger in all such lists of characteristics is the tendency to assume, or at least look for, all of those characteristics in all of the children considered to be in the category. This danger is especially acute in the case of learning disabilities. To give you some idea of the extent of this problem—a notion of just how different from one another learning disabled children are—consider this: A national task force found 99 separate characteristics of learning disabled children described in the literature (Clements, 1966).

Mercer (1987) notes that since Clements's (1966) report of the most frequently cited characteristics of learning disabled children, there has been little systematic research on the relative incidence of the various characteristcs, and the list is no longer accurate. For example, the first four characteristics on Clements's list were hyperactivity, perceptual-motor impairments, emotional ups and downs, and general coordination deficits. Specific academic difficulty, the fundamental defining characteristic of learning disabilities today, was ranked only eighth on the Clements list.

Several major studies of the characteristics of students with learning disabilities have been reported (Cone, Wilson, Bradley, & Reese, 1985; Kirk & Elkins, 1975; Norman & Zigmond, 1980; Sheppard & Smith, 1981). The most recent, Cone et al. (1985), examined the demographic, intellectual, and achievement data for 1,839 students enrolled in K–12 learning disabilities programs in Iowa. They found that (1) males outnumbered females by a 3:1 ratio across primary, elementary, and secondary age levels, (2) 75% of the students were initially identified as learning disabled in the elementary grades, (3) the mean IQ for the sample was 95, (4) students exhibited more academic deficiencies in reading and spelling than in mathematics, and (5) students' relative level of academic achievement decreased progressively as their grade level increased.

Other researchers have investigated the social acceptance of students labeled learning disabled, their classroom deportment, and their ability to attend to a task. The results of this research are far from conclusive, perhaps partly because of the heterogeneous nature of learning disabilities and partly because of the lack of agreement in and inconsistent application of identification criteria. For example, the conclusion reached by most researchers who have investigated the social status of students with learning disabilities has been that low social acceptance is common (Bryan & Bryan, 1978; Gresham, 1982). However, after reviewing the published studies on the social status of learning disabled individuals, Dudley-Marling and Edmiaston (1985) concluded that as a group learning disabled individuals may be at greater risk for attaining low social status but that some learning disabled students are, in fact, popular. Two subsequent studies continued the contradictory findings on peer acceptance. Gresham and Reschly (1986) report that they found significant deficits in the social skills and peer acceptance of 100 mainstreamed learning disabled children when compared to 100 nonhandicapped children. But in the same journal issue Sabornie and Kauffman (1986) report their more optimistic findings that there was not a significant difference in the sociometric standing of 46 mainstreamed learning disabled high school students and 46 nonhandicapped peers. Moreover, they discovered that some of the learning disabled students enjoyed socially rewarding experiences in the mainstream classrooms. One interpretation of these contradictory results is that social acceptance is not so much a characteristic of learning disability as it is an outcome of the different social climates created by teachers, parents, and other caregivers with whom learning disabled students interact.

Read page 139 to learn how one learning disabilities resource room teacher helps her students stay on task while working at their desks.

Attention deficit—the inability to attend to a task—has also been frequently cited as a characteristic of learning disabled children (e.g., Keogh & Margolis, 1976). However, in a well-controlled experiment that included both classroom and laboratory tasks, Samuels and Miller (1985) failed to find any differences between learning disabled children and normal children in attention to task.

The type and incidence of classroom behavior problems exhibited by children with learning disabilities have been the subject of considerable research. Epstein and Cullinan at Northern Illinois University have conducted a series of studies that have revealed a higher-than-normal rate of behavior problems among learning disabled students (Epstein, Bursuck, & Cullinan, 1985; Epstein, Cullinan, & Lloyd, 1986; Epstein, Cullinan, & Rosemier, 1983). They point out that although their data definitely show increased behavior problems among learning disabled children, the relationships between the problem behavior and academic difficulty of these students are not known. In other words it cannot be said that either the academic deficits or the behavior problems cause the other difficulty. It must also be pointed out that the data from these studies summarize large groups of students. Many children with learning disabilities exhibit no behavior problems at all.

Regardless of the inter-relationships of these characteristics, teachers and other caregivers responsible for planning educational programs for students with learning disabilities must be skilled in dealing with social and behavioral difficulties as well as academic skill deficits.

Because of the many learning and behavioral characteristics that have been associated with learning disabilities and the inability to create an accurate profile of characteristics for persons labeled learning disabled, some professionals are suggesting that distinct subtypes of learning disability exist and should be classified. McKinney (1985) states that the literature, collectively, argues against a "single syndrome" theory of learning disability and that it is feasible to create more homogeneous diagnostic subgroups within this presently broad and ill-defined category of exceptional children. It is much too early to predict whether the search for subgroups among learning disabled individuals will have any legitimate implications for education and treatment.

On pages 161–62 one woman shares some of her experiences and frustrations in coping with a learning disability, both as a child and as an adult.

Another perspective on the characteristics of individuals with learning disabilities is the life-span view. Table 4.1 presents Mercer's (1987) summary of the major problem areas most likely to occur, the purposes of assessment and treatment, and the treatments most recommended in five different age spans.

In concluding this discussion, we must stress that the single, fundamental characteristic of children with learning disabilities is a specific and significant achievement deficiency in the presence of adequate overall intelligence. Some learning disabled children are also hyperactive (or any of the other cited characteristics), and some are not. And children with any of these other characteristics who do not also have deficits in achievement are not considered learning disabled.

PREVALENCE

Learning disabilities is the largest of all special education categories. During the 1984–85 school year 1,839,292 children aged 3 to 21 were identified as learning disabled

TABLE 4.1

A life-span view of learning disabilities summarizing likely problem areas, purposes of assessment and treatment, and the treatments most recommended at five different age levels.

	Preschool	Grades K–1	Grades 2–6	Grades 7–12	Adult
Problem Areas	Delay in developmental milestones (e.g., walking) Receptive language Expressive language Visual perception Auditory perception Short attention span Hyperactivity	Academic readiness skills (e.g., alphabet knowledge, quantitative concepts, directional concepts, etc.) Receptive language Expressive language Visual perception Auditory perception Gross and fine motor Attention Hyperactivity Social skills	Reading skills Arithmetic skills Written expression Verbal expression Receptive language Attention span Hyperactivity Social-emotional	Reading skills Arithmetic skills Written expression Verbal expression Listening skills Study skills (metacognition) Social-emotional-delinquency	Reading skills Arithmetic skills Written expression Verbal expression Listening skills Study skills Social-emotional
Assessment	Prediction of high risk for later learning problems	Prediction of high risk for later learning problems	Identification of learning disabilities	Identification of learning disabilities	Identification of learning disabilities
Treatment Types	Preventative	Preventative	Remedial Corrective	Remedial Corrective Compensatory Learning strategies	Remedial Corrective Compensatory Learning strategies
Treatments with Most Research and/or Expert Support	Direct instruction in language skills Behavioral management Parent training	Direct instruction in academic and language areas Behavioral management Parent training	Direct instruction in academic areas Behavioral management Self-control training Parent training	Direct instruction in academic areas Tutoring in subject areas Direct instruction in learning strategies (study skills) Self-control training Curriculum alternatives	Direct instruction in academic areas Tutoring in subject (college) or job area Compensatory instruction (i.e., using aids such as tape recorder, calculator, computer, dictionary) Direct instruction in learning strategies

Source: From *Students with Learning Disabilities* (3rd ed., p. 44) by C. D. Mercer, 1987. Columbus, OH: Merrill. Reprinted by permission.

and received special education services under P.L. 94–142 (U.S. Department of Education, 1986). This figure represents 42% of all handicapped children served in the United States. And the number has grown tremendously in recent years. The 1984–85 figure represents an increase of 131% over the 797,213 learning disabled children receiving special education in 1976–77. During this same period the total number of children served in special education increased by only 18%. Among the reasons cited by the U.S. Department of Education (1986) for the growth in the number of children with learning disabilities are "eligibility criteria that permit children with a wide range of learning problems to be classified as learning disabled; social acceptance and/or preference for the learning disabled classification; the reclassification of some mentally retarded children as learning disabled; and the lack of general education alternatives for children who are experiencing learning problems in regular classes" (p. 5).

Because of the many ways in which the definition of learning disabilities can be interpreted, the different means of diagnosing and identifying learning disabled children from one state to the next, and the unreliable assessment instruments used to diagnose learning disabilities, it is impossible at present to give a true incidence rate of learning disabilities. Estimates have ranged anywhere from 1% to 30% of the school-age population. In reviewing 21 different surveys of school populations, Bryant (1972) found that learning disabled children were cited as comprising anywhere from 3% to 28% of a school's total enrollment. Based on P.L. 94–142 child count data reported by the states, the number of children with learning disabilities represented 4.57% of the total U.S. population aged 3 to 21 during the 1983–84 school year (U.S. Department of Education, 1985).

CAUSES OF LEARNING DISABILITIES

In almost every case, exactly how a child comes to have a learning problem is unknown. However, a variety of causes of learning disabilities have been proposed. These etiological factors generally fall into three categories—brain damage, biochemical imbalance, and environmental factors.

Brain Damage

Some professionals believe that learning disabled children suffer from some form of brain injury. The suspected brain damage is not considered extensive enough to cause a generalized and severe learning problem across all kinds of intellectual development, so the children are often referred to as minimally brain damaged. In cases where actual evidence of brain damage cannot be shown (and this is the situation with the majority of learning disabled children), the term *minimal brain dysfunction* is often used. This phrase implies brain damage by asserting that the child's brain does not function well. The term is still used by some in the field of learning disabilities, especially by physicians.

SIGNALING FOR HELP

A resource room for students with learning disabilities is a busy place. Students come and go throughout the day, each according to a schedule that specifies the amount of time to be spent in the resource room. Each student with a learning disability who comes to the resource room does so because of a need for intensive individualized instruction in one or more academic areas. The IEP objectives of the students in a resource room at any one time often cover a wide range of skill deficits. Because of the varied skill levels and the ever-changing student groupings in the resource room, it is often necessary for the resource room teacher to manage several types and levels of instruction at one time. To accomplish this, students are sometimes assigned individualized instructional materials. While students work at their desks, the teacher moves about the room providing prompts, encouragement, praise, and/or corrective feedback to individual students as needed.

But this arrangement presents resource room teachers with a difficult challenge: the need to be in several places at once. While in the resource room, students are usually working on those skills in which they need the most help. The resource room teacher must have an effective and efficient system

This student raises his flag to get his teacher's attention.

for students to signal for assistance. Hand-raising, the typical attention-getting signal, poses several problems. It is difficult to continue to work while holding one's hand in the air, a situation that results in a great deal of "down" time as students wait for the teacher to get to them. In addition, if several students are waving their hands in competition for the teacher's attention, it is distracting to other students and to the teacher. If unsuccessful in getting the teacher's help, students may give up trying whenever they run into difficulty. Even worse, students who are unsuccessful in obtaining the teacher's assistance may stop discriminating their need for help and simply continue to practice errors.

One solution is both simple and effective. Students need an easy, quiet means of signaling for help that allows them to keep working, with the assurance that their teacher will recognize their need for help. In Ronni Hochman's resource room for learning disabled middle school students, each student has a small flag made of colored felt, a dowel rod, and a 1¼-inch cube of wood. When one of Ronni's students needs assistance or wants her to check completed work, the student simply stands the flag up on his desk. While waiting for the teacher, the student can either go on to another item or work on materials in a special folder. With this simple and inexpensive system, down time is greatly reduced, and neither Ronni nor her students are distracted by hand waving or calling out.

Ronni asked her students to write what they thought of the flag signal system after they had used it for about 3 months.

This is one of the best way to work in sted of raising your hand you raise your flag and keep on working but if you raise you hand you can't keep working. That is speicel because I get more work done. If she is working with some on els you raise it and she will get to you as fast as she can.
—Brent

The flags in Miss Hochmans room are used for assistance from the teacher. When Miss Hochman is working you rais you flag and she will help you as soon as she has time. But you keep on working, like going on the the next problem.
—Pam

Most educators in the field of learning disabilities place little value on brain dysfunction as an explanation of the difficulties experienced by learning disabled persons. As Smith and Robinson (1986) state, "The evidence linking behavioral characteristics to brain dysfunction is circumstantial, speculative, and in most cases clearly not documentable. Identifying brain damage does not lead to sets of instructional or remediation strategies that produce guaranteed or uniform results" (p. 223).

There are two major problems with current etiological theories linking learning disabilities to brain damage. The first problem is a lack of evidence. All learning disabled children do not display clinical (medical) evidence of brain damage. And not all brain-damaged children are learning disabled. Boshes and Myklebust (1964) reported the results of EEG readings given to 200 normal and 200 learning disabled children. Results showed that 29% of the normal children and 42% of the learning disabled children displayed abnormal brain wave patterns. Even though more learning disabled children were rated abnormal, certainly these results prove that there is not a direct, one-to-one relationship between brain injury and learning disability.

The second problem with the brain-damage assumption is that it serves as a powerful, built-in excuse for failure to teach the child. If the child doesn't learn, it is thought to be no one's fault; she has a brain injury that "prevents" her learning. Unfortunately, given the traditional association of the term *learning disability* with the idea of brain damage, some teachers react the same way to that diagnosis.

Nevertheless, some learning disabled children do show definite signs of brain damage, which may well be the cause of their learning problems.

The existence of brain damage is shown by test results from an **electroencephalograph (EEG)**. An EEG measures and makes a graph of brain waves. Brain damage can be inferred from the presence of abnormal brain waves.

Biochemical Imbalance

Some researchers claim that biochemical disturbances within a child's body are the cause of learning disabilities. Dr. Benjamin Feingold (1975a, 1975b, 1976) has received much publicity for his claims that artificial colorings and flavorings in many of the foods children eat can cause learning disabilities and hyperactivity. He recommends a treatment for learning disabilities that consists of a diet with no foods containing synthetic colors or flavors.

In 1965 Feingold, a San Francisco allergist, treated a woman with an acute case of hives. The woman was put on a diet that removed all salicylates—a group of natural compounds found in certain fruits and vegetables. In less than 2 weeks the hives had disappeared, and the woman reported that she did not feel as aggressive or hostile as she had before (Feingold, 1975b). Feingold then tried the elimination diet on 25 hyperactive children in one school system and claimed that 16 of the children responded favorably. On the basis of this and several other uncontrolled studies, Feingold held a news conference and announced that "hyperactivity can be greatly reduced by the elimination of artificial food coloring and flavoring" from children's diets and that the diet "brings hope to thousands of parents who have been distressed by the need to cope with the problem of hyperactivity by giving their children prescribed drugs" (Spring & Sandoval, 1976). Newspaper and magazine articles, more press conferences, a popular book (Feingold, 1975b), and appearances on television talk shows followed. In an article in the *Journal of Learning Disabilities*, Feingold (1976) wrote,

The "demonstration study" of hyperactive children was never published in a scientific journal.

Artifical food colors and flavors have the capacity to induce adverse reactions affecting every system of the body. Of all these adverse reactions, the nervous system involvement, as evidenced by behavioral disturbances and learning disabilities, is the most frequently encountered and most critical, affecting millions of individuals in this country alone.

The K-P diet, which eliminates all artificial food colors and flavors as well as foods with a natural salicylate radical, will control the behavioral disturbance in 30% to 50% (depending on the sample) of both normal and neurologically damaged children. (p. 558)

The K-P diet is Feingold's name for his diet.

Public response to Feingold's claims has been intense. As Divoky (1978) writes, "Along comes Feingold. Not only is he going to get hyperactive kids off drugs, but

Finding the key to a motivational problem can sometimes solve a student's learning problem as well.

he's going to do it with a wonderfully appealing treatment: additive-free, healthful food" (p. 56). Today the Feingold Association has a membership of over 10,000 people (mainly parents) in 120 local groups.

A number of research studies have been conducted to test the Feingold diet, some claiming positive results (Connors, Goyette, Southwick, Lees, & Andrulonis, 1976; Cook & Woodhill, 1976). However, in a comprehensive review of diet-related studies, Spring and Sandoval (1976) concluded that there is very little evidence in support of Feingold's theory. Many of the studies were poorly conducted, and the few experiments that were scientifically sound concluded that only a small portion of hyperactive children might be helped by the special diet. However, in a more recent, well-controlled study employing "double-blind" procedures, Rose (1978) found that two 8-year-old girls who had been on the Feingold diet for at least 11 months spent less time on-task and more time out of their seats when they had eaten cookies that contained a yellow artificial food coloring just before going to school.

The controversy over the theory and diet treatment continues, with a great need for continued research (Adler, 1978). The American Council on Science and Health, in a 1979 publication, issued the following statement:

> Hyperactivity will continue to be a frustrating problem until research resolves the questions of its cause, or causes, and develops an effective treatment. The reality is that we still have a great deal to learn about this condition. We do know now, however, that diet is not the answer. It is clear that the symptoms of the vast majority of the children labeled "hyperactive" are not related to salicylates, artificial food colors, or artificial flavors. The Feingold diet creates extra work for the homemakers and changes the family lifestyle . . . but it doesn't cure hyperactivity. (p. 5)

Cott (1972) hypothesized that learning disabilities can be caused by the inability of a child's bloodstream to synthesize a normal amount of vitamins. Based on his contention, some physicians began megavitamin therapy with learning disabled children. Megavitamin treatment consists of massive daily doses of vitamins in an effort to overcome the suspected vitamin deficiencies.

Two studies designed to test the effects of megavitamin treatment with learning disabled and hyperkinetic children found that huge doses of vitamins did not improve the children's performance (Arnold, Christopher, Huestis, & Smeltzer, 1978; Kershner, Hawks, & Grekin, 1977). And several researchers have cautioned against the potential risks of large doses of vitamins. Toxic effects such as scurvy, cardiac arrhythmia, headaches, and abnormalities of the liver may result, especially from megadoses of certain B vitamins (Eastman, 1978; Golden, 1980).

Environmental Factors

Lovitt (1978) cites three types of environmental influences that he feels are related to children's learning problems: emotional disturbance, lack of motivation, and poor instruction. Many children with learning problems have behavior disorders as well. Whether one causes the other or whether both are caused by some other factor(s) is uncertain at this time. In addition, it is difficult to identify reinforcing activities for

The girls ate a yellow cookie each day, but neither they nor the observers knew whether the cookies contained artificial coloring on any certain day. Thus, the girls' responses and the observers' measurements were not affected by their expectations. This is a double-blind procedure.

Many learning disabled children are given daily doses of medication in an effort to treat attention deficits and hyperactivity. Although a discussion of the use of psychotropic medication—behavior- and/or mood-altering drugs—is beyond the scope of this text, the book by Gadow (1986) is an excellent source of information on this important topic for educators.

some learning disabled students; they may not be interested in many of the things other children like. Some research studies have shown that finding a key to the child's motivational problem can sometimes solve the learning problem as well (Lovitt, 1977).

One variable that is likely to be a major contributor to children's learning problems is the quality of instruction they receive. Lovitt (1978) states it this way:

> [A] condition which might contribute to a learning disability is poor instruction. Although many children are able to learn in spite of poor teachers and inadequate techniques, others are less fortunate. Some youngsters who have experienced poor instruction in the early grades never catch up with their peers. (p. 169)

Engelmann (1977) is even more direct.

> Perhaps 90 percent or more of the children who are labeled "learning disabled" exhibit a disability not because of anything wrong with their perception, synapses, or memory, but because they have been seriously mistaught. Learning disabilities are made, not born. (pp. 46–47)

Lovitt and Engelmann are among a growing number of educators who feel that the best way to help a child with learning problems is to emphasize the assessment and training of those specific behaviors (e.g., reading and arithmetic skills) that are troublesome for that particular child. Mounting evidence indicates that many students' learning problems can be remediated by direct, systematic instruction. However, it would be naive to think that the learning problems of all children stem from inadequate instruction. Perhaps Engelmann's other 10% are those children whose learning disability is caused by a malfunctionoing central nervous system. In any event, from an educational perspective, good, systematic instruction should be the treatment of first choice.

At present there is much more speculation than hard evidence, and the search for the real causes of children's learning problems must go on. Only through positive identification of the causes of learning disabilities can prevention become a realistic alternative.

ASSESSMENT

In education the word *assessment* is synonymous with *testing*. Literally hundreds of tests have been developed to measure virtually every motor, social, or academic response children make (Buros, 1978). Unfortunately, much of the testing in education has been conducted primarily for the purpose of identifying children for certain special education categories and placement. Certainly, assessment for identification is important. As Myers and Hammill (1982) point out,

For an excellent discussion of systematic assessment for instructional planning—that is, for using assessment to determine *what* to teach and *how* to teach—see Zigmond and Miller (1986).

> At some point along the continuum of services provided by the school, there must be a cutoff that dictates which children will be served by special education and which will remain totally the responsibility of the general education program. Obviously, the vast majority of children who have trouble in school will have to stay in regular classes. In any event, the type of assessment that deals with identification is

of the utmost importance in states where laws, policies, or traditions make it mandatory that children be classified according to type of handicap before they can qualify for special services. (p. 44)

However, because of the complex way that learning disability is defined, the task of identifying the true LD child guarantees that a battery of tests will be administered. One study of 14 school districts in Michigan found that, on the average, three to five different tests were given to each student referred for learning disabilities (Perlmutter & Parus, 1983). When Shepard and Smith (1981) examined how the determination of a learning disability was made in 1,000 individual cases in Colorado, they discovered that one-half of the school district funds available for services to learning disabled students were expended on identification alone. As a result of these assessment practices, learning disabled children have been called the "most diagnosed" of all types of exceptional children (Lovitt, 1982). Even though identification and placement are appropriate and important functions of educational testing, assessment has a much more important purpose: to provide information for planning and implementing an instructional program for the child.

At least five different types of tests are commonly used in the assessment of learning disabilities: norm-referenced tests, process tests, informal reading inventories, criterion-referenced tests, and direct daily measurement. Of these five types norm-referenced tests and process tests are *indirect* assessment devices. That is, the child's general ability along various dimensions is measured. Informal reading inventories, criterion-referenced tests, and direct daily measurement can all be classified as *direct* assessment techniques. In direct assessment the specific skills and behaviors that a child is to be taught are measured. The choice between direct and indirect assessment is largely determined by the approach to instructional remediation taken by a given school program, which is discussed later in this chapter.

For a critical examination of how assessment of learning disabled children is conducted, see Ysseldyke et al. (1983), who contend that too many tests are administered that produce little data of use in planning instruction. The authors make a strong case for spending less time and fewer resources on assessment for classification and diagnosis and more resources on instruction.

Two good texts that describe special education assessment practices in detail and examine many widely used tests are McLoughlin and Lewis (1986) and Salvia and Ysseldyke (1985).

Norm-Referenced Tests

Norm-referenced tests are designed so that one child's score can be compared with those of other children of the same age who have taken the same test. Because deficits in academic achievement are the major characteristic of learning disabled children, standardized achievement tests are commonly used. Some standardized achievement tests—like the Iowa Tests of Basic Skills (Hieronymus & Lindquist, 1978), the Peabody Individual Achievement Test (Dunn & Markwardt, 1970), and the Wide Range Achievement Test (Jastak & Jastak, 1965)—are designed to measure children's overall academic achievement. Scores on these tests are reported by grade level; a score of 3.5, for example, means that a child is performing at the level of the average child halfway through the third grade. Other norm-referenced tests measure a child's achievement in certain academic areas. Some of the frequently administered reading achievement tests are the Durrell Analysis of Reading Difficulty (Durrell, 1955), the Gates-McKillop Reading Diagnostic Test (Gates & McKillop, 1962), the Gray Oral Reading Tests (Gray, 1963), the Spache Diagnostic Reading Scales (Spache, 1963), and the Woodcock Reading Mastery Tests (Woodcock, 1974). The KeyMath Diagnostic Arithmetic Test (Connolly, Natchman, & Pritchett, 1973) and the Stanford Diagnostic Arithmetic Test (Beatty, Madden, & Gardner, 1966) are often used to test arithmetic achievement.

Process Tests

The concept of process, or ability, testing was created by the field of learning disabilities. It grew out of the belief that learning disabilities are caused by a basic, underlying difficulty of the child to process, or use, environmental stimuli in the same way that normal children do. These general abilities are categorized under headings such as visual perception, auditory perception, and eye-motor coordination. The developers and users of these tests believe that if the specific perceptual problems of the child can be identified, treatment programs can then be designed to improve those problems, and the child's learning disability will be remediated.

A number of process tests have been developed. We will briefly discuss the two process tests most widely used in the diagnosis and assessment of learning disabilties: the Illinois Test of Psycholinguistic Abilities (ITPA) (Kirk, McCarthy, & Kirk, 1968) and the Marianne Frostig Developmental Test of Visual Perception (Frostig, Lefever, & Whittlesey, 1964).

No other test has been as strongly associated with the assessment of learning disabilities as the Illinois Test of Psycholinguistic Abilities. First published in 1961 and later revised in 1968, the ITPA consists of 12 subtests, each designed to measure some aspect of psycholinguistic ability considered by Kirk and his colleagues to be central to learning. Results of the test are depicted on a profile (see Figure 4.1), showing in which of the 12 areas a child demonstrates weaknesses.

Many remedial education programs and activities for learning disabled children have been based on the psycholinguistic or information-processing model. Although research on the effectiveness of these training programs has not validated their effectiveness, one major contribution of the ITPA to educational assessment cannot be denied. The ITPA was developed and has been used for gathering data that can be translated directly into an educational program designed to meet the individual needs of a specific child.

For reviews of this research see Hammill and Larsen (1974, 1978).

The Marianne Frostig Developmental Test of Visual Perception (Frostig et al., 1964) was developed by Dr. Frostig and her colleagues in order to measure certain dimensions of visual perception that they considered crucial to a child's ability to learn to read. The Frostig test is comprised of five subtests designed to pinpoint the kinds of perceptual difficulties a child has. These five areas are eye-motor coordination, figure-ground discrimination, constancy of shape, position of objects in space, and spatial relationships.

Informal Reading Inventories

Teachers' growing awareness of the inability of formal achievement tests and process tests to provide truly useful information for planning instruction has led to an increased use of teacher-developed and -administered informal tests, particularly in the area of reading. An informal reading inventory usually consists of a series of progressively more difficult sentences and paragraphs that a child is asked to read aloud. By directly observing and recording aspects of the child's reading skills—such as mispronounced vowels or consonants, omissions, reversals, substitutions, and comprehension—the teacher can determine the level of reading material that is best suited for the child and the specific reading skills that require remediation.

Criterion-Referenced Tests

Criterion-referenced tests differ from norm-referenced tests in that a child's score on a criterion-referenced test is compared to a predetermined criterion, or mastery level,

Profile of Abilities

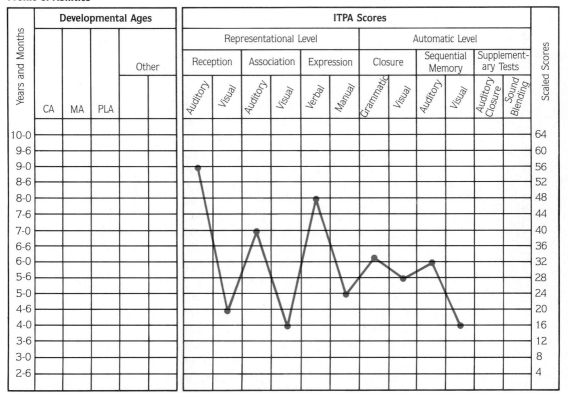

FIGURE 4.1

ITPA profile of abilities. This child was evaluated on 10 measures, involving levels of organization (representational and automatic), psycholinguistic processes (reception, association, etc.), and channels of communication (auditory, visual, etc.). In addition, some children are tested on two supplementary subtests.

Source: From the Illinois Test of Psycholinguistic Abilities (rev. ed.) by S. A. Kirk, J. J. McCarthy, and W. D. Kirk, 1968, Urbana: University of Illinois Press. Copyright by the Board of Trustees of the University of Illinois. Reprinted by permission.

Task: Names each of the eight basic colors when shown

Materials: One box of crayons (to include eight basic colors). One scoring sheet.

Directions (to student): "Say the name of each crayon as I hold it up. You have only three seconds to give me your answer, so pay close attention. (Pick up the first crayon.) What color is this?" Repeat procedure for each of the eight colors. Do not tell the subject if she is correct or incorrect. Do not let the student see what you are marking. Use a stopwatch or a sweep second hand out of the subject's field of vision. Timing should begin immediately following the word *this* in the direction.

Scoring: Wait 3 seconds for response. If the response is incorrect, put the crayon back in the box and mark "incorrect" on the scoring sheet. If the response is correct, put the crayon back in the box and mark "correct" on the scoring sheet. If the child hesitates, wait the full 3 seconds before putting the crayon back in the box and mark "incorrect."

CAP: 100% accuracy

Skill: Knowledge of the eight basic colors
Task: Names each of the eight basic colors when shown
Subject _____ Age _____
Examiner _____ Date _____

Stimulus	Response (check one)	
	Correct	Incorrect
1. red	1 _____	1 _____
2. blue	2 _____	2 _____
3. yellow	3 _____	3 _____
4. green	4 _____	4 _____
5. black	5 _____	5 _____
6. orange	6 _____	6 _____
7. brown	7 _____	7 _____
8. purple	8 _____	8 _____

FIGURE 4.2
Sample criterion-referenced test and scoring sheet.

Source: *Evaluating Exceptional Children: A Task Analysis Approach* (pp. 97–98) by K. W. Howell, J. S. Kaplan, and C. Y. O'Connell, 1979. Columbus, OH: Merrill. Reprinted by permission.

rather than to normed scores of other students. The value of criterion-referenced tests is that they identify the specific skills the child has already learned and the skills that require instruction. Some commercially distributed curricula now include criterion-referenced test items for use both as a pretest and as a posttest. The pretest assesses the student's entry level in order to determine what aspects of the program he is ready to learn, and the posttest evaluates the effectiveness of the program. Of course, criterion-referenced tests can be, and often are, informally developed by classroom teachers. A sample criterion-referenced test developed to determine a child's knowledge of the eight basic colors is shown in Figure 4.2.

Direct Daily Measurement

Direct daily measurement means observing and recording, every day, a child's performance on the specific skill that is being taught (Lovitt, 1975a, 1975b). For example, in a program teaching multiplication facts, the student's performance of multiplication facts would be assessed every day. Measures such as correct rate (number of facts stated correctly per minute), error rate, and percentage correct are often recorded. The advantages of direct daily measurement are clear. First, it gives information about the child's performance on the skill being taught. Second, this information is available on a continuous basis so that the teacher can change the child's program because of changing (or perhaps unchanging) performance, not because of intuition, guesswork,

Garrett's graph shows a clear record of his daily academic performance.

or the results of a test that measures something else. Direct daily measurement is the cornerstone of the behavioral approach to education introduced in chapter 3. It is becoming an increasingly popular assessment and evaluation technique in all areas of special education (Howell, Kaplan, & O'Connell, 1979). One teaching approach used by many learning disabilities teachers is based entirely on direct daily measurement; it is called **precision teaching.**

Precision Teaching

Precision teaching is a system of direct daily measurement of children's performances originated by Ogden R. Lindsley. It is now being used with children of all ages and skill levels.

Lindsley, who had worked with B. F. Skinner at Harvard, sought to translate much of the traditional operant (behavioral) terminology into language that sounded more natural in the schools. Thus, precision teachers look at *behavior* as *movement,* at *antecedent and consequent events* as *events before and after* the child's movement, at *reinforcement schedules* as *arrangements of the events* that follow a movement, and so on. Then, he sought to develop a set of simple but effective procedures that teachers could follow to identify, monitor, and make decisions about critical movements children need to succeed in school. Finally, based on extensive data indicating that children take bigger and bigger steps as they become more proficient at a movement, Lindsley devised the Standard Behavior Chart to show graphically how the child progresses from day to day.

Since its inception precision teaching has been refined and improved by many teachers and researchers. As it is presently practiced, precision teaching consists of the steps summarized here (and illustrated in Figure 4.3).

1. Precisely pinpoint the movement the child must make to learn the skill required—writing digits, saying words, and so on.
2. Next, observe the child's performance of the movement, noting both accuracy and fluency (speed), and chart the results.
3. Using the information from a few days' observation, set an aim (objective) for the child—in terms of both accuracy and fluency—and note it on the chart.
4. Connect the average performance from the first few days with this aim, producing a line on the chart that represents the minimum progress the child must make each day to reach the aim in the time available.
5. As the days and weeks pass, continue to measure the child's performances every day, charting the information every day.
6. Paying careful attention to the chart, follow certain decision rules that tell when the program should be changed—to prevent the child from slipping below the line of minimum progress.
7. Whenever a program change (phase change) is needed, note the change on the chart, draw a new aim and a new minimum progress line, and begin again—before the child has had a chance to fail.

For more information about precision teaching, see the *Journal of Precision Teaching;* Haring, Lovitt, Eaton, and Hansen (1978); White (1986); and White and Haring (1980). In addition, Hasselbring and Hamlett (1983) have authored a microcomputer program designed to help teachers implement precision teaching procedures.

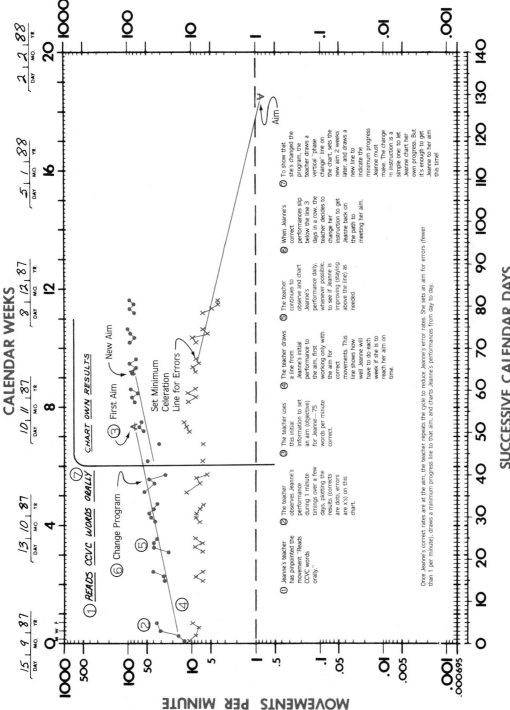

FIGURE 4.3

A standard behavior chart used in precision teaching.

Source: Adapted from *Exceptional Teaching* (p. 276) by O. White and N. Haring, 1976, Columbus, OH: Merrill. Reprinted by permission.

In describing precision teaching, White (1986) writes,

> Essentially, in order to be responsive to the pupil's needs *the teacher must be a student of the pupil's behavior,* carefully analyzing how that behavior changes from day to day and adjusting the instructional plan as necessary to facilitate continued learning. Precision Teaching offers a set of procedures designed to assist in that process. (p. 522)

EDUCATIONAL APPROACHES

Most learning disabilities specialists believe in a diagnostic-prescriptive approach, in which the results of diagnosis (assessment) lead directly to a prescription (plan) for teaching. However, there is still great disagreement over what is to be diagnosed, and there are many approaches to how the problem is to be treated.

Ysseldyke and Salvia (1974) outline two major models of instructional remediation within the overall framework of the diagnostic-prescriptive approach. These two models are the ability training (or process) model and the skill training (or task-analysis) model. Although there is not complete agreement among practitioners following either of the two models as to what constitutes the single, best approach, there are fundamental differences between the two models. We will describe the basic assumptions, some of the teaching strategies, and some of the research on the effectiveness of each model.

Ability Training

Ability trainers believe that a child's observed performance deficit (learning problem) is due to weakness in a particular ability thought necessary to perform a given task. That is, a particular child may have difficulty reading because of a visual-perceptual disorder. These abilities are usually classified as perceptual-motor, sensory, or psycholinguistic. Educational remediation involves testing the child (e.g., with the ITPA or Frostig tests) to determine disabilities and then prescribing instructional activities designed to remediate those disabilities. If deficits in basic abilities cause the child's learning problem, remediating those deficits should result in improved achievement. The logic is sound.

A number of distinct approaches can be identified within the ability-training model. The most popular of these approaches are psycholinguistic training, based on the ITPA; the visual-perceptual approach (Frostig & Horne, 1973); and the perceptual-motor approach (Kephart, 1971). According to Kephart, motor development precedes visual development; lack of proper perceptual-motor development, such as eye-hand coordination, is often a cause of reading difficulty. In Kephart's program four areas of motor development are taught: balance and posture, locomotion, contact, and receipt and propulsion.

Another approach to teaching children with learning disabilities is the multisensory approach. Although in this approach teachers are more likely to work directly on academic skills, it is still based primarily on an information-processing model. As its name suggests, the multisensory approach employs as many of the child's senses as possible in an effort to help him learn. The most notable multisensory programs are those developed by Fernald (1943) and Slingerland (1971). Fernald's method is known as the VAKT technique. In learning a new letter, for example, the child would see the letter (visual), hear the letter (auditory), and trace the letter (kinesthetic and tactile). Little scientific research has been conducted on the multisensory method.

There is not much research to support the effectiveness of ability training. Hammill, Goodman, and Wiederholt (1974) reviewed the results of studies conducted on the Kephart and Frostig approaches. They concluded that 13 of the 14 studies evaluating the Frostig reading materials produced unimpressive results. Of 15 studies using Kephart's perceptual-motor training program, only 6 reported significant improvements (intelligence, school achievement, and language functioning were measured in these studies). In addition, only 4 of 11 studies measuring visual-motor functioning reported that the training significantly improved visual-motor performance. In another review Myers and Hammill (1976) found that, in general, the Frostig materials improved children's scores on the Frostig Developmental Test of Visual Perception (Frostig et al., 1964), but whether their reading achievement improved was still in question. Two more-recent comprehensive reviews have also found the effectiveness of the perceptual-motor approach wanting. Kavale and Mattison (1983) reanalyzed 180 studies that investigated the effectiveness of the perceptual-motor approach and concluded that it is "not effective and should be questioned as a feasible intervention technique for exceptional children" (p. 165). After reviewing the results of 85 perceptual-motor training studies, Myers and Hammill (1982) state,

The CLD has published a position statement opposing the measurement and training of perceptual and perceptual-motor functions as part of educational services for individuals with learning disabilities (see *Learning Disability Quarterly*, Summer 1986, p. 247). The organization cites lack of scientific evidence in support of the claimed benefits of perceptual and perceptual-motor training.

> As a consequence of our reviews of these systems, we would recommend that perceptual-motor training in the schools be carefully reevaluated. Unlike a decade ago, when research on the topic was sparse, one can no longer assume that these kinds of activities will be beneficial to the children who engage in them. In fact, in the long run they may even be somewhat harmful because (1) they may waste valuable time and money and (2) they may provide a child with a placebo program when the child's problems require a real remedial effort. We would suggest that when these programs are implemented in the schools, they be considered as highly experimental, nonvalidated services that require very careful scrutiny and monitoring. (p. 416)

In a major review of 38 studies of ITPA-based psycholinguistic training, Hammill and Larsen (1974, 1978) conclude that "the overwhelming consensus of research evidence concerning the effectiveness of psycholinguistic training is that it remains essentially nonvalidated" (1978, p. 412). Critics of Hammill and Larsen's ITPA review (e.g., Lund, Foster, & McCall-Perez, 1978) claim that they were not justified in their conclusions because many of the original studies were poorly controlled. Kavale (1981) reanalyzed the Hammill and Larsen studies and contends that his investigation "appears to answer affirmatively" that psycholinguistic training is effective.

In a different response to the Hammill and Larsen (1974) review, Minskoff (1975) suggests that the earlier psycholinguistic research was not a good basis on which to evaluate the approach because it tended to be incomplete and methodologically inadequate. She goes on to specify criteria for future psycholinguistic research, presumably so that its effectiveness will be more clearly understood. Sowell, Packer,

Poplin, and Larsen (1979) followed Minskoff's criteria in a study designed to evaluate the effectiveness of psycholinguistic training with 63 first graders. They found the psycholinguistic training program to be unsuccessful and concluded their study with this comment:

> In summary, the amount of time, effort, and monies currently devoted in the schools to improving psycholinguistic abilities needs to be reevaluated. At best, psycholinguistic training should be viewed as experimental and not be employed extensively until its usefulness can be effectively demonstrated. In reality, the onus of documenting the value of psycholinguistsic training procedures falls primarily to those individuals who produce and/or advocate them. Until such time as experimental validation for this approach is forthcoming, educators are well advised to utilize other strategies in attempting to stimulate academic and/or language skills in children under their care. (p. 76)

Skill Training

Skill trainers believe that a child's demonstrated performance deficit *is* the problem; it is not the sign of an underlying disability, but the result of the child's not having had an appropriate opportunity to learn. For example, if a child cannot master a complex behavior (such as reading a sentence) and she has had sufficient opportunity and she wants to succeed, a skill trainer would conclude that she has not learned the necessary prerequisite skills (such as reading single words, reading letter sounds, and so on).

Task analysis and direct instruction can be used to teach more than traditional school subjects. See page 155 to find out how one teacher prepared a group of high school learning disabled students to take their driver's license examination on road signs and traffic laws.

Skill trainers use (1) precise, operational definitions of the specific behaviors they intend to teach, (2) task analysis to break down complex skills into smaller units, or subskills, requiring the learner to master only one component of the task at a time, (3) direct teaching methods that require the learner to practice the new skill many times, and (4) direct daily measurement to monitor the child's progress and evaluate instruction. Applied behavior analysis, direct instruction, and precision teaching are some of the skill-training approaches. All are closely related to one another, and all systematically manipulate aspects of the child's environment (materials, instructions, cues, rewards, and so on) in an attempt to facilitate the child's acquisition and retention of the new skill.

For a description of the DISTAR method and a review of the research conducted on it, see Harring, Bateman, and Carnine (1977).

One skill-training teaching program is the Direct Instructional System for Teaching Arithmetic and Reading (DISTAR), developed by Siegfried Engelmann and his colleagues. DISTAR programs are available for arithmetic, reading, and language. Each DISTAR program consists of a highly sequenced series of skills, materials, and activities designed to help children practice those skills and precise instructions for the teacher. The teacher works with a small group of children (4 to 10) who respond both individually and in unison to a fast-paced series of teacher-generated prompts and cues. Sometimes the teacher uses hand signals to direct and guide the children's responses. Corrective feedback for incorrect responses and praise for correct responses are also used. Unlike the ability-training instructional approaches, DISTAR has an impressive body of research demonstrating its effectiveness. A nationwide evaluation of the DISTAR program conducted by Follow Through and involving more than 8,000 children in 20 communities showed that children made significant gains in academic achieve-

JUST LIKE WE LEARNED IN CLASS

In most states a temporary learner's permit is a prerequisite to a driver's license. Obtaining the permit involves passing a test on road signs and traffic laws. Driver education courses usually focus instruction on how to operate the car. Students are expected to read the state motor vehicle digest and pass the test for the learner's permit. This poses a serious handicap to learning disabled students with poor reading skills.

Cheryl Hoagland, a high school learning disabilities teacher in Hilliard, Ohio, decided to teach the six students in her eighth period class the road signs and traffic laws included in the Ohio Department of Motor Vehicles (ODMV) Digest. Several of her students were hoping to get temporary permits in the coming months. "The reading ability of most of my ninth grade students is closer to that of a fifth grader. We always talk about teaching relevant skills. Here was one, and an important rite of passage as well that LD students should have an opportunity to achieve. But the wording, the vocabulary, and the sentence structure of the Digest make it automatically intimidating for my students."

Cheryl began with a road signs and traffic laws instructional program that had already been established as effective (Test & Heward, 1983). The program had been developed for use in a special classroom called the Visual Response System (see photo on p. 158), where students respond on overhead projectors built into their desks (Heward, 1978). Cheryl, however, modified the instructional program so it could be used in a conventional classroom setting.

Cheryl needed to create a means for every student to respond to every question in a manner that would enable her to provide immediate feedback. "In the Visual Response System, students respond by placing transparency response slides on or writing directly on the stage of their overhead projectors. Every student responds, and the teacher can easily see each student's answer. But there is only one overhead projector in my classroom—the teacher's. So I made each student a set of response cards, small squares of cardboard with traffic signs, "true," "false," "yes," "no," and so forth on them. I projected the instructional transparencies from the original program and had each student hold up a response card to every question. They also traced the movement of their cars through traffic situations and held them up for me to see. By wiping off their marks, we could use the same street scene over and over." Cheryl gave each student a small hand-held counter to keep track of their correct answers. After each class session the students recorded their numbers in a folder.

Throughout the 4-week unit, an average of .8 responses per minute per student were made during each 40-minute period. That translates into a total of 192 individual learning trials each period. The students answered correctly 92% of all questions during those instructional sessions.

To evaluate her program, Cheryl gave a series of tests designed to simulate the actual ODMV test as closely as possible. Criterion for passing the ODMV test is 15 correct on each of the two 20-question parts. On the simulation tests Cheryl's students averaged 90% correct. "I knew they would do well. They really loved the program. They would finish their math early during seventh period and set up the classroom for the driver ed unit so we could start right on time. I knew they were motivated by the content of the unit in the beginning, but it was the active pace and immediate feedback that kept them going for a month. It wouldn't be hard to teach this material in a boring, ineffective way."

Shortly after the unit was completed, one of the students turned 16 and took the ODMV test. She scored a passing 85% on each part. Returning to school the next day, she said, "It was a cinch, Ms. Hoagland. Everything was just like we learned in class."

Follow Through is a nationwide comprehensive educational program for economically disadvantaged children, kindergarten through third grade. Many Head Start children enter Follow Through programs. See chapter 13.

ment (Becker & Englemann, 1976). These children caught up to or even surpassed the national norms on several arithmetic, reading, and language skills, as measured by the Wide Range Achievement Test (Jastak & Wilkinson, 1984) and the Metropolitan Achievement Test (Balow, Farr, Hogan, & Prescott, 1978). On other skills, such as spelling, the DISTAR students finished a little below the national norm but still showed significant gains. None of the other educational approaches evaluated by the Follow Through program were as effective as DISTAR.

SCHOOL SERVICES

Most public schools offer a range of service delivery and placement alternatives for learning disabled students. The most common arrangements are the regular classroom, the consultant teacher model, the itinerant teacher model, the resource room, and the self-contained special class.

The Regular Classroom

Current legislation requires that handicapped children are to be educated with their nonhandicapped peers to the maximum extent possible and that they should be removed from normal settings only to the extent that their disability necessitates. This means that some learning disabled children remain in the regular classroom, and others are placed there for some time each day. Several factors combine to help make the regular classroom an effective learning environment for many learning disabled children today. These factors include the increased use of individualized instruction, teacher aides, and peer-tutoring programs in many regular classrooms. In addition, school districts are providing more in-service teacher-training programs, many of which focus on the identification, assessment, and remediation of children's learning problems. It may be unrealistic to think that the regular classroom is the best educational environment for children with severe learning disabilities (Reger, 1974). However, as Wallace and McLoughlin (1979) point out,

One peer tutoring program is described on pages 47–48.

> The practice of considering the regular classroom as a realistic service delivery system is also one aspect of the intention to *prevent* learning disabilities. As we have discussed previously, instructional factors may cause or at least compound the learning difficulties of some children. By including the regular classroom setting as one of the key delivery systems, we may be channeling the necessary information and skills where they are most needed. (p. 365)

In two other service delivery models, the consultant teacher and the itinerant teacher models, the learning disabled student stays in the regular classroom, but he and/or his teacher receive additional help.

The Consultant Teacher

A consultant teacher provides support to regular classroom teachers and other school staff who work directly with learning disabled children. The consultant teacher helps the regular teacher select assessment devices, curriculum materials, and instructional activities for the learning disabled children in that teacher's classroom. The consultant may even demonstrate new teaching methods or behavior management strategies. The major advantage of this model is that the consultant teacher can work with several teachers and thus indirectly provide special education services to many children. The major drawback is that the consultant has little or no direct contact with the children. Heron and Harris (1982) have described procedures that consultant teachers can use to increase their effectiveness in supporting mainstreamed children.

The Itinerant Teacher

The itinerant teacher is a combination consultant teacher and learning disabilities tutor "on wheels." An itinerant teacher serves several schools in a given district or geographical area. She acts as a consultant to the regular classroom teachers on her route and also serves as a tutor, providing direct assessment and instruction for some children. The itinerant teacher model attempts to combine the consultant teacher model and the resource room concept in areas where one school does not have enough learning disabled children to warrant its own program. In some rural areas, where learning disabled children are spread over a large area, this may be the only realistic way to provide special education services and allow learning disabled children to remain in the regular classroom.

The Resource Room

The resource room is the most widely used service delivery model for educating children with learning disabilities. A resource room is a specially staffed and equipped classroom where learning disabled children come for one or several periods during the school day to receive individualized instruction (Harris & Schutz, 1986; Wiederholt, 1974b).

The resource teacher is a specially trained and certified learning disabilities specialist whose primary role is to teach needed skills to those children who are referred to the resource room. Most of the children are in their regular classrooms for most of the school day, and they come to the resource room only for specialized instruction in the academic skills—usually reading or mathematics—or social skills they need to smooth their integration into the regular classroom. Other children may receive all of their academic instruction in the resource room and attend the regular classroom only for such periods as art, music, and social studies. In addition to teaching learning disabled children, the resource teacher also works closely with each student's regular teacher to suggest and help plan the child's program in the regular classroom.

Ronni Hochman, a middle school learning disabilities resource room teacher, offers suggestions for placing a learning disabled child in the regular classroom.

> I think a key to a resource room is identifying where the child's successes are and initially putting him back into the regular classroom only in the areas in which he can experience a great amount of success. I use the child's time in the resource

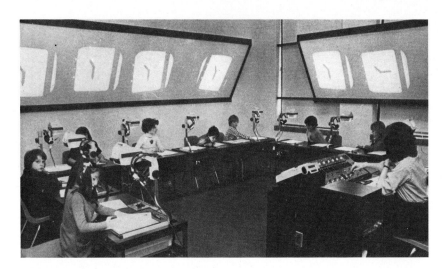

The Visual Response System is a resource room specially designed for small-group instruction. The teacher can easily see each student's response, enabling her to provide immediate feedback (Heward, 1978).

room to build those skills he needs to learn to be completely integrated into the regular classroom—whether it's learning to read better or simply learning to complete a task.

Some advantages of the resource room model are that (1) the children do not lose their identity with their peer group, so there is a smaller chance they will be stigmatized as "special"; (2) the children can receive the intense, individualized instruction they need every day, which might be impossible for the regular teacher to provide (with 29 other students); and (3) flexible scheduling allows the resource room to serve a fairly large number of learning disabled students (Mayhall & Jenkins, 1977; Wiederholt, Hammill, & Brown, 1983). A survey of resource room teachers found that their biggest concerns were over unclear role descriptions, variable expectations of administrators and regular classroom teachers, and insufficient time for planning, consulting, and observing students (McLoughlin & Kelly, 1982). Although the resource room concept is increasingly popular, its success depends on the skills of the resource teacher and the administrative practices used by the school. In particular, procedures must be determined that will help the learning disabled child generalize the skills learned in the resource room to the regular classroom.

The Self-Contained Classroom

In a self-contained classroom the learning disabilities teacher is responsible for all the educational programming for a group of 6 to 12 learning disabled children. The academic achievement deficiencies of some learning disabled children are so severe that they need to be full-time in a learning setting with a specially trained teacher. In addition, their poor work habits and inappropriate social behaviors make some learning disabled children candidates for the self-contained classroom, where distractions can be minimized and individual attention stressed. However, it is important that placement in a self-contained class not be considered permanent. Children should be placed in a self-contained class only after unsuccessful attempts to serve them adequately in other less-restrictive environments. As Wallace and McLoughlin (1979) suggest,

> It is preferable that the basis for placing a child in a special class be diagnostic and instructional experience in the resource room model. In this way, the special class system can be used only for the child who needs the most support. Hopefully, after a period in a highly structured environment and under a consistent intervention program, the child can develop communication and social skills to a satisfactory level and be moved back into a less isolated setting. (pp. 369–70)

A follow-up study of 10 high school students 5 to 6 years after they had been enrolled for a year in a self-contained learning disabilities program showed them to be performing as well as nonhandicapped students in a comparison group (Leone, Lovitt, & Hansen, 1981). Even though the students' performances varied considerably, their oral reading ability, free-time and occupational interests, and general success in high school were within the normal range. The results of the follow-up study suggest that placement in a self-contained special class because of significant academic deficits in the elementary grades does not preclude success in high school.

Secondary Programs

During the first 10 years of the learning disabilities movement, programs and services expanded greatly, but almost exclusively at the elementary level. In 1975 a survey across 37 states found that only 9% of the districts offered educational programming for secondary-level learning disabled students (Scranton & Downs, 1975). Many reasons have been cited for the lack of secondary programs, among them the fact that in many states students can drop out of school after completing the eighth grade or after reaching the age of 16. In addition, some believe that elementary learning disabilities programs are successful in remediating the achievement deficits of some students so that they can succeed in high school without special help. In spite of these factors, each year thousands of young men and women leave our nation's high schools with few, if any, marketable skills. Some learning disabled teenagers, who might have been able to attend college had they been given the help they needed in high school, are unable to find jobs of any consequence.

Marsh, Gearheart, and Gearheart (1978) predicted that the increasing awareness of the need for good secondary programs would result in much more activity in secondary schools by learning disabilities professionals in the near future. Fortunately, this trend has already begun. In 1978 McNutt and Heller surveyed 301 school districts and found that only 22.5% did *not* provide any programming for learning disabled adolescents. This number was a significant improvement over the survey results just 3 years earlier.

Deschler, Lowrey, and Alley (1979) conducted a nationwide survey of junior and senior high school learning disabilities teachers and found five different models or program options predominant.

1. *Basic skills remediation model.* This model provides developmental or remedial instruction for basic academic skill deficits. Reading and mathematics deficits receive the most attention.
2. *Tutorial model.* This model emphasizes instruction in academic content areas. Areas of instruction are usually those in which the student is experiencing difficulty or failure. The teacher's major responsibility is to help keep the LD student in the regular curriculum.
3. *Functional curriculum model.* Emphasis is on equipping students to function in society. The focus of instruction is on consumer information, completion of application forms, banking and money skills, and life-care skills such as grooming. In addition, this approach often attempts to relate academic content to career concepts.
4. *Work-study model.* Instruction in job- and career-related skills and on-the-job experience is emphasized. Students typically spend half the day on the job and the remainder of the day in school studying compatible material.
5. *Learning strategies model.* Instruction is designed to teach students how to learn rather than to teach specific content. For example, the teacher might present techniques for organizing material that has to be memorized for a history test, rather than teaching the actual history content.

Recent research on the learning strategies model by Deschler and Schumaker and their colleagues at the University of Kansas Research Institute on Learning Disabilities has proven very promising (Deschler, Schumaker, & Lenz, 1984; Schumaker, Deschler, Alley, & Warner, 1983). They have developed, field-tested, and validated a learning strategies curriculum with learning disabled adolescents. Information on that curriculum can be obtained by writing the Kansas Research Institute at the address given at the end of this chapter.

In their study Deschler and colleagues (1979) found that 51% of the existing secondary learning disabilities programs followed the basic skills remediation model. The other models, in order of their presentation here, were used by 24%, 17%, 5%, and 3% of the programs. Since programming for secondary learning disabled students is such a new phenomenon, it remains to be seen which of these models, or combination of approaches, will prove the most useful. Each of the five models has specific advantages and disadvantages (Alley & Deschler, 1979), and no one approach is apt to be the best for all learning disabled students.

CURRENT ISSUES/FUTURE TRENDS

Learning disabilities is such a dynamic and relatively young field that an entire book could be devoted to a discussion of current issues. Some of these issues include what terminology should be used (is a reading disability the same as a learning disability?), where learning disabled children should be taught (least restrictive environment), what kind of training learning disabilities teachers should receive, how federal and state funds should be appropriated, and what should be done about the proliferation of controversial "cures" for learning disabilities (megavitamin regimes and diets free of food additives). We will discuss here the continuing debate over the definition of learning disabilities and the concern for the special needs of adults with learning disabilities.

YES, I'M STILL LEARNING DISABLED

Elisabeth Wiig

I grew up in a time when we didn't have all the labels that we have now for disabilities. When I look at my life, I realize I had a bona fide learning disability. When I entered the third grade, I was a nonreader. My auditory memory skills had helped me so much that it was impossible to catch me before. Everybody thought I was reading from the page; but I was actually reciting, utilizing other cues such as pictures, and getting my buddies to give me the key words that started the sentences. If I got the key word that started the sentence, I could rattle off the rest. But in the third grade they took the pictures away from the readers. I hadn't started to associate text and topics and sentences with page numbers up in the corner. So I was just lost. But reading was not the only problem I had.

I couldn't do math either. My problem is visual-spatial orientation; and when you put a math problem down on paper, the numbers have to be lined up properly. I knew what it meant to subtract, and

to multiply and divide; and I could handle it as long as it was verbal—"7 times 7" or "6 times 3." Basically I learned the problems by heart. But once you get past the two-digit numbers and up into the hundreds, all of a sudden you have to put it down on paper. I couldn't place a number that had to be subtracted beneath the column it had to be subtracted from. Nor could I do problems where you have to carry. I couldn't put the carried-over digits in the right place; they hung all over the place. It was impossible for me to do even a simple sum. When they finally found out it was not the basic operations I had problems with they modified their approach. I was introduced to little grids that helped me set the problems up, and that countered my visual problems just fine.

I went through all kinds of things. I was in a classroom for the mentally retarded for a while. Yet when I look back on the early years, I did not realize how different I was. When I went to nursery school, at age 5, my mother was still dressing me. I didn't know that other kids could dress themselves.

I was constantly in trouble. The teacher would come over to me and I would start singing, because it would make her so mad that I would get thrown out of the room. If I could just get the teacher to expel me from the room, I could fantasize my whole day away. If I started singing when I wasn't supposed to, by 9:15 I could be out of the room. So I had all of the nonadaptive strategies, things kids learn how to do to get out of the mess they're in. And as long as you can get out of the mess, you can have a modicum of self-esteem.

I still consider myself learning disabled because there are times when I fail because of my problems. As long as there are very specific times when you fail, you still have a learning and perceptual problem.

One example occurred when I was up for my driver's test. I forgot I had to take directions from the policeman. He used "right," and "left," and I didn't know which way to turn. He yelled and screamed at me and took me back and failed me. The second time I went, I told the policeman about my problem head on. I said, "I'm confused when people say 'right' and 'left,' and I know you'll be telling me to turn right and left. Can I paste these letters on my hands?" He said yes. So I stuck big letters on the backs of my hands where I could see them while holding the wheel. By facing my problem head on, I did fine.

It's almost a daily occurrence. When I have to go places, the first few times I cannot find my way. I build in an extra half hour whenever I have to go someplace new. I'm OK on the freeway; but if there's any opportunity for failure, I get lost. I still get lost on campus, because there are parts that aren't familiar to me. To hold a map, you have to know where you are and which way you're facing. I go the wrong way anyway. One time I attended a professional meeting in Las Vegas, and I couldn't find anyplace. By the time I got there, the meetings were always over. I ended up sitting in my hotel room and crying. I went home three days early.

I've learned to overcome failure by knowing where I need support systems. For example, I'm an author who cannot spell. So I have a secretary who knows what my spelling error patterns are. Without her, I cannot write.

When I travel professionally, I don't rent a car because I'd get lost. So if people want me to speak, they have to pick me up. If I must travel by car, I stay in motels right by major roads. Otherwise, who knows if I'll ever get on the road again? I could be driving in the opposite direction. It's happened often.

Support systems are absolutely essential. I make sure I earn enough to pay for my support systems. Early in my career, my payments for support systems were exorbitant in relation to my salary. But I knew I had to pay to succeed.

Anxiety attacks used to leave me exhausted, like when I got lost and had to go back. These days I say, "So what? I can't find it? They're waiting for me. I'll call and they can come and get me." It's easy in the role of success, but it's totally different for young adults on the way up. Once you've "arrived," you can ask those who want things from you to help you. You don't feel so terrible about not always being quite with it.

My self-esteem has grown with every success, but it took me until I was 40 or older until I had reconciled who I was, until I no longer had anxiety attacks and nightmares. Since I reached 40, with every gain toward inner equanimity I have moved ahead. My growth has been tremendous.

Elisabeth H. Wiig is now professor of speech pathology at Boston University. Dr. Wiig is the author of three textbooks, four language assessment tests, and over 50 research articles dealing with language disorders in children and adolescents. She speaks six languages fluently. We are grateful to Dr. Wiig for her willingness to share some of her experiences with us.

Who Are the Learning Disabled?

The widely differing findings of prevalence studies (from 5% to 30% of the school-age population) indicate that there is no one standard, operational definition of learning disabilities. Some prominent special educators believe that the trend toward expanding the learning disabilities classification to include more and more children indicates a misunderstanding of the concept and only detracts from and weakens services to children who have severe learning problems (Larsen, 1978; Myers & Hammill, 1982; Wallace & McLoughlin, 1979).

Hammill (1980), in an address to the Council for Learning Disabilities, said,

> I know some people in our field who say the incidence of learning disabilities is 35% to 40%, depending on whether you want to throw in delinquents. I know people that see dyslexics under every bed; dysgraphics at every desk. Some people see all children who don't read too well as being learning disabled. And I know a few people who bounce back and forth on the incidence-definition question depending on how much federal and state funding is available. Eventually, we will have to decide just who and what LD is. (p. 4)

Clearly, there is no consensus regarding who is learning disabled. Two studies have shown that educators identify certain children as learning disabled even when all of their evaluative data are in the normal range, and that the single most reliable variable predicting whether a child will be identified is the *amount* of information presented on the child—the more information, the more likely the student will be identified—rather than the type of information or its relationship to usual identification critera (Algozzine & Ysseldyke, 1981; Ysseldyke, Algozzine, Richey, & Graden, 1982).

Although all agree that children who have any learning difficulty, major or minor, should receive help, special education services for learning disabled students should be reserved for those children with *severe* and *specific* learning difficulties (Wallace & McLoughlin, 1979). Kirk (1978a) suggests one solution to this problem. He says that all regular classroom teachers should have access to consultants for assistance with the 10% of all children in any classroom that need some degree of additional help. Such consultants might serve between 20 and 40 children at a given time. A second group of special educators could be highly trained learning disabilities specialists who would work with only those children who require more intensive, direct help. These teachers might serve only five or six students each day.

The discussion of what constitutes a true learning disability is likely to go on for some time. We believe that what a child's learning problem is called is not so important; what *is* important is that schools provide an educational system responsive to the individual needs of all children who have difficulty in learning.

Adults with Learning Disabilities

Discovering appropriate and effective programs and services to help young people with handicaps make a successful transition from school to adult life is one of the major challenges for all of special education today. The task is made even more difficult in the learning disabilities field because so little is known about adults with learning disabilities. As Smith and Robinson (1986) point out, "The field does not know what becomes of the LD students served in secondary schools: what percentage attend college, find successful employment, enter job training programs, or are unsuccessful in making the transition to adulthood?" (p. 242). According to a U.S. Department of Education fact sheet, 1% of all college freshmen in 1984 reported that they were learning disabled. Both Cordoni (1982) and Corbin Sicoli (1985) have described some of the support services that are available for college students with learning disabilities.

One learning disabled adult tells some of her story on pages 161–62.

Those studies that have been conducted have revealed a greater concern among adults with learning disabilities for self-perceived deficits in social and occupational skills rather than in the academic skills that caused their primary problems during their school years (Chelser, 1982; White, 1985). Kokaska and Skolnik (1986) surveyed 10 adults with learning disabilities to seek their suggestions for attaining a positive employment situation. Those adults were generally optimistic about future career success, although several indicated anxieties about their jobs. They suggested that adults with learning disabilities should select jobs in which personal strengths and personal initiative are emphasized, and they should accept the need to improve interpersonal skills, to work harder and longer than others to maintain good job performance, and to understand their own limitations.

We expect to witness a substantial increase in the number and range of educational, training, counseling, and other support services that will be available for adults with learning disabilities.

SUMMARY

1. Learning disabilities is a relatively new, rapidly growing field in special education.
   a. The term *learning disabilities* was first used in 1963 by S. A. Kirk to describe children who have serious learning problems in school but no other obvious handicaps.
   b. During the late 1960s two growing organizations—ACALD and DCLD—helped bring about federal legislation providing funds for learning disabilities programs.
   c. Today, learning disabilities is a handicapping condition included in P.L. 94–142.
2. There is no one, universally agreed-upon definition of learning disabilities. However, most definitions incorporate three criteria that must be met for a child to be labeled learning disabled.
   a. Learning disabled children must have a severe discrepancy between potential or ability and actual achievement.
   b. Learning disabled children must have learning problems that cannot be attributed to other handicapping conditions, such as blindness or mental retardation.
   c. Learning disabled children must need special educational services to succeed, services that are not needed by their nonhandicapped peers.
   d. No matter what definition is used, educators should focus on each child's specific skill deficiencies for assessment and instruction.
3. Characteristics of learning disabled children vary widely.
   a. Learning disabilities are not physically apparent. These children look like all other children.

    b. The single common characteristic is a specific and significant achievement deficiency in the presence of adequate overall intelligence.

4. Because definitions of learning disabilities and assessment and diagnosis procedures vary so widely, there are no reliable prevalence figures. During the 1983–84 school year the number of children with learning disabilities represented 4.57% of the U.S. population aged 3 to 21, making it the largest category in special education.

5. Although the actual cause of a specific learning disability is seldom known, the suspected causes can be grouped into three categories.

    a. Learning disabilities may be caused by brain damage. However, the majority of children with learning disabilities show no evidence of brain damage.

    b. Other researchers believe that various types of biochemical imbalance cause learning disabilities. Although research has failed to prove this contention, it is still a matter of considerable debate.

    c. Many special educators believe that environment—including quality of instruction—is a major cause of learning problems. They stress direct instruction in problem skill areas as the best approach to remediation.

6. Most learning disabilities professionals take a diagnostic-prescriptive approach to assessment. That is, results of assessment on any of a variety of types of tests lead directly to a plan for classroom instruction.

    a. Norm-referenced tests compare a child's score with the scores of other age-mates who have taken the same test.

    b. Process tests are designed to measure a child's ability in different perceptual or psycholinguistic areas. Two widely used process tests are the Illinois Test of Psycholinguistic Abilities and the Frostig Developmental Test of Visual Perception.

    c. Teachers use informal reading inventories to observe directly and record a child's reading skills.

    d. Criterion-referenced tests compare a child's score to a predetermined mastery level.

    e. Direct daily measurement involves regularly assessing a child on the specific skill being taught. One instructional system based on direct daily measurement is precision teaching.

7. There are two basic approaches to educating learning disabled children.

    a. Ability training involves prescribing instructional activities designed to remediate a child's weakness in underlying basic abilities.

    b. Psycholinguistic training, the visual-perceptual approach, the perceptual-motor approach, and the multisensory approach are all types of ability training.

    c. There is not much research to support the effectiveness of ability training. However, this approach is still advocated and used by some educators in the field.

    d. Skill training, the second approach, is based on the belief that the performance deficit is the problem, not a sign of an underlying disability.

    e. In skill training, remediation is based on direct instruction of precisely defined skills, many opportunities to practice, and direct measurement of a child's progress.

    f. Research has shown the skill-training approach—including applied behavior analysis DISTAR, and precision teaching—to be effective.

8. There are several different arrangements used in educating learning disabled children.

    a. Some learning disabled children are educated in the regular classroom.

    b. In some schools a consultant teacher helps regular classroom teachers deal with learning disabled children.

    c. In other districts an itinerant teacher serves as a consultant to teachers in several schools and also acts as a tutor for some children.

    d. In the resource room, which is the most common service delivery model for educating children with learning disabilities, a specially trained teacher works with the children on particular skill deficits for one or more periods a day. The children remain in the regular classroom for the rest of the day.

    e. A few learning disabled children attend separate self-contained classes. However, this placement should be used only after attempts to serve the child in a less restrictive setting have failed, and it should not be considered permanent.

9. Learning disabilities programs in the secondary schools are rapidly expanding. We do not yet know which of several current models will prove most useful.

10. Even though it may be difficult, if not impossible, to determine what is a true learning disability, the important point is that schools must respond to the individual needs of any child who has learning problems.

11. Increasing efforts should be directed toward the development of educational, training, counseling, and other support services for adults with learning disabilities.

FOR MORE INFORMATION

Journals

Academic Therapy. Published five times a year by Academic Therapy Publication, 20 Commercial Boulevard, Novato, CA 94947. Publishes articles describing specific ideas that teachers and parents of individuals with learning disabilities can implement.

Journal of Learning Disabilities. Published 10 times a year by Professional Press. Publishes research and theoretical articles relating to learning disabilities.

Journal of Precision Teaching. Published quarterly by Plain English Publications, P.O. Box 7224, Kansas City, MO 64113. A multidisciplinary journal dedicated to a science of human behavior that includes direct, continuous, and standard measurement. Publishes both formal and informal articles describing precision teaching projects.

Learning Disabilities Research and *Learning Disabilities Focus.* Each is published twice a year by the Division for Learning Disabilities, Council for Exceptional Children, 1920 Association Drive, Reston, VA 22091.

Learning Disability Quarterly. Published four times a year by the Council for Learning Disabilities. Emphasizes practical implications of research and applied research dealing with learning disability populations and settings.

Books

Alley, G., & Deschler, D. (1979). *Teaching the learning disabled adolescent: Strategies and methods.* Denver: Love.

Harris, W. J., & Schutz, P. N. B. (1986). *The special education resource room: Rationale and implementation.* Columbus, OH: Merrill.

Kauffman, J. M., & Hallahan, D. P. (Eds.). (1976). *Teaching children with learning disabilities: Personal perspectives.* Columbus, OH: Merrill.

Lewis, R. B., & Doorlag, D. H. (1987). *Teaching special students in the mainstream* (2nd ed.). Columbus, OH: Merrill.

Mercer, C. D. (1987). *Students with learning disabilities.* (3rd ed.). Columbus, OH: Merrill.

Myers, P. I., & Hammill, D. D. (1982). *Learning disabilities: Basic concepts, assessment practices, and instructional strategies.* Austin, TX: Pro-Ed.

Smith, D. D. (1981) *Teaching the learning disabled.* Englewood Cliffs, NJ: Prentice-Hall.

Wallace, G., & Kauffman, J. M. (1986). *Teaching children with learning problems* (3rd ed.). Columbus, OH: Merrill.

Organizations

Association for Children and Adults with Learning Disabilities, 5255 Grace Street, Pittsburgh, PA 15236. An active organization of parents and educators that serves as an advocate for learning disabled children.

Council for Learning Disabilities, Department of Special Education, University of Louisville, Louisville, KY 40292. An organization for professionals who work with learning disabled individuals. Publishes *Learning Disabilities Quarterly,* holds an annual conference to disseminate research and information, and promotes standards for learning disabilities professionals.

Division for Learning Disabilities, Council for Exceptional Children, 1920 Association Drive, Reston, VA 22091. Includes teachers, teacher educators, researchers, and other members of CEC who work with or on behalf of individuals with learning disabilities.

Learning Disability Research Institutes

Addresses for the five federally funded learning disabilities research institutes and their primary area(s) of research interest follow:

☐ Research Institute for the Study of Learning Disabilities (language comprehension)
Box 118
Teachers College, Columbia University
New York, NY 10027

☐ Chicago Institute for Learning Disabilities (social adjustment, language)
University of Illinois at Chicago Circle
Box 4348
Chicago, IL 60680

☐ Research Institute in Learning Disabilities (LD adolescents, learning strategies)
University of Kansas
Room 313 Carruth-O'Leary
Lawrence, KS 66045

☐ Institute for Research on Learning Disabilities (identification, assessment, and placement)
350 Elliot Hall
75 East River Road
University of Minnesota
Minneapolis, MN 55455

☐ Learning Disabilities Research Institute (attentional deficits, self-activated learning strategies)
University of Virginia
Department of Special Education
152 Ruffner Hall
Charlottesville, VA 22903

5

BEHAVIOR DISORDERS

Childhood is supposed to be a happy time—a time for playing, growing, learning, and making friends—and for most children it is. But for some children, life seems to be a constant turmoil. They are in conflict, often serious, with others and themselves. Or they are so shy and withdrawn that they seem to be in their own worlds. In either case playing with others, making friends, and learning all the things a child must learn are extremely difficult for these children. They are children with behavior disorders. These children are referred to by a variety of terms—*emotionally disturbed, socially maladjusted, psychologically disordered, emotionally handicapped,* or even *psychotic* or *autistic* if their behavior is extremely abnormal or bizarre.

Behavior disordered children are seldom really liked by anyone—their peers, teachers, brothers or sisters, even parents. Sadder still, they often do not even like themselves. They are difficult to be around, and attempts to befriend them may lead only to rejection, verbal abuse, or even physical attack. With some emotionally withdrawn children, all overtures seem to fall on deaf ears; and yet these children are not deaf.

Many nonhandicapped children act in the same ways as children with behavior disorders—but not as often or with such intensity. And of course, behavior disordered children can be likable.

Although behavior disordered children are not physically handicapped, their noxious or withdrawn behavior can be as serious a handicap to their development and learning as the mentally retarded child's slowness to learn. Behavior disordered children make up a significant portion of those needing special education.

DEFINING BEHAVIOR DISORDERS

Currently there is no definition of behavior disorders that is generally agreed upon. There are several reasons for the lack of a clear definition. First, there are measurement problems. Second, there is no clear agreement about what constitutes good mental health. Third, different theories of emotional disturbance use their own terminology and definitions. Cultural influence is another problem. The expectations and norms for appropriate behavior are often quite different across ethnic and cultural groups. In addition, frequency is a concern. All children behave inappropriately at certain times. Finally, disordered behavior sometimes occurs in conjunction with other handicapping conditions (most notably mental retardation and learning disabilities), making it difficult to tell whether one condition is the result or the cause of the other.

In spite of, or perhaps because of, these problems, many efforts have been made to define emotional disturbance in children. According to Hewett and Taylor (1980), a definition of emotional disturbance should ideally (1) help us accurately identify the type of child we are concerned with so the problem can be diagnosed, (2) permit communication with individuals and agencies who determine educational, administrative, and funding policies for behavior disordered children, and (3) help in research by enabling precise specification of the characteristics of disturbed children serving as subjects so that studies can be replicated and findings generalized.

Although numerous definitions have been proposed, the one written by Eli Bower (1969, 1981) has had by far the most impact on special education. Bower's definition, with only a few changes, was adopted by the U.S. Department of Education as the definition of seriously emotionally disturbed children, one of the categories of handicapping conditions covered by P.L. 94–142.

> Seriously emotionally disturbed is defined as follows:
> (i) The term means a condition exhibiting one or more of the following characteristics over a long period of time and to a marked degree, which adversely affects educational performance.
> > (a) An inability to learn which cannot be explained by intellectual, sensory, and health factors;
> > (b) An inability to build or maintain satisfactory interpersonal relationships with peers and teachers;
> > (c) Inappropriate types of behavior or feelings under normal circumstances;
> > (d) A general pervasive mood of unhappiness or depression; or
> > (e) A tendency to develop physical symptoms or fears associated with personal or school problems.
> (ii) The term includes children who are schizophrenic or autistic.
> > The term does not include children who are socially maladjusted unless it is determined that they are seriously emotionally disturbed. (*Federal Register, 42* (163), August 23, 1977, p. 42478).

Although the definition specifies the types of behavioral characteristics to be found in disturbed children, it is vague and leaves much to the subjective opinion of the authorities (usually teachers) surrounding the child. How does one operationalize such terms as *satisfactory, normal, inappropriate,* and *pervasive?* And how is the determination to be made that some behavior problems represent social maladjustment whereas others are indicative of true emotional disturbance? This determination is critical because children who are socially maladjusted are not considered handicapped and are therefore ineligible for special education services under P.L. 94–142. It should be noted that Bower's original definition did not include any mention of social maladjustment, and he and others have criticized the inclusion in the federal definition of this seemingly illogical criterion (Bower, 1982). It is difficult to conceive of a child

---

The federal definition has been amended to move autism from this category to "other health impaired." See pages 188–94 for more on autism.

The Council for Children with Behavior Disorders (CCBD), the major professional organization concerned with the education and treatment of children with behavior disorders, has adopted the position that the term *behaviorally disordered* is more appropriate than the term *seriously emotionally disturbed.* The CCBD endorses use of the term *behaviorally disordered* because (1) it does not suggest any particular theory of causation or set of intervention techniques, (2) it is more representative of the students who are handicapped by their behavior and are being served under P.L. 94–142, and (3) it is less stigmatizing (Huntze, 1985).

The behavior disordered child's noxious or withdrawn behavior is a serious impediment to learning.

who is sufficiently socially maladjusted to have received that label but who does not display one or more of the five characteristics (especially *b*) included in the federal definition.

Although P.L. 94–142 clearly mandates that all handicapped children receive individualized special education services, the definition included in the law may be partially responsible for the great disparity between the estimated prevalence of children with behavior disorders and the number of such children receiving special education (Bower, 1982; Knitzer, 1982; Kauffman, 1985, 1986; Wood, 1985). The uncertain meaning of many aspects of the definition allows the determination of whether a child is considered behaviorally disordered to be more a function of a school district's available resources (i.e., its ability to provide the needed services) than a function of the child's actual needs for such services.

Still, Bower's definition is a good one for special education because it describes the relevant behavior problems of school children. As we will show throughout this chapter, special education with behaviorally disordered children is most effective when it focuses on what they actually do and what the environmental conditions are in which they misbehave, rather than attempting to define and classify some inner disturbance.

Other definitions of behavior disorders have been proposed (e.g., Kauffman, 1977; Ross, 1974). Although each definition is somewhat different, all agree that a child's behavior, to be considered disordered, must differ markedly (extremely) and chronically (over time) from current social or cultural norms.

The Role of Teacher Tolerance in Defining Children's Behavior Disorders

Even though none of the definitions of emotional disturbance proposed so far have provided a consistent, universally agreed-upon standard for identification, diagnosis, communication, and research, they all place the concept of behavior disorders in a "conceptual ballpark" (Hewett & Taylor, 1980). And the key player in that ballpark seems to be teacher tolerance. A number of studies have shown that a student's identification as behaviorally disordered is largely a function of the teacher's notion of the expected or acceptable behavior of children. In a **longitudinal study** Rubin and Balow (1978) found that 59% of all children who had received three or more annual ratings had been identified as behavior disordered by at least one teacher at some time between kindergarten and sixth grade. Of course, this study suggests another important conclusion as well—that a great many children do experience some type of behavioral problem during their early school years. Although they do go away, these problems are identified by teachers at the time as an indication of emotional disturbance.

The role of teacher tolerance in identifying children as emotionally disturbed is significant. Algozzine (1980) found that, as a group, regular classroom teachers rated certain behaviors as more disturbing than did a comparison group of special education teachers. In a subsequent study Curran and Algozzine (1980) found teachers with varying levels of tolerance for immature or defiant behaviors differentially rated a hypothetical child's likelihood of success in the regular classroom. These studies suggest that "emotional disturbance is a function of the perceiver. . . . What is disturbance to one teacher may not be to another" (Whelan, 1981, pp. 4–5).

Defining Disordered Behavior

Perhaps the most functional way to look at behavior disorders is to describe how children who are called emotionally disturbed actually act. What dimensions of their behavior are different from those of their normal peers? We can analyze or measure several dimensions of children's behavior—its rate, duration, topography, and magnitude.

Rate refers to how often a particular behavior is performed. Almost all children cry, get into fights with other children, and sulk from time to time; yet we are not apt to label them emotionally disturbed. The primary difference between behavior disordered children and normal children is the rate at which these kinds of undesirable activities occur. Although the disturbed child often does nothing that a normal child does not do, she does certain undesirable things much more often (e.g., crying, hitting others, playing alone).

Closely related to rate is **duration.** Duration is a measure of how long a child engages in a given activity. Again, even though normal and behavior disordered children may do the same things, the amount of time the behavior disordered child spends in certain activities is often markedly different from that of the normal child—either longer or shorter. For example, many young children have temper tantrums, but they generally last no more than 5 or 10 minutes. A behavior disordered child may have a tantrum for an hour or more. Sometimes the problem is one of too short a duration, as with paying attention or working independently. Some behavior disordered children cannot stick to one task for more than several seconds at a time.

Topography refers to the physical shape or form of an action. For instance, throwing a baseball and rolling a bowling ball involve different topographies. Although both involve the arm, each activity requires a different movement. The responses emitted by a behavior disordered child may be of a topography seldom, if ever, seen in normal children. These behaviors are often maladaptive or dangerous to the child or others (e.g., twirling a small object in a bizarre manner close to the eye, pulling out hair).

Finally, behavior is sometimes characterized by its **magnitude** or force. It may be either too soft (for example, talking in a volume so low that you cannot be heard) or too hard (such as slamming the door).

Disturbed children also have difficulty discriminating when and where certain behaviors are appropriate. Learning that kind of **stimulus control** is a major task of growing up, which most children master naturally through socialization. They pick it up from their friends, siblings, parents, and other adults. However, some behavior disordered children often appear unaware of their surroundings. They do not learn the proper time and place for many actions without being carefully instructed.

There are two other important aspects of children's behavior disorders. First, these children usually exhibit a variety of problems across several different areas of functioning. Hewett and Taylor (1980) refer to this as "clustering," the exhibition of two or more types of problem behaviors that increase the chance that the child's behavior will exceed the teacher's range of tolerance. The authors illustrated clustering with the case of Bobby, a child who, in one "infamous morning," destroyed school property, stole a classmate's lunch money and punched that student in the stomach, defied the teacher, and used obscene language. Another important aspect is that behavior disordered children have long-standing problems that require extensive treatment rather than brief intervention.

The advantage of defining behavior disorders in terms of these behavioral dimensions is that identification, assessment, treatment strategies, and evaluation of the effects of treatment can all revolve around the objective measurement of these dimensions. This approach leads to a direct focus on the child's problem—the inappropriate behavior—and ways of dealing with it, as opposed to concentrating on some problem within the child. If the child can learn new, socially acceptable ways to behave, he need no longer be called behavior disordered.

PREVALENCE

Because there is no one operational definition of behavior disorders that can be applied uniformly in all instances, estimates of how many children have behavior disorders vary tremendously. The U.S. Department of Education has traditionally used the figure of 2% of the school-aged population in its estimates for funding and personnel needs for behavior disordered children. During the 1984–85 school year the federal government reported that 373,207 emotionally disturbed children aged 3 to 21 received special education under P.L. 94–142. Although this figure marked the greatest number of behavior disordered children ever served and ranked emotional disturbance as the fourth largest category of special education, it represented considerably less than half of the 2% estimate. Kauffman (1985) believes that social policy and economic factors are related to the fact that the government has now reduced its estimate of the prevalence of behavior disorders to a range of 1.2% to 2%.

> The government would prefer for obvious reasons not to allow wide discrepancies to exist between prevalence estimates and the actual number of children served. It is easier to cut prevalence estimates in half than to double the number of children served. (p. 28)

Morse (1975) reviewed a number of surveys and found that anywhere from 0.1% to 30% of the school-age population was considered behavior disordered. With such widely varying estimates, it is obvious that people are using different criteria for deciding whether a child is behavior disordered. Kelly, Bullock, and Dykes (1977) report that teachers identified about 20% of their students as suffering from some kind of emotional disturbance. Based on his survey of California schools, Bower (1981) concluded that two or three children in the average classroom (about 10%) can be expected to show signs of emotional disturbance. In the Rubin and Balow (1978) longitudinal study cited earlier, 7.4% of all of the children in their sample ($n = 1,586$) were considered to have a behavior problem by *every* teacher who rated them over the 3-year period.

Wood and Zabel (978) suggest that the difference in prevalence figures stems as much from the manner in which the figures are collected as it does from the use of different definitions. Most surveys ask teachers to identify students in their classes who are behavior problems at that point in time. Many children display inappropriate behavior for short periods of time, and such one-shot screening procedures will identify them, as in the Rubin and Balow (1978) study in which more than half of all students were identified as behavior problems by at least one teacher at some time during their elementary school careers. As Hewett and Taylor (1980) observe,

> In our experience, when you walk into any elementary classroom, you can usually pick out two or three children who are "not with it" and who are visible enough to stand out from other members of the class in terms of their problem behavior. And

if you stay long enough, you can usually determine if they "fit" within the teacher's range of tolerance for behavioral differences. Whether they would be the same children a week or semester later is debatable. Thus, we get almost no meaning from incidence figures. The U.S. Office of Education's 2 percent is undoubtedly very conservative and may be most accurate in relation to the moderately and severely emotionally disturbed. In general, the more severe the problem behavior the child exhibits, the more likely we are to obtain accurate, stable, and reliable estimates. (p.42)

Regardless of what prevalence study one turns to, it is evident that there are many thousands of school children whose disordered behavior is handicapping their educational progress but who are presently not receiving the special education they need.

Sex

Boys are much more likely to be identified as behavior disordered than girls (Morse, Cutler, & Fink, 1964; Rubin & Balow, 1971; Schultz, Salvia, & Feinn, 1974; Werry & Quay, 1971). In one study conducted in a large metropolitan school district, 82% of the children referred for evaluation for behavior disorders were boys (Mendelsohn & Jennings, 1986). Boys labeled disturbed are likely to be aggressive and act out, whereas behavior disordered girls are typically shy, anxious, and withdrawn. Among severely disturbed children (i.e., autistic and schizophrenic), boys outnumber girls anywhere from 2:1 to 5:1 (Hingtgen & Bryson, 1972; Morse, 1975).

Age

There is relatively little emotional disturbance reported in the early grades, with a sharp increase and peak during the middle grades, and a decline in prevalence beginning in junior high school and continuing through high school (Morse et al., 1964). However, arrest rates for juvenile delinquency, one type of behavior disorder, increase sharply during the junior high years. This pattern probably reflects both the greater harm adolescents can cause to society as a result of their inappropriate behavior and the fact that younger children are often not arrested (and therefore do not show up on the records) for committing the same acts that lead to the arrest of an older child. However, younger children are now committing more serious and violent crimes than in years past (Cavan & Ferdinand, 1975).

Juvenile Delinquency

Each year approximately 3% of all children in this country are referred to juvenile courts (Achenbach, 1974; Cavan & Ferdinand, 1975). In 1979 more than 500,000 youth were admitted to juvenile detention and correctional facilities (Heim et al., 1980). Although the word *delinquent* is a legal term, the offenses an adolescent commits to be labeled delinquent constitute a behavior disorder. The rate and seriousness of crimes committed by juveniles have been increasing significantly (Cohen, 1973). Although boys have generally committed crimes involving aggression (such as assault

In a national survey of juvenile correctional facilities, Rutherford, Nelson, and Wolford (1985) found that 28% of the residents were identified as handicapped (e.g., displaying mental retardation, learning disability). Recent studies have revealed that many handicapped juvenile offenders receive few or no special education services. See the May/June 1986 special issue of *Remedial and Special Education* for a series of articles on special education in juvenile correctional facilities.

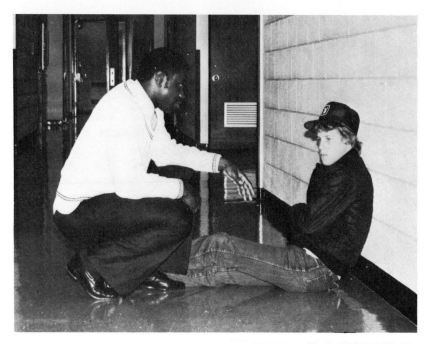

One-to-one counseling plays an important role in working with juvenile offenders.

and burglary) and girls have been associated with sex-related offenses (such as prostitution), more and more violent offenses are being committed by girls (Cavan & Ferdinand, 1975). Offenses involving the use of illegal drugs have also increased tremendously over the past 2 decades.

Severely Disturbed Children 500,000

The National Association for Mental Health has estimated that more than 500,000 children in the United States are severely emotionally disturbed. These children are commonly diagnosed and referred to as autistic, psychotic, or schizophrenic. The National Society for Autistic Children (1977) has estimated that autism occurs in approximately 5 of every 10,000 children. Although autism is quite rare, it is actually more common than blindness in children (Lotter, 1966; Rutter, 1965). Kauffman (1980) suggests that 0.5% of all children (or 1 in 200) are being served as severely disturbed.

CLASSIFICATION OF CHILDREN'S BEHAVIOR DISORDERS

As we mentioned in chapter 1, classifying observed phenomena within a given field in different categories is an important scientific task. In the area of behavior disorders a reliable and valid classification system would foster accurate communication among researchers, diagnosticians, and teachers. Better communication could result, most importantly, in a child's receiving the educational placement and treatment that have been proven most effective for her specific behavior problem. Unfortunately, as yet we are far from having such a workable classification system.

One system of classifying behavior disorders is the *Diagnostic and Statistical Manual for Mental Disorders* (DSM-III) developed by the American Psychiatric Association (1980). The DSM-III is an elaborate and vast classification system consisting of 230 separate diagnostic categories, or labels, used to identify the various types of disordered behavior noted in clinical practice. Because of its more precise language, its use of more examples, and the greater amount of information it requires about the person being diagnosed, the DSM-III represents an improvement in clinical classification over earlier versions (DSM-I, 1952; DSM-II, 1968). However, even though the DSM-III classification system is used quite regularly in the mental health professions, it is not very useful for educational purposes. One problem is its lack of reliability. Even with the more precise language it is not uncommon for one psychiatrist or psychologist to classify a child in one category and a second examiner to place the same child in a completely different category (Epstein, Detwiler, & Reitz, 1985).

But an even greater problem is that putting a child in a given category provides no guidelines for treatment. Knowing that a child has been diagnosed as fitting a certain category in the DSM-III provides a teacher with virtually no useful information on what intervention or therapy is needed.

Another well-known classification system was developed by Quay and his co-workers (Quay, 1975, 1979). Quay collected a wide range of data—including behavior ratings by parents and teachers, life histories, and responses on questionnaires by the children themselves—for hundreds of behavior disordered children. By statistically analyzing all of this information, the researchers found that children's behavior disorders tend to appear in groups, or clusters. Children who showed some of the behaviors in a given cluster had a high likelihood of also showing the other traits and behaviors in that cluster. Quay calls the four types conduct disorder, personality disorder, immaturity, and socialized aggression.

Children described as having a **conduct disorder** are likely to be disobedient and/or disruptive, get into fights, be bossy, and have temper tantrums. A **personality disorder** in children is identified by social withdrawal, anxiety, depression, feelings of inferiority, guilt, shyness, and unhappiness. **Immaturity** is characterized by a short attention span, extreme passivity, daydreaming, preference for younger playmates, and clumsiness. The fourth dimension, **socialized aggression,** is marked by truancy, gang membership, theft, and a feeling of pride in belonging to a delinquent subculture. Although Quay's system has proven quite reliable—the same four clusters of behavior and personality traits have been found in many samples of behavior disordered children (Quay, 1979)—it does not provide treatment information. Therefore, its usefulness is limited primarily to describing the major types of children's behavior disorders.

Hewett and his colleagues have developed a classification scheme based on "levels of learning competence" (Hewett, 1964, 1968; Hewett & Forness, 1977; Hewett & Taylor, 1980). Hewett and Taylor (1980) describe an actual episode that led them to seek better ways of classifying behavior disorders. Donald, an 11-year-old boy, was completely immobilized—he would not walk, talk, eat, or care for himself. He was fed with a stomach tube at first but later began to swallow juice, his only observable response. At this point Donald's psychiatrist felt that going to school might help him. He introduced him to the teacher by saying,

> "This is Donald. He is in a catatonic schizophrenic stupor with severe psychomotor retardation. Good luck."
>
> Such a description was a bit unsettling for the teacher and is an excellent example of the alien and essentially useless contribution such labels and diagnostic terms have to make in educational settings. As long as the teacher was intimidated by this pathetic little boy in a "catatonic schizophrenic stupor," it was doubtful that any worthwhile program could be provided by the school. But once she set aside the psychiatric jargon and took a long, hard look at Donald, things got better. Here was this immobilized student. We had heard what his psychiatric problem was. Now, what was his educational problem? Simple. Donald *was a severe response problem* in educational and learning terms. He did not move. To learn you must respond. Donald was a candidate for a response curriculum. He was no longer a mysterious alien with catatonic schizophrenia. He was now a learner, and it would be the role of the school to teach him to respond as the initial educational task. (p. 96)

Hewett's classification system includes six levels of learning competence. The attention level has to do with children making contact with their environment; the response level, with active motor and verbal participation; the order level is concerned with teaching children to follow instructions and routines; the exploratory level has children accurately and thoroughly investigate their environment; the social level focuses on interactions with others; and the mastery level involves skills related to self-care, academics, and vocational interests. Table 5.1 shows how the classification scheme views behavior problems along a continuum of too little to too much in respect to the six levels of learning competence.

Hewett and Taylor (1980) contend that this classification system is both descriptive and functional, that classifying a child's behavior problem within the system "provides a direct link to the setting of curriculum goals" (p. 99). In the case of Donald, for instance, his nearly total lack of response was the first order of business for the teacher. Hewett's classification system is a considerable advance over systems that provide descriptive labels only, labeling the child without relating to useful educational strategies.

See journals such as *Behavior Therapy, Behavioral Disorders,* and *Journal of Applied Behavior Analysis.*

It is much easier to classify behaviors objectively than to classify children. In addition, there is an ever-growing body of research literature indicating that certain strategies are often successful in changing certain types of behaviors. Thus, objectively pinpointing the specific inappropriate things that a disturbed child does can lead to treatment strategies. And labeling behaviors rather than children is optimistic; it implies that the child will be normal as soon as he learns more socially adaptive actions to replace his disordered behavior. This attitude might help to alleviate some of the permanent stigma that often comes from labeling children.

Another method of classifying behavior disordered children is by degree of severity. Although emotionally disturbed children have sometimes been referred to as displaying mild, moderate, and severe behavior problems, at least one study suggests

TABLE 5.1
Classification of disturbed children by negative variants of six levels of learning competence.

Too Little	Optimal			Too Much
Disturbances in sensory perception	Excessive daydreaming Poor memory Short attention span In a world all his or her own	Attention	Selective attention	Fixation on particular stimuli
Immobilization	Sluggishness Passivity Drowsiness Clumsiness Depression	Response	Hyperactivity Restlessness	Self-stimulation
Failure to develop speech	Failure to use language for communication	Response	Extremely talkative	Uses profanity Verbally abusive
Self-injurious Lawlessness Destructiveness	Disruptiveness Attention seeking Irresponsibility Disobedience	Order	Overly conforming	Resistance to change Compulsive
Bizarre or stereotyped behavior Bizarre interests	Anxiety Preoccupation Doesn't know how to have fun Behaves like an adult Shyness	Exploratory	Plunges into activities	Tries to do everything at once
Preoccupation with inanimate objects Extreme self-isolation Inability to relate to people	Social withdrawal Alienates others Aloofness Prefers younger playmates Acts bossy Secretiveness Fighting Temper tantrums	Social	Hypersensitivity Jealousy Overly dependent	Inability to function alone
Blunted, uneven or fragmented intellectual development	Lacks self-care skills Lacks basic school skills Laziness in school Dislike for school Lacks vocational skills	Mastery	Preoccupation with academics	Overintellectualizing

Source: From *The Emotionally Disturbed Child in the Classroom: The Orchestration of Success,* (pp. 100—101, 2nd ed.) by F. M. Hewett and F. D. Taylor, 1980, Boston: Allyn & Bacon. Reprinted by permission.

that this three-level distinction is not supported in practice. Olson, Algozzine, and Schmid (1980) found that teachers of emotionally handicapped children regularly identified only two levels, or degrees, of behavioral disturbance: mild and severe. Mildly emotionally disturbed children were seen as those children who could respond to interventions provided in regular classrooms by regular class teachers, with the support of guidance counselors or consulting teachers. Severely disturbed children were viewed as those needing intense treatment programs and residential placement.

Most behavior disordered children have mild or moderate problems that are often fairly short-lived and can be treated effectively in the regular classroom and at home by knowledgeable teachers and parents. Children who are severely disturbed—often called **psychotic, schizophrenic,** or **autistic**—require intensive, specially designed programming, usually in a highly supervised environment such as a special class or residential treatment center. However, classification by degree of severity is primarily after the fact. Important decisions as to the type of programming a child needs and the environment in which it should be delivered should be based on an objective assessment of the individual needs of the child, rather than on someone's opinion that the child is either mildly or severely disturbed.

CHARACTERISTICS OF CHILDREN WITH BEHAVIOR DISORDERS

We have already described some of the characteristics of behavior disordered children. In this section we will discuss the intellectual ability and academic achievement of these children, as well as the two general types of behavior they display—aggression and social withdrawal. We will also describe the dominant characteristics of childhood autism.

Intelligence and Achievement

See chapter 3 for a discussion of IQ tests.

Contrary to one popular myth, most emotionally disturbed children are not bright, intellectually above-average children who are bored with their surroundings. Many more behavior disordered children than normal children score in the slow learner or mildly retarded range on IQ tests. A score of about 90 is average for behavior disordered children. Many severely disturbed children are untestable; for those who can be tested the average IQ score is about 50. Occasionally, a severely disturbed child scores very high on an IQ test, but this is a rare exception.

Whether behavior disordered children actually have any less real intelligence than normal children is difficult to say. An IQ test measures only how well a child performs certain tasks. It is possible that the disturbed child's inappropriate behavior has interfered with past opportunities to learn the tasks included on the test, but the child really has the necessary intelligence to learn them. In any event, IQ tests are good indicators of school achievement, and behavior disordered children are noted for their problems with learning and academic achievement. Based on his review of research related to the intelligence of emotionally disturbed children, Kauffman (1985) has hypothesized that, as a group, their IQ scores are distributed as shown in Figure 5.1.

A.M. CLUB: JOGGING AS THERAPY FOR BEHAVIOR DISORDERED STUDENTS

The use of vigorous physical exercise has been proposed as effective therapy for children with behavior disorders, possibly resulting in reduced rates of disruptive classroom behavior and improved self-esteem. Allen (1980) noted significantly fewer classroom disruptions after jogging sessions; Evans, Evans, Schmid, and Pennypacker (1985) found that jogging and touch football resulted in fewer talkouts and increased academic production in the classroom; and Kern, Koegel, and Dunlap (1984) discovered that 15 minutes of vigorous jogging reduced stereotypic responding. The following story is excerpted from one teacher's description of a systematic program of running that she used with behaviorally disordered junior high school students.

The information came rushing into my head and tumbled into a box marked, "Yep, that's right!" Therapeutic jogging for behaviorally impaired kids: Whoopee—what a right idea! And A.M. Club was conceived. The administration was receptive *and* supportive. We began to consider the when, where, and how aspects of the program. It was suggested that we might consider running the three-story stairs in our junior high building before school each morning. But it seemed to me that I remembered my son's tennis season and how they called running the stairs the suicide run! So as a concession to myself, I did not choose the three flights as the site. How about the grassy lot across the street from the junior high each morning? But these kids have enough trouble with peer relations without adding being a spectacle. A.M. Club was having labor pains. The site finally selected was the YMCA, a new facility with a running track.

The local runners with whom I talked spoke about the joy of running, the runner's high, the inside thrill. With these kids, I might address these lofty issues later; in the meantime, they needed a tangible reward, something they could hold in their hand, carry with them, or put on the refrigerator

The physical exercise and group cohesiveness fostered by the A.M. club can help cut down disruptive classroom behavior and improve self-esteem.

at home. Ribbons! Any kid works for a ribbon. So design a ribbon with the club logo and for every three attendances present them with a ribbon. After eight ribbons they earn a T-shirt with the club logo on the front. We were recognizable. A.M. Club had an identity.

The biggest concern was how to structure the program to decrease inappropriate behaviors such as fighting or leaving the exercise area. How do we foster appropriate behaviors, a feeling of helping others, of being part of a team effort and giving encouragement? And how would we get kids to work on improvement of physical condition? We wrote into the IEP three rules tied to a reward which would act as an incentive.

1. No physical fighting or namecalling.
2. Stay in the designated area.
3. Continuous forward movement during the 12-minute exercise period.

If all members followed the rules for 2 weeks, we would have breakfast together at McDonald's on the second Friday on the way back to school. A.M. Club was born.

As I write this, after several months the following facts can be stated: Of the 4 original members, 3 have never missed; our group now numbers 12 students; 3 of the members have signed up for the eighth grade track team. And students are actively engaged in encouraging others in the group. They can be seen running in pairs, with one behind the other running at his shoulder saying, "Come on, one more lap."

I am not naive enough to believe a program such as A.M. Club is appropriate for every student with behavior problems, nor do I believe there is a "magic cure" which comes for those students who participate. This program is only one small part of a larger, comprehensive program tailored to the specific needs of our students. But let me tell you, there is real joy in this small group. We hear parents speak of the commitment their child shows to the group and to their own self-improvement. As a teacher I frequently follow the philosophy when working with kids, "If it looks good, try it. If it works, try it again." And that is why A.M. Club started. Physical exercise and group cohesiveness looked good as a concept, and it worked.

Source: From "A.M. Club" by Evelyn Anderson, 1985, *Teaching Behaviorally Disordered Youth, 1,* pp. 12–16. Copyright by the Council for Children with Behavior Disorders. Reprinted by permission.

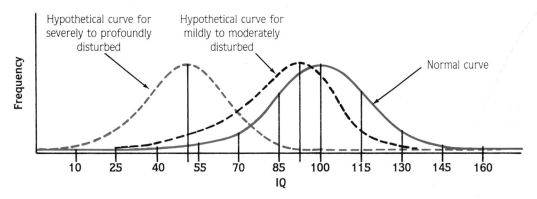

FIGURE 5.1

Hypothetical frequency distributions of IQ for mildly to moderately, and severely to profoundly disturbed children compared to a normal frequency distribution.

Source: From *Characteristics of Children's Behavior Disorders* (3rd ed., p. 142) by J. M. Kauffman,
1985, Columbus, OH: Merrill. Reprinted by permission.

Even when IQ scores are taken into account, however, behavior disordered children achieve less than their scores indicated that they should. Glavin and Annesley
(1971), in a study of 130 behavior disordered children, found that 81% were underachieving in reading and 72% were achieving less than would be expected in math.

Data obtained by the state of Florida on a total of 193 eleventh grade students
classified as emotionally disturbed or socially maladjusted indicated that almost 50%
of these students could not read well enough to pass a functional literacy test. Approximately 75% of the sample did not have the mathematics skills necessary for a
high school diploma (reported in Cawley & Webster, 1981). A survey of correctional
institutions found 34% of incarcerated delinquents to be functionally illiterate (Clearinghouse for Offender Literacy Programs, 1975). Oliver (1974), in a national survey
of 12- to 17-year-old public school students, found that over 80% of those who
needed frequent discipline were behind in their academic achievement.

Usually, the behavior disordered child is an acting-out child in the classroom, See pages 181–82 for
constantly defying the teacher's instructions and classroom rules and procedures. the story of how one
Walker and Buckley (1974) have suggested that the behavior disordered child's aca- teacher used a before-
demic deficits can, at least in part, be explained in terms of the large amount of time school jogging program
the child spends on nonacademic matters (such as running around the room or fight- to help her behaviorally
ing), at the expense of learning. Hops, Beickel, and Walker (1976) list the following form better in the class-
behaviors as characteristic of the acting-out child in the classroom. room.

1. Is out of seat
2. Yells out
3. Runs around room
4. Disturbs peers
5. Hits or fights
6. Ignores teacher
7. Complains
8. Fights excessively
9. Steals
10. Destroys property
11. Does not comply with adult com-
    mands or directions.

12. Argues (talks back)
13. Ignores other teachers
14. Distorts the truth
15. Has temper tantrums

16. Is excluded from activities by peers
17. Does not follow directions
18. Does not complete assignments

Many educators have noted the close association of learning disabilities and behavior disorders (e.g., Stephens, 1977; Wallace & McLoughlin, 1979). Many children with behavior disorders also have the problems in learning described in chapter 4.

Aggressive Behavior

Aggression is the major characteristic of Quay's conduct disorder and socialized aggression categories.

The most common characteristics of behavior disordered children are aggression and acting out. Even though all children sometimes cry, hit others, and refuse to comply with the requests of their parents and teachers, disturbed children do so frequently. Also, the aggressive behavior of behavior disordered children often occurs with little or no provocation. Aggression takes many forms—verbal abuse toward adults and other children, destructiveness and vandalism, physical attacks on others. These children seem to be in continuous conflict with those around them. Their own aggressive outbursts often cause others to strike back in attempts to punish them. It is no wonder that these children are not liked by others or that they establish few friendships.

Patterson and his co-workers have conducted considerable research on childhood aggression (Patterson, Reid, Jones, & Conger, 1975). Through intensive observations of many aggressive children at home and in school, they have identified 14 different classes of noxious behaviors often shown by behavior disordered children. Table 5.2 shows the different rates at which behavior disordered and normal children

Aggression and acting out are the most common characteristics of children with behavior disorders.

TABLE 5.2
Noxious behaviors in aggressive and nonaggressive children.

Noxious Behavior	Description	Average No. of Mins. Between Occurrences*	
		Aggressive Children	Nonaggressive Children
Disapproval	Disapproving of another's behavior by words or gestures	7	12
Negativism	Stating something neutral in content but saying it in a negative tone of voice	9	41
Noncompliance	Not doing what is requested	11	20
Yell	Shouting, yelling, or talking loudly; if carried on for sufficient time it becomes extremely unpleasant	18	54
Tease	Teasing that produces displeasure, disapproval, or disruption of current activity of the person being teased	20	51
High rate activity	Activity that is aversive to others if carried on for a long period of time (e.g., running in the house or jumping up and down)	23	71
Negative physical act	Attacking or attempting to attack another with enough intensity to potentially inflict pain (e.g., biting, kicking, slapping, hitting, spanking, throwing, grabbing)	24	108
Whine	Saying something in a slurring, nasal, high-pitched, or falsetto voice	28	26
Destructive	Destroying, damaging, or trying to damage or destroy any object	33	156
Humiliation	Making fun of, shaming, or embarrassing another intentionally	50	100
Cry	Any type of crying	52	455
Negative command	Commanding another to do something and demanding immediate compliance, plus threatening aversive consequences (explicitly or implicitly) if compliance is not immediate; also directing sarcasm or humiliation at another	120	500
Dependent	Requesting help with a task the child is capable of doing alone (e.g., a 16-year-old boy asking his mother to comb his hair)	149	370
Ignore	The child appears to recognize that another has directed behavior toward him but does not respond in an active fashion	185	244

*Minutes between occurrences are expressed as approximations of reported average rates per minute (e.g., for aggressive children's whine, reported rate per minute equals 0.0360, or approximately once every 28 minutes).

Source: From *Characteristics of Children's Behavior Disorders* (3rd ed., pp. 214–215) by J. M. Kauffman, 1985, Columbus, OH: Merrill, as adapted from *A Social Learning Approach to Family Intervention: Vol. 1. Families with Aggressive Children* (p. 5) by G. R. Patterson, J. B. Reid, R. R. Jones, and R. E. Conger, 1975, Eugene, OR: Castilia. Reprinted by permission.

emit these inappropriate behaviors. The data in the table were taken from observations in the homes of aggressive and nonaggressive children. Observations in the classroom indicated similar patterns (Patterson, Cobb, & Ray, 1972).

As many behavior disordered children grow older, their aggressive behavior causes conflict in the community, leading to run-ins with law enforcement officials and arrests for criminal offenses. Teenage delinquency is a serious problem in the United States today. Youth under the age of 18 are responsible for a large number of each year's criminal arrests (Arnold & Brungardt, 1983).

To add to the problem, as we mentioned earlier, the incidence of serious and violent crimes committed by juveniles is increasing (Cavan & Ferdinand, 1975). In 1981, 9% of all people arrested for murder and nonnegligent manslaughter were under 18. And younger children are being arrested; in 1981 over 600,000 arrests were made of children under 15. A total of 205 of those arrests were for murder and nonnegligent manslaughter (U.S. Department of Justice, 1982).

The total number of criminal offenses committed by youths against others and property is, of course, impossible to determine. Many crimes go unreported or unsolved, leaving identification of the perpetrator unknown. However, the information in Table 5.3 indicates the possible extent of the problem and the many crimes often committed by individual juvenile offenders. Originally intended to show the ability of positive peer-culture counseling groups to provide confidentiality and to generate a feeling of trust among the youths and their adult leader, this table gives further information on the characteristics of juvenile offenders.

Many believe that most children who exhibit deviant behavior patterns will grow out of them with time and become normally functioning adults. Although this popular wisdom may hold true for many children with emotional problems such as withdrawal, fears, and speech impairments (Rutter, 1976), research indicates that it is not so for children who display consistent patterns of aggressive, coercive, antisocial, and/or delinquent behavior (Robins, 1979; Wahler & Dumas, 1986). Robins (1966) conducted a follow-up study of over 500 adults who as children had been seen by a clinic because of behavior problems. Robins used structured interviews to gather such information as work history, alcohol and drug use, performance in the armed services, arrest, social relationships, and marital history. A control group of 100 adults who grew up in the same community as the subjects was used for comparison. The results were significant. Of those adults who had been referred to a clinic for behavior problems as children, 45% had five or more antisocial traits. Only 4% of those in the control group showed that many antisocial characteristics. In analyzing the results further, Robins found that those children who had been referred to the clinic for antisocial behavior—theft, fighting, discipline problems in school, truancy, and the like—had the most difficulty adjusting as adults. Furthermore, those children as adults tended to raise children who had a higher incidence of problem behaviors than normal, thus continuing the cycle.

Withdrawn Behavior

These children make up Quay's personality disorder and immaturity dimensions.

Some behavior disordered children are anything but aggressive. Their problem is the opposite—too little social interaction with others. Although children who consistently

TABLE 5.3
Juvenile offenses known to the court and offenses not known to the court but admitted in a group counseling program.

Offenses Known to Court	Offenses Not Known to Court, Discussed in Group
Student A Petty larceny; brutality (holding 9-year-old boy over burning trash barrel).	Auto theft; breaking and entering.
Student B Beyond control of parent; sexual intercourse with 12-year-old sister.	Auto theft; attempted rape; stealing; shoplifting; breaking and entering; vandalism; sexual acts with animals; incest with mother.
Student C Shoplifting; disorderly conduct; grand larceny; breaking and entering; destroying private property; truancy.	Habituation to drugs; grand larceny; petty larceny; arson; auto theft; carrying concealed weapons.
Student D Curfew violation; auto theft; breaking and entering; public intoxication; operating motor vehicle without license.	Carrying deadly weapon; robbery; arson; auto theft; multiple breaking and entering; three instances assault and battery.
Student E Truancy; runaway; obtaining merchandise under false pretenses.	Habituation to drugs; shoplifting; auto theft; vandalism; "rolling queers" for money (assault, battery, robbery).
Student F Petty larceny; contempt of court; curfew violation; breaking and entering.	Malicious cutting and wounding; housebreaking; stealing; forgery; shoplifting.
Student G Breaking and entering; attempted safe burglary; safe burglary.	Carrying a deadly weapon; malicious cutting and wounding; burglary; concealing stolen property; fraud; stealing from automobiles.
Student H Shoplifting; runaway; violation of probation.	Breaking and entering; stealing.
Student I Public intoxication; petty larceny; carrying concealed deadly weapon; burglary; attempted safecracking.	Shoplifting; driving without license; breaking and entering.

Source: From *Positive Peer Culture* (2nd ed., p. 84) by H. H. Vorrath and L. K. Brendtro, 1985, Hawthorne, NY: Aldine de Gruyter. Reprinted by permission.

act immature and withdrawn do not present the threat to others that aggressive children do, their behavior still creates a serious impediment to their development. These children seldom play with other children their own age. They usually do not have the social skills necessary to make friends and have fun and often retreat into their own daydreams and fantasies. Some are fearful of things without reason, frequently complain of being sick or hurt, and go into deep bouts of depression. Obviously, these behavior patterns limit the child's chances to take part in and learn from the school and leisure activities that normal children participate in.

See pages 189–90 for a case study involving a kindergarten girl who was so withdrawn that she did not speak at school. For information on teaching social skills to children, see Cartledge and Milburn (1986), Stephens (1978), and Strain, Guralnick, and Walker (1986).

Jeff's inability to interact with others is of great
concern to his teachers and parents.

Happily, for the mildly or moderately disturbed child who is withdrawn and
immature and who is fortunate enough to have competent teachers and other school
professionals responsible for her development, the outlook is fairly good. Carefully
outlining the social skills the child should learn and gradually and systematically arranging opportunities for and rewarding those behaviors often prove successful.

Autism

Autism refers to a set of behavioral characteristics common to many profoundly disturbed children. Mildly and moderately behavior disordered children usually are not
labeled as having a problem during their preschool years; many are not considered
behavior disordered by anyone until they reach their middle elementary years at

WORKING WITH DENISE—AN ELECTIVE MUTE

Some children become so shy and withdrawn that they refuse to speak at school, even though they use normal speech in other places or in the presence of other people. The clinical term for this behavior disorder, speaking normally in one setting and not speaking in another, is *elective mutism.*

Denise was a 5-year-old kindergarten student who spoke only to her parents and brother when at home. Throughout her first 6 months at school no one there heard Denise talk, laugh, cry, or make any vocalizations whatsoever. Yet her speech at home was reportedly fluent. Denise was described by her mother as generally happy and helpful around the house. Denise completed some school assignments at home, but she never attempted any work in school. She rarely took part in any group activities and sometimes stood in one spot for long periods of time unless she was coaxed to do otherwise.

Because Denise spoke freely at home but was mute at school, it was decided to use a treatment program that united the two environments. A **token economy** was chosen for this purpose, whereby desired behaviors could be rewarded with some tangible item that could be accumulated and traded in for a variety of back-up reinforcers. Because any treatment program bridging home and school would require full cooperation from Denise's parents, a meeting was arranged. The teacher explained to the parents that when Denise did certain things at school, she would be given gold stars to take home and "buy" things with, provided she had enough stars to cover the cost of the desired item. Denise's parents then made a list of items and activities their daughter liked. In addition to vocalizations, behaviors that would increase the likelihood of speech were also listed to be rewarded. Those behaviors requiring Denise to speak earned her the most stars.

A chart illustrating the available rewards and their relative cost in stars was constructed and taped to the refrigerator door in Denise's house. She also got a folder in which she could save and carry home the gummed stick-on stars.

The teacher explained to Denise's classmates (in Denise's absence) that they were going to play a game, the object of which was to get Denise to talk at school. Even the promise of the possibility of Denise's talking to them was a strong incentive for her peers to cooperate. The teacher then asked Denise's classmates to "try to pay more attention to Denise when she is doing one of these things" and read the list of desired behaviors to them. They were also told to ignore her at other times.

Denise made rapid progress with this program. Whereas she had earned only one star on the first day, for joining story time, by Day 30 she took part in all group activities, said "Hi," and answered seven questions from the teacher. She had accumulated the 40 stars she needed for a new doll.

It is important to note that behaviors other than those that involve speech were rewarded. To get the token economy started, some behaviors Denise was already doing were included for reinforcement. In this case simply waiting for Denise to speak would probably have been futile and frustrating. By increasing the frequency of behaviors that required Denise to confront other people (such as joining group activities), she had many more occasions for speaking.

Another important factor was the behavior of Denise's classmates. Before the program they would answer questions for her, frequently ask her whether she was all right, and get things for her. She received a lot of attention for *not* talking. During the program, however, this attention was withheld; and Denise's classmates were very good at paying attention to her only when she was participating.

In Denise's case the ice was broken just before the end of the school year, and it was feared that her muteness might return again in the fall. To help prevent that, Denise was enrolled in a 6-week summer school session with the same classroom teacher. During that session social praise and special privileges (such as wiping the blackboard, feeding the class turtle) were substituted for the home reward menu and were given at school for doing the same list of behaviors. Gold stars were again used as token reinforcers until the last week and a half of the summer session. Denise's rate of speech and social activity in general continued to increase during the summer.

A year after Denise's original program, she was described by her new teacher as a child who talks "a mile a minute." She had been retained in kindergarten because her extreme withdrawal during the first 7 months of school had prevented her from acquiring most of the prerequisite skills for the first grade. At the end of her first kindergarten year, Denise could not identify any shapes, colors, or numbers and knew only a few letters of the alphabet.

At the beginning of her second year, Denise would not answer a question unless she felt sure of the right answer. Her teacher dealt immediately with this temporary muteness by walking away and ignoring her. After 2 days Denise began to answer "I don't know" to questions she did not understand. Three months later she was answering in complete sentences in front of the class, beginning conversations, initiating play with other children, and learning in school.

Source: From a case study reported by W. L. Heward, H. T. Eachus, and J. Christopher, 1974.

school. This is not true for autistic children. An autistic child often seems different from normal children even during the first 2 years. Lovaas and Newsom (1976) have described six common characteristics of autistic children.

1. *Apparent sensory deficit.* We may move directly in front of the child, smile, and talk to him, yet he will act as if no one is there. We may not feel that the child is avoiding or ignoring us, but rather that he simply does not seem to see or hear. The mother also reports that she did, in fact, incorrectly suspect the child to be blind or deaf. . . . As we get to know the child better, we become aware of the great variability in this obliviousness to stimulation. For example, although the child may give no visible reaction to a loud noise, such as a clapping of hands directly behind his ears, he may orient to the crinkle of a candy wrapper or respond fearfully to a distant and barely audible siren.

2. *Severe affect isolation.* Another characteristic that we frequently notice is that attempts to love and cuddle and show affection to the child encounter a profound lack of interest on the child's part. Again, the parents relate that the child seems not to know or care whether he is alone or in the company of others.

3. *Self-stimulation.* A most striking kind of behavior in these children centers on very repetitive **stereotyped** acts, such as rocking their bodies when in a sitting position, twirling around, flapping their hands at the wrists, or humming a set of three or four notes over and over again. The parents often report that their child has spent entire days gazing at his cupped hands, staring at lights, spinning objects, etc.

4. *Tantrums and self-mutilatory behavior.* Although the child may not engage in self-mutilation when we first meet him, often the parents report that the child sometimes bites himself so severely that he bleeds, or that he beats his head against walls or sharp pieces of furniture so forcefully that large lumps rise and his skin turns black and blue. He may beat his face with his fists. . . . Sometimes the child's aggression will be directed outward against his parents or teachers in the most primitive form of biting, scratching, and kicking. Some of these children absolutely tyrannize their parents by staying awake and making noises all night, tearing curtains off the window, spilling flour in the kitchen, etc., and the parents are often at a complete loss as to how to cope with these behaviors.

5. *Echolalic and psychotic speech.* Most of these children are mute; they do not speak, but they may hum or occasionally utter simple sounds. The speech of those who do talk may be echoes of other people's attempts to talk to them. For example, if we address a child with the question, "What is your name?" the child is likely to answer, "What is your name?" (preserving, perhaps, the exact intonation of the one who spoke to him). At other times the **echolalia** is not immediate but delayed; the child may repeat statements he has heard that morning or on the preceding day, or he may repeat TV commercials or other such announcements.

6. *Behavior deficiencies.* Although the presence of the behaviors sketched above is rather striking, it is equally striking to take note of many behaviors that the autistic child does *not* have. At the age of 5 or 10, he may, in many ways, show the behavioral repertoire of a 1-year-old child. He has few if any self-help skills but needs to be fed and dressed by others. He may not play with toys, but put

them in his mouth, or tap them repetitively with his fingers. He shows no understanding of common dangers.*

Clearly, children who act as Lovaas and Newsom (1976) describe are profoundly
disturbed. Their management and treatment often require intensive behavioral programming to reduce the frequency of self-injurious and/or self-stimulatory behaviors.
Even after years of extensive intervention in which substantial progress has been
made, unless systematic programming is continued to maintain those gains, some autistic children revert to their earlier forms of behavior (Lovaas, Koegel, Simmons, &
Long, 1973).

On the brighter side, however, a great deal of exciting and promising research
may lead to better futures for children with autism (Valcante, 1986). For example,
the recent work of Lovaas (1982) and his colleagues at the University of California at
Los Angeles indicates the tremendous potential of early intervention with autistic children. He reports that 50% of a group of autistic children who were provided with an
early intervention program of intensive, one-to-one behavior modification for more
than 40 hours per week prior to the age of 3½ years made a complete recovery.
That is, they were later able to advance from first to second grade in a regular
classroom, attained normal IQ scores, and were considered by their teachers to be
well adjusted. Another 40% of the group was said to have made substantial improvement.

Researchers are also discovering successful procedures for using sensory stimulation (e.g., movement, visual and/or auditory feedback, vibration) to reduce self-
stimulation and to reinforce desired responses (Ferrari & Harris, 1981; Rincover,
Cook, Peoples, & Packard, 1979). More effective methods of programming important
aspects of instruction for autistic children, such as scheduling learning tasks and varying reinforcers, are being experimentally demonstrated (Dunlap & Koegel, 1980; Egel,
1981). Still other researchers are teaching autistic children to communicate through
sign language (Barrera & Sulzer-Azaroff, 1983; Bonvillian & Nelson, 1976) and to use
social interaction skills with nonhandicapped peers (Gaylord-Ross, Haring, Breen, &
Pitts-Conway, 1984).

Russo and Koegel (1977) carried out an impressive case study showing that an
autistic child could be successfully mainstreamed in a regular classroom. A 5-year-old
girl with a primary diagnosis of autism was placed in a regular public school kindergarten with 20 to 30 normal children and one teacher. For the first 12 weeks (after
a 3-week **baseline** period), a therapist was also in the classroom to provide a treatment program of token reinforcement, verbal praise, and prompts for desired behaviors. For the remaining 10 weeks of the school year, the kindergarten teacher, who
had been trained by the therapist, carried out the treatment program alone and kept
the autistic child in the classroom. Figure 5.2 shows the number of desirable social
interactions, amount of stereotypic self-stimulatory behavior (such as rocking and

*From "Behavior Modification with Psychotic Children" by O. I. Lovaas and C. D. Newsom (1976) in
Handbook of Behavior Modification and Behavior Therapy by Harold Leitenberg (Ed.), (pp 308–309).
Englewood Cliffs, NJ: Prentice-Hall. Reprinted by permission.

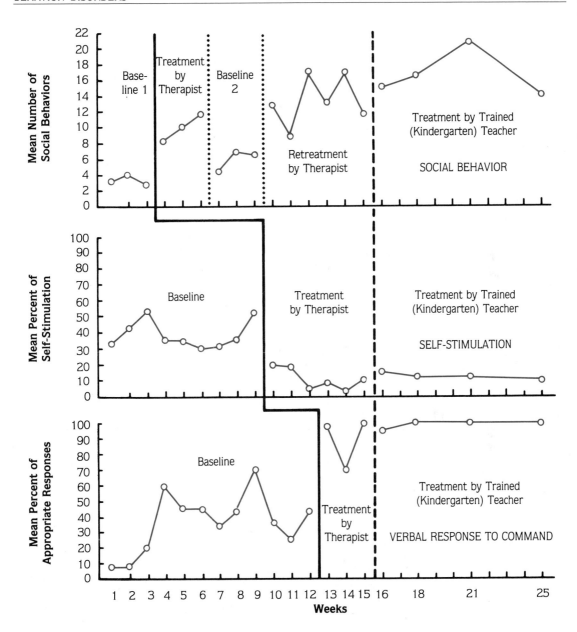

FIGURE 5.2

Social behavior, self-stimulation, and verbal response to command in the normal kindergarten classroom during baseline, treatment by the therapist, and treatment by the trained kindergarten teacher; all three behaviors were measured simultaneously.

Source: From "A Method for Integrating an Autistic Child in a Normal Public-School Classroom" by D. C. Russo and R. L. Koegel, 1977, *Journal of Applied Behavior Analysis, 10,* p. 585. Copyright by the Society for the Experimental Analysis of Behavior, Inc. Reprinted by permission.

rhythmic manipulation of small objects), and percent of appropriate responses to questions (such as "What color is this?") asked by the therapist or teacher.

During the next school year the girl was placed in a regular first grade classroom with another teacher. At the beginning of first grade, she was emitting fewer social behaviors and the frequency of self-stimulatory behavior had increased over the levels obtained by the end of kindergarten. However, in-class retreatment by the therapist and training of the first grade teacher resulted in improvements similar to those of the kindergarten year. Russo and Koegel state that no further problems were reported by the school throughout the remainder of the first grade or during the child's second and third grade years. The researchers report that four other autistic children were also successfully placed in regular classrooms (three in kindergarten and one in the fifth grade) using the same procedures.

Russo and Koegel's (1977) research is critically important for two reasons. First, they discovered at least some of the variables that can be controlled to help an autistic child function in a regular classroom. Second, their successful results offer real hope and encouragement for the many teachers and parents working to learn more about helping autistic children.

For more on mainstreaming autistic children, see Knoblock, 1982.

CAUSES OF BEHAVIOR DISORDERS

Several theories and conceptual models have been proposed to explain abnormal behavior. Regardless of the conceptual model from which behavior disorders are viewed, the suggested causes of disordered behavior can be grouped into two major categories—physiological and psychological.

Physiological Factors

For the vast majority of behavior disordered children, there is no evidence of organic injury or disease. That is, they appear to be biologically healthy and sound. Some experts believe that all children are born with a biologically determined temperament. Although a child's inborn temperament may not in itself cause a behavior problem, it may predispose the child to problems. Thus, certain events that might not produce abnormal behavior in a child with an easy-going temperament might result in disordered behavior by the child with a difficult temperament (Thomas & Chess, 1984; Thomas, Chess, & Birch, 1968).

Possible biological causes are more clearly evident in severely and profoundly disturbed children. Many autistic children show signs of neurochemical imbalance (Rimland, 1964, 1971), and other physiological causes of autism—including pre- and postnatal infections, chromosomal disorders, auditory impairments, and central nervous system dysfunction—have been suspected (Ciaranello, Vandenberg, & Anders, 1982; Garreau, Parthelmy, Sauvage, Leddet, & LeLord, 1984; Menolascino & Eyde, 1979; Ritvo, Ritvo, & Brothers, 1982). Genetics have been shown to play a role in childhood schizophrenia (Buss, 1966; Heston, 1970; Meehl, 1969). However, even when there is a clear biological impairment, no one has been able to say with certainty whether the physiological abnormality actually causes the behavior problem or is just associated with it in some unknown way.

Psychological Factors

Psychological factors involve events in the child's life that affect the way she acts. Psychological factors are considered important in the development of behavior disorders in all conceptual models (except a strict physiological stance, which few adhere to). However, the kinds of events seen as important and the ways in which they are analyzed are viewed differently by professionals with different approaches (e.g., a psychoanalyst and a behavior analyst). The two major settings in which these events take place are a child's home and school.

We know that the relationship children have with their parents is critical to the way they learn to act, particularly during their early years. Observation and analysis of parent-child interaction patterns shows that parents who treat their children with love, are sensitive to their children's needs, and provide praise and attention for desired behaviors tend to have normal children with positive behavioral characteristics. Aggressive, behavior-problem children often come from homes in which parents are inconsistent disciplinarians, use harsh and excessive punishment, and show little love and affection for good behavior (Becker, 1964; Martin, 1975).

Because of the research on the relationship between parental child-rearing practices and behavior problems, many mental health professionals have been quick to pin all of the blame for children's behavior problems on parents. But the relationship between parent and child is a dynamic, reciprocal one. In other words, the behavior of the child may affect the behavior of the parents just as much as the parents' actions affect the child (Patterson, 1980; Sameroff & Chadler, 1975). Therefore, it is not practical, at the least, and wrong, at the worst, to place all blame for abnormal behavior in young children on their parents. Instead, professionals must work with the parents to help them systematically change certain aspects of the parent-child relationship in an effort to prevent and modify these problems (Heward, Dardig, & Rosset, 1979).

See chapter 13 for an in-depth discussion of working with parents.

School is the place where children spend the largest portion of their time outside the home. Therefore, it makes sense to observe carefully what takes place in schools in an effort to identify other events that may cause problem behavior. Also, because most behavior disordered children are not identified as such until they are in school, it seems reasonable to question whether the school actually contributes to the incidence of behavior disorders. Some professionals have gone further than simply questioning; they feel that the schools are the major cause of behavior disorders in children. However, there is no evidence to support this contention. As with physiological or family causes, we cannot say for sure whether a child's school experiences are the lone cause of the behavior problems, but we can identify ways in which the school can influence or contribute to the child's emotional disturbance (e.g., through inappropriate expectations, inconsistent management).

Several studies have demonstrated that what takes place in the classroom can maintain and actually strengthen deviant behavior patterns, even though the teacher is trying to help the child (Bostow & Bailey, 1969; Thomas, Becker, & Armstrong, 1968; Walker & Buckley, 1973). Walker (1979) concludes,

> It is apparent that a child's behavior pattern at school is the result of a complex interaction of (1) the behavior pattern the child has been taught at home, including attitudes toward school, (2) the experiences the child has had with different teachers in the school setting, and (3) the relationship between the child and his/her current teacher(s). Trying to determine in what proportion the child's behavior pattern is attributable to each of these learning sources is an impossible and unnecessary task. Deviant child behavior can be changed very effectively without knowing the original causes for its acquisition and development. (p. 7)

Kauffman (1981a) suggests five ways in which schools should treat children in order to help prevent the development of behavior problems.

1. Have a fair attitude toward individual differences in interests and abilities; do not force every child to fit a narrow mold.
2. Have appropriately average expectations for behavior and academic achievement. If too low, expectations become self-fulfilling prophecies; if too high, expectations frustrate children.
3. Manage a child's behavior consistently; just as the parent's being too lax or too rigid encourages disordered behavior, inconsistent school discipline can have the same negative result.
4. Include areas of study that have relevance to the child; not to do so invites truancy or misbehavior.
5. Reward desired behaviors and do not reinforce inappropriate behaviors; from the viewpoint of behavioral psychology, failure to do this contributes to disturbance.

IDENTIFICATION AND ASSESSMENT

Few school districts use any systematic method for identifying disturbed children. Some have speculated that systematic screening and identification methods are not used because the schools would identify many more children than they could provide special education services for. Another reason may be that they are not needed. If only a portion of the children with behavior problems can be served, those children with the more obvious and severe disturbances will receive the services, and they are clearly identifiable without formal methods.

In fact, most behavior disordered children are readily identifiable. They stand out. This does not mean, however, that identification is always a sure thing. With younger children identification of emotional disturbance is more difficult because the behavior of all young children changes quickly and often. Also, some withdrawn children go undetected because their problem does not draw the attention of parents and teachers. Aggressive children, on the other hand, seldom go unnoticed. Research has shown that informal teacher ratings are relatively reliable and valid in selecting behavior disordered children (Bower, 1981; Cosper & Erickson, 1984; Nelson, 1971).

Although there are no reliable tests for determining emotional disturbance, several **screening** devices have been developed. Children identified in the screening are then either watched closely for further signs or given a more intensive examination. The most widely used screening test for behavior disorders is A Process for In-School Screening of Children with Emotional Handicaps (Bower & Lambert, 1962). This device employs ratings of the child's behavior by his teacher, his peers, and the child himself. If the child is rated negatively by the teacher and his classmates or by himself, it is suggested that he be evaluated further. The instrument has three different forms: one with rating scales and questions appropriate for kindergarten through third grade, one for fourth through seventh grade, and one for eighth through twelfth grade. Simpson (1981) suggests that a thorough screening/identification process for behavior disordered students should include (1) an interview with the parent(s) or guardian, (2) at least one behavior rating scale, (3) direct classroom observation, (4) peer evaluation, and (5) self-evaluation.

Traditionally, assessment of behavior disordered children has relied heavily on the results of psychological tests and interviews. However, the results of **projective tests** (e.g., Rorschach Ink Blot [Rorschach, 1942], Draw-A-Man Test [Goodenough & Harris, 1963]) have proven to be of minimal value in prescribing an appropriate intervention. Children often do not respond in a testing or interview situation in the same way they would in the classroom or at home. Also, results of these assessment procedures test only a limited sample of a child's behavior and, importantly, do not assess how the child typically acts over a period of time. One-time measures are not sufficient to use as a basis for planning treatment.

In recent years direct and continuous measurement has become more and more popular as a method for assessing children with behavior disorders. With this method the actual behaviors that cause a child to be considered disturbed in the first place are clearly specified and observed in the setting where they normally occur (e.g., the classroom) every day. In this way precise statements can be made about what problem behaviors must be weakened and what adaptive behaviors should be performed with greater frequency. In addition to providing specific information on the frequency of occurrence of the problem, direct and continuous measurement also enables the teacher to observe systematically and note what events normally surround the behavior(s) of concern—both before and after it. As we stressed in the chapter on learning disabilities, the primary purpose of assessment is not to determine whether the child has something called a behavior disorder, but to see whether the child's behavior is different enough to warrant special services and, if so, to indicate what those services should consist of. Kauffman (1985) makes a strong case for direct and continuous measurement with behavior disordered children.

For a detailed explanation of procedures for the direct and continuous measurement of behavior, see Cooper (1987).

Disturbed children are considered to need help *primarily because they exhibit behavioral excesses or deficiencies.* Not to define precisely and measure these behavioral excesses and deficiencies, then, is a fundamental error: It is akin to the malpractice of a nurse who decides not to measure vital signs (heart rate, respiration rate, temperature, and blood pressure), perhaps arguing that he/she is too busy, that subjective estimates of vital signs are quite adequate, that vital signs are only superficial estimates of the patient's health, or that vital signs do not signify the nature of the underlying pathology. The teaching profession is dedicated to the task of changing behavior—changing behavior demonstrably for the better. What can one say, then, of educational practice that does not include reliable and forthright measurement of the behavior change induced by the teacher's methodology? I believe this: *It is indefensible.* (pp. 339–340)

Behaviorally oriented educators are concerned with the social significance of behavior change (Baer, Wolf, & Risley, 1968). It is not enough just to demonstrate that one can alter a child's behavior; teachers must show that the changes they bring about have **social validity** (Van Houten, 1979; Wolf, 1978). One measure of social validity is whether newly acquired behaviors are really worthwhile for the child; that is, whether the new behavior will be viewed as significant by others, by those people who deal with the child. Walker and Hops (1976) describe one approach for evaluating the effects of treatment on the classroom behavior of elementary school students referred to an experimental class because of inappropriate behavior. Instead of merely demonstrating that the children's behavior could improve in the special class, Walker and Hops compared the behavior of their special students with the actual classroom behavior of their peers in the regular classroom. Figure 5.3 shows the results for one of the three groups in the study.

The special students received a treatment program consisting of systematic social and token reinforcement in the classroom. It produced behavior that was actually

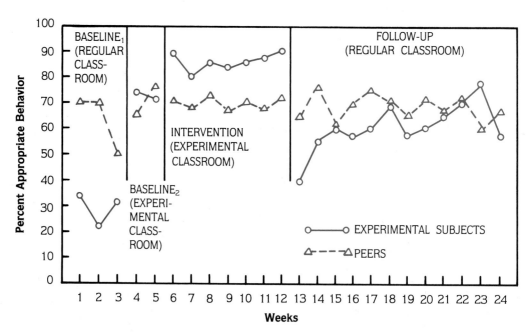

FIGURE 5.3

Appropriate behavior of disruptive students compared to their normal peers before, during, and after treatment.

Source: From "Use of Normative Peer Data as a Standard for Evaluating Classroom Treatment Effects" by H. M. Walker and H. Hops, 1976, *Journal of Applied Behavior Analysis, 9*, p. 165. Copyright by the Society for the Experimental Analysis of Behavior, Inc. Reprinted by permission.

better than that of the students' peers during the same period back in the regular classroom. Continued observation of the students during a 12-week follow-up period after their return to the regular classroom revealed that they maintained appropriate behavior within the normal limits defined by their peers' behavior. Walker and Hops demonstrated not only that their treatment program improved the disruptive students' behavior, but also that the improvements were socially valid (i.e., the special students now acted as well as their normal classmates) and were maintained during a 3-month follow-up.

For a series of articles describing assessment and evaluation of programs for behaviorally disordered children, see the Fall 1985 issue of *Education and Treatment of Children.*

EDUCATIONAL APPROACHES FOR BEHAVIOR DISORDERED CHILDREN

There are several different approaches to educating emotionally disturbed children, each with its own definitions, purposes of treatment, and types of intervention. Based on the work of Rhodes and his colleagues (Rhodes & Head, 1974; Rhodes & Tracy, 1972a, 1972b), Kauffman (1985) lists six categories of models.

1. *Biogenic.* This model suggests that deviant behavior is a physical disorder with genetic or medical causes. It implies that these causes must be cured to treat the emotional disturbance. Treatment may be medical or nutritional.
2. *Psychodynamic.* Based on the idea that a disordered personality develops out of the interaction of experience and internal mental processes (ego, id, and superego) that are out of balance, this model relies on psychotherapy and creative projects for the child (and often the parents) rather than academic remediation.
3. *Psychoeducational.* This model is concerned with "unconscious motivations and underlying conflicts yet stresses the realistic demands of everyday functioning in school and home" (Kauffman, 1985, p. 30). Intervention focuses on therapeutic discussions to allow the children to understand their behavior rationally and plan to change it (Rich, Beck, & Coleman, 1982).
4. *Humanistic.* This model suggests that the disturbed child is not in touch with her own feelings and cannot find self-fulfillment in traditional educational settings. Treatment takes place in an open, personalized setting where the teacher serves as a nondirective, nonauthoritarian "resource and catalyst" for the child's learning.
5. *Ecological.* This model stresses the interaction of the child with the people around him and with social institutions. Treatment involves teaching the child to function within the family, school, neighborhood, and larger community.
6. *Behavioral.* This model assumes that the child has learned disordered behavior and has not learned appropriate responses. To treat the behavior disorder, a teacher uses applied behavior analysis techniques to teach the child appropriate responses and eliminate inappropriate ones.

Few programs or teachers use only the techniques suggested by one of these models; most programs employ methods from several of the approaches. And the models themselves are not entirely discrete; they overlap in certain areas. Sometimes the difference is primarily a matter of wording; the actual classroom practices may be quite similar.

Our main purpose here is to make you aware of these different approaches. It is beyond the scope of this text to do justice to a description of each model and to compare and contrast them. We will say, however, that there is little empirical evidence to attest to the effectiveness of treatment approaches based on underlying subconscious causes of children's problems (Levitt, 1957, 1963). On the other hand, a growing body of research literature supports the effectiveness of the ecological and behavioral models, which analyze and modify the ways in which a child interacts with the environment.

For reviews of some of this research, see Burchard and Harig, 1976; Hobbs, 1982; Lovaas and Newsom, 1976; Montgomery and Van Fleet, 1978; and Walker, 1979.

CURRENT ISSUES/FUTURE TRENDS

Teaching Self-Management Skills

An increasing amount of research has been conducted on teaching self-control or self-management skills to children, and the results of much of this work is encouraging (O'Leary & Dubey, 1979; Rosenbaum & Drabman, 1979). Self-management, when taught as a social skill in its own right, includes five elements: (1) self-selection and definition of the target behavior to be managed, (2) self-observation and recording of the target behavior, (3) specification of the procedures to be used to change the behavior, (4) implementation of those procedures, and (5) evaluation of the self-control effort (Heward, 1979; Sulzer-Azaroff & Mayer, 1977).

Many behavior disordered children think they have little control over their lives. Things just seem to happen to them, and being disruptive is their means of reacting to a world that is inconsistent and frustrating. Children who learn self-management skills find out that they can have some control over their own behaviors and, as a result, over their environment.

When children learn to observe and record their own behavior, they can see for themselves the effects of various events on their performance. They can also be taught to influence certain events themselves. In one study Drabman, Spitalnik, and O'Leary (1973) taught a group of eight 9- and 10-year-old emotionally disturbed children to evaluate and record their own social and academic work behaviors. Initially, they were rewarded with tokens when their own evaluations matched those of the teacher; then, just teacher praise was given for accurate evaluations; finally, the students rated themselves and decided how many tokens they had earned during the day. A classroom token economy was operating during this study. Spot checks showed that the children evaluated themselves accurately and honestly. Disruptive behavior decreased, and academic achievement increased.

See Heward, 1987a, for a review of self-management procedures.

Numerous research studies have since demonstrated that children with behavior problems can effectively use self-monitoring as well as a number of other self-management techniques to help regulate their own behavior. Self-monitoring can be aided by a prompt to record the target behavior. For example, a prerecorded tone from a cassette tape player might serve as the cue to monitor and record one's behavior. Lovitt (1984) describes the use of "countoons," which remind children of not only

FIGURE 5.4

A countoon that can be taped to a student's desk as a reminder of the target behavior, the need to self-record it, and the consequence.

Source: From *Tactics for Teaching* (p. 202) by T. C. Lovitt, 1984, Columbus, OH: Merrill. Reprinted by permission.

what behavior to record, but also what consequence they are to self-deliver. Figure 5.4 shows a countoon that was taped to an elementary student's desk, showing her what behavior to monitor (finger snapping), how to record it (by putting an *X* through the next number on the countoon), and what her self-delivered consequence would be each time (solving 25 arithmetic problems).

In another study Marshall and Heward (1979) taught self-management skills to a group of eight boys in an institution for juvenile delinquents. The boys met as a group for one period each school day in a specially designed resource room. During this class period the students were taught basic principles of behavior modification, such as defining a target behavior, recording behavior, graphing behavior, positive reinforcement, setting personal goals, and standards for behavior. During the program each student selected a behavior he wanted to change and designed and conducted a self-management program to accomplish that goal. Students displayed their data and discussed and modified their projects as needed during the 4-week program. At the end of study, seven of the eight students believed they had successfully changed their behavior with the methods they had learned.

Figure 5.5 shows the results of one student's self-management project. This student had trouble interacting with others. He thought that one reason for his problem was a tendency to "dip," or interrupt, other people's conversations (this apparently had been brought to his attention on numerous occasions). When he counted the target behavior during the baseline phase of the project, he dipped others an average of 15.9 times per day. When he started his intervention program, he decided to reward himself with a box of raisins at the end of each day in which he had eight or fewer dips. During the project he lowered this criterion twice, to six and then to four or fewer dips per day. His average number of dips throughout his self-manage-

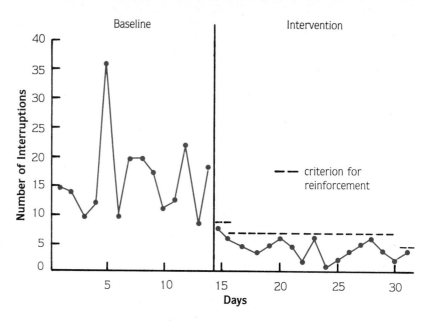

FIGURE 5.5
Sample self-management project showing number of verbal interruptions during baseline and self-administered reward.

Source: "Teaching Self-Management to Incarcerated Youth" by A. E. Marshall and W. L. Heward, 1979, *Behavioral Disorders, 4,* p. 222. Reprinted by permission.

ment program was 4.6 per day. At the end of the 8 weeks, he believed that his self-management project had been very successful and that he could use the skills learned in the program to change other behaviors.

Although a great deal more research is needed, teaching behavior disordered children and adolescents to have some control over their own lives by giving them the skills to make changes in their behavior is a promising approach.

Teacher Skills

A continuing concern in the field of behavior disorders is teacher skills—that combination of professional competencies and personal characteristics that produces the best teaching of emotionally disturbed children. It goes without saying that a teacher of disturbed children must be effective and creative, able to adapt curriculum materials and activities to the individual needs of the students. And although behavior disordered children require the help of a specially trained teacher to work on their specific behavior problems, the teaching of academic skills cannot be neglected. Most behavior disordered children are already achieving at a rate below that of their age-mates. Ignoring the three Rs would only put them at a bigger disadvantage. Reading, writing, and arithmetic are as important to behavior disordered children as they are to any child who hopes to function normally in our society.

Lon

However, the primary task of the teacher of behavior disordered children is to teach improved social skills—helping the students replace their maladaptive behaviors with more socially appropriate responses. This task is often difficult and demanding, particularly because the teacher seldom, if ever, knows all of the factors that affect the children's behavior. There are sometimes a host of contributing factors over which the teacher can exert little or no control (e.g., the delinquent friends with whom the child associates after school). However, it does little good to bemoan the child's past (which no one can alter) or to use all of the things in the child's environment that cannot be changed as an excuse for failing to help the child in the classroom. Special

Establishing a healthy teacher-student relationship is a key to effective teaching of children with behavior disorders.

educators should focus attention and efforts on those aspects of a child's life that they can effectively control (Kerr & Nelson, 1983; Wood, 1985). Kauffman (1985) says it like this:

> The *focus* of the special educator's concern should be on those contributing factors *which can be altered by the teacher.* Factors over which the teacher has no control may indeed come into the picture in that they may determine how the child is approached initially. However, the teacher of disturbed children is called upon to begin working with children *after* behavior disorders have appeared. The special educator has two primary responsibilities: first, to make sure that he or she does no *further* disservice to the child; and second, to manipulate the child's present environment in order to cause more appropriate behavior to develop *in spite of* past and present circumstances that cannot be changed. The emphasis must be on the present and future, not the past, and on the classroom environment. It is certainly true that it may be profitable for teachers to extend their influence beyond the classroom, perhaps working with parents to improve the home environment or using community resources for the child's benefit. But talk of influence beyond the classroom, including such high-sounding phrases as *ecological management,* is patent nonsense until the teacher has demonstrated that he or she can make the *classroom* environment productive of improved behavior. (p. 341)

Explanation of these behavior management techniques is beyond the scope of this book. For more information, see Alberto and Troutman, 1986; Cooper, Heron, & Heward, 1987; Sulzer-Azavoff & Mayer, 1986; Walker, 1979.

Managing the classroom environment to successfully change the behavior patterns of disturbed children requires a teacher highly skilled in techniques used to change behavior. Procedures such as contingency contracting; ignoring disruptive behavior **(extinction);** reinforcing any behavior *except* the undesirable response, which must be weakened **(differential reinforcement of other behavior);** removing the child from all chances for reward for a brief time following an inappropriate behavior **(time-out);** and requiring the child to make restitution beyond the damaging effects of her behavior (**overcorrection**), as when a child who takes another child's cookie must return it plus one of her own—these are just some of the many behavior management skills that a competent teacher of behavior disordered children needs. And we have already stressed the importance of direct and daily measurement as the means to monitor and evaluate the effects of the teacher's efforts.

But the effective teacher of behavior disordered children must have skills that go beyond arranging environmental variables and measuring behavior. With behavior disordered children, the way in which assignments, expectations, and consequences for behavior are communicated to the child can be as important as the consequences themselves. Rothman (1977) stresses the importance of avoiding a win-lose situation, in which the teacher gains status by dominating the child. Rather, a win-win arrangement is the goal—when the child wins, the teacher wins.

In addition to having instructional and behavior management skills, the teacher of behavior disordered children must be able to establish healthy child-teacher relationships. Morse (1976) believes teachers must have two important affective characteristics in order to relate effectively and positively to emotionally disturbed children. He calls these traits differential acceptance and an empathetic relationship. Differential acceptance means that the teacher can receive and witness frequent and often extreme acts of anger, hate, and aggression from children without responding similarly. This is

RE-EDUCATING TROUBLED CHILDREN

Pressley Ridge School in Pittsburgh is a private school licensed by the Pennsylvania Departments of Education and Mental Health to provide special education and treatment services for 120 emotionally disturbed children and youth. Students are referred to Pressley Ridge by local school districts following a determination that the districts cannot provide appropriate educational services. The most common referral problems include hyperactivity, lack of impulse control, verbal and physical aggression, social withdrawal, depression, truancy/runaway, and poor social interaction skills. In addition, though the students typically have normal or near-normal intelligence, they are generally 3 to 4 years below grade level academically. A large number of students also come from multiproblem families in which their siblings or parents are receiving, or in need of, special social, psychological, or educational services. Students range in age from 6 to 18, with a mean age of 14. Approximately 80% of the students are male, and about 40% are black. Students typically attend the program for 1½ to 2 years. Upon discharge the majority of students return to the public schools, with smaller percentages moving into vocational training programs, competitive employment, or other treatment programs.

The school's professional staff is composed of 20 teacher/counselors, assigned to 10 classrooms of 12 students each; 7 family and community liaison workers; specialists in the areas of speech and language, physical education, career education, and educational diagnostics; psychological and psychiatric consultants; 4 supervisors; and the program director.

The program's treatment model is based on a combination of re-education philosophy (Hobbs, 1982) and principles of behavior analysis (Cooper, Heron, & Heward, 1987). These approaches emphasize that behavior, both positive and negative, is learned. The program does not look within the child for the causes of negative, troubling behaviors (i.e., for personality disorders, disabilities, or other pathologies). Instead the focus is on the child's ecological system, which is seen as supporting the maladaptive behaviors. Treatment, then, focuses less on traditional psychotherapy and medical intervention and more on restructuring the child's environment to teach and support new, more adaptive behavior. Specific treatment interventions are the result of carefully pinpointing the child's problem areas (academic, personal, and/or social), analyzing the relevant antecedent and consequent conditions that are

Discussing progress toward each person's goals

maintaining the problem behaviors, and then re-structuring the environment to facilitate the development of more adaptive, functional behaviors.

In addition to each child's individual academic and treatment programs, the daily operation of every classroom consists of two major components designed to promote successful adjustment in the school, home, and community. The first is group process, which consists of frequent group interactions between students and teachers, designed to teach students to (1) set reasonable goals for themselves and structure their environment to help achieve those goals, (2) identify and resolve interpersonal conflict, (3) realistically evaluate their own and others' behavior, and (4) cooperate and actively assist each other in goal achievement. The second component is a behavior management system that enables students to earn daily privileges by following a set of rules regarding appropriate personal and interpersonal behavior.

The following comments about the program were made by a teacher/counselor and a recent graduate of the program, respectively.

> Our kids are lost, with no sense of direction. They believe that if a person cares about them, they will set no boundaries or limits. But after a few months here, they see that limits and boundaries are set to help them. We give the kids the sense that we really care about them and their development. Even if they leave under less than happy circumstances, we continue to care about them and they are always welcome to return. We use all the parts of our system—individualized academics, group process, point systems, individualized treatment interventions—to try to help meet each student's needs.

One of the real strengths of Pressley Ridge is the cohesiveness of all the staff, the way we work together and support each other. This is what keeps us going even when the job seems just too hard to manage.

> My name is Wendy and I am almost 19 years old. I came to Pressley Ridge School at the beginning of my junior year in high school. No other school would accept me because of my behavioral problems. I was kicked out of high school twice and no one seemed able to help me. I was sent to several schools and hospitals but instead of getting better I just got worse. I rebelled against all authority, was filled with hatred and depression, and even tried to kill myself. In September of 1981 I came to Pressley Ridge. The first 6 months I rebelled and caused a lot of trouble. I didn't like myself and in my mind they didn't like me either, so I wouldn't listen to them. But they didn't stop trying; they cared and wanted to help me. Finally I stopped fighting. I started listening and working to better myself. I made straight A's in all my subjects, including English, geometry, biology, and Spanish. I also talked and tried to work out some of my problems. I still had some setbacks, but I didn't stay down like I used to. I got up and tried again. Pressley Ridge has taught me not to give up but to keep on trying. They gave me self-confidence and courage to go out and make something of myself, with the understanding that they will always be there if I need them. I left Pressley Ridge in February 1983, with the hope that I'll be somebody important. I have just finished a course in college for emergency medical technicians and work full-time with an ambulance company as crew chief. My future goal is to be a physician's assistant. I only hope that future kids at Pressley Ridge will benefit from their help like I did.

much easier said than done. But the teacher of emotionally disturbed children must view disruptive behavior for what it is—behavior that reflects the child's past frustrations and conflict with himself and those around him—and try to help the child learn better ways of behaving. This acceptance should not be confused with approving of or condoning disturbed behavior—the child *must* learn that he is responding inappropriately. Instead, this concept calls for understanding without condemning. Having an empathetic relationship with a child refers to a teacher's ability to recognize and understand the many nonverbal cues that often are the keys to understanding the individual needs of emotionally disturbed children.

Kauffman (1985) stresses the importance of teachers communicating directly and honestly with behaviorally troubled children. Many of these children have already had experience with supposedly helpful adults who have not been completely honest with them. Emotionally disturbed children can quickly detect someone who is not genuinely interested in their welfare.

See pages 205–6 for a description of a program for behavior disordered children that combines behavior analysis principles and Hobbs's (1982) philosophy of re-education.

The teacher of behavior disordered children must also realize that her actions serve as a powerful model for the children. Therefore, it is critical that the teacher's actions and attitudes be mature and demonstrate self-control. Hobbs (1966) describes the kind of person he believes would make a good teacher and model for disturbed children. In his view, and ours, the effective teacher is

> a decent adult; educated, well trained; able to give and receive affection, to live relaxed, and to be firm; a person with private resources for the nourishment and refreshment of his own life; not an itinerant worker but a professional through and through; a person with a sense of the significance of time; of the usefulness of today and the promise of tomorrow; a person of hope, quiet confidence, and joy; one who has committed himself to children and to the proposition that children who are emotionally disturbed can be helped by the process of re-education. (pp. 1106–7)

SUMMARY

1. There is no single, widely used definition of behavior disorders.
   a. However, most definitions agree that a child's behavior must differ significantly and over time from current social or cultural norms to be considered disordered.
   b. Teacher tolerance of children's behavior has a definite effect on whether a particular child will be identified as behavior disordered.
   c. We can describe behavior disorders in terms of their rate, duration, topography, and magnitude. A child's disordered behavior may differ from his peers' behavior in one or more of these four dimensions.
   d. Most behavior disordered children have a variety of problems in more than one area.
   e. Describing behavior disorders in terms of objective dimensions implies that we can deal with a specific, measurable problem rather than with a disturbance or illness. We can teach a child to act more appropriately.
2. The U.S. Department of Education has traditionally estimated that children with behavior disorders comprise 2% of the school-age population. However, even though

behavior disorders is the fourth largest category in special education, the number of children served is less than half of the 2% estimate.

   a. Boys are much more likely to be labeled as behavior disordered than girls. Disturbed boys are likely to be aggressive and act out; girls are likely to be shy, anxious, and withdrawn.
   b. Most behavior disorders seem to appear in the middle grades and fall off in junior high school.
   c. However, juvenile delinquency seems to increase sharply during the junior high years and after, even though more younger children are committing more serious crimes than in the past.

3. As of yet there is no widely accepted system for classifying behavior disorders.
   a. One system describes four clusters of behavior problems: conduct disorders, personality disorders, immaturity, and socialized delinquency.
   b. A second classification system describes six levels of learning competence, ranging from an attention level to a mastery level.
   c. Most behavior disordered children have mild to moderate problems that can be treated effectively in the regular classroom and at home.
   d. Severely disturbed children—often called psychotic, schizophrenic, or autistic—require intensive programming, usually in a more restrictive setting.
   e. Any system for classification should be based on classifying behaviors rather than children so that the label can lead to specific strategies to replace the disordered behavior with more appropriate ones.

4. On the average, behavior disordered children score somewhat below normal on IQ tests. Their school achievement is even lower than their scores would predict, and many have learning problems.

5. There are two general types of disordered behavior.
   a. Some children are overly aggressive and frequently act out. They seem to be in constant conflict.
   b. Many of these children become delinquents as adolescents.
   c. They also seem to have difficulty adjusting as adults and may have children with problem behaviors.
   d. Other behavior disordered children are overly withdrawn. They do not have the social skills they need.
   e. For these children the outlook is fairly good. They can often be taught the needed social skills and can learn to be comfortable with other people.

6. Autistic children, who are often identified while they are toddlers, usually show one or more of these characteristics: apparent sensory deficit, severe affect isolation, self-stimulation, tantrums and self-mutilation, muteness or psychotic speech, and behavior deficiencies.
   a. Although behavior modification techniques have helped control the destructive actions of many autistic children, even with intensive programs some autistic children remain functionally retarded.
   b. Although many autistic children require a supervised environment throughout their lives, some autistic children are being successfully mainstreamed in regular classes. The outlook for autistic children is gradually getting better.

7. There are two groups of causes suggested for behavior disorders.
   a. Physiological factors, including inborn temperament, may predispose some children to problems.

   b. Psychological factors, including parent-child interactions and specific events, are clearly important in the development of behavior disorders.
   c. Because of its central role in a child's life, the school can also be an important contributing factor to a behavior problem.
   d. We can never pinpoint an exact, lone cause of a child's behavior problems, so we must try to identify ways in which physiological factors, the family, and the school influence or contribute to a problem.

8. There are no completely reliable methods to identify emotional disturbance.
   a. Although aggressive children stand out, withdrawn children may go unnoticed.
   b. Several screening tests for emotional disturbance have been developed.
   c. Although they have been widely used for assessment of behavior problems, psychological tests and interviews have limited practical value.
   d. Direct and continuous observation and measurement of specific problem behaviors, within the classroom, is becoming more and more popular. It is an assessment technique that indicates directly what intervention is needed.

9. There are at least six approaches to educating emotionally disturbed children: biogenic, psychodynamic, psychoeducational, humanistic, ecological, and behavioral.
   a. Although each approach has a distinct theoretical basis and suggests types of treatment, many teachers use techniques from more than one of the models.
   b. A growing body of research supports the behavioral and ecological models, which analyze and modify the ways a child interacts with her environment.

10. Teaching behavior disordered children to control their own behavior with self-management skills is one new and promising approach.

11. The primary goal of the teacher of behavior disordered children is to help the children replace inappropriate behaviors with more socially acceptable ones by modifying those factors in the teacher's control.
   a. To be successful, the teacher must be skilled in changing behavior.
   b. The teacher must also be able to interact with these demanding children, understanding and accepting them without condoning disturbed behavior.

FOR MORE INFORMATION

Journals

Behavioral Disorders. Published quarterly by the Council for Children with Behavior Disorders, Council for Exceptional Children. Publishes research and discussion articles dealing with behavior disorders in children.

Behavior Therapy. Published five times a year by Academic Press for the Association for the Advancement of Behavior Therapy.

Journal of Applied Behavior Analysis. Published quarterly by the Society for the Experimental Analysis of Behavior, Lawrence, Kansas. Publishes original experimental studies demonstrating improvement of socially significant behaviors. Many studies involve behavior disordered children as subjects.

Journal of Autism and Developmental Disorders. A quarterly journal that publishes multidisciplinary research on all severe psychopathologies in childhood.

Books

Braaten, S., Rutherford, R. B., Jr., & Kardash, C. A. (Eds.). (1984). *Programming for adolescents with behavior disorders.* Reston, VA: Council for Exceptional Children.

Brown, G., McDowell, R. L., & Smith, J. (Eds.). (1981). *Educating adolescents with behavior disorders,* Columbus, OH: Merrill.

Cartledge, G., & Milburn, J. F. (1986). *Teaching social skills to children* (2nd ed.). New York: Pergamon Press.

Coleman, M. (1986). *Behavior disorders: Theory and practice.* Englewood Cliffs, NJ: Prentice-Hall.

Epanchin, B. C., & Paul, J. L. (1987). *Emotional problems of childhood and adolescence.* Columbus, OH: Merrill.

Hewett, F. M., & Taylor, F. D. (1980). *The emotionally disturbed child in the classroom: The orchestration of success* (2nd ed.). Boston: Allyn & Bacon.

Hobbs, N. (1982). *The troubled and troubling child.* San Francisco: Jossey-Bass.

Kauffman, J. M. (1985). *Characteristics of children's behavior disorders* (3rd ed.). Columbus, OH: Merrill.

Kauffman, J. M., & Lewis, C. D. (Eds.). (1974). *Teaching children with behavior disorders: Personal perspectives.* Columbus, OH: Merrill.

Kerr, M. M., & Nelson, C. M. (1983). *Strategies for managing behavior problems in the classroom.* Columbus, OH: Merrill.

Koegel, R. L., Rincover, A., & Egal, A. L. (Eds.). (1982). *Educating and understanding autistic children.* San Diego, CA: College Hill.

Paul, J. L., & Epanchin, B. C. (1982). *Emotional disturbance in children.* Columbus, OH: Merrill.

Swanson, H. L., & Reinhert, H. R. (1984). *Teaching strategies for children in conflict.* St. Louis: Mosby.

Walker, H. M. (1979). *The acting-out child: Coping with classroom disruption.* Boston: Allyn & Bacon.

Ziontz, P. (1985). *Teaching disturbed and disturbing students.* Austin, TX: Pro-Ed.

Organizations

American Association for the Advancement of Behavior Therapy, 420 Lexington Avenue, New York, NY 10017. Includes psychologists, educational researchers, and educators (primarily at the university level).

Council for Children with Behavior Disorders, Council for Exceptional Children, 1920 Association Drive, Reston, VA 22091. Includes teachers and teacher educators interested in behavior disorders. Produces an annual publication titled *Teaching: Behaviorally Disordered Youth.*

National Society for Autistic Citizens, 621 Central Avenue, Albany, NY 12206.

6

COMMUNICATION DISORDERS

Have you ever tried to go through an entire day without speaking? If so, you surely had a great deal of difficulty making contact with other people. And you probably experienced frustration when your needs and feelings were not understood by others. By the end of the day, you may even have felt exhausted, humiliated, and incapable of functioning adequately in the world.

Even though relatively few people with communication disorders are completely unable to express themselves, an exercise such as that just described can be helpful in increasing your awareness of some of the problems and frustrations faced every day by children and adults who cannot communicate effectively or acceptably. Language is central to human existence—"the most powerful, fascinating skill that humans possess" (Reed, 1986, p. vii). Children who cannot absorb information through listening and reading or who cannot express their thoughts in spoken words are virtually certain to encounter difficulties in their schools and communities. If communication disorders persist, it may be hard for children to learn, to develop, and to form satisfying relationships with other people. As Richmond and McCroskey (1985) observe, "Even though computers are playing and will continue to play a significant role in our lives, they will not replace basic human interaction. . . . live communication between humans will still be the fuel that makes our world go around" (p. 1).

Before proceeding to our discussion of specific communication disorders, a few definitions of basic terms will be helpful.

COMMUNICATION, LANGUAGE, AND SPEECH

Communication, in its broadest sense, is any interaction that transmits information. It is not necessary for spoken or written words to be used; however, in order for true communication to exist, there must be both a sender and a receiver. We observe, and take part in, literally thousands of communicative interactions every day. An infant cries, and her mother reacts by picking her up. A dog barks, and its owner responds by letting it out of the house. A teacher smiles, and his student knows that an assignment has been accomplished well. In each of these interactions there has been (1) a message, (2) expressive communication by the sender, and (3) receptive communication by the receiver.

Lindfors (1987) has enumerated several important functions served by communication, particularly between teachers and children.

1. *Narrating.* Children need to be able to tell (or follow the telling of) a "story;" that is, a sequence of related events, connected in an orderly, clear, and interesting manner. Five-year-old Cindy tells her teacher, "I had a birthday party. I wore a funny hat. Mommy made a cake and Daddy took pictures." Fourteen-year-old David tells the class about the events leading up to Christopher Columbus's first voyage to America.
2. *Explaining/informing.* Teachers expect children to interpret the explanations of others in speech and in writing and also to put something they understand into words so that their listeners or readers will be able to understand it, too. In typical classroom settings children must respond to teachers' questions frequently: "Which number is larger?" "How do you suppose the story will end?" "Why do you think George Washington was a great president?"
3. *Expressing.* It is important for children to express their personal feelings and opinions and to respond to the feelings of others. Speech and language can convey joy, fear, frustration, humor, sympathy, anger. A child writes, "I have just moved. And it is hard to find a friend because I am shy." Another tells her classmates, "Guess what? I have a new baby brother!" Through such communicative interactions children gradually develop a sense of self and an awareness of other people.

Some investigators maintain that animals, such as gorillas and dolphins, use language. However, it is usually considered an ability unique to human beings.

Language is a system used by a group of people for giving meaning to sounds, words, gestures, and other symbols to enable communication with each other. Bloom and Lahey (1978) have defined language as the "knowledge of a code for representing ideas about the world through a conventional system of arbitrary signals for communication" (p. 4). A child may learn to identify a familiar object, for example, by hearing the spoken word *tree,* by seeing the printed word *tree,* by viewing the sign language gesture for *tree,* or by encountering a combination of these signals. When we hear, speak, read, or write with language, we transmit information.

The rules of all languages are essentially arbitrary, and spoken English is no exception. The arbitrariness of language means that there is usually no logical, natural, or required relationship between a set of sounds and the object, concept, or action it represents. The word *whale,* for example, brings to mind a large mammal that lives in the sea, but the sound of the word has no apparent connection with the creature. *Whale* is merely a symbol we use for this particular mammal. A small number of onomatopoetic words—such as *tinkle, buzz,* and *hiss*—are considered to sound like what they represent, but most English words have no such relationship with what they represent.

There are several different kinds of elements used to convey meaning in language. The English language uses 36 different sound elements, called **phonemes.** Only the initial phoneme prevents the words *pear* and *bear* from being identical, for example; yet in one case we think of a fruit and in the other a large animal. The smallest elements of language that carry meaning are called **morphemes.** The word *baseball,* for example, consists of two morphemes—*base* and *ball.* The *-s* added to make *baseballs* would be a third morpheme, because it changes the meaning.

There are also several kinds of language rules. Phonological rules describe how sounds in a language can be combined. Morphological rules are concerned with how morphemes can be strung together. Morphology is part of **syntax,** the system or rules governing the meaningful arrangement of words. For example, "Help my chicken eat" conveys a meaning much different from "Help eat my chicken." Finally, rules of **semantics** relate phonology and syntax to meaning; that is, semantics describes how people use language to convey meaning.

One model of language, developed by Bloom and Lahey (1978), describes three components of language—form, content, and use—that make up an integrated system. The form of the language connects sound and meaning. The content is based on knowledge of the world and our feelings about it. Thus, the form of language allows us to express content. The use of language refers to the ways that language functions in communication. It includes both our purposes in communicating and the way in which we choose a specific form to express a particular message.

This model can be helpful in understanding and treating a child's communication disorder.

Speech is the actual behavior of producing a language code by making appropriate vocal sound patterns (Hubbell, 1985). Although it is not the only possible vehicle for producing language—gestures, manual signing, pictures, and written symbols can also be used to convey ideas and intentions—speech is surely the most complex and difficult. Speech production requires the precise coordination of nerves and muscles in several locations to perform the important processes of respiration (breathing by the lungs), phonation (the production of sound by the larynx and vocal folds), and articulation (the formation of specific, recognizable speech sounds by the tongue, lips, teeth, and mouth). Figure 6.1 shows the normal speech organs. Thus, people hear these

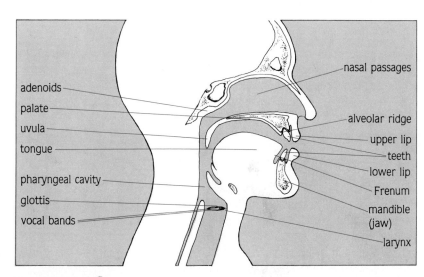

FIGURE 6.1
The normal speech organs.

sounds and interpret them as words (McCormick & Schiefelbusch, 1984; Reed, 1986). Most languages start out in oral form, developed by people speaking to each other. Reading and writing can be viewed as oral language in a different form.

Despite the complexity of our language system—with its phonemes, morphemes, and syntax—most children learn to understand language and then to speak during the first few years of life, without any formal instruction. They integrate form, content, and use to communicate. The process of learning language is a remarkable one, one that is not fully understood. As Leonard (1982) points out, an understanding of how young, normally developing children acquire language is helpful to the teacher or specialist working with children who have delayed or disordered communication. A knowledge of normal language development can help the specialist determine whether a particular child is simply developing language at a slower-than-normal rate or whether the child shows an abnormal pattern of language development.

Normal Language Development

Parents, teachers, and scholars have been fascinated for centuries by the phenomenon of language acquisition in children.

> Whether a child grows up in a "traditional" society or in a "technological" one; whether in a large extended family or in a small nuclear one; whether on a Pacific island, in an urban ghetto, or in a tribal farm compound; whether in a villa, a straw hut, an apartment, or a tent; whether with or without formal schooling; whether in a wet, dry, hot, or cold climate—the child will acquire the language of his community. Humans vary in which languages and dialects they acquire, in how rapidly they acquire them. . . in how talkative they are, in what they use language for, and in how effectively they express themselves in speech and/or writing. But virtually all of them acquire at least one linguistic system for relating meanings. . . . Further, there is striking similarity in how all children learn their language. (Lindfors, 1987, p. 91)

Children whose hearing is impaired have a special set of problems in learning language. See chapter 7.

We will present, in some detail, a summary of normal language development. However, the ages at which a normal child acquires certain speech and language skills are not rigid and inflexible. Children's abilities and early environments vary widely, and all of these factors affect communication. Nevertheless, most investigators agree that most children follow a relatively predictable sequence in their development of speech and language.

Birth to 6 Months

The infant first communicates by crying, which involves breath, muscles, and vocal chords. She soon learns that her crying produces a reliable consequence in the form of parental attention. Within a few months the baby develops different types of crying—a parent can usually tell from the baby's cry whether the child is wet, tired, or hungry. Babies also make comfort sounds—coos, gurgles, and sighs—that contain some vowels and consonants. The comfort sounds develop into babbling, sounds that in the beginning are apparently made for the enjoyment of feeling and hearing them.

Vowel sounds, such as /i/(pronounced "ee") and /ə/ (pronounced "uh") are produced earlier than consonants, such as /m/, /b/, and /f/. At this stage the infant does not attach meaning to the words she hears from others, but she may react differently to loud and soft voices. She turns her eyes and head in the direction of a sound.

Phonemes are represented by letters or other symbols between slashes. For example, the phoneme /ŋ/ represents the "ng" sound in *sing*; /i/ represents the long "e" as in *see*.

6 to 12 Months

Before the first year, baby develops **inflection;** her voice rises and falls. She may seem to be giving you a command, asking a question, or expressing surprise. She appears to understand certain words at this stage. She may respond appropriately to "no," "bye-bye," or her own name and may perform an action, such as clapping her hands, when told to. When parents say simple sounds and words, such as "mama," the baby will repeat them.

12 to 18 Months

By 18 months most children have learned to say several words with appropriate meaning (although their pronunciation is far from perfect). The baby may say "tup" when you point to a cup, or "goggie" when she sees a dog. She will probably be able to tell you what she wants by pointing and perhaps saying a word or two. She will respond to simple commands such as "Give me the cup" and "Open your mouth."

18 to 24 Months

Most children go through a stage of echolalia, in which they simply repeat, or echo, the speech they hear. If father says, "Do you want some milk?" the baby will repeat, "Want some milk?" Echolalia is a normal phase of language development, and most children outgrow it by about the age of 2½. There is a great spurt in the acquisition and use of speech during this stage. Children usually begin to combine words into short sentences, such as "Daddy bye-bye" and "Want cookie." The child's receptive vocabulary—the words she understands—grows even more rapidly. By 2 years of age she may understand more than 1,000 words. She understands such concepts as "soon" and "later" and makes more subtle distinctions between objects, such as cats and dogs, and knives, forks, and spoons.

2 to 3 Years

The 2-year-old child talks. She can say sentences like "I won't tell you" and can ask questions like "Where my daddy go?" She may have an expressive vocabulary of up to 900 different words, averaging three to four words per sentence (Weiss & Lillywhite, 1976). She is learning how to participate in conversations with the people around her. She can identify colors, use plurals, and tell simple stories about her experiences. She is able to follow compound commands such as "Pick up the doll and bring it to me." The 2-year-old child uses most of the vowel sounds and some consonant sounds correctly. The earliest consonant sounds learned are generally /p/, /b/, and /m/.

3 to 4 Years

The normal 3-year-old has lots to say, speaks rapidly, and asks many questions to obtain information. Her sentences are longer and more varied: "Cindy's playing in water"; "Mommy went to work"; "The cat is hungry." She is able to use speech to request, protest, agree, and make jokes. The 3- to 4-year-old child can understand children's stories, grasp such concepts as *funny, bigger,* and *secret* and complete simple analogies, such as "In the daytime it is light; at night it is _____." She typically substitutes certain sounds, such as saying "baf" for "bath," or "yike" for "like." Many 3-year-olds repeat sounds or words ("b-b-ball," "l-l-little"). Their repetitions and hesitations are normal and do not indicate that the child will develop a habit of stuttering.

We will discuss dysfluencies (stuttering) later in this chapter.

4 to 5 Years

By age 4, children have an average vocabulary of over 1,500 words and use sentences averaging five words in length (Leonard, 1982). They are generally able to make themselves understood, even to strangers. The 4-year-old begins to show the ability to modify her speech for the listener; for example, she uses longer and more complex sentences when talking to her mother than when addressing a baby or a doll. She can define words like *hat, stove,* and *policeman* and can ask questions like "How did you do that?" or "Who made this?" She uses conjunctions such as *if, when,* and *because.* She can recite poems and sing songs from memory. Children at this age may say, "I almost fell," or "Let's do something else." They may still have difficulty with such consonant sounds as /r/, /s/, and /z/ or with blends like "tr," "gl," "sk," and "str."

After 5 Years

Language continues to develop steadily, though less dramatically, after age 5. The child acquires more vocabulary and is able to use more sophisticated grammatical forms. A 6-year-old child, in fact, normally uses most of the complex forms of adult English. Some of the consonant sounds and blends, however, are not mastered until age 7 or 8. By the time a child enters first grade, her grammar and speech patterns usually match those of her family, neighborhood, and region. A 6-year-old from rural Alabama has different pronunciation and rhythms from a 6-year-old who lives in Boston.

As the preceding descriptions indicate, children's words and sentences often differ from adult forms while the children are learning language. Lindfors (1987) points out that children who use such structures as "All gone sticky" and "Where he is going?" or pronunciations like "cwackers" and "twuck" or word forms like "comed," "goed," or "sheeps" gradually learn to replace them with acceptable adult forms. The early developmental forms drop out as the child matures, usually without any special drilling or direct instruction.

It is also worth noting that children's production of speech sounds is often inconsistent. The clarity of a sound may vary according to such factors as where the sound is placed within a word and how familiar the word is to the child. Although speech sounds generally become clearer as the child grows older, there are exceptions to this rule of gradual progress. Kenney and Prather (1986), for example, found that

Structured play activities are not only fun, they encourage language development.

3½-year-old children made fewer errors on the *s* sound than did children aged 4 to 5½. The reasons for such reversals in accuracy are not clear.

DEFINING COMMUNICATION DISORDERS: SPEECH AND LANGUAGE

As we have said, the development of speech and language is a highly individual process. No child conforms exactly to precise developmental norms; some are advanced, some are delayed, and some acquire language in an unusual sequence. Unfortunately, some children deviate from the normal to such an extent that they have serious difficulties in learning and in interpersonal relations. People who are not able to make themselves understood or who cannot comprehend ideas that are spoken to them by others are

Specific speech and language disorders are discussed later in this chapter.

likely to be greatly handicapped in virtually all aspects of education and adjustment. They need specialized help. These kinds of problems, called communication disorders, occur frequently among children in regular and special education classes.

When does a communication *difference* become a communication *disorder?* In making such judgments, Emerick and Haynes (1986) emphasize the impact that a communication pattern has on a person's life. A communication difference would be considered a handicapping condition, they note, when

For children whose native language is not English, the distinction between a difference and a disorder is critical. Chapter 12 contains guidelines for the assessment of children from multicultural backgrounds.

☐ the transmission and/or perception of messages is faulty
☐ the person is placed at an economic disadvantage
☐ the person is placed at a learning disadvantage
☐ the person is placed at a social disadvantage
☐ there is a negative impact upon the emotional growth of the person
☐ the problem causes physical damage or endangers the health of the person (pp. 6–7)

Most specialists in the field of communication disorders make a distinction between speech impairments and language disorders. Children with impaired speech have difficulty producing sounds properly, maintaining an appropriate flow or rhythm in speech, or using the voice effectively. Speech impairments are impairments in language form. Children with impaired language have problems in understanding or expressing the symbols and rules people use to communicate with each other. A child may have difficulty with language form, content, and/or use. Speech and language are obviously closely related to each other. Some people find it helpful to view speech as the means by which language is most often conveyed. A child may have a speech impairment or a language disorder or both.

Speech Impairments

A child's speech is considered to be impaired if it is unintelligible, abuses the speech mechanism, or is culturally or personally unsatisfactory (Perkins, 1977). The most widely quoted definition of a speech impairment is probably that of Charles Van Riper, who states that "speech is abnormal when it deviates so far from the speech of other people that it calls attention to itself, interferes with communication, or causes the speaker or his listeners to be distressed" (Van Riper & Emerick, 1984, p. 34). A general goal of professional specialists in communication disorders is to help the child speak as clearly and pleasantly as possible so that a listener's attention will be drawn to what the child says, rather than how she says it.

It is always important to keep the speaker's age, education, and cultural background in mind when determining whether speech is impaired. A 4-year-old girl who says, "Pwease weave the woom," would not be considered to have a speech impairment, but a 40-year-old woman would surely draw attention to herself with that pronunciation, because it differs markedly from the speech of most adults. A traveler unable to articulate the /l/ sound would not be clearly understood in trying to buy a bus ticket to Lake Charles, Louisiana. A male high school student with an extremely high pitched voice might be reluctant to speak in class for fear of being mimicked and ridiculed by his classmates.

Language Disorders

Some children have serious difficulties in understanding language or in expressing themselves through language. A child with a receptive language disorder may be unable to learn the days of the week in proper order or may find it impossible to follow a sequence of commands, such as "Pick up the paint brushes, wash them in the sink, and then put them on a paper towel to dry." A child with an expressive language disorder may have a limited vocabulary for his age, be confused about the order of sounds or words ("hostipal," "aminal," "wipe shield winders"), and use tenses and plurals incorrectly ("Them throwed a balls"). Children with difficulty in expressive language may or may not also have difficulty in receptive language. For instance, a child may be able to count out six pennies when asked and shown the symbol *6* but may not be able to say the word *six* when shown the symbol. In that case the child has an expressive difficulty, but his receptive language is adequate. He may or may not have other disorders of speech or hearing.

Leonard (1986) has noted that children with impaired language frequently play a passive role in communication. They may show little tendency to initiate conversations. When language disordered children are asked questions, "their replies rarely provide new information related to the topic" (p. 114).

Children with serious language disorders are likely to have problems in school and social development. It is often difficult to detect children with language disorders; their performance may lead people to mistakenly label them as mentally retarded, hearing impaired, or emotionally disturbed, when in fact these descriptions are neither accurate nor appropriate. A recent study of peer perceptions (Gies-Zaborowski & Silverman, 1986) found that an 11-year-old girl with a neurological impairment affecting her speech and language production was perceived as "frightened, nervous, tense, and unlovable" by nonhandicapped fifth and sixth grade children. These perceptions "obviously could have a negative impact on her self-concept" (p. 143).

Language is so important in academic performance that it can be impossible to differentiate a learning disability from a language disorder. Again, emphasis should be placed on remediating children's skill deficits rather than on labeling them.

A child may also be markedly delayed in language development. Even though a relatively wide range of language patterns and age milestones is considered normal, some children do not acquire speech or the ability to understand language until much later than would be normally expected. A 6-year-old child who cannot tell you what a key is used for or who is not able to use such pronouns as *I, you,* and *me* would be regarded as having a serious delay in language development. In rare cases children who have no other impairment may even fail to speak at all.

Dialects and Differences

The way children speak reflects their culture. Before entering school, most children have learned patterns of speech and language appropriate to their families and neighborhoods. Every language contains a variety of forms called **dialects** that result from historical, geographical, and social factors. The English language, for example, includes such variations as standard American English (as used by most teachers, employers, and public speakers), black English, Appalachian English, southern English, a New York dialect, and Spanish-influenced English. A child who uses these variations should not be treated as having a communication disorder. However, it is certainly possible for a child to have a communication disorder within her dialect. The American Speech-Language-Hearing Association (1983) considers it essential for a specialist to be able to "distinguish between dialectal differences and communicative disorders" and to "treat only those features or characteristics that are true errors and not attributable to the dialect" (p. 24). A speech or language *difference* from the majority of children, then, is not necessarily a communication disorder in need of treatment. Problems may arise in the classroom and in parent-teacher communication if the teacher does not accept natural communication differences among children and mistakenly assumes that a speech or language impairment is present (Bankson, 1982; Reed, 1986).

PREVALENCE

Estimates of the prevalence of communication disorders in children vary widely. Reliable figures are hard to come by, as investigators often employ different definitions of speech and language disorders and sample different populations. As Culton (1986) observes, surveys are often based on interviews of questionable validity, and there is a likely tendency to underreport the presence of communication disorders.

Fein (1983) reviewed various prevalence studies of school-age populations and concluded that speech impairments serious enough to warrant special attention are present in approximately 4.2% of children. This represents a large population when compared to other categories of exceptional children. A 4.2% prevalence rate means that between 2 and 3 million American children have communication disorders. Fein reported that speech impairments tend to be more prevalent among males than females, more prevalent among nonwhite persons than white persons, and about the same in each of the major geographical regions of the United States. Similarly, the National Center for Health Statistics (1981) reported that approximately twice as many boys as girls have speech impairments.

Figures on the prevalence of language disorders are less reliable. Reed (1986) notes that about 1% of school-age children are considered to have language disorders. However, since definitions of learning disabilities place strong emphasis on an understanding and usage of spoken and written language (see chapter 4), a sizable percentage of children who are served in special education programs for learning disabled students could also be regarded as having language disorders.

The major types of communication disorders will be discussed in the next section of this chapter.

Some figures are available on the incidence and prevalence of specific types of communication disorders. In the recent past, **articulation** disorders, which involve difficulties in producing speech sounds accurately, were by far the most common type of speech problem found in children. In 1961 the American Speech-Language-Hearing Association (ASHA) estimated that 80% of the school-age population with communication disorders had articulation disorders. However, changing emphasis and improved assessment techniques have led to changes in the relative number of children treated for speech and language disorders. A 1982 ASHA survey indicated that "54% of speech-language pathologists' clients were primarily exhibiting language impairments" (cited in Fein, 1983, p. 37). The speech problems of hearing impaired persons are also significant; the 1971 National Health Interview Survey found that 15.2% of the speech impaired population also had hearing impairments (National Center for Health Statistics, 1975).

The prevalence of communication disorders does not remain the same throughout the life span. As Culton (1986) observes, "Age-specific prevalence data are more meaningful than overall prevalence data" (p. 6). The percentage of children with speech and language disorders, although rather high, decreases significantly from the earlier to the later school grades. For example, Hull, Mielke, Willeford, and Timmons (1976) found that about 7% of all first grade boys were reported as having "extreme articulation deviations," but only 1% of third grade boys and 0.5% of twelfth grade boys fell into that category. Culton (1986) studied more than 30,000 college freshmen who had undergone screening tests over a 13-year period and found that 2.42% exhibited speech disorders, with an additional 2.34% reporting that they had recovered from earlier speech disorders. The largest part of the speech/language impaired population is composed of young children with articulation problems. Many of these disorders, although significant enough to merit professional attention, are apparently not severe enough to persist into adulthood. They respond favorably to intervention and/or maturation.

TYPES AND CAUSES OF COMMUNICATION DISORDERS

There are many recognized types of communication disorders and numerous possible causes. A speech impairment may be organic; that is, attributable to a specific physical cause. Examples of physical factors that frequently result in communication disorders include cleft palate, paralysis of the speech muscles, absence of teeth, craniofacial abnormalities, enlarged adenoids, and neurological impairments. Organic speech impairments may be regarded as a child's primary handicapping condition or may be secondary to other handicapping conditions, such as delayed intellectual development, impaired hearing, and cerebral palsy.

See chapters 3, 7, and 9 for discussions of these conditions.

Most communication disorders, however, are not considered organic but are classified as functional. They cannot be ascribed to a specific physical condition and their origin is not clearly known. As Winitz (1977) points out, decades of research on the causes of many speech and language impairments have produced only uncertainty. A child's surroundings provide many opportunities for him to learn appropriate and inappropriate communication skills; some specialists believe that functional communication disorders derive mainly from environmental influences. It is also possible that some speech impairments are caused by disturbances in the motor control system and are not fully understood.

However, regardless of whether a communication disorder is considered organic or functional, a child with speech or language that is substantially different from that of others in her age and cultural group requires special training procedures to correct or improve the impairment.

Articulation Disorders

As we have noted, articulation disorders are the type of speech impairment most prevalent among school-age children. The correct articulation, or utterance, of speech sounds requires us to activate a complicated system of muscles, nerves, and organs. Haycock (1933), who compiled a classic manual on teaching speech, describes how the speech organs are manipulated into a variety of shapes and patterns, how the breath and voice must be "molded to form words." For example, here is Haycock's description of how the /v/ sound is correctly produced.

> The lower lip must be drawn upwards and slightly inwards, so that the upper front teeth rest lightly on the lip. Breath must be freely emitted between the teeth and over the lower lip, and voice must be added to the breath.

Should any part of this process function imperfectly, a child will have difficulty articulating the /v/. Clearly, in such a complicated process there are many different types of possible errors.

Children may *omit* certain sounds, as in saying "cool" for *school*. They may drop consonants from the ends of words as in "pos" for post. Most of us leave out sounds at times, but an extensive omission problem can make speech impossible to understand.

Children may *substitute* one sound for another, as in saying "train" for *crane* or "doze" for *those*. Children with this problem are often certain they have said the correct word and may resist correction. Substitution of sounds can cause considerable confusion for the listener.

Children may *distort* certain speech sounds, while attempting to produce them accurately. The /s/ sound, for example, is relatively difficult to produce; children may produce the word *sleep* as "schleep," "zleep," or "thleep." Some speakers have a lisp; others a whistling /s/. Distortions can cause misunderstanding, though parents and teachers often become accustomed to a child's use of them.

Children may also *add* extra sounds, making comprehension difficult. They may say "buhrown" for *brown* or "hamber" for *hammer*.

Like all communication disorders, articulation problems vary in the degree of severity. Many children have mild or moderate articulation disorders. It is usually possible to understand their speech, but they may mispronounce certain sounds or use immature speech, like that of younger children. These problems often disappear as a child matures. If a mild or moderate articulation problem does not seem to be improving over an extended period or if it appears to have a negative effect on the child's interaction with others, referral to a communication disorders specialist may be indicated.

A severe articulation disorder is present when a child pronounces many sounds so poorly that his speech is unintelligible most of the time. In that case even the child's parents, teachers, and peers cannot easily understand him. As Liebergott and colleagues (1978) point out, the child with a severe articulation disorder may "chatter away and sound as though he or she is talking gibberish" (p. 17). He may say, "Yeh me yuh a wido," instead of "Let me look out the window," or perhaps "Do foop is dood" for "That soup is good." The fact that articulation disorders are prevalent does not mean that teachers, parents, and specialists should regard them as simple or unimportant. On the contrary, as Emerick and Haynes (1986) observe, "An articulation disorder severe enough to interfere significantly with intelligibility is . . . as debilitating a communication problem as many other disorders . . . articulation disorders are not simple at all, and they are not necessarily easy to diagnose effectively" (p. 153).

Voice Disorders

Voice disorders occur when the quality, loudness, or pitch of the voice is inappropriate or abnormal. Such disorders are far less common in children than in adults. Considering how often some children shout and yell without any apparent harm to their voices, it is evident that the vocal cords can withstand heavy use (Renfrew, 1972). In some cases, however, a child's voice may be difficult to understand or may be considered unpleasant. As Moore (1982) observes, a person's voice may be considered disordered if it differs markedly from what is customary in the voices of others of the same age, sex, and cultural background. Moore uses the term *dysphonia* to describe any condition of poor or unpleasant voice quality and notes that a voice—whether good, poor, or in between—is closely identified with the person who uses it.

The voice disorders most frequently found among children of school age are hoarseness, breathiness, and nasality. An unusually hoarse voice sounds husky and

Mark's teacher recognizes and rewards his efforts to communicate.

strained most of the time. It can have organic causes, such as growths or irritations on the vocal cords, but hoarseness is most frequently due to chronic vocal abuse such as yelling, imitating noises, or habitually talking while under tension. A breathy voice is unpleasant because it is low in volume and fails to make adequate use of the vocal cords.

Nasality results if too many sounds come out through the air passages of the nose (hypernasality) or, conversely, if there is not enough resonance of the nasal passages (hyponasality). The hypernasal speaker may be perceived as talking through her nose or having an unpleasant twang. A child with hypernasality has speech that is excessively nasal, neutral, or central-sounding rather than oral, clear, and forward-sounding (Cole & Paterson, 1986). A child with hyponasality (sometimes called de-nasality) may sound as though he constantly has a cold or a stuffed nose, even when he does not. As with other voice disorders, the causes of nasality may be either organic (e.g., cleft palate, swollen nasal tissues, hearing impairment) or functional (perhaps resulting from learned speech patterns or behavior problems).

Fluency Disorders

Normal speech makes use of rhythm and timing. Words and phrases flow easily, with certain variations in speed, stress, and appropriate pauses. **Fluency** disorders interrupt the natural, smooth flow of speech with inappropriate pauses, hesitations, or repetitions. One type of fluency disorder is known as cluttering, a condition in which speech is very rapid and clipped, to the point of unintelligibility. The best known—and probably least understood—fluency disorder, however, is **stuttering.** This condition is marked by "rapid-fire repetitions of consonant or vowel sounds, especially at the beginning of words; and complete verbal blocks" (Jonas, 1976). The cause of stuttering remains unknown, although the condition has been studied extensively with some interesting results. Stuttering is far more common among males than females. And it occurs more frequently among twins. The prevalence of stuttering is about the same in all Western countries: regardless of what language is spoken, about 1% of the general population has a stuttering problem. Stuttering is much more commonly reported among children than adults; prevalence estimates in school-age populations are in the 5% range (Ham, 1986; Martin & Lindamood, 1986). Stuttering is considered a disorder of childhood; it rarely begins in persons past the age of 6 (Emerick & Haynes, 1986). According to Jonas (1976), stuttering typically makes its first appearance between the ages of 3 and 5, "*after* the child has already made great strides toward fluency. . . . The trouble comes later, just as speech is becoming less of a feat and more of a habit."

All children experience some dysfluencies—repetitions and interruptions—in the course of developing normal speech patterns. It is important not to overreact to children's dysfluencies and insist on perfect speech; some specialists believe that stuttering can be caused by pressures placed on a child when parents and teachers react to normal hesitations and repetitions by labeling the child a stutterer. Lingwell (1982) explains that stuttering is not just one specific disorder but many, which may be why there are several conflicting theories about its cause. According to Lingwell, stuttering can be caused by neurological, psychological, or allergic factors or can result from rhythmic control or faulty learning patterns.

Stuttering is situational; that is, it appears to be related to the setting or circumstances of speech. A child may be likely to stutter when talking to the people whose opinions matter most to him—such as parents and teachers—and in situations like being called on to speak in front of the class. Most people who stutter are fluent about 95% of the time; a child with a fluency disorder may not stutter at all when singing, talking to his pet dog, or reciting a poem in unison with others. The reactions and expectations of parents, teachers, and peers clearly have an important effect on any child's personal and communicative development.

Several researchers and clinicians have explored the effects of social pressures on stuttering, by examining its incidence in cultures other than our own. Gerald Jonas, who himself was affected by stuttering, derives insights from a comparison of American Indian tribes. He observes that certain tribes, such as the Utes and the Bannocks of the Rocky Mountain region, have an unusually permissive attitude toward children's speech and have virtually no stuttering problems. Other tribes, such as the Cowichans of the Pacific Northwest, are highly competitive, expecting children to take part in complicated rituals at a young age, and have a high incidence of stuttering. Jonas (1976) suggests that the reason the Ute and Bannock children do not stutter may be that no one ever tries to "make them speak correctly." But he acknowledges that this theory fails to explain "why in so many other cultures some children of nagging parents turn into stutterers while others do not" (p. 14). Van Riper (1972) reflects on the importance of cultural attitudes toward stuttering in the following passage:

> Once, on Fiji in the South Pacific, we found a whole family of stutterers. As our guide and translator phrased it: "Mama kaka; papa kaka; and kaka, kaka, kaka, kaka." All six persons in that family showed marked repetitions and prolongations in their speech; but they were happy people, not at all troubled by their stuttering. It was just the way they talked. We could not help but contrast their attitudes and the simplicity of their stuttering with those which would have been shown by a similar family in our own land, where the pace of living is so much faster, where defective communication is rejected, where stutterers get penalized all their lives. To possess a marked speech disorder in our society is almost as handicapping as to be a physical cripple in a nomadic tribe that exists by hunting. (p. 4)

Language Disorders

Language disorders are usually classified as either receptive or expressive. As described earlier in this chapter a receptive language disorder interferes with the understanding of language. A child, for example, may be unable to comprehend spoken sentences or to follow a sequence of directions. An expressive language disorder interferes with the production of language. The child may have a very limited vocabulary, may use incorrect words and phrases, or may not even speak at all, communicating only through gestures. A child may have good receptive language when an expressive disorder is present or may have both expressive and receptive disorders in combination.

To say that a child has a language delay does not necessarily mean that she has a language disorder. As Reed (1986) explains, a language delay implies that a child is slow to develop linguistic skills but acquires them in the same sequence as normal children. Generally, all features of language are delayed at about the same rate. On the other hand, a language disorder suggests a disruption in the usual rate and sequence of specific emerging language skills. A child who consistently has difficulty in responding to who, what, and where questions but otherwise displays language skills appropriate for her age would likely be considered to have a language disorder.

Chaney and Frodyma (1982) list several factors that can contribute to language disorders in children.

Learning disabilities (see chapter 4) and autism (see chapter 5) are viewed by some professionals primarily as language disorders.

1. Cognitive limitations or retardation
2. Environmental deprivation
3. Hearing impairments
4. Emotional deprivation or behavior disorders
5. Structural abnormalities of the speech mechanism

Environmental influences are thought to play an important part in delayed, disordered, or absent language. Some children are rewarded for their efforts at communication, whereas others, unfortunately, are punished for talking, gesturing, or otherwise attempting to communicate. A child who has little stimulation at home and has few chances to speak, listen, explore, and interact with others will probably have little motivation for communication and may well develop disordered patterns of language. Children who have had little exposure to words and experiences may need the teacher's help in encouraging communication. Active participation in experiences gives children the opportunity to learn and use appropriate vocabulary.

Some severe disorders in expressive and receptive language result from impairments of the brain. The term *aphasia* is frequently used to describe a "breakdown in the ability to formulate, or to retrieve, and to decode the arbitrary symbols of language" (Holland & Reinmuth, 1982, p. 428). Aphasia is one of the most prevalent causes of language disorders in adults, most often occurring suddenly, following a cardiovascular accident (stroke). Aphasia can also occur in children, however, either as a congenital or an acquired condition. Head injury is considered to be a significant

A congenital disorder is one that is present at birth.

cause of aphasia in children. Aphasia may be either expressive or, less commonly, receptive. Children with mild aphasia have language patterns that are close to normal but may have difficulty retrieving certain words and tend to need more time than usual to communicate (Linebaugh, 1986). Children with severe aphasia, however, are likely to have a markedly reduced storehouse of words and language forms. They may not be able to "use language for successful communicative interchange" (Horner, 1986, p. 892).

DEVELOPMENT OF THE FIELD
OF COMMUNICATION DISORDERS

Although there have always been people with speech and language disorders, special education and treatment for this population are relatively recent developments. Hewett and Forness (1977) report that the first special class for "speech defective" children in the U.S. was established in New York in 1908. Special education for other groups of children—including deaf children, blind children, and those with mental retardation—was begun much earlier, suggesting that communication disorders have historically been considered less severe and less easily recognized than other disabilities.

During the 19th century some treatment was provided at clinics and hospitals for people with communication disorders. The earliest specialists were college and university professors who, in the course of their study of normal speech processes, became interested in people with irregular patterns of speech, particularly stuttering and articulation disorders. Although American therapists concentrated primarily on the correction of speech defects, European specialists (largely physicians) had developed a considerable body of scientific knowledge about communication disorders prior to World War II (Boone, 1977). The postwar years saw a proliferation of clinical services and research efforts. Many speech pathologists became especially interested in the rehabilitation of military personnel who had developed communication disorders because of damage to the brain or to the physical speech mechanisms. Speech and hearing clinics and centers were established in many cities, often operating in cooperation with hospitals or universities.

In recent years there has been a notable expansion of services in the regular public schools to children with speech and language disorders. Professionals who provide remedial services to children with communication disorders are today usually called speech-language pathologists or communication disorders specialists, rather than speech therapists. In 1978 the name of the major professional organization involved with communication disorders was changed to the American Speech-Language-Hearing Association (though it is still abbreviated as ASHA). These changes in terminology reflect a current awareness of the interrelationships among speech, language, and other aspects of learning, communication, and behavior. Speech is no longer viewed as a narrow specialty concerned with disorders to be corrected in isolation. Increasingly, speech-language pathologists who work in school settings now function as team members concerned with the overall education and development of children. As Matthews (1982) observes, there is a trend for remedial procedures to be carried out in the regular classroom, rather than in a special speech room, and the speech-language pathologist often provides training and consultation for the child's regular teacher, who may do much of the direct work with a child with communication disorders.

ASSESSMENT AND EVALUATION

"Don't worry, she'll grow out of it."
"Speech therapists can't help a child who doesn't talk."
"He'll be all right once he starts school."

These "misguided and inaccurate remarks" are indicative of widely held attitudes toward communication disorders, according to Thompson (1984). Such attitudes, she contends, are "at best worrying and annoying, at worst positively destructive to the child's social, emotional, and intellectual development" (p. 86).

In order to avoid the consequences of unrecognized or untreated speech and language disorders, it is especially important for children to receive professional assessment and evaluation services. When assessing or diagnosing a child suspected of having a communication disorder, the specialist seeks to meet the following objectives, as delineated by Emerick and Haynes (1986):

1. *To describe the problem.* What are the dimensions of the communicative disturbance with respect to voice, fluency, language, and articulation?
2. *To estimate its severity.* How large a problem is it?
3. *To identify factors that are related to the problem.* What are the antecedents and consequences of it?
4. *To estimate prospects for improvement.* What estimate can we make of the extent of possible recovery and the time frame of treatment?
5. *To derive a plan of treatment.* What are the specific targets for therapy, and how can the client best be approached? (p. 50)

Most professional speech and language assessments begin with the collection of case history information from the child and the parent. This typically involves completing a biographical form that includes such diverse information as the child's birth and developmental history, illnesses, medications taken, scores on achievement and intelligence tests, and adjustment to school. The parent may be asked when the child first crawled, walked, and uttered words. Social skills, such as playing readily with other children, may also be considered.

The specialist examines the child's mouth carefully, noting whether there are any irregularities in the tongue, lips, teeth, palate, or other structures that may affect speech production. If the child has an organic speech problem, the specialist refers the child for possible medical intervention. Testing procedures vary according to the type of functional disorder suspected. Often the specialist conducts broad screenings to detect areas of concern and then moves to more detailed testing in those areas. A comprehensive evaluation to detect the presence of a communication disorder would likely include the following general components:

1. *Articulation test.* The speech errors the child is making are assessed. A record is kept of the sounds that are defective, the way in which they are being mispronounced, and the number of errors made. Examples of published tests include the Templin-Darley Test of Articulation (Templin & Darley, 1969) and the Test of Minimal Articulation Competence (Secord, 1981).

2. *Hearing test.* Hearing is generally tested to determine whether a hearing problem is the cause of the speech disorder.

3. *Auditory discrimination test.* This test is given to determine whether the child is hearing sounds correctly. If he is unable to recognize the specific characteristics of a given sound, he will not have a good model to imitate. The Wepman Auditory Discrimination Test (Wepman, 1958) and the Templin Speech Sound Discrimination Test (Templin, 1957) are two examples.

4. *Language development test.* This is administered to help determine the amount of vocabulary the child has acquired, because vocabulary is generally a good indication of intelligence. Frequently used tests include the Peabody Picture Vocabulary Test

(Dunn, 1965), which is a measure of receptive vocabulary, and the Carrow Elicited Language Inventory (Carrow, 1974).

A fifth evaluation used more and more frequently is an overall language test, which assesses the child's understanding and production of language structures (e.g., important syntactical elements like conjunctions showing causal relationships). An example is the Clinical Evaluation of Language Functions (Semel & Wiig, 1980).

The effective examiner does not merely ask, "Does the child talk?" but rather asks, "How does the child communicate?" (Ulrey, 1982, p. 123). An important part of any evaluation procedure is obtaining a language sample, an accurate example of the child's expressive speech and language. The examiner considers such factors as the intelligibility and fluency of speech, the voice quality, and the use of vocabulary and grammar. Some speech-language pathologists use structured tasks to elicit language samples. They may, for example, ask a child to describe a picture, tell a story, or answer a list of questions. Most specialists, however, use informal conversation as their

Comprehensive assessment includes both formal and informal measures of language and communication.

preferred procedure to obtain language samples (Atkins & Cartwright, 1982). They believe that the child's language sample will be more representative if the examiner uses natural conversation rather than highly structured tasks. Emerick and Haynes (1986) advise examiners to tape-record language samples instead of taking notes, which can be distracting to the child. Open-ended questions, such as "Tell me about your family," are suggested rather than yes-no questions or questions that can be answered with one word, such as "What color is your car?"

Behavioral observation is becoming increasingly important in the assessment of communication disorders. As Schiefelbusch and McCormick (1981) observe, objective recording of children's language competence in social contexts has added much to our knowledge of language acquisition. It is imperative that the observer have experience in reliably recording speech and language and that the child's behavior be sampled across various settings, rather than limited to a clinic or examining room. For young children a parent-child observation is frequently arranged. The specialist provides appropriate toys and activities and requests the parent to interact normally with child.

After the assessment procedures have been completed, the speech-language pathologist reviews the results of the case history, formal and informal tests, language samples, behavioral observations, medical records, and other available data. A treatment plan is then developed in cooperation with the child's parents and teachers, to set up realistic communication objectives and to determine the methods that will be used. Kelly and Rice (1986) suggest that parents be given an opportunity to question and react to the recommendations and to discuss their willingness to follow through with the treatment plans. It is also appropriate, they note, to inform parents of the frequency of therapy, the costs involved, and the availability of resources in the community.

TREATMENT AND REMEDIATION OF COMMUNICATION DISORDERS

Various approaches are employed in the treatment of speech and language disorders. Medical, dental, or surgical procedures can help many children whose speech problems result from organic causes. The profession of speech-language pathology addresses both organic and nonorganic causes and encompasses practitioners with numerous points of view and a wide range of accepted intervention techniques. Some specialists employ structured exercises and drills to correct speech sounds; others emphasize speech production in natural language contexts. Some perfer to work with children in individual therapy sessions; others believe that group sessions are advantageous for language modeling and peer support. Some encourage children to imitate the therapist's speech; others prefer to have the child listen to tapes of her own speech. Some specialists follow a highly behavioral approach, in which target speech behaviors are precisely prompted, recorded, and reinforced; others favor less structured methods. Some speech-language therapists focus their efforts exclusively on a child's expressive and receptive communication; others devote attention to other aspects of the child's behavior and environment, such as self-confidence or interactions with parents and classmates. Clearly, there are many possible options to explore in devising an appropriate treatment plan for a child with a communication disorder. We will briefly describe some current approaches.

Articulation Disorders

Speech-language pathologists, according to Bernthal and Bankson (1986), feel more comfortable and competent when dealing with articulation disorders than with other types of speech and language impairments. This response is probably attributable, they note, to the fact that articulation disorders can be broken down into identifiable segments more readily than can disorders of voice, fluency, or language. Also, a child can logically progress from articulating simple sounds in isolation to syllables, words, phrases, sentences, and sustained conversation. A large percentage of functional articulation disorders are either successfully treated or simply fade away as the child matures.

Four models of treatment are widely used in the treatment of articulation disorders (Bernthal & Bankson, 1986; Newman, Creaghead, & Secord, 1985). In the discrimination model emphasis is placed on developing the child's ability to listen carefully and detect the differences between similar sounds (such as the *t* in *take* and the *c* in *cake*). The child learns to match his speech to that of a standard model, using auditory, visual, and tactual feedback. The phonologic model seeks to identify a child's pattern of sound production and to teach her to produce gradually more acceptable sounds. A child who tends to omit final consonants, for example, might be taught to recognize the difference between word pairs like *two* and *tooth* and then to produce them more accurately. The sensory-motor model emphasizes the repetitive production of sounds in various contexts, with special attention given to the motor skills involved in articulation; frequent exercises are employed to produce sounds with differing stress patterns. The operant conditioning model seeks to define antecedent events, present specific stimuli, and shape articulatory responses by providing reinforcing consequences. An instructional objective might be stated as "Wayne will say the *k* in the final position of 10 words after being shown 10 pictures by the therapist. The *k* sound must be produced correctly in 9 of the 10 words."

There is a generally consistent relationship between children's ability to recognize sounds and their ability to articulate them correctly (Newman, Creaghead, & Secord, 1985). Whatever treatment model(s) are used, the specialist may have the child carefully watch how sounds are produced and then use a mirror to monitor his own speech production. Children are expected to accurately produce problematic sounds in syllables, words, sentences, and stories. They may tape-record their own speech and listen carefully for errors. It is sometimes helpful for children to learn to recognize the difference between the way they produce a sound and the way other people produce it. As in all communication training, it is important for the teacher, parent, or specialist to provide a good language model, to reward the child's positive performance, and to encourage the child to talk.

Voice Disorders

In the case of a child with a voice disorder, a medical examination should always be sought. Organic causes often respond to surgery or medical treatment. In addition, communication disorders specialists sometimes recommend environmental modifications; a person who is consistently required to speak in a noisy setting, for example, may benefit from the use of a small microphone to reduce vocal straining and shouting (Moore, 1982). Most remedial techniques, however, offer direct vocal rehabilitation, which helps the child with a voice disorder gradually learn to produce more acceptable and efficient speech. Depending on the type of voice disorder and the child's overall circumstances, vocal rehabilitation may include such activities as exercises to increase breathing capacity, relaxation techniques to reduce tension, or procedures to increase or decrease the loudness of speech.

Visi-pitch is an example of a visual speech display. It can be used with Apple and IBM computers.

The principles of applied behavior analysis have had a profound impact on the treatment of voice disorders in recent years, according to Johnson (1986). Because many voice problems are directly attributable to vocal abuse, behavioral principles are frequently used to pinpoint abusive vocal behaviors and then to shape and modify them. Many children and adults have thus been able to break habitual patterns of vocal misuse. Computer technology has also been successfully applied in the treatment of voice disorders. Some instruments enable speakers to see visual representations of their voice patterns on a screen or printout; speakers are thus able to monitor their own vocalizations visually as well as auditorily and to develop new patterns of using their voices more naturally and efficiently (Bull & Rushakoff, 1987).

Fluency Disorders

The treatment of stuttering and other fluency disorders varies widely according to the orientation of the client and the therapist. Over the course of history, people who stutter have been subjected to countless treatments, some of them unusual, to say the least. Past treatments included holding pebbles in the mouth, sticking fingers in a light socket, talking out of one side of the mouth, eating raw oysters, speaking with the teeth clenched, taking alternating hot and cold baths, and speaking on inhaled rather than exhaled air (Ham, 1986). For many years it was widely thought that stuttering was caused by a tongue that was unable to function properly in the mouth. It was not uncommon for early physicians to prescribe ointments that would blister or numb the tongue or even to remove portions of the tongue through surgery!

Today's methods of treatment tend to emphasize one of two general approaches (Ham, 1986). One approach might be termed symptom modification. Using various techniques, the therapist takes aim at the stuttering itself and/or the underlying emotional dimensions of the stutterer. The principal goal of such therapy is to develop the person's ability to control the stuttering and to behave appropriately in situations where communication is required. The other prevalent approach could be labeled fluency reinforcement. A therapist employing this methodology would regard stuttering as a learned response and would seek to eliminate it by establishing and encouraging fluent speech.

The application of behavioral principles has strongly influenced recent practices in the treatment of fluency disorders. Hegde (1986) observes that the punishment of stuttering is socially undesirable as well as ineffective and tends to generate emotional side effects, but the "positive reinforcement of nonstuttered utterances can be an attractive alternative" (p. 521). Children may learn to manage their stuttering by deliberately prolonging certain sounds or by speaking slowly to get through a "block." They may increase their confidence and fluency by speaking in groups, where pressure is minimized and successful speech is positively reinforced. They may learn to monitor their own speech and reward themselves for periods of fluency. They may learn to speak to a rhythmic beat or with the aid of devices that mask or delay their ability to hear their own speech. Tape recorders are often used for drills, simulated conversations, and documentation of progress.

Effective programs of treatment do not focus on only one aspect of stuttering, but instead identify and alter its communicative, behavioral, and emotional components (Emerick & Haynes, 1986). The importance of **generalization** of the targeted speech behaviors to natural settings—that is, outside the clinic—is emphasized by Hegde (1986). A therapist might, for example, "accompany the stutterer to a store or a restaurant, and manage the treatment contingencies in a subtle manner" (p. 532). Parents, teachers, siblings, and peers may be invited to the treatment sessions and may be trained to reinforce stutter-free patterns of speech at home or school.

When interacting with a child who stutters, it is recommended that a teacher pay primary attention to what the child is saying, rather than to his difficulties in saying it. This focus will help the child develop a more positive attitude toward himself and toward communication with others. When the child experiences a verbal block, the teacher should be patient and calm, say nothing, and maintain eye-to-eye contact with the child until he finishes what he wants to say.

In many cases, children learn to control their stuttering and to produce increasingly fluent speech as they mature. No single method of treatment has been recognized as most effective. Stuttering frequently decreases when children enter adolescence, regardless of which treatment method was used. The problem even disappears with no treatment at all in some cases. Martin and Lindamood (1986) studied the phenomenon of spontaneous recovery from stuttering and concluded that approximately 40% to 45% of children diagnosed as stutterers apparently outgrow or get over their dysfluencies without formal intervention.

Although a variety of programs to treat stuttering are likely to continue, it is important for teachers, parents, and clients to evaluate the effectiveness of such programs. Sacco (1986) has established six essential criteria for the successful treatment of stuttering.

1. Lessens tension in the speech mechanism
2. Reduces rates of speech production
3. Eliminiates accompanying struggle behaviors
4. Creates a more healthy attitude about speaking
5. Reduces the client's perception of stress
6. Produces speech that is more natural (p.81)

Language Disorders

Treatments for language disorders are also extremely varied. Some programs center around precommunication activities that encourage the child to explore and that make the environment conducive to the development of receptive and expressive language. Clearly, children must have something they want to communicate. And because children learn through imitation, it is important for the teacher or specialist to talk clearly, use correct inflections, and provide a rich variety of words and sentences. The presence of other children in the classroom or clinical setting also appears to play a useful role in language development. Lowenthal (1981) found that preschool children with language impairments learned most effectively when they were taught in groups of three or four children. Larger groups, with 10 children, were less effective in encouraging the development of vocabulary and comprehension skills.

Chaney and Frodyma (1982) describe two different methods used to encourage language development in preschool children with various handicapping conditions: the precision method and the experiential method. In the precision method children are placed in groups according to their ability levels in each of several areas, such as language, cognition, motor skills, self-help skills, and social skills. Group lessons and activities about 20 minutes long emphasize language through tasks that a child has not yet learned, and extensive data on each child's performance are maintained. The experiential method uses groups of children with varying levels of language ability; children with higher language skills serve as models for those whose language is not as well developed. Different demands and expectations are placed on each child, and each day's activities are presented around a unified theme or experience. Activities for one day, for example, might revolve around clothing. The children might discuss what clothes they are wearing, paste clothes on paper dolls, wash clothes, and learn concepts of size and color using articles of clothing.

Some specialists in language disorders do a great deal of written and verbal labeling to help the child develop language content; that is, attach meaning to important objects in the environment. In many instances children's language skills improve when they become better able to pay attention. The specialist may reinforce the child for imitating facial expressions or body movements or simply for maintaining eye contact. Some speech-language pathologists emphasize the pairing of actions with words, teaching the natural gestures that go along with such expressions as "up," "look," and "goodbye." D'Angelo (1981) recommends the use of wordless picture books as a means of building vocabulary, conversational skills, and positive attitudes with language disordered children. Questions such as "What is happening in the picture?" and "What things do you see?" can be used by a parent or teacher in initiating conversations with a child.

Programs for children with language disorders, although acknowledging the importance of oral speech, are currently moving away from an exclusive emphasis on spoken communication. Sign language has been successfully used to develop communicative skills in several children who, though their hearing was not impaired, were apparently unable to develop expressive or receptive language through normal channels. For example, Bonvillian and Nelson (1976) were able to teach sign language to an autistic child who had previously been considered mute and nonresponsive. Sign language, gestures, and symbol systems have also been successfully taught to children whose language disorders are attributed to mental retardation, aphasia, or behavior disorders. These approaches should, however, be viewed as supplements to speech rather than as *replacements* for speech. Children who are able to initiate communication through signs, gestures, or symbols may be able to transfer to speech as they learn and develop their communicative abilities. Speech is always a desirable goal for children whose cognitive and physical abilities enable them to achieve it.

Children with severe language disorders tend to require highly structured programs of intervention. The teacher's verbal or nonverbal prompts and the student's acceptable responses are defined and measured very specifically. For example, when Cindy's teacher asks, "Do you want more juice?" Cindy must clearly articulate at least the syllable *mo* (for *more*) within 5 seconds in order to receive a sip of juice. Sounds and partial sentences, such as "want cookie," may be regarded as suitable vocal responses. Cavallaro and Poulson (1985) defined a system of communicative prompts, ranging from least assistance to most assistance, for teachers to use to encourage language development in children with severe handicaps (see Table 6.1).

No matter what approach to treatment is used, it is clear that children with language disorders need to be around children and adults with something interesting to talk about. As Reed (1986) points out, for many years it was assumed that a one-to-one setting was the most effective format for language intervention. Emphasis was

TABLE 6.1
Prompts used in incidental teaching, listed in order from least assistance to most assistance.

Prompt	Clarification	Used When
Nonvocal prompt	The teacher looked at the child and remained silent for at least 3 sec.	Always used as first prompt.
Question	The teacher asked a question which provided no assistance, such as "What do you want?"	When the child was able to produce the response without prompting.
Request for terminal response	"Say the whole thing," or "Tell me what you want."	When the child could produce the response without a model.
Partial model	The teacher presented a model of part of the desired response, such as "Say, want . . ."	When the child could reliably imitate a full model.
Full model	The teacher modeled the entire response, and requested imitation, such as "Say, want cookie."	When the child could not reliably produce the response.

Source: From "Teaching Language to Handicapped Children in Natural Settings" by C. C. Cavallaro & C. L. Poulson, Winter 1985, *Education and Treatment of Children, 8*(1) p. 10.

placed on eliminating distracting stimuli and focusing a child's attention on the desired communication task. Today, however, the importance of language as an interactive, interpersonal behavior is generally recognized, and small-group intervention formats can expose children with language disorders to "a variety of stimuli, experiences, contexts, and people that are not available in one-to-one situations" (Reed, 1986, p. 276).

Whether they use individual or group therapy, effective speech-language pathologists establish specific goals and objectives, keep precise records of their students' behaviors, and structure the teaching situation so that each child's efforts at communication will be rewarded and enjoyable.

Facilitating Communication

All good teachers—whether they are specifically trained as language specialists or not—are also good communication facilitators who encourage children's communication skills and motivation. The effective teacher speaks with feeling and animation and listens to children with genuine interest. When a child makes an error, the teacher can correct it by naturally rephrasing it.

> Child: "Them boys has football helmets."
> Teacher: "Yes, those boys have football helmets."

See chapter 14 for a review of several strategies used by teachers of handicapped preschool children to increase speech and language skills. The FOCUS feature that follows highlights one particular strategy and gives specific suggestions.

Interactions like this may be considered a form of behavioral modeling, and over a period of time the child will be expected to use patterns of speech and language that more closely approximate the appropriate usage. However, a child's attempts at communication should *never* be rejected. When unable to understand a child's speech, the teacher may say, "Show me what you mean," or attempt to draw more information from the child by asking who, what, when, or where questions. The good teacher creates a classroom atmosphere that offers many chances for relaxed communication and makes each child feel that she has an important contribution to make. The teacher is a person of primary importance in the development of children's speech and language skills. And effective communication in the classroom enriches the learning situation for all students.

Patterns of Service

Although there are some self-contained special classes specifically designed for children with speech or language impairments, the regular classroom is by far the most prevalent setting for school-age children with communication disorders. There is an increasing tendency for communication disorders specialists to serve as consultants for regular and special education teachers (and parents), rather than spending most of their time providing direct services to individual children. All of these people are important in the development and practice of speech and language skills. The specialist concentrates his efforts on assessing communication disorders, evaluating progress, and providing materials and techniques. Teachers and parents are encouraged to follow the specialist's guidelines.

ASHA can provide further information about the training, qualifications, and responsibilities of speech-language pathologists. The address of ASHA is given in the listing of resources at the end of this chapter.

Recent surveys of members of the American Speech-Language-Hearing Association (Mansour, 1985; Shewan, 1986) have found that speech-language pathologists

FOCUS

DEVELOPING LANGUAGE AND LEADERSHIP

Young children with impaired speech or language often are frustrated by the difficulty they experience in asking questions, expressing their needs, or conveying their wishes to other people. When unable to make themselves understood, some children may resort to physical communication (such as pulling, pushing, or hitting classmates), whereas others become so frustrated that they stop trying to communicate.

Judith Hurvitz, Sarah Pickert, and Donna Rilla believe that teachers can help children develop language skills by encouraging them to assume leadership roles in the classroom. Activities that carry responsibility, power, and prestige, they maintain, are useful in promoting language and social interaction. Here are some suggestions developed for Karen, a hypothetical 5-year-old with a communication disorder.

☐ Ask Karen to sit on a chair while the rest of the children are seated on the floor.

☐ Allow Karen to wear a special hat or badge.

☐ Give Karen the authority to distribute rewards, such as stars or tokens, to other children.

☐ Let Karen lead circle-time activities by taking attendance, directing group songs, and greeting others ("Hi, Judy").

☐ Allow Karen to assign daily classroom jobs to other children ("Barry, mats" "Ron, get snack").

☐ Have Karen act as class messenger, especially when the recipient of the message is familiar with the meaning to be conveyed (she might say to the librarian, "Need book").

☐ Permit Karen to choose how class members will participate in a particular activity; for example, designating whether boys or girls will go first in line ("Boys first").

☐ Give Karen a picture to hold up and ask her to call on a child to describe the picture ("Donna, what this?").

☐ Let Karen lead the group in a movement activity by calling out actions ("March!" "Walk!" "Sit!").

☐ Suggest words that Karen can use to solve a problem herself when she asks for teacher intervention. Say, "Go to Anthony and tell him, 'I want my block'" or "Take your puzzle to Glen and say, 'Help me.'"

☐ Encourage Karen to work together with another child in such tasks as cleaning up after snack time or moving a bulky table.

☐ Invite Karen to talk with a classmate using a pair of toy telephones. (This often generates enthusiasm.)

Activities such as these can help children use language more effectively and with greater variety. They also enable children to experience the pleasure and power of using language to control their environments.

Source: Adapted from "Promoting Children's Language Interaction" by J. A. Hurvitz, S. M. Pickert, and D. C. Rilla, 1987, *Teaching Exceptional Children, 19*(3), pp. 12–15. Reprinted by permission.

are employed in a wide variety of settings, with the largest single group—about 37%—working in schools. Other settings include hospitals, speech and hearing clinics, nursing homes, physicians' offices, and private practice. The caseloads of these professionals vary widely according to the setting and the types and severity of communication disorders among their clients. In schools the most prevalent pattern of service delivery is a specialist working with a child for two sessions each week. The most prevalent communication disorders among children served by school speech-language pathologists are, in order of frequency, language disorders (52.2% of a typical caseload), articulation disorders (34.8%), hearing impairments (4.5%), fluency disorders (4.1%), and voice disorders (2.4%) (Shewan, 1986).

In some programs the specialist visits schools according to a regular schedule and gives individual or group therapy to the children. However, this approach is becoming somewhat less common today. Communication is seen as occurring most ap-

COMMUNICATION RULES

ADULT SHOULD . . .

* Keep child for more turns.
* Act and communicate like the child and sometimes a little higher (not in adult ways.)
* Talk with sensible words that describe the child's world (not with adult or academic words).
* Frequently play and communicate just for fun (not only to teach or direct).

CHILD SHOULD . . .

* Keep playing for longer turns
* Communicate habitually in old and new ways (rather than "the easy way").

* Stay in longer turns on the same topic with new words.

* Frequently communicate to be playful (rather than only for needs).

CONTACT MORE - STAY LONGER - BE CHILDLIKE & PLAYFUL

This chart gives guidelines for facilitating communication in a preschool classroom.

propriately in the natural environment rather than in the clinical setting. Consequently, some professionals believe that it is impossible to adequately serve the child with a speech or language disorder in a program consisting of only one or two 30-minute sessions each week with a specialist. In fact, this approach has been described as a futile attempt to "sweep back a river with a broom" (Hatten & Hatten, 1975).

The speech and language specialist may also act as a resource room teacher. Based in a regular school, she may then serve a variety of children on a regular basis, while also maintaining contact with their regular teachers. Students with communication disorders are seldom placed in self-contained classrooms or special schools unless the disorder is extremely severe (as in the case of a completely nonverbal child) or the child has multiple physical, intellectual, or behavioral impairments.

Tomes and Sanger (1986) surveyed the attitudes of classroom teachers toward the services provided by speech-language pathologists in their schools. Although the attitudes were generally positive, there was some confusion about the specialists' roles and responsibilities. It was recommended that speech-language pathologists encourage teachers to observe treatment sessions and that they obtain suggestions from teachers regarding the kinds of in-service training they would find most helpful.

Administrators and parents are also encouraged to observe treatment procedures.

CURRENT ISSUES/FUTURE TRENDS

The future will probably find specialists in communication disorders functioning even more indirectly than they do today. They will continue to work as professional team members, assisting teachers, parents, physicians, and other specialists in recognizing potential communication disorders and in facilitating communication skills. In-service training will become an ever more important aspect of the specialist's responsibilities.

Speech-language pathologists who work in schools are likely to find themselves working with an increasing percentage of children with severe and multiple handicaps who previously did not receive specialized services from communication disorders specialists. In some school districts increasing caseloads are already arising, along with financial restrictions that make it virtually impossible for all students with communication disorders to receive adequate services from the relatively few specialists who are employed. Even though all handicapped students are supposed to receive all of the special services they need, the schools' financial problems may necessitate difficult decisions at the local level. Some programs may choose to provide special services only to those students with the most severe speech and language impairments. Others may concentrate their professional resources on higher-functioning students who are considered to have the best potential for developing communication skills. Parents, advocates, and professional organizations will play an instrumental role in determining which children are to receive specialized speech and language services.

Paraprofessional personnel may, in the future, be more widely trained to work directly with children who have speech and language disorders, while professionals concentrate their efforts on diagnosis, prescriptive programming, evaluation, and the use of technology. Peer tutoring or therapy approaches using nonhandicapped students as language models are likely to become more prevalent. These approaches may allow more students to receive specialized help.

"I HAVE A LOT OF THINGS TO SAY. . . .

Susan M. Bolton is a speech-language pathologist in the Fountain Valley School District, Fountain Valley, California. Much of Sue's work has been in an innovative project to use new communication technology with nonoral students at Plavan School, where students with and without disabilities are educated together. Sue agreed to discuss some recent developments in augmentative communication—and several of her students also had some things to tell us.

The ability to communicate through speech is something that most of us take for granted. Yet many children and adults either fail to acquire or lose the ability to use this most precious of human communicative skills.

Widespread use of sign language among deaf people is evidence of the success of augmentative (supplemental to speech) systems for individuals with speech handicaps. Children with severe physical handicaps, however, often find that their ability to use sign language is limited by the same disabilities that prevent them from acquiring oral speech.

Fortunately, modern technology has enabled many of these individuals to communicate without speech in a variety of ways. Some of the systems, such as communication boards (also known as language or conversation boards), have been widely used with this population. These boards are often customized for the person's needs and are usually inexpensive to develop. In some cases, such as with individuals with low cognitive functioning, the boards adequately meet the needs of the person. But many people require more extensive vocabulary in a personal, portable system.

The answer to their needs came as a result of the microchip revolution. These tiny units of information storage provide the capability of almost limitless vocabulary compacted into systems that can be transported right along with the speech impaired person.

For the past 6 years, I have worked with children of all ages who require augmentative communication systems in various forms. A look of the eye or a facial expression often told us that these children had much to say. Yet, as a speech-language pathologist, I had experienced many frustrating moments because I could not develop the kind of oral speech in these children that I knew society would demand. As soon as appropriate systems were developed and fitted to these children, I obtained some interesting comments from them that I would like to share with you.

Although these children use a variety of systems (small minitypewriters, scanners, personal computers, and so on), the common thread is strong: before acquiring their systems, limited speech also limited their ability to interact with people, to express feelings, to show humor, or to do many other things we normally expect of children (and ourselves).

Six students, ranging in age from 11 to 19, were asked to address the topic "What My Communication Aid Means to Me." Here are their responses.

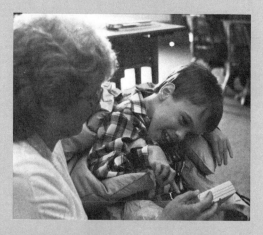

Jay with a Canon Communicator.

Jay H. is 11 years old. About all he can say is a resemblance to "yes/no." After 2 years of working on his personal computer, Jay wanted us to know some of his feelings.

I was sad. Mom and I are happy [to get my computer].

Jim T., age 14, reminded us that his oral speech was not very understandable outside family and friends.

It was hard to get the words out but when I got the [communicator] it got eseer [easier].

Of course, Jim still has to improve his spelling so that the community will understand him, but it's remarkably better than having people guess at his intentions!

Monica and her Porta-Tel.

Jim and his Canon Communicator.

One student, Monica S., age 14, acknowledges that her small minitypewriter now allows her the freedom to be quite verbal.

One day my father brought me a [communicator]. It opened my life because I can talk with it to any-one who can't intertian [understand] me. I have CP [cerebral palsy] and it infecks [affects] my vocter code [vocal cords].

I am in gril [girl] scout [s]. I stop all of my talking and tell you my name. My name is Monica. I have alot of things to say and I love my [communicator]. I hope I helped you with my grabing [gabbing].

John producing synthetic speech.

A high school student, John M., age 19, was a little reluctant to share his recent successes in communicating with girls, but he was willing to tell us this.

Before I got my [communicator] it was hard for me to talk to people who were not my family and my teachers. I got a [communicator] when I started high school. At first was hard for me to use it. Now it is easy. I think the [communicator] is a great machine. It help me talk to people.

Ivan with an experimental computer.

In addition to communication, another student, Ivan K., age 18, told me that his system was versatile enough to allow him to demonstrate skills in other ways.

Since the summer of 1982 I have had . . . [a] computer. Since I got it, I have been able to express myself more than ever. I can draw to show how I feel. The computer has been a great help to me.

Personal computer-based communication systems, like any custom-fitted aids, may not be appropriate for everyone with limited oral speech. Some factors, such as language delay or cognitive impairment, may prevent the acquisition of necessary prerequisite skills. In some cases language boards are more appropriate and can be considered precursors to the use of more sophisticated systems. The best decision, however, rests in the combined agreement of an interdisciplinary team comprised of parents, educators, speech-language pathologists, and appropriate allied health professionals such as doctors and physical and occupational therapists. Often the child can contribute ideas that determine the best fit.

No matter what the system, the desired outcome is the same: to produce an individual capable of communicating to the best of his or her potential with the greatest number of those in society willing to take time to listen. Granted, these are strange and new ways compared to the familiarity of speech. One unknown author showed considerable foresight in commenting:

Communicate—from me to you
Is socially the thing to do
And as the means to do it changed
Society was re-arranged!

Advances in technology have already resulted in the widespread use of computers and other assistive devices designed to help children with virtually every kind of speech and/or language disorder. Bull and Rushakoff (1987) report that about half of all professionals in speech and hearing currently use computers in their work. Some computers can be programmed with synthetic speech to enable previously nonspeaking children to express themselves by operating a keyboard or communication board. Other devices "understand" vocal commands. In addition, sophisticated software programs allow professionals to analyze a child's speech patterns and verbal language samples precisely so that appropriate programs of intervention can be devised. And computers and electronic communication aids appear to have a positively reinforcing value for many students and may encourage them to communicate more effectively even when they are not using the aid directly. Applications of technology in the field of communication disorders are sure to continue.

See the FOCUS feature on pages 242–44.

Currently, speech and language intervention programs are heavily oriented toward the preschool and school-age population. Although early detection and intervention will clearly remain a high priority among communication disorders specialists, there is a need for long-term studies to document the effectiveness of early intervention on later speech and language development. Relatedly, professionals are gradually becoming aware of the special speech and language needs of adolescents and adults, many of whom have untreated communication problems. The future will likely see increased attention on the assessment and treatment of speech and language disorders caused by the aging process.

SUMMARY

1. Communication is extremely important in human interaction.
2. Communication is any interaction that transmits information.
   a. Narrating, explaining, informing, and expressing are major communicative functions.
   b. A language is an arbitrary symbol system used to enable a group of people to communicate.
   c. Each language has rules of phonology, morphology, syntax, and semantics that describe how users put sounds together to convey meaning.
   d. Language can also be described in terms of its form, content, and use.
   e. Speech is the vocal response mode of language. It is the basis on which language develops.
3. Normal language development follows a relatively predictable sequence. Most children learn to use language without direct instruction.
   a. Infants soon learn to make sounds to communicate and to react to people's voices.
   b. They learn to babble, develop inflection, and can respond to familiar words and commands by the age of 1.
   c. By 1½ most babies can say several words; they use words and gestures to communicate certain needs.
   d. During the next 6 months many children go through a stage of echolalia. They learn to use short sentences, and their receptive vocabulary grows rapidly.

e. After the age of 2, vocabulary use increases greatly. Most preschool children learn to use progressively longer and more complex sentences. Correct pronunciation, however, takes longer to develop.

f. By the time most children enter first grade, their grammar and speech patterns match those of the adults around them.

4. Difficulties with speech and language can cause learning, behavioral, and social problems.

   a. A child has a speech disorder if his speech draws unfavorable attention to itself, interferes with the ability to communicate, or causes social or interpersonal problems.

   b. Some children have trouble understanding language (receptive language disorders); others have trouble using language to communicate (expressive language disorders). Still other children have language delays.

   c. Many language disordered children play a passive role in communication.

   d. Speech or language differences based on cultural dialects should not be considered communication disorders. However, children with dialects may also have speech or language disorders.

5. Children with communication disorders make up a large group of handicapped children. However, the number of these children decreases significantly as they get older. Many articulation disorders appear to resolve themselves as children mature.

6. Although some speech disorders have physical (organic) causes, most are considered functional disorders. They cannot be directly attributed to physical conditions.

7. There are several types of communication disorders.

   a. Articulation disorders, which are common, involve repeated incorrect utterances of speech sounds. They include omissions, substitutions, distortions, and additions of sounds.

   b. Voice disorders involve inappropriate or abnormal quality, loudness, or pitch of the voice. The most common are hoarseness, breathiness, and nasality.

   c. Fluency disorders, including stuttering, interrupt the normal rhythm or flow of speech.

   d. Language disorders include both receptive and expressive difficulties. A child may have either or both types. Children with language disorders do not follow the usual rate and sequence of language acquisition.

8. Treatment of communication disorders is a relatively new field.

   a. The professionals who work with communication disorders are called communication disorders specialists or speech-language pathologists, reflecting awareness of the interrelationships among speech, language, and learning.

   b. Today, intervention is being carried out increasingly in the regular classroom. The specialist works with the teacher rather than directly with the child.

9. Assessment of a child who is suspected of having a communication disorder may include some or all of the following components, depending on the nature of the disorder:

   a. case history

   b. physical examination

   c. articulation test

    d. hearing test

    e. auditory discrimination test

    f. language development test

    g. language test

    h. conversation with the child or language sample

    i. behavioral observation

    j. observation of parent-child interaction.

10. The different types of communication disorders call for different approaches to remediation. Behavioral approaches are frequently used.

    a. Children with articulation disorders are often taught to discriminate between sounds and practice making them correctly.

    b. Some voice disorders are treated medically; others, through educational programs involving auditory discrimination, self-monitoring, and modeling.

    c. Stuttering can be treated in several different ways. Some treatments seek to enable people to control their stuttering whereas others aim for the elimination of stuttering. It is important to help children feel comfortable and relaxed when speaking.

    d. Language disorders can also be treated in more than one way, but again it is important to reward children for any attempt at communication, to help them feel relaxed, and to encourage them to converse with other children. Both individual and group approaches are used.

    e. Effective teachers of children with communication disorders should encourage them to communicate by being genuinely interested in them, correcting errors unobtrusively, and making the children feel comfortable and important.

11. Most children with speech and language problems attend regular classes. The largest single group of communication disorders specialists are employed in schools.

    a. Some children receive special help from their regular teachers, special education teachers, and/or parents, who work with the communication disorders specialist. The specialist concentrates on assessment, evaluation, and guidelines for teachers and parents.

    b. In other programs the communication disorders specialist travels from school to school and gives direct individual or group therapy to the children. However, because this means that therapy is delivered in a clinical (rather than a natural) setting and only at certain times each week, this method is becoming less common.

    c. The speech and language specialist may also serve as a resource room teacher and may provide consultation to regular teachers.

12. In the future, communication disorders specialists will probably provide largely consultative services and in-service training, rather than direct one-to-one therapy. They will help train parents, teachers, and paraprofessionals to work with most children, while they concentrate on diagnosis, programming, and direct intensive services to a few children with special needs.

13. Advances in technology will spread the use of special devices to help individuals with communication disorders. Electronic devices are now widely used in analyzing children's speech and language and in providing instruction.

14. Older youths and adults with untreated speech and language problems represent a sizable population. It is hoped that they will receive more services in the coming years.

FOR MORE INFORMATION

Journals

Communication Outlook. Emphasizes the use of augmentative communication techniques and technology. Published quarterly by Artificial Language Laboratory, Computer Science Department, Michigan State University, East Lansing, MI 48824.

Journal of Speech and Hearing Disorders. Published quarterly by the American Speech-Language-Hearing Association (ASHA). Includes articles dealing with the nature, assessment, and treatment of communication disorders.

Language, Speech, and Hearing Services in the Schools. Also published quarterly by ASHA; focuses on practical applications of speech and language training and provides activities for teachers and specialists consistent with current research and theory.

Books

Berko Gleason, J. (1985). *The development of language.* Columbus, OH: Merrill.

Costello, J. M., & Holland, A. L. (Eds.). (1986). *Handbook of speech and language disorders.* San Diego: College-Hill.

Emerick, L. L., & Haynes, W. O. (1986). *Diagnosis and evaluation in speech pathology* (3rd ed.). Englewood Cliffs, NJ: Prentice-Hall.

Lindfors, J. W. (1987). *Children's language and learning* (2nd ed.). Englewood Cliffs, NJ: Prentice-Hall.

McCormick, L., & Schiefelbusch, R. L. (1984). *Early language intervention: An introduction.* Columbus, OH: Merrill.

McLauchlin, R. M. (Ed.). (1986). *Speech-language pathology and audiology: Issues and management.* Orlando, FL: Grune & Stratton.

Newman, P. W., Creaghead, N. A., & Secord, W. (1985). Assessment and remediation of articulatory and phonological disorders. Columbus, OH: Merrill.

Reed, V. A. (1986). *An introduction to children with language disorders.* New York: Macmillan.

Shames, G. H., & Rubin, R. (1986). *Stuttering then and now.* Columbus, OH: Merrill.

Van Riper, C., & Emerick, L. (1984). *Speech correction: An introduction to speech pathology.* Englewood Cliffs, NJ: Prentice-Hall.

Organizations

American Speech-Language-Hearing Association, 10801 Rockville Pike, Rockville, MD 20852. The major professional organization concerned with speech and language. Serves as a certifying agency for professionals who provide speech, language, and hearing services. Publishes several journals, sponsors research in communication disorders, and provides a comprehensive *Guide to Professional Services,* which also includes information on accredited training programs. Also sponsors the National Student Speech, Language, Hearing Association, which has chapters on many college and university campuses.

Division for Children with Communication Disorders, Council for Exceptional Children, 1920 Association Drive, Reston, VA 22091. Includes teachers and communication disorders specialists who work with exceptional children. Sponsors sessions at state, provincial, and national conferences. Publishes the *Journal of Childhood Communication Disorders* twice yearly.

Trace Research and Development Center, 314 Waisman Center, University of Wisconsin, Madison, WI 53706. Offers publications, in-service training, and information relating primarily to nonoral communication strategies for persons with severe speech and language impairments.

7

HEARING IMPAIRMENT

Nature attaches an overwhelming importance to hearing. As unborns we hear before we can see. Even in deep comas, people often hear what is going on around them. For most of us, when we die, the sense of hearing is the last to leave the body.

—Lou Ann Walker, *A Loss for Words*

As Lou Ann Walker, the child of deaf parents, observes in her recent autobiography, people who have normal hearing usually find it difficult to fully appreciate the enormous importance of the auditory sense in human development and learning. Many of us have simulated blindness by closing our eyes or donning a blindfold, but it is virtually impossible to switch off our hearing voluntarily.

Children learn a great deal by using their hearing, starting at birth. Newborn infants are able to respond to sounds by startling or blinking. At a few weeks of age, infants with normal hearing can listen to quiet sounds, recognize their parents' voices, and pay attention to their own gurgling and cooing sounds. During the first year of life, infants acquire much information by listening. They can recognize sounds of familiar people and objects, discriminate meaningful sound from background noise, and localize and imitate sounds (Lowell & Pollack, 1974).

As hearing children grow, they develop language by constantly hearing language used and by associating these sounds with innumerable activities and events. They learn that people convey information and exchange their thoughts and feelings by speaking and hearing. They attach meaning to sound. By the time hearing children reach school age, they are likely to have a vocabulary of over 5,000 words. And they have already had perhaps 100 million meaningful contacts with language (Napierkowski, 1981).

As we saw in the previous chapter, the process of language acquisition and development, though complex, occurs naturally and spontaneously in most children with normal hearing. Children with a hearing impairment, however, are not able to participate in this process without special help. They may acquire a good deal of information about the world but have few symbols or patterns available to help them in sending and receiving messages. They miss out on many early and critical opportunities for developing basic communication skills. Hans Furth (1973), a psychologist who devoted much of his career to studying the language development of hearing impaired people, suggests that a good way to approximate the experience of a child who is deaf from birth or early childhood is to watch a television program in which a foreign language is being spoken—with the sound on the TV set turned off! You would be faced with the double problem of reading lips and understanding an unfamiliar language.

Hearing is vital in every aspect of our daily existence. If you were unable to hear, you would, at best, find it difficult to participate fully in the activities of your school or college, your job, your neighborhood, and even your own family, unless some special adaptations were made. At worst, you might find that our society's great reliance on hearing and speech as avenues of communication made it virtually impossible for you to function effectively.

As Hoemann and Briga (1981) point out, the educational, vocational, and social development of a hearing impaired child is influenced by many factors in addition to the type and degree of hearing loss. These include the age at which the hearing impairment began, the attitudes of the child's parents and siblings, the opportunities available for the child to develop oral and manual communication skills, and the presence or absence of other disabilities. A child's potential can certainly not be predicted from a hearing test alone.

Today, many children with impaired hearing are identified in early childhood. They are often helped through surgery or the use of hearing aids. They may learn to communicate with their families and friends by using speech, speech reading, sign language, or other techniques. Many hearing impaired people achieve high levels of educational, professional, and personal success. But it is impossible to truly compensate or make up for the loss of hearing. The information and understanding that come through the auditory channel can never be fully replaced.

DEFINITIONS, TYPES, AND MEASUREMENT OF HEARING LOSS

There is no legal determination of the hearing impaired population. When we speak of a person with normal hearing, we generally mean that she has enough hearing to understand speech. Assuming that the listening conditions are adequate, a person with normal hearing does not need to rely on any special device or technique to interpret speech in everyday situations.

Deafness has been defined as a sensory deficiency that prevents a person from receiving the stimulus of sound in all or most of its forms (Katz, Mathis, & Merrill, 1978) and as a condition in which perceivable sounds (including speech) have no meaning for ordinary life purposes (Wolfe & Rawlings, 1986). A deaf person is not able to use his hearing to understand speech, although some sounds may be perceived. Even with a hearing aid the hearing loss is too great to allow a deaf person to understand speech through the ears alone. Quigley and Paul (1984) maintain that the

A deaf child's language development depends heavily on early identification and intervention.

term *deaf* should be applied only to those persons who process language by eye, rather than by ear.

A **hard-of-hearing** person has a significant hearing loss that makes some special adaptations necessary. However, as Berg (1986) points out, it is possible for a hard-of-hearing child to respond to speech and other auditory stimuli. "Communicatively, the hard-of-hearing child is more like the normal hearing child than like the deaf child, because both use audition rather than vision as the primary mode for speech and language development" (p. 3). In other words, the hard-of-hearing child's speech and language skills, though they may be delayed or deficient, are developed mainly through the auditory channel. Hard-of-hearing children are able to use their hearing to understand speech, generally with the help of a hearing aid.

Both deaf and hard-of-hearing children are said to be **hearing impaired.** This term, used mainly in education, indicates a child who needs special services because of a hearing loss. Most children in classes for the hearing impaired do have some degree of **residual hearing.**

When a hearing impairment goes undetected, some hard-of-hearing students are mistakenly considered to have learning disabilities or behavior disorders.

Even very slight levels of residual hearing can be useful.

A hearing impairment may also be described in terms of its age of onset. It is important to consider whether a hearing loss is congenital (present at birth) or **adventitious** (acquired later in life). A child who, from birth, is unable to hear the speech of other people will not be able to learn speech and language spontaneously, as do children with normal hearing. A child who acquires a hearing impairment after speech and language are well established will need help in adjusting to the hearing loss and in maintaining the ability to speak clearly.

Educators often use the term **prelingual** to refer to a hearing impairment that is present at birth or occurs before the development of speech and language, as opposed to a **postlingual** hearing impairment, which occurs after speech and language skills have been acquired through the sense of hearing. The educational program of a prelingually deaf child usually focuses on the acquisition of language and communication, whereas that of a postlingually deaf child usually emphasizes the maintenance of intelligible speech and appropriate language patterns.

Types of Hearing Impairment

There are two main types of hearing impairments, conductive and sensorineural. A **conductive hearing loss** results from obstructions or interference in the transmission of sound from the outer or middle ear into the inner ear. Figure 7.1 shows the parts of the human ear. A buildup of excessive wax in the auditory canal can cause a conductive hearing loss, as can a disease that leaves fluid or debris. Some children are born with incomplete or malformed auditory canals. As its name implies, a conductive hearing impairment involves a problem with conducting, or transmitting, sound vibrations to the inner ear. Because the rest of the auditory system is generally intact, conductive hearing losses can often be corrected through surgical or medical treatment. Hearing aids are usually helpful.

A **sensorineural hearing loss** can result from damage to the auditory nerve fibers or other sensitive mechanisms in the inner ear. The cochlea converts the physical characteristics of sound into corresponding neural information that the brain can process and interpret (Berg, 1986); impairment of the cochlea may mean that sound is delivered to the brain in a distorted fashion or is not delivered at all. Amplification—making the source of sound louder—may or may not help the person with a sensorineural hearing impairment. Unfortunately, most sensorineural hearing impairments cannot be corrected by surgery or medication.

It is possible for a child to have a mixed hearing loss, including both conductive and sensorineural impairments. Diagnosis of a mixed hearing loss is especially difficult, as there are problems with both the conduction and the processing of sound. Treatment must focus on both types of hearing loss.

Hearing impairment is also described in terms of its being unilateral (present in one ear only) or bilateral (present in both ears). Most children in special programs for the hearing impaired have bilateral losses, although the degree of impairment may not be the same in both ears. Children with unilateral hearing impairments generally learn speech and language without major difficulties, although they tend to have problems localizing sounds and listening in noisy or distracting settings. There is some recent

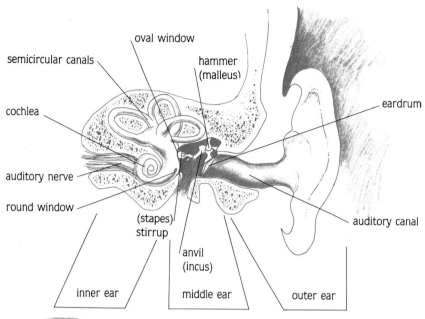

FIGURE 7.1

Parts of the human ear. The external part of the ear and the auditory canal make up the outer ear. The middle ear includes the eardrum, hammer, anvil, and stirrup. The inner ear includes the round window, the oval window, the semicircular canals, and the cochlea. Damage to any part can cause a hearing loss.

evidence to suggest that children with unilateral hearing impairments may be at a disadvantage in acquiring certain academic skills (Keller & Bundy, 1980).

Measuring Hearing Loss

Sound is measured in units that describe its intensity and frequency. Both are important in considering the needs of a child with impaired hearing. The intensity or loudness of sound is measured in **decibels (dB).** Zero dB represents the smallest sound the person with normal hearing can perceive. Larger dB numbers represent increasingly louder sounds. A low whisper 5 feet away registers about 10 dB, an automobile about 65 dB, and Niagara Falls about 90 dB. Conversational speech 10 to 20 feet away registers about 30 to 65 dB. A sound of about 125 dB or louder will cause pain to the average person. A person may have a loss of up to 25 dB (i.e., not be able to hear any sound of less than 25 dB) and still be considered to have hearing within the normal range (Davis & Silverman, 1970). The 25 dB level is often used in screening school children for hearing loss, although as Berg (1986) points out, such testing may fail to identify a sizable percentage of hard-of-hearing children.

In addition to the dB loss, it is always important to consider the listening environment, because background noise may cause additional problems for a child with a hearing impairment. Northern and Lemme (1982) observe that, for normally hearing adults, speech needs only to be 10 to 15 dB louder than background noise for them to listen and understand comfortably. For children with impaired hearing, it is likely that speech must be significantly louder than background noise, or they will not be able to attend to the message being transmitted.

The frequency, or pitch, of sounds is measured in cycles per second, or **hertz** units **(Hz).** One hertz is equal to one cycle per second. The lowest note on a piano has a frequency of about 30 Hz, middle C about 250 Hz, and the highest note about 4,000 Hz. Human beings are able to hear frequencies ranging from about 20 to 20,000 Hz (Davis & Silverman, 1970), but many of these audible sounds are outside the speech range, the frequency range where ordinary conversation takes place. A person who cannot hear very low sounds (such as foghorn) or very high sounds (such as a piccolo) may perhaps suffer some inconvenience but will not be significantly handicapped in education and everyday life. A person with a serious hearing loss in the speech range, however, is at a great disadvantage in communication.

The frequency range generally considered most important for hearing conversational speech is from 500 to 2,000 Hz. The sounds of English speech vary in their frequency level. For example, the /s/ phoneme (as in the word *sat*) is a high frequency sound, typically occurring between 4,000 and 8,000 Hz (Northern & Lemme, 1982). A child whose hearing loss is more severe in the higher frequencies will thus have particular difficulty in discriminating the /s/ sound. Conversely, phonemes such as /dʒ/ (the sound of the *j* in *jump*) and /m/ occur at low frequencies and will be more problematic for a person with a low-frequency hearing impairment. As you might expect, a student with a high-frequency impairment tends to hear men's voices more easily than women's voices.

IDENTIFICATION AND ASSESSMENT

An audiologist specializes in the evaluation of hearing ability and the treatment of impaired hearing.

The science of **audiology** has made many advances in recent years. The development of sophisticated instruments and techniques has enabled audiologists to detect and describe hearing impairments with increasing precision, even in infants and very young children. Most instruments used to test hearing now incorporate computers into their design (Kelly, 1987).

Two relatively recent audiological techniques have proven helpful in identifying hearing loss in infants and children. Evoked-response audiometry uses electrodes to sense slight electric signals that the auditory nerve generates in response to sound stimulation. Thus, the audiologist can detect hearing impairments in infants or in others who may not respond to conventional testing, because a voluntary response is not required. Impedance audiometry tests a child's middle ear function by inserting a small probe and pump to detect sound reflected by the eardrum. It is especially useful in detecting middle ear problems that can result in temporary or permanent conductive hearing loss (MacCarthy & Connell, 1984).

The earlier a hearing impairment is identified, the better are a child's chances for receiving treatment and thus developing good communication skills, appropriate behaviors, and satisfying social relationships. If a child's hearing impairment goes un-

In determining whether an infant has a hearing impairment, it is helpful for parents and teachers to have a knowledge of the normal sequence of auditory development. Audiologist Linda Cleeland has provided the following guide to behaviors that may be expected at certain ages. If a young child is not displaying these behaviors, it is advisable to have the child's hearing professionally tested.

1 Month

☐ will jump or startle in response to loud noises
☐ will begin to make gurgling sounds

3 Months

☐ will make babbling sounds
☐ will be aware of voices
☐ may quiet down to familiar voices close to ear
☐ stirs or awakens from sleep when there is a loud sound relatively close

6 Months

☐ makes vocal sounds when alone
☐ turns head toward sounds out of sight or when name is called and speaker is not visible
☐ vocalizes when spoken to directly

9 Months

☐ responds differently to a cheerful versus angry voice

☐ turns head toward sounds out of sight or when name is called and speaker is not visible
☐ tries to copy the speech sounds of others

12 Months

☐ can locate a sound source by turning head (whether the sound is at the side, above, or below ear level)
☐ ceases activity when parent's voice is heard
☐ recognizes own name
☐ uses single words correctly
☐ vocalizes emotions
☐ laughs spontaneously
☐ disturbed by nearby noises when sleeping
☐ attempts imitation of sounds and words
☐ understands some familiar phrases or words
☐ responds to music or singing
☐ increases babbling in type and amount

24 Months

☐ has more than 50 words in vocabulary
☐ uses two words together
☐ responds to rhythm of music
☐ uses voice for a specific purpose
☐ shows understanding of many phrases used daily in life
☐ plays with sound-making objects
☐ uses well-inflected vocalizations
☐ refers to himself/herself by name

FIGURE 7.2
Expected auditory behaviors.
Source: From "The Function of the Auditory System in Speech and Language Development" by L. K. Cleeland in *The Hearing-Impaired Child in School* (pp. 15–16) by R. K. Hull and K. I. Dilka (Eds.), 1984, Orlando, FL: Grune & Stratton. Reprinted by permission.

detected until the age of 5 or 6—the age at which children typically enter school—a great many valuable opportunities for learning will surely have been lost. Figure 7.2 offers a guide to auditory behaviors that should be present in infants with normal hearing. Failure to demonstrate these responses may mean that an infant's hearing is impaired.

Despite modern audiological techniques, hearing impairment still goes undetected in many children. All infants, hearing and deaf alike, babble, coo, and smile. Later on, deaf children tend to stop babbling and vocalizing because they cannot hear themselves or their parents, but a baby's silence may be mistakenly attributed to other causes. Unfortunately, many hearing impaired children have been erroneously labeled mentally retarded or emotionally disturbed. Some have even spent years inappropriately placed in institutions because nobody realized that their problem was deafness, rather than mental retardation or emotional disturbance. To avoid such misplacements in the future, efforts are continually made to conduct screening tests for hearing impairment and to educate doctors, teachers, and parents to recognize the signs of hearing loss in children.

Degrees of Hearing Impairment

When hearing is formally tested, the examiner exposes the child to sounds at different levels of intensity and frequency. The device that generates these sounds is called an **audiometer,** and the child's responses are recorded on a chart called an **audiogram.** The test seeks to determine how loud each sound must be before the child is able to hear it. A child with a hearing impairment does not begin to detect sounds until a high level of loudness—measured in decibels—is reached. For example, a child who has a 60 dB hearing loss cannot begin to detect a sound until it is at least 60 dB loud, in contrast to a child with normal hearing, who would detect that same sound at a level between 0 and 10 dB. To obtain a hearing level on an audiogram, the child must be able to detect a sound at that level at least 50% of the time.

An individual's hearing impairment is usually described by the terms slight, mild, moderate, severe, and profound, depending on the average hearing level, in decibels, throughout the frequencies most important for understanding speech (500 to 2,000 Hz). Table 7.1 presents the decibel levels associated with these degrees of hearing impairment and lists some likely effects of the hearing impairment on children's speech and language development, as well as considerations for educational programs.

No two children have exactly the same pattern of hearing, even if their responses on a hearing test are similar. Just as a single intelligence test does not provide sufficient information to plan a child's educational program, so a child's needs cannot be determined from an audiometric test alone. Success in communication and school achievement cannot be predicted simply by looking at an audiogram. Children hear sounds with differing degrees of clarity, and the same child's hearing ability may vary from day to day. Some children with very low levels of measurable hearing are able to benefit from hearing aids and can learn to speak. On the other hand, some children with less apparent hearing loss are not able to function well through the auditory channel and need to rely on vision as their primary means of communication.

The level of hearing loss required for children to be considered deaf for educational placement purposes has changed considerably over the past 20 years (Connor, 1986). In the 1960s many children with average hearing losses of 50, 60, or 70 dB

TABLE 7.1
Effects of hearing impairments.

Faintest Sound Heard	Effect on the Understanding of Language and Speech	Probable Educational Needs and Programs
27 to 40 dB (slight loss)	☐ May have difficulty hearing faint or distant speech ☐ Will not usually have difficulty in school situations	☐ May benefit from a hearing aid as loss approaches 40 dB ☐ Attention to vocabulary development ☐ Needs favorable seating and lighting ☐ May need speechreading instruction ☐ May need speech correction
41 to 55 dB (mild loss)	☐ Understands conversational speech at a distance of 3 to 5 feet (face to face) ☐ May miss as much as 50% of class discussions if voices are faint or not in line of vision ☐ May have limited vocabulary and speech irregularities	☐ Should be referred to special education for educational follow-up ☐ May benefit from individual hearing aid through evaluation and training in its use ☐ Favorable seating and possible special class placement, especially for primary-age children ☐ Attention to vocabulary and reading ☐ May need speechreading instruction ☐ Speech conservation and correction, if indicated
56 to 70 dB (moderate loss)	☐ Can understand loud conversation only ☐ Will have increasing difficulty with school group discussions ☐ Is likely to have impaired speech ☐ Is likely to have difficulty in language use and comprehension ☐ Probably will have limited vocabulary	☐ Likely to need resource teacher or special class ☐ Should have special help in language skills, vocabulary development, usage, reading, writing, grammar, etc. ☐ Can benefit from individual hearing aid through evaluation and auditory training ☐ Speechreading instruction ☐ Speech conservation and speech correction
71 to 90 dB (severe loss)	☐ May hear loud voices about 1 foot from the ear ☐ May be able to identify environmental sounds ☐ May be able to discriminate vowels but not all consonants ☐ Speech and language likely to be impaired or to deteriorate ☐ Speech and language unlikely to develop spontaneously if loss is present before 1 year of age	☐ Likely to need a special education program for hearing impaired children, with emphasis on all language skills, concept development, speechreading, and speech ☐ Needs specialized program supervision and comprehensive supporting services ☐ Can benefit from individual hearing aid through evaluation ☐ Auditory training on individual and group aids ☐ Part-time regular class placement as profitable

TABLE 7.1
continued

Faintest Sound Heard	Effect on the Understanding of Language and Speech	Probable Educational Needs and Programs
91 dB or more (profound loss)	☐ May hear some loud sounds but is aware of vibrations more than tonal pattern ☐ Relies on vision rather than hearing as primary avenue for communication ☐ Speech and language likely to be impaired or to deteriorate ☐ Speech and language unlikely to develop spontaneously if loss is prelingual	☐ Will need a special education program for deaf children, with emphasis on all language skills, concept development, speechreading, and speech ☐ Needs specialized program supervision and comprehensive supporting services ☐ Continuous appraisal of needs in regard to oral or manual communication ☐ Auditory training on individual and group aids ☐ Part-time regular class placement may be feasible

were routinely enrolled in special schools and classes for deaf children. Today, however, those children are regarded as hard-of-hearing rather than deaf, thanks to improved methods of testing, amplification, and teaching. According to Connor (1986), "Only children with losses greater than 90 dB who had prelingual losses should be considered deaf in the mid-1980s" (p. 124).

Figure 7.3 shows the audiogram of Vicki, a child with a *mild* hearing impairment. Vicki is able to understand face-to-face conversation with little difficulty but misses much of the discussion that goes on in her classroom—particularly if several children are speaking at once or if she cannot see the speaker clearly. Most of her friends are unaware that she has a hearing impairment. Vicki benefits from wearing a hearing aid and receives occasional speech and language assistance from a speech-language pathologist.

Figure 7.4 shows the audiogram of Raymond, a child with a *moderate* hearing impairment. Without his hearing aid Raymond can hear conversation only if it is loud and clear. He finds male voices easier to hear than female voices, because his loss is less severe in the lower frequencies. Raymond's teacher attempts to arrange favorable seating for him, but most class discussions are impossible for him to follow. Raymond attends a part-time special class for hearing impaired children and is in a regular classroom for part of the day.

Figure 7.5 shows the audiogram of Brenda, a child with a *severe* hearing impairment. Brenda can hear voices only if they are very loud and 1 foot or less from her ear. She wears a hearing aid, but it is uncertain how much she is gaining from it. She can distinguish most vowel sounds but hears only a few consonants. She can hear a door slamming, a vacuum cleaner, and an airplane flying overhead. She must always pay close visual attention to a person speaking with her. Brenda attends a full-time

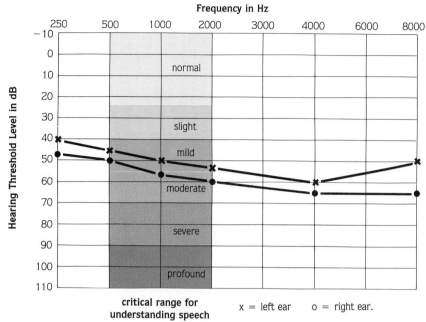

FIGURE 7.3

Audiogram for Vicki (mild hearing impairment).

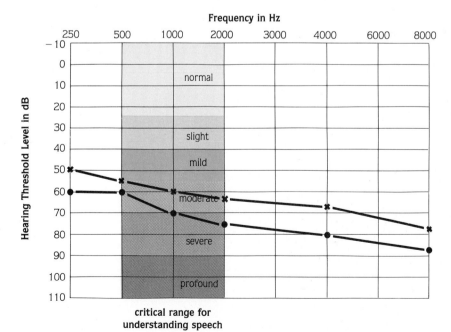

FIGURE 7.4

Audiogram for Raymond (moderate hearing impairment).

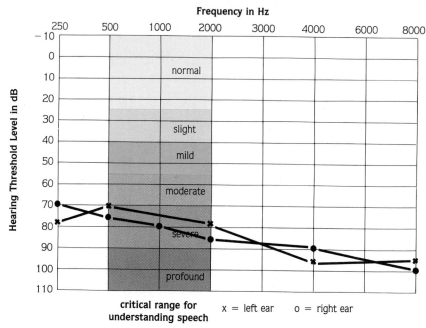

FIGURE 7.5
Audiogram for Brenda (severe hearing impairment).

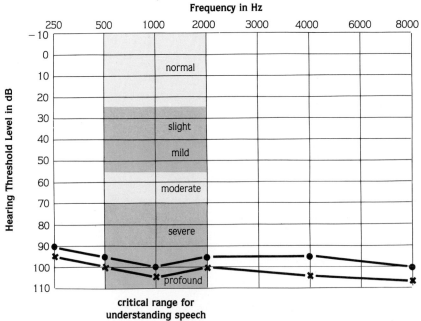

FIGURE 7.6
Audiogram for Steve (profound hearing impairment).

special class for hearing impaired children in a regular public school and interacts with nonhandicapped children in several activities.

Figure 7.6 shows the audiogram for Steve, a child with a *profound* hearing impairment. Steve cannot hear conversational speech at all. His hearing aid seems to help him be aware of certain loud sounds, such as a fire alarm or a bass drum. Steve's hearing impairment is congenital, and he has not developed intelligible speech. He attends a residential school for deaf children and uses sign language as his principal means of communication.

PREVALENCE

Several authorities have concluded that approximately 5% of all school-age children have hearing impairments (Bensberg & Sigelman, 1976; Davis & Silverman, 1970). However, many of these impairments are not considered severe enough to require special education services. Hoemann and Briga (1981) estimate that only about 0.2% of the school-age population (i.e., 1 child in 500) has a severe or profound hearing impairment. A recent report (Ries, 1986) estimated that there were 129,000 school-age children in the United States who could "at best hear and understand shouted speech" and included among these 22,000 who "could not hear and understand any speech" (p. 8). Males, black students, and children aged 6 to 11 were found to be somewhat overrepresented in the hearing impaired group, in comparison to their proportions in the general population.

For every child identified as deaf, there are probably six or seven children who are hard-of-hearing and who may need certain special education services. Surveys suggest that although over 90% of the children in the United States identified as deaf are receiving special services, the percentage of hard-of-hearing children receiving special services may be only 20% or less (Berg, 1986; Moores, 1987). It is likely, then, that a significant number of hearing impaired students in regular classes may not be receiving the special assistance they need for effective learning and adjustment. One educator describes the hard-of-hearing child as "the most neglected exceptional child in our public day school system other than the gifted" (Gonzales, 1980, p. 20). Most school districts do not have many hearing impaired students among their population and may find it difficult to provide a wide range of supportive services, personnel, and materials.

Refer to chapter 2 for guidelines on placing students in the least restrictive environment.

CAUSES OF HEARING IMPAIRMENT

There are many causes of hearing impairment. These vary somewhat from region to region and have changed over the years. According to Brown (1986), four prevalent causes of deafness and severe hearing impairment in children warrant special attention.

1. *Maternal rubella*. This is the single greatest cause of deafness in the current population of children and youth in the United States. Although rubella (also known as German measles) has symptoms that are relatively mild, it has been shown to cause

deafness, visual impairment, heart disorders, and a variety of other serious disabilities when it affects a woman during pregnancy, particularly during the first 3 months. A major epidemic of rubella took place in the United States and Canada between 1963 and 1965. The children who were born with disabilities at that time are now young adults who are gradually leaving special education programs. However, maternal rubella continues to be a significant cause of hearing impairment. An effective vaccination for rubella is available, but many women of childbearing age fail to receive it.

2. *Hereditary causes.* There is strong evidence that congenital hearing impairment runs in some families. A tendency toward certain types of adventitious hearing loss may also be inherited. Various surveys have found that a high percentage of deaf students have relatives who are also hearing impaired; Moores (1987) places this number at about 30% of the school-age population of deaf students. More than 50 types of hereditary or genetic deafness have been identified. Brown (1986) considers this to be "the most internally varied group" (p. 53) and one in which additional handicapping conditions are not frequent.

3. *Prematurity* and *complications of pregnancy.* These factors appear to increase the risk of deafness and other disabling conditions. It is difficult to precisely evaluate the effects of prematurity on hearing impairment, but early delivery and lower birth weight have been found to be more common among deaf children than among the general population. Complications of pregnancy arise from a variety of causes.

4. *Meningitis.* The leading cause of adventitious hearing impairment is **meningitis.** It is a bacterial or viral infection that can, among its other effects, destroy the sensitive acoustic apparatus of the inner ear. Difficulties in balance may also be present. Brown (1986) reports that children whose deafness is caused by meningitis generally have profound hearing losses but are not likely to have additional handicapping conditions.

Another significant cause of hearing impairment is **otitis media,** an infection or inflammation of the middle ear. If untreated, otitis media can result in a buildup of fluid and a ruptured eardrum, causing permanent conductive hearing impairment.

Causes of hearing impairment that appear to have declined in recent years because of improved medical treatment include blood (Rh) incompatibility between mother and child, mumps, and measles. On the other hand, the percentages of students with deafness caused by meningitis, heredity, and otitis media appear to be increasing. In addition, some factors related to people's environments and activities are regarded as growing causes of hearing loss. Noise pollution—repeated exposure to loud sounds, such as industrial noise, jet aircraft, guns, or amplified music—is increasing as a cause of hearing impairment. Damage to hearing can also result from frequent deep-sea diving; Edmonds (1985) found that more than 70% of professional divers had evidence of sensorineural high-frequency deafness.

Hearing impairment occurs more often than would be expected among certain other populations of handicapped children. Down syndrome often involves irregularities in the auditory canal and a tendency for fluid to accumulate in the middle ear; as

See chapter 10 for more information on children with multiple handicaps.

many as 75% of children with Down syndrome may also have significant hearing impairments (Northern & Lemme, 1982). Among children with cerebral palsy, there is also a substantially higher-than-normal incidence of hearing impairment. It is always advisable to test the hearing of any child who is referred for special education services.

BACKGROUND OF THE FIELD

Deaf children and adults have long been a source of fascination and interest. One of the earliest educational programs for exceptional children of any kind was a school for the deaf children of noble families that was established in Spain around 1578 by Pedro Ponce de León. In order for children to be recognized as persons under the law and be eligible to inherit their families' titles and fortunes, it was necessary for them to be able to speak and read. Ponce de León reportedly achieved success in teaching speech, writing, reading, arithmetic, and foreign languages to some deaf students (Hewett & Forness, 1977; Sacks, 1986). During the 18th century, schools for deaf children were set up in England, France, Germany, Holland, and Scotland. Both oral and manual methods of instruction were used.

Deaf children were among the first groups of handicapped individuals to receive special education in the United States, also. The American Asylum for the Education of the Deaf and Dumb opened in Hartford, Connecticut, in 1817. The original name of this institution indicates the prevailing philosophy of the early 19th century, when deaf persons were viewed as dumb, or mute, incapable of benefiting from oral instruction. At that time deaf students were considered most appropriately served in asylums, special sanctuaries removed from normal society. Many of the private, public, and parochial schools for the deaf founded in the 19th century were, in fact, located in small towns, away from major centers of population. For the most part these were residential institutions.

This school, more than 170 years old, is now known as the American School for the Deaf.

During the second half of the 19th century, instruction in speech and speech-reading became widely available to deaf students throughout the United States. In fact, oral approaches to education of hearing impaired students came to dominate professional thought to such a great degree that the use of sign language in schools was officially prohibited at an international conference held in 1880. A particularly influential figure during this era was Alexander Graham Bell, the inventor of the telephone, who had a lifelong interest in deafness. His mother was deaf, and his father and grandfather were teachers of speech and articulation. Bell himself married Mabel Hubbard, a deaf student whom he had tutored. Before the end of the 19th century, several day schools for deaf students were established. In general, however, the late 19th century brought about an "increasing isolation of deaf children from their families and from society at large" (Moores & Kluwin, 1986, p. 106). And it was not until many years later that most schools relaxed their restrictions against the use of sign language.

Decibels are named for Alexander Graham Bell.

Today, few schools strictly prohibit deaf students from using sign language.

Educational opportunities for deaf children in regular public schools have become widespread only in recent years. In most areas of the United States, parents now have the option of choosing between local public school programs and residential school placement, in accordance with the least-restrictive-environment concept. Today, more than 60% of the deaf children in the United States attend local school programs, and most of these children are integrated into regular classrooms at least part of the time (Moores, 1987; Quigley & Paul, 1986). About one-third of the children who attend residential schools do so as day students (Schildroth, 1986); that is, they live at home with their families while attending the special school program.

Today, increasing attention is given to the needs of hearing impaired students with additional handicapping conditions, such as mental retardation, learning disabilities, behavior disorders, and physical, health, and visual impairments. Around 30% of the children currently enrolled in schools and classes for hearing impaired students are considered to be multihandicapped (Orlansky, 1986; Schildroth, 1986). Many programs also seek to meet the needs of the sizable population of hearing impaired children from culturally diverse backgrounds. The challenge of teaching communication skills to a deaf child when a language other than English is spoken in the home is particularly complex.

Over the years many special methods and materials have been developed for and used with hearing impaired children, and much research has been conducted. Techniques, theories, and controversies have proliferated, often with passionate proponents. Today, interest in deaf people is as high as ever. Yet we still do not fully understand the effects of hearing impairment on learning, communication, and personality, nor have we solved the most difficult problem inherent in educating deaf students: *teaching language to children who cannot hear.*

The present state of special education for hearing impaired children is not a happy one. Many deaf students leave school unable to read and write English proficiently. According to Quigley and Paul (1986), there has been no general improvement in the academic achievement levels of hearing impaired students in recent years: "The average deaf student completing a secondary education program is still performing at a level similar to the average 9 or 10 year old hearing student" (pp. 81–82). Many deaf students are not able to communicate effectively, perhaps not even with schoolmates or members of their own families. Many parents are given confusing, contradictory information and advice when it is discovered that their children have hearing impairments; identification of a deaf child is often devastating for parents. The rate of unemployment and underemployment among deaf adults is shockingly high, and their wages are often lower than those of the hearing population. Many questions remain unanswered, and many challenges remain to be faced in the education of children with hearing impairments.

Chapter 12 contains further information about children from bilingual backgrounds.

AMPLIFICATION AND AUDITORY TRAINING

Deafness is often mistakenly considered to be a total lack of hearing. In years past it was assumed that deaf children simply did not hear at all; that they were "stone deaf." This view was incorrect. We now know that hearing loss occurs in many different degrees and patterns. Nearly all children who are classified as deaf have some amount of residual hearing. With help, they need not grow up in a "silent world."

Modern methods of testing hearing and improved electronic technology for the amplification of sound enable many hearing impaired children today to use their residual hearing productively. Even children with severe and profound hearing impairments can benefit from hearing aids in the classroom, home, and community, regardless of whether they communicate primarily in an oral or manual mode. Ross (1986) considers residual hearing to be the "biologic birthright" of every hearing impaired child, and one that "should be used and depended on to whatever extent possible" (p. 51). It is important for teachers and audiologists to cooperate with each other in reaching this goal.

A hearing aid is an amplification instrument; that is, it functions to make sounds louder. Levitt (1985) describes the hearing aid as "the most widely used technological aid of all. . . . a low cost, acoustic amplification system that can be programmed to best match the needs of each user" (pp. 120–121). There are dozens of different kinds of hearing aids; they can be worn behind the ear, in the ear, on the body, or in eyeglasses. Children can wear hearing aids in one or both ears (monaural or binaural aids). Today's hearing aids are generally smaller and lighter in weight than older models, yet they are also more powerful and versatile. Whatever its shape, power, or size, a hearing aid picks up sound, magnifies its energy, and delivers this louder sound to the user's ear and brain. In many ways the hearing aid is like a miniature public address system, with a microphone, an amplifier, and controls to adjust volume and tone (Clarke & Leslie, 1980).

Although recent advances in hearing aid design have been remarkable, it is important to keep in mind that the aids have certain limitations. No hearing aid can cure a hearing loss or by itself enable a deaf child to function normally in a regular classroom. Some deaf students, even with the best available hearing aids, are unable to hear speech because of the kind and degree of their hearing loss. Learning to use residual hearing effectively is a difficult and demanding process, but one that pays worthwhile dividends for the many hearing impaired students who are able to develop an awareness of sound through good amplification, training, and practice. These procedures can also enable many hearing impaired students to improve the quality of their own speech.

Group hearing aids, or classroom amplification systems, are widely used also. In most systems a radio link is established between the teacher and the hearing impaired children, with the teacher wearing a small microphone-transmitter (often on the lapel, near the lips) and each child wearing a receiver that doubles as a personal hearing aid (Ross, 1986). An FM radio frequency is usually employed, and wires are not required; so the teacher and students can move freely around the classroom area. Classroom amplification systems are used both in special classes and in mainstream settings where hearing impaired students are integrated with nonhandicapped students.

Hearing aids can be helpful to many children in increasing their awareness of sound. The aids make sounds louder, but not necessarily clearer. Thus, children who hear sounds with distortion will still experience distortion with hearing aids. The effect is similar to turning up the volume on a cheap transistor radio—you can make the music louder, but you cannot make the words clearer. And even the most powerful hearing aids generally cannot enable children with severe and profound hearing losses to hear speech sounds beyond a distance of a few feet. In all cases it is the wearer of the hearing aid—not the aid itself—that does most of the work in interpreting conversation.

To derive the maximum benefit from a hearing aid, a child should wear it throughout the day. Residual hearing cannot be effectively developed if the aid is removed or turned off outside the classroom. It is important for the child to hear sounds while eating breakfast, shopping in the supermarket, or riding the school bus. Financial assistance from local or state agencies is often available for the purchase and maintenance of hearing aids.

The earlier in life a child can be fitted with an appropriate hearing aid, the more effectively she will learn to use hearing for communication and awareness. Today it is not at all unusual to see hearing aids worn by infants and preschool children; the improved listening conditions become an important part of the young child's speech and language development. A worthwhile goal is to provide for a child a sense of hearing that is "integrated into the personality" (Lowell & Pollack, 1974).

Auditory training helps children make better use of their residual hearing. All hearing impaired children, whatever their preferred method of communication, should participate in lessons and activities that help them improve their listening ability and, especially, recognize speech sounds. As Ross (1981) observes, many hearing impaired children have much more auditory potential than they actually use, and their residual hearing can be most effectively developed in the context of actual communication and daily experiences. An auditory training program should not be limited to artificial exercises in the classroom.

Teachers can help parents recognize opportunities for auditory training around the house.

An auditory training program for a young hearing impaired child is likely to emphasize the awareness of sound. Parents might direct their child's attention to such sounds as a doorbell ringing or water running. They might then focus on the localization of sound, for example, by hiding a radio somewhere in the room and encouraging the child to look for it. Discrimination of sounds is another important concept; a child might learn to notice the differences between a man's voice and a woman's voice, between a fast song and a slow song, or between the words *rack* and *rug*. Recognition of sounds comes when a child is able to identify a sound, word, or sentence through listening.

Some teachers find it helpful to conduct formal auditory training sessions, in which a child is required to use *only* hearing—he would have to recognize sounds and words without looking at the speaker. In actual practice, however, the student gains useful information from vision and the other senses to supplement the information received from hearing. Consequently, all senses should be effectively developed and constantly used.

Speechreading

Conversely, as chapter 8 explains, visually impaired children rely heavily on their sense of hearing.

Hearing impaired children, whether they have much or little residual hearing and whether they communicate primarily through oral or manual means, use their vision to help them understand speech. Some sounds are readily distinguished by watching the lips of the speaker. For example, the word *pail* begins with the lips in a shut position, whereas in the word *rail* the lips are somewhat drawn together and puckered at the corners. Paying careful attention to a speaker's lips may help a hearing impaired person derive important clues—particularly if she is also able to gain some information through residual hearing, signs or gestures, facial expressions, and familiarity with the context or situation.

Speechreading, or lipreading, however, is difficult and has many limitations. As Walker (1986) observes, even the best speechreaders detect only about 25% of what is said through visual clues alone; "the rest is contextual piecing together of ideas and expected constructions" (p. 19). To make matters worse, about half of all English words have some other word(s) that appear the same in pronunciation; that is, they may sound quite different, but they look alike on the lips. Words such as *bat*, *mat*, and *pat*, for example, look exactly alike and simply cannot be discriminated by watching the speaker's lips.

The frustrations of lipreading are graphically described in this passage by Shanny Mow (1973), a teacher who is deaf.

> Like the whorls on his fingertips, each person's lips are different and move in a peculiar way of their own. When young, you build confidence as you guess correctly "ball," "fish," and "shoe" on your teacher's lips. This confidence doesn't last. As soon as you discover there are more than four words in the dictionary, it evaporates. Seventy percent of the words when appearing on the lips are no more than blurs. Lipreading is a precarious and cruel art which rewards a few who have mastered it and tortures the many who have tried and failed. (pp. 21–22)

And many speakers are virtually unintelligible through speechreading; they may seem not to move their lips at all. In addition, it is extremely tiring to watch lips for a long period of time, and it may be impossible to do so at a distance, such as during a lecture.

Despite the problems inherent in speechreading, it can be a valuable adjunct in the communication of a hearing impaired person. According to Moores (1987), few new techniques have been developed recently, and little research has been done into the most effective ways of teaching speechreading. Although speechreading cannot take the place of hearing, improved methods might well enable many hearing impaired people to make better use of their vision in decoding messages.

In the future, technology may become available to facilitate speechreading.

EDUCATIONAL APPROACHES

Teaching hearing impaired children is one of the most "special" areas of special education. As Samuel Kirk (1981) observes,

> Special education has been defined as that education which is unique, uncommon, or of unusual quality and is in addition to the procedures used with the majority of children. The special techniques that have been developed over the years to assist deaf children in processing information without the sense of hearing are certainly unique, ingenious, and highly specialized. (p. xi)

Effects of Hearing Impairment on Language, Education, and Social Development

See "Jennifer: A Mother's Story" on pp. 271–72 for a parent's description of her hearing impaired child's development.

The effects of hearing impairment—especially if severe and present from birth—are so complex and pervasive that special techniques, materials, and people are indeed called for. It is perhaps impossible for a person with normal hearing to fully comprehend the immense difficulties faced by a deaf child trying to learn language. Hearing children typically acquire a large vocabulary and a knowledge of grammar, word order, idiomatic expressions, fine shades of meaning, and many other aspects of verbal expression by listening to others and to themselves from early infancy. A child with a hearing impairment, however, is exposed to verbal communication only partially or not at all.

According to Moores (1985), four conditions appear to be most closely related to the academic success of hearing impaired students.

1. *The severity of the hearing impairment.* The greater the hearing loss, the more likely the child is to experience difficulty in learning language and academic skills.
2. *The age at the onset of the hearing loss.* A child who is hearing impaired from birth or who loses his hearing before acquiring speech and language is at a greater disadvantage than a child with a postlingual hearing impairment.
3. *The socioeconomic status of the family.* A hearing impaired child whose parents are affluent and college educated is more likely to achieve academic success than a child from a low-income, less-educated family.
4. *The hearing status of the parents.* A deaf child with deaf parents is considered to have better chances for academic success than a deaf child with normally hearing parents—particularly if the deaf parents are highly educated.

Hearing impaired children—even those with superior intelligence and abilities— are at a great disadvantage in acquiring language skills. When standard measures of reading and writing achievement are used with deaf students, examiners typically find that the students' vocabularies are smaller and their sentence structures are simpler and more rigid than those of hearing children of the same age or grade level (Meadow, 1980). However, caution should always be used in comparing the test scores of deaf and hearing children. Geers (1985) notes that the relatively poor performance of deaf children on tests that were normed on hearing children has led teachers to expect too little of these children. For many deaf children "it is more informative to define their strengths and weaknesses in relation to other hearing impaired children than in relation to their age mates with normal hearing" (Geers, 1985, p. 57).

As Norris (1975) points out, the grammar and structure of English often do not follow logical rules, and a prelingually hearing impaired person must put forth a great deal of effort to read and write with acceptable form and meaning. For example, if the past tense of *talk* is *talked*, then why doesn't *go* become *goed*? If the plural of *man* is *men*, then shouldn't the plural of *pan* be *pen*? It is far from easy to explain the difference between the expressions "He's in" and "He's all in" to a person who has never had normal hearing.

JENNIFER: A MOTHER'S STORY

Jennifer, (not her real name) has a severe congenital hearing impairment. She is now in her mid-twenties, successfully employed as a clerk with a government agency. In this account Jennifer's mother recalls some of her early experiences.

Jennifer was my first child. Just as many people learn parenting with their first child, I was flying blind all the way with her. Parents' initial reactions vary only in the ways we declare our ignorance. I remember another mother who said that, when they learned of their child's hearing loss, her husband's first remark was, "Where will we ever find a deaf Jewish boy for her?" I thought a hearing aid and school for the deaf would be the answer.

My daughter was born 9 weeks early, so the fact that she was late developing in many ways didn't alarm me or the doctor. When she had no speech at age 2½, I began taking her to specialists, and I was always told to return in 6 months.

When Jennifer was 3½, I took her to a medical center in Toronto, expecting at best a cure and at worst an accurate diagnosis. She was seen by a neurologist, a speech therapist, and an ophthalmologist. They told me her main problem was receptive aphasia, complicated by a high-frequency hearing loss. They recommended speech therapy and assured me she was not mentally retarded.

So Jennifer began having speech therapy—half an hour a week. It was about as significant as putting a pail of water on an acre of potatoes, but she enjoyed it and seemed to try very hard.

At age 5 Jennifer really had no speech, so we arranged with a nursery school teacher to have her in her class. She wasn't accepted by the other children, but she loved going. The next year she still wasn't ready for public school, and we couldn't get her back into the nursery school, so we appealed to the parochial school system. With perhaps a 25-word vocabulary she certainly wasn't ready for first grade, but they took her.

By the time Jennifer was 10 years old, she was struggling unsuccessfully with fourth grade work. At this point I had six younger children and no time to give her much help. I was quite devastated by this; I didn't realize that what she missed from me, she gained from her constant exposure to other children. She became a very good lipreader by being continually exposed to oral speech.

We had never considered the school for the deaf for Jennifer, because the speech therapists advised strongly against sending her there. And we still were thinking of her main problem as brain damage (aphasia). At about this time she was seen by a specialist who said her problem was hearing loss only and not aphasia. He told us to send her to the school for the deaf. It was called an oral school, but signing was used almost exclusively. The pupils—most of whom had been there since age 5—did not communicate orally.

Jennifer was at the school for the deaf for 4 months. There she learned to sign, which was good for her, since most people in the deaf community are not oral. She was very unhappy at the school for the deaf, though. She couldn't relate to the silent atmosphere. She wasn't accepted by the other pupils because she could speak and they couldn't. If we had left her there, she would have lost her speech from lack of use.

We next heard that special classes for hearing impaired children were starting in our home town. My husband made several inquiries but was unable to find out anything concrete. At the beginning of the following school year, we kept Jennifer home as a form of protest. She was so upset that she made herself ill. She always wanted to go to school, and we couldn't communicate with her well enough to explain the situation. We tried tutoring and various private schools.

When Jennifer was 13, we learned through a friend that outreach classes for hearing impaired children had been started in the public schools. That September my husband delivered her to school, prepared to insist that she be admitted.

They took her in, just as though they had been expecting her. So at 13 years old, Jennifer began her first meaningful schooling.

Jennifer's first teacher was an outstanding middle-aged woman who knew, from hard experience, how to reach her pupils. Most of the other teachers were younger women, and Jennifer related to them very well. She was the oldest pupil there, and she enjoyed helping with the younger children.

Jennifer received a ninth grade equivalency certificate, but she was not encouraged to go to high school, as no resource help was available. The vocational teacher thought a course in child care might be beneficial, so Jennifer took one the next year. She worked at a day-care center but felt she was being exploited—cleaning pet cages, bathrooms, and so on. She then had a series of simple jobs. Finally she took a course to become a clerk-typist. But she was unable to obtain a job, because most offices demand that employees use the telephone. She spent months at home, pursuing her job placement officer. Eventually she took a temporary job with the Civil Service Commission that got extended. Now, a year later, she is on the permanent staff and has received a couple of promotions.

I think my daughter is well adjusted. She enjoys her work and the people at her office. She is the first hearing impaired person to be employed by the local Civil Service Commission and is very proud to be able to do the work. She feels she is accepted by the staff and not labeled specially.

Today's educational opportunities seem quite wonderful to me, compared to what was available back then. And it is a delight for me to see the changes in educators' attitudes, compared with the uninformed people I dealt with a decade or two ago. Then I was afraid of being at all forceful, for fear of jeopardizing my child's situation or being classed as overprotective and biased. The situation today is healthier and allows a beneficial mutual exchange of information.

If I were my daughter, I'd be asking, "Why was I born too soon, to miss all these advantages?" Jennifer is aware of what is happening, as she keeps in touch with her former teachers and the young students she helped with. She is only happy for them.

The hearing impaired people I have known have more empathy for our problems than we have for theirs. They are warm, caring people. I think these exceptional children become exceptional adults when we give them a chance. If we could walk in their shoes, they would have an easier time living in our world.

Many deaf students tend to write sentences that are short, incomplete, or improperly arranged. They may omit endings of words, such as the plural -s, -ed, or -ing. They may have difficulty in differentiating questions from statements. The following excerpts from papers written by deaf high school students illustrate some language problems directly attributable to impaired hearing.

> She is good at sewing than she is at cooking.
> Many things find in Arkansas.
> To his disappointed, his wife disgusted of what he made.
> I was happy to kiss my parents because they letted my playing football. (Fusfeld, 1958, cited in Meadow, 1980, p. 33)

Because language development is closely related to reading and to achievement in all academic areas, many investigators have found that hearing impaired children are, as a group, significantly behind normally hearing children on standardized tests of reading and academic achievement. Reading is clearly central to educational achievement and to obtaining information throughout life; we must continue to seek more effective ways of teaching reading and writing to hearing impaired students. However, it is important that we not equate verbal performance with intelligence. Most deaf children have normal intellectual capacity, and it has been repeatedly demonstrated that their scores on nonverbal intelligence tests are approximately the same as those of the general population. Deafness "imposes no limitations on the cognitive capabilities of individuals" (Moores, 1987). The problems that deaf students often experience in their education and adjustment may be largely attributable to a bad fit between their perceptual abilities and the demands of spoken and written English (Hoemann & Briga, 1981). Command of English is only one indicator of a person's intelligence and ability.

Social and Psychological Factors

Impaired hearing can also influence a child's behavior and social-emotional development. Research has not provided clear insights into the effects of hearing impairment on behavior. However, it appears that the extent to which a hearing impaired child successfully interacts with family members, friends, and people in the community depends largely on the attitudes of others and the child's ability to communicate in some mutually acceptable way. Deaf children of deaf parents are thought to have higher levels of social maturity, adjustment to deafness, and behavioral self-control than do deaf children of hearing parents, largely because of the early use of manual communication between parent and child that is usually found in homes with deaf parents. In the opinion of Schlesinger (1985) and other psychologists, "Most deaf parents welcome their deaf children and are not rendered powerless or helpless by them" (p. 108).

Feelings of depression, withdrawal, and isolation are frequently expressed by hearing impaired persons, particularly those who experience adventitious loss of hearing (Meadow-Orlans, 1985). A study of more than 1,000 deaf adolescents who were considered to be disruptive in the classroom (Kluwin, 1985) found that the most important related factor was reading ability; that is, students who were poorer readers were more likely to exhibit problem behaviors in school. Some observers have noted that deaf people often tend to associate primarily with other deaf people; this may be mistakenly viewed as clannishness. Certainly, communication plays a major role in any person's adjustment.

Most hearing impaired people are fully capable of developing positive relationships with their hearing peers when a satisfactory method of communication can be used. A number of deaf children do have serious behavior disorders that require treatment. Unfortunately, however, there are relatively few specialists in the identification and treatment of behavior disorders who are able to communicate easily and directly with deaf people, so the special needs of this population remain largely unmet.

Special Methods

Educational programs and techniques for hearing impaired students are special primarily because of the many challenges involved in teaching communication to children who cannot hear normally. Educators, scientists, philosophers, and parents—both hearing and deaf—have for many years debated the most appropriate instructional methods for deaf children. Today, this controversy is as lively as ever.

The fundamental disagreement concerns the extent to which deaf children should express themselves through speech and perceive the communication of others through speechreading and residual hearing. Some educators insist that a purely oral method is best for helping deaf students develop speech and language-related skills. These oralists often discourage the use of sign language and gestures. Other educators believe that sign language, gestures, cues, fingerspelling, and other manual means used along with speech are a more natural way of communicating and enable hearing impaired children to express themselves more fully and to understand other people.

Virtually no responsible educator today would argue that speech is unimportant or that manual communication should be used *in place of* speech. Speech is, of course, the principal way that people communicate; it can be of great value to a deaf person in moving into a less restrictive educational and living environment. We view the controversy over instructional methods as a difference of opinion over the *degree* to which speech should be emphasized in the education of hearing impaired children.

Oral Approaches

Educational programs with an **oral** emphasis view speech as essential for the deaf person's integration into the hearing world. Training in producing and understanding speech and language is incorporated into virtually all aspects of the child's education. Currently, a predominantly oral approach is used in about one-third of the educational programs for hearing impaired children in the United States (Reagan, 1985). Connor (1986) observes that the use of speech and the development of oral receptive skills have declined markedly in recent years as more and more educational programs for hearing impaired students rely on sign language systems to transmit instructional information.

A hearing impaired child who attends a program with an oral emphasis typically uses several means to develop residual hearing and the ability to speak as intelligibly as possible. Auditory, visual, and tactual methods of input are frequently used. Much attention is given to amplification, auditory training, speechreading, the use of technological aids, and—above all—talking. Parent and family involvement tends to be strongly emphasized in oral education. A few schools and classes maintain a purely oral environment and may even prohibit children from pointing, using gestures, or spelling out words to communicate. In these programs the children must express themselves and learn to understand others through speech alone. Other programs also emphasize speech but are more flexible. They may use a variety of approaches to help the students produce and understand spoken language.

Cued speech is a method of supplementing oral communication. It seeks to supply a visual representation of spoken language by adding cues, in the form of hand signals near the chin, to assist the deaf person in identifying sounds that cannot be distinguished through speechreading. The hand signals must be used in conjunction with speech; they are neither signs nor manual alphabet letters and cannot be read alone. Eight different hand shapes are used to identify consonant sounds, and four different locations identify vowel sounds. A hand shape coupled with a location gives a visual indication of a syllable. See Figure 7.7 for a representation of cued speech.

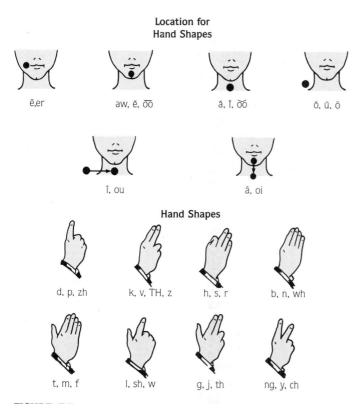

FIGURE 7.7

Total communication is emphasized in many educational programs.

According to Cornett (1974), who developed the system, cued speech can clarify the patterns of spoken English and give intensive language input to young children. It does not disrupt the natural rhythm of speech. Of course, the cues must be learned by the child's parents and teachers and preferably by her peers as well. Reportedly, cued speech can be learned in 10 to 20 hours of instruction. Although it is advocated by a number of active parent groups, the system has not become highly popular in the United States (Calvert, 1986). It is widely used in educational programs for hearing impaired children in Australia.

Educators who use an oral approach acknowledge that teaching speech to hearing impaired children is difficult, demanding, and time-consuming for the teacher, the parents, and—most of all—the student. Speech comes hard to the deaf child, and no recent breakthrough has made the task any easier (Calvert, 1986). The rewards of successful oral communication, however, are thought to be worth all the effort. And indeed, many hearing impaired children and adults are able to learn speech well enough to communicate effectively with hearing people.

Total Communication

Educational programs with an emphasis on **total communication** use a variety of methods to assist the hearing impaired child in expressing, receiving, and developing language. Practitioners of total communication maintain that the simultaneous presentation of signs (including fingerspelling when necessary) and speech (through speech-reading and residual hearing) makes it possible for children to use either one or both types of communication (Ling, 1984). Total communication is now "the predominant method of instruction in schools for the deaf" (Luterman, 1986, p. 263). According to a recent survey (Wolk & Schildroth, 1986), the percentage of deaf students who both speak and sign (62.2%) is far greater than that of those who speak only (21.1%) or who sign only (16.7%). The communication method used may depend on the setting: even though many hearing impaired students use sign language in their classes, they are less likely to do so outside school, because signs are not usually understood by the general public.

Sign language uses gestures to represent words, ideas, and concepts. Many signs convey meaning by motions that appear to imitate or act out their message. In making the *cat* sign, for example, the signer seems to be stroking feline whiskers on his face; in the sign for *eat*, the hand moves back and forth into an open mouth (see Figure 7.8). Many other signs, however, have little or no resemblance to the objects or actions they represent. If sign language were simply a form of pantomime, then most nonsigners would be able to understand it with relatively little effort. But several studies have shown that the majority of signs cannot be guessed by people who are unfamiliar with that particular sign language (Klima & Bellugi, 1979).

American Sign Language (often referred to as ASL or Ameslan) is a language widely used by hearing impaired people in the United States and Canada. There has been a great deal of recent interest in the study of ASL; psychologists, linguists, and educators now generally view ASL as a complex and legitimate language in its own

FIGURE 7.8
Sign language for *cat* (left) and *eat* (right).

right, rather than an imperfect variation of spoken English. In ASL the shape, location, and movement pattern of the hands, the intensity with which motions are made, and the signer's facial expressions all communicate meaning and content. Interestingly, ASL is a language that is often passed on from children to other children (usually in residential schools), rather than the more common pattern of parents to children. Only about 12% of deaf children have deaf parents (Reagan, 1985).

Because ASL has its own vocabulary, syntax, and grammatical rules, it does not correspond exactly to spoken or written English. Articles, prepositions, tenses, and plurals may be left out, and the word order may be different from that of standard English. It is difficult to make precise word-for-word translations between ASL and English, just as it is difficult to translate many foreign languages into English word for word.

See "Around the World in Sign Language" for examples of signs used in other countries.

Teachers who practice total communication generally speak as they sign and make a special effort to follow the form and structure of spoken English as closely as possible. Several sign language systems have been designed primarily for educational purposes, with the intention of facilitating the development of reading, writing, and other language skills in hearing impaired students. These sign systems incorporate many features of ASL, while also seeking to follow correct English usage and word order. The term "Pidgin Sign English" is sometimes used to describe the use of ASL signs in English word order, and Manually Coded English is the term applied to several educationally oriented sign systems, such as Seeing Essential English (Anthony, 1971), Signing Exact English (Gustason, Pfetzing, & Zawolkow, 1980), and Signed English (Bornstein, 1974). Hearing impaired students often use two or more sign language systems, depending on the person with whom they are communicating.

Fingerspelling, or the manual alphabet, consists of 26 distinct hand positions, one for each English letter. A one-hand manual alphabet is used in the United States

AROUND THE WORLD IN SIGN LANGUAGE

Is sign language universal? Students frequently ask, "When deaf people from other countries get together, can they understand each other?" Sign language is not universal. Dictionaries of sign languages have been published in several countries, and there appears to be little uniformity of signs. The photos we have here, for example, show how differently the sign for *mother* is made in six different countries.

Just as there are different dialects among hearing people in different parts of the United States, so there are regional differences in sign language. However, a deaf traveler does have certain advantages in communicating with deaf people in other regions or countries. A traveler accustomed to using signs, gestures, and body language will probably be able to work out some ways of communicating with a foreign deaf person. Indeed, hearing travelers often devise their own sign language to convey information and ask questions when they do not know the oral language of the country they are visiting.

United States

Denmark

China

Brazil

England

Finland

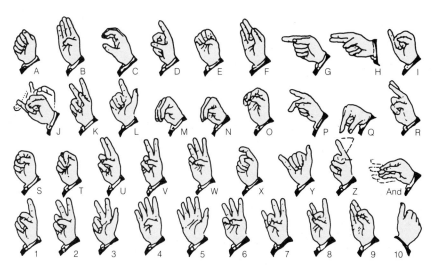

FIGURE 7.9
The manual alphabet.

and Canada (see Figure 7.9). Some manual letters—such as *C, L,* and *W*—resemble the shape of printed English letters, whereas others—such as *A, E,* and *S*—have no apparent similarity. As in typewriting, each word is spelled out letter-by-letter.

Fingerspelling is often used in conjunction with other methods of communication. A user of sign language relies on fingerspelling to spell out proper names for which no sign exists and to clarify meanings that may be unclear. The Rochester Method uses a combination of oral communication and fingerspelling but does not use sign language. The teacher fingerspells every letter of every word as she speaks, and the hearing impaired student learns to use the same means of expression. The Rochester Method also emphasizes reading and writing; its advocates believe that this approach facilitates the acquisition of correct language patterns. Fingerspelling is also used by many people who are both deaf and visually impaired; the manual alphabet can be used at close distances or felt with the hand if a person is totally blind.

Supporters of total communication methods believe that this approach is the best way to provide a "reliable receptive-expressive symbol system," especially in the preschool years when communication between parent and child is vitally important (Denton, 1972). Several researchers have found that even very young children are able to produce and understand signs effectively (e.g., Maestas y Moores & Moores, 1980; Orlansky & Bonvillian, 1985; Prinz & Prinz, 1979).

Although there is no firm evidence that deaf children's use of sign language inhibits their acquisition of speech (Moores, 1987; Rooney, 1982; Sacks, 1986), some specialists contend that it is difficult for hearing impaired children to process signs and speech when they are presented together. "Even for experts it is not easy to combine signs and speech effectively," writes Daniel Ling (1984, p. 11), noting that they are usually produced at different rates of speed. In Ling's view the simultaneous use of

Some children as young as 5 months of age can respond to and produce certain signs.

signs and speech is likely to impair the quality of speech, or signs, and/or language. It may be better, he suggests, for children to learn oral and manual skills separately, rather than at the same time.

Total communication appears to be gaining wide acceptance in educational programs for hearing impaired students. Luterman (1986), however, regards the effects of the movement toward total communication as unproven. Many educators consider total communication to have facilitated parent-child and teacher-child communication and to have enhanced children's self-esteem, but these supposed gains cannot be easily documented. Luterman (1986) further observes that "total communication has not made any substantial changes in the depressingly low academic achievement of deaf children" (p. 263).

Language Instruction

Many techniques and materials have been developed to help hearing impaired children acquire and use written language. The relationship between written and spoken expression is obviously a close one, but there is no exact correspondence between the type of communication method a child uses (oral-only or total communication) and the method of language instruction that a particular school or class employs.

Instructional programs in language for hearing impaired students are generally classified as either structured or natural. A well-known structured method, developed more than 50 years ago but still widely used, is the Fitzgerald Key (Fitzgerald, 1929). This method provides several labeled categories, such as who, what, where, and when. The child learns to generate correct sentences by placing words into the proper categories. An example of a natural method is Natural Language for Deaf Children (Groht, 1958). This method emphasizes language development through modeling and conversation; games and activities are preferred to formal drills and exercises. Moores and Maestas y Moores (1981) provide a helpful review of methods of language instruction, noting that virtually no research has been conducted to evaluate the advantages of one approach over the other and that most educational programs today tend to use a combination of structured and natural methods.

Controversy and Choices

The controversies over communication and instructional methods for hearing impaired students are likely to continue well into the future. Research has not provided—and probably never will provide—a definitive answer to the question of which communication method is best. There is general agreement, however, that our educational programs leave much room for improvement.

See "Tips for facilitating communication" on pp. 283–84.

Different children communicate in different ways. Some hearing impaired children, unfortunately, have experienced deep frustration and failure because of rigid adherence to an oral-only program. They have left their programs without having developed a usable avenue of communication. Equally unfortunate is the fact that other hearing impaired children have not been given an adequate opportunity to develop their auditory and oral skills, because they were placed in educational programs that did not provide good oral instruction. In both cases children have been unfairly

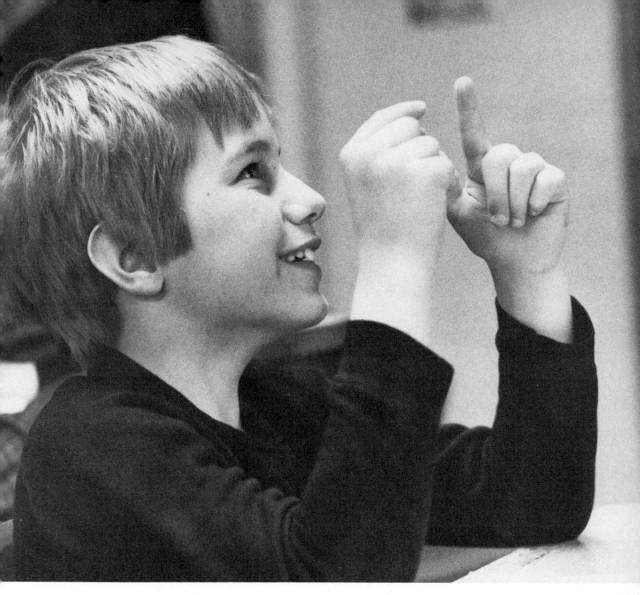

Derrick must use his vision to understand others.

penalized. Every hearing impaired child should have access to an educational program that uses a communication method appropriate to his unique abilities and needs.

EDUCATIONAL SERVICE ALTERNATIVES

Early detection of hearing loss and early intervention with the hearing impaired child and the family are generally recognized as critical. Many schools, speech and hearing clinics, and other agencies provide educational programs for preschool children. Usually the child's hearing is tested, an amplification aid is provided, and the program emphasizes communication with adults and other children. Parent groups and home visits are an important part of a preschool program; through these efforts parents may be helped to communicate with their child more effectively. A hearing impaired child who

The passage of P.L. 99–457 in 1986 has led to increased emphasis on serving handicapped infants and preschoolers (see chapter 2).

receives no specialized assessment, amplification, or training until the age of 5 or 6 will undoubtedly be at a great disadvantage in communication and general development.

Educational programs for hearing impaired children are available in residential schools, special day schools, and regular public schools. Schildroth (1986) notes that enrollment in the more than 60 public residential schools for hearing impaired children in the United States has declined sharply in the past decade, as public school programs have become more widely available and as the majority of students whose deafness was caused by the rubella epidemics of the mid-1960s have departed from the school-age population. Over 90% of the students currently enrolled in residential schools are those with severe and profound prelingual hearing impairments. Nearly one-third of the hearing impaired students now served in residential schools are considered to be multihandicapped, and nearly one-third come from minority ethnic backgrounds.

Educational programs for hearing impaired children in local public schools have expanded in recent years, in response to federal legislation, improvements in hearing aids and other technology, and an increased demand by parents and deaf citizens for services at the local level (Davis, 1986). Hearing impaired children in regular schools may attend self-contained classes or may be integrated with nonhandicapped children for all or part of the school day. Quigley and Paul (1986) report that about 45% of hearing impaired students are integrated into regular classrooms to some degree; most of these students have average hearing losses of less than 90 dB. According to Davis (1986), the most important ingredients for the hearing impaired child's success

Most students served by residential schools have severe or profound prelingual hearing impairments.

TIPS FOR FACILITATING COMMUNICATION

Hearing impaired people are increasingly participating in community life. It is no longer unusual for a businessperson, bank teller, student, police officer, or anyone else to have the opportunity to communicate with a deaf person. Yet many people with normal hearing are still unsure of themselves. They may try to avoid communicating with deaf people altogether or may use ineffective and frustrating strategies.

The following tips for facilitating communication with deaf people were suggested by the Community Services for the Deaf program in Akron, Ohio. These tips provide basic information about three common ways in which deaf people communicate: through speechreading, written communication, and the assistance of a sign language interpreter. Usually a deaf person will indicate the approach she is most comfortable with. If the deaf person relies mainly on speechreading (lipreading), here are things you can do to help.

☐ Face the deaf person and stand or sit no more than 4 feet away.
☐ The room should have adequate illumination—but don't seat yourself in front of a strong or glaring light.
☐ Try to keep your whole face visible.
☐ Speak clearly, naturally, and not too fast. Don't exaggerate your mouth movements.
☐ Don't raise the level of your voice.
☐ Some words are more easily read on the lips than others. If you are having a problem being understood, try substituting different words.
☐ It may take a while to become used to the deaf person's speech. If at first you can't understand what he is saying, don't give up.
☐ Don't hesitate to write any important words that are missed.

If the deaf person communicates best through sign language (and you do not), it will probably be necessary to use an interpreter. Here are some considerations to keep in mind.

- ☐ The role of the interpreter is to facilitate communication between you and the deaf person. The interpreter should not be asked to give opinions, advice, or personal feelings.
- ☐ Maintain eye contact with the deaf person and speak directly to her. The deaf person should not be made to take a back seat in the conversation. For example, say "How are you today?" instead of "Ask her how she is today."
- ☐ Remain face-to-face with the deaf person. The best place for the interpreter is behind you and a little to the side of you. Again, avoid strong or glaring light.
- ☐ Remember, it is the interpreter's job to communicate *everything* that is said by you and the deaf person. Don't say anything that you don't want interpreted for the person.

Written messages can be helpful in exchanging information. Consider the following:

- ☐ Avoid the temptation to abbreviate your communication.
- ☐ Write in simple, direct language.
- ☐ The deaf person's written English may not be grammatically correct, but you will probably be able to understand it. One deaf person, for example, wrote "Pay off yesterday, finish me" to convey the message "I paid that loan off yesterday."
- ☐ Use visual aids, such as pictures, diagrams, and business cards.
- ☐ Don't be afraid to supplement your written messages with gestures and facial expressions.
- ☐ Written communication has limitations—but it is often more effective than no communication at all.

Remember that the language of many deaf people may be quite different from standard English. They are deprived of a great deal of information because they cannot hear. Language is not an accurate reflection of a person's intelligence or ability to function independently.

"Where's the nearest bank?"

in the regular classroom are (1) good oral communication skills, (2) strong parental support, (3) average or above-average intelligence, (4) self-confidence and other personal qualities, and (5) adequate support services, such as tutoring, audiological consultation, and speech therapy.

The specialized needs of children with severe hearing impairments make special services necessary in virtually all cases. In an integrated public school setting, special services for a hearing impaired child may include

□ smaller class size
□ regular speech, language, and auditory training instruction from a specialist
□ amplification systems
□ services of an interpreter if the child uses manual communication
□ special seating in the classroom to promote speechreading
□ captioned films
□ good acoustics and reduction of background noise
□ special tutoring or review sessions
□ someone to take notes in class so that the hearing impaired student can pay more constant attention
□ instruction for teachers and nonhandicapped students in sign language or other communication methods used by the hearing impaired student
□ counseling

It may be difficult for public schools in rural areas to provide all of these services. Several school districts may need to cooperate with each other.

Several recent publications (Dale, 1984; Kampfe, 1984; Lynas, 1986; J. Z. Orlansky, 1979; Webster & Ellwood, 1985) provide helpful guidelines, practical suggestions, and descriptions of programs that have successfully integrated hearing impaired students into regular classes.

Teacher Competencies

Teachers of hearing impaired students must complete specialized training programs and meet the certification standards established by the states and by national professional organizations. Usually, this training includes the study of speech and hearing anatomy, audiology, language assessment and development, reading, curriculum, and use of technology. Most college and university preparation programs require the teacher to become competent in both oral and manual communication methods. Sass-Lehrer (1986) surveyed 150 supervisors of instructional programs for hearing impaired students in both regular and special schools and found that the following competencies were among those considered "most critical to the effective teaching of hearing impaired students" (p. 230):

□ providing language instruction
□ teaching small groups of hearing impaired students who function on different levels
□ developing and adapting instructional materials
□ guiding students in the development of a positive self-concept
□ using information from various assessment procedures to develop an IEP
□ dealing with crises calmly and effectively

Teachers must design instruction for hearing impaired
students who are functioning on different levels.

Postsecondary Education

A growing number of educational opportunities are available to hearing impaired students after completion of a high school-level program. The oldest and best-known of
these is Gallaudet University in Washington, D.C., which offers a wide range of undergraduate and graduate programs in the liberal arts, sciences, education, business, and
other fields. Hearing impaired students from throughout the United States, Canada,
and other countries compete for admission. All classes at Gallaudet are taught in simultaneous communication, through speech and sign language. In addition, the National Technical Institute for the Deaf (NTID), located at the Rochester (New York)
Institute of Technology, provides wide-ranging programs in technical, vocational, and
business-related fields such as computer science, hotel management, photography, and
medical technology. Both Gallaudet and NTID are supported by the federal government
and enroll approximately 1,500 hearing impaired students each.

> Gallaudet also has pro-
> grams to train teachers
> of deaf children. Both
> deaf and hearing stu-
> dents are accepted into
> these programs.

More than 100 other institutions of higher education, although not dedicated to
serving hearing impaired students exclusively, have developed special programs of supportive services for them. Among these are four regional postsecondary programs
that enroll substantial numbers of hearing impaired students: St. Paul (Minnesota)

Technical-Vocational Institute, Seattle (Washington) Central Community College, the Postsecondary Education Consortium at the University of Tennessee, and California State University at Northridge.

The percentage of hearing impaired students who attend postsecondary educational programs has risen dramatically in the past 20 years. Today, about 40% of all hearing impaired students go on to receive higher education (Connor, 1986). Enrollment has increased most sharply in areas of study related to business and office careers (Rawlings & King, 1986). It is hoped that the increase in postsecondary programs will expand vocational and professional opportunities for deaf adults.

CURRENT ISSUES/FUTURE TRENDS

As more hearing impaired children come to be educated in regular public school settings, it appears likely that oral methods of instruction will hold a position of great importance. Speech, after all, is the most widely used form of communication among teachers and students in regular classes. Concurrently, however, manual communication will probably become more familiar to the general public. Training in sign language is already offered to children with normal hearing in some schools, and an increasing number of people who contact the public in the course of their jobs—such as police officers, firefighters, flight attendants, and bank tellers—will learn to communicate manually with deaf individuals. Television programs, films, concerts, and other media using interpreters or printed captions are already becoming more widely available. No longer is it unusual to see a sign language interpreter standing next to a public speaker or performer.

Despite the recent expansion of postsecondary programs of education and training, many hearing impaired adults still find limited opportunities for appropriate employment and economic advancement. Recent court decisions regarding the rights of hearing impaired students have had mixed results. In one case (*Barnes* v. *Converse College*, 1977) a court ordered a private college to provide, at its own expense, an interpreter for a deaf student. In another case (*Southeastern Community College* v. *Davis*, 1979) the U.S. Supreme Court decided that a college could not be compelled to admit a hearing impaired student into its nursing program. A widely publicized Supreme Court case (*Rowley* v. *Hendrick Hudson School District*, 1982) resulted in a local school district's not being required to provide, at its expense, a sign language interpreter for a deaf child who was performing adequately without one in the regular classroom. Similar cases are certain to arise in the future, as hearing impaired people become increasingly aware of their civil rights and seek access to education, employment, and other rights.

The *Rowley* case was also discussed in chapter 2. It was the first Supreme Court case to be argued by a deaf lawyer.

Technological advances are already having a significant impact on the educational programs of many hearing impaired students. In addition to the sophisticated techniques now used to detect hearing losses and to make use of even slight amounts of residual hearing, a number of devices known as speech production aids help deaf persons monitor and improve their own speech (Calvert, 1986). Microcomputers are also being used increasingly in language and academic instruction of hearing impaired students. Prinz and Nelson (1985), for example, describe a successful microcomputer

A deaf person can use the telephone with the aid of a TTY.

program that uses pictures and representations of ASL signs to improve deaf children's reading and writing skills; Tomlinson-Keasey, Brawley, and Peterson (1986) report that an interactive videodisc system helped deaf students make significant progress in language skills and also increased their motivation.

Some employers were reluctant to hire deaf people, because the ability to use the telephone is needed in many jobs.

Other developments in electronics and computer technology are making the telephone and television more accessible to people with hearing impairments. The telephone has long served as a barrier to deaf people in employment and social interaction, but acoustic couplers now make it possible to send immediate messages over conventional telephone lines in typed or digital form. Telecommunication devices for deaf persons (often called TTY or TDD systems) are now widely used and relatively inexpensive. Similarly, closed captioning is being used on more and more television programs; thus, a hearing impaired person who has a special decoding device is able to read captions or subtitles on the television screen. Another recent form of technology, known as real-time graphic display, facilitates the rapid captioning of live presentations, such as public lectures.

Future technological advances may enable educators to analyze and track the language development of hearing impaired students with much greater precision than is now possible and to use this information in planning appropriate language instruction for each child (Levitt, 1985). Among the most intriguing concepts is the possibility that an automatic speech recognition system may someday be perfected. Such a system could enable a deaf person to recognize instantly the speech of other people, perhaps through a small, portable printout device that would be activated by the speaker's voice. The research required to develop a speech recogniton system is highly complex, because human speech patterns differ immensely. Nevertheless, improvements in technology, coupled with a concern for individual needs and rights, will enable people with impaired hearing to participate more fully in a broad range of educational, vocational, social, and recreational activities in their schools and communities.

SUMMARY

1. Hearing is extremely important in a child's development, learning, and everyday life. The loss or severe impairment of hearing has far-reaching effects on communication.

2. There are many different levels of hearing ability.
   a. A deaf person is not able to understand speech through the ears alone.
   b. A hard-of-hearing person is able to use hearing to understand speech, generally with the help of a hearing aid.

3. Hearing impairments can be classified in several ways.
   a. A congenital hearing impairment is present at birth; an adventitious hearing impairment is acquired later in life.
   b. A prelingual hearing impairment occurs before the child has developed speech and language; a postlingual hearing impairment occurs after that time.
   c. A hearing impairment can be conductive or sensorineural, depending on the type and location of the impairment.
   d. A hearing impairment can be unilateral (in one ear) or bilateral (in both ears).

4. Sounds are measured in units of intensity and frequency.
   a. Intensity is measured in decibels. A person can have a loss of up to 25 dB and still be considered to have hearing in the normal range.
   b. Frequency is measured in hertz. It is important to note the frequency range of speech (about 500 to 2,000 Hz).

5. Audiologists seek to detect hearing impairments, especially in young children.
   a. A formal hearing test generates an audiogram, which graphically shows the intensity of the faintest sound an individual can hear at various frequencies.
   b. Hearing impairments can be classified as mild, moderate, severe, or profound, depending on the degree of hearing loss.
   c. The audiogram is only one source of information about hearing ability. Useful information can also be gained from observing children's behavior at home and school.
   d. Generally today, only children with hearing losses greater than 90 dB are considered deaf for educational placement purposes.

6. Hearing impairment is a low-prevalence disability.
   a. About 5% of all school-age children have some form of hearing impairment, but many of these do not require special education.
   b. Only about 1 child in every 500 has a severe or profound hearing impairment.
   c. Although most deaf children participate in special education programs, only about 20% of hard-of-hearing children receive special services.

7. There are many causes of hearing impairment, but four are especially prevalent today.
   a. maternal rubella
   b. hereditary causes
   c. prematurity and complications of pregnancy
   d. meningitis

8. The education of deaf students has a long history.
   a. Efforts to teach deaf children were made in Europe as early as the 16th century.
   b. Deaf children were among the first handicapped children to receive education in the United States. The first American school opened in 1817.
   c. Instruction in speech and speechreading became widespread during the latter half of the 19th century.
   d. Traditionally, most deaf children were educated in residential schools. Today, however, more than 60% attend classes in local public schools.
   e. Many hearing impaired students have multiple handicaps, and many are from culturally diverse backgrounds.

9. Amplification and auditory training seek to enable hearing impaired students to use their residual hearing more effectively.
   a. Hearing aids make sounds louder but cannot eliminate the distortion of sounds.
   b. Both individual and group hearing aids are used.
   c. Hearing aids should be fitted as early as possible in a child's life and should be worn throughout each day.
   d. Speechreading provides useful visual information but also has many limitations. Most English sounds cannot be distinguished through vision alone.

10. Many special techniques and materials are used in the education of hearing impaired students.
    a. Deaf children experience many difficulties in acquiring language and academic skills, particularly reading.
    b. Deafness may also have significant effects on a child's behavior, personal development, and social adjusment.
    c. Some educators utilize a primarily oral approach to the education of hearing impaired students, emphasizing the development of speech and related skills.
    d. Cued speech is a method of supplementing oral communication by using hand signals near the mouth.
    e. Other educators utilize a total communication approach, combining sign language and fingerspelling with speech. They usually speak and sign simultaneously.
    f. There are several different sign language systems. Some follow the forms of standard English closely, whereas others do not.
    g. Some educators contend that it is difficult for deaf children to process sign language and speech when they are presented together.
    h. Methods of language instruction can be classified as either structured or natural.
    i. Questions of education and communication are controversial. There is no clear indication that any one method is best for all hearing impaired children.

11. There are several different options for educating hearing impaired students.
    a. Early detection of hearing loss and preschool education are important.
    b. Enrollment in residential schools has declined sharply in the past decade.
    c. In regular schools hearing impaired children may attend regular or self-contained classes or a combination of these.
    d. Many specialized services and resources are required to adequately meet the needs of hearing impaired students.
    e. A growing number of postsecondary educational opportunities are available. About 40% of all hearing impaired students go on to other educational programs after high school.

12. Sign language is becoming more widely used and accepted in society generally.

13. Technology holds much promise for addressing the communication problems faced by deaf persons.
   a. Microcomputers are often used in educational programs.
   b. Telecommunication devices enable many hearing impaired persons to use the telephone, television, and other devices.
   c. Research into speech recognition technology is continuing. In the future it may be possible for deaf people to recognize the speech of others more rapidly and efficiently.

FOR MORE INFORMATION

Journals

American Annals of the Deaf. Published bimonthly by the Convention of American Instructors of the Deaf and the Conference of Executives of American Schools for the Deaf. Presents articles dealing with education of deaf and hearing impaired students.

Journal of Rehabilitation of the Deaf. Published by the Professional Rehabilitation Workers with the Adult Deaf. Focuses on research, innovations, patterns of service, and other topics related to deaf adults.

Sign Language Studies. Published quarterly by Linstok Press, Silver Spring, MD. Contains research and practical articles related to sign language and manual communication.

The Volta Review. Published nine times a year by the Alexander Graham Bell Association for the Deaf. Encourages teaching of speech, speechreading, and use of residual hearing to deaf persons. Advocates oral approach.

Books

Hull, R. H., & Dilka, K. I. (Eds.). (1984). *The hearing-impaired child in school.* Orlando, FL: Grune & Stratton.

Luterman, D. M. (Ed.). (1986). *Deafness in perspective.* San Diego: College-Hill.

Lynas, W. (1986). *Integrating the handicapped into ordinary schools: A study of hearing-impaired pupils.* London: Croom Helm.

Mindel, E. D., & Vernon, M. (1986). *They grow in silence: Understanding deaf children and adults* (2nd ed.). San Diego: College-Hill.

Moores, D. F. (1987). *Educating the deaf: Psychology, principles, and practices* (3rd ed.). Boston: Houghton Mifflin.

Quigley, S. P., & Paul, P. V. (1984). *Language and deafness.* San Diego: College-Hill.

Schildroth, A. N., & Karchmer, M. A. (Eds.). (1986). *Deaf children in America.* San Diego: College-Hill.

Van Cleve, J. V. (Ed.). (1986). *Gallaudet encyclopedia of deaf people and deafness.* New York: McGraw-Hill.

Walker, L. A. (1986). *A loss for words: The story of deafness in a family.* New York: Harper & Row.

Organizations

Alexander Graham Bell Association for the Deaf, 3417 Volta Place, NW, Washington, DC 20007. Provides brochures, books, software, audiovisual materials, and other information on hearing impairment, with an auditory-oral emphasis. Publishes *The Volta Review* for professionals, *Our Kids Magazine* for parents, and *Newsounds* newsletter. Sponsors organizations for teachers, parents, researchers, and oral deaf adults.

Gallaudet University, 800 Florida Ave, NE, Washington DC 20002. Has in its bookstore one of the most complete collections of professional and popular literature about hearing impairment, communication, education, psychology, and related topics. Also has children's sign language books that appeal to many readers. Provides free catalogs of book lists; arranges tours of the Gallaudet campus for Washington visitors.

National Association of the Deaf, 814 Thayer Avenue, Silver Spring, MD 20910. A clearinghouse for information about education, employment, legal issues, communication, technological aids, and other topics. Sponsors activities for deaf adults, children, and parents.

National Cued Speech Association, P. O. Box 31345, Raleigh, NC 27622. Provides information, training, and publications on the cued speech system of identifying sounds and supplementing speechreading skills.

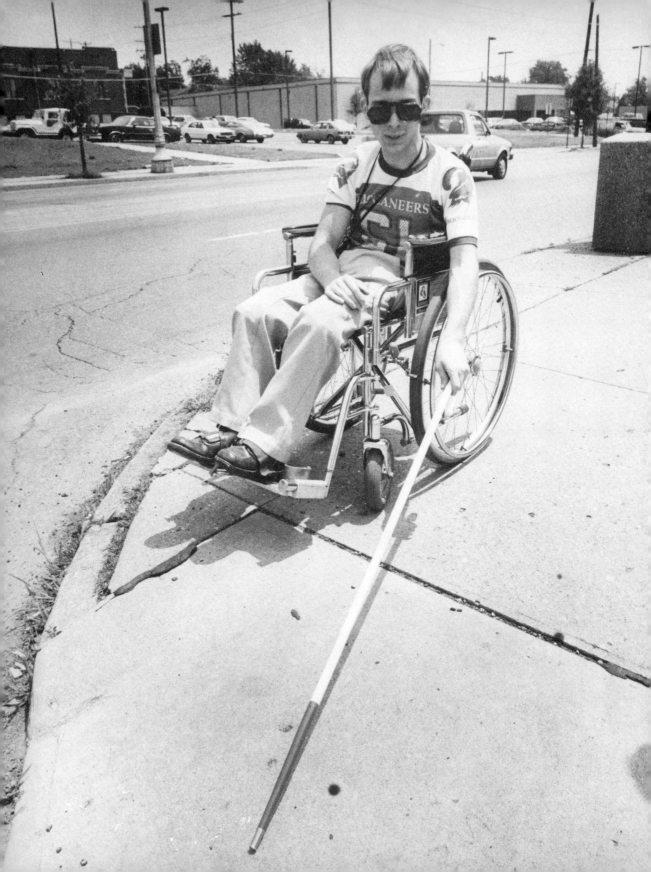

8

VISUAL IMPAIRMENT

Sixteen-year-old Maria is a bright, college-bound student who has been totally blind since birth. She recently took a series of intellectual and psychological tests and generally performed well, scoring at about her expected age and grade level. Something unusual, however, happened on one test. The examiner handed Maria an unpeeled banana and asked, "What is this?" Maria held the banana for minutes and took several guesses but could not answer correctly. The examiner was astonished, as were Maria's teachers and parents. After all, this section of the test was intended for young children. Maria had eaten bananas many times but had missed out on one important aspect of the banana experience: she had never held and peeled a banana by herself.

This true story (adapted from Swallow, 1978) illustrates the tremendous importance of vision in obtaining accurate and thorough information about the world in which we live. Visually impaired students are "a small group of handicapped pupils who are more similar to than different from their nonhandicapped peers" (Scholl, 1987, p. 36). The major difference is in the visually impaired students' need for compensatory education to help them overcome the absence of vision, an extremely important means of sensory input. Thus, teachers who work with visually impaired children find it necessary to plan and present a great many firsthand experiences. Many of the concepts that children with normal vision seem to acquire almost effortlessly may not be learned at all by visually impaired children—or may be learned incorrectly—unless someone deliberately teaches the concepts to them. Often, the best teachers are those who enable visually impaired children to learn by doing things for themselves.

Visually impaired students display a wide range of visual abilities, ranging from total blindness to relatively good residual (remaining) vision. The one characteristic that all these students have in common is "a visual restriction of sufficient severity that it interferes with normal progress in a regular educational program without modifications" (Scholl, 1986, p. 29).

Even when information is deliberately presented to visually impaired children, they may not learn it in exactly the same way that children with normal vision would. Visually impaired students may learn to make good use of their own senses. Hearing, touch, smell, and taste can be useful channels of sensory input, but they do not totally compensate for the loss of vision. Touch and taste cannot tell children much about things that are far away from them—or even just beyond the length of their own arms. Hearing can tell them a good deal about the near and distant environment, but it seldom provides information that is as complete, as continuous, or as exact as the information people obtain from seeing their surroundings.

> Blind people are not gifted with an extraordinary sense of touch. Rather, they may learn to use their sense of touch to gain information about the environment.

The classroom is one important setting in which vision is critical for successful learning and development. In school normally sighted children are routinely expected to exercise several important visual skills. They must be able to see clearly. They must focus on different objects, shifting from near to far as needed. They must have good eye-hand coordination and must be able to remember what they have seen. They must discriminate colors accurately. They must be able to see and interpret many things simultaneously. They must be able to maintain visual concentration. Without any of these skills, children find it difficult to learn and need special procedures or materials to let them function effectively in school.

DEFINING VISUAL IMPAIRMENT

There are both legal and educational definitions of visual impairment. The legal definition of blindness relies heavily on measurements of **visual acuity,** which is the ability to clearly distinguish forms or discriminate details at a specified distance. Most frequently, visual acuity is measured by reading letters, numbers, or other symbols from a chart 20 feet away. The familiar phrase "20/20 vision" simply indicates that at a distance of 20 feet the eye can see what a normally seeing eye should be able to see at that distance. As the bottom number increases, visual acuity decreases.

If a person's visual acuity is 20/200 or less in the better eye, even after the best possible correction with glasses or contact lenses, then he is considered **legally blind.** If Jane has 20/200 vision while wearing her glasses, she needs to stand at a distance of 20 feet to see what most people can see from 200 feet away. In other words Jane must get much closer than normal to see things clearly. Her legal blindness means that Jane will likely find it difficult to use her vision in many everyday situations, but there is a good chance that a child with 20/200, or even 20/400, vision will be able to succeed in a regular classroom with special help. Some students are unable to perceive fine details at any distance, even while wearing glasses or contact lenses.

A person may also be considered legally blind if her **field of vision** is extremely restricted. When gazing straight ahead, a normal eye is able to see objects within a range of approximately 180 degrees. If David's field of vision is only 10 degrees, he is able to see only a limited area at any one time (even though his visual acuity in that small area may be quite good). Some people with limited fields of vision describe their perceptions as viewing the world through a narrow tube or tunnel; they have good central vision but poor **peripheral vision** at the outer ranges of the visual field. Some eye conditions, on the other hand, make it impossible for people to see things clearly in the central visual field but allow relatively good peripheral vision.

Whether the visual field impairment is central or peripheral, a person can be considered legally blind if he is restricted to an area of 20 degrees or less from the normal 180-degree field. It is common for the visual field to decrease slowly and for the decrease to go undetected in children and adults. A thorough visual examination should always include measurement of the visual field, as well as visual acuity.

Legally blind children are eligible to receive a wide variety of educational services, materials, and benefits from governmental agencies. They may, for example, obtain records (known as "Talking Books"), tapes, and record players from the Library of Congress. Their schools may be able to buy books and educational materials from the American Printing House for the Blind, because the federal quota system allots states and local school districts a certain financial allowance for each legally blind student (Chase, 1986b). A person who is legally blind is also entitled to vocational training, free U.S. mail service, and an additional income tax exemption.

Even though all of these services and benefits are important to know about, the legal definition of blindness is not especially useful to teachers. Some children, although they are not legally blind, have visual impairments severe enough to require special educational techniques and materials. Other students, whose vision qualifies them as legally blind, find little or no use for many of these specialized services. The educational definition of visual impairment considers the extent to which a child's vision affects learning and makes special methods or materials necessary. Educators often differen-

One of these two high school wrestlers is totally blind.

tiate between **blind** and **low vision** students. This distinction does not rely on precise measurements of visual acuity or visual field.

Braille is a system of representing letters, numbers, and other symbols with combinations (patterns) of six raised dots. It also uses special abbreviations for certain common words and parts of words (see page 306).

A blind child is totally without sight or has so little vision that she learns primarily through the other senses. Most blind children, for example, use their sense of touch to read **braille.** A low vision child, on the other hand, is able to learn through the visual channel and generally learns to read print. Today, the great majority of children enrolled in educational programs for the visually impaired have useful vision; low vision students comprise between 75% and 80% of the school-age visually impaired population (Bryan & Jeffrey, 1982).

Barraga (1983) uses the term *visual efficiency* to denote how well a person can *use* whatever vision he has. Visual efficiency cannot be determined by measuring a child's visual acuity or visual field, nor can it be predicted. Some children have severe visual impairments but are able to use their vision very capably. Other children have relatively minor visual impairments but are unable to function as visual learners; they may even behave as though they were blind. Barraga and her colleagues have shown that systematic training in visual recognition and discrimination can help many visually impaired children use their remaining vision more efficiently.

Although the most frequently mentioned visual impairments are in visual acuity and field of vision, there are several other significant ways in which a person's vision may be impaired. **Ocular motility,** the eye's ability to move, may be impaired. This impairment can cause problems in **binocular vision,** which is the ability of the two eyes to focus on one object and fuse the two images into a single clear image (Ward, 1986). Binocular vision is actually a complicated process, requiring good vision in each eye, normal eye muscles, and smooth functioning of the coordinating centers of the brain (Miller, 1979).

Several conditions make it difficult or impossible for a child to use her eyes together effectively. **Strabismus** is a term that describes an inability to focus on the same object with both eyes, because of an inward or outward deviation of one or both eyes. The colloquial terms *squint, cross-eyed,* and *wall-eyed* have been applied to children with strabismus.

If left untreated, strabismus and other disorders of ocular motility can lead to permanent loss of vision. When the two eyes cannot focus simultaneously, the brain avoids a double image by suppressing the visual input from one eye. Thus, the weaker eye—usually the one that turns inward or outward—can actually lose its ability to see. **Ambylopia** refers to this reduction in or loss of vision in the weaker eye from lack of use, even though no disease is present. The usual treatment for ambylopia is to place a patch over the stronger eye so that the weaker eye is forced to develop better vision through training and experience. This treatment is most effective if started in early childhood. Eye muscle surgery may also help to correct the muscle imbalance and prevent further loss of vision in the weaker eye (Batshaw & Perret, 1986).

Other kinds of visual impairments include problems in **accommodation,** in which the eye cannot adjust properly for seeing at different distances. A child with difficulty in accommodation may have trouble shifting from reading a book to looking at the chalkboard and back again. Some visually impaired children have a condition known as **nystagmus,** in which there is a rapid, involuntary back-and-forth movement of the eyes in a lateral, vertical, or rotary direction. Nystagmus is generally not discernible by the person with the impairment (Chase, 1986b). Severe nystagmus can cause problems for a child in focusing and reading.

Some children's eyes are unusually sensitive to light; this condition is known as **photophobia.** The child may need to wear tinted glasses and avoid areas of strong light or glare. Children with **albinism** almost always have photophobia because their eyes (and skin and hair) lack normal pigmentation.

Color vision can also be impaired. A child with deficient color vision is not actually color-blind; that is, he does not see only in black and white. However, he may find it difficult to distinguish certain colors. Red-green confusion is most common, occuring in about 8% of all males and 0.4% of females (Ward, 1986). Deficient color vision does not get better or worse as a child gets older, and it is usually not considered an educationally significant visual impairment.

Age at Onset

Like other disabilities, visual impairment can be congenital or adventitious. It is useful for a teacher to know the age at which a student acquired a visual impairment. A child who has been blind since birth naturally has quite a different view of the world from that of a child who became blind at 12 years of age. The first child has a background of learning through hearing, touch, and the other nonvisual senses, whereas the second child has a background of visual experiences to draw on. Many adventitiously blind people retain a visual memory of things they formely saw. And this memory can be helpful in a child's education; an adventitiously blind child may, for instance, remember the appearance of colors, maps, and printed letters. At the same time, however, her need for emotional support and acceptance may be greater than that of the congenitally blind child, who does not have to make a sudden adjustment to the visual impairment.

TYPES AND CAUSES OF VISUAL IMPAIRMENT

The basic function of the eye is to collect visual information from the environment and transmit it to the brain. A simplified diagram of the eye appears in Figure 8.1. The eye is stimulated by light rays, reflected from objects in the visual field. In the normal eye these light rays come to a clear focus on the central part of the **retina.** This multilayered sheet of nerve tissue at the back of the eye has been likened to the film in a camera: for a clear image to be transmitted to the brain, the light rays must come to a precise focus on the retina. The **optic nerve** is connected to the retina. It conducts visual images to the brain.

In the process of vision, light rays must pass through several structures and substances in the eye itself. Each of these bends the light a little bit in order to produce the ideal image on the retina. The light first hits the **cornea,** the curved transparent membrane that protects the eye (much as an outer crystal protects a wristwatch). It then passes through the **aqueous humor,** a watery liquid that fills

Human Eye

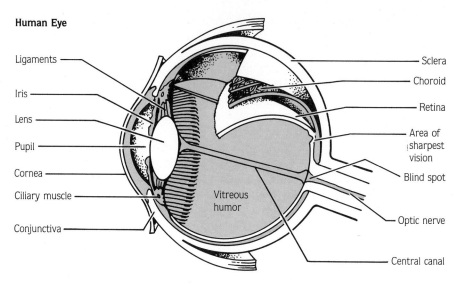

Ligaments — ... — Sclera

Iris — ... — Choroid

Lens — ... — Retina

Pupil — ... — Area of sharpest vision

Cornea — ... — Blind spot

Ciliary muscle — ...

Vitreous humor

Conjunctiva — ... — Optic nerve

— Central canal

FIGURE 8.1
The human eye.

the front chamber of the eye. Next, the light passes through the **pupil,** a circular hole in the center of the colored **iris;** the pupil contracts or expands to regulate the amount of light entering the eye. The light then passes through the **lens,** a transparent, elastic structure suspended by tiny muscles that adjust its thickness so that both the near and far objects can be brought into sharp focus. Finally, the light passes through the **vitreous humor,** a jellylike substance that fills most of the eye's interior. Disturbances of any of these structures can prevent the clear focusing of an image on the retina.

Refractive Errors

Refraction is the process of bending light rays when they pass from one transparent structure to another. As just described, the normal eye refracts light rays so that a clear image is perceived on the retina; no special help is needed. However, for many people—perhaps half the general population (Miller, 1979)—the size and shape of the eye prevent refraction from being perfect. That is, the light rays do not focus clearly on the retina. Refractive errors can usually be corrected by glasses or contact lenses; but if severe enough, they can cause permanent visual impairment.

In **myopia,** or nearsightedness, the eye is larger than normal from front to back. The image conducted to the retina is thus somewhat out of focus. A child with myopia can see near objects clearly, but more distant objects—such as a blackboard or a movie—are blurred or are not seen at all. The opposite of myopia is **hyperopia,** commonly called farsightedness. The hyperopic eye is shorter than normal, preventing the light rays from converging on the retina. A child with hyperopia has difficulty seeing near objects clearly but is able to focus well on more distant objects. **Astigmatism** refers to distorted or blurred vision caused by irregularities in the cornea or other surfaces of the eye; both near and distant objects may be out of focus. Glasses or contact lenses can correct many refractive errors by changing the course of light rays to produce as clear a focus as possible.

Other Causes of Visual Impairment

Blindness or impaired vision can result from many causes, only a few of which will be discussed here. A **cataract** is a cloudiness in the lens of the eye that blocks the light necessary for seeing clearly. Vision may be blurred, distorted, or incomplete. Some people with cataracts liken their vision to looking through a dirty windshield. If the cataract is extremely cloudy or dense, a person may be unable to perceive any details at all. Cataracts are common in older people but may also occur in children. Most children born with cataracts have their cloudy lenses surgically removed. They must then wear special postcataract eyeglasses or contact lenses and usually need to wear bifocals or have one pair of glasses for distance vision and another pair for reading, because the glasses or contact lenses cannot change focus as a natural lens does. A permanent lens is sometimes implanted into the eye after cataract surgery, but this procedure is not yet universally accepted by ophthalmologists.

Glaucoma is a prevalent disease marked by abnormally high pressure within the eye. There are various types of glaucoma, all related to disturbances or blockages of the fluids that normally circulate within the eye. Central and peripheral vision are impaired—or lost entirely—when the increased pressure damages the optic nerve. Although glaucoma can be extremely painful in its advanced phase, it frequently goes undetected for long periods, and children may not even be aware of the small, gradual changes in their vision. If detected in its early stages, glaucoma can often be treated successfully with medication or surgery. Figure 8.2 shows how the world might look to people with cataracts or glaucoma.

Several important causes of visual impairment and blindness involve damage to the retina, the light-sensitive tissue that is so critical for clear vision. The retina is rich in blood vessels and is affected by disorders of the circulatory system. One such disorder is **diabetes;** children and adults with diabetes frequently have impaired vision due to hemorrhages and the growth of new blood vessels in the area of the retina. This condition, known as **diabetic retinopathy,** is the leading cause of blindness for people between 20 and 64 years of age. Surgery with lasers has been helpful in some instances, but there is no effective treatment as yet. However, the American Academy of Ophthalmology (1985) recently advised that up to half of all cases of diabetic retinopathy could be prevented through early diagnosis and treatment. All children and adults with diabetes should receive regular, detailed eye examinations.

Chapter 9 includes further information on diabetes in children.

Retinitis pigmentosa (RP) is the most common of all inherited retinal disorders. This disease causes a gradual degeneration of the retina. The first symptom is usually difficulty in seeing at night, followed by loss of peripheral vision. A small amount of central vision may be maintained. In most cases RP is not treatable, although recent research has helped to identify families at high risk of having affected children (Kaiser-Kupfer & Morris, 1985). RP sometimes occurs in congenitally deaf people. The unfortunate combination of congenital deafness and gradual retinitis pig-

(a) Shaded area indicates normal field of vision. Dark spot near center is the *macula*, or area of the sharpest central vision.

(b)

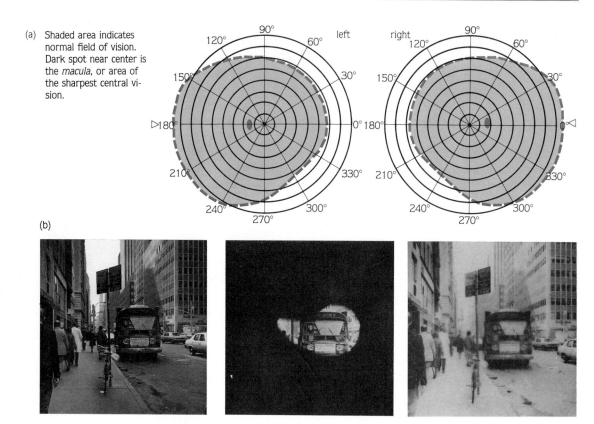

FIGURE 8.2
(a) Charts used to record field of vision. (b) The same street scene as might be viewed by a person with normal vision, advanced glaucoma, or cataracts.
Source: The Lighthouse, New York Association for the Blind, New York. Reprinted by permission.

mentosa is known as **Usher's syndrome,** a significant cause of deaf-blindness among adolescents and adults.

Macular degeneration is a fairly common condition in which the central area of the retina (the macular area) gradually deteriorates. In contrast to retinitis pigmentosa, the child with macular degeneration usually retains peripheral vision but loses the ability to see clearly in the center of the visual field.

Detached retinas result when the retina becomes partially or totally separated from the outer layers of tissue in the eye. Such a condition may accompany several diseases of the eye or can result from trauma. Detached or torn retinas can frequently be repaired by surgery.

Retinopathy of prematurity (ROP), formerly referred to as retrolental fibroplasia, affected thousands of children in the 1940s and 1950s. These children, born prematurely, actually had normal visual potential at birth. However, they were routinely placed in incubators and given high levels of oxygen. When the infants were later removed from the oxygen-rich incubators, the change in oxygen levels resulted in an abnormally dense growth of blood vessels and scar tissue in the eyes, often leading to retinal detachment and total blindness. Today, the amount of oxygen given to premature infants is much more carefully regulated, and ROP is no longer a leading cause of visual impairment. However, it still occurs when infants are born at extreme risk and need massive doses of oxygen in order to survive.

ROP is one example of how medical technology can have both positive and negative effects.

A familiarity with a student's visual impairment can be an asset to a teacher. It is useful to know, for example, that Linda has difficulty reading under strong lights, that Richard has only a small amount of central vision in his right eye, or that Ella sometimes experiences eye pain. Basic knowledge of the conditions described here can help a teacher understand some aspects of a child's learning and behavior and decide when to refer a child for professional vision care.

PREVALENCE

Visually impaired children constitute a small percentage of the school-age population— approximately one child in a thousand. The prevalence of these children within the population of children requiring special education services is also small—about 1% of all handicapped children (Kirchner, 1985). Recent advances in early detection, medical care, and optical correction have enabled many students who would formerly have been classified as visually impaired to attend regular classes without special help.

The American Printing House for the Blind conducts a detailed annual census of legally blind students in the United States. In a recent year 45,221 visually impaired students were enrolled in formal educational programs (American Printing House for the Blind, 1985). About 74% of these students received their education in regular public schools, whereas just over 10% attended schools for the blind. Most of the remaining 16% of visually impaired students were served in programs for multihandicapped students and in vocational rehabilitation programs. The actual number of visually impaired students is probably somewhat higher than the American Printing House census indicates, because not all schools and agencies report their students to this agency. Still, it is doubtful that visually impaired students exceed 0.1% of the entire school-age population.

Surveys of the reading methods used by visually impaired students give some insight into the heterogeneity and changing nature of this population. The 1985 American Printing House census identified 36% of visually impaired students as visual readers, who primarily use large-print or regular-print materials. The next largest group (23%) was comprised of auditory readers, who use recorded or taped materials or are read to aloud. In addition, there are nonreaders (20%), braille readers (15%), and prereaders (6%). These figures are consistent with the observation that a sizable percentage of blind and visually impaired students have other significant disabilities. According to Scholl (1986), recent reports from the field indicate that approximately one-third of the school-age population of visually impaired students have at least one additional impairment.

Nonreaders, as used here, refers to multihandicapped students, whereas prereaders are children who are expected to follow an academic program.

Visual impairment is thus considered a **low-prevalence disability.** There are comparatively few visually impaired students, even relative to other populations of

Small school districts often cooperate with each other in employing special teachers for visually impaired students.

exceptional children. Educators and parents of visually impaired children frequently express concern about this low prevalence. When financial resources are limited, they fear, visually impaired students may not receive adequate services from specially trained teachers. It may be particularly difficult for a local public school to provide comprehensive services for a visually impaired child who resides in a rural area.

BACKGROUND OF THE FIELD

Blind and visually impaired people, although not a large population, have been a conspicuous group throughout history. In most countries education of blind children is viewed as a high priority; schools and other special programs for blind children have historically been established before those for other groups of disabled children. Today, over 1,000 separate organizations exist to provide special services to visually impaired people in the United States. There are so many resources, in fact, that it is advisable for a blind person to take a special course in how to identify and use the most appropriate services, products, and information available (Winer, 1978).

There are several possible explanations for the special attention given to blind and visually impaired people. Blindness is usually readily apparent to the observer and evokes feelings of pity and sympathy in many people. It is perhaps the most feared of any disability. There are also many widely held stereotypes and misconceptions about blind people. One study found that sighted people considered the blind to have "nice," "sweet," and "charming" personalities (Klinghammer, 1964). Other old but persistent assumptions are that blind children are naturally gifted in music, that they have a sixth sense enabling them to detect obstacles, that they have better-than-normal hearing, and that they have superior memory skills.

In contrast, disabilities that are less visible, such as learning disabilities, have a comparatively short history.

Valentin Haüy (1745–1822) is given credit for starting the first school for blind children, the *Institution des Jeunes Aveugles* in Paris, which opened in 1784. Haüy had been shocked at seeing blind people performing as jesters and beggars on the streets of Paris and resolved to teach them more dignified ways of earning a living. The subjects taught at Haüy's school included reading and writing (using embossed print), music, and vocational skills. The competence demonstrated by Haüy's blind students impressed citizens in France and elsewhere in Europe. By the early 19th century residential schools for blind children had been established in several other countries, including England, Scotland, Austria, Germany, and Russia (Koestler, 1976; Roberts, 1986).

American educators, influenced by the European institutions, established private residential schools for blind children in Boston, New York, and Philadelphia around 1830. Within the next few decades most states had opened public residential schools for visually impaired children. Such schools continued to educate the great majority of visually impaired children until the mid-20th century (Koestler, 1976).

The first American public school class for totally blind children opened in Chicago in 1900; the first class for low vision children began in Boston in 1913; and the first itinerant teaching program for visually impaired children attending regular classes was implemented in Oakland, California, in 1938 (Ward, 1979). The mainstreaming of visually impaired children thus has a relatively long and successful history.

Sight-Saving Classes

For a good part of this century, many children with low vision were educated in special sight-saving classes, both in regular public schools and residential schools for the blind. It was generally believed that a child's remaining vision should be conserved by not using it too much. In extreme instances children with impaired but useful vision were even blindfolded or educated in dark rooms so that their precious vision would not be lost. Today, a dramatically different approach prevails. Eye specialists agree that vision, even if imperfect, *benefits* from being used; thus, educational programs for visually impaired children concentrate on helping them develop and use their visual abilities as much as possible.

This trend parallels the emphasis on teaching hearing impaired children to use their residual hearing as much as possible (see chapter 7).

A Wave of Visually Impaired Children

In the 1940s and 1950s thousands of infants became blind or severely visually impaired because of retinopathy of prematurity, described earlier in this chapter. This unfortunate medical occurrence, however, had a beneficial side effect in expanding the educational opportunities available to visually impaired children. Because the residential schools then in existence were unable to accommodate the large, sudden influx of children affected by ROP and because many parents did not want their children to attend distant residential schools, educational programs and services for visually impaired students became much more widely available in the regular public schools during the 1950s and 1960s. Although the majority of children blinded by ROP are now adults, public school programs for visually impaired children have continued to develop and diversify. Today, in most regions of the United States and Canada, parents may choose between public school and residential school education for their visually impaired children.

EDUCATIONAL APPROACHES

Teachers of visually impaired children are often thought of in conjunction with specialized equipment and materials, such as braille, canes, tape recorders, and magnifying devices. Media and materials do play an important role in the education of children with impaired vision. But the effective teacher must know a great deal more than how to use these special devices.

Because they are frequently called on to teach skills and concepts that most children acquire through vision, teachers of visually impaired students must be knowledgeable, competent, and creative. They must plan and carry out activities that will help their students gain as much information as possible through the nonvisual senses and by participation in active, practical experiences.

Many educators and psychologists have described the obstacles to learning imposed by blindness or severe visual impairment. Lowenfeld (1973), for example, observes that a blind child may hear a bird singing but gets no "concrete idea of the bird itself" from this sound alone. A teacher interested in teaching such a student about birds—to follow up on Lowenfeld's example—might plan a series of activities that would have the student touch birds of various species and manipulate related objects such as eggs, nests, and feathers. The student might assume the responsibility

Of course, even though opportunities for first-hand discovery and exploration are particularly vital for visually impaired children, they are also useful and appropriate for children with normal vision.

for feeding a pet bird at home or in the classroom. Perhaps a field trip to a poultry farm could be arranged. Through experiences such as these, visually impaired children can gradually obtain a more thorough and accurate knowledge of birds than they could if their education were limited to reading books about birds, memorizing vocabulary, or feeling plastic models.

There are virtually no limits on the extent to which a visually impaired child may participate in a full, well-rounded school program. Educators should ensure that the visually impaired student's IEP "includes the full range of instructional areas: those studied with nonhandicapped peers, those that require special instruction, and those outside of the school curriculum that are essential to enable them to compete with their nonhandicapped peers when they move into the adult world" (Scholl, 1987, p. 36). Successful accomplishment of this goal, however, requires that special educators provide support, consultation, and materials to regular teachers with visually impaired students in their classes.

Special Adaptations for Blind Students

Braille is a system of reading and writing in which letters, words, numbers, and other systems are made from arrangements of raised dots. The system was developed around 1830 by Louis Braille, a young Frenchman who was blind. Although the braille system is over 150 years old, it is by far the most efficient approach to reading by touch and is still an essential skill for people who have too little vision to read print. Blind students can read braille much more rapidly than they could the raised letters of the standard alphabet. Figure 8.3 shows the braille alphabet and numerals.

The braille system is complex. In many ways it is like the shorthand used by secretaries. Abbreviations, called *contractions,* help save space and permit faster reading and writing. For example, when the letter *r* stands by itself, it means *rather.* The word *myself* in braille is written *myf.* Frequently used words—such as *the, and, with,* and *for*—have their own special contractions. For example, the *and* symbol (⠯) appears four times in the following sentence:

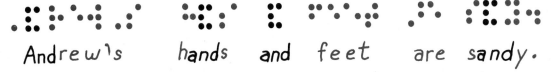

Many similar abbreviations assist in the more efficient reading and writing of braille. Mathematics, music, foreign languages, and scientific formulas all can be put into braille. When blind children attend regular public school classes, a specially trained teacher provides individual instruction in braille reading and writing. Cooperative planning with the regular classroom teacher is critical so that books can be ordered or prepared in advance. The regular classroom teacher is not usually expected to learn braille, but some teachers find it helpful and interesting to do so. The braille system is not as difficult to learn as it first appears to be.

Most blind children are introduced to braille when they are at about the first grade level. The majority of teachers introduce contractions early in the program,

The six dots of the Braille cell are arranged and numbered thus:

$$1\ \bullet\bullet\ 4$$
$$2\ \bullet\bullet\ 5$$
$$3\ \bullet\bullet\ 6$$

The capital sign, dot 6, placed before a letter makes it a capital. The number sign, dots 3, 4, 5, 6, placed before a character, makes it a figure and not a letter.

1	2	3	4	5	6	7	8	9	0
a	b	c	d	e	f	g	h	i	j
k	l	m	n	o	p	q	r	s	t
u	v	w	x	y	z	Capital Sign	Number Sign	Period	Comma

FIGURE 8.3
The braille system for representing numbers and letters.
Source: From the Division for the Blind and Physically Handicapped, Library of Congress, Washington, DC 20542.

rather than having the child learn to write out every word, letter by letter, and later have to unlearn this approach. Of course, it is important for the blind child to know the full and correct spelling of words, even if every letter does not appear separately in braille. It usually takes several years for children to become thoroughly familiar with the system and its rules. The speed of braille reading varies a great deal from student to student, but it is almost always much slower than the speed of print reading.

Young children generally learn to write braille using a brailler, a six-keyed device that somewhat resembles a typewriter. Older students are usually introduced to the slate and stylus, in which the braille dots are punched out one at a time by hand, from right to left. The slate and stylus method has certain advantages in note-taking; it is much smaller and quieter than the brailler.

The widely used Perkins Brailler has six keys, one for each dot of the braille cell.

Technology and Other Special Aids

These new devices enable many blind students to function more independently in regular classrooms, universities, and employment settings. Kelly (1987), Ruconich (1984), and Todd (1986) provide further information about the promising technological applications of braille.

Several recent devices have applied technology to make braille more efficient. Typically, braille books are large, expensive, and cumbersome. It can be difficult for blind students to retrieve information quickly when they must tactually review many pages of braille books or notes. One system, known as VersaBraille, is paperless: braille is stored on small cassette tapes and can be efficiently retrieved when the tape is placed into a special device. Other devices, such as the Cranmer Modified Perkins Brailler, allow students to send information to a computer and receive brailled output on paper. These and other systems offer blind students the advantages of word processing; written materials can be readily reviewed or altered without reading or rewriting entire pages in braille.

Typewriting is an important means of communication between blind children and their sighted classmates and teachers and is also a useful skill for further education and employment. Instruction in typing should begin as early as is feasible in the child's school program. Today, handwriting is less widely taught to totally blind students. One noteworthy exception is that it is necessary for children to learn to sign their own names so that they can assume such responsibilities as maintaining a bank account, registering to vote, and applying for a job.

A wide range of specialized materials and devices has been specially developed or modified for the instruction of blind students. Most of these educational materials are available from state instructional materials centers for the visually impaired or from the American Printing House for the Blind.

Mathematical aids for blind students include the Cranmer Abacus. The abacus, long used in Japan, has been adapted to assist blind students in learning number concepts and making calculations. Manipulation of the abacus beads is particularly useful in counting, adding, and subtracting. For more advanced mathematical functions the student is likely to use the Speech-Plus talking calculator, a small electronic instrument that performs most of the operations of any standard calculator. It "talks" by voicing entries and results aloud and also presents them in digital form visually. This is only one of many instances in which the recent development of synthetic speech technology has helpful implications for blind people. Talking clocks and spelling aids are also available.

Further information about these programs is available from the organizations listed at the end of this chapter.

In the sciences and social studies, several adaptations have been designed to encourage blind students to use their tactile and auditory senses for firsthand manipulation and discovery. Examples include embossed relief maps and diagrams, three-dimensional models, and electronic probes that give an audible signal in response to light. Curriculum modification projects such as MAVIS (Materials Adaptation for Visually Impaired Students in the Social Studies) and SAVI (Science Activities for the Visually Impaired) emphasize how visually impaired students can, with some modifications, participate in learning activities along with normally sighted students.

The Optacon (*optical-to-tactile converter*) is a small electronic device that converts regular print into a readable vibrating form for blind people. When the tiny camera of the Optacon is held over a printed *E*, for example, the user feels on the tip of one finger a vertical line and then three horizontal lines. The Optacon does not

George places the Optacon's tiny camera on his book and feels the raised letters with the fingertip of his other hand.

convert print into braille but into a configuration of raised "pins" representing the letter being viewed by the camera. Although extensive training and practice are required, many blind children and adults are able to read regular print effectively with the aid of the Optacon. It can allow students to work with typewriters, calculators, computer terminals, and small print.

The Kurzweil Reading Machine is another recent technological development with exciting implications for visually impaired and other disabled students. This sophisticated computer actually reads books and other printed matter aloud, using synthetic speech. The reader can regulate the speed and tone of the voice and can even have the machine spell out words letter by letter if desired. The machines are costly and require considerable training. However, the "intelligence" of the Kurzweil Reading Machine is constantly being improved, and the machines are in use at most residential schools and also in many public school programs, large public libraries, rehabilitation centers, and colleges and universities.

The cost of such a device may be as much as $30,000.

Special Adaptations for Students with Low Vision

As previously noted, the great majority of children enrolled in educational programs for the visually impaired have some potentially useful vision. Their learning need not be restricted to touch, hearing, and other nonvisual senses. Currently, there is great emphasis on developing children's abilities to use their residual vision as effectively as possible. Recent research has shown that structured programs of visual assessment, training, and evaluation can dramatically improve these abilities; the earlier in life such programs are begun, the more likely they are to be successful (Corn, 1986; Fellows,

Leguire, Rogers, & Bremer, 1986; Ferrell, 1985). The current emphasis on utilization of low vision is largely attributable to the influential work of Natalie Barraga (1964, 1970, 1980, 1983). She demonstrated that children—even those with extremely limited visual acuity or visual field—could be helped to improve their visual efficiency dramatically.

Visual efficiency, as defined by Barraga, includes such skills as controlling eye movements, adapting to the visual environment, paying attention to visual stimuli, and processing visual information rapidly. The fundamental premise in developing visual efficiency is that children *learn to see* and must be actively involved in using their own vision. Merely furnishing a classroom with attractive things for children to see is not sufficient. A low vision child may, without training, be unable to derive much meaningful information through vision. Forms may be perceived as vague masses and shapeless, indistinct blobs. Training has helped many children learn to use their visual impressions intelligently and effectively, to make sense out of what they see. Barraga's Program to Develop Efficiency in Visual Functioning, including a helpful *Source Book on Low Vision* (which can be purchased separately), is available from the American Printing House for the Blind.

> These materials may also be useful with other children who, though not visually impaired, require instruction on basic pre-reading and visual discrimination skills.

Many children with low vision are able to benefit from special optical aids. These may include glasses and contact lenses that are worn on or in the eyes, small telescopes that are held in the hand, or magnifiers placed on top of printed pages. Such aids cannot give normal vision to visually impaired children but may help them to perform better at certain tasks, such as reading small print or seeing distant objects.

Optical aids are usually specialized, rather than, all-purpose. Juanita might, for example, use her glasses for reading large print, a magnifier stand for reading smaller print, and a monocular (one-eye) telescope for viewing the blackboard. A usual disadvantage of corrective lenses and magnifiers is that the more powerful they are, the more they tend to distort or restrict the peripheral field of vision. Some field-widening lenses and devices are now available for students with limited visual fields. These include prisms and fish-eye lenses, designed to make objects appear smaller so that a greater area can be perceived on the unimpaired portions of a student's visual field. Instruction in vision utilization should not be taught only in isolated time blocks but should be incorporated into all parts of the low vision student's curriculum (Corn, 1986). For example, a child learning daily living skills might be encouraged to use his vision to identify and reach for his toothbrush.

> Children whose vision is extremely limited are more likely to use monocular (one-eye) than binocular (two-eye) aids, especially for seeing things at a distance.

Today, a large number of ophthalmologists, optometrists, and clinical facilities specialize in the assessment and treatment of low vision. A professional examination can help determine which types of optical aids, if any, are appropriate for a particular student. It is usually a good idea to furnish optical aids on a trial or loan basis so that the student can gradually learn to use and evaluate them in natural settings. A follow-up session should then be scheduled.

Many books and other materials are available in large print for children with low vision. Although these are helpful in many cases, large print materials have certain disadvantages. When print is made very large, the number of letters and words that can be seen at any one time is sharply reduced; it thus becomes more difficult for a student to read smoothly, with a natural sweep of eye movements. It is generally

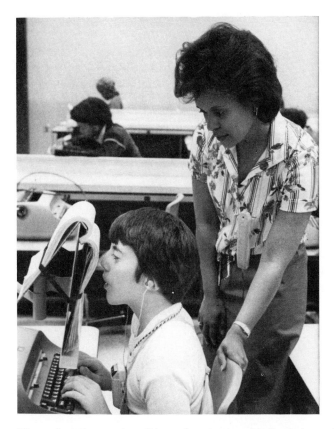

Minor adaptations, such as this reading stand, enable Randy to use his vision as effectively as possible in school.

agreed that a visually impaired child should use the smallest print size that she can read comfortably. A child may be able to transfer from large print to smaller print as reading efficiency increases, just as most normally sighted children do.

A significant number of children with low vision are able to learn to read using regular-sized print, with or without the use of optical aids. This situation permits a much wider variety of materials and eliminates the added cost of obtaining large print books or enlarging texts with special duplicating machines. Although the size of print is an important variable, other equally important factors to consider with low vision students are the quality of the printed material, the contrast between print and page, the spacing between lines, and the illumination of the setting in which the child reads.

Some educational programs use closed circuit television systems to enable low vision students to read regular-sized printed materials. These systems usually include a sliding table on which a book is placed, a television camera with a zoom lens mounted above the book, and a television monitor nearby. The student is able to adjust the size, brightness, and contrast of the material and can select either an ordinary black-on-white image or a negative white-on-black image, which is preferred by

LOW VISION

What does a child with low vision actually see? It is difficult for us to know. We may try to obtain some idea of total blindness by wearing a blindfold—but the majority of visually impaired children are not totally blind. Even if two children share the same cause of visual impairment, it is unlikely that they see things in exactly the same way. And each child may see things differently at different times.

We asked a few people with low vision to describe how they see. Here are some excerpts from what they told us.

Have you ever been out camping in a strange place? When it's dark and you're trying to find your way from the tent to the bathroom, and you can't wear your glasses or contact lenses—that's like the way I see.

I'm pretty much nearsighted. I can *see* a far object, I mean I know the image is there, but I can't *distinguish* it. I can see a house. It is just a white blob out there. I couldn't tell you what color is the roof trim, or where the windows are.*

Put on a pair of sunglasses. Then rub vaseline all around the central part of each lens. Now try reading a book. Or crossing a street.

I never see blackness. . . . If I am looking at a picture, it's not like I see a hole in the middle. I fill something in there, but it wouldn't necessarily be what is *really* there. That's how I describe it to people—take a newspaper, hold it up, and look straight ahead. Now describe what you see here, off to the side . . . that's what I see all the time.*

The following suggestions for teachers of students with low vision were made by the Vision Team, a group of specialists in visual impairment who work with regular class teachers in 13 school districts in Hennepin County, Minnesota. Glenda Martin has permitted us to share the suggestions with you.

☐ Using the eyes does not harm them. The more children use their eyes, the greater their efficiency will be.

☐ Holding printed material close to the eyes may be the low vision child's way of seeing best. It will not harm the eyes.

☐ Although eyes cannot be strained from use, a low vision child's eyes may tire more quickly. A change of focus or activity helps.

☐ Copying is often a problem for low vision children. The child may need a longer period of time to do classwork, or a shortened assignment.

☐ It is helpful if the teacher verbalizes as much as possible while writing on the chalkboard or using the overhead projector.

☐ A few low vision children use large print books, but most do not. As the child learns to use vision, it becomes more efficient, and the student can generally read smaller print.

☐ Dittoes can be difficult for the low vision child to read. Giving that child one of the first copies or the original from which the ditto was made can be helpful.

☐ The term *legally blind* does not mean educationally blind. Most children who are legally blind function educationally as sighted children.

☐ Contrast, print style, and spacing can be more important than the size of the print.

☐ One of the most important things a low vision child learns in school is to accept the responsibility of seeking help when it is needed—rather than waiting for someone to offer help.

☐ In evaluating quality of work and applying discipline, the teacher best helps the low vision child by using the same standards that are used with other children.

Perhaps most important of all, an attitude of understanding and acceptance can help the student with low vision succeed in the regular classroom.

Children who have low vision aids—such as special eyeglasses, magnifiers, and telescopes—may need instruction and assistance in learning how to

*From *Voices: Interviews with Handicapped People* by M. D. Orlansky and W. L. Heward (Columbus: Merrill, 1981).

312

Some magnifiers come with a built-in light, but most times you will have to use another light. A desk lamp is best. (The overhead light casts a shadow on your book or paper as you get close enough to see it.) Be sure the light is along your side, coming over your shoulder.

☐ Be sure to keep your aids clean. Dust, dirt, and fingerprints are hard to see through. Clean the lenses with a clean, soft cloth (never paper). If you have contact lenses clean them with a special solution, *following your doctor's instructions carefully.* Always be sure your hands are clean to begin.

☐ Keep your aids in their cases when you are not using them. They will be more protected and always ready to be taken with you wherever you go.

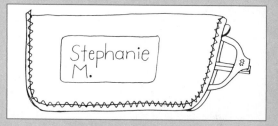

use them most effectively. Here are some tips written especially for children and designed to help them become accustomed to low vision aids.*

☐ Low vision aids take time to get used to. At first it seems like just a lot more things to take care of and carry around, but each aid you have will help you with a special job of seeing. You will get better with practice. In time, reaching for your telescope to read the blackboard will seem as natural as picking up a pencil or pen to write. *It's all a matter of practice.*

☐ Lighting is very important. Always work with the most effective light for you. It makes a big difference in how clear things will look.

☐ Carry your low vision aids with you. Most of them are small and lightweight. That way, you will have them when you need them. If you have aids you use only at school, you may want to ask your teacher to keep them for you in a safe place.

☐ Experiment in new situations. Can you see the menu at McDonalds? watch the football game? see prices on toys? find your friend's house number? The more often you use your low vision aid, the better you will get at using it.

☐ Try out different combinations of aids with or without your glasses or contact lenses. This way you will find the combination that works best for you.

*From *A Closer Look at Low Vision Aids* by Marybeth Dean with illustrations by Gail Feld. Available from the Connecticut State Board of Education and Services for the Blind, Division of Children's Services, 170 Ridge Road, Wethersfield, CT 06109.

many students. The teacher may also have a television monitor that lets him see the student's work without making repeated trips to the student's desk. A disadvantage of closed circuit television systems—in addition to their cost—is that they are usually not portable, so that the student who uses television as a primary reading medium is largely restricted to the specially equipped classroom.

See "Low Vision" on pages 312–13.

Other classroom adaptations for low vision students are often minor but can be very important. Many students benefit from desks with adjustable or tilting tops so that they can read and write at close range without constantly bending over and casting a shadow. Most regular classrooms today have adequate lighting, but special lamps may still be helpful for some children. Writing paper should have a dull finish to reduce glare; an off-white color such as buff or ivory is generally better than white. Some teachers have found it helpful to give low vision students chairs with wheels so that they can easily move around the blackboard area or other sections where instruction is taking place, without constantly getting up and down. Dittoed worksheets in light purple or other poorly contrasting colors are difficult for most low vision students to use; an aide or classmate could first go over the worksheet with a dark pen or marker. Many other modifications can be made by a teacher, using common sense and considering the needs of the individual student with low vision.

Listening

Visually impaired children—both those totally blind and those with low vision—must obtain an enormous amount of information through the sense of hearing. A great deal of time in school is devoted to speaking and listening to others. Visually impaired students also make frequent use of recorded materials, particularly in high school. Recorded books and magazines and the equipment to use them can be obtained through the Library of Congress, the American Printing House for the Blind, the Canadian National Institute for the Blind, Recording for the Blind, and various other organizations, usually on a free-loan basis. Each state has a designated library that provides books and materials for blind readers.

Because many visually impaired students are able to process auditory information at a faster rate than that of average conversational speech, devices are available to increase the rate at which tapes are played back without significantly distorting the quality of the speech. The ever-increasing use of synthetic speech equipment probably means that listening skills will become even more important to visually impaired students in the future. The ability of blind students to comprehend synthetic speech was investigated by Rhyne (1982), who found that the aural (listening) mode was a generally efficient way to learn and that the students' comprehension increased as they gained more experience listening to synthetic speech.

Because there are so many useful opportunities for learning through listening, an important component of the educational program of virtually every visually impaired child is the systematic development of listening skills. Children do not automatically develop the ability to listen effectively simply by being placed in a regular classroom, nor are visually impaired students necessarily better listeners than normally sighted students.

Listening involves several components, including attention to and awareness of sounds, discrimination, and assignment of meaning to sound (Heinze, 1986). Good listening skills tend to broaden a student's vocabulary and to support the development of speaking, reading, and writing abilities. Learning-to-listen approaches can take an almost unlimited variety of forms. Young children, for example, might learn to discriminate between sounds that are near and far, loud and soft, high-pitched and low-pitched. A teacher might introduce a new word into a sentence and ask the child to identify it. Older students might learn to listen for important details while there are distracting background noises, to differentiate between factual and fictional material, or to respond to verbal analogy questions.

Some structured programs for developing listening skills have been developed (Alber, 1974; Stocker, 1973; Swallow & Conner, 1982). Instruction in this area can be among the most useful parts of a visually impaired student's curriculum.

Recreational activities in the community, such as bowling, can provide opportunities for visually impaired students to develop self-confidence.

Practical Living and Social Skills

Some educators of visually impaired students suggest that academic achievement has traditionally been overemphasized at the expense of important basic living skills. Hatlen (1976), for example, calls for "the most urgent attention" to be given to such areas as cooking, grooming, shopping, financial management, decision making, recreational activities, personal hygiene, and social behavior. Specific instruction in these skills can facilitate a student's eventual independence as an adult. The specially trained teacher, the regular class teacher, other specialists, the parents, and the student should all participate in planning and providing instruction that will be practical and relevant to the student's needs and future objectives.

Hatlen (1978) further recommends that, if necessary, visually impaired students be taught how to deal with strangers, how to interpret and explain their visual impairments to other people, and how to make socially acceptable gestures in conversation. It is also important for students to be aware of the range of career opportunities available to them and to be informed about services, resources, and responsibilities in their communities.

Another area of some concern to educators is special mannerisms—repetitive body movements or other behaviors, such as rocking, eye-poking, hand-waving, and head-rolling. Although not necessarily harmful in themselves, mannerisms can place a visually impaired person at a social disadvantage, because such actions are conspicuous and call attention to the person as different or handicapped. It is not clearly known why many visually impaired children engage in manneristic behaviors. Tooze (1981) attributes them to a child's being under stress or having a "desire to move coupled with a fear of moving forward" (p. 29). It is generally suggested that children be kept busy and active so that they will have less time to indulge in mannerisms. Applied behavioral programs have also been used with visually impaired children to modify head-drooping during conversation (Raver, 1984) and various off-task behaviors that interfere with learning (Barton & LaGrow, 1985).

Huebner (1986) provides an excellent set of guidelines for teaching social skills. She emphasizes the importance of developing socially acceptable behaviors, which in turn facilitate independence, self-confidence, and acceptance by others in school, community, and employment settings. Even though a visually impaired child may perform a task safely and independently, she may not be doing so in a traditional, socially acceptable manner—for example, the child who likes to eat oatmeal by scooping it up to her mouth with her fingers!

Human Sexuality

Sighted children typically learn a great deal about human sexuality through vision. They see people establish social and sexual relationships with each other; they can see their own bodies and those of others. Blind children, however, may grow up with serious knowledge gaps or misconceptions about sexuality and reproduction, particularly if parents and teachers fail to provide information and explanations. "I know girls have breasts," a blind adolescent told his counselor, "but I don't know where they are!" (Elliott, 1979). Modesty makes it difficult for blind children to learn by touching the bodies of others, and it is sometimes mistakenly assumed that blind people are uninterested in sex. In some European countries live human models are used to familiarize blind students with anatomy and sexuality, but this practice has not been widely adopted in North America. In addition to providing accurate biological information, instructional programs should also consider the emotional aspects of sexual experience and the possible genetic implications of a student's visual impairment.

Some kinds of visual impairments can be passed from parents to children.

Issues in Assessment

There is a continuing concern about the use (and possible misuse) of intelligence tests with visually impaired children. Intelligence tests, standardized on sighted children, are often based largely on visual concepts. They may include such questions as "Why do people have hedges around their homes?" or "What should you do if you see a train approaching a broken track?" The results of these tests may well give an inaccurate picture of a visually impaired child's abilities and needs. Regrettably, many blind and low vision children have been placed in inappropriate educational programs because of strict reliance on standardized test performance.

Few tests have been developed for and standardized on visually impaired children. However, even if such tests were more readily available, they would be of questionable value because of the diversity and small size of the population. Helpful reviews of assessment procedures and guidelines for the appropriate use of tests with visually impaired learners have recently been provided by Chase (1986a, 1986b) and Hall, Scholl, and Swallow (1986). A number of instruments, although not specifically designed for visually impaired students, may nevertheless be useful in assessing certain aspects of their performance. In gathering information that will be helpful in developing educational goals for a visually impaired child, a variety of formal and informal procedures should be used. The results of developmental or intelligence tests should always be supplemented by careful observations of the child's behavior in school and play situations (Chapman, 1978). Teachers and parents are usually in the best position to observe the child's communication, exploration, and social interaction over an extended period. Their contributions should play a major part in planning a visually impaired child's educational program.

Orientation and Mobility

The educational program of a visually impaired child could hardly be considered complete or appropriate if it failed to include instruction in orientation and mobility. **Orientation** is defined as the ability to establish one's position in relation to the environment through the use of the remaining senses. **Mobility** is the ability to move safely and efficiently from one point to another (Lowenfeld, 1973). For most students more time and effort is spent in orientation training than in learning specific mobility techniques. It is extremely important that, from an early age, visually impaired children be taught basic concepts that will familiarize them with their own bodies and their surroundings. For example, they need to be taught that the place where the leg bends is called a knee and that rooms have walls, doors, windows, corners, and ceilings.

O&M specialists are called peripatologists in some states.

Orientation and mobility (O&M) instruction is a well-developed subspecialty in the education and rehabilitation of blind and visually impaired persons. There are many specific techniques involved in teaching visually impaired students to understand their environment and maneuver through it effectively. Training in such skills should be given by qualified O&M specialists. Until recently, formal O&M instruction was seldom given to children younger than about 12 years of age. However, the importance of early development of travel skills and related concepts is now generally recognized. Today, it is not at all unusual for preschool children to benefit from the services of an O&M instructor.

The long cane is the device most widely used by visually impaired persons for independent travel. The traveler does not "tap" the cane but sweeps it lightly in an arc while walking, to gain information about the path ahead. Properly used, the cane enables the traveler to detect obstacles such as curbs, stairs, doors, holes, and parking meters. Changes in the travel surface (e.g., from grass to concrete or from a rug to a wooden floor) can also be detected one step in advance. However, even though mastery of cane skills can do much to increase a person's independence and self-esteem, there are certain disadvantages to cane use (Tuttle, 1984). The cane cannot detect overhanging obstacles such as tree branches, and provides only fragmentary information about the environment, particularly if the blind person is in new or unfamiliar surroundings.

A small percentage of visually impaired people (about 1% to 3%) travel with the aid of guide dogs (Hill & Jacobson, 1985). Like the cane traveler, the guide dog user must have good O&M skills to select the route to be taken and to be aware of the environment. The dog wears a special harness and has been trained to follow several basic verbal commands, to avoid obstacles, and to ensure the traveler's safety. Several weeks of intensive training at special guide dog agencies are required before the person and dog can work together effectively. Misunderstandings sometimes arise when blind people with guide dogs are refused entry into restaurants, hotels, airplanes, or other places that normally do not permit animals; state and local regulations permit guide dogs to have access to these places. Guide dogs are especially helpful when a person must travel over complicated or unpredictable routes, as in large cities. They are not usually available to children under 16 years of age or to people with multiple disabilities.

In the area of mobility most visually impaired people find it necessary occasionally to rely on the assistance of others. The sighted guide technique is a simple method of helping a visually impaired person travel. The visually impaired person should lightly grasp the sighted person's arm just above the elbow and walk half a step behind in a natural manner. In situations where visually impaired students attend regular classes, it may be a good idea for one of the students and the O&M specialist to demonstrate the sighted guide technique for classmates.

Never pull or push a blind person when you are serving as a sighted guide.

Several recently developed electronic travel aids may facilitate orientation and independent travel for blind and visually impaired persons. These include a laser beam cane, which emits a sound to signal objects in the path of a traveler as well as hazards overhead and drop-offs below. Other devices, designed to be used in conjunction with a standard cane or guide dog, send out sound waves to bounce off objects and give the trained traveler information about the environment through auditory or tactual channels. Electronic travel aids have even been used with blind infants as young as 6 months of age, in an attempt to enhance their early learning and awareness by enabling them to explore their environment more thoroughly and independently (Ferrell, 1984). Disadvantages of electronic travel aids include their high cost, the extensive training required, and possible problems in adverse weather conditions. Hill and Jacobson (1985) noted that users of electronic travel aids found them helpful in orienting themselves to new settings but tended to use the aids less after they had become familiar with the environment.

Whatever the preferred method of travel, most visually impaired students can generally learn to negotiate familiar places, such as school and home, on their own. Good orientation and mobility skills have many positive effects. The visually impaired child who can travel independently is likely to develop more physical and social skills and more self-confidence than the child who must continually depend on other people to get around. Good travel skills also expand a student's opportunities for employment and independent living in the community.

EDUCATIONAL ALTERNATIVES FOR VISUALLY IMPAIRED STUDENTS

Public Schools

In the past, most children with severe visual impairments were educated in residential schools for blind children. Today, however, most visually impaired children attend regular public school classes with their normally sighted peers. Supportive help is usually given by itinerant teacher-consultants, sometimes called vision specialists. These specially trained teachers may be employed by a residential school, a school district, a regional education agency, or a state or province. Their roles and caseloads vary widely from program to program. In general, however, the itinerant teacher-consultant may be expected to assume some or all of the following responsibilities:

See the special feature on page 321 for a description of the responsibilities of one itinerant teacher.

- ☐ instruct the visually impaired student directly (within the classroom and/or individually elsewhere)
- ☐ obtain or prepare specialized learning materials
- ☐ put reading assignments into braille, large print, or tape-recorded form or arrange for readers
- ☐ interpret information about the child's visual impairment and visual functioning to other educators and parents
- ☐ suggest classroom and program modifications that may be advisable because of the child's vision
- ☐ help plan the child's educational goals, initiate and maintain contact with various agencies, keep records of services provided
- ☐ consult with the child's parents and other teachers

Some itinerant teacher-consultants specialize in work with visually impaired infants and preschool children.

The itinerant teacher-consultant may or may not provide instruction in orientation and mobility. Some programs—particularly in rural areas—employ dually certified teachers who are also orientation and mobility specialists. Other programs employ one teacher for educational support and another for orientation and mobility training.

Some public school programs have special resource rooms for visually impaired students. In contrast to the itinerant teacher-consultant, who travels from school to school, the resource room teacher remains in one specially equipped location and serves visually impaired students for part of their school day. Resource rooms for visually impaired students are usually found only in large school districts.

The amount of time that the itinerant teacher-consultant or resource room teacher spends with a visually impaired student who attends regular classes varies considerably. Some students may be seen every day because they require a great deal of specialized assistance. Others may be seen weekly, monthly, or even less frequently because they are able to function well in the regular class with less support.

Public school education for visually impaired children has many advocates. McIntire (1985) writes that "the least restrictive environment for blind children is in the local public school regular classroom with nonhandicapped children" (p. 163);

Working together with his sighted classmates helps Paul maintain a high level of achievement in the regular classroom.

HELP WANTED: ITINERANT TEACHER OF VISUALLY IMPAIRED STUDENTS

An itinerant teacher travels from school to school providing instruction, materials, and supportive services to visually impaired students. Because most of these students attend regular classes in public schools, the itinerant teacher frequently consults with other teachers, parents, and rehabilitation specialists in planning to meet these students' needs. Students on an itinerant teacher's caseload may range from infants to young adults and may include blind, low vision, and multihandicapped children. In rural areas the itinerant teacher often spends a great deal of time on the road in order to visit and work with each student. The following job description gives a realistic indication of the varied and challenging responsibilities assumed by itinerant teachers of visually impaired children. The description was shared with us by High Plains Special Education Co-op in Garden City, Kansas.

The High Plains Special Education Cooperative, providing services in 19 rural southwest Kansas school districts, has a vacancy for an itinerant teacher of the visually impaired. We feel that salary and fringe benefits are excellent.

The new teacher would be based in Ulysses, a town of approximately 4,000. He/she would be responsible for providing services to both braille and print reading students of all grade levels in our co-op.

The student requiring the most direct service is a very bright braille-reading student in Ulysses. He is just completing first grade. He has useful vision and does math and some reading workbook assignments with an electronic visual aid in his classroom. He is near the top of his class. Also in Ulysses, we have recently become aware of a 9-month-old with several handicaps, including visual impairment. Information is sketchy at this time. We would hope the teacher would be willing to serve as a resource person and to do some work with the parents and child.

In Liberal, a town of 20,000, located 60 miles southeast of Ulysses, is an albino girl, just completing second grade. She is a large print reader. She does well but needs assistance in math and fine motor skills.

There is a sixth grade boy in Elkhart, 60 miles southwest of Ulysses, who needs to be checked on periodically. His main difficulty is in the area of social relationships. He will be using regular print materials for the coming year.

We have just received word that a student currently attending the State School for the Visually Handicapped will be entering public school in Johnson this fall. Johnson is 20 miles from Ulysses. This seventh grade girl is also a print reader.

In Copeland there is a high school student who uses all the regular school materials. He has not required any direct services for 2 years.

We have an Optacon and several other electronic aids. We contract with an orientation/mobility instructor for services in that area.

Ability to work cooperatively with classroom teachers and a willingness to drive perhaps 100 miles per day are essential. Travel expenses are reimbursed. The teacher is given a lot of freedom in setting up his/her schedule and program. Most teachers, parents, administrators, and students are enjoyable to work with.

Cruickshank (1986) maintains that "the blind child is perhaps the easiest exceptional child to integrate into a regular grade in the public schools" (p. 104). To make this integration successful, however, a full program of appropriate educational and related services must be provided. As Griffing (1986) observes, "No category of handicap requires greater coordination and cooperation among resources than the area of the blind and visually impaired" (p. 5). A key person in the visually impaired child's program is the regular classroom teacher. In fact, an extensive study of the "components of success in mainstreaming" (Bishop, 1986) found that "an accepting and flexible regular classroom teacher" was considered to be the single most important factor in the successful placement of visually impaired children in public school classes. Other aspects of the school situation that were rated as highly important were peer acceptance and interaction, the availability of support personnel, and adequate access to special supplies and equipment.

Regular classroom teachers are important in other areas of special education, too, of course.

Residential Schools

Residential schools also serve many visually impaired children from low-income, culturally diverse, and non-English-speaking backgrounds (see chapter 12).

Residential schools continue to meet the needs of a sizable number of visually impaired children. There are 52 such schools operating in the United States today. The current population of residential schools consists largely of visually impaired children with additional disabilities, such as mental retardation, hearing impairment, behavior disorders, and cerebral palsy. Some parents are not able to care for their children adequately at home, and others prefer the greater concentration of specialized personnel, facilities, and services that the residential school usually offers.

Parents and educators who support residential school education for visually impaired children frequently point to the leadership that such schools have provided over a long period, with their "wealth and broad range of expertise" (Miller, 1985, p. 160). A residential school can be the least restrictive environment for many visually impaired and multihandicapped students, these supporters argue. A follow-up study of visually impaired students at a state school for the blind (Livingston-White, Utter, & Woodard, 1985) found that parents, local education agencies, and the students themselves generally considered the residential school placement to have been appropriate and beneficial. Among the advantages cited were specialized curriculum and equipment, participation in extracurricular activities, individualized instruction, small classes, and improved self-esteem.

See chapter 10 for information on multihandicapped and deaf-blind children.

A child's placement in a residential school program need not be regarded as permanent. Many visually impaired children move from residential schools into public schools (or vice versa) as their needs change. Some students in residential schools attend nearby public schools for all or part of their school day. Most residential schools encourage parent involvement and have recreational programs that bring visually impaired students into contact with nonhandicapped peers. Independent living skills and vocational training are important parts of the program at virtually all residential schools.

See pages 323–24 for a description of the services provided by a residential school.

In several states and provinces there is close cooperation between public school and residential school programs that serve visually impaired children. Thurman (1978), for example, reports that in Canada's Atlantic provinces the residential school employs

PERKINS SCHOOL FOR THE BLIND: A RESIDENTIAL SCHOOL MEETS NEW CHALLENGES

Perkins School for the Blind, located in Watertown, Massachusetts, was chartered in 1829. One of the oldest and best-known schools of its kind, Perkins has served a wide variety of blind, deaf-blind, and multihandicapped students over the years. Perhaps the most famous teacher-student combination in American history—Anne Sullivan and Helen Keller—spent several years at Perkins. The school also has a long history of providing training for teachers from around the world.

For the more recent history of Perkins, we asked Kevin J. Lessard, Director of Perkins School for the Blind, to describe the school's current programs and services.

During the past 10 years the on-campus enrollment of the school has decreased in size, and the functional ability of the population has changed. Perkins has adapted its programs, curricula, teaching methodologies, and facilities to serve an increasing number of multihandicapped students and clients.

The on-campus programs, serving 200 day and residential students, are as follows: Preschool services, lower school program, secondary services, severe impaired program, deaf-blind program, and adult services. Each program focuses on the development and implementation of reality-based IEPs for each student, which include a number of off-campus, community-based services as an integral

Helen Keller and Anne Sullivan were at the Perkins school for several years. Helen was probably about 12 years old when this picture was taken.

part of each student's program. Community-based services include orientation and mobility training, community experience curricular, prevocational and vocational placements within business and industry, and a wide range of support services and recreation programs.

As Perkins's population has changed and as the curricula have emphasized community-based programming, the school has also developed a significant number of community and outreach services to help meet the needs of today's population.

1. *Community living services.* Perkins is presently operating two community residence programs, one intermediate care facility, and five independent living apartments in which blind, multihandicapped blind, and deaf-blind adults can live.
2. *Infant/toddler services.* Home-based services are provided to 35 infants, toddlers, and their families in many different communities.
3. *Preschool services.* A few Perkins staff members are providing services in a number of cities and towns to blind preschool students, through a contract between Perkins and local education agencies.
4. *Projects with industry program.* For blind adults Perkins staff members provide on-the-job training and job placements within a large number of businesses and industries throughout New England.
5. *Outreach services to public school students.* A number of teen weekends during the regular school year and summer program services are available to blind students enrolled full-time in public schools throughout New England.
6. *Diagnostic evaluation services.* Perkins provides a three-day diagnostic evaluation program for those who are seeking admission to Perkins or who are in need of comprehensive evaluation.
7. *New England regional center for deaf-blind services.* Perkins operates a federally funded program that provides consultation and some direct services to deaf-blind students and their families throughout New England.
8. *Regional library for the blind.* The school serves over 12,000 blind adults each year by providing regional library services. Many books, recordings, and other materials are mailed to readers in the region.
9. *Teacher training program.* Perkins has an affiliation with the special education program at Boston College, and the school provides a teacher training program for 15 or 20 American and foreign trainees every year.
10. *Outreach services for professionals in New England.* For the past 4 years Perkins has planned and operated inservice training workshops for itinerant teachers and other professionals in New England.
11. *Howe Press.* Perkins operates the Howe Press and provides products and materials to over 7,000 blind individuals each year.

A residential school for the blind today has an opportunity to work closely with consumers, parents, professionals, and funding agencies in the development of a wide array of community-based services. Cooperative working relationships and creative short- and long-term planning efforts have the potential to generate positive and reality-based services that respond to present-day needs within the context of community integration. Residential schools, primarily because of the expertise of their staff but also because of their location, centralization of resources, and availability of facilities, have the potential to become responsive resource centers on regional and state levels. It is important that the private sector, consumers, all professionals working with the blind in a given state, and state education and rehabilitation agencies work closely together in developing comprehensive plans to best serve an ever-increasing blind population.

For further information contact Perkins School for the Blind, 175 North Beacon Street, Watertown, Massachusetts 02172.

a network of itinerant teacher-consultants who provide instruction, materials, and assistance to visually impaired children attending regular public schools. These professionals offer regular consultation to the various teachers who also work with the visually impaired students. In this region it is expected that most visually impaired children will gradually be integrated into their local public schools and that the residential school will serve mainly multihandicapped students and young visually impaired children who require training in basic skills.

Residential schools have long played an important role in the training of teachers of visually impaired children, both on a preservice and an inservice basis. The residential school is usually well equipped to serve as a resource center for instructional materials and as a place where visually impaired students can receive specialized evaluation services. An increasing number of residential schools now offer short-term training to visually impaired students who attend regular public schools. One example is a summer workshop emphasizing braille, mobility, and vocational training.

CURRENT ISSUES/FUTURE TRENDS

As we have noted, visually impaired children constitute only a small portion of the school-age population, but they have many unique needs. Although the current trend toward greater integration of visually impaired children into regular public school classes is generally welcomed, some educators caution against the wholesale placement of visually impaired children in regular schools without adequate support. Most vision professionals tend to resist noncategorical special education programs, at least for visually impaired students. It is unrealistic, they argue, to expect regular teachers or teachers trained in other areas of special education to be competent in such specialized techniques as braille, mobility, and visual efficiency.

Although financial restrictions may require some public school and residential school programs for visually impaired children to close down or consolidate with programs for children with other disabilities, there is strong support for the continuation of highly specialized services. Both public and residential programs for visually impaired children will continue to operate well into the future, occasionally challenging each other for the privilege of serving the relatively small number of available students. The results of this competition may well prove favorable, if both types of schools are encouraged to improve the quality of their educational services.

As more infants and preschool children with impaired vision are identified, there will be an increased emphasis on specialized programs of early intervention (Ferrell, 1986). Older students will receive more systematic instruction in skills related to employment and independent living, and there will be continuing efforts to improve the coordination of services between educational programs and postschool rehabilitation agencies. The current interest in low vision children will extend beyond the area of vision utilization and into many other aspects of education and development. Some evidence suggests that low vision children may have a more difficult time than totally blind children in being socially accepted by sighted children in public schools (Corn, 1986; Spenciner, 1972); thus, new programs will be designed to address the psychosocial needs of low vision children.

New technological and biomedical developments will continue to aid visually impaired students, particularly in the areas of mobility, communication, and use of low vision. In the not-too-distant future it may even be possible to provide a form of artificial sight to certain totally blind people, by implanting electrodes into the brain and connecting them to a miniature television camera built into an artificial eye. Research in artificial sight is in the early experimental stages at present but suggests much promise (Dobelle, 1977; Marbach, 1982). Other systems of electronic vision substitution rely on tactual images projected onto an area of the body, such as the back or abdomen, enabling the blind person to perceive a visionlike sensation.

Like other groups of disabled individuals, blind and visually impaired people are becoming increasingly aware of their rights as citizens and consumers and are beginning to fight discrimination based on their disabilities. As Willoughby (1980) observes, many people—some of whom work with the visually impaired—tend to underestimate the capacities of their students and deny them a full range of occupational and personal choices. The future will probably bring a gradual shift away from some of the vocational settings in which visually impaired people have traditionally worked—such as piano tuning, sheltered workshops, and rehabilitation counseling—in favor of a more varied range of employment opportunities. These and other trends will be appropriately reflected in future programs of education and training for visually impaired children.

SUMMARY

1. Vision is a critical sense that children use in obtaining information about the world in which they live. Without it they need special materials and attention if they are to learn and develop to their full potential.

2. There are both legal and educational definitions of visual impairment.
   a. A person whose visual acuity is 20/200 or less in the better eye after correction is legally blind.
   b. A person whose field of vision is extremely restricted (20 degrees or less) is also considered to be legally blind.
   c. An educational definition considers the extent to which a visual impairment makes special education materials or methods necessary.
   d. Blind children have so little vision that they learn primarily through their other senses. Most blind children read braille.
   e. Low vision children can learn through the visual channel and usually can learn to read print.
   f. Besides impairments in visual acuity and field of vision, a child may have problems with ocular motility or visual accommodation, photophobia, or defective color vision.
   g. Regardless of whether a visual impairment is congenital or adventitious, the age of onset may affect the child's educational and emotional needs.

3. The eye collects light reflected from objects, focuses the objects' image on the retina, and transmits the image to the brain. Difficulty with any part of this process can cause vision problems. Common types of visual impairment include

a. myopia (nearsightedness)

b. hyperopia (farsightedness)

c. astigmatism (blurred vision caused by irregularities in the cornea or other eye surfaces)

d. cataract (blurred or distorted vision caused by cloudiness in the lens)

e. glaucoma (loss of vision caused by high pressure within the eye)

f. diabetic retinopathy, retinitis pigmentosa, macular degeneration, and retinal detachment (all caused by problems with the retina)

g. retinopathy of prematurity (retrolental fibroplasia) (caused by administration and withdrawal of high doses of oxygen to premature infants in incubators)

4. Visual impairment is a low-prevalence disability, affecting less than 0.1% of the school-age population. About one-third of all visually impaired students have additional disabilities.

5. Educating blind students is one of the oldest fields of special education, perhaps because blindness is readily apparent and provokes strong emotions.

a. The first school for blind children was started by Haüy in Paris in 1784. By the early 19th century several other European countries had started residential schools for blind children.

b. The first American schools for blind children were private residential schools, established around 1830. Public residential schools began to be opened soon afterward.

c. Until recently, children with low vision were encouraged to not use their sight in order to conserve it. Today they are taught to concentrate on developing and using their vision as much as possible.

d. The influx of children with blindness caused by retinopathy of prematurity led to the expansion of regular public school programs for visually impaired children in the 1950s and 1960s.

e. Most parents today can choose between public day and residential schools for their visually impaired children. Neither placement need be considered permanent.

6. Teachers of visually impaired children need to have many specialized skills and be knowledgeable, competent, and creative in working with the needs of individual children.

a. Visually impaired children need as many active, participatory experiences as possible.

b. Most blind children learn to read braille and write with a brailler and a slate and stylus. They may also learn to type and use special equipment for mathematics, social studies, and listening to or feeling regular print.

c. Children with low vision should learn to use their residual vision as efficiently as possible. Many use optical aids and large print to read regular type. They may need special adaptations such as closed-circuit television to let them benefit as much as possible from the materials and physical setting of the regular classroom.

d. All visually impaired children need to develop their listening skills.

e. Visually impaired students also may need special instruction in practical daily living skills, in dealing with other people, and in human sexuality.

f. Many visually impaired children need help to avoid developing distinctive mannerisms.

g. The teacher must use observation and a variety of informal and formal procedures in assessing visually impaired children. Standardized intelligence tests are often inappropriate.

    h. For blind or severely visually impaired children, orientation and mobility instruction is a must. From an early age the children must be made familiar and comfortable with their own bodies and their surroundings if they are eventually to develop the skills to travel independently. Long canes, electronic aids, and guide dogs are used.

7. Today, most visually impaired children attend regular classes with their sighted peers.
    a. In many districts a specially trained itinerant vision specialist provides extra help for students and regular class teachers.
    b. Some programs also have separate orientation and mobility instructors or separate resource rooms for visually impaired students.
    c. Many visually impaired children—especially those with other handicapping conditions—attend residential schools.

8. Visually impaired children are likely to receive specialized services in the future in both regular and residential schools.

9. There will be increased emphasis on intervention with visually impaired infants and young children and on training older students for independence.

10. Low vision children will receive more attention in the coming years, and it is hoped that all visually impaired people will benefit from new technological and biomedical developments. Artificial sight may be possible in the future.

11. Career opportunities for visually impaired persons will likely expand as these individuals become more aware of their legal and human rights.

FOR MORE INFORMATION

Journals

Education of the Visually Handicapped. Published quarterly by the Association for Education and Rehabilitation of the Blind and Visually Impaired. Includes practical articles, research studies, interviews, and other features relevant to teachers of visually impaired students, orientation and mobility specialists, rehabilitation workers, administrators, and parents.

Journal of Visual Impairment and Blindness. Published 10 times per year by the American Foundation for the Blind. An interdisciplinary journal for practitioners and researchers concerned with the education and rehabilitation of blind and visually impaired children and adults. Includes regular updates on technological and legislative developments.

The Sight-Saving Review. Published quarterly by the National Society to Prevent Blindness. Empahsizes new developments in the assessment and treatment of visual impairments, low vision aids, eye safety, and health education.

Books

Ferrell, K. A. (1985). *Reach out and teach.* New York: American Foundation for the Blind.

Heller, B. W., Flohr, L. M., & Zegans, L. S. (Eds.). (1987). *Psychosocial interventions with sensorially disabled persons.* Orlando, FL: Grune & Stratton.

Jose, R. (1983). *Understanding low vision.* New York: American Foundation for the Blind.

Kirchner, C. (1985). *Data on blindness and visual impairment in the United States.* New York: American Foundation for the Blind.

Scholl, G. T. (Ed.). (1986). *Foundations of education for blind and visually handicapped children and youth: Theory and practice.* New York: American Foundation for the Blind.

Tuttle, D. W. (1984). *Self-esteem and adjusting with blindness: The process of responding to life's demands.* Springfield, IL: Charles C Thomas.

Organizations

American Foundation for the Blind, 15 West 16th Street, New York, NY 10011. Provides many publications and films about blindness. Distributes aids and appliances for people with impaired vision. Publishes *Journal of Visual Impairment and Blindness* and *Directory of Agencies Serving the Visually Handicapped in the United States.*

American Printing House for the Blind, 1839 Frankfort Avenue, Louisville, KY 40206. Provides books, magazines, and many other publications in braille, large print, and recorded form. Distributes educational materials and aids specially designed for the blind and helpful publications for teachers. Attempts to register all legally blind U.S. children through state departments of education or residential schools. Also provides recordings and computer materials.

Association for Education and Rehabilitation of the Blind and Visually Impaired, 206 North Washington Street, Alexandria, VA 22314. Emphasizes educational, orientation, mobility, and rehabilitation services. Holds regional and national conferences in the United States and Canada. Publishes *Education of the Visually Handicapped* and a *Yearbook* compiling recent literature in this field.

Canadian National Institute for the Blind, 1921 Bayview Avenue, Toronto, Ontario M4G 3E8. The central agency for information, materials, and supportive services for visually impaired people in Canada. Maintains regional and local offices in all provinces. Effectively depicts the growth and development of a young blind child in a film, *Shelley.*

Division for the Visually Handicapped, Council for Exceptional Children, 1920 Association Drive, Reston, VA 22091. Presents sessions of interest to educators at international, state, and provincial conferences of the Council for Exceptional Children. Publishes a quarterly journal on educational topics.

National Association for Parents of the Visually Impaired, 2011 Hardy Circle, Austin, TX 78756. Provides practical information for parents. Sponsors parent groups in several areas. Holds conferences and workshops for parents and teachers.

National Federation of the Blind, 1800 Johnson Street, Baltimore, MD 21230. The largest organization of blind people in the United States, with many state and local chapters. Provides publications and films that emphasize the rights and capabilities of blind people. Seeks to involve blind people in education and employment and to avoid discrimination. Also sponsors activities and publications for parents of blind children.

9

PHYSICAL AND HEALTH IMPAIRMENTS

Children with physical and health impairments are an extremely varied population. It would be impossible to describe all of them with a single set of characteristics, even if we used very general terms. Their physical disabilities may be mild, moderate, or severe. Their intellectual functioning may be normal, below normal, or above normal. Children may have a single impairment or a combination of impairments. They may have lived with their physical or health impairment since birth, or they may have suddenly acquired it. The children whose special needs we will consider in this chapter have a great many individual differences; there is no typical case of anything. We can make general statements about some physical and health-related conditions—such as cerebral palsy or epilepsy—but there are numerous variations in the degree and severity of such conditions and in the ways they may affect a child.

Many students with physical and health impairments adjust to their conditions well. They present no unusual behavior problems and are fully capable of learning in the regular classroom and interacting successfully with their nondisabled peers. As Pieper (1983) observes, "Just as the concept that children with disabilities should be dependent on charity for their education is fast giving way, so too are we questioning the belief that medical settings and medically oriented staff are appropriate to foster academic learnings, life skills or social behaviors" (p. 21). Today's methods of medical treatment enable many children with physical and health impairments to attend school regularly. Hospital stays tend to be shorter, physical therapy can be provided in school settings, and surgery can often be scheduled during vacation periods.

The current trend to educate students with physical and health impairments in regular school settings makes it important for teachers (and often for other students as well) to have an understanding of how a particular condition may affect a child's learning, development, and behavior. Linda, for example, has had long periods of hospitalization and finds it difficult to keep up with her academic work. Gary takes medication that controls his seizures most of the time but also tends to make him drowsy in the classroom. Teachers are entitled to accurate, up-to-date information about the

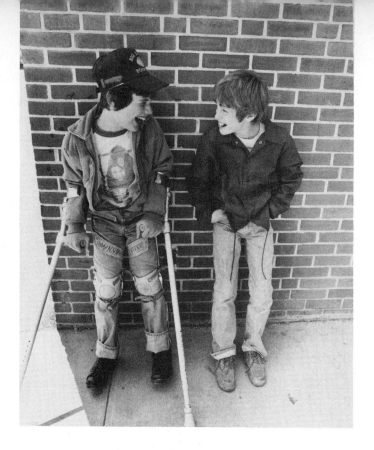

Friends have all things in common.

Plato

physical and health conditions of their students. Pieper (1983) offers some examples of questions that may be asked by teachers to obtain such information.

☐ Does he have movement in his legs? Can he bear his own weight? What aids does he need for standing or walking?
☐ Does she have sensation (feeling) in her legs? Has she learned to be careful of hot objects, such as radiators, or of scraping her legs on hard surfaces? Should she wear long pants in gym?
☐ Does he have control of his bladder? Has he learned to lift and reposition himself?
☐ Is it advisable for her to lie down for brief periods during the day? Does she develop pressure sores from sitting in one position too long? What should we look for on her skin?

Because of their disabilities or illnesses, children with physical and health impairments may require modifications in the physical environment, in teaching techniques, in communication, or in other aspects of their educational programs. Teachers need to understand the conditions that affect their students' behavior or performance in school. Today, children with physical and health impairments are generally included in educational programs on the basis of their particular learning needs, not according to their specific disability or disease. Therefore, teachers can expect to have more students with specialized medical and physical management requirements (Mullins, 1979).

Physical and health problems can give rise to special needs in the school setting. In defining the population of handicapped children according to P.L. 94–142, the

Disabilities may also necessitate special considerations outside the school setting. The following FOCUS feature identifies helpful approaches and accommodations that might enable disabled citizens to exercise a basic right.

federal government emphasizes that a child's educational performance may be adversely affected by severe orthopedic impairments (including those caused by cerebral palsy, amputation of limbs, fractures, and burns) or by other serious or long-standing health problems that limit the child's strength, vitality, or alertness.

Some children with physical and health impairments are extremely restricted in their activities and intellectual functioning, whereas others have no major limitations on what they can do and learn. Some are entirely normal in appearance, others have disabilities that are immediately apparent. Some children must use special devices or equipment that call attention to their disabilities; others display behaviors that are not under voluntary control. Some disabilities are always present, whereas others occur only from time to time. Over an extended period of time, the degree of a child's disability may increase, decrease, or remain about the same.

In school the special problems encountered by children with physical and health impairments also vary in kind and degree. Brian, who uses a wheelchair for mobility, is disappointed that he is not able to compete with his classmates in football, baseball, and track. Yet he participates fully in all other aspects of his high school program with no special modifications other than the addition of a few ramps in the building and a newly accessible washroom. Most of Brian's teachers and friends, in fact, do not think of him as needing special education at all.

In this chapter we will focus on information that is helpful to the teacher in understanding the nature and effects of various physical and health impairments. Many conditions, after all, can affect a child's school experience in important ways. Janice, for example, becomes tired easily and attends school for only 3 hours a day. Kenneth uses a specially designed chair to help him sit more comfortably in the classroom. It is important to emphasize, however, that special modifications or alterations should not be any more restrictive than necessary. A bright child who uses a wheelchair should not be totally removed from the regular school program and placed in a class where she can interact only with other disabled children.

With some conditions possible complications or emergencies may arise in the classroom; it is important for the teacher to know how to manage the situation effectively and when and how to seek help from others. Thus, general information and suggested guidelines will shape our basic approach to the topic of children with physical and health impairments.

TYPES AND CAUSES

Orthopedic and Neurologic Impairments

An **orthopedic impairment** involves a child's skeletal system; that is, the bones, joints, limbs, and associated muscles. A **neurologic impairment** involves the nervous system, affecting a child's ability to move, use, feel, or control certain parts of the body. Orthopedic and neurologic impairments are two distinct and separate types of disabilities but may cause similar limitations in movement (Shivers & Fait, 1985). Many of the same educational, therapeutic, or recreational activities are likely to be appro-

DISABLED CITIZENS AT THE POLLS

According to the National Organization on Disability, an estimated 20 million Americans with disabilities are eligible to vote. Most of them, however, do not exercise this privilege of citizenship because of physical, attitudinal, or administrative barriers, such as inaccessible polling places, inconvenient registration procedures, lack of information on when and where to vote, and unavailability of transportation or parking.

P.L. 98–435, the Voting Accessibility for the Elderly and Handicapped Act, was passed by Congress in 1984 and took full effect in 1986. This law requires election officials at all levels of government to make registration and voting places accessible to people with temporary or permanent physical disabilities and to elderly people. The following guidelines and suggestions were prepared by the National Easter Seal Society and the National Organization on Disability to assist in making voting more accessible to citizens with physical impairments and other disabilities.

COMMON COURTESIES AND GUIDELINES

☐ Be considerate of the extra time it might take for a person who is disabled or elderly to get things done, and give unhurried attention to a person who has difficulty speaking.

☐ Speak directly to the person who has a disability rather than to a companion who may be along.

☐ Speak calmly, slowly, and directly to a person with a hearing problem. Your facial expressions, gestures, and body movements help in understanding. Don't shout or speak in the person's ear. If full understanding is doubtful, write a note to the person with a hearing problem.

☐ Before pushing someone in a wheelchair, ask whether you may do so and how you should proceed.

☐ Greet a person who is visually impaired by letting the person know who and where you are. Provide a guiding device such as a ruler or card for signing forms. When offering walking assistance, allow the person to take your arm and alert the person when you are approaching steps or inclines.

☐ Be aware that dogs who assist people with disabilities should be admitted into all buildings. Such dogs are highly trained and need no special care other than that provided by their owners.

☐ Be aware that federal law allows voters with disabilities to be accompanied by and to receive assistance from another person in the voting booth.

☐ Remember that all voters deserve courteous attention in exercising their rights as citizens.

SUGGESTIONS FOR MAKING VOTING PLACES ACCESSIBLE AND USABLE

☐ Use temporary signs to identify handicapped parking and directions to entries for people with disabilities.

☐ Use a temporary ramp if your voting place has steps at the entrance, but be sure the incline is not too steep.

☐ If your voting place has heavy doors, someone should be available to assist those who need help.

☐ A 32-inch clearance at nonrevolving doors enables a person using a wheelchair to enter the building.

☐ Smooth and hard floor surfaces or those covered with a tightly woven carpet with no pad or a thin pad are best for wheelchair users and others.

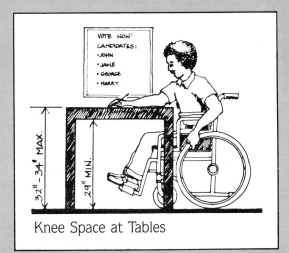

Knee Space at Tables

radio and TV, as well as in the newspapers, is the most effective way to reach people with disabilities.

☐ When choosing voting locations in your community, select buildings that are more apt to be accessible, that is, schools, libraries, community centers, firehouses, park buildings, court houses, post offices, other government buildings, and places of worship. Polling places can be moved from inaccessible sites to accessible ones.

For further information an illustrated manual entitled *Disabled Citizens at the Polls: A Guide for Election Officials* is available from the National Organization on Disability, 2100 Pennsylvania Avenue, NW, Washington, DC 20037.

☐ Tables to be used by people in wheelchairs should have a clear knee space underneath that is at least 29 to 34 inches high.

☐ Printed instructions enable persons who are hearing impaired to vote. Printed instructions in simple, large lettering help persons who are vision impaired to vote. Pictures or symbols help everyone. For example, arrows or a hand pointing is easier for everyone to understand than a sign saying "Voters' Entrance at the East Side."

☐ For persons unable to operate voting machines, paper ballots make voting possible.

☐ At least one punch card machine should be available with enough knee clearance to allow voting from a seated position.

☐ You will increase voter turnout if you inform people with disabilities that voting places are accessible. A public service announcement on

Chairs

priate for students with orthopedic and neurologic impairments. And there is a close relationship between the two types. For example, a child who is unable to move his legs because of damage to the central nervous system (neurologic impairment) may also develop disorders in the bones and muscles of his legs (orthopedic impairment)—especially if he does not receive proper therapy and equipment.

Whatever their cause, orthopedic and neurologic impairments are frequently described in terms of the parts of the body that are affected. The term *plegia* (derived from the Greek "to strike") is often used in combination to indicate the location of limb involvement. **Quadriplegia** means that all four limbs (both arms and legs) are affected; movement of the trunk and face may also be impaired. **Paraplegia** indicates a motor impairment of the legs only. A child with **hemiplegia** is affected on one side of the body; for example, the left arm and the left leg may be impaired. **Diplegia** refers to a major involvement of the legs, with less severe involvement of the arms. Less frequent forms of involvement include **monoplegia** (only one limb is affected), **triplegia** (three limbs are affected), and double hemiplegia (major involvement of the arms, with less severe involvement of the legs).

It is difficult to establish precise criteria for describing the degree or extent of motor involvement in orthopedic and neurologic impairments. Children's difficulties in performing motor-related tasks may vary from time to time, depending on such factors as positioning, fatigue, and medication. The terms *mild, moderate,* and *severe* are often used. Jones (1983) for example, describes mild motor impairment as being marked by "very little limitation of activity or incoordination." A child with moderate impairment has disabilities "severe enough to be a handicap in ambulation, self-help, and communication, but not sufficient to disable entirely," whereas a child with severe impairment has disabilities that, without treatment, are "almost totally incapacitating" (p. 43). All three terms can be used to describe the functioning of children with a wide variety of physical and health impairments.

Cerebral Palsy

Cerebral palsy is one of the most prevalent physical impairments found in children of school age. It is a long-term condition that involves damage to the brain or an abnormality of brain growth that causes paralysis or a motion disorder of the limbs (Bleck, 1979; Gillham, 1986). Cerebral palsy is actually a variety of symptoms and subtypes; as Cruickshank (1986) points out, it is often a multiply handicapping condition and "probably the best example we have of the unevenness of development in children" (p. 52). Cerebral palsy is not contagious. It can be treated but not cured; the impairment usually does not get progressively worse as a child ages. Cerebral palsy is not fatal and, in the great majority of cases, is not inherited.

The causes of cerebral palsy are varied and not clearly known. It has often been attributed to the occurrence of injuries, accidents, or illnesses that are **prenatal** (before birth), **perinatal** (at or near the time of birth), or **postnatal** (soon after birth). Recent improvements in obstetrical delivery and neonatal care, however, do not seem to have decreased the incidence of cerebral palsy, which has remained steady over the past 20 years or so at about 4 in every 1,000 births. An extensive study of children with cerebral palsy (Nelson & Ellenberg, 1986) found that the factors most likely to be associated with cerebral palsy were mental retardation of the mother, premature birth (i.e., gestational age of 32 weeks or less), low birth weight, and a delay of 5 minutes or more before the baby's first cry. The researchers concluded that cerebral palsy does not appear to be caused by a single factor and that complications of labor and delivery are not so important in causing cerebral palsy as was previously thought. Prevention of cerebral palsy, then, is likely to prove extremely difficult.

Children with cerebral palsy have disturbances of their voluntary motor functions. These disturbances may include paralysis, extreme weakness, lack of coordination, involuntary convulsions, and other motor disorders. Children with cerebral palsy may have little or no control over their arms, legs, or speech, depending on the type and degree of impairment. They may also have impaired vision or hearing.

Intellectual impairments *may* accompany cerebral palsy. Nelson and Ellenberg (1986) found in their study that 41% of the children with cerebral palsy scored below 70 on a standardized IQ test. The probability of mental retardation appears greater when a seizure disorder is present also (Smith, 1984). Other surveys (e.g., Verhaaren & Connor, 1981) have estimated that about one-third of children with cerebral palsy have intelligence within or above the normal range. Caution should be used in interpreting any such estimates, however. As Levine (1986) points out, students with cerebral palsy often have motor and/or speech impairments that limit the appropriateness of standardized intelligence tests; thus, an IQ score should never serve as the sole descriptor of a child's actual or potential ability. It is also important to bear in mind that no clear relationship exists between the degree of motor impairment and the degree of intellectual impairment (if any) in children with cerebral palsy. A student with only mild motor impairment may experience severe developmental delays, whereas a student with severe motor impairments may be intellectually gifted.

Seizure disorders are described later in this chapter.

Cerebral palsy has traditionally been classified into several types, according to characteristic patterns of motor behavior. Among children the most common types are **spasticity, athetosis,** and **ataxia** (Gillham, 1986). **Rigidity** and **tremor** are additional but less common types of cerebral palsy. Children may also be described as having mixed cerebral palsy, consisting of more than one of these types, particularly if their impairments are severe.

Children with spastic cerebral palsy have tense, contracted muscles. Their movements may be jerky, exaggerated, and poorly coordinated. They may be unable to grasp objects with their fingers. If they try to control their movements, they may become even more jerky. If they are able to walk, it may be with a scissors gait, standing on their toes with their knees bent and pointing inward.

Children with athetoid cerebral palsy make large, irregular, twisting movements that they cannot control. When they are at rest or asleep, there is little or no abnormal motion. An effort to pick up a pencil, however, may result in wildly waving arms, facial grimaces, and an extension of the tongue. These children may not be able to control the muscles of their lips, tongue, and throat and may drool. They may also seem to stumble and lurch awkwardly as they walk. At times their muscles may be tense and rigid, whereas at other times they may be loose and flaccid. Extreme difficulty in expressive oral language often accompanies this form of cerebral palsy.

Children with ataxic cerebral palsy have a poor sense of balance and body position. They may appear to be dizzy while walking and may fall easily if not supported. Their movements tend to be jumpy and unsteady, with exaggerated motion patterns. They seem to be constantly attempting to overcome the effect of gravity and to stabilize their bodies.

Children with the rare rigidity type of cerebral palsy display extreme stiffness in the affected limbs; they may be fixed and immobile for long periods. Tremor cerebral palsy, also rare, is marked by rhythmic, uncontrollable movements—the tremors may actually increase when the children attempt to control their actions.

The more severe forms of cerebral palsy are often identified in the first few months of a child's life, but in many other cases cerebral palsy is not detected or diagnosed until later in childhood. Parents may be the first to notice that their child is having difficulty crawling, balancing, or standing. According to Bleck (1979), about 80% of children with cerebral palsy are capable of learning to walk, although many need to use wheelchairs, braces, and other assistive devices, particularly for moving around outside the home.

Infants and children with cerebral palsy may experience problems in being fed. They may at first be unable to suck or swallow and may choke on their food or regurgitate it. Such difficulties can be overcome with early physical therapy; the therapist can show parents how to best position the child and how to give the appropriate types and amounts of food. In this and various other areas it is obviously important that therapy and parent education begin as early as possible in a child's life. Another problem, muscle tension, can sometimes be partially controlled by medications, braces, and special adaptive equipment. Orthopedic surgery may be done to increase a child's range of motion or to avoid such complications as hip dislocations and permanent muscle contractions. Edginton (1976) advises that children with cerebral palsy should be made to feel physically secure at all times—they should never be seated in a precarious position. Those children who use wheelchairs should change their position from time to time by standing, lying down, stretching, sitting on a mat, or walking with assistance.

Gillham (1986) describes cerebral palsy as the result of "not just a brain with a bit missing, but a reorganised brain, working to its own rules" (p. 64). Because cerebral palsy is such a complex condition, it is most effectively managed through the cooperative involvement of physicians, teachers, physical therapists, occupational therapists, communication specialists, counselors, and others who work directly with children and families. Regular exercise and careful positioning in school settings help the child with cerebral palsy to move as fully and comfortably as possible and prevent or minimize progressive damage to the muscles and limbs.

The interdisciplinary approach is discussed later in this chapter.

Spina Bifida

Spina bifida, another relatively prevalent condition that causes physical impairments in children, is a congenital defect in the development of the spinal cord. A portion of the spinal cord and the nerves that normally control muscles and feeling in the lower part of the body fail to develop normally. If the lining of the spinal cord bulges

Like other children with spina bifida, Mike exercises daily to develop strength and flexibility in his upper body.

through an opening in the infant's back at birth, the condition is properly called **meningocele.** If the spinal lining, spinal cord, and nerve roots all protrude, the child is said to have **myelomeningocele.** This is the most serious condition, carrying a high risk of paralysis and infection. In general, the higher the location of the lesion on the spine, the greater the effect on the body and its functioning (Pieper, 1983). The term *neural tube defect* is sometimes used to describe spina bifida and similar impairments.

The protruding spinal cord and nerves are usually tucked back into the spinal column shortly after birth. However, spina bifida is generally accompanied by hydrocephalus, the accumulation of cerebrospinal fluid in tissues surrounding the brain. If left untreated, this condition can lead to head enlargement and severe brain damage. Surgeons are now able to treat hydrocephalus by inserting a **shunt,** a one-way valve that diverts the cerebrospinal fluid away from the brain and into the bloodstream. Replacements of the shunt are usually necessary as a child grows older. Teachers who work with children who have shunts should be aware that blockage, disconnection, or infection of the shunt may result in increased intracranial pressure; warning signs such as drowsiness, vomiting, headache, irritability, and squinting should be heeded. Shunts have become safer and more reliable in recent years and can be removed in many school-age children when the production and absorption of cerebrospinal fluid are brought into balance (Gillham, 1986).

Usually, children with spina bifida have some degree of paralysis of the lower limbs and lack full control of their bladder and bowel functions. In most cases these children have good use of their arms and upper body (although fine-motor problems are not uncommon). Children with spina bifida usually walk with braces, crutches, or walkers; they may use wheelchairs for longer distances. Some children need special help in dressing and toileting, whereas others are able to manage these tasks on their own. Most children with spinal bifida need to use a **catheter** (tube) or bag to collect their urine; a method known as intermittent catheterization is often taught to these children so that they can empty their bladders at convenient times. According to Pieper (1983), this technique is effective with both boys and girls, works best if used every 3 to 4 hours, and does not require an absolutely sterile environment.

The Tatro case, described later in this chapter, concerns intermittent catheterization.

Muscular dystrophy

Muscular dystrophy refers to a group of long-term diseases that gradually weaken and waste away the body's muscles. There are several different types. The *Duchenne*, or *progressive*, form of muscular dystrophy, which affects boys much more frequently than girls, is the most likely to be seen in children of school age. The child is apparently normal at birth, but muscle weakness is usually evident by the age of 4 or 5. Slowness or clumsiness in walking is an early sign of muscular dystrophy. The child may walk with an unusual gait, showing a protruding stomach and a hollow back. The calf muscles of a child with muscular dystrophy tend to appear unusually large because the degenerated muscle has been replaced by fatty tissue.

Children with muscular dystrophy often have difficulty getting to their feet after lying down or playing on the floor. They may fall easily. Some doctors and therapists recommend the early use of electrically powered wheelchairs, whereas others adopt a more aggressive approach to prolong walking as long as possible, with special braces and other devices. The child gradually loses the ability to walk; the small muscles of the hands and fingers are usually the last to be affected.

Unfortunately, at present there is no known cure for most cases of muscular dystrophy, and the disease is often fatal. A good deal of independence can be maintained, however, by regular physical therapy, exercise, and the use of appropriate aids and appliances. In school a teacher should be careful not to lift a child with muscular dystrophy by the arms—even a gentle pull may cause the child's limbs to become dislocated. The teacher may also need to help the child deal with the gradual loss of physical abilities and the possibility of death.

Osteogenesis Imperfecta

Osteogenesis imperfecta is an inherited condition marked by bones that are extremely brittle. The skeletal system does not grow normally, and the affected child's bones are easily fractured. Children with osteogenesis imperfecta are literally fragile and must be protected. Wheelchairs are usually used, although the children may be able to walk for short distances with the aid of braces, crutches, and protective equipment. Like other children with orthopedic impairments, the child with osteogenesis imperfecta may have frequent hospitalizations for treatment and surgery. Some children, understandably, are reluctant to be touched or handled. Usually children with osteogenesis imperfecta have adequate use of their hands and can participate in most classroom activities if they receive appropriate physical support and protection. As the children mature, their bones may become less brittle, requiring less attention.

Spinal Cord Injuries

Spinal cord injuries usually stem from accidents. Injury to the spinal column is generally described by letters and numbers indicating where the damage occurred. For example, a *C5–6* injury means that the damage occurred at the level of the fifth and sixth cervical vertebrae—a flexible area of the neck susceptible to injury from whiplash and diving or trampoline accidents. A *T12* injury occurs at the twelfth thoracic (chest) vertebra and an *L3* at the third lumbar (lower back) area. In general, there is paralysis and loss of sensation below the level of the injury.

Children who have sustained spinal cord injuries usually use wheelchairs for mobility. Motorized wheelchairs, although expensive, are recommended for those with quadriplegia, whereas self-propelled wheelchairs can be used by paraplegic children. Children with quadriplegia may have severe breathing problems because the muscles of the chest, which normally govern respiration, are affected. In most cases children with spinal cord injuries lack bladder and bowel control and need to follow a careful management program to maintain personal hygiene and avoid infection and skin irritation.

Rehabilitation programs for children and adolescents who have sustained spinal cord injuries usually involve physical therapy, the use of adaptive devices for mobility and independent living, and psychological support to help them adjust to a sudden disability. With supportive teachers and peers, these students can participate fully in the school program. Adolescents and adults are often particularly concerned about sexual function. Even though most spinal cord injuries do affect sexuality, with understanding partners and positive attitudes toward themselves, these individuals are often able to enjoy varied and satisfying sexual relationships. Many counselors now specialize in addressing the sexual concerns of people who have been disabled by spinal cord injury or other conditions.

Head Trauma

Injuries to the head are common in children and adolescents. According to Rosen and Gerring (1986), in the United States about 20,000 persons under the age of 21 have survived a head injury severe enough to require 3 weeks or more of hospitalization. Significant causes of head trauma include automobile, motorcycle, and bicycle accidents, falls, assaults, and child abuse. Although relatively few studies have been done on the educational effects of head trauma, it is known that many children who have suffered serious head injury experience subsequent problems in learning, behavior, and adjustment. Temporary or lasting symptoms may include cognitive and language deficits, memory loss, seizures, and perceptual disorders. Inappropriate or exaggerated behaviors may be displayed, ranging from extreme aggressiveness to apathy. Children may also have difficulty paying attention and retaining new information.

A *coma* is an abnormal deep stupor that can result from severe head trauma. The individual affected may be impossible to arouse by external stimuli for an extended period of time (Kleinberg, 1982). Although P.L. 94–142 does not specifically mention the needs of children who have experienced head trauma and/or coma and few educational programs have been specifically designed for this population, these children may well be in need of special education services. As Rosen and Gerring (1986) observe, head-injured students reenter school with deficits from their injuries compounded by an extended absence from school. These students are likely to require academic, psychological, and family support; and methods developed for students with other disabling conditions may not be applicable.

Amputations

Amputations or missing limbs affect a significant number of students. Artificial limbs are often used to facilitate balance, to enable the children to participate in a variety of tasks, and to create a more normal appearance. Some students or their parents, however, prefer not to use artificial limbs. Children may become quite proficient at using their remaining limbs. Some children who are missing both arms, for example, learn to write, eat, and perform vocational tasks with their feet. They have a much greater

Batter-up!

feeling of being in contact with objects and people than they would if they used prosthetic limbs. Unless children have other impairments in addition to the absence of limbs, they should be able to function in a regular classroom without major modifications.

Chronic Illness and Other Health-Related Conditions

There are many conditions that can affect a child's health, whether permanently, temporarily, or intermittently. In general, the conditions discussed in this section are *chronic;* that is, they are present over long periods of time and tend not to get better or disappear. Children with chronic illnesses are not usually confined to beds or hospitals, except during occasional flare-ups of their diseases; but "even with good control and years of remission, the threat of a recurrent crisis is everpresent" (Kleinberg, 1982, p. 5).

An *acute* illness, in contrast, is severe but of short duration.

The usual and proper course of action for children and families affected by chronic health-related conditions is to seek medical treatment. In many instances, however, an illness or health impairment can significantly affect a child's school performance and social acceptance; consequently, it is important for a teacher to be aware of it. Although chronic illnesses and other health-related conditions are generally less visible than the orthopedic and neurologic impairments discussed previously, their effects on a child may be just as great.

Seizure Disorders (Epilepsy)

Some children of school age have *seizures*, which are disturbances of movement, sensation, behavior, and/or consciousness caused by abnormal electrical activity in the brain. Theoretically, anyone can have a seizure. It is not uncommon for seizures to occur in people when they have high fevers or drink excessive alcohol or experience a blow to the head. When seizures occur chronically and repeatedly, however, the condition is called **epilepsy.** With proper medical treatment and the support of parents, teachers, and peers, most children with epilepsy lead full and normal lives. Most have normal intelligence and need not be considered disabled or handicapped. Epilepsy itself constitutes a disorder only while a seizure is actually in progress.

Seizure disorders are common in children with severe and multiple handicaps. The next chapter discusses this population.

Epileptic seizures may be largely or wholly controlled by anticonvulsant medications. Some children require such heavy doses of medication that their learning and behavior are adversely affected. And some medications have undesirable side effects, such as drowsiness, nausea, weight gain, or thickening of the gums.

The specific causes of epilepsy are not clearly known. It is likely that people become seizure-prone when a particular area of the brain becomes electrically unstable. This condition may result from an underlying lesion caused by scar tissue from a head injury, a tumor, or an interruption in blood supply to the brain (Gillham, 1986). In many cases the origin of seizure activity cannot be traced to a particular incident. Epilepsy can occur at any stage of life but most frequently begins in childhood. A wide variety of psychological, physical, and sensory factors are thought to trigger seizures in susceptible persons—for example, fatigue, excitement, anger, surprise, hyperventilation, hormonal changes (as in menstruation or pregnancy), withdrawal from drugs or alcohol, or exposure to certain patterns of light, sound, or touch. During a seizure a dysfunction in the electrochemical activity of the brain causes a person to lose control of her muscles temporarily. Between seizures—that is, most of the time—the brain functions normally. Many unfortunate misconceptions about epilepsy have circulated in the past and are prevalent even today. Negative public attitudes, in fact, have probably been more harmful to people with epilepsy than the condition itself.

It is important for teachers, school health care personnel, and perhaps classmates to be aware that a child is affected by epilepsy, so that they can be prepared to deal with a seizure if one should occur in school. There are several classifications of seizures, three of which are relatively common. The **grand mal,** or generalized tonic-clonic, seizure is the most evident and serious type of epileptic seizure. A grand mal seizure can be disturbing and frightening to someone who has never seen one. The affected child has little or no warning that a seizure is about to occur, the muscles become stiff, and the child loses consciousness and falls to the floor. Then the entire body shakes violently as the muscles alternately contract and relax. Saliva may be forced from the mouth; legs and arms may jerk; the bladder and bowels may be emptied. After a few minutes the contractions diminish, and the child either goes to sleep or regains consciousness in a confused or drowsy state. Grand mal seizures may occur as often as several times a day or as seldom as once a year. They are more likely to occur during the day than at night.

The Epilepsy Foundation of America (1974) recommends that a teacher remain calm and explain to other students that the seizure is painless to the affected child and is not contagious. The following procedures are suggested in case a grand mal seizure occurs in the classroom.

1. Ease the child to the floor and loosen his collar. You cannot stop the seizure. Let it run its course and do not try to revive the child.
2. Remove hard, sharp, or hot objects that may injure the child, but do not interfere with movements.
3. Do not force anything between the child's teeth. If the child's mouth is already open, you might place a soft object, like a handkerchief, between the side teeth. Be careful not to get your fingers between the teeth.
4. Turn the head to one side for release of saliva. Place something soft under the child's head.
5. When the child regains consciousness, let him rest if he wishes.
6. If the seizure lasts more than a few minutes or if the child seems to pass from one seizure to another without gaining consciousness, call the school nurse or doctor for instructions and notify the parents. This rarely happens but should be treated immediately.

The **petit mal seizure** (sometimes called an absence) is far less severe than the grand mal but may occur much more frequently—as often as 100 times per day in some children. Usually there is a brief loss of consciousness, lasting anywhere from a few seconds to half a minute or so. The child may stare blankly, flutter or blink his eyes, grow pale, or drop whatever he is holding. He may be mistakenly viewed as daydreaming or not listening. The child may or may not be aware that he has had a seizure, and no special first aid is necessary. The teacher should keep the child's parents advised of seizure activity and may also find it helpful to explain it to the child's classmates.

A **psychomotor seizure** may appear as a brief period of inappropriate or purposeless activity. The child may smack her lips, walk around aimlessly, or shout. She may appear to be conscious but is not actually aware of her unusual behavior. Psychomotor seizures usually last for a few minutes but go on as long as several hours in some cases. The teacher should keep dangerous objects out of the child's way and, except in emergencies, should not try to physically restrain her. Some children may respond to spoken directions during a psychomotor seizure.

In some children petit mal and psychomotor seizures can go undetected for long periods. An observant teacher can be instrumental in detecting the presence of a seizure disorder and in referring the child for appropriate medical help. The teacher can also assist parents and physicians by noting both the effectiveness and the side effects of any medication taken by a child with a seizure disorder.

Many children experience a warning sensation, known as an *aura*, a short time before a seizure. The aura takes different forms in different people; distinctive feelings, sights, sounds, tastes, and even smells have all been described. Frequently, such a warning enables the child to remove himself from a class or group before the seizure actually occurs. Cruickshank (1986) considers the aura to be a useful safety valve that often helps children feel more secure and comfortable about themselves.

Today, the majority of children with epilepsy can be helped with medication. Drugs can sharply reduce or even eliminate seizures in many cases. All children with epilepsy benefit from a realistic understanding of their condition and from accepting attitudes on the part of teachers and classmates.

Diabetes

Juvenile diabetes mellitus is a disorder of metabolism; that is, it affects the way in which the body absorbs and breaks down the sugars and starches in foods. Without proper medical management the diabetic child's system is not able to obtain and retain adequate energy from food. Not only does the child lack energy, but many important parts of the body—particularly the eyes and the kidneys—can be affected by untreated diabetes. Early symptoms of diabetes in children include thirst, headaches, loss of weight (despite a good appetite), frequent urination, and cuts that are slow to heal.

Diabetic retinopathy is a leading cause of blindness in adults.

Children with diabetes have insufficient insulin, a hormone normally produced by the pancreas and needed for the proper metabolism and digestion of foods. Insulin must be injected daily under the skin to regulate the condition. Most children with diabetes learn to inject their own insulin—in some cases as frequently as four times per day—and to determine the amount of insulin they need by testing the level of sugar and other substances in their urine. It is also important that children with diabetes follow a specific and regular diet prescribed by a physician or nutrition specialist. A regular exercise program is also usually suggested.

Teachers should be aware of the symptoms of insulin reaction, also called *diabetic shock*. It can result from taking too much insulin, from unusually strenuous exercise, or from a missed or delayed meal (the blood sugar level is lowered by insulin and exercise and raised by food). The symptoms of insulin reaction include faintness, dizziness, blurred vision, drowsiness, and nausea. A child may appear irritable or have a marked personality change. In most cases giving the child some form of concentrated sugar—such as a sugar cube, glass of fruit juice, or candy bar—ends the insulin reaction within a few minutes. The child's doctor or parents should inform the teacher and school health personnel of the appropriate foods to be given in case of insulin reaction.

A *diabetic coma* is more serious. It indicates that too little insulin is present; that is, the diabetes is not under control. Its onset is gradual, rather than sudden. The symptoms of diabetic coma include fatigue; thirst; dry, hot skin; deep, labored breathing; excessive urination; and fruity-smelling breath. A doctor or nurse should be contacted if a child displays such symptoms.

Cystic Fibrosis

Cystic fibrosis is a serious chronic disease of children and adolescents. A thick mucus is secreted by the exocrine glands of the body; it can block the lungs and parts of the digestive system. Children with cystic fibrosis may have difficulty breathing and are susceptible to coughs and respiratory infections. They may also have large and frequent bowel movements, because food passes through the system only partially digested.

Medications prescribed for children with cystic fibrosis include enzymes to facilitate digestion and solutions to thin and loosen the mucus in the lungs. During vigorous physical exercises some children may need help from teachers, aides, or classmates to clear the lungs and air passages.

Research has not clearly established the cause of cystic fibrosis. It appears to be hereditary and is found mainly among Caucasian children, both male and female. The symptoms may be due to a missing chemical or substance in the body, but no reliable cure for cystic fibrosis has yet been found. Nonetheless, many children and young adults with this condition are able to lead active lives. With continued research and treatment techniques, the long-range outlook for children affected by cystic fibrosis is improving.

Hemophilia

In **hemophilia** the blood does not clot as quickly as it should. The most serious consequences are usually internal, rather than external, bleeding; contrary to popular opinion, minor cuts and scrapes do not usually pose a serious problem. However, internal bleeding can cause swelling, pain, and permanent damage to a child's joints, tissues, and internal organs and may necessitate hospitalization for blood transfusions. It is thought that emotional stress may intensify episodes of bleeding (Verhaaren & Connor, 1981). A child with hemophilia may need to be excused from some physical activities and may use a wheelchair during periods of susceptibility. However, as with most children who have health-related impairments, good physical condition is important for development and well-being, so the restrictions on activities should not be any greater than necessary.

Burns

Burns are a leading cause of injury in childhood. Most often, burns result from household accidents, but sometimes they are caused by child abuse. As Yurt and Pruitt (1983) point out, the skin is the largest organ in the human body and one of the most important; serious burns can cause complications in other organs, long-term physical limitations, and psychological difficulties. Children with serious burn injuries usually experience pain, scarring, limitations of motion, lengthy hospitalizations, and repeated surgery. Some children with severe burns on their faces and other areas wear sterilized elastic masks to protect and soften the skin. The disfigurement caused by severe burns can affect a child's behavior and self-image, especially if teachers and peers react negatively. When a child is returning to class after prolonged absence resulting from an extensive burn injury, it may be advisable for the teacher, parents, or other involved person (such as a social worker or physical therapist) to explain to classmates the nature of the child's injury and appearance (Yurt & Pruitt, 1983).

Other Health Problems and Related Concerns

There are, of course, many other significant physical and health-related conditions that can influence a child's learning and behavior at school. Heart disease, asthma, cancer, and juvenile rheumatoid arthritis are conditions that generally do not require the use of special teaching techniques or adaptive equipment. Yet they may cause variations in the child's performance, as a direct result of not only the condition itself, but also the child's frequent absences from school, the effects of medication, fatigue, and pain.

The child with a physical or health impairment may be afraid of going to the hospital and being separated from her parents. She may look and feel different from her classmates. An older student may resent medication, therapy, prohibitions on activities, and other restrictions that limit independence and may worry about an uncertain future. The family of a child with a physical or health impairment may encounter many demands on time and energy, as well as financial problems from long-term medical care and equipment costs, which are often not covered by insurance. A teacher's concern and familiarity with a student's physical or health impairment can do much to improve the quality of that student's school experience. Specific information about a student's condition can usually be obtained from the student's parents or physician or directly from the student. The references listed at the end of this chapter may also be useful to teachers.

IMPORTANT VARIABLES TO CONSIDER

In assessing the effects of a physical or health impairment on a child's development and behavior, many factors should be taken into consideration. Important among these are the severity and visibility of the impairment and the age at which the disabling condition was first acquired.

Severity

Most children learn by exploring their surroundings, interacting with other people, and having a wide variety of experiences in their homes, neighborhoods, schools, and communities. A minor or transient physical or health impairment—such as those experienced by most children while growing up—is not likely to have lasting effects, but a severe, long-standing impairment can greatly limit a child's range of experiences. Many such disabling conditions seriously restrict a child's mobility and independence, much as a severe visual or hearing impairment would. The child may not be able to travel alone at all and may have few opportunities to explore the environment by seeing, hearing, touching, smelling, or tasting things. He may spend most of the time at home or in a hospital. Some children are in virtually constant pain or become tired after any sort of physical exertion. Some take medications that decrease their alertness and responsiveness. Some may be physically fragile and afraid of injury or death.

Visibility

Some physical impairments are highly visible and conspicuous. The way in which children think about themselves and the degree to which they are accepted by others often are affected by the visibility of a condition. Some children need to rely on a variety of special orthopedic appliances, such as wheelchairs, braces, crutches, and adaptive tables. They may ride to school with other disabled children on a specially equipped bus or van. In school they may need assistance using the toilet or may wear prominent helmets. Although such special devices and adaptations do help children meet important needs, they often have the unfortunate side effect of increasing the visibility of the physical impairment and making the child look even more different from nondisabled peers. Many disabled people report that their hardware—wheelchairs, artificial limbs, communication devices, and other apparatus—creates a great deal of curiosity and leads to frequent, repetitive questions from strangers. For many children, learning to explain their disabilities and respond to questions can be an appropriate component of their educational programs. They may also benefit from discussing such concerns as when to ask for help from others and when to decline offers of assistance.

Age at Acquisition

As with virtually all exceptionalities, it is important for the teacher to be aware of the age of the child at the time the physical or health impairment was originally acquired. A child who has not had the use of her legs since birth may have missed out on some important developmental experiences, particularly if early intervention services were not provided. In contrast, a teenager who suddenly loses the use of his legs in an accident has likely had a normal range of experiences throughout childhood but may need considerable support from parents, teachers, specialists, and peers in making a successful adaptation to life with this newly acquired disability.

PREVALENCE

Because there are numerous different physical and health impairments and no universally accepted definition of this population, it is difficult to obtain accurate and meaningful prevalence statistics. As Bigge and Sirvis (1986) observe, physical disabilities and health impairments often occur in combination with other handicapping conditions, so children may be counted under other categories, such as learning disabilities, speech impairment, or mental retardation. According to Dykes and Venn (1983), for special education placement purposes a diagnosis of mental retardation usually takes precedence over a diagnosis of physical impairment. Also, many of the approximately 250,000 children born each year with significant birth defects are not considered disabled or handicapped by the time they reach school age, thanks to improved medical and surgical treatment or to the results of successful early intervention programs (Grove, 1982).

A survey of 3- through 21-year-old handicapped children served in special education programs during the 1984–85 school year placed the number of orthopedically impaired children at 58,835 and the number of other health impaired children at 69,118 (U.S. Department of Education, 1986). Together, these categories would represent about 3% of all children receiving special education services. However, as noted earlier, the number of children with physical and health impairments included under other special education categories is not known but is probably sizable.

See chapter 1 for an indication of how this prevalence rate compares with those of other areas of exceptionality.

The children most frequently placed in special education programs for physical, orthopedic, or health impairments are those with cerebral palsy. In some programs half or more of the students considered physically impaired have cerebral palsy. Spina bifida and muscular dystrophy also account for relatively high percentages of the students receiving such services (Bigge & Sirvis, 1986; Dykes & Venn, 1983).

Current Incidence Trends

The causes of physical disabilities and health impairments have changed somewhat over the years. Medical detection, genetic counseling, and vaccination programs have significantly reduced the incidence of numerous diseases that formerly affected many children. Additionally, it is now possible to correct or control a variety of orthopedic, neurologic, and health impairments—through early surgery, physical therapy, medication, and the use of artificial internal or external body parts—to the point where many conditions formerly regarded as crippling, disabling, or disfiguring no longer are so.

On the other hand, medical and technological advances (particularly in neonatal and emergency care) mean that more infants and children with serious physical and health impairments are surviving. Many of these children require special education services. It also appears that the numbers are increasing for children and young adults who suffer physical and health impairments as the result of motor vehicle accidents, child abuse and neglect, and drug and alcohol abuse. Many individuals and families affected by these factors are likely to need specialized educational and emotional support.

HISTORICAL BACKGROUND

Perhaps because there are so many different types of physical and health impairments, it is difficult to trace the development of services for this population with any precision. Before there were public school educational opportunities, which began around the turn of this century, most children with severely disabling conditions were kept at home, in hospitals, or in institutions. If local public schools were willing to accept them and make any necessary modifications, some physically disabled children probably attended regular classes, especially if their handicaps were less severe and their intellectual functioning was not impaired.

The first special public school class for physically handicapped children in the United States was established in Chicago around 1900. Two American physicians, Winthrop Phelps and Earl Carlson, made noteworthy contributions to the understanding and acceptance of physically disabled children. Phelps demonstrated that children could be helped through physical therapy and the effective use of braces, whereas Carlson (who himself had cerebral palsy) was a strong advocate of developing the intellectual potential of physically disabled children through appropriate education (Hewett & Forness, 1977).

As the 20th century progressed, the educational needs of children with physical and health impairments were gradually recognized. A dual system of special education prevailed for many handicapped children throughout most of this century—that is, virtually all children with disabilities such as blindness, deafness, and mental retardation were served either in state-run residential schools or in local schools and classes (Cruickshank, 1986). However, this dual system did not apply to physically impaired children; hardly any state residential schools were established for them. Instead, emphasis has long been placed on making services available at the community level. Children who were kept at home or in hospitals for reasons of health were served by homebound or hospital teachers, who traveled from place to place. Special self-contained classes for children with physical impairments were set up in many regular public schools. Large school districts frequently maintained special schools solely for children with physical impairments. These special classes or schools typically had such modifications as ramps, adapted toilets, special gymnasiums, and space for wheelchairs in school cafeterias.

Many special classes and schools still exist for children with physical and health impairments. Today, however, there is a trend toward increased integration of these students in regular public school classes. The implementation of P.L. 94–142 and Section 504 of the Rehabilitation Act of 1973—as well as numerous court cases requiring architectural accessibility, appropriate educational programs for children in the least restrictive environment, and an end to discrimination against persons with disabilities—have had a positive impact on this integration. No longer may a child be

See chapter 2 for a description of these laws.

denied the right to attend her local public school simply because there is a flight of stairs at the entrance, or bathroom or locker facilities are not suitable, or school buses are not equipped to transport wheelchairs. The local school district now has the responsibility of providing suitable programs, facilities, and services to meet each child's needs. Today, many thousands of children with physical and health impairments are successfully attending regular classes.

EDUCATIONAL IMPLICATIONS

Alternative Settings

Children with physical and health impairments are served in a wide variety of educational settings, ranging from regular classrooms to homes and hospitals. Special educators address the needs of these students from infancy to young adulthood, in cooperation with parents, other educators, and specialists.

Early intervention programs are important for all exceptional children, especially those with physical and health impairments. Programs for infants and preschool children are increasingly available through local school districts—in part as a response to the Education of the Handicapped Act Amendments of 1986—as well as in hospitals, clinics, university-affiliated facilities, and specialized community agencies (such as United Cerebral Palsy). The services may be directed exclusively to at-risk or disabled children or may include nondisabled children as well. Usually, early intervention programs for children with physical and health impairments emphasize assessment of a child's performance in many areas and seek to systematically develop the child's motor, self-help, social, and communication skills. A good early intervention program can be of enormous help to the child and family in providing information and support.

Chapters 2 and 14 contain further information on P.L. 99–457.

Regular public school classes, in which school-age children with physical and health impairments are educated along with nondisabled children, are the educational settings preferred by many parents and educators. The amount of supportive help that may be required to enable a physically impaired student to function effectively in a regular class varies greatly, according to each child's condition, needs, and level of functioning. Some children require comparatively minor modifications—such as ramps and altered seating arrangements—whereas others require special equipment and considerable assistance in mobility, eating, using the toilet, administering medication, and performing other daily activities. An effective program in an integrated school setting can encourage independence, communication, and social development and can make nondisabled students more aware of their peers with disabilities.

The continuum of educational services, as described in chapter 2, is especially applicable to children with physical and health impairments.

Special classes for children with physical disabilities are also found in many public schools. Some districts have entire schools designed especially for physically disabled students, whereas in others self-contained special classrooms are housed within regular elementary or secondary school buildings. Special classes usually provide smaller class size, more adapted equipment, and easier access to the services of important professionals, such as physicians, physical and occupational therapists, and specialists

Bobby's classmates are learning that a physical impairment need not stand in the way of full participation in the regular classroom

in communication disorders and therapeutic recreation. Some parents and educators believe that it is desirable for physically impaired children to associate with other disabled children and to be served closely by teachers and therapists familiar with their special needs.

Homebound or hospital education programs are available to children with especially severe physical and health impairments. If a handicapped child's medical condition necessitates hospitalization or treatment at home for a lengthy period (generally 30 days or more), the local school district is obligated to draw up an individualized education program and provide appropriate educational services to the child through a qualified teacher. This is usually regarded as the most restrictive level of special education service, because little or no interaction with nondisabled students is possible in a home or hospital setting. Most large hospitals and medical centers employ educational specialists who cooperate with the hospitalized student's home school district in planning and delivering instruction. Homebound children are visited regularly by itinerant teachers. Some hospital-based and homebound educational programs also offer special counseling to help children and their families deal with the problems of chronic and/or terminal illness.

The Interdisciplinary Approach

Children with physical and health impairments usually come into contact with a great many teachers, physicians, therapists, and other specialists, both in and out of school. It is important that both regular and special educators make informed decisions about each child's needs, in cooperation with parents and other professionals. There are many opportunities for members of an interdisciplinary team to share information about a child from their individual vantage points. The team approach has special relevance to a child with a physical or health impairment. Medical, educational, therapeutic, vocational, and social needs are important and complex and frequently interact with each other. Communication and cooperation among educational and health care personnel are especially crucial if the diverse needs of each child are to be met. For example, in devising appropriate toileting procedures for Richard, a pediatrician may recommend a diet and a schedule, following a medical examination of bowel and bladder functioning. A biomedical technician may then design an adaptive device to facilitate Richard's transfer from his wheelchair to the toilet; and a physical therapist may help him use the device, while demonstrating proper bracing and muscle-strengthening techniques to Richard's parents and teachers.

Sirvis (1982) suggests that an interdisciplinary team of professionals and parents should work toward achieving four general goals in the educational program of a student with a physical or health impairment.

1. physical independence, including mastery of daily living skills
2. self-awareness and social maturation
3. academic growth
4. career education, including constructive leisure activities

Two specialists of particular importance to many children with physical and health impairments are the physical therapist and the occupational therapist. Each of these specialists must complete a specialized training program and must meet rigorous professional standards. Their work frequently takes them into contact with physically and health impaired children, and they are often called on to provide practical suggestions and training to teachers and parents.

Physical therapists use specialized knowledge to plan and oversee a child's program in making correct and useful movements. They may prescribe specific exercises to help a child increase control over muscles and use specialized equipment, such as braces, effectively. Massage and prescriptive exercises are perhaps the most frequently applied procedures, but physical therapy can also include swimming, heat treatment, special positioning for feeding and toileting, and other techniques. Physical therapists encourage children to be as motorically independent as possible, help develop muscular function, and reduce pain, discomfort, or long-term physical damage. They may also suggest dos and don'ts for sitting positions and activities in the classroom and may suggest exercise or play programs that a disabled child can enjoy along with other children.

Occupational therapists are concerned with a child's participation in activities, especially those that will be useful in self-help, employment, recreation, communication, and other aspects of daily living. They may help a child learn (or relearn) such diverse motor behaviors as drinking from a modified cup, buttoning clothes, tying shoes, pouring liquids, cooking, and typing on a computer keyboard. Such activities can enhance a child's physical development, independence, vocational potential, and self-concept. Occupational therapists conduct specialized assessments and make recommendations to parents and teachers regarding the effective use of appliances, materials, and activities at home and school. Many occupational therapists also work with vocational rehabilitation specialists in helping students find opportunities for work and independent living after completion of an educational program.

Additional specialists who frequently offer services to children with physical and health impairments include *prosthetists*, who make and fit artificial limbs; *orthotists*, who design and fit braces and other assistive devices; *biomedical engineers*, who develop or adapt technology to meet a student's specialized needs; and *medical social workers*, who assist students and families in adjusting to disabilities. Korabek and Cuvo (1986) state that *applied behavior analysts* often have a useful role to play in working with physically disabled students. Some children, they note, display self-injurious behaviors and may inflict serious wounds on parts of their bodies where they cannot feel physical sensations or pain.

APPROACHES TO INTERVENTION

The educational programs of children with physical and health impairments are often similar to those of nonhandicapped children or children with other exceptionalities (depending, of course, on individual needs and educational settings). For many children, particularly those with physical impairments that affect their motor functioning, some treatment of the disability takes place in school. Blasco (1986) observes that treatment of motor impairments usually falls into one of four general categories.

1. *Hands-on therapy.* Physical, occupational, and other specialists provide direct hands-on treatment. Because the amount of time therapists can spend with individual children is usually limited, they often show teachers and parents how to correctly implement such techniques as positioning, bracing, and exercising. Thus, children can receive the benefits of more frequent and regular therapy, still under the supervision of the specialist.
2. *Assistive devices.* Braces and splints (usually made of molded plastic) are used to give a child movement with stability, to correct abnormal postures, and to control involuntary motions. Special inserts or wedges can help children sit or stand in positions that are comfortable and suitable for instructional tasks. In addition, technological aids for movement and communication are increasingly used today. Assistive devices are specially designed and fitted, as appropriate to each child's developmental level and needs in the home, school, and community. The teacher is generally not involved in prescribing or fitting them but can help evaluate their effectiveness and can suggest changes that may be necessary as a child grows.
3. *Medication.* Medicines can sometimes help reduce spasticity and rigidity but generally are of only limited usefulness in improving the muscle tone of children with

physical disabilities (Batshaw & Perret, 1986). More often, medications are used to manage problems related to the physical or health impairment, such as antibiotics to prevent bladder infections or anticonvulsant drugs to control seizures (Blasco, 1986). Because many medications have side effects (e.g., drowsiness, nausea, weakness), teachers can help parents and physicians by keeping them informed of a student's classroom performance.

4. *Surgery.* Orthopedic or neurologic surgery, although often regarded as a last resort in the treatment of physical impairments, can become necessary if other approaches are not successful in improving a child's ability to function. There is always a potential risk. A child who undergoes major surgery is likely to be absent from school for an extended period; the teacher should take this into consideration in educational planning. Also, the child may have fears and concerns regarding hospitalization, pain, and the outcome of the surgery.

Special Devices and Appliances

Many children with physical disabilities use special orthopedic devices to increase their mobility and help their bones, joints, and muscles develop. A **prosthesis** is an artificial replacement of a missing body part (most frequently an arm, leg, or eye). Teachers of students who use prostheses or such devices as canes, leg or hip braces, walkers, and wheelchairs should be familiar with the purpose and function of these devices. The teacher is in a good position to observe the ways in which a student uses and cares for a device or prosthesis and to encourage the student to use it appropriately in school. The teacher can also keep parents informed of any problems or malfunctions that may occur, including discomfort caused by poorly fitting appliances.

A helpful series of checklists for teachers to use in evaluating orthopedic and prosthetic devices is provided by Venn, Morganstern, and Dykes (1979). They point out that the same devices may function differently for different children. For example, braces are typically used for control in children with cerebral palsy and for support in children with spina bifida. Support braces tend to be smaller and lighter in weight than control braces.

Wheelchairs, probably more than any other device, are closely associated in the public mind with physical and health impairments. Persons who spend most or all of each day sitting in a wheelchair face several problems (Zacharkow, 1984). These include pressure sores, discomfort, poor posture, and damage to muscles, spinal column, and bones. A working knowledge of techniques associated with wheelchair use can be helpful to a teacher in reducing some of these problems and in making classrooms and school buildings accessible.

See pages 356–57 for guidelines on wheelchair use.

Incidentally, a student should not be described as being "confined to a wheelchair." This expression suggests that the person is restrained, or even imprisoned. Actually, most students leave their wheelchairs from time to time to exercise or lie down. It is preferable to say that a student "has a wheelchair" or "uses a wheelchair to get around."

Wheelchairs have various parts and specialized functions and children are generally instructed in their safe and efficient use and maintenance by an orthopedist or

CHECKLISTS FOR THE CLASSROOM

John Venn, Linda Morganstern, and Mary K. Dykes have prepared information and checklists that may be helpful to the teacher who works with children using braces, prostheses, or wheelchairs in the classroom. Here is a portion of the material on wheelchairs.

WHEELCHAIRS

Wheelchair locomotion is prescribed by a physician for individuals who are unable to ambulate or for those whose ambulation is unsteady, unsafe, or too strenuous. A wheelchair may also be needed by those who can ambulate but cannot rise unassisted from sitting to standing. Those who need crutches to ambulate but have to carry things from one place to another may also require the use of a wheelchair (Hirschberg, Lewis & Thomas, 1964).

The most commonly used type of wheelchair is made of metal and upholstery and has four wheels. The two back wheels are large and have a separate rim that can be grasped to propel the chair while the two small front wheels are casters that pivot freely. The casters are attached to the wheelchair by a fork and stem assembly that allows them to pivot 360°. Since wheelchairs are fitted to individuals, and not individuals to wheelchairs, the special parts and features are numerous. Such special features include detachable armrests, which are fitted with a locking device to secure them in place; footrests, which often have nylon heel loops to hold the foot on the footrest; leg rest panels to support the leg in proper position; and a folding device that allows the wheelchair to be folded for easier storage (Ellwood, 1971). After it has been decided that a wheelchair is needed, the wheelchair dealer, often in conjunction with a physical therapist, measures the child to ensure an individual prescription that will properly fit the child. The dealer also provides instruction in the use and care of the wheelchair.

Recent wheelchair developments include increasing use of lightweight, adaptive wheelchairs as well as motorized wheelchairs. The lightweight chairs are primarily designed for children. Fea-

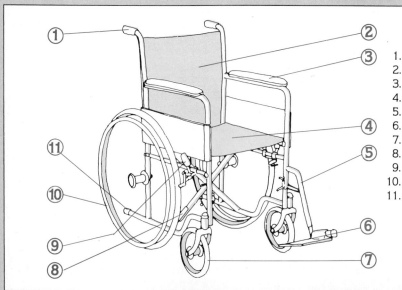

1. handgrips/push handles
2. back upholstery
3. armrests
4. seat upholstery
5. front rigging
6. footplate
7. casters
8. crossbraces
9. wheel locks
10. wheel and handrim
11. tipping lever

tures include such things as a travel chair with a unique folding mechanism that allows it to double as a stroller and a car seat. Accessories include adjustable Velcro fasteners for lap belts, pads, attachable trays, and head restraints. In addition, motorized wheelchairs of various designs may be precribed for individuals unable to propel themselves independently. Wheelchair transporters such as modified golf charts are available for relatively long driving ranges (Peizer, 1975).

The Role of the Teacher

The primary role of the teacher regarding ambulation devices is daily observation of the student's use and care of his or her equipment. Teachers should keep parents apprised of special problems and needs when they arise. The teacher, along with other special education support personnel, is responsible for designing a barrier-free classroom and also for obtaining the special equipment and materials that will allow the student to participate in classroom activities. In conjunction with the physical therapist and the family, the teacher should develop a program to encourage maxi-

mum use of ambulation devices in the classroom, the school, the home, and the community. Therefore, the teacher's role extends beyond the school's boundaries and into the home and the community.

Use of the Checklists

A checklist for use in the classroom is provided to enable the teacher to monitor the condition and function of wheelchairs. The items on each checklist are marked with "yes" and "no" answers. If the device is in proper working condition and fitted correctly, all items should be marked in the "yes" column. "No" answers indicate problems with the device that require attention. A section for comments about specific needs is provided for each item.

The classroom teacher may use these checklists for preliminary evaluations but should refer the child to a physical therapist for reassessment or request that parents seek physical therapist assistance/reassessment before assuming that his or her (the teacher's) evaluation is correct or referring the child to a specialist.

	No	Yes	Comments		No	Yes	Comments
With the student out of the wheelchair				3. When the chair is folded fully are the front post slides straight and round?			
A. Arms				D. Wheel locks			
1. Are the armrests and side panels secure and free of sharp edges and cracks?				1. Do the wheel locks securely engage the tire surfaces and prevent the wheels from turning?			
2. Do the armlocks function properly?				E. Large wheels			
B. Backs				1. Are the wheels free from wobble or sideplay when spun?			
1. Is the upholstery free of rips and tears?							
2. Is the back taut from top to bottom?				2. Are the spokes equally tight and without any missing spokes?			
3. Is the safety belt attached tightly and not frayed?				3. Are the tires free from excessive wear and gaps at the joined section?			
C. Seat and frame							
1. Is the upholstery free of rips and tears?							
2. Does the chair fold easily without sticking?							

Source: (Wheelchair Prescriptions, 1968, 1976)

Source: From "Checklists for Evaluating the Fit and Function of Orthoses, Prostheses, and Wheelchairs in the Classroom" by J. Venn, L. Morganstern, & M. K. Dykes, 1979, *Teaching Exceptional Children, 11*, pp. 51–56. Copyright by the Council for Exceptional Children. Reprinted by permission. Drawing courtesy of Everest and Jennings.

a physical therapist. Necessary techniques involved in wheelchair operation include using footrests, handbrakes, and rims; turning safely; traveling over rugs, doorways, curbs, and mud; and transferring from the wheelchair to a chair, car, or toilet. Propelling a wheelchair takes up to five times more energy than normal walking (Mullins, 1979); some wheelchairs are motorized, thereby reducing the effort involved but adding a substantial amount of additional weight. Swack (1969) observes that there are two basic causes of accidents involving wheelchairs in the classroom: (1) classmates pushing a wheelchair too rapidly and (2) wheelchairs rolling away when left unlocked. Strict enforcement of no-speeding rules and locking the brakes on wheelchairs when they are not in motion should reduce classroom mishaps.

A prosthesis replaces a missing body part, whereas an adaptive device modifies or replaces a body function.

Children with physical and health impairments also use **adaptive devices** in many everyday activities. Special eating utensils, such as forks and spoons with custom-designed handles or straps, may enable children to feed themselves more independently. New technological aids for communication are used increasingly with children whose physical impairments prevent them from speaking clearly. For students who are able to speak but have limited motor function, there are voice input/output products that enable them to access computers (Esposito & Campbell, 1987). Such developments allow students with physical impairments to communicate expressively and receptively with others and to take part in a wide range of instructional programs.

See chapter 6 for a discussion of nonverbal communication aids.

Modifying the Environment

Teachers of children with physical and health impairments frequently find it necessary to adapt equipment, schedules, or settings so that their students can participate in educational and recreational activities. Although we usually think first of barrier-free architecture as a way to increase the accessibility of programs, there are many other ways in which useful adaptations can be made at little or no cost. The U.S. Commission on Civil Rights (1983) suggests several examples of such adaptations that are applicable to school settings.

1. changing desk and table tops to appropriate heights for students who are very short or use wheelchairs
2. providing a wooden pointer to enable a student to reach the upper buttons on an elevator control panel
3. installing paper cup dispensers near water fountains so that they can be used by students in wheelchairs
4. moving a class or activity to an accessible part of a school building so that a student with a physical impairment can be included.

Physical and recreational activities are important; they can strengthen children's muscles, increase flexibility, and provide enjoyable opportunities for interaction with other children. Shivers and Fait (1985) suggest the following examples of relatively minor adaptations that can enable students with physical and health impairments to participate:

1. substituting a different body position from the one normally used (as in lying on a mat to play checkers)

2. modifying equipment—for example, adding a longer handle to a tennis racket or a rake so that it can be used from a wheelchair
3. developing alternative techniques for accomplishing activities, such as having two-handed tasks performed with one hand, with the feet, or with the teeth
4. decreasing the distances a student must move or reducing the size of a court on which a game is played
5. providing more frequent rest periods than usual.

Importance of Positioning

A working knowledge of positioning techniques can be helpful to the teacher of students with physical and health impairments. Students' head and arm control, coordination, comfort, and muscle tone can vary greatly according to various positions. Restricting a student to one position for long periods can lead to poor circulation, muscle tightness, pressure sores, and other problems; thus, "every student should have a minimum of two (and preferably more) ways of being positioned in the classroom" (Campbell, 1987, p. 177). Parents, physical therapists, or the individual student is usually able to specify how long sitting or standing can be comfortable without repositioning. Many students need to change position every 20 or 30 minutes to be comfortable and maintain good circulation, digestion, respiration, and physical development (Parette & Hourcade, 1986).

A general guideline is that any sitting, standing, or other positioning device should provide adequate support without locking the child into a static position. The child should be able to maintain the recommended posture while still having an opportunity to move (Kasari & Filler, 1981). Physical therapists can assist in prescribing, maintaining, and evaluating devices such as adaptive chairs, standing tables, wedges, and inflatable support equipment.

The positioning of a physically disabled child can also have significant effects on how the child is perceived and accepted by other people. A recent study (Brown, 1982) found that postural adjustment had a major influence on teachers' attitudes toward physically disabled children; well-positioned children were rated more positively than poorly positioned children. Simple adjustments in posture may greatly improve the appearance and acceptance of children with physical disabilities.

Attitudes

The ways in which parents, teachers, classmates, and others react to a child with physical disabilities are at least as important as the disability itself. Many disabled children suffer from excessive pity, sympathy, and overprotection, whereas others are cruelly rejected, stared at, teased, and excluded from participation in activities with nondisabled children. All children—disabled or not—need to develop respect for themselves and to feel that they have a rightful place in their family, school, and community.

Children with physical disabilities should be given the chance to participate in activities and to experience success and accomplishment. Effective parents and teachers accept these children as worthwhile individuals, rather than as disability cases. They encourage the children to develop a positive, realistic view of themselves and their physical conditions. They expect the children to meet reasonable standards of performance and behavior. They help the children cope with their disabilities wherever possible and realize that, beyond their physical impairments, these children have many qualities that make them unique individuals.

Many nondisabled people tend to feel uncomfortable in the presence of a person with a visible disability and react with tension and withdrawal (Allsop, 1980). This response is probably attributable to a lack of previous contact with disabled individuals; people may fear that they will say or do the wrong thing. A study by Belgrave and Mills (1981) found that when disabled people specifically mentioned their disabilites in connection with a request for help ("Would you mind sharpening my pencil for me? There are just some things you can't do from a wheelchair"), they were perceived more favorably than they were when no mention was made of the disability.

The classroom can be a useful place to discuss disabilities and to encourage understanding and acceptance of a child with a physical or health impairment. Some teachers find that simulation or role-playing activities are helpful. Nondisabled children might, for example, have the opportunity to use wheelchairs, braces, or crutches to increase their awareness of some barriers faced by a disabled classmate. Pieper (1983) notes that most children with physical and health impairments are "neither saintly creatures nor pitiable objects" (p. 8). She suggests that teachers emphasize cooperation rather than competition by choosing tasks that require students to work together. It is important to give praise when earned but not to make the child with a physical impairment a teacher's pet who will be resented by other students. Factual information can also be helpful in building a general understanding of an impairment. Classmates should learn to use accurate terminology and to offer the correct kind of assistance when needed.

A child should *never* be equated with a disability label, as in "He's a C.P." or "She's an epileptic."

CURRENT ISSUES/FUTURE TRENDS

There is currently an increasing trend toward integrating children with physical and health impairments into regular educational programs as much as possible. No longer is it believed that the regular classroom is an inappropriate environment for a child with physical limitations. Although architectural and attitudinal barriers still exist in some areas, integrated public school programs are gradually becoming more accessible.

This integration of students with physical and health impairments, however, has raised several controversial issues. Many questions center on the extent of responsibility properly assumed by teachers and schools in caring for a child's physical and health needs. In a well-publicized case (*Irving Independent School District v. Tatro,* 1984) the U.S. Supreme Court decided that a school district was obligated to provide clean, intermittent catheterization service to a young child with spina bifida. This procedure, required every 3 or 4 hours, drains urine through a tube that is inserted into the bladder. The Court considered catheterization to be a related service, necessary for the child to remain in the least restrictive educational setting and able to be performed by a trained layperson. Some educators and school administrators believe that services such as catheterization are more medical than educational and should not be the school's responsibility. The expense of such services and the availability of insurance pose potential problems for school personnel. Nevertheless, the *Tatro* case probably means that "handicapped children with medical problems who were once excluded from school programs may now be provided access since certain medical services can be provided by qualified personnel who are not physicians" (Vitello, 1986, p. 356). Similar questions have been raised with regard to the equipment and special services that may be needed by physically or health impaired children in regular schools. Who should bear the cost of an expensive computerized communication system for a child with cerebral palsy, for example—the parents, the school, both, or some other agency?

The future will likely see a continuation of the present trend to serve children with physical and health impairments in regular classrooms as much as possible. Therapists and other support personnel will come into the classroom to assist the teacher, child, and classmates. This appears to be a more effective and economical use of professional time and skill than removing a disabled child from the classroom and providing services in an isolated setting.

Recent developments in technology and biomedical engineering hold exciting implications for many children with physical disabilities. People with paralysis due to spinal cord injury and other causes are already benefiting from sophisticated microcomputers able to stimulate paralyzed muscles by bypassing damaged nerves. In 1982 Nan Davis became the first human being ever to walk with permanently paralyzed muscles; she was able to control a computer with her brain and transmit impulses to sensors placed on her paralyzed muscles. Such systems are likely to become more efficient and widespread in the future, helping many people with varied kinds of physical impairments. Improved medical treatment will also alleviate some physical and health-related conditions.

The use of animals to assist people with physical disabilities has also engendered much recent interest. Trained dogs are now frequently used to give physical assistance and support to people with physical impairments; they can help people stand, walk, carry objects, and even propel wheelchairs. Monkeys have been trained to perform such complex tasks as opening doors, preparing food, and turning the pages of books (MacFadyen, 1986). Sometimes technological and animal assistance are used together, as when a person uses a laser beam (emitted from a device held in the mouth) to show a monkey which light switch needs to be turned on. In addition to providing practical assistance and enhancing the independence of people with disabilities, animals also appear to have social value as companions.

See "A Canine Helper" on page 362 for an example of animal assistance.

Students with physical limitations will continue to be encouraged to develop as much independence as possible. Often, well-meaning teachers, classmates, and parents tend to do too much for a child with a physical or health impairment. It may be difficult, frustrating, and/or time-consuming for the child to learn to care for his own needs, but the confidence and skills gained from independent functioning are well worth the effort in the long run. Nevertheless, most persons with physical disabilities find it necessary to rely on others for assistance at certain times, in certain situations. Effective teachers can help their students cope with their disabilities, set realistic expectations, and accept help gracefully when it is needed.

FOCUS

A CANINE HELPER

There are many ways in which animals can be of help to children and adults with disabilities. Nearly everyone is familiar with guide dogs, who can help blind people travel independently. Some agencies also train hearing dogs to assist deaf persons by alerting them to sounds. Another recent and promising approach to the use of animals with disabled people is that of a "helping dog." Depending on a person's needs, dogs can be trained to perform the following tasks:

☐ Picking up objects
☐ Turning light switches on or off
☐ Opening doors
☐ Picking up telephone receivers
☐ Carrying books and other objects (in saddle bags)

Dogs can also be used for balance and support—for example, in helping a person propel a wheelchair up a steep ramp or in helping a person stand up from a seated position. And dogs can be trained to contact family members or neighbors if the disabled person is in need of help. Frequently, people report that dogs serve as an ice-breaker in opening up conversations and contacts with nondisabled people in the school and community. In addition, assuming the responsibilities of caring for an animal is a worthwhile experience for many people, with or without disabilities.

Jim Ward is a 21-year-old man who was injured in a diving accident at the age of 17. He lost the use of both legs and arms (although he has limited mobility in his left arm). Several months after his injury, Jim became a client of Happy Canine Helpers, Inc. The agency provided and trained for him a German shepherd called Lady. In the following letter Jim's mother, Barbara Ward, describes what Lady has meant to Jim and his family.

> I would like to tell you about Lady, our Happy Canine Helper. She has become an important part of our family.
>
> When Jim Ward, my son, came home from the hospital, he was very depressed and unmotivated. He was unable to do anything for himself.
>
> Lady has changed all that. She can open doors for Jim and turn the light switch and TV on and off. She retrieves things that Jim drops on the floor.
>
> More importantly, I think, she has motivated Jim into returning to life. Jim is trying harder through therapy to work with Lady. He is more willing to meet the public with Lady at his side. He talks more and is developing better social skills.
>
> Lady sleeps by Jim's bed, so Jim sleeps better at night knowing he can send Lady for me if he becomes sick or needs help. We rest better knowing Lady is taking care of Jim.
>
> We are so grateful for such a wonderful dog. Lady was provided for us *free* of charge from Happy Canine Helpers, Inc. What a wonderful organization to work with. The support and love they have given us have made a fantastic change in Jim's life. I pray they will be able to continue providing dogs for the handicapped community. God bless them all.
>
> Sincerely,
>
> Barbara Ward

For more information Happy Canine Helpers, Inc. may be contacted at 16277 Montgomery Road, Johnstown, Ohio 43031. Financial assistance is often provided through local community agencies and charitable groups or special fund-raising projects.

*mylomonirgocule
meningocule*

The future will need to focus on several areas in which progress has been made but improvement is still needed. Even though physical education is an important need of most disabled people—and is specifically required by P.L. 94–142 to be included in the educational program of every handicapped child—many schools do not provide adapted physical education programs for their disabled students, thus excluding them from participation in most athletic and recreational activities.

Another area of concern is employment, which is one of the most critical aspects of any adult's life. Many studies have shown that successful and remunerative work is among the most important variables in enabling disabled people to lead satisfying, productive, and independent lives. Yet negative attitudes persist on the part of many employers. Vocational and professional opportunities must be expanded to include disabled individuals more adequately. While children are in school, their education should help them investigate practical avenues of future employment, and there should be ongoing contact between educators and vocational rehabilitation specialists.

There is also a need for improved programs of education and counseling for students with terminal illnesses. These programs should give realistic support to the child and family in dealing with death and in making the best possible use of the time available to them. When a child dies, teachers and classmates may also be seriously affected, and their needs should also be considered and talked about.

Many self-help groups of people with disabilities now exist. These can be very helpful in providing information and support to children affected by similar disabilities. It is usually encouraging for a child and parent to see capable, independent adults with severe disabilities, and worthwhile, helping relationships can be established. Some groups operate centers for independent living, which emphasize adaptive devices, financial benefits, access to jobs, and provision of personal care attendants. Other groups are active as advocates for social change, countering instances in which disabled people are excluded from meaningful participation in society.

There is every indication that the years ahead will find children and adults with physical and health impairments participating more fully in schools, colleges, and virtually all other facets of everyday community life. However, we still need better physical access to public buildings, improved public attitudes, and greater support to parents early in the lives of their disabled children. As these needs are met, the opportunities open to people with physical and health impairments will be greatly expanded.

A comprehensive guide to special adaptations in physical education for disabled students is provided by French and Jansma (1982).

SUMMARY

1. Children with physical and health impairments are a widely varied population, and the degree to which their conditions require special instruction, equipment, or placement also varies greatly.
    a. Some children are extremely restricted in their activities, whereas others have few limitations.
    b. It is important for teachers to understand how a child's physical or health impairment may affect learning, development, or behavior.

2. There are many types of physical and health conditions that may make some sort of special education services necessary.

   a. An orthopedic impairment involves a child's skeletal system; a neurologic impairment involves the nervous system.

   b. Physical impairments are described in terms of the type of limb involvement (e.g., quadriplegia, paraplegia, hemiplegia, diplegia).

   c. Impairments are also described in terms of their severity, such as mild, moderate, and severe.

   d. Cerebral palsy is a long-term condition, arising from impairment to the brain and causing disturbances in voluntary motor functions. Its causes are varied and not clearly known. Children with cerebral palsy may have normal, above normal, or below normal intelligence. The most common types of cerebral palsy are spasticity, athetosis, and ataxia. Other types are rigidity and tremor. Cerebral palsy, like other physical and health impairments, is most effectively managed by a team of professionals.

   e. Spina bifida is a congenital condition that may cause loss of sensation and severe muscle weakness in the lower part of the body. A shunt is often used to drain fluid that might lead to head enlargement and brain damage. Usually, children with spina bifida can participate in most classroom activities. They need assistance in toileting.

   f. Muscular dystrophy is a long-term condition that weakens and wastes the muscle tissue. Most children with progressive muscular dystrophy gradually lose the ability to walk independently.

   g. Other orthopedic and neurologic conditions that can affect a child's classroom performance include osteogenesis imperfecta, spinal cord injuries, and amputations or missing limbs.

   h. Head injuries, sometimes leading to coma (an abnormal period of deep stupor), are a significant cause of neurologic impairments and learning problems.

   i. Seizure disorders produce disturbances of movement, sensation, behavior, and/or consciousness because of abnormal electrical activity in the brain. Epilepsy is a term that describes chronic and repeated seizures. Seizure disorders can usually be controlled with medication. Some drugs, however, have undesirable side effects. Three common types of seizures are grand mal, petit mal, and psychomotor. Teachers and classmates of children with seizure disorders should be familiar with the condition and with procedures to follow during a seizure. Understanding and acceptance are important to children with seizure disorders.

   j. Diabetes is a disorder of metabolism that can often be controlled with injections of insulin. Teachers should learn to recognize the symptoms of insulin reaction and diabetic coma.

   k. Children with cystic fibrosis, hemophilia, severe burns, or other health conditions may need modifications in their education or activities or other special services, such as counseling.

3. The severity of the impairment, its visibility to other people, and the age at which it was acquired are important variables to consider in providing appropriate services to a student with a physical or health impairment.

4. Prevalence statistics are difficult to obtain, because there is no universally agreed-upon definition of the physically and health impaired population. In addition, many children counted under other categories of exceptionality have physical or health impairments also.

    a. Approximately 3% of children receiving special education services are classified as having orthopedic or other health impairments.

    b. Cerebral palsy accounts for the largest single group of physically impaired children.

    c. Disease-related disabilities and orthopedic impairments are decreasing in prevalence because of better medical and surgical treatments. However, more children with multiple impairments are surviving infancy, and more children are developing physical disabilities as a result of accidents, child abuse, alcoholism, and other factors.

5. Public school programs for children with physical disabilities began around the turn of the century. Two physicians, Phelps and Carlson, were influential advocates for the education and acceptance of children with physical disabilities.

    a. In contrast to the historical development of educational services for children with other disabilities, few state-run residential schools were ever established for children with physical and health impairments.

    b. Children with physical and health impairments have largely been served in special public schools or separate classes. More recently, they have been more widely integrated into regular classes, with architectural and programmatic modifications as necessary.

6. There are many different factors to be considered in developing an educational program for a physically or health impaired child.

    a. Early intervention programs are important for the child and family. They are becoming increasingly available.

    b. Many disabled students are served in regular classes, which have the potential to encourage independence, social development, and communication with nondisabled peers.

    c. Special classes for children with physical disabilities are also found in many public schools. They offer the advantage of easier access to specialized professionals and equipment.

    d. Some children with severe physical and health impairments are educated at home or in hospitals. As in other settings, individualized education programs are required.

7. Children with physical and health impairments typically require interdisciplinary services from a team of professionals. Specialists such as a teacher, physician, physical therapist, occupational therapist, vocational specialist, and others work together in planning and delivering services; they also consult with each other.

8. The treatment of physical impairments usually includes one or more of the following approaches: hands-on therapy, assistive devices, medication, and surgery.

9. Many physically disabled children need special devices, such as braces, wheelchairs, prostheses, modified eating appliances, and other equipment.

10. Adaptations to the physical environment and to classroom activities can enable physically or health impaired students to participate more fully in the school program.

11. The ways in which students are positioned throughout the day should be carefully considered. Proper positioning can enhance physical and social development.

12. Students who use wheelchairs should be taught to operate them safely and efficienctly. Classmates should also be aware of safety rules.

13. Teachers can do much to encourage the development of positive attitudes toward children with physical and health impairments.

14. The current trend toward educating physically impaired children in the regular classroom is likely to continue. Recent court cases suggest that more children who need

medical attention will be served in public schools. The question of who will pay for equipment and special services is often controversial.

15. Recent developments in technology and biomedical engineering hold much promise for persons with physical disabilities. The use of animals to assist people with physical needs is also increasing.

16. Generally, programs for students with physical and health impairments seek to develop as much independence as possible, while relying on others for assistance at certain times.

    a. Physical education and vocational preparation are important components of an educational program.
    b. Independent living centers and self-help groups are active and are improving the long-range outlook for people with physical and health impairments.

17. Although many services for this population have been developed, there is room for improvement in such areas as public attitudes, access to buildings, and services to parents of young children with physical and health impairments.

FOR MORE INFORMATION

Journals

ACCENT on Living (P.O. Box 700, Bloomington, IL 61701). A quarterly journal of practical information, with articles on varied topics, including employment, aids to independent living, architectural barriers, and family concerns. Primarily written by and about people with physical and health impairments. Also sponsors an extensive catalog of assistive devices and a computerized information retrieval system.

The Disability Rag (P.O. Box 145, Louisville, KY 40201). Described as "a spicy, irreverent journal." A bimonthly publication tackling controversial issues affecting people with disabilities and serving as a forum for opinion and debate. Features articles on such topics as telethons, legal battles, sexuality, and media portrayals of people with disabilities.

Disability Studies Quarterly (Department of Sociology, Brandeis University, Waltham, MA 02254). Regularly prints abstracts of current research projects, book reviews, announcements of conferences, resources, and grants. Focuses on social and psychological issues, as well as advocacy, economics, and attitudes of and toward persons with physical and other disabilities.

Disabled USA (President's Committee on Employment of the Handicapped, 1111 20th Street, NW, Suite 600, Washington, DC 20036). A quarterly publication reporting on current developments in employment, rehabilitation, and independent living. Seeks to document progress in employment and to encourage new opportunities for workers with disabilities.

Rehabilitation Literature (National Easter Seal Society, 2023 West Ogden Avenue, Chicago, IL 60612). An interdisciplinary monthly publication containing abstracts of current research and practice, with an emphasis on children and adults with orthopedic, neurological, and other physical and health-related impairments. Regularly features reviews of recent books.

Books

Batshaw, M. L., & Perret, Y. M. (1986). *Children with handicaps: A medical primer* (2nd ed.). Baltimore: Paul H. Brookes.

Bleck, E. E., & Nagel, D. A. (Eds.). (1981). *Physically handicapped children: A medical atlas for teachers* (2nd ed.). Orlando, FL: Grune & Stratton.

Goldfarb, L. A., Brotherson, M. J., Summers, J. A., & Turnbull, A. P. (1986). *Meeting the challenge of disability or chronic illness: A family guide.* Baltimore: Paul H. Brookes.

Hanson, M. J., & Harris, S. R. (1986). *Teaching the young child with motor delays: A guide for parents and professionals.* Austin, TX: Pro-Ed.

Kleinberg, S. B. (1982). *Educating the chronically ill child.* Rockville, MD: Aspen.

Pieper, E. (1983). *The teacher and the child with spina bifida* (2nd ed.). Rockville, MD: Spina Bifida Association of America.

Rosen, C. D., & Gerring, J. P. (1986). *Head trauma: Educational reintegration.* San Diego: College-Hill.

Zacharkow, D. (1984). *Wheelchair posture and pressure sores.* Springfield, IL: Charles C Thomas.

Organizations

A large number of national agencies and organizations provide information, educational programs, and community services to children and adults with specific physical and health impairments and to their parents and teachers. Many of these have state and local chapters. Listed here are some of the largest organizations that disseminate publications and encourage research into the causes and treatment of physical and health impairments.

Cystic Fibrosis Foundation, 6000 Executive Boulevard, Rockville, MD 20852.

Epilepsy Foundation of America, 4531 Garden City Drive, Landover, MD 20785.

Juvenile Diabetes Association, 23 East 26th Street, New York, NY 10010.

Muscular Dystrophy Asociation, 810 Seventh Avenue, New York, NY 10019.

National Easter Seal Society, 2023 West Ogden Avenue, Chicago, IL 60612.

Spina Bifida Association of America, 343 South Dearborn Street, Chicago, IL 60604.

United Cerebral Palsy Associations, Inc., 66 East 34th Street, New York, NY 10016.

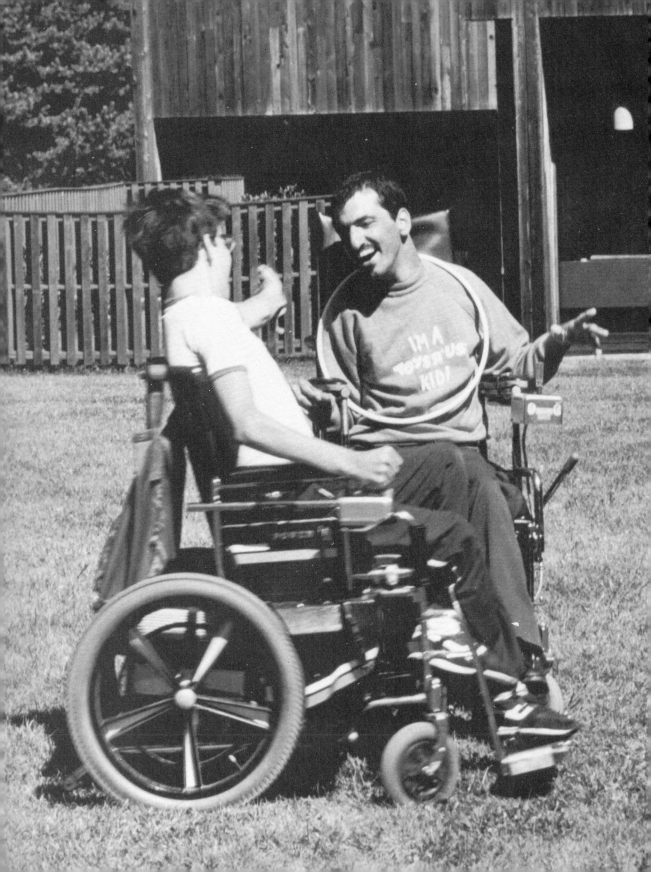

10

SEVERE HANDICAPS

Five-year-old Zack is learning to feed himself with a spoon. A teacher is showing 13-year-old Toni that it is more appropriate to shake hands than to hug a person when first introduced. Martha, who is 20, is learning to ride a city bus to her afternoon job at a cafeteria, where she clears tables and sorts silverware. Zack, Toni, and Martha have severe and multiple handicaps. They have little in common, except for their dependence on other people and their need for instruction in skills usually acquired at a younger age by nonhandicapped children. They belong to a group that has been called "the most seriously impaired of all disabled people" (Haring & Smith, 1978). The behaviors and skills of students with severe handicaps are highly diverse, and "when appropriate intervention is absent, maladaptive behavior is likely to predominate" (Snell & Renzaglia, 1986, p. 274).

Because of their intense physical, intellectual, and behavioral limitations, children with severe handicaps tend to grow, learn, and develop much more slowly than any other group of children (including other children who are considered disabled or handicapped). Indeed, without intensive training many persons with severe handicaps would probably be unable to perform the most basic tasks necessary for human survival, such as eating, toileting, communicating, and finding shelter.

Despite the severity and multiplicity of their disabilities, however, it has been shown conclusively that students with severe handicaps *can* and *do learn*. This realization has come about only recently. In the past, children with severe handicaps were a neglected population; it was widely believed that they were incapable of acquiring useful skills. They were often placed in institutions as infants and were considered to be beyond the responsibility of our public educational system. They usually received no education or training at all and were given only the most basic care required to sustain life.

Although the exclusion of severely handicapped students from educational programs—and from normal society in general—was widely practiced in the past, a philosophy of inclusion now prevails. It is supported by laws requiring free, appropriate

Are all children educable, regardless of the severity of their handicaps? See pages 397–98 for several viewpoints.

369

programs of public education for *all* handicapped students and by a rapidly growing body of evidence indicating that students with severe handicaps can learn and function effectively in integrated public school and community settings. "The goals of education apply equally to them as to nonhandicapped children, even though the specific educational objectives may have to be stated differently" (Alter, Gottlieb, & Gottlieb, 1986, p. 124).

DEFINITION AND CHARACTERISTICS

We will review several approaches to the description and definition of students with severe handicaps. Because this field is so young and because it focuses on people with such a wide variety of characteristics, no single, universally accepted definition of the severely handicapped population has yet emerged. In examining definitions, we must keep in mind that children with severe handicaps constitute a heterogeneous group. They differ from nonhandicapped children "in degree, not in kind" (Sontag, Smith, & Sailor, 1977). As Guess and Mulligan (1982) point out, the differences among students with severe handicaps are greater than their similarities.

Students with severe handicaps often have intense and complex combinations of disabilities. These may include extreme deficits in intellectual functioning, motor development, speech and language, adaptive behavior, and visual and auditory functioning. Many have medical and physical problems that require frequent attention. The severely handicapped population usually is said to encompass students with severe and profound mental retardation, severe behavior disorders, and/or physical/sensory impairments combined with marked developmental delay.

In recent years the most familiar and widely used definition has been that of the U.S. Department of Education, Office of Special Education Programs.

> Severely handicapped children are those who because of the intensity of their physical, mental, or emotional problems, or a combination of such problems, need educational, social, psychological, and medical services beyond those which are traditionally offered by regular and special education programs, in order to maximize their potential for useful and meaningful participation in society and for self-fulfillment. (21 U.S. Code 1407[7]; 45 Code of Federal Regulations 121.1)

Some educators prefer to take a developmental approach to the definition of severe handicaps. Justen (1976), for example, proposes that "those individuals age 21 and younger who are functioning at a general developmental level of half or less than the level which would be expected on the basis of chronological age" (p. 5) be considered severely handicapped. Others maintain that developmental levels have little relevance to this population and instead emphasize that the severely handicapped student—regardless of age—is one who "requires instruction in basic skills," such as getting from place to place independently, communicating with others, controlling bowel and bladder functions, and self-feeding (Sontag, Smith, & Sailor, 1977). Most children without disabilities are able to acquire these basic skills in the first 5 years of life, but the student with severe handicaps needs special instruction in order to do so. The basic-skills definition implies that education for students with severe handicaps should not be restricted to traditional academic instruction.

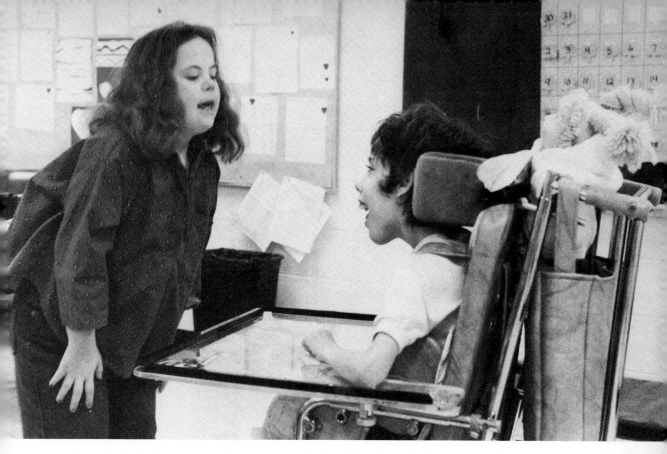

Students with severe handicaps often have complex combinations of disabilities.

We should always exercise caution in defining children's abilities and limitations. Day-to-day educational practices often lag behind the rapidly developing state of the art.

> Children who were once considered incapable of speaking now can not only speak but sometimes can learn to read and write. Adults who were once considered incapable of self-care now can not only dress and groom themselves but sometimes can participate in gainful employment. Unfortunately, not every severely handicapped student experiences this level of success; and when educational gains do occur, it is often only after intensive efforts. (Ludlow & Sobsey, 1984, 22–23)

Traditional methods of intelligence testing are virtually useless with most severely handicapped children. If tested, they tend to be assigned IQs at the extreme lower end of the continuum. However, knowing that a particular student has an IQ of 25 is of little value in designing an appropriate educational program. Educators of students with severe handicaps tend to focus on the specific skills that a child needs to learn, rather than on her intellectual level. Because students with severe handicaps can master basic skills and can learn new behaviors, "the state of being severely handicapped is a changing one; that is, a child could be considered severely handicapped at one point in his or her life and not severely handicapped at another point" (Stainback & Stainback, 1985, p. 4).

Imagine the difficulty of giving an IQ test to a 5-year-old who cannot hold his head up straight or point, let alone talk.

371

More important to the teacher than the student's IQ or the precise cause of the handicapping condition is an accurate understanding of the student's behavior (or, in many cases, *lack* of behavior). Because of their severe and multiple impairments, severely handicapped children often look noticeably different from nonhandicapped children, and their behavior may be considered deviant or extreme, particularly by people who are not familiar with them. No specific set of behaviors is common to all severely handicapped children. Each child has a different set of physical, intellectual, and social characteristics, and each has lived in a different environment. Educators of children with severe handicaps generally agree, however, that the following behaviors are frequently observed (Abt Associates, 1974; Guess & Mulligan, 1982; Haring, 1978; Tawney, 1977).

1. *Little or no communication.* Almost all children with severe handicaps are greatly limited in their ability to express themselves and to understand others. Many cannot talk or gesture meaningfully; they do not respond when communication is attempted. Of course, this makes education and social interaction extremely difficult. The children may not be able to follow even the simplest commands.
2. *Delayed physical and motor development.* Most severely handicapped children have limited physical mobility. Many cannot walk or even sit up by themselves. They are slow to perform such basic tasks as rolling over, grasping objects, or holding their heads up. Physical deformities are common and may be worsened by lack of therapy and lengthy stays in bed.
3. *Frequent inappropriate behavior.* Many children with severe handicaps do things that appear to have no constructive purpose. These activities have been described as ritualistic (e.g., rocking back and forth, waving fingers in front of the face, twirling the body), self-stimulatory (e.g., masturbating, grinding the teeth, patting the body), and self-injurious (e.g., head banging, hair pulling, eye poking, hitting or scratching or biting oneself). Although some of these behaviors may not be considered abnormal in and of themselves, the high frequency with which some children perform these activities is a serious concern, because these behaviors interfere with teaching and with social acceptance.
4. *Deficits in self-help skills.* Severely handicapped children are often unable to care for their most basic needs, such as dressing, eating, exercising bowel and bladder control, and maintaining personal hygiene. Such children usually require special training to learn these basic skills.
5. *Infrequent constructive behavior and interaction.* Nonhandicapped children and those whose handicaps are less severe typically play with other children, interact with adults, and seek out information about their surroundings. Most children with severe handicaps do not. They may appear to be completely out of touch with reality and may not show normal human emotions. It may be difficult to capture a severely handicapped child's attention or to evoke any observable response.

Descriptions of behavioral characteristics, such as those just presented, may give an overly negative impression of students with severe handicaps. These students may also possess many positive characteristics, in spite of their severely handicapping conditions (Stainback & Stainback, 1985)—including warmth, persistence, determination, sense of humor, sociability, and various other desirable traits. Many teachers have found great satisfaction in working with students who have severe handicaps and in observing their progress in school, home, and community settings.

Learning to do something that would be taken for granted by a nonhandicapped person can greatly impact the life of a child with severe handicaps (see pages 375–76).

Multiple Handicaps

Most severely handicapped students have more than one disability. Even with the best available methods of diagnosis and assessment, it is often difficult to identify the nature and intensity of a child's multiple handicaps or to determine the ways in which combinations of disabilities affect a child's behavior. For example, many severely handicapped children do not respond in any observable way to visual stimuli, such as bright lights or moving objects. Is the child blind because of eye damage, or is he able to see but unable to respond because of damage to the brain? Such questions arise frequently in planning educational programs for students with severe handicaps of all types. What is the most appropriate way to teach language to a deaf child with severe handicaps? How can we help a nonambulatory, nonverbal child learn to display appropriate social behaviors in public?

Children with severe handicaps often have combinations of obvious and not-so-obvious disabilities that require special additions or adaptations in their education. But the fact that a child is considered severely handicapped does not necessarily preclude meaningful achievements. Today, many students with severe handicaps are learning useful skills and are interacting with nonhandicapped persons in schools, neighborhoods, and workplaces. Appropriate programs of instruction can enable students with severe handicaps to engage in a wide variety of useful, worthwhile, and personally satisfying activities.

PREVALENCE

Because there is no universally accepted definition of severe handicaps, there are no accurate and uniform figures on the prevalence of the condition. Authorities have estimated that anywhere from .1% to 1% of the population can be considered to have severe handicaps (Ludlow & Sobsey, 1984); Snell (1987) uses a prevalence figure of .05%. If we accept the widely quoted prevalence of profound mental retardation as about 1 in every 1,000 school-age children, we would conclude that approximately 55,000 children in the United States fall into this category and constitute part of the population with severe handicaps. Although many children with moderate and severe mental retardation and with multiple disabilities are also considered severely handicapped for educational placement purposes, they may be counted among other categories of exceptionality. In 1976 the National Association for Retarded Citizens estimated that there were perhaps 300,000 severely handicapped children who were not receiving adequate educational services.

Although the existing prevalence figures are not wholly reliable, they do indicate the current uncertainties surrounding the definition and classification of severely handicapped students. The available information suggests that this is neither a small nor an isolated population; in fact, the severely handicapped population consists of several different subgroups of students, whose needs are not always the same. Today, most school districts have among their students some children with severe and multiple handicaps.

BACKGROUND OF THE FIELD

Little is known about the treatment of severely handicapped individuals throughout most of history. Because severe handicaps so often occur in conjunction with medical and physical disabilities, many of these children probably did not live past infancy. In many earlier societies—and in some parts of the world today—a philosophy of survival of the fittest prevailed. The abandonment or deliberate killing of children with severe impairments is thought to have been a common practice (Anderson, Greer, & Rich, 1982).

To say that humane treatment and education of children with severe handicaps did not begin until the 20th century would be an oversimplification. As Scheerenberger's (1983) comprehensive review points out, efforts were made throughout history to understand the causes of severe handicaps and, at times, to provide care and training. In the 19th century, physicians Jean Itard, Edouard Seguin, and Samuel Gridley Howe achieved notable advances in systematically teaching communication and self-help skills to children with severe handicaps. Certainly, many other dedicated teachers, parents, and caregivers sought to help people with severe handicaps; unfortunately, their names have been lost in history.

During the second half of the 19th century, hundreds of state-operated residential institutions were established in the United States for the confinement and custodial care of severely handicapped children and adults. An optimistic philosophy—strongly influenced by the efforts of pioneering physicians—prevailed at the outset, and some severely handicapped individuals were, in fact, successfully educated and returned to their home communities (Wolfensberger, 1976).

At first, many institutional programs were called asylums for the feebleminded. Later they came to be called hospitals, state schools, and training centers. But despite these titles, education and training usually were not provided to the more severely handicapped residents in these institutions. Many observers have commented on the bleak, unstimulating environments, the lack of adequate care, and the prevailing attitude of pessimism found in most large residential institutions. And once placed in an institutional program, a severely handicapped child was unlikely ever to leave it. Unless parents were able to provide care and training at home or to afford an expensive private school education, there were virtually no opportunities for severely handicapped children to learn useful skills or to lead satisfying lives.

In the last 15 years or so, several judicial decisions and new laws have had important effects on the development of educational services for severely handicapped children. Particularly significant to this population was the case of *Pennsylvania Association for Retarded Children v. Commonwealth of Pennsylvania* (1972). Before the

LITTLE CHANGES WITH BIG IMPACTS:
REACTIONS TO PROGRESS BY STUDENTS WITH SEVERE HANDICAPS

Michael F. Giangreco is the coordinator of the Department of Special Education for the Cayuga-Onondaga Board of Cooperative Educational Services in Auburn, New York. Mike has been a leader in integrating students with severe and multiple handicaps into regular public school classes. We asked Mike to share some of his thoughts about the students, teachers, and families with whom he works.

Teachers and therapists are people who want to make a difference, people who hope that what they do will improve the quality of life for the students and families with whom they work. Laura is one such teacher. Over the past couple of years Laura has been working with a heterogeneous group of students with challenging needs at East Middle School. One aspect of the educational program there is to teach skills that will allow students to participate more fully in the community with non-handicapped individuals. There have been times when Laura has gotten discouraged because the rate of progress by some of her more severely handicapped students has seemed low. She started asking, "Am I really helping?" "Am I really making a difference?"

One day Laura received the following letter from a parent regarding her daughter Jackie, a 13-year-old girl with Down syndrome, functioning in the severe range of mental retardation and diagnosed as legally blind.

Dear Laura,

After school we went grocery shopping, me, Jackie, and Sheldon (the baby). On our way home Jackie said, "Mom, you forgot Italian bread." She was right. I said we would have to go without—I was not hauling the baby out of the car again. Jackie said, "I can buy it myself at P & C." I said, "I don't know, Jackie." "Yes Mom, my teacher helped me." She was so sure she could do it that I didn't

want to defeat her—so off to P & C. I pulled up in front with mounting panic. Jackie was still positive she could do it. I explained that the bread was back by the meat and bakery—we had bought it here before, but not recently. Jackie said, "I know—it has a light." I then gave Jackie $2 and let her go. Four minutes later (it seemed like two hours) she was back at the car with her Italian bread in a shopping bag and her change tight in her hand. I couldn't believe it—talk about the taste of success—I think that was the best bread we have ever had! Be proud, teacher—Mom is!

When Laura shared the letter with me, it was clear that this seemingly small achievement had a big impact. It reminded me of a similar experience I had had as a teacher. Tom was one of the most challenging students I had ever encountered. Several years earlier he had suffered a severe brain stem injury in a bicycle-auto accident. The injury left Tom profoundly mentally retarded, severely physically handicapped, and blind. Tom was nonverbal and nonambulatory and had no functional use of his limbs or hands. He slept a lot and seemed alert only for short periods during the day. For a couple of years after his accident Tom was fed through a plastic tube that was inserted in his stomach. Tom's family had worked very hard to teach him to eat by mouth again. When I met Tom, he was able to be fed pureed foods by mouth, but he still had the gastrostomy tube in his stomach as a precaution because he was prone to dehydration during the summer.

In a meeting with Tom's parents to plan his IEP, his dad said, "We'd like him to learn something, anything, so we know that he *can* learn." We agreed that one goal would be to try to teach Tom to follow a simple direction, "Open up," so that he could be fed, have his teeth brushed, and accept medicine. With an instructional procedure called time-delay, Tom began responding to the direction.

Although this tiny achievement did little for Tom directly, it had a major impact on the quality of his life indirectly. For the first time in a long time people at home and at school were encouraged because Tom had learned. This hopeful experience resulted in Tom's receiving more frequent and positive interaction from others.

Seemingly small accomplishments hold the potential for tremendous positive impact. Professionals in schools *can* make a difference when they work collaboratively with families to select and teach meaningful skills designed to enhance a student's quality of life at home, at school, and in the community.

Mastery of an everyday task that most of us take for granted can make a tremendous difference in the lives of students with severe handicaps.

PARC case many states had laws allowing public schools to deny educational services to so-called ineducable severely handicapped children. In the PARC case the court decided against such exclusion and noted in its decision that education could be useful to severely handicapped individuals.

> Without exception, expert opinion indicates that all mentally retarded persons are capable of benefitting from a program of education. . . . The vast majority are capable of achieving self-sufficiency and the remaining few, with such education and training, are capable of achieving some degree of self-care; that the earlier such education and training begins, the more thoroughly and more efficiently a mentally retarded person will benefit from it and, whether begun early or not, that a mentally retarded person can benefit at any point in his life and development from a program of education. *(PARC v. Commonwealth of Pennsylvania,* 1972)

Many other cases—including *Wyatt v. Stickney* (1971), *Halderman v. Pennhurst State School and Hospital* (1978), *Armstrong v. Kline* (1979), and *Irving Independent School District v. Tatro* (1984)—have since upheld the right of students with severe handicaps to receive a free, appropriate program of education at public expense. The provisions of P.L. 94–142 fully apply to children with severe handicaps; they must have access to an educational program in the least restrictive setting possible, and their parents or guardians must be involved in the development and implementation of an appropriate IEP. In addition, the law gives priority to identifying and serving children who have been unserved or underserved, and this provision clearly applies to the severely handicapped population. These legal and judicial developments, coupled with an increasing awareness of the potential of severely handicapped students, are bringing about a dramatic expansion of educational programs in public schools, vocational facilities, and other community-based settings. Even the severely handicapped children who continue to be served in institutions are entitled to a free and appropriate educational program.

Today, education of persons with severe handicaps is one of the most exciting and dynamic fields in special education. Its rapid growth is illustrated by the history of The Association for Persons with Severe Handicaps (TASH). Started in 1975 by a few dozen special educators, TASH now has a membership of more than 7,000 educators, parents, and other concerned individuals. The past few years have also witnessed a dramatic increase in the number of books, research studies, curricula, and other materials directed at meeting the needs of children and adults with severe handicaps.

CAUSES

Severe handicaps can be caused by a wide variety of conditions, largely biological, that may occur before, during, or after birth. In most cases the brain is damaged. A significant percentage of severely handicapped children are born with chromosomal abnormalities, such as Down syndrome, or with genetic or metabolic disorders that can cause serious problems in a child's physical or intellectual development. Complications of pregnancy—including prematurity, Rh incompatibility, and infectious diseases contracted by the mother—can contribute. It is also believed that women who are poorly nourished during pregnancy or who consume excessive amounts of alcohol or drugs may give birth to children who are severely handicapped. In general, children with severe handicaps are more frequently identified at or shortly after birth than are children with milder disabilities, because their impairments tend to be more extreme and more readily observable.

The birth process itself involves certain hazards and complications: infants are particularly vulnerable to oxygen deprivation and brain injury during delivery. Severe handicaps may also develop later in life from head trauma caused by vehicular accidents, falls, assaults, or abuse (see Rosen & Gerring, 1986, for descriptions of educational approaches for head-injured students). Malnutrition, neglect, ingestion of poisonous substances, and certain diseases that affect the brain (such as meningitis and encephalitis) can also cause severe handicaps.

Although hundreds of medically related causes of severe handicaps have been identified, there are many cases in which the cause of a child's disabilities cannot be clearly determined. Severe handicaps are usually considered to be less closely associated with socioeconomic status than are milder handicaps (Snell & Renzaglia, 1986). However, a child's access to good medical care, early identification of disabling conditions, education, and a stimulating home environment may be influenced by a family's level of education, income, and other socioeconomic factors.

Deaf-Blind Children

A particularly challenging group of children with multiple disabilities, usually considered severely handicapped, are the several thousand children in the United States and Canada who are deaf-blind. Many of these children were born with visual, hearing, and other impairments after an epidemic of rubella affected thousands of pregnant women in the mid-1960s. The U.S. federal government established a special network of regional and state centers in 1968 and allocated several million dollars for the education of deaf-blind children, thus making this the first group of exceptional children to receive special education under federal mandate and with substantial federal financial assistance. Several years later, when P.L. 94–142 was passed, the law included a section on deaf-blind children, defined as those who have

> both auditory and visual handicaps, the combination of which causes such severe communication and other developmental and educational problems that they cannot properly be accommodated in special education programs solely for the hearing handicapped child or for the visually handicapped child.

As the definition points out, deaf-blind children have a combination of sight and hearing impairments but are not necessarily totally blind or profoundly deaf. An educational program for deaf children is often inappropriate for a child who also has limited vision, because many methods of instruction and communication rely heavily on the use of sight. Programs for visually impaired students, on the other hand, usually require good hearing because much instruction is auditory. Most students who are classified as deaf-blind do have some residual vision and/or hearing. However, they frequently have other physical, intellectual, and behavioral disabilities along with their impaired sight and hearing.

The intellectual level of deaf-blind students ranges from giftedness (as in the famous case of Helen Keller, who lost her sight and hearing at about 16 months of age) to severe mental retardation. The majority of children who have both visual and hearing impairments at birth experience major difficulties in acquiring communication and motor skills, mobility, and appropriate social behavior. A vivid description of the importance of sight and hearing in a child's learning and development is offered by Robert Smithdas (1981), a deaf-blind man.

> The senses of sight and hearing are unquestionably the two primary avenues by which information and knowledge are absorbed by an individual, providing a direct access to the world in which he lives. . . . When these senses are lost or severely limited, the individual is drastically limited to a very small area of concepts, most of which must come to him through his secondary senses or through indirect information supplied by others. The world literally shrinks; it is only as large as he can reach with his fingertips or by using his severely limited sight and hearing, and it is only when he learns to use his remaining secondary senses of touch, taste, smell, and kinesthetic awareness that he can broaden his field of information and gain additional knowledge. (p. 38)

Educational programs for deaf-blind children who require instruction in basic skills are generally similar to those for other children with severe handicaps. There is likely to be a strong emphasis on communication—most often involving some form of sign language or gestures but including speech and tactual speechreading for some students. Van Dijk (1983) has provided a detailed description of approaches to assessment and skill development in a population of deaf-blind children handicapped by maternal rubella. With the rubella children of the mid-1960s now young adults, many efforts are currently directed toward the teaching of vocational and self-help skills that will enable them to live and work as independently as possible. Persons with multiple sensory impairments have the potential to achieve success in employment and independent living, but they require suitable training to facilitate communication, generalization of skills, and development of appropriate behaviors (Bullis & Bull, 1986). It is also important to help such students effectively use any residual vision or hearing.

In 1968 fewer than 100 deaf-blind children were being served in specialized educational programs, virtually all of which were located at residential schools for blind children. Today, about 6,000 deaf-blind children are being educated in the United States, in hundreds of different programs, including those located at schools for deaf children, early childhood developmental centers, vocational training centers, and regular public schools (Dantona, 1986). Deaf-blind students who progress to high school and postsecondary levels are usually integrated into educational programs for students with other disabilities or into programs for nonhandicapped students, with supportive assistance provided by special teachers, intervenors, interpreters, or tutors.

APPROACHES TO THE EDUCATION
OF STUDENTS WITH SEVERE HANDICAPS

General Principles of Educational Programming

Care and concern for the well-being of students with severe handicaps and assurance that they have access to educational programs are important. By themselves, however, they are not enough. Students with severe handicaps need more than love, care, and classroom placement if they are to learn and develop effectively. They cannot acquire complex skills solely through imitation and observation. They are not likely to blossom on their own.

In the not-too-distant past, educators tended to focus largely on the so-called mental or developmental ages of their students. Although this approach may be helpful in identifying skills that a student can and cannot perform, it may also detract from the most effective use of instructional time, for it "assumes that those sequences of behavior typical of nonhandicapped students are relevant for the student with severe or profound handicaps" (Brown, 1987, p. 43). Strict reliance on a developmental approach may lead to an emphasis on teaching prerequisite skills that are not really essential for later steps (Ludlow & Sobsey, 1984) and may contribute to the perception of students with severe handicaps as eternal children (Bellamy & Wilcox, 1982). Today, most educators of individuals with severe handicaps consider it important to be familiar with the normal sequences of child development but recognize that their students often do not acquire skills in the same way that nonhandicapped students do and believe that developmental guides should not be the only basis for determining teaching procedures. For example, a 16-year-old student who is just learning to feed and toilet himself should not be taught in exactly the same way or with the same materials as a nonhandicapped 2-year-old child who is just learning to feed and toilet himself. The past experiences, the present environments, and the future prospects of these two individuals are, of course, quite different, even though their ability to perform certain skills may be similar. A thoughtful critique of the developmental sequencing strategy is offered by Freagon (1982).

> When the developmental curricular strategy is employed, severely handicapped students have considerable impediments to achieving a postschool adult life-style that is similar to those of nonhandicapped persons. In the first place, when instructional activities are based on mental, language and social, and gross and fine motor ages, severely handicapped students rarely, if ever, gain more than 1 or 2 developmental years over the entire course of their educational experience. Therefore, 18-year-old students are relegated to performing infant or preschool or elementary nonhandicapped student activities. They are never seen as ready to engage in 18-year-old activities. In the second place, little, if any, empirical evidence exists to support the notion that severely handicapped students need to learn and grow along the same lines and growth patterns as do nonhandicapped students in order to achieve the same goal of education. (p. 10)

A recent review of instructional programs (National Association of State Directors of Special Education, 1986) concluded that contemporary curriculum content for students with severe handicaps is marked by an emphasis on interpersonal interactions and the acquisition of employment skills. Educational programs are future-oriented in their efforts to teach skills and behaviors that will enable students with severe handicaps to be as independent and productive as possible after they leave school. The following principles are generally considered important in designing and carrying out instructional activities for students with severe handicaps (Bellamy & Wilcox, 1982; Freagon, 1982; Ludlow & Sobsey, 1984; Snell, 1987; Wehman, Renzaglia, & Bates, 1985).

Functionality

A *functional* skill is one that is immediately useful to a student and is frequently demanded in her natural environment. The skill should employ real materials and enhance the student's ability to perform as independently as possible. Placing pegs in a pegboard would not be considered functional, because this task is seldom required in the natural environment of most people. Learning to ride a public bus and learning to purchase items from coin-operated vending machines are examples of more functional skills.

Chronological Age-Appropriateness

Wherever possible, students with severe handicaps should participate in activities that are appropriate for and acceptable to nonhandicapped students of their own chronological age. Severely handicapped adolescents need not use the same materials as young nonhandicapped children—in fact, when handicapped teenagers are seen doing things like sitting on the floor playing clap-your-hands games or cutting and pasting large snowmen, their differences are highlighted and integration is discouraged. It is more appropriate to teach recreational skills such as bowling and tape-recorder operation or to engage the students in holiday projects such as printing greeting cards. Teachers of adolescent students with severe handicaps should avoid decorating classroom walls with child-oriented characters such as Big Bird or Mickey Mouse and should not refer to their students as boys, girls, or kids when young men, young women, or students is clearly more age-appropriate.

Interaction with Nonhandicapped People

Contact with nonhandicapped students should be regularly scheduled as a part of the educational program of students with severe handicaps. This contact may take several forms, such as riding school buses together, sharing lunchroom facilities, playing games together in the gym, and peer tutoring. Such interactions can be mutually beneficial. They tend to encourage handicapped students to learn socially acceptable behaviors and to help nonhandicapped students become more aware of people who experience disabilities. Stainback and Stainback (1985) offer numerous suggestions for facilitating interactions between severely handicapped and nonhandicapped students.

This neighborhood store frequently serves as Peter's "classroom."

Directed Toward the Community

A long-range goal should be to assist the severely handicapped student in living and working in the community as independently as possible. It is often necessary for teachers to identify specific skills that are required in the community and then to proceed to teach those skills. For example, to buy a carton of milk, the student must be able to (1) arrive at the supermarket, (2) locate the area where milk is kept, (3) select the desired size and type of milk, (4) transport the milk to the check-out counter, (5) pay for the milk with the correct amount of money (usually receiving some change), and (6) take the milk home. Some students are able to learn all these steps, whereas others need to rely on certain adaptations—such as carrying a picture of the milk and requesting the assistance of store personnel in locating it or using a backpack to carry the milk home. Such partial participation enables the student to take part in a much wider variety of productive activities and increases his chances of moving into a satisfying community-based setting, even if some extra help continues to be required.

Structure and Precision in Assessment and Teaching

The learning and behavior problems of students with severe handicaps are so extreme and so significant that extensive structure and careful planning are required if we are to adequately meet the needs of these students. "Precise behavioral objectives, task analysis, and other individualized instructional techniques combine to form a powerful teaching process" for students with severe handicaps (Ludlow & Sobsey, 1984, p. 22). Indeed, structure and precision are essential. The teacher must know what skill to teach the student, why it is important for this skill to be taught, how the skill will be taught to the student, and when the teacher will know that the skill has been achieved or performed by the student.

An effective teacher of students with severe handicaps learns to use task analysis (described in chapter 3), in which skills are broken down into a series of specific, observable steps, and the student's performance of each step is carefully monitored. Table 10.1 provides an example of an important skill—washing one's hands—broken down into small, precise steps. Some students might require even more specific steps than the 19 illustrated here, whereas others might need fewer steps. Before any instruction begins, the teacher needs to accurately assess a student's performance of the task. Judy might be able to perform all the steps up to Step 15, turning off the water, whereas Sam might not even be able to demonstrate Step 1, going to the sink. Such assessment helps the teacher determine where to begin instruction. She can gradually teach each required step, in order, until the student can accomplish the entire task independently. Without this sort of structure and precision in teaching, a great deal of time is likely to be wasted.

Most educational programs for severely handicapped students are not held in conventional classrooms. Instead, the rooms may have mats for physical therapy, special tables and chairs to provide adequate support, clothes for teaching dressing skills, and interesting items for the students to see, hear, smell, and taste. Whenever possible, the teacher should see that skills are taught in natural settings. Getting dressed and

TABLE 10.1
Task analysis for hand washing.

1. Go to bathroom sink.
2. Grasp the cold water faucet.
3. Turn on the water.
4. Wet your hands.
5. Pick up the soap (with the dominant hand).
6. Rub the soap on the other hand.
7. Put the soap down.
8. Rub palms together.
9. Rub back of hand (with palm of opposite hand).
10. Rub back of other hand (with palm of opposite hand).
11. Put hands underwater.
12. Rinse palm of hands (until all visible suds removed).
13. Rinse back of hands (until all visible suds removed).
14. Grasp the cold water faucet.
15. Turn off the water.
16. Pick up towel.
17. Dry your palms.
18. Dry the back of your hands.
19. Hang towel over rack.

Source: From *Systematic Instruction of Persons with Severe Handicaps*, third edition (p. 75) by M. E. Snell (Ed.), 1987, Columbus, OH: Merrill.

undressed, for example, usually does not take place in a classroom but is appropriate in a child's home or domitory. Communication and cooperation with a student's parents (or with staff members if the student lives in a group home or other residential program) are essential to ensure that skills are being consistently taught and practiced. Careful attention should be given to the following components of an instructional program for a student with severe handicaps.

1. *The student's current level of performance must be precisely assessed.* Is Karen able to hold her head up without support? For how many seconds? Under what conditions? In response to what verbal or physical signal? Unlike traditional assessment procedures, which may rely heavily on standardized scores and developmental levels, assessment of a severely handicapped child emphasizes the learner's ability to perform specific, observable behaviors. Figure 10.1 presents an example of some assessment items that might be used in determining a severely handicapped student's instructional needs. Assessment should not be a one-shot procedure but should take place at different times, in different settings, and with different persons. The fact that a severely handicapped student does not demonstrate a skill on one particular assessment does not mean that he is incapable of demonstrating that skill. Precise assessment of current performance is of great value in determining which skills are to be taught and at what level the instruction can start.

2. *The skill to be taught must be defined clearly.* "Ian will feed himself" is too broad a goal for many severely handicapped children. A more appropriate statement might be "When applesauce is applied to Ian's right index finger, he will move the finger to his mouth within 10 seconds." A clear statement like this would enable the teacher and other observers to determine whether Ian had attained this objective. If, after repeated trials, he had not, it would be advisable to try a different method of instruction.

3. *The skills must be ordered in an appropriate sequence.* The teacher must be able to arrange "a relationship between the student and his environment which results in positive experiences for the student and small positive changes in skill acquisition" (Sailor & Haring, 1977, p. 73). This does not imply that severely handicapped students will always acquire skills in exactly the same order as nonhandicapped students, but it is useful to consider that some skills logically come before others, and some groups of skills are naturally taught at the same time. A carefully sequenced procedure for teaching a severely handicapped child to walk was described by Meyerson, Kerr, and Michael (1967). First, the child was required to stand for 5 to 10 seconds, without support. Then she learned to pull herself up to a standing position, using chairs that were supported by adults. The child was then taught to move from one chair to another, taking several unaided steps as the distance between the chairs was gradually increased. After that she learned to walk holding an adult's hand. Finally, the child was able to walk across the room unsupported.

4. *The teacher must provide a clear cue or instruction to the child.* It is important for the child to know what action or response is expected of him. A cue can be verbal, as when the teacher says, "Bev, say *apple*," to indicate what Bev must do before she will receive an apple. Or a cue can be physical, as when the teacher points to

Social/Self Help Record Sheet

Circle around category key indicates a basic skill.

		IEP	Testing Date __/__/__ Tester ___ +/- note	__/__/__ ___ +/- note	__/__/__ ___ +/- note	__/__/__ ___ +/- note

Feeding

RF 1. Ⓞ suck liquid from bottle
2. Ⓞ self-feed cracker
3. Ⓞ drink from cup
4. O hold cup and drink
5. Ⓞ bring spoon to mouth
6. Ⓞ eat solid food with spoon
7. Ⓞ turn faucet on/off
8. Ⓞ carry ¾ filled cup
9. Ⓞ pour liquid from pitcher to cup
10. Ⓞ spread with knife
additional IEP objectives

Set | Mastered | Mastered | Mastered | Mastered

Dressing

11. Ⓞ cooperate while being dressed
12. Ⓞ self-remove sock
13.   remove coat
    Ⓞ a. with help
    Ⓞ b. without help
14. Ⓞ pull down pants
15. Ⓞ pull up pants
16. Ⓞ put coat on
17. Ⓞ unzip
18. Ⓞ pull on shoe
19. Ⓞ pull on pullover shirt
20. Ⓞ button and unbutton
21. Ⓞ snap and unsnap
22. Ⓞ zip including thread zipper
additional IEP objectives

Set | Mastered | Mastered | Mastered | Mastered

Toileting

23. Ⓞ sit on toilet
24. Ⓞ use toilet 50%
25. Ⓞ indicate must use toilet
26. Ⓞ use toilet independently
additional IEP objectives

Set | Mastered | Mastered | Mastered | Mastered

Washing, Grooming

27. Ⓞ wash, dry hands
28. Ⓞ wash, dry face
29. Ⓞ brush teeth
30. Ⓞ brush, comb hair
additional IEP objectives

Set | Mastered | Mastered | Mastered | Mastered

FIGURE 10.1
One page of the UPAS record form.

Testing Date   / /   / /   / /   / /
Tester

	IEP	+/− note	+/− note	+/− note	+/− note

Play

31. interact appropriately with materials
   - (O) a. in group activities
   - (O) b. in 1:1 or small group
   - (O) c. during free choice
32. interact with peers
   - (O) a. low social behavior
   - (O) b. high social behavior
33. claim and defend possessions
   - (O) a. physically
   - (O) b. verbally
34. O independent play 20 minutes
35. (O) take turns and share
36. C use "props" in dramatic play
37. C dress-up and pretend
38. O play organized games
39. O has preferred playmate

additional IEP objectives

Set   Mastered   Mastered   Mastered   Mastered

Personal Information

40. (C) tell age
41. (O) tell first, last name
42. (O) tell address
43. (O) tell phone number

additional IEP objectives

Set   Mastered   Mastered   Mastered   Mastered

Classroom Work Skills

44. (O) follow group directions
45. O work independently on paper
   and pencil task

additional IEP objectives

Set   Mastered   Mastered   Mastered   Mastered

Total Nonadapted % = $\dfrac{100 \times ①}{45}$ = $\dfrac{\quad}{45}$ =   %

Total Adapted % = $\dfrac{100 \times (① + ② + ④)}{45 - ③}$ = ____ =   %

FIGURE 10.1 *continued*

Source: *Uniform Performance Assessment System: Record Form* by N. G. Haring, O. R. White, E. B. Edgar, J. Q. Affleck, and A. H. Hayden with R. G. Munson and M. Bendersky, Eds., 1981, Columbus, OH.: Merrill. Reprinted by permission.

a light switch, to indicate that Bev should turn the light on. It may also be necessary for the teacher to demonstrate an activity many times and to physically guide the child through some or all of the tasks required in the activity.

5. *The child must receive feedback and reinforcement from the teacher.* Students with severe handicaps must receive clear information about their performance, and they are more likely to repeat an action if it is immediately followed by a reinforcing consequence. Unfortunately, it can be quite difficult and time-consuming to determine what items or events a noncommunicative child finds rewarding. Many teachers devote extensive efforts to reinforcer sampling; that is, they attempt to find out which items and activities are reinforcing to a particular child, and they keep careful records of what is and is not effective. Striefel worked with a severely handicapped child for more than 2 years in order to find an effective reinforcer he could use in an instructional program. The items Striefel tried are listed in Table 10.2 (Spradlin & Spradlin, 1976).

6. *The teacher should include strategies to facilitate generalization of learning.* It is well known and documented that students with severe handicaps often have difficulty in generalizing the skills they have learned. As Horner, McDonnell, and Bellamy (1986) explain, "Education for students with severe handicaps is relevant only to the extent that the knowledge and behaviors that the students acquire become part of their daily routine" (p. 289). Thus, an effective teacher has students perform tasks in several different settings and with different instructors, cues, and materials before concluding with confidence that the student has acquired and generalized a skill.

Principles and guidelines for facilitating generalization are provided by Baer (1981), Heward (1987b), Horner, McDonnell, and Bellamy (1986), and Browder and Snell (1987).

7. *The child's performance must be carefully measured and evaluated.* Because students with severe handicaps often make progress in very small steps, it is important to measure their performance precisely. Careful measurement helps the teacher plan instruction that will be appropriate to the child's needs and evaluate the program's effectiveness. Change in performance is shown most clearly when data on the child's efforts are collected every day. When working on dressing skills, for example, a teacher might measure the number of seconds it takes a child to remove a sock from her right foot when given the cue "Donna, take off your sock." Over a period of time, Donna should perform the task more rapidly. If she does not, some aspect of the instructional program may have to be changed. Accurate information about a child's performance increases the teacher's ability to design an appropriate educational program. In some programs videotaped records are kept of severely handicapped students' performance on specific tasks. This can add an important dimension to documenting behavior changes over extended periods.

Increasing Socially Acceptable Behavior

As students with severe handicaps are being increasingly served in integrated school and community settings, there have been notable changes in the ways that teachers manage behaviors considered disruptive, aggressive, or socially unacceptable. In the recent past a student who displayed "excess" behaviors, such as stereotypic head-

TABLE 10.2
Items used in an attempt to find an effective reinforcer for a child with severe handicaps.

A. Social
   1. Praise
   2. Pat on knee
   3. Hug
   4. Hand-squeeze
   5. Tickling ribs
   6. Stroking face
   7. Verbal comments such as "Good girl," "That's the way," "Great"
   8. Another child getting reinforced for correct responses

B. Liquids
   1. Tang (orange and grape)
   2. Lemonade
   3. Kool-Aid (variety of flavors)
   4. Soda (variety of flavors)
   5. Water

C. Edibles
   1. Ice cream (variety of flavors)
   2. Candy
   3. Marshmallows
   4. M & M's
   5. Mints
   6. Cheetos
   7. Pretzels
   8. Candy corn
   9. Peanuts
   10. Butterscotch candy
   11. Corn chips
   12. Potato chips (plain and barbecue)
   13. Dry cereals (variety)
   14. Sweet and sour candy
   15. Pudding (chocolate and butterscotch)
   16. Chocolate-covered peanuts
   17. Lollipops
   18. Dried fruits (variety)
   19. Cookies (variety)

D. Toys
   1. Magazines
   2. Picture books
   3. The Farmer Says (talking toy)
   4. Music box
   5. Noisemaker
   6. Horns
   7. Teddy bear
   8. Barking-walking dog
   9. Balls
   10. Toy adding machine
   11. Santa Claus
   12. Dolls
   13. Helicopter
   14. Wind-up monkey
   15. Chatter telephone
   16. Cars
   17. Trucks
   18. Scissors and paper
   19. Play dough

E. Tokens (backups included)
   1. Wide variety of nickel candy
   2. Wide variety of penny candy
   3. Wide variety of carnival-type toys

F. Other
   1. Mirror
   2. Tape-recorded music (wide variety)
   3. Video tapes (children's programs, commercials, feedback of self)

Source: From "Developing Necessary Skills for Entry into Classroom Teaching Arrangements" by J. E. Spradlin and R. R. Spradlin in *Teaching Special Children* (p. 241) by N. G. Haring and R. L. Schiefelbusch (Eds.), 1976, New York: McGraw-Hill. Reprinted by permission.

weaving, would likely have been subjected to an unpleasant and undignified procedure, such as having his head restrained or perhaps having a teacher manipulate his head up and down for several minutes (Gast & Wolery, 1987). Some maladaptive behaviors of students with severe handicaps were "treated" with the application of aversive consequences (e.g., being sprayed with cold water) or with an extended time-out from instruction. These were "modes of intervention which most people would reject as absolutely unacceptable if they were used with a person who does not have disabilities" (Center on Human Policy, 1986, p. 4).

With today's emphasis on respect for the individual student and on preparation for independent living, a growing number of educational programs deal with challenging, excessive, or unacceptable behaviors in more functional and dignified ways. Specifically, they attempt to (1) understand the meaning that a behavior has for a student, (2) offer the student a positive alternative behavior, (3) utilize nonintrusive intervention techniques, and (4) use strategies that have been validated and are intended to be used in integrated community settings (Center on Human Policy, 1986). More detailed descriptions of such strategies are provided by Gast and Wolery (1987), LaVigna and Donnellan (1987), and Meyer and Evans (1986).

Making Choices

Traditionally, persons with severe handicaps have simply been cared for and taught to be compliant. Emphasis was placed on establishing instructional control over students. In the past, students with severe handicaps were given few opportunities to make choices and decisions or to express their preferences.

> Some caregivers might feel that to complete tasks for persons with disabilities is easier and faster than allowing them to do it for themselves; while others may have the attitude that the person already has enough problems coping with his or her disability. Regardless of what the underlying intention is, the result can be to overprotect, to encourage learned helplessness, and to deprive the individual of potentially valuable life experiences. (Guess, Benson, & Siegel-Causey, 1985, p. 83)

Today, efforts are being made to help students with severe handicaps learn to function more independently and make decisions about matters that will affect them, such as the types of settings in which they will live and work, the foods they will eat, the partners they will socialize with, and so on. Shevin and Klein (1984) offer several suggestions for incorporating choice-making activities into the classroom programs of students with severe handicaps. For example, a child might be presented with pictures of two activities and asked to point to the one she would rather engage in. Another child might be asked, "Whom would you like to be your partner?" Or the teacher might say, "Should we do this again?" Of course, in presenting such choices, the teacher must be prepared to accept whichever alternative is selected by the student and to follow through accordingly.

Communication Skills

Recently, there has also been a good deal of interest in specialized methods of teaching communication skills to children and youth with severe handicaps. Considerable data exist to indicate that basic communication skills are highly important for students' successful functioning in vocational and independent living programs (Orlansky, 1986; Rusch, Chadsey-Rusch, & Lagomarcino, 1987). Many students with severe handicaps are able to learn to understand and produce spoken language; speech is always a desirable goal, of course, for those who can attain it. A student who can communicate verbally is likely to have a wider range of educational, employment, residential, and recreational opportunities than a student who is unable to speak.

Some students with severe handicaps—because of their sensory, motor, cognitive, or behavioral limitations—may not learn to speak intelligibly, even after extensive training. Many systems of augmentative communication have proven useful for such students. These include gestures, various sign language systems, pictorial communication boards, symbol systems, and electronic communication aids. Although these systems are not as widely used as speech in the general community, they do enable many students with severe handicaps to receive and express basic information, feelings, needs, and wants. Sign language and other communication systems can also be learned by a student's teachers, peers, parents, and employers, thus encouraging use outside the classroom. Some students—after learning basic communication skills through sign language, communication boards, or other strategies—are later able to acquire speech skills. Reichle and Keogh (1986) discuss rules for decision-making in selecting the most appropriate method(s) of communication for students with severe handicaps.

An overview of augmentative communication systems and their applicability to severely handicapped students is provided by Miller and Allaire (1987).

Vocational Training

An especially important curriculum area for most students with severe handicaps is skills that will enable them to work in competitive employment in the community or in workshops. In the past few years there has been a greatly increased effort to provide appropriate vocational training opportunities for severely handicapped students. Much has been recently learned about methods of training complex vocational skills and about effective procedures to manage inappropriate behaviors. It is now widely believed that even the most severely handicapped person "has an untapped vocational potential that can be translated into productive and independent work" (Rusch & Mithaug, 1980, p. xv).

Precise methods of teaching vocational skills to people with severe handicaps have largely evolved from the task analytic approach of Gold (1980) and his colleagues. Careful attention is given to the physical arrangement of the work setting, the cues provided by the trainer, and the gradual attainment of acceptable rates of production and accuracy.

Teachers and others who are involved in designing vocational programs for severely handicapped students should first investigate what specific skills and behaviors are required in settings where their students might realistically be employed. Because job requirements change from time to time and from place to place, it may be advisable to survey potential employers and workshops to determine what skills are necessary for employment or for acceptance into a more advanced vocational training program. For example, in a survey of activity centers and sheltered workshops, Mithaug and Hagmeier (1978) found that a great majority of workshop supervisors considered it important or necessary for a client to be able to communicate basic needs (such as hunger, pain, and toileting) and to move safely about the shop. On the other hand, relatively few supervisors required their clients to be able to use the telephone book to look up names and numbers or to have basic arithmetic skills. Assessment of current job prerequisites is thus the first step in designing a program of vocational instruction.

With each passing month more evidence documents that severely handicapped children and adults are capable of performing useful and remunerative work in a wide variety of settings. Some teachers combine classroom instruction and practical experience in the community for children of school age. Winkler, Armstrong, Moehlis, Nietupski, and Whalen-Carrell (1982) describe a successful program in which severely handicapped students prepared and delivered classified advertising guides in their community. Most students improved in their ability to attend to tasks such as folding, collating, and packing; and many students learned money management skills with their earnings from the project. Wehman, Hill, Goodall, Cleveland, Brooke, and Pentecost (1982) offer a detailed report on a project in which severely handicapped adults were placed in community employment—mostly in utility jobs, such as wiping tables in restaurants or sweeping floors. After a 3-year period 67% of the clients were still employed. Their absenteeism and tardiness rates were generally as good as those of nonhandicapped workers, and the predominant attitude of co-workers was one of "indifference as long as the client performs his/her job acceptably" (p. 12). The wages and benefits earned by the handicapped workers were substantially greater than those they would have earned in sheltered workshops. Thus, rather than being dependent on public financial assistance, these workers were earning money and paying local, state, and federal taxes.

See chapter 15 for more on employment of adults with handicaps.

Recreational and Leisure Skills

Most children develop the ability to play and later to occupy themselves constructively and pleasurably during their free time. But children with severe handicaps may not learn appropriate and satisfying recreational skills unless they are specifically taught. As a survey by Pancsofar and Blackwell (1986) found, many persons with severe handicaps do not use their unstructured time appropriately; rather than participating in enjoyable pursuits, they may spend excessive time sitting, wandering, or looking at television. In response, a variety of programs to teach recreational and leisure skills have recently been developed; and this area is now generally acknowledged to be an important part of the curriculum for most students with severe handicaps.

Horst, Wehman, Hill, and Bailey (1981) describe how several severely handicapped students, aged 10 to 21, were taught age-appropriate leisure skills. The activities were selected "largely on the basis that many nonhandicapped peers regularly engage in these types of activities" (p. 11). Precise teaching procedures were followed in the assessment and teaching of (1) throwing and catching a Frisbee, (2) operating a cassette tape recorder, and (3) playing an electronic bowling game. All students were able to increase their skills in these activities. Teaching appropriate leisure and recreational skills helps severely handicapped individuals interact socially, maintain their physical skills, and become more involved in community activities. Additional guidelines for selecting and teaching recreational and leisure activities are provided by Moon and Bunker (1987) and Wehman, Renzaglia, and Bates (1985).

Teacher Competencies and Qualities

Teaching students with severe handicaps is difficult and demanding. The teacher must be well-organized, firm, and consistent. He must be able to manage not just a classroom, but a complex educational operation, which usually involves the supervision of paraprofessional aides, student teachers, peer tutors, and volunteers. The teacher must be knowledgeable about individualized and group instructional techniques and must work cooperatively with other professionals, such as physicians, psychologists, physical therapists, social workers, and language specialists. He must maintain accurate records and must be constantly planning for the future needs of the students. Effective communication with parents (or residential staff), school administrators, vocational rehabilitation personnel, and community agencies is also important.

Students with severe handicaps sometimes give little or no apparent response, so their teacher needs to be sensitive to small changes in student behavior. The effective teacher is consistent in designing and implementing strategies to improve learning and behavior (even if some of the students' previous teachers were not). The effective teacher should not be too quick to remove tasks that are difficult—it is better to teach students to request assistance (Durand, 1986).

Some people might consider it undesirable to work with students with severe handicaps, because of their serious and multiple disabilities; yet this field can offer many highly rewarding teaching experiences. There is much satisfaction in teaching a child to feed and toilet herself independently, helping a student make friends with nonhandicapped peers, and assisting a young adult to live, travel, and work independently in the community. The challenge and the rewards of teaching students with severe handicaps are great.

Individual or Group Instruction?

In many educational programs for students with severe handicaps, instruction is largely or wholly one-to-one; that is, a teacher works with one student at a time. In a review of professional literature, Favell, Favell, and McGimsey (1978) found that about 90% of the articles about teaching or modifying the behavior of severely handicapped students described a one-to-one approach. Some professionals, in fact, may argue that such training is the *only* effective method for producing changes in the behavior of students with severe handicaps.

Recently, however, a number of researchers have investigated the effectiveness of small-group teaching with students who have severe handicaps. The results of some of these studies are encouraging. For example, Mansdorf (1977) found that group training was effective in teaching the use of a token system. Storm and Willis (1978) found that severely handicapped students in groups of four could learn to imitate motor tasks as well as they could in individualized settings. In addition, Curran (1983) and Orelove (1982) found that severely handicapped students were capable of incidental learning of vocabulary. That is, when words were presented to a certain student in a small group, other students in the group could also learn to understand them. Edwards (1986) advocates the use of heterogeneous groupings, because the needs of students who require high levels of caretaking are "more easily handled when their presence is in smaller numbers in a classroom" (p. 10).

Group training of students with severe handicaps thus appears to be promising, although much research remains to be done. Group instruction allows teachers to use their time more effectively, gives students the benefit of increased training time, and encourages the children to socialize. Should research continue to find group instruction effective, future programs of education and training for severely handicapped learners will most likely include a combination of group and one-to-one instructional techniques.

See Polloway, Cronin, and Patton (1986) and Reid and Favell (1984) for reviews of research on group instruction.

Educational Alternatives

What is the least restrictive and most appropriate educational setting for students with severe handicaps? This question is the subject of much current debate and discussion. Many educators have called for the abolition of *all* institutional placements, arguing that institutions cannot provide a natural or effective learning environment. According to Brown (1986), "When required to function within segregated environments, people with severe intellectual disabilities could not achieve in reasonable accordance with capacities and could not even begin the quest for the personal freedoms and dignities that most others enjoy" (p. xii).

At the present time a significant number of persons with severe handicaps continue to be served in institutional settings. This population represents "the group most difficult to teach" (Warren, 1986, p. 65). Fortunately, the educational programs within many institutions are increasing in number and quality. Warren contends that institutional placement can be the least restrictive environment for some students, particularly if they have rare or serious medical or behavioral problems, if they are from sparsely populated areas where a suitable educational program is not available, or if their families are not able to cope with the massive needs of one member with severe handicaps. Institutions can also be used for short-term training, for example, in the reduction of self-injurious behavior. In most states there is a trend toward reducing the size of institutions, providing individualized education programs for residents, increasing parent and community involvement, and developing plans for some residents to move into community-based settings. Residential institutions need not necessarily be bleak and inhuman.

In the FOCUS feature that follows, the parent of a child with severe handicaps argues that institutions are not always a terrible placement for a child with severe handicaps. What do you think?

The public schools, which until recently excluded most severely handicapped children, are now beginning to provide educational opportunities for them on a large scale. The most prevalent model of public school programming is the self-contained special class for severely handicapped students. Especially when a self-contained class is located in a regular public school, this approach is seen as much more desirable and less restrictive than institutional placement (Guess & Mulligan, 1982). Although their highly specialized needs make placement in a regular classroom unlikely, severely handicapped students who are educated in public schools have opportunities to come into contact with their nonhandicapped peers—for example, on the school bus, in the corridors, or in selected activities in school. It is widely assumed that these interactions result in improved social relationships between handicapped and nonhandicapped chil-

INSTITUTION IS NOT A DIRTY WORD

Deinstitutionalization has become widely practiced across the nation. Yet, like every social movement, its effects are not necessarily 100% positive. Here is a different perspective—one parent's story.

I watched Phil Donahue recently. He had on mothers of handicapped children who talked about the pain and blessing of having a "special" child. As the mother of a severely handicapped 6-year-old boy who cannot sit, who cannot walk, who will be in diapers all of his days, I understand the pain. The blessing part continues to elude me—notwithstanding the kind and caring people we've met through this tragedy.

What really makes my jaws clench, though, is the use of the word "special." The idea that our damaged children are "special," and that we as parents were somehow picked for the role, is one of the myths that comes with the territory. It's reinforced by the popular media, which present us with heartwarming images of retarded people who marry, of quadriplegics who fly airplanes, of those fortunate few who struggle out of comas to teach us about the meaning of courage and love. I like these stories myself. But, of course, inspirational tales are only one side of the story. The other side deals with the daily care of a family member who might need more than many normal families can give.

STOICISM

Parents who endure with silent stoicism or chin-up good humor are greeted with kudos and applause. "I don't know how you do it," the well-wishers say, not realizing, of course, that no one has a choice in this matter. No one would consciously choose to have a child anything less than healthy and normal. The other truth is not spoken aloud: "Thank God, it's not me."

One mother on the Donahue show talked about how difficult it was to care for her severely brain-damaged daughter, but in the end she said serenely, "She gives much more than she takes from our family." And no, she would never institutionalize her child. She would never "put her away." For "she is my child," the woman firmly concluded as the audience clapped in approval. "I would never give her up."

Everyone always says how awful the institutions are. Don't they have bars on the windows and children lying neglected in crowded wards? Aren't all the workers sadists, taking direction from the legendary Big Nurse? Indeed, isn't institutionalizing a child tantamount to locking him away? Signing him out of your life forever? Isn't it proof of your failure as a parent—one who couldn't quite measure up and love your child, no matter what?

No, to all of the above. And love is beside the point.

Our child Zachariah has not lived at home for almost 4 years. I knew when we placed him, sorry as I was, that this was the right decision, for his care precluded any semblance of normal family life for the rest of us. I do not think that we "gave him up," although he is cared for daily by nurses, caseworkers, teachers, and therapists, rather than by his mother and father. When we come to visit him at his "residential facility," a place housing 50 severely physically and mentally handicapped youngsters, we usually see him being held and rocked by a foster grandma who has spent the better part of the afternoon singing him nursery rhymes. I do not feel that we have "put him away." Perhaps it is just a question of language. I told another mother who was going through the difficult decision regarding placement for her retarded child, "Think of it as going to boarding school rather than institutionalization." Maybe euphemisms help ease the pain a little bit. But I've also seen enough to know that institution need not be a dirty word.

The media still relish those institution horror stories: a page-one photo of a retarded girl who was repeatedly molested by the janitor on night duty. Oh, the newspapers have a field day with something like that. And that is how it should be, I suppose. To protect against institutional abuse, we need critical reporters with sharpened pencils and a keen investigative eye. But there are other scenes from the institution as well. I've seen a young caseworker talk lovingly as she changed the diapers of a teen-age boy. I've watched as an aide put red ribbons into the ponytail of a cerebral-palsied woman, wipe away the drool, and kiss her on the cheek. When we bring Zach back to his facility after a visit home, the workers welcome him with hugs and notice if we gave him a haircut or a new shirt.

The reporters don't make news out of that simple stuff. It doesn't mesh with the anti-institutional bias prevalent in the last few years, or the tendency to canonize the handicapped and their accomplishments.

SURVIVAL

This anti-institutional trend has some very frightening ramifications. We force mental patients out into the real world of cheap welfare hotels and call it "community placement." We parole youthful offenders because "jails are such dangerous places to be," making our city streets dangerous places for the law-abiding. We heap enormous guilt on the families that need, for their own survival, to put their no-longer-competent elderly in that dreaded last stop—the nursing home.

Another danger is that in a time of economic distress for all of us, funds could be cut for human-service programs under the guise of anti-institutionalization. We must make sure, before we close the doors of those "awful" institutions, that we have alternative facilities to care for the clientele. The humanitarians who tell us how terrible institutions are should be wary lest they become unwilling bedfellows to conservative politicians who want to walk a tight fiscal line. It takes a lot of money to run institutions. No politician is going to say he's against the handicapped, but he can talk in sanctimonious terms about efforts to preserve the family unit, about families remaining independent and self-sufficient. Translated, this means, "'You got your troubles, I got mine."

Most retarded people do not belong in institutions any more than most people over 65 belong in nursing homes. What we need are options and alternatives for a heterogeneous population. We need group homes and halfway houses and government subsidies to families who choose to care for dependent members at home. We need accessible housing for independent handicapped people; we need to pay enough to foster-care families to show that a good home is worth paying for. We need institutions. And it shouldn't have to be a dirty word.

Source: From "My Turn," by Fern Kupfer, *Newsweek*, December 13, 1982, p. 17. Reprinted by permission.

dren, but this assumption has not yet been conclusively supported by research (Peck & Semmel, 1982). Merely placing a severely handicapped student in a public school class does not ensure that she is receiving the most appropriate education possible. "Classrooms are not necessarily instructional environments. It is time to attend to the quantity and quality of instruction in these classes" (Tawney & Smith, 1981, p. 15).

Educational, vocational, and residential programs for severely handicapped individuals are also expanding rapidly in their home communities. This trend is strongly supported by many; "there is no service or program that can be provided in a large institution that cannot be provided better, and possibly for less money, in a community setting" (Larsen, 1976, p. 129). It is especially critical for education to begin as early as possible; a severely handicapped child who receives no formal training until the age of 5 or 6 will surely be at a great disadvantage and may well have developed a repertoire of inappropriate behaviors that will be difficult to deal with. Thus, it is extremely important for a severely handicapped child's family to receive information and supportive services that will help them to encourage their child's development and maintain as normal a family life as possible. Any successful community program for a child with severe handicaps must also serve that child's family.

See chapter 14 for a detailed discussion of the critical importance of early intervention.

CURRENT ISSUES/FUTURE TRENDS

The current extension of public education and community-based services to severely handicapped children is a tremendously important and challenging development. Those people who are providing instruction to severely handicapped students can rightfully be called pioneers on an exciting new frontier of special education. Professionals involved in the education of severely handicapped children "can look back with pride, and even awe, at the advances they have made. In a relatively brief period, educators, psychologists, and other professionals have advocated vigorously for additional legislation and funds, extended the service delivery model into the public schools and community, and developed a training technology" (Orelove, 1984, p. 271).

Future research will increase our understanding of the ways in which students with severe handicaps acquire, maintain, and generalize functional skills. Better techniques of measuring and changing behavior are constantly being developed; these are balanced with an increasing concern for the personal rights and dignity of individuals with severe handicaps.

Technology will find increasing applications for the education and habilitation of persons with severe handicaps.

> The microcomputer can bring the gift of speech to persons who are nonverbal, telephone use to persons with hearing impairments, voice to persons with vision impairments, and environmental control to those who experience physical handicaps. It can remove the paper and pencil blockade and improve the quality of life for people with varying abilities in a number of ways. (Effertz-Tougas, 1986, p. 3)

Microswitches, scanning devices, interactive video, communication aids, data management systems, and various other forms of educational technology are currently being successfully used with students who have severe and multiple disabilities and are sure

ARE ALL CHILDREN EDUCABLE?

Some educators, other professionals, and citizens question the wisdom of spending large amounts of money, time, and human resources attempting to train severely handicapped children, many of whom have such serious disabilities that they may never be able to function independently. Some people would prefer to see our resources spent on children who have higher apparent potential—especially when economic conditions limit the availability of educational services for all children in the public schools. "Why bother with children who fail to make meaningful progress?" they might ask.

Accelerating a response rate may indeed be a worthy first goal in an educational program if there is reasonable hope of shaping the response into a meaningful skill. Nevertheless, after concerted and appropriate effort by highly trained behavior therapists, for a reasonable period of time, a child's failure to make significant progress toward acquisition of a meaningful skill could reasonably be taken as an indication that the child is ineducable. . . . Granted, all children probably are educable if education is defined as acceleration of any operant response. But such a definition trivializes the meaning of the term *education* and, even without consideration of benefit, moots the question of educability. Formulating consensual definitions of *education, meaningful skill*, and *significant progress* will be difficult, but it is a task we cannot avoid. . . . We suggest that public response to the questions "What is education?" "What skills are meaningful?" "What rate of progress is significant?" and "What cost/benefit ratios are acceptable?" sampled with sufficient care, could be invaluable in deciding who is educable and who is not. (Kauffman & Krouse, 1981, pp. 55–56)

A special educator who is also the parent of a daughter with severe handicaps disagrees.

If anyone were to be the judge of whether a particular behavior change is "meaningful," it should certainly not be only the general taxpayer, who has no idea how rewarding it is to see your retarded 19-year-old acquire the skill of toilet flushing on command or pointing to food when she wants a second helping. I suspect that the average taxpayer would not consider it "meaningful" to *him* or *her* for Karrie to acquire such skills. But in truth, it is "meaningful" to that taxpayer whether he recognizes it or not, in the sense that it is saving him or her the cost of Karrie's being institutionalized, which she certainly would have been by now if she never showed any progress; thus it is functional for the taxpayer even though his or her answer to the question "Is this meaningful?" might well be "No" or "Not enough to pay for."

The complexity, cost, and hopelessness of evaluating fairly the "meaningfulness" of various behavior changes leads me to conclude that no one should be denied an education. . . . I would be very resistant to the idea that we should now, at this infant stage of the science and technology of education for severely retarded students, give up intensive skill training for anyone. (Hawkins, 1984, p. 285)

How far can she go?

In many ways our knowledge of the learning and developmental processes of severely handicapped children is still primitive and incomplete. We do know, however, that children with severe handicaps are capable of benefiting significantly from appropriate and carefully implemented educational programs. Even in cases where little or no progress has been observed, we cannot conclude that the student is incapable of learning. It may instead be that our teaching methods are imperfect and that the future will bring improved methods and materials to enable that student to learn useful skills. Children, even if severely impaired, have the right to the best possible public education and training that we can offer them.*

Virtually every parent of a child with severe handicaps has heard a host of negative predictions from educators, doctors, and concerned friends and family. The parents are often offered such discouraging forecasts as "Your child will never talk" or "Your child will never be toilet-trained." Yet in many instances the gains of those children who *are* taught far exceed the original predictions of the professionals. Despite predictions to the contrary, many children *have* learned to walk, talk, toilet themselves, and perform other "impossible" tasks.

*Readers wishing to learn more about the educability debate are referred to Heward, Heron, Hill, and Trap-Porter (1984); Kauffman (1981b); Noonan, Brown, Mulligan, and Rettig (1982); and Ulicny, Thompson, Favell, and Thompson (1985).

There are still many unanswered questions in the education of children with severe handicaps. Even though their opportunities for education and training are rapidly expanding, nobody really knows their true learning potential or the extent to which they can be successfully integrated into the nondisabled population. What we do know is that they will go no further than we let them; it is up to us to open doors and raise our sights, instead of creating additional barriers.

Some of us have ignored both the thesis that all retarded persons are educable and the thesis that some retarded persons are ineducable, and instead have experimented with ways to teach some previously unteachable people. Over a few centuries, those experiments have steadily reduced the size of the apparently ineducable group relative to the obviously educable group. Clearly, we have not finished that adventure. Why predict its outcome, when we could simply pursue it, and just as well without a prediction? Why not pursue it to see if there comes a day when there is such a small class of apparently ineducable persons left that it consists of one elderly institution resident who is put forward as ineducable. If it comes, that will be a very nice day, and the next day will be even better. (Baer, 1984, p. 299) to be used even more widely in the future (Effertz-Tougas, 1986; Esposito & Campbell, 1987; Hofmeister & Friedman, 1986).

As more and more people with severe handicaps leave large residential institutions, it is especially important that adequate care and supportive services be provided in the community. There is currently a pressing need for good, well-staffed group homes or small community residences that can accommodate severely handicapped individuals. Group homes can vary considerably in the quality of care they provide, and objective evaluations of their services are needed (Pratt, Luszcz, & Brown, 1980). Employment settings with appropriate tasks, good working conditions, fair wages, and adequate supervision must be further developed. Finally, we must make much better efforts at encouraging awareness and acceptance of severely handicapped individuals by the general public and must help these individuals become as self-sufficient and socially acceptable as possible.

See chapter 15 for more on residential and work settings for adults with handicaps.

SUMMARY

1. Despite their limitations children with severe handicaps can and do learn.
2. There is no universally agreed-upon definition of the severely handicapped population.
   a. The child with severe handicaps needs instruction in self-help, motor, perceptual, social, cognitive, and communication skills.
   b. Traditional intelligence tests are useless in assessing the child with severe handicaps; instead, the teacher needs to observe the unique abilities and limitations of each child.
   c. Although each child exhibits an individual set of physical, intellectual, and social characteristics, children with severe handicaps frequently show some or all of the following behaviors: little or no communication, delayed physical and motor development, frequent inappropriate behavior, deficits in self-help skills, and infrequent constructive behavior and interaction.
   d. These children almost always have multiple disabilities, including physical problems. They usually look and act markedly different from normal children.
3. Although prevalence figures are not precise because definitions vary so widely, we do know that this population is neither small nor isolated. Most communities include some children with severe and multiple handicaps.
4. Education of persons with severe handicaps is a recent innovation.
   a. Throughout most of history these children probably died in infancy.
   b. During the 19th century hundreds of state-run custodial asylums were established. They offered little or nothing in the way of education and training for their residents.
   c. Within the last 15 years court cases and laws have mandated public education for these children for the first time, recognizing that *all* children—regardless of disabilities—can benefit from education.
5. Severe and profound handicaps most often have biological causes, including chromosomal abnormalities, genetic and metabolic disorders, complications of pregnancy and prenatal care, birth trauma, and later brain damage.

     a. In many cases the cause is unknown.

     b. A rubella epidemic caused many cases of deaf-blindness in children born during the mid-1960s. Deaf-blind children, regardless of intellectual functioning, have too little hearing to benefit from programs for visually impaired students (which rely on auditory instruction) and too little sight to benefit from programs for deaf students (which rely on visual instruction).

6. Students with severe handicaps should be taught skills that are functional, age-appropriate, and directed toward the community. Interaction with nonhandicapped students should occur regularly as part of the educational program for students with severe handicaps.

7. Effective instruction of students with severe handicaps requires structure and precision.

     a. Skills to be taught must be broken down into small steps.

     b. Special equipment, furniture, and materials may be needed.

     c. The child's current performance must be precisely assessed, and the target skill stated clearly.

     d. Skills must be taught in an appropriate sequence.

     e. The child needs a clear cue from the teacher before performing the skill and immediate feedback and reinforcement afterward.

     f. The teacher must program for generalization of learning.

     g. The child's progress must be carefully measured and evaluated regularly.

8. Educators are seeking strategies for dealing with the excessive or socially unacceptable behaviors sometimes exhibited by students with severe handicaps. Effective approaches seek to

     a. understand the meaning the behavior may have for the student

     b. offer the student a positive alternative behavior

     c. use nonintrusive intervention techniques

     d. utilize strategies validated and intended for use in integrated community settings

9. Traditionally, persons with severe handicaps have simply been cared for and taught to be compliant. Today, however, some educators are teaching choice-making skills to students with severe handicaps.

10. Students who can learn speech should do so. A system of augmentative communication is an appropriate option for those who have not learned speech even after training.

11. Through training, most students with severe handicaps can learn to perform useful vocational skills.

12. Students with severe handicaps should also be taught age-appropriate recreation and leisure skills.

13. Teachers of children with severe handicaps must be highly competent, able to work with many different kinds of people, and well organized.

14. Although most students with severe handicaps are taught in one-on-one settings, there is now evidence that small-group training may be effective for some tasks.

15. Although many persons with severe handicaps are still in residential institutions, where they are receiving more and better education than in the past, community-based programs are expanding.

     a. Education for children with severe handicaps should begin in infancy if possible.

b. More and more children with severe handicaps are being educated in self-contained classrooms within the regular school so that they have the opportunity to have contact with both handicapped and nonhandicapped peers.

c. Most children and adults with severe handicaps are able to live in group homes or small community residences and to work in supervised settings.

16. As more children and adults with severe handicaps leave institutions, we must be careful to provide adequate residential facilities, educational programs, and employment opportunities to meet their needs. We also need to increase public understanding and acceptance of this group of exceptional people.

17. We still do not know much about how children with severe handicaps learn and develop. We do know, however, that the achievements of these children often surpass the predictions of professionals. Thus, we must be optimistic and open doors for them, instead of setting limited goals.

FOR MORE INFORMATION

Journals

Analysis and Intervention in Developmental Disabilities. Published quarterly by Pergamon Press. Includes articles on theory and behavioral research related to people "who suffer from severe and pervasive developmental disabilities."

Journal of The Association for Persons with Severe Handicaps. Published quarterly by The Association for Persons with Severe Handicaps. Publishes articles dealing with useful information regarding how to develop, implement, and evaluate educational programs for severely handicapped persons, including policy statements and research.

Books

Browder, D. M. (1987). *Assessment of individuals with severe handicaps: An applied behavioral approach to life skills assessment.* Baltimore: Paul H. Brookes.

Evans, I. M., & Meyer, L. H. (1985). *An educative approach to behavior problems: A practical decision model for interventions with severely handicapped learners.* Baltimore: Paul H. Brookes.

Gaylord-Ross, R. J., & Holvoet, J. F. (1985). *Strategies for educating students with severe handicaps.* Boston: Little, Brown.

Horner, R. H., Meyer, L. H., & Fredericks, H. D. B. (Eds.). (1986). *Education of learners with severe handicaps: Exemplary service strategies.* Baltimore: Paul H. Brookes.

Lazarus, P. J., & Strichart, S. S. (Eds.). (1986). *Psychoeducational evaluation of children and adolescents with low-incidence handicaps.* Orlando, FL: Grune & Stratton.

Orelove, F. P., & Sobsey, D. (1987). *Educating children with multiple disabilities: A transdisciplinary approach.* Baltimore: Paul H. Brookes.

Perske, R., Clifton, A., McLean, B. M., & Stein, J. I. (Eds.). (1986). *Mealtimes for persons with severe handicaps.* Baltimore: Paul H. Brookes.

Snell, M. E. (Ed.). (1987). *Systematic instruction of persons with severe handicaps* (3rd ed.). Columbus, OH: Merrill.

Wilcox, B., & Bellamy, G. T. (1987). *The activities catalog: An alternative curriculum for youth and adults with severe disabilities.* Baltimore: Paul H. Brookes.

Organizations

ABLENET, 360 Hoover Street, NE, Minneapolis, MN 55413. Offers information and publications on the use of automated learning devices, microswitches, and other technology with persons who have severe handicaps. Has available for purchase a book by Jackie Levin and Lynn Scherfenberg, *Breaking Barriers: How Children and Adults with Severe Handicaps Can Access the World Through Simple Technology.*

The Association for Persons with Severe Handicaps, 7010 Roosevelt Way, NE, Seattle, WA 98115. Through its journal and monthly newsletter, disseminates a wide variety of useful information to teachers, parents, administrators, researchers, and others. Through its annual convention provides the major professional forum for the exchange of new developments relating to the education of persons with severe handicaps. Through its many state and local chapters also sponsors conferences and activities.

Center on Human Policy, 724 Comstock Avenue, Syracuse, NY 13244. Provides reports and other resources on the integration of people with severe handicaps into community life. Also distributes materials encouraging the development of positive attitudes about persons with disabilities in schools and the media.

Department of Specialized Educational Services, Madison Metropolitan School District, 545 West Dayton Street, Madison, WI 53703. In cooperation with the Department of Studies in Behavioral Disabilities at the University of Wisconsin, has been especially active in developing programs of instruction for severely handicapped children and in seeking to facilitate integration with nondisabled individuals. Has available for purchase a number of curriculum guides and other materials.

Helen Keller National Center for Deaf-Blind Youths and Adults, 111 Middle Neck Road, Sands Point, NY 11050. Offers training programs for persons with impaired vision and hearing and consultation to agencies providing services to this population. Publishes *Directory of Agencies and Organizations Serving Deaf-Blind Individuals,* curriculum manuals, and other informational materials about deaf-blindness.

11

GIFTED AND TALENTED STUDENTS

Raymond H. Swassing
Ohio State University

O ur study of exceptional children thus far has focused on children with intellectual or physical disabilities-children who require special methods and materials in order to derive maximum benefit from their educational programs. Gifted and talented children may also find that a traditional curriculum is inappropriate; it may not provide the advanced and unique challenges they require to learn most effectively. Gifted and talented children represent the other extreme on the continuum of academic, artistic, social, and scientific abilities. They, too, need special educational opportunities if they are to reach their potential.

> The term *exceptional children* includes both children who experience difficulties in learning and children whose performance is so superior that special education is necessary if they are to fulfill their potential.

Although the regular classroom is viewed as the least restrictive environment for many exceptional children with handicaps, the standard curriculum and usual school activities are often highly inappropriate and restrictive for gifted children. When the school year begins in September, intellectually gifted students may already have all of the skills their grade-level peers are supposed to learn during the year. Thus, a school program that does not allow gifted children to explore areas of individual interest or to learn things beyond the basic curriculum would be restrictive. Children with special talents should be given opportunities to develop those abilities further; an appropriate education for gifted and talented children must include special curriculum and instruction.

Even though P.L. 94–142 does not apply to gifted and talented children, they are easily seen as exceptional students in need of special education. To reach his or her potential and to succeed fully in school, the gifted and talented child needs specially trained teachers; special instruction, materials, and resources; and perhaps a special classroom placement for part or all of the school day. Issues such as assessment, family involvement, placement, expectations for achievement, and the child's unique abilities are just as important for an effective individualized education program for a gifted and talented student as they are for that of a student with handicaps. Programs tailored to individual needs are beneficial to *all* exceptional children.

DEFINITION AND PREVALENCE OF
GIFTED AND TALENTED CHILDREN

Numerous definitions of gifted and talented children have been proposed and debated over the years. Terman (1925), one of the pioneers in the field, defined the gifted as those who score in the top 2% on standardized tests of intelligence. Witty (1940), recognizing the value of including special skills and talents, described gifted and talented children as those "whose performance is consistently remarkable in any potentially valuable area" (p. 516). Both viewpoints are included within the definitions of gifted and talented children most widely used today. Federal legislation defines gifted and talented children as

> children who give evidence of high performance capability in areas such as intellectual, creative, artistic, leadership capacity, or specific academic fields, and who require services or activities not ordinarily provided by the school in order to fully develop such capabilities. (Sec. 582, P.L. 97-35)

An earlier federal definition included a sixth area of giftedness—psychomotor ability. This category included students gifted in the use of gross and fine motor development (e.g., diving, gymnastics), but Congress believed that schools' existing athletic programs served such students adequately.

The areas in which children can show outstanding performance or unusual potential in order to be considered gifted and talented cover almost the full range of human endeavor. Overall intellectual ability and specific academic aptitude are only two areas. General intellectual ability refers to overall performance on intelligence or achievement tests. Children who meet this criterion usually do, or can, perform well in most academic areas. Children with specific academic aptitude have outstanding ability in one or two areas. For example, Reggie, who has specific academic aptitude, performs extremely well in science; however, his work in social studies and English is no better than that of most of his age peers.

Leadership ability has been included in the definition of giftedness only recently; the ability to demonstrate leadership had not been recognized in most previous definitions of gifted and talented students. The framers of the current definition were aware of society's need to develop leadership potential. Such problems as pollution, population control, nutrition, and peacekeeping require the efforts not only of scientists and economists, but also of those people who can bring groups of people together and lead them toward common goals. Answers to pressing problems may be provided by scientists, and the source of the resources may be suggested by economists. But if we have no leaders to implement the scientists' and economists' solutions, the problems remain at least as critical as when first identified.

The federal definition, essentially unchanged for several years, has received fairly widespread acceptance and has been adopted by many states (Zettel, 1979). However, most states limit their definition of giftedness to the three areas of general intellectual ability, creativity, and leadership (Sisk, 1984). Renzulli has offered an alternative definition that has gained considerable attention.

> Giftedness consists of an interaction among three basic clusters of human traits— these clusters being above average general abilities, high levels of task commitment, and high levels of creativity. Gifted and talented children are those possessing or capable of developing this composite set of traits and applying them to any potentially valuable area of human performance. Children who manifest or are capable of

developing an interaction among the three clusters require a wide variety of educational opportunities and services that are not ordinarily provided through regular instructional programs. (p. 184)

Renzulli's definition brings together the three features of ability (actual or potential), task commitment, and creative expression and requires that all three be jointly applied to a valuable area of human endeavor. Like the federal definition, Renzulli's provides a great deal of freedom in determining who is considered gifted and talented, depending on the interpretation of "valuable" human performance.

Prevalence

The identification of gifted children requires a comparison with normative standards. To be considered gifted or talented for special education programs, a student is often identified as performing in the top 3% to 5% of the school-age population (Marland, 1971). Outstanding ability is based on the performance of the individual as compared to the usual performance of age-mates on a given task or skill.

Given the estimates that gifted children comprise 3% to 5% of the school-age population, there would be approximately 1,450,000 to 2,415,000 children in the nation's schools who meet the federal criteria. In fiscal year 1981 the 50 states and the District of Columbia served approximately 909,437 students in gifted and talented programs (Mitchell, 1981, pp. 6–7), making gifted and talented students the third largest subgroup of exceptional children served by the schools. However, only 17 states mandated these programs.

HISTORICAL PERSPECTIVE

Historically, the concept of giftedness has been neither as broad nor as inclusive as the definitions we currently use. Early 19th-century works, including a classic study by Sir Francis Galton (1869), focused on the concept of genius. Galton was the first to offer a definition of genius that used observable characteristics or outcomes. His study was based on famous adults, however, and contributed little to the identification and nurturing of potential in children. Furthermore, Galton felt that genius was genetically determined. Although Galton's work has been heavily criticized, his book *Hereditary Genius* is recognized as a major contribution to the better understanding of people of genius.

In the United States, special education for gifted and talented children can be traced back as far as 1867. In that year the St. Louis public schools initiated a plan of flexible promotion. For the next 30 years, schools instituted various plans for promoting high-achieving students at various rates. Around 1900, rapid advancement classes were established, in which children could complete 2 years' worth of academic work in 1 year, or 3 years' work in 2.

One of the earliest enrichment programs for gifted children began in the early 1920s in Cleveland, Ohio (Goddard, 1928). In 1922 a group of "publicly spirited" women organized to promote classes for gifted students. H. H. Goddard, their advisor, published a description of the program in a 1928 textbook. The Cleveland program remains one of the longest-running, continuous programs for gifted children in the United States.

In order to separate individuals into groups according to intellectual abilities, educators needed effective measuring devices. During the last quarter of the 19th century, several instruments designed to measure intellectual ability were developed. In Paris in 1905 two French psychologists, Alfred Binet and Theophile Simon, published a graduated series of tests called a Measuring Scale of Intelligence. Their system was intended to classify children according to their intellectual abilities in order to facilitate their education. The Binet-Simon scale was transported to the United States, where several translations were made. The translation by Terman (1916) at Stanford University became the edition that dominated the field. Known as the Stanford-Binet Intelligence Scale, it was published in 1916 and was most recently revised in 1973 (Terman & Merrill, 1973). It has become the scale against which all other measures of intelligence have been compared.

In addition to translating the Stanford-Binet test, Lewis Terman conducted a famous long-term study that contributed greatly to our knowledge of the characteristics of gifted individuals. From 1925 through 1959, five volumes of the *Genetic Studies of Genius* were published—periodic reports of a study of approximately 1,500 gifted individuals from childhood into midlife. Numerous articles and papers have also been developed by Terman's colleagues and students. Two of the most recent papers reported on the life satisfaction of some of the original subjects (Sears, 1977, 1979).

To be included in the Terman study, a child had to have an intelligence quotient (IQ) of 140 or above, as measured by the 1916 Stanford-Binet. Measures were taken in a number of areas, including social and physical development, achievement, character traits, books read, and play interests. This long-term study refuted certain myths about gifted individuals, including "early ripe, early rot," "genius and insanity go hand in hand," and the stereotype of the gifted child as a little adult.

Another important contribution was made by Leta S. Hollingsworth, an educational psychologist who tested a child with a score of more than 180 on the Stanford-Binet. This was the beginning of a series of case studies Hollingsworth conducted with children of extremely high intelligence. In her book *Children Above IQ 180* (1942, 1975), Hollingsworth reported the case histories of 12 such children from the New York City area. The school histories of these children varied considerably. One factor that differentiated the successful from the unsuccessful in school was early recognition of their superior talents and the willingness of parents and school personnel to act on that awareness. Some of the case studies revealed that these gifted children were frustrated and felt stifled by regular school procedures. Early identification, guidance, personal interest in the children, and special programs contributed to helping these youngsters adjust and accept learning as a rewarding challenge (Hollingsworth, 1975).

Although certain myths were dispelled by the early studies, problems were also evident. A narrow view of giftedness dominated by an IQ score prevailed for many years. It is probable that many children with special gifts and talents were not recognized or given the opportunity to develop fully. The IQ score came to be relied on excessively as an identification tool and as a predictor of success in life (Witty, 1930, 1962). Giftedness was restricted to high IQ scores and came to be associated with

High verbal ability at a young age is one indicator of giftedness.

only the white, urban, middle- and upper-class segments of society (Witty, 1940). In the early 1950s Guilford, a psychologist noted for his work in the area of analyzing and categorizing mental processes, challenged the field to look beyond traditional conceptions of intelligence and to view the IQ score as a small sample of mental abilities (Guilford, 1956). Since that challenge the concept of giftedness has developed in several directions to involve many forms of intellectual activity.

During the 1960s attention was turned to creativity and other alternatives to the traditional IQ score for identification of gifted and talented children (Frierson, 1969). Some efforts were initiated to identify and develop talent among the culturally diverse; this movement continued to expand during the 1970s (Torrance, 1977). Also, during the 1970s the gifted and talented among females and handicapped students came to be more widely recognized (Fox, 1977; Maker, 1977).

Current definitions have grown out of our awareness that IQ alone does not define all of the possible areas of giftedness. We have realized that some people have advanced talents in socially valued endeavors that cannot be measured by intelligence tests; that intelligence tests are, as Guilford suggested, only a small sample of intellectual activity in limited areas of human endeavor. The concept of giftedness has expanded to include many talents that contribute substantially to the quality of life—for both the individual and society.

CHARACTERISTICS OF GIFTED AND TALENTED CHILDREN

Physically, gifted children do not differ substantially from other children their age. The widely held stereotype of the gifted child—a little adult in horn-rimmed glasses, arms laden with volumes of Homer, Plato, Descartes, and Einstein—is not based in reality. Any one gifted child may be taller or shorter than her age-mates. The child may weigh more, about the same, or less than her peers. In other words, on a class picnic the gifted and talented child would not be easily identifiable.

Giftedness is a complex concept covering a wide range of abilities and traits. Some children have special talents. They may not be outstanding in academics, but

What are some of your beliefs about the characteristics of gifted and talented children? Find out by responding to the statements in the Focus feature that follows.

they may have special abilities in music, literature, or leadership. Other children may have intellectual abilities found only in one child in a thousand, or one child in 10 thousand.

Clark (1983) describes the characteristics of gifted children across five domains: cognitive, affective, physical, intuitive, and societal (see Table 11.1). She contends that the special education needs of gifted and talented students are a function of the characteristics that differentiate them from typical learners.

TABLE 11.1
Differentiating characteristics of the gifted.

I. The Cognitive Domain

Extraordinary quantity of information; unusual retentiveness

Advanced comprehension

Unusually varied interests and curiosity

High level of language development

High level of verbal ability

Unusual capacity for processing information

Accelerated pace of thought processes

Flexible thought processes

Comprehensive synthesis

Early ability to delay closure

Heightened capacity for seeing unusual and diverse relationships

Ability to generate original ideas and solutions

Early differential patterns for thought processing (e.g., thinking in alternatives, abstract terms, sensing consequences, making generalizations)

Early ability to use and form conceptual frameworks

An evaluative approach to themselves and others

Persistent goal-directed behavior

II. The Affective Domain

Large accumulation of information about emotions that has not been brought to awareness

Unusual sensitivity to the expectations and feelings of others

Keen sense of humor—may be gentle or hostile

Heightened self-awareness, accompanied by feelings of being "different"

Idealism and a sense of justice that appear at an early age

Earlier development of an inner locus of control and satisfaction

Advanced levels of moral judgment

High expectations of self and others, which often lead to high levels of frustration with self, others, and situations

Unusual emotional depth and intensity

Sensitivity to inconsistency between ideals and behavior

III. The Physical Domain

Unusual discrepancy between physical and intellectual development

Low tolerance for the lag between their standards and their physical capacity

Cartesian split—can include neglect of physical well-being and avoidance of physical activity

IV. The Intuitive Domain

Early involvement and concern for intuitive knowing, psychic and metaphysical ideas and phenomena

Open to experiences in this area; will experiment with psychic and metaphysical phenomena

Creativity apparent in all areas of endeavor

Acceptance and expression of a high level of intuitive ability, especially with the highly gifted

V. The Societal Domain

Strongly motivated by self-actualization needs

Advanced cognitive and affective capacity for conceptualizing and solving societal problems

Source: From *Growing Up Gifted* (2nd ed., pp. 195, 201, 202, 208, 211) by B. Clark, 1983, Columbus, OH: Merrill. Reprinted by permission.

EXAMINE YOUR BELIEFS

These questions allow you to look at your beliefs regarding gifted and talented children. Before each statement place the number that most closely describes your reaction to the notion it presents. Be as open as you can.

1—I strongly agree 4—I disagree
2—I agree 5—I strongly disagree
3—I have no opinion

_____ 1. The term *gifted* can mean different things to different people and often causes much confusion and miscommunication.

_____ 2. Intelligence can be developed and must be nurtured if giftedness is to occur.

_____ 3. We seldom find very highly gifted children or children we could call geniuses; therefore, we know comparatively little about them.

_____ 4. Thinking of, or speaking of, gifted children as superior people is inaccurate and misleading.

_____ 5. Gifted children, although interested in many things, usually are not gifted in everything.

_____ 6. Difficulty conforming to group tasks is often the result of the unusually varied interests and curiosity of a gifted child.

_____ 7. Because gifted children have the ability to think in diverse ways, teachers often see them as challenging their authority, disrespectful, and disruptive.

_____ 8. Some gifted children have been found to use their high level of verbal skill to avoid difficult thinking tasks.

_____ 9. The demand for products or meeting of deadlines can inhibit the development of a gifted child's ability to integrate new ideas.

_____ 10. Work that is too easy or boring frustrates a gifted child just as work that is too difficult frustrates an average learner.

_____ 11. Most gifted children in our present school system are underachievers.

_____ 12. Commonly used sequences of learning are often inappropriate and can be damaging to gifted learners.

_____ 13. Gifted children often expect others to live up to standards they have set for themselves, with resulting problems in interpersonal relations.

_____ 14. The ability of gifted learners to generalize, synthesize, solve problems, and engage in abstract thinking most commonly differentiates gifted from average learners. Therefore, programs for gifted children should stress utilization of these abilities.

_____ 15. The persistent goal-directed behavior of gifted children can result in others perceiving them as stubborn, willful, and uncooperative.

_____ 16. If not challenged, gifted children can waste their ability and become mediocre, average learners.

_____ 17. Gifted children often express their idealism and sense of justice at a very early age.

_____ 18. Not all gifted children show creativity, leadership, or physical expertise.

_____ 19. People who work with, study, and try to understand gifted children have more success educating the gifted than those who have limited

If not challenged, gifted children can waste their ability and become mediocre, average learners.

contact and have not educated themselves as to the unique needs of these children.

_____ 20. I would be pleased to be considered gifted, and I enjoy people who are.

The questionnaire you have just completed presents opinions of gifted children that are supportive to their educational growth. The more "I strongly agree" (1) answers you were able to give, the more closely your opinions match those of individuals who have devoted their energy to understanding gifted children.

Source: Adapted from *Growing Up Gifted*, (2nd ed., pp. 4–5) by B. Clark, 1983, Columbus, OH: Merrill. Reprinted by permission.

An analysis of those characteristics can provide us with a model for organizing educational programs. Programs that relate clearly to the differentiating characteristics of this population can most effectively meet the educational needs and nurture the high-level abilities of gifted pupils. While all students have unique needs, some generalizations about needs that result from highly developed intelligence can be made. (Clark, 1983, p. 194)

Characteristics that relate to curriculum frequently focus on learning and intellectual skills. According to Gallagher (1981), gifted children possess a rich supply of the following abilities:

1. the ability to relate one idea to another
2. the ability to make sound judgments
3. the ability to see the operation of larger systems of knowledge than are seen by the ordinary citizen
4. the ability to acquire and manipulate symbol systems

Although the most common symbol system is language, there are numerous other symbol systems, such as scientific notation, music and dance notation, mathematics, and engineering symbols. These systems can be incorporated into creative endeavors as well as academic and intellectual areas. We must remember that the characteristics presented here are generalizations about the population of gifted and talented children, not the description of any single individual. We may meet a gifted child who does not neatly match these characteristics. It may be the child's giftedness that makes him unique, and this uniqueness may defy any attempt to categorize it into a neat, well-ordered compartment. We must also realize that many lists of gifted characteristics portray gifted children as having only virtues and no flaws (Gallagher, 1975b). However, the very attributes by which we identify gifted children can cause some problems. High verbal ability, for example, may prompt gifted children to talk themselves out of troublesome situations or to dominate class discussions. High curiosity may give them the appearance of being aggressive or just snoopy, as they pursue anything that comes to their attention. The two lists presented in Table 11.2 describe both positive and not-so-positive aspects of intellectual giftedness. List A describes the positive side; List B identifies some of the problems that may occur as a result of these positive traits. The lists were developed with the assistance of graduate students at Ohio State University.

Awareness of individual differences is also important in understanding gifted students. Like other children, gifted children show both **interindividual** and **intraindividual** differences. For example, if three children were given the same reading achievement test and each obtained a different score, we could speak of interindividual differences in reading achievement. Or a child who obtains a high reading achievement score may obtain a much lower score on an arithmetic achievement test. That child has an intraindividual difference across the two areas of performance.

A graph of any child's abilities would reveal some high points and some lower points; scores would not be the same across all of the dimensions measured. However,

TABLE 11.2
Two sides to the behavior of gifted and talented students.

List A	List B
1. Expresses ideas and feelings well	1. May be glib, making fluent statements based on little or no knowledge or understanding
2. Can move at a rapid pace	
3. Works conscientiously	
4. Wants to learn, explore, and seek more information	2. May dominate discussions
5. Develops broad knowledge and an extensive store of vicarious experiences.	3. May be impatient to proceed to next level or task
	4. May be considered nosey
6. Is sensitive to the feelings and rights of others	5. May choose reading at the expense of active participation in social, creative, or physical activities
7. Makes steady progress	
8. Makes original and stimulating contributions to discussions	6. May struggle against rules, regulations, and standardized procedures
9. Sees relationships easily	7. May lead discussions "off the track"
10. Learns material quickly	8. May be frustrated by the apparent absence of logic in activities and daily events
11. Is able to use reading skills to obtain new information	
12. Contributes to enjoyment of life for self and others	9. May become bored by repetitions
	10. May use humor to manipulate
13. Completes assigned tasks	11. May resist a schedule based on time rather than task
14. Requires little drill for learning	12. May lose interest quickly

the gifted child's pattern of performance may be well above the average for that grade and/or age (see Figure 11.1).

Creativity

Creativity has been called "the highest expression of giftedness" (Clark, 1983, p. 30). There is, however, no universally accepted definition of creativity. The many possible approaches to creativity reflect the complex nature of the concept. Because it is one of the more intriguing aspects of human behavior, creativity has been studied from several points of view. Gowan (1972) lists five different approaches to an understanding of creativity: (1) cognitive, rational, and problem-solving aspects; (2) personality traits, family, and environmental origins; (3) mental health, psychological openness, and self-actualization; (4) a Freudian view; and (5) existential, psychedelic, and irrational aspects. In addition, we can add the behavior analysis approach to creativity (Glover & Gary, 1976; Goetz, 1982; Goetz & Baer, 1973; Vargas & Moxley, 1979) and Clark's (1983) integrated model, which represents a holistic view of creativity.

Guilford, in his much-cited work *Traits of Creativity* (1959), describes four dimensions of creative behavior.

1. *Fluency.* Many words, associations, phrases and/or sentences, and ideas are produced.
2. *Flexibility.* A wide variety of ideas, unusual ideas, and alternative solutions are offered.
3. *Originality.* Low probability, unique words and responses are used.
4. *Elaboration.* The ability to provide details is evidenced.

Another type of creativity is sensitivity, the awareness that a problem exists (Carin & Sund, 1978). And motivation and the willingness to work and persevere are personality traits of many creative people. Thus, we could consider creative children as those who can identify problems, come up with a wide variety of ideas and possible solutions (some of them original), examine those ideas, fill out the most likely one(s) with the necessary details, and then follow through on the most promising.

To be creative, a child must have some knowledge, examine it in a variety of ways, critically analyze the outcomes, and be able to communicate her ideas (Keating,

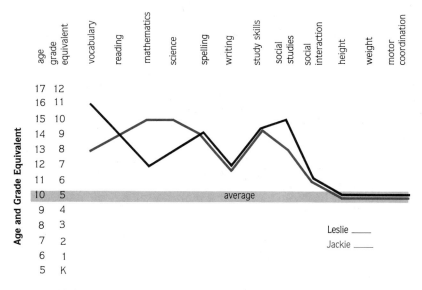

FIGURE 11.1
Profiles of two gifted 10-year-olds. Leslie and Jackie are both 10 years old and are in the fifth grade. For their age and grade placement, they are performing well above what might be expected. Only in social interactions, height, weight, and physical coordination are the two students similar to their average 10-year-old peers.

The overall abilities of Leslie and Jackie are similar. Leslie, however, performs higher in vocabulary and social studies than Jackie does, and Jackie shows higher performance in science and mathematics than Leslie. These are interindividual differences. Each student also has intraindividual differences in scores. For example, Leslie has the vocabulary of an eleventh grader, but scores only at a seventh grade equivalent in mathematics. And Jackie earned grade equivalents of tenth grade in science and mathematics and seventh grade in writing.

1980). There are numerous ways to communicate—such as through literature, mathematics, music, poetry, and dance—but the communication skills must be adequate for the idea.

IDENTIFICATION

In recent years many educators of gifted and talented children have been critical of the intelligence testing movement, especially because it has led to a one-dimensional

Creativity can be expressed in many ways.

concept of giftedness that emphasizes intellectual performance exclusively. However, it is important to remember that Binet and Simon made a significant contribution to the education of gifted children by developing the first instrument that could predict school success. A standardized objective measure, however crude, makes it possible to identify some children with above-average academic potential. Intelligence tests offered the first means of locating bright children, and plans for meeting their special needs could then be developed.

The use of the IQ as the sole criterion for giftedness has been out of favor with some professionals for many years (Witty, 1940). After Terman's (1925) first report, educators and psychologists raised serious doubts about the ability of an IQ test taken during childhood to predict success in adult life. Far more than IQ is involved in gifted performance. Furthermore, intelligence tests do not always identify gifted persons in all socioeconomic and culturally diverse groups. IQ measures tend to identify giftedness more readily in middle- and upper-middle-class, urban, white populations. During the 1960s it was recognized that the usual intelligence measures are inappropriate for any child who is not representative of the normative population (Maker, 1977; Tor rance, 1977).

Measures of intelligence may be a part of the identification process, but no single index or procedure can identify all gifted and talented children. Identification usually involves a combination of procedures, including

- ☐ intelligence scores
- ☐ creativity measures
- ☐ achievement measures
- ☐ teacher nomination
- ☐ parent nomination
- ☐ self-nomination
- ☐ peer nomination

The measures and procedures used for identification should be determined by the definition of giftedness developed for each program. Knowing what to look for helps to determine where to look and how to recognize it. Test instruments, checklists, observation forms, and other approaches are ultimately tied to the definition of giftedness being used by a given program (Frazier, 1980; Hagen, 1980).

Stephens and Wolf (1978) suggest that identification of gifted students should be linked directly to the goals of the program in which they will be placed. Their approach involves five steps.

1. Establish program goals.
2. Develop objectives.
3. Specify requisite student characteristics.
4. Locate students.
5. Assign students.

Linking identification to program goals helps increase the chances of a good student-to-program match. Students can be assigned to special programs that have objectives consistent with their individual interests and abilities. However, with this approach giftedness is limited to those who meet the program's goals; other gifted and talented children may not be identified and adequately served.

One alternative to identification by goals is to develop a comprehensive definition of giftedness and try to identify all the children who are gifted and talented. The school would then try to offer a complete and comprehensive program, meeting the needs of all of the children identified. Identification by goals does allow for systematic program growth: one set of goals and its respective program can be developed, then another, then another (Swassing, 1985). But until all program goals are developed, some children will go unidentified and unserved. Comprehensive identification, on the other hand, locates *all* children who show actual or potential special abilities or talents and then relies on the school, given whatever resources are available, to develop a comprehensive program serving all of the identified gifted and talented students.

In any case identification procedures should not be used to exclude youngsters from programs for the gifted and talented. That is, any one measure may identify some number of children to be placed in a certain program, but it should not be used to keep everyone else out. A second measure, a third, and so on should be used to include other children in special programs. School districts that provide only one or two programs may not be providing all the children in the system with the appropriate educational experiences. Gifted and talented students who do not have the specific requisite characteristics will be kept from appropriate educational opportunities, a situation that is inconsistent with the concept of equal educational opportunities for all children. For this reason program planners need to know about their entire school population before they establish hard and fast program goals.

EDUCATIONAL APPROACHES

The overall goal of educational programs for gifted and talented students should be the fullest possible development of every child's actual and potential abilities. In the broadest terms the goals of education for these youngsters are no different from the goals of education for all children. Feelings of self-worth, self-sufficiency, civic responsibility, and vocational and avocational competence are important for everyone. However, there are also some specific educational outcomes that are especially desirable for gifted and talented students.

Gallagher (1981) has classified the educational objectives of programs for gifted students into two areas: (1) mastering the knowledge structure of disciplines and (2) heuristic skills. Knowledge structures include both basic principles and systems of knowledge; heuristic skills include problem solving, creativity, and use of the scientific method. In other words, gifted students need both content knowledge and the abilities to use and develop that knowledge effectively.

Feldhusen and Sokol (1982) refer to the cognitive, affective, and generative needs of gifted students. They believe important cognitive skills for gifted students include basic thinking skills, a broad store of knowledge, disciplined and in-depth inquiry, methods of research and analysis, and organizational theories and ideas. In affective terms gifted students need stimulation through association with peers, interaction with adult models, a strong self-concept, social learning skills, and acceptance of their own abilities. Gifted students also need certain generative characteristics, including an acceptance of their roles as producers of knowledge and creative products, motivation and habits of inquiry and research, creative activity, early and continuous experience in research, and independence in investigation.

Of course, these cognitive and affective skills are appropriate for all students to some degree. The generative skills, however, emphasize the special roles that individuals with gifts and talents can play. Not only are gifted and talented students consumers of artistic, scientific, and creative products; they are potential creators of these products, which enrich the lives of all of us (Renzulli, 1977). Generative skills require high levels of motivation and may lead to life-styles that differ markedly from those of most other people. A glacier geologist may spend months at a time studying ice formations in remote Arctic areas; a cultural anthropologist may spend years living among the inhabitants of remote islands; a concert pianist may spend most of his waking hours practicing.

There are some who say that the skills of reading, writing, and arithmetic need not be taught, that gifted youngsters will learn them when they need them. In fact, however, no one will be called on to use these skills more than gifted children, so it is essential that they master the basic tool skills. The issue is determining the appropriate time and emphasis. Not all gifted children should be taught the same skills at the same time. After all, some gifted youngsters enter school with many basic skills. It is unreasonable to expect them to review that learning for 3 or 4 or more years. Then again, some gifted children enter school with few, if any, of the basic skills. For these children, teaching the basic skills is most important. Through direct assessment, teachers can determine which skills to teach to which students. Furthermore, basic skills need to be taught—not over and over, but until mastered. For some youngsters this means a 30-second lesson to explain the concept or principle. For other children it means a sequenced set of instructional activities to develop and practice a particular skill.

For gifted and talented students the three Rs alone do not comprise the basics. A fourth R, research skills, should also be systematically taught as part of the curriculum. The skills of systematic investigation are fundamental abilities that gifted students use throughout a lifetime of learning. These skills include use of references, use of the library, information (data) gathering, and reporting findings in a variety of ways. These skills may ultimately be used in diverse settings, such as law and medical libraries, museums, chemical and electrical laboratories, theatrical archives, and national parks.

Curriculum Organization—Enrichment and Acceleration

The processes of identification and goal setting mean little if the children in programs for the gifted do not receive unique learning opportunities. These experiences can be considered differentiated education. Curricula that incorporate higher cognitive concepts should be presented by specifically prepared teachers, using strategies that accommodate the learning styles of the students. Group arrangements may include special classes, honors classes, seminars, resource rooms, and other flexible approaches to grouping and scheduling. Two widely used approaches to educational programming for gifted students are enrichment and acceleration.

Enrichment experiences are those that let youngsters investigate topics of interest in much greater detail than is ordinarily possible with the standard school curriculum. Topics of investigation may be based on the ongoing activities of the classroom but may permit students to go beyond the limits of the day-to-day instructional offerings.

Enrichment is not a do-your-own-thing approach with no structure or guidance. Children involved in enrichment experiences should not be released to do a random, haphazard (and thus inefficient) project. A basic framework that defines limits and sets outcomes is necessary. Projects should have purpose, direction, and specified outcomes. A teacher should provide guidance where necessary—and to the degree that is necessary—to keep the youngsters efficient (Renzulli, 1977).

Several administrative or placement options may be followed to implement enrichment programs.

☐ special experiences within the regular classroom
☐ special groupings in the regular classroom
☐ special classes
☐ resource rooms

Enrichment opportunities may be offered through a variety of special activities, such as

☐ field trips and special camps
☐ hobby clubs
☐ extra-school programs
☐ summer camps and programs
☐ guest instructors
☐ mentorships

Some gifted students participate in competitions in which problem-solving skills, creativity, and/or academic excellence are evaluated. See page 442 for a description of four such programs.

There is little evidence yet to suggest which, if any, of the alternatives is best. The decision should be based on the resources and needs of the local school, the community, and the children involved.

Acceleration means providing a child with learning experiences that are usually given to older children; that is, speeding up the usual presentation of content without modifying that content or method of presentation. Approaches to acceleration include

☐ early admission to school
☐ grade skipping
☐ concurrent enrollment in both high school and college
☐ advanced placement tests
☐ early admission to college
☐ content acceleration (giving youngsters the opportunity to move through a particular curricular sequence at their own rates)

Enrichment activities, such as this plant propagation project, enable gifted students to investigate topics in greater detail than is possible in the standard curriculum.

One noted educator of gifted children, Sidney Pressey, advocated acceleration because it allows children to reduce the time spent in training and gives more years of productivity. In this way both society and the individual benefit (Pressey, 1962). Research suggests that wisely practiced acceleration does not cause the problems of social and emotional adjustment often attributed to it (Gallagher, 1975a). Instead,

> it improves the motivation, confidence and scholarship of gifted students. Second, it prevents the development of habits of mental laziness. Third, it allows for earlier completion of professional training, and fourth, it reduces the total cost of education particularly at the collegiate level for parents and for the students themselves. (Van Tassel–Baska, 1986, p. 184)

The study of mathematically precocious youth (Stanley, Keating, & Fox, 1974) at Johns Hopkins University has demonstrated the effectiveness of acceleration in mathematics. The project identified seventh and eighth grade students with exceptional ability in mathematical reasoning and accelerated their mathematics experiences. Some even took college courses during the first or second years in high school.

COMPETITIONS FOR GIFTED AND TALENTED STUDENTS

Programs in which students or teams of students from different schools compete with one another on academic, problem-solving, or creative tasks have become increasingly popular in recent years. For some gifted students these competitions provide an enjoyable and productive enrichment experience. Following are descriptions of four competitions held throughout the country.

ACADEMIC COMPETITIONS

Contact: National Academic Association
P.O. Box 14798
Columbus, OH 43214
(614) 846–7101

Synopsis: Academic competitions involve high school students and operate on county, state, and national levels. Typically, teams are formed on a try-out basis, and four members compete in each match or tournament. Quick recall of academic facts is needed to answer questions in categories such as mathematics, literature, history, fine arts, sciences, government, and quotations. The program seeks to recognize academic excellence, encourage participation, and promote sportsmanship.

COMMISSION ON PRESIDENTIAL SCHOLARS

Contact: White House Commission on Presidential Scholars
Office of Elementary and Secondary Education
U.S. Department of Education
400 Maryland Avenue, SW
Washington, DC 20202
(202) 245–8720

Synopsis: After initial screening by the Educational Testing Service on the basis of college entrance examination scores, the commission evaluates each candidate on additional criteria, including participation in community activities and leadership ability. Two scholars are selected from each state, recognized with a monetary award of $1000 from the National Endowment for the Arts, and given the opportunity to participate in other activities.

FUTURE PROBLEM SOLVING PROGRAM

Contact: St. Andrews College
Laurinburg, NC 28352
(919) 276–8361

Synopsis: The Future Problem Solving Program (FPSP) involves teams of four students and is open to students in Grades 4 through 12. During the year the teams work with a coach on three practice problems. The completed problems are mailed to evaluators who critique the solutions and offer suggestions. Teams with exceptional solutions are invited to participate in FPSP bowls each spring. The program also offers other options, which include community problem solving, scenario-writing competitions, and a noncompetitive primary division. Several informational and supportive publications are available, and an international FPSP conference is held annually.

ODYSSEY OF THE MIND

Contact: OM Association, Inc.
P. O. Box 27
Glassboro, NJ 08028
(609) 881–1603

Synoposis: Formerly Olympics of the Mind, the OM program is open to students from the primary level through college and seeks to promote problem-solving, brainstorming, and creative skills. During the fall, students are involved in a practice period. Seven students are later chosen to be on a team, and each team is given a problem. The problems are organized according to subject matter and include history, science, language, computer science/technology, and balsa wood construction. The competitions, which involve the prepared problems and also a spontaneous task, are held on local, regional, state, and international levels.

Neither enrichment nor acceleration will have particular merit if the experiences provided are not appropriate for the gifted and talented children served in the program. Clark (1983) has suggested attending to the following dimensions when differentiating curriculum for gifted and talented students.

☐ accelerated or advanced content
☐ more complex understanding of generalizations, principles, theories, and the structure of the content area
☐ abstract concepts and thought processes or skills
☐ level and type of resources used to obtain information, acquire skills, and develop products
☐ appropriation of longer/shorter time span for learning
☐ generating new information and/or products
☐ transfer of learning to new/different disciplines, and situations.
☐ development of personal growth and sophistication in attitudes, appreciations, feelings, intuition
☐ independence of thought and study (p. 214)

Currently, 17 states require IEPs and due process procedures for gifted students (Zirkel & Stevens, 1986). The prescriptive elements of an IEP allow considerable planning flexibility based on the assessed needs of each student. Renzulli and Smith (1979) have proposed a detailed model for developing IEPs for gifted and talented students; the model is consistent with Renzulli's (1977) definition of giftedness and incorporates ability, creativity, and task commitment.

Talent Development

The contributions and skill levels of our most talented scientists, artists, musicians, athletes, and political leaders receive much attention. Unfortunately, the interest in their accomplishments far exceeds the research available to guide us in encouraging and nurturing exceptional talent in young people. Two important investigations into the development of highly skilled persons do, however, offer some guidance, and the findings of both studies are clear and consistent. Pressey (1955) studied the careers of musicians, scientists, and Olympic swimmers. He identified five common factors in the backgrounds of his subjects.

1. Excellent early opportunities for the ability to develop and encouragement from family and friends.
2. Superior early and continuing individual guidance and instruction
3. The opportunity frequently and continually to practice and extend their special ability and to progress as they were able.
4. Close association with others in the field, which greatly fostered the abilities of all concerned.
5. Many opportunities for real accomplishment, within their possibilities but of increasing challenge; the precocious musician or athlete has had the stimulation of many and increasingly strong success experiences—and his world acclaimed these successes. (p. 124)

Recently, Bloom (1985) studied the development of 120 highly talented individuals in three areas: athletic/psychomotor skills (Olympic swimmers and world class professional tennis players), aesthetic/musical/artistic talent (concert pianists and sculptors), and cognitive/intellectual achievement (mathematicians and research neurologists). The study revealed three phases of talent development. The first phase emphasized playful exploration and "messing around," which enticed the learner into further involvement. Instruction was informal, with high rates of personal interaction and reinforcement of the learner's enjoyment of the activity. The second phase emphasized the acquisition of skills and attention to detail. Practice became more rigorous, with frequent evaluations based on precision and technique. In the third phase of talent development, a commitment to excellence was made. The learner was almost always taught by a highly skilled mentor who held high expectations for performance. Practice and instruction were extremely time-consuming and demanded a considerable sacrifice. Rewards were infrequent but powerful, such as winning contests, public acclaim, and the acknowledgment of peers.

Teaching–Learning Models

Several teaching-learning models (Renzulli, 1986) typically are used to guide the development of differentiated education for gifted and talented students. We will describe five of those models. A given program may be based on any one of these approaches or a combination of two or more.

These students are using mathematical modeling to estimate the potential of solar energy.

Bloom's Taxonomy of Educational Objectives

Bloom and others (1956) developed the *Taxonomy of Educational Objectives: Cognitive Domain* to provide a hierarchy for writing and classifying learning objectives for testing purposes. Following are the six levels of objectives within the cognitive domain, along with examples of items that might be used to test each level.

1. Knowledge:
   "Name the continents."
   "Distinguish between a cross-section and a longitudinal section."
   "Place these seven objects in their proper categories."
   "Name the systems of the human body."
2. Comprehension:
   "Repeat the story."
   "Tell me in your own words."
3. Application:
   "How could you measure this room with 15th-century measuring devices?"
   "Write a short story."
4. Analysis:
   "What are the parts of this problem?"
   "How do the cardiovascular and lymphatic systems relate to each other?"
5. Synthesis:
   "What are some solutions to this problem?"
   "Prepare an article to explain the issues to your readers."
6. Evaluation:
   "Will this new product meet the requirements established for judging its effectiveness?"
   "Tell us about the qualities of this poem that may make it a classic."

Bloom's emphasis on a range of learning beyond the reiteration of facts and figures has been the basis of the taxonomy's use in enrichment programs. For example, the taxonomy has been used effectively in developing learning centers. Some activities in a learning center are appropriate and required for all children in a class, and others are intended for selected students only. Children with varying interests and abilities are asked to do individually specified tasks. In some instances the tasks vary according to those interests and abilities. In other instances gifted students are asked to do only those tasks at the higher levels of the taxonomy.

A classroom learning center on outer space travel might include activities from all six levels of the taxonomy. All children might be required to read the directions and a preliminary information sheet and to view a slide-tape presentation. Some students might then be asked to answer a series of posttest questions (knowledge level). Others might be asked to write a newspaper article (synthesis). Still others might be required to read about the Bernoulli principle (regarding objects moving through fluids) and to demonstrate that principle in an experiment (analysis).

The next activity in the learning center might be to examine human energy and nutritional requirements in space. Again, all students would receive the preliminary information, in this case via a NASA video cassette. Some students might be asked to develop a display of the basic food groups (comprehension). Some might design a new food capsule for prolonged space exploration (synthesis). Still other students might design meals based on color, texture, and nutritional requirements (evaluation). Using the taxonomy allows a teacher to provide one set of materials but organize instruction at various levels with tasks appropriate for the differing ability levels of students in the class.

Guilford's Structure of Intellect Model

The Structure of Intellect (SOI) is a three-dimensional model (Guilford, 1956). The three major dimensions of the SOI model are content, operations, and products. In other words, there is some content or material upon which an individual performs an operation; the outcome of that operation is a product. Guilford uses this model (see Figure 11.2) to describe human intelligence. He further identifies four subcategories of content, five subcategories of operations, and six subcategories of products. Thus, according to Guilford's model, a given task can be described as the intersection of three points on the model—for instance, evaluating a semantic relationship, as in comparing.

See examples of activities to encourage creativity, drawn from the University of Illinois Preschool Gifted Program, and described on pages 434–35.

The SOI model has had its greatest impact on programs to identify and nurture creativity in children (Karnes, Shwedel, & Williams, 1983; Khatena, 1976). However, diagnostic-prescriptive instructional activities have also been developed from the model (Gurcsick, 1981; Meeker, 1969). In addition, Navarre (1983) has used the SOI model to identify careers that capitalize on an individual's strongest intellectual abilities, as described by the model. For example, a person with exemplary skills in cognition of figural units might take special advantage of those talents in photography or graphic design. Divergent production of figural units, on the other hand, emphasizes creativity with objects and shapes, which is useful for printing and layout illustrators, designers, and architects.

Williams's Cognitive-Affective Model

The cognitive-affective model of Williams (1970) combines (1) curriculum or subject matter, (2) pupil behaviors, both cognitive and affective, and (3) teaching strategies into a comprehensive approach to teaching and learning. The affective domain has been built into the model as as integral instructional sphere.

Williams (1970) gives several examples of how this model can be used for instruction. To encourage "original thinking and imagination" in social studies through "provocative questions and visualization skills," children were asked to list everything they might see if they flew through the air on a kite string. In addition, they were asked to identify ways to return to the ground (p. 23). In another example designed to encourage "fluent and original thinking" in language arts through an "organized random search and creative writing skill," the children took a field trip to a dairy and then were asked to make a treasure chest of all the descriptive phrases that might be used to refer to their trip. Later they were to write a story using those phrases (p. 270).

Products

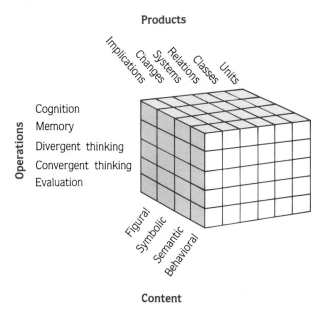

Implications
Changes
Systems
Relations
Classes
Units

Operations

Cognition
Memory
Divergent thinking
Convergent thinking
Evaluation

Figural
Symbolic
Semantic
Behavioral

Content

FIGURE 11.2

Guilford's Structure of Intellect Model.

Source: From *The Nature of Human Intelligence*, by J. P. Guilford, 1967, New York: McGraw-Hill. Reprinted by permission.

Renzulli's Enrichment Triad Model

Renzulli (1977, 1982) developed the Enrichment Triad Model (ETM) to guide the planning of enrichment activities for gifted and talented children. It is based on three levels, or types, of enrichment. General exploratory activities (Type I) are those that let students survey a variety of topics to gain ideas for further study. Students are introduced to a subject and its components, in search of areas of interest. Group training activities (Type II) involve students in exercises designed to provide the skills, knowledge, and attitudes necessary for future in-depth study; that is, to learn how to learn within the content area of interest. Type III enrichment activities consist of individual and small-group investigations of real problems. Students are to assume the posture of a real investigator in the process of adding to the knowledge base in the selected area of interest. It is considered important that, as true investigators, students address real problems—those that are not imposed by the teacher but that have meaning to the children in light of the subject matter and the circumstances around which the problems have been defined. The teacher should explain to the students, however, that as fledgling investigators they may not be at the forefront of the given area of study, although, as Renzulli (1977) points out, at times they may actually make discoveries that have far-reaching impacts.

    Reis and Cellerino (1983), teachers of gifted students, use a revolving-door identification model (Renzulli, Reis, & Smith, 1981) that allows all children in their

Independent projects can develop original thinking and insight.

resource room program to participate in Type I and Type II enrichment activities. Only students who show serious interest in a specific topic evolve into Type III investigations. Students are never compelled to begin Type III investigations; it is their option.

When a student does indicate a particular area of interest, the teacher must determine whether the student's interest is serious enough to warrant launching an in-depth investigation or whether it is only a temporary, superficial interest. Reis and Cellerino (1983) conducted an interview with Michael, a second grade student in their gifted program who, as a result of Type I and Type II activities, expressed a strong interest in Tchaikovsky, the composer. The following questions were asked:

1. Michael, will you tell me a little about Tchaikovsky and how you became interested in knowing more about him?
2. Have you read any books about him and his music?
3. How long have you been interested in studying about Tchaikovsky?
4. Do you like looking in different books to find information?
5. Do you have any ideas about what you would like to do with the information you find? (p. 137)

Michael's responses during the interview showed his interest in Tchaikovsky to be genuine. After specifying objectives for his research, Michael's teachers helped him set up a management plan for his investigation. Potential sources of information were identified and a timeline developed. Then Michael was encouraged to come up with a specific idea for a product of his investigation and to consider an audience for his product. Michael's product, a children's book of 30 typed pages and an audio-taped version that plays selections of Tchaikovsky's music, is now part of both his school's and his local public library's collection. On the first page of his book, Michael wrote,

> Some of you may wonder why a second grader would want to write a book about Tchaikovsky. People get interested in different things for different reasons. For example, I got interested in Tchaikovsky because I like his music. I play the piano and have a whole book of his music. At Christmas I saw the ballet of the Nutcracker Suite. His music can be both cheerful and sad at the same time. I wondered how music can be both happy and sad at the same time so I decided to learn about Tchaikovsky's life.
>
> I wondered if when he was sad he wrote sad music, and if when he was happy he wrote happy music. In this book you will get to know a little bit more about Tchaikovsky, how he lived and about the music he wrote. (Reis & Cellerino, 1983, p. 139).

Maker's Integrated Curriculum Model

Maker (1982) analyzed the major contributions of the various teaching-learning models and integrated what she considered the best components of each. Maker's model involves a four-dimensional approach to curriculum modification for gifted and talented students: content, process, product, and environment. To provide enrichment, a teacher can modify any one or more of the four dimensions.

Content modifications emphasize complex, abstract, and varied organization of the ideas, concepts, and facts presented. Process modifications address the method of presenting the material, emphasizing the higher levels of thinking. Product modifications are aimed at what might be expected of gifted and talented children. The product varies according to the process used to arrive at the product and the audience for whom it is intended. Environmental modifications focus on the conditions under which learning is to take place, the role of the teacher in the activities, and individual students' learning styles. The teacher as facilitator, complex activities, and open, independent learning environments are emphasized. Maker's integrated model incorporates many variables into a comprehensive approach to educational programming for gifted and talented students.

In science, for example, a lesson for the entire class might involve a basic understanding of rain forests, their levels, flora, and fauna. Content modification for the gifted students might encourage them to study the interactions of plants and animals and symbiosis and to draw parallels between plant, animal, and human behavior in a rain forest environment. The learning process might be independent study or inquiry lessons. The products would be real. They might include a slide-tape presentation for the school and/or local library, a newspaper account, a videotaped report, or a presentation to the entire science class. The final modification would be in the learning environment. It must be open, so the students are free to divert from usual procedures. The teacher must be willing to remain in the background, available when needed, ready to encourage and praise an insight, but seldom directive.

Teachers of the Gifted

No instructional theory or approach is more important than the teacher who implements it. One of the first questions asked is, Does the teacher have to be gifted in order to teach gifted children effectively? The answer is Not necessarily—in the sense of giftedness used in this chapter. All teachers should be gifted, regardless of whom they teach. And teachers should be gifted in different ways to teach different children. Nonetheless, teachers of gifted children do need to have some particular qualities.

1. Be willing to accept unusual and diverse questions, answers, and projects.
2. Be intellectually curious.
3. Be systematic and businesslike.
4. Have a variety of interests.
5. Appreciate achievement (Bishop, 1968).
6. Be well prepared in instructional techniques.
7. Be well prepared in content area.
8. Want to teach gifted students (Gallagher, 1975b).
9. Be aware that the teacher may not know as much about some specific topics as the children do, and be comfortable with that situation.

CURRENT ISSUES/FUTURE TRENDS

Many questions remain in the education of gifted and talented children. We need much research in a variety of areas, including the nature of intelligence, learning, creativity, the roles of parents and families, cultural diversity, sex roles, and the impact of high technology on the education and lives of gifted and talented people. An examination of future trends suggested by *Megatrends* (Naisbitt, 1982) provides much food for thought. The new society sketched by Naisbitt has significant implications for education in general and several points have special meaning for gifted and talented children.

We are rapidly moving from an industrial society to an information-processing, high-technology society. We can no longer remain isolated and self-sufficient as individuals or as a nation. Long-range social goals and instantaneous information based on informal human networks rather than complex political systems are an aspect of social change, personally and politically. Clearly, as Naisbitt points out, the future will call for the best human resources available.

In this vein we must capitalize on the resources found in special populations—women, people who are handicapped, individuals from culturally diverse groups, and those not achieving up to their potential. The first major issue affecting these groups is the ability of educational planners to identify the gifted and talented individuals among them. The usual testing procedures are often inappropriate or incomplete (Bruch, 1975; Callahan, 1979; Fox, 1977; Maker, 1977). The instruments commonly

Teachers of the gifted must be able to share their students' enthusiasm for learning.

used (intelligence and achievement tests) seem to penalize anyone who is not like the group that was used to develop the tests' norms. We say that a test or instrument is culturally biased if different groups have different opportunities to learn the skills it measures. For example, do boys and girls have the same opportunities to learn vocabulary? Do children who are handicapped have the same opportunities to engage in sequential motor skills or experiences as do nonhandicapped children? If the opportunities are not the same, the test is biased and individuals from such special populations may be at a disadvantage when taking the test. The question of cultural bias in commonly used intelligence tests has led to much study. Although the evidence of bias is not as substantial as was first expected (Sattler, 1982), the fact remains that for a given child the effects of any bias may be enough to preclude that child from being considered for a gifted and talented program.

Callahan (1979) has summarized the literature on gifted and talented women. In comparisons of gifted males and females, the literature is generally inconclusive except in mathematics, where a greater proportion of males are identified as gifted. Cultural barriers, test and social biases, organizational reward systems, sex-role stereotyping, and conflicts between career and marriage and family all continue as external impediments to the advancement of gifted and talented women (Kerr, 1985). In reviewing the topic of gifted women, Silverman (1986) points out that the history of genius and women's roles have been contradictory (eminent contributions cannot be made from a subservient status) and that identification procedures reflect masculine (product oriented) versus feminine (development oriented) concepts of giftedness. Silverman (1986) presents recommendations for improving the special education of gifted girls.

☐ Hold high expectations for girls.
☐ Believe in their logical and mathematical abilities.
☐ Expose both boys and girls to female role models.
☐ Actively recruit girls for advanced placement math and science classes.
☐ Encourage and deal with girls' multiple interests and talents.
☐ Use nonsexist texts, language, and communication.
☐ Form support groups for girls.
☐ Encourage independence.

Maker (1977) raises a particularly salient point about looking for giftedness among handicapped students, challenging the seeming dichotomy between the concepts of disability and giftedness. When all handicapped children are viewed as below average, those who are also gifted are cast into a stereotype that disavows their true abilities. A loss of mobility, for example, does not imply reduced intellectual functioning, nor does deafness reduce one's artistic abilities. Recognition of intraindividual differences is important, emphasizing skills rather than deficits. Whitmore and Maker (1985) have identified four obstacles to the identification of gifted handicapped students: stereotypic expectations for disabled persons that restrict the ability to recognize giftedness, developmental delays in specific abilities, incomplete information about these children, and no opportunities for them to display their intellectual abilities or special talents. Maker (1977) suggests using checklists and Meeker's (1969) approaches to testing for the identification of the gifted handicapped.

We have known for some time that there are gifted and talented persons among culturally diverse groups (Frierson, 1965; Torrance, 1977; Witty & Jenkins, 1934). But until recent years the identification and development of those individuals received little attention. Work in this important area is now increasing dramatically (Baldwin, Gear, & Lucita, 1978; Malone, 1978; Torrance, 1977). Baldwin (1978) has listed some descriptors of culturally diverse gifted children.

1. Depend on controls from their environment rather than control from "within"
2. Loyal to peer group
3. Able to "rebound" from environmental hardships
4. Verbally persuasive; humor rich with symbolism; language rich in imagery
5. Logical reasoning and problem-solving ability
6. Socially intelligent and active regarding justice
7. Sensitive and alert to movement (p. 47)

Underachieving gifted students represent another complex problem. Delisle (1982) has described the phenomenon of "learning to underachieve." Some gifted and talented children learn to perform below their potential because

☐ it is socially safe; that is, teachers and peers do not single the child out
☐ there is nothing to learn that is interesting or challenging
☐ peer and parent relationships are not based on expectations of superior achievement.

Whitmore (1980) has described underachievement as mild to moderate and moderate to severe. She also discusses the unknown underachiever; that is, the child who is performing normally so that no one knows of the child's hidden exceptional abilities. High aptitude scores with low grades or high standardized achievement scores with low grades may indicate two other kinds of underachievement. Effective remediation involves increasing the child's motivation, working on self-perceptions, and modifying classroom instruction, environment, and curriculum. Guidance and counseling are integral to improved self-concept and self-esteem (VanTassel-Baska, 1983).

Counseling is an important concern for all gifted children. Blackburn and Erickson (1986) have identified a number of predictable crises in the lives of gifted and talented students. Differences between their intellectual and emotional and physical growth, particularly for boys, can result in conflicts between their cognitive competence and their ability to perform. As previously mentioned, underachievement is a cause for counseling. Fear of success, particularly for adolescent girls, or meeting failure for the first time can also be helped by appropriate counseling. In addition, because gifted students have so many options, they often need help in sorting through the choices available to them.

There are still other moments when professional counseling may be required. Beyond the stresses of growing up that are experienced by all children, gifted and talented individuals must sometimes deal with conflicts caused by the expectations that others or they themselves hold for their achievement. Conflicting expectations may concern the present—perhaps grades, extracurricular activities, or home life—or they may have to do with future career or life-style choices. Gifted students can benefit from guidance and counseling that helps them adjust to their special abilities and the ways in which those abilities affect their lives.

Finally, as we have seen with other groups of exceptional children, to improve the future for gifted and talented children, we must improve society's attitudes toward them. The stereotype of the gifted child as a socially ineffectual "brain," hidden indoors behind a huge stack of books, is not only inaccurate, but it can be destructive and stultifying. Furthermore, many people—including some educators—believe that gifted

ACTIVITIES FOR PRESCHOOLERS

These activities were developed to demonstrate a method by which the creative and productive thinking of gifted preschool children can be integrated into an informal setting, such as an open classroom. The activities are designed to be freely chosen by individual children; after receiving instructions from a teacher, each child should be able to complete the activity independently, with minimal teacher supervision. All the activities encourage children to engage in divergent thinking—that is, creative and original thinking—as defined in Guilford's SOI model.

Mark Williams, Polly Kemp, Michael Marks, and Rebecca Hansen of the University of Illinois preschool program for gifted children created these activities.

SPACE OBJECTS

Materials: five numbered pictures of "space objects"; cassette recorder and blank tape

Directions:

Pretend that you are the captain of a spaceship which is exploring outer space. You are close to a planet which you think has some sort of people on it, so you send down a scouting party to see what they can find.

When they return to the ship, the scouting crew members report that they couldn't find any people on the planet, but that they did find all kinds of strange objects. They didn't want to disturb these objects because they didn't know what they were, so they took pictures of them with their cameras and brought back the pictures to show to you. What do you think these strange objects could be? Look at each picture, and record on the tape recorder all the ideas you have of what it might be. Don't forget to say the number of the picture before you give your ideas so everyone will know which picture you are talking about. Think of as many ideas as you can for each picture.

To Make Materials:

On a separate piece of white heavy card-stock paper, draw each of the following "space objects" as shown. Be sure to number each prominently so that the child can record the number of the object he or she is thinking about. Cover each card with clear contact paper.

RAINBOW MENU

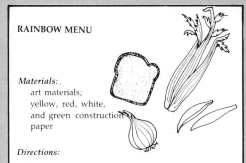

Materials:.
art materials;
yellow, red, white,
and green construction
paper

Directions:

Pretend that you just became the owner of the biggest and best restaurant in the whole world. You decide that you want a new menu that is different from any other restaurant's menu, so you decide to group all of your foods according to color. Each page of your menu will be a different color and will only list foods that are that color. What are all the foods that would be on the yellow page? List all of the yellow foods you can think of, and I will write them down.

Now think of all the red foods you can. (Repeat with white foods and green foods.) Now it is time for you to make your menu. Take one sheet each of yellow paper, red paper, white paper, and green paper, and draw the foods that will be on your menu. I will remind you of foods you named if you forget.

MODERN INVENTIONS

Materials: art materials; construction materials (boxes, etc.)

Directions:

An inventor is a person who makes new things which nobody has ever made before. Inventors make new things to solve special problems, for example, garage doors that you can open without getting out of your car.

Be an inventor and make something that no one has ever made before. Use whatever material you need to make a garbage can that a dog would especially like. Before you begin, be sure to think about what a dog would like a garbage can to be like.

Substitutions:

- a trap to catch insects alive without harming them
- a mail box that does more than hold letters and packages
- a bed that is extremely convenient for a sick person
- a television set that helps with the housework

ACTIVITIES FOR A NEW CHILD

Materials: art materials

Directions:

Pretend that tomorrow morning we will be getting a new child in our classroom. She will be very different from you and all the other children, because she will be coming here from another planet somewhere in outer space. Everything here will be very new to her—the furniture, the weather, the plants, how we talk.

What activities do you think this new child would choose to do? I'm sure they would be very different from the activities that you children sign up for, because she has so much new to learn. Make an activity sheet for the new child. Give her a choice of at least six activities—be sure to try to think of things that *she* would be interested in doing.

Substitutions:

- activity sheet for a little baby
- activity sheet for an adult
- activity sheet for a new teacher
- activity sheet for a family pet

SHOE STORY

Materials none (art materials optional)

Directions:

Did you ever hear someone complaining that her feet hurt because she'd been standing or walking all day? Well, did you ever stop to think how badly that person's *shoes* must be feeling too? What if shoes could have thoughts and feelings like people? What do you suppose a shoe might think about? If a shoe could talk, what would it say?

Make up a story about a whole day in the life of a shoe, from the time it wakes up in the closet in the morning till it goes back into the closet for the night. Dictate your story to a teacher; draw pictures to go with your story if you like.

Substitutions:

- wristwatch
- wallet
- key
- pair of glasses

children, by their very nature, do not need special education; they can make it on their own. This attitude can be seen from the local level to the federal government, which no longer monitors programs for gifted and talented children. In reality, gifted and talented children *do* need special education if they are to reach their potential. Too many gifted children are bored and frustrated in school; some even drop out altogether, and even more are made to settle for less than they deserve. The quality of our collective future may depend in large measure on our ability to develop this valuable human resource.

SUMMARY

1. Like other exceptional children, gifted and talented students need special education provisions to reach their full potential.
2. Gifted and talented children have unusual intellectual, creative, artistic, specific academic, or leadership ability, which requires special school services.
    a. To be considered gifted, a student must perform in the top 3% to 5% of the school-age population.
    b. A 1981 report found that only 17 states mandated IEPs and due process procedures for gifted and talented students.
3. Although some gifted children are outstanding in many areas, others have special talents in only one or two fields. Gifted children are by no means perfect, and their unusual talents and abilities may make them difficult to manage.
4. Many gifted children are creative. Although there is no universally accepted definition of creativity, we know that creative children have knowledge, examine it in a variety of ways, critically analyze the outcomes, and communicate their ideas.
5. Identifying gifted and talented children usually involves several procedures, Including intelligence, creativity, and achievement testing and nomination by teachers, parents, peers, and even the children themselves.
    a. It is best to match students to the goals of the programs in which they will be placed.
    b. Any single indentification procedure should be used only to identify certain successful students for special programs; it should not be used to keep other children from receiving special services.
    c. Most school districts need to have more than one type of program for gifted and talented children.
6. The concept of giftedness has evolved over the years. The current concept is broader than traditional definitions.
    a. Early 19th-century works focused on genius, which was thought to be genetically determined.
    b. Standardized intelligence tests, beginning with the Stanford-Binet, have been used during most of this century to predict school success and to identify unusually bright children. Reliance on these tests has tended to restrict giftedness to high IQ scores, which are associated with white, urban, middle- or upper-class society.
    c. The research of Terman and Hollingsworth did much to increase our knowledge of the gifted and to dispel popular myths.

    d. In the early 1950s Guilford first suggested that more than IQ should be considered in determining who is gifted.

    e. Since then, the concept of giftedness has expanded to include creativity and other alternatives to traditional IQ scores. We have also come to recognize giftedness among the culturally diverse, among females, and among handicapped children.

7. Education of gifted and talented students should be geared toward the fullest possible development of each child's abilities.

    a. Gifted students need both content knowledge and the abilities to use and develop that knowledge effectively.

    b. Gifted and talented children need to know basic skills, including how to conduct research and how to continue to learn after they have left school.

    c. Two common approaches to educating the gifted are enrichment and acceleration.

    d. Five models for teaching gifted students are

        (1) Bloom's Taxonomy of Educational Objectives

        (2) Guilford's Structure of Intellect Model

        (3) Williams's Cognitive-Affective Model

        (4) Renzulli's Enrichment Triad Model

        (5) Maker's Integrated Curriculum Model

    e. Teachers of the gifted must be flexible, curious, tolerant, competent, and self-confident.

8. Many questions remain in the education of gifted and talented children. We need research in a variety of areas if these children are to grow up to be leaders in our rapidly changing society.

9. The importance of identifying gifted and talented children among females, diverse cultural groups, and handicapped students is now being recognized. We need better procedures for identifying, assessing, teaching, and encouraging these children.

10. As we have seen with other exceptional children, we must improve society's attitudes toward gifted and talented children if we are to improve their futures.

FOR MORE INFORMATION

Journals

The Gifted Child Quarterly. Published four times per year by the National Association for Gifted Children. Publishes articles by both parents and teachers of gifted children.

Gifted Child Today (formerly *G/C/T*). Published six times per year by GCT, Inc. Publishes articles with ideas aimed at parents and teachers of gifted, talented, and creative youngsters.

Gifted International. Published semi-annually by the World Council for Gifted and Talented Children. Devoted to international communication among educators, researchers, and parents.

Journal for the Education of the Gifted. Published quarterly by the Association for the Gifted, the Council for Exceptional Children. Presents theoretical, descriptive, and research articles presenting diverse ideas and different points of view on the education of gifted and talented students.

Roeper Review. Published quarterly by the Roeper City and County School. Publishes articles by teachers, researchers, and students in gifted education.

Books

Barbe, W. B., & Renzulli, J. C. (1981). *Psychology and education of the gifted* (3rd ed.). New York: Irvington.

Clark, B. (1983). *Growing up gifted* (2nd ed.). Columbus OH: Merrill.

Cox, J., Daniel, N., & Boston, B. O. (1985). *Educating able learners: Programs and promising practices.* Austin: University of Texas Press.

Gallagher, J. J. (1985). *Teaching the gifted child* (3rd ed.). Boston: Allyn & Bacon.

Kramer, A. H., Bitan, D., Butler-Or, N., Eryatar, A., & Landau, E. (Eds.). (1981). *Gifted children: Challenging their potential.* New York: World Council for Gifted and Talented Children.

Maker, C. J. (1982). *Curriculum development for the gifted.* Rockville, MD: Aspen.

Maker, C. J. (Ed.). (1986). *Critical issues in gifted education: Defensible programs for the gifted.* Rockville, MD: Aspen.

Sisk, D. (1987). *Creative teaching of the gifted.* New York: McGraw-Hill.

Swassing, R. H. (Ed.). (1985). *Teaching gifted children and adolescents.* Columbus, OH: Merrill.

Tannenbaum, A. J. (1983). *Gifted children: Psychological and educational perspectives.* New York: Macmillan.

Organizations

Association for the Gifted, the Council for Exceptional Children, 1920 Association Drive, Reston, VA 22091. A growing division of CEC that includes teachers, teacher educators, administrators, and others interested in gifted and talented children.

Gifted Child Society, Suite 6, 190 Rock Road, Glen Rock, NJ 07452. An organization for parents, also offering information and in-service training for educators.

National Association for Gifted Children, 4175 Lovell Road, Suite 140, Circle Pines, MN 55014. An organization of parents, professionals, and interested lay persons.

World Council for Gifted and Talented Children, HMS 412, University of South Florida, Tampa, FL 33620. The organization's purpose is to promote worldwide communication on issues related to the education and development of gifted children.

PART THREE
CULTURAL, FAMILY, AND LIFE-SPAN ISSUES IN SPECIAL EDUCATION

12

CULTURAL DIVERSITY IN SPECIAL EDUCATION

Exceptional students, their families, and special educators are first and foremost human beings whose rich diversity of culture, race, ethnicity, religion, geography, economic and social condition, language, and gender must be addressed with respect. (Weintraub, 1986, p. 2)

Demographic information indicates that this country's population is growing older and less White. Its children are less secure financially. Public school students are increasingly likely to be minority, and to come from homes where a language other than English is spoken. (Yates, 1986, p. 8)

There is a bitter irony in the fact that an English-speaking student may earn college credit for learning to speak another language, while a language minority child is encouraged not to use, and therefore lose, the same skill. (Ada, 1986, p. 387)

Many of the teachers of black children have roots in other communities and do not often have the opportunity to hear the full range of their students' voices. I wonder how many of Philadelphia's teachers know that their black students are prolific and "fluent" writers of rap songs. I wonder how many teachers realize the verbal creativity and fluency black kids express every day on the playgrounds of America as they devise new insults, new rope-jumping chants and new cheers. Even if they did hear them, would they relate them to language fluency? (Delpit, 1986, p. 383)

These wide-ranging observations suggest some of the challenges facing special educators today as they seek to provide a relevant, individualized education to exceptional students from culturally diverse backgrounds. Our public school system, after all, is based on a philosophy of equal educational opportunity. In the preceding chapters we have emphasized the importance of assessment, educational planning, direct instruction, family involvement, and other factors that contribute to meeting the needs of each exceptional student. We hope to equip all of our students with skills and confidence so that they can lead satisfying and productive lives.

The Education for All Handicapped Children Act of 1975 (P.L. 94–142) is only one of many recent significant steps toward the implementation of equal educational opportunity. In addition to prohibiting discrimination in schools because of a child's intellectual or physical disability, court decisions and legislation have forbidden discrimination in education and employment on the basis of a person's race, nationality, sex, or inability to speak English. Special programs now provide financial support and assistance to schools that serve refugee and migrant students and that provide self-determination in education for Native Americans.

Despite these important efforts, equal opportunity for all is not yet a reality. Many exceptional students still experience discrimination or receive a less-than-adequate education because of their race, social class, or other differences from the majority. In addressing ourselves to this issue, we do not mean to imply that belonging to a cultural or linguistic group that is different from that of the majority culture is a handicap or disability. On the contrary, a great strength of the United States is its cultural diversity. Our society is made up of immigrants from many lands, and we have benefited from the contributions of many ethnic groups.

> Ethnic diversity enriches the nation and increases the ways in which its citizens can perceive and solve personal and public problems. This diversity also enriches a society by providing all citizens with more opportunities to experience other cultures and thus to become more fulfilled as human beings. When individuals are able to participate in a variety of ethnic cultures, they are more able to benefit from the total human experience. (James Banks, 1977, p. 7)

Even though cultural diversity is a strength of our society, being a member of a minority too often means discrimination and misunderstanding, closed doors, and lowered expectations. Fortunately, this situation is improving; closed doors are opening.

Currie (1981) notes that a policy of multiculturalism is officially pursued by the government of Canada; although English and French are the two official languages, no ethnic group takes precedence over any other. He recalls a native Canadian parent who likened multiculturalism to a bouquet that is "more beautiful because of the diversity of flowers, all of which add to the total beauty, and yet, each is beautiful in its own right. . . . It is the differences which must be recognized and accepted instead of being ignored or rejected" (p. 165).

Garcia (1981) outlines three basic concepts of membership in cultural groups that can serve as a worthwhile point of departure for our consideration of the special needs of culturally diverse exceptional students.

1. Every person needs to belong to, or have a sense of belonging to, a group. A child's ethnic or cultural group provides a system of values and behaviors and is important in developing self-concept. Group membership should be a source of strength and social sustenance rather than a source of shame or anxiety.
2. Ethnic groups have both similarities and differences. Students should be encouraged to explore the characteristics of various groups; teachers can strive for cross-

cultural communication and understanding. For example, students can discuss the social implications of racial differences.

3. Segregated people develop myths, prejudices, and stereotypes about each other. Conflicts can occur when different groups first come into contact. Students may consider the consequences of separation and integration.

As special educators, we believe strongly in the importance of interindividual and intraindividual differences, even within the context of our own widely used categories. We know, for example, that two students affected by Down syndrome may display

Stereotyping has been defined as the "arbitrary assigning of certain habits, abilities, and expectations to people solely on the basis of group membership, regardless of their attributes as individuals" (Campbell, 1979, p. 1).

Mei is served by a resource room program for students with learning disabilities.

widely different academic abilities, social behavior, and personality traits. We have seen that one blind child may read braille fluently and play the piano well, whereas another blind child does neither. Similarly, two members of the same racial or cultural group may function, quite differently in school; we should always be objective observers of students' behavior and avoid stereotypes based on race or culture.

INTERNATIONAL PERSPECTIVES

The principal focus of this chapter is on understanding and meeting the needs of exceptional children in our own country who come from diverse ethnic and cultural backgrounds. However, it is also worth noting that special education, like other fields, is increasingly global in scope. Through international travel, conferences, and publications, American educators have learned about approaches to the education and employment of exceptional individuals in many other countries and in some cases have incorporated aspects of these techniques into their own programs. For example, our approaches to normalization—integrating people with disabilities into their own communities—are derived largely from Scandinavian countries. At a time when most Americans with severe mental retardation were in large, impersonal institutions, "the Danish and Swedish institutions and community residences were more like well-kept, comfortable, and pleasant homes" (Goldstein, 1984, p. 80). The concept of the *educateur*—a professional who plays an active, varied role in the education and adjustment of children with emotional disorders—originated in France and is now widely adopted in the United States and Canada. The order, discipline, and academic emphasis seen in Japanese schools have attracted the interest of many American educators (Ohanian, 1987). Others have studied methods of communication used with deaf and deaf-blind children in the Netherlands, approaches to the diagnosis and treatment of learning disabilities in the Soviet Union, and techniques for teaching reading to non-English-speaking native children in Australia and New Zealand.

An international perspective is also evident in the growing number of American special educators who have worked in the developing regions of the world, principally in Africa, Asia, and Latin America. They have assisted host-country colleagues in such tasks as assessing handicapped children, setting up special education programs, and training teachers and parents. More than 70% of the world's total population of disabled persons is found in the developing countries (Marfo, 1986). Opportunities for international service can be arranged through governmental agencies—such as the Peace Corps, the Agency for International Development, or the U.S. Department of Education Teacher Exchange Programs—or through private, charitable, or religious organizations.

REASONS FOR CONCERN

Recent surveys have reported that a sizable percentage of students in special education programs are members of culturally diverse groups. This situation reflects current population patterns in general education; all but 2 of the 25 largest public school systems in the United States now have a majority of minority students enrolled. In addition, bilingual children constitute an unusually high percentage of special education classes (Willig & Greenberg, 1986), and dropout rates are high. In the 15-to-19-year-old population, it is estimated that 15% of white youth, 21% of black youth, and 39% of Hispanic youth dropped out of school in a recent year. The public schools of New York City and Chicago have dropout rates estimated at 45% and 55%, respectively (Bernick, 1986).

Data on the prevalence of handicapped students in the United States indicate that a disproportionate number of them come from culturally diverse backgrounds (Salend, Michael, & Taylor, 1984). Kamp and Chinn (1982) report that about one-third of the entire population of students in special education programs in the United States come from multicultural backgrounds. Black students account for more than 28% of students identified as mentally retarded, although the percentage of black students in the overall school population is only about 18%. Black children are also somewhat overrepresented in the emotionally disturbed/behavior disordered category, but to a lesser extent (Wolff & Harkins, 1986). Schildroth (1986) has documented the steadily increasing percentage of black and Hispanic students in residential schools for the deaf and the "precipitous decline in the number of white, non-Hispanic students" (p. 100). Cummins (1986) contends that the currently favored diagnostic category for minority students is learning disabilities and that Hispanic students are greatly overrepresented in classes for learning disabled children, despite the absence of "any intrinsic processing deficit unique to Hispanic children" (p. 9).

Many observers maintain that culturally diverse children are not only overrepresented in classes for handicapped students, but are also correspondingly underrepresented in programs for gifted and talented students. Chinn and McCormick (1986), for example, point out that "gifted children from minority cultures possess a variety of talents that are valued and nurtured within their own cultures but are often ignored in school" and back up this observation with the fact that ethnic minority students constitute about 26.7% of the general school population but only about 18% of the population identified as gifted (p. 103).

The fact that culturally diverse children constitute a high percentage of special education students is not, in itself, a problem. Students with special needs *should* be served in special programs, whatever their ethnic background. However, the presence of large numbers of culturally diverse students raises several important concerns for special educators, such as the following:

☐ *Adequacy of assessment and placement procedures.* Have students received fair and multifaceted assessments before being placed in special education programs? Is referral based on a child's documented special needs, rather than on value judgments about her background? Are there opportunities for periodic reassessment and for parent and student involvement in program planning? Are culturally diverse students and disabled students included in screenings for gifted and talented children?

☐ *Provision of appropriate supportive services.* Special efforts may help improve the education and adjustment of students from culturally diverse backgrounds; such services may be provided either by the school or by other agencies. Examples of special efforts that may be appropriate include (1) bilingual aides to assist non-English-speaking students in the classroom and to translate correspondence sent home, (2) in-service training for teachers, to encourage sensitivity toward different cultures and to enhance appropriate educational planning, and (3) multiethnic education for students, to increase awareness of their own and other backgrounds and to reduce the potential for conflict and misunderstanding in the classroom.

☐ *Interactions between school and cultural background.* Schools generally require or expect certain behaviors of their students. For example, it is assumed that most children will learn to respond to the teacher's instructions and will be positively motivated by verbal praise. Children, however, are strongly influenced by their early contacts with family members, neighbors, and friends. If the expectations and values of home and school environments are vastly different, children may have serious problems. Many children appear to "think, act, and be motivated appropriately in activities out of school, yet do not demonstrate these same behaviors in school. . . . many school-related problems of minority children seem to be the results of conflict between the hidden curriculum and cultural preparation" (Chan & Rueda, 1979, p. 427). Such conflicts can interfere with a child's learning and behavior and are thus a legitimate concern of special educators.

TERMINOLOGY

Many terms have been applied to members of culturally diverse populations. As we have learned elsewhere in this book, it is difficult to use labels effectively. Although labels serve a useful purpose in identifying certain traits, they may also convey misleading or inaccurate generalizations. This unfortunate effect is especially evident in several terms that have been used to refer to children who come from different cultural backgrounds.

A *minority* group implies that the population of that group is small, and the term carries some "negative connotations of being less than other groups with respect to power, status, and treatment" (Chinn & Kamp, 1982, p. 383). In many regions, however, blacks, Hispanics, and Native Americans are not a minority at all but constitute the predominant population of a particular school or locality. And members of these groups are involved as teachers, clinicians, and administrators of educational programs. A black child in Detroit, a Mexican-American child in El Paso, and a Navajo child on a reservation in Arizona could be considered part of a "minority" only in respect to the population of the nation as a whole, a comparison that would have little relevance to the child's immediate environment.

Terms such as *culturally deprived* and *culturally disadvantaged* have also been used to describe children from various backgrounds. Although these labels recognize the influence of children's environments on their education and achievement, they also make the unfortunate suggestion that a background that is different from that of the majority or of more widely accepted groups is somehow inferior or lacking. A 1966 report, for example, used the terms *deprived* and *disadvantaged* in referring to a population of preschool black children in a southern town. This report also noted, however, that most of the children's families had been in the vicinity for at least three generations and that only 2 of 87 families dropped out of a 3-year-long research and demonstration project (Gray, Klaus, Miller, & Forrester, 1966, p. 1). Such information strongly suggests the presence, not absence, of a stable cultural environment in the family and community. As Sue (1981) observes, it is now acknowledged that all people inherit some cultural background, and the fact that a culture may differ from white middle-class norms does not mean that it is deviant, impoverished, or in need of reform.

Culturally diverse is the term we have elected to use when referring to children whose background is different enough to require, at times, special methods of assessment, instruction, intervention, or counseling. This term implies no judgment of a culture's value and does not equate cultural diversity and disability. We view membership in a cultural group as an opportunity for an enriching experience rather than as a disadvantage. We hope that this chapter's examination of issues in the education of culturally diverse exceptional children will help teachers and others to "free children from the damaging effects of premature, inaccurate, or prejudiced estimates and interpretations of their behavior that are culturally induced" (Spindler, 1974, p. 38).

ASSESSMENT OF CULTURALLY DIVERSE EXCEPTIONAL CHILDREN: PROBLEMS AND SUGGESTED SOLUTIONS

Tests are frequently used in placing exceptional children, in planning their educational programs, and in evaluating their progress. However, the procedures used in schools for testing and placing students from culturally diverse backgrounds have often unfairly subjected them to a second-class status: "An intelligence test given in English to a Spanish-speaking student may, but is not likely to, test accurately the student's potential to be successful in school or in his or her inherent or acquired skills" (H. R. Turnbull, 1986, p. 94). Brown (1982) discusses several ways in which tests—traditionally standardized on white, English-speaking, middle-class children—may discriminate against those from different cultural backgrounds.

1. The tests use formats and items that are more germane to one group than another. For example, the test may include restrictive time limits, vocabulary tasks that require the child to read the word, items that require a child to read in a task designed to measure listening comprehension ability, and so on.
2. Children have differing amounts of "test wiseness," which is more likely to be a problem with the preschool-aged child than with the school-aged child. For example, white, middle class preschool-aged children tend to be familiar with question-and-answer formats, with puzzles, and with pointing and naming tasks often included on tests. The same degree of familiarity cannot be assumed when evaluating a disadvantaged child.
3. The skills reflected by the test items may not be relevant to the skills demanded by the disadvantaged and culturally different child's environment . . . the tests, rather than assessing the disadvantaged child's ability, measure the extent to which such children have assimilated aspects of the dominant culture. (p. 164)

An influential study of a large California school district, reported by the sociologist Jane Mercer in 1973, is often cited as evidence that race and culture may play an unfair role in determining whether a child is placed in special classes and, if so, what type of services he will receive. Mercer found that black and Mexican-American children were much more likely to be placed in classes for the educable mentally retarded than were Anglo-American children: only 1.8% of all Anglo-American children in the school district were enrolled in EMR classes, whereas 12.9% of the black children and 18.6% of the Mexican-American children were (Mercer, 1973a). These figures can be interpreted as meaning that a Mexican-American child was 10 times more likely than an Anglo-American child to receive the EMR label, which at that time led to placement in special classes for much or all of the school day. Another study of racial imbalance in special education classes yielded somewhat different findings, however. Gottlieb, Agard, Kaufman, and Semmel (1976) reported that, although many children in a Texas school district were placed in EMR classes that were "very heavily overrepresented with children of their own race" (p. 212), this situation generally reflected the racial composition of the schools as a whole, rather than bias on the part of school officials.

Issues in IQ testing were discussed more fully in chapter 3.

The practice of placing children in special education programs for handicapped or gifted students solely because of their performance on standardized intelligence tests is rapidly disappearing. It is widely believed that, in the past, overreliance on IQ tests resulted in the inappropriate labeling and placement of many students from diverse cultural backgrounds; IQ tests do not present a fair or complete measure of the intelligence of culturally diverse students.

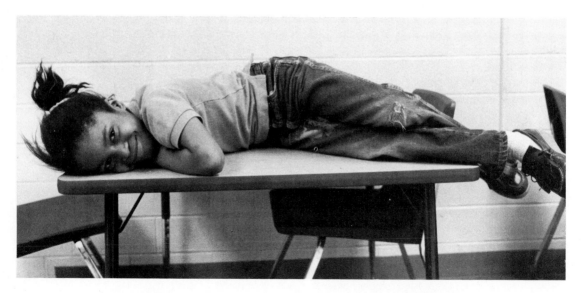

Special education placement should be based on each child's individual learning needs, not on race or culture.

Hilliard (1975) calls attention to sources of cultural bias in several widely used tests of cognitive ability. These tests appear to be based on the faulty premise that every child comes to the test with a similar background of life experiences. The following examples of potentially unfair test items are cited:

> On one test, a child must be familiar with such words as *wasp, captain, hive, casserole, shears, cobbler,* or *hydrant.* On another test, a child must know the distance from Boston to London [and] why icebergs melt. . . . The child, in order to get the answers correct, must assume that women are weak and need protection, that policemen are always nice, that labor laws are just. How is the examiner to distinguish ignorance from disagreement? (Hilliard, 1975, p. 22)

Samuda (1976) also finds an "Anglocentric" bias in many intelligence tests and contends that, when IQ scores are "interpreted with the knowledge that sociocultural factors contaminate them" and when a child's adaptive behavior is considered, "racial imbalance in classes for the mentally retarded disappears" (pp. 70–71). As Brown (1982) notes, limited use of language is not synonymous with limited intellectual ability: "Some culturally different children are virtually silent in the testing situation, and the examiner may need to listen to the child in play with other children to hear a representative sample of the child's language" (p. 170). Standardized tests in English, obviously, are not likely to give an accurate picture of a child's abilities if she comes from a non-English-speaking home. "If the student's primary language is Spanish, Navajo, or Thai, the only justification for testing in English is to determine the student's facility in this second language" (Lewis & Doorlag, 1987, p. 331).

P. L. 94–142 specifies that assessment for the purpose of identifying and placing handicapped children must be conducted in the child's native langauge. Unfortunately, there are not many reliable tests available in languages other than English, and the translation or adaptation of tests into other languages poses certain problems. Alzate (1978), for example, reviewed several studies of the performance of Spanish-speaking children on translated versions of English tests and concluded that translated tests are generally unreliable. DeAvila (1976) points out the great variety in language within Hispanic populations and notes that when Mexican-American children were given a test in Spanish that was developed with a population of Puerto Rican children, they performed even more poorly than on an admittedly unfair English test. To illustrate the confusion that may result from inappropriate translations, DeAvila observes that a Spanish-speaking child may use any one of several words to describe a kite, depending on the family's country of origin: *cometa, huila, volantín, papalote,* or *chiringa.* Thus, although the translation of tests and other materials into a child's native language may be helpful in many instances, great caution must be taken because an improper translation may actually do a disservice to the linguisitically different child.

Bias and discrimination can also occur in the referral process, when children's records are reviewed and decisions are made about the type of services to be provided. In the opinion of some educators, a child's race, family background, and economic circumstances—rather than actual performance and needs—unfairly influence the label he is likely to receive and the degree to which he will be removed from the

The law also requires that notice of IEP and placement meetings and other important conferences be given to parents in their native language.

See the Focus feature on page 453 for an illustration of possible cultural bias in assessment.

regular classroom. Two children with similar performance may be treated quite differently by school personnel because of racist attitudes.

> If a black and a white child are not learning well, the chances are that the black will be called *mentally retarded* and the white will be called *learning disabled*. The latter term has much more of a positive image, suggesting that the learning disabled white child is average but needs extra remedial help to fulfill his potential. The black child is seen as inferior and needs much less of a challenge. (Silberberg & Silberberg, 1974, p. 56)

How can bias in testing and decision making be reduced or eliminated? The current emphasis on interdisciplinary assessment of exceptional children, using a variety of formal and observational evaluation techniques and involving a team of professionals, is a healthy one that should reduce inappropriate labeling and placement. The evaluation process must concern itself with identifying a child's specific, observable skills and deficits. According to Duffey, Salvia, Tucker, and Ysseldyke (1981), "The problem of bias in assessment will not be resolved until educators can operationally specify the criteria to be used in decision making. Until this time, attempts to eliminate bias will be as effective as applying a bandaid to a hemorrhage" (p. 433).

Mercer (1981) suggests that the observation of a child's behavior outside school, in the family and neighborhood, may be more valuable than formal tests in determining her abilities and needs and in particular may help differentiate learning disabled from mentally retarded students. If a child is "learning the skills needed to cope intelligently with the nonacademic world, then s/he may be ignorant of the skills needed to succeed in school but is not mentally retarded" (Mercer, 1981, p. 101). The importance of precise descriptions of behaviors—including antecedents and consequences—is emphasized by Dent (1976). In certain cultures and settings loud talking is not always equivalent to boisterous or aggressive behavior. And hitting and name-calling may not be hostile—they may represent a sign of respect or affection (Dent, 1976, pp. 89–90). Interpretations and value judgments should not be used in reporting children's behavior.

There is some interesting evidence that indicates that a child's performance in testing situations may be heavily influenced by the environment and the examiner. Labov (1975) presents a case study of the verbal behavior of an 8-year-old black child named Leon. When Leon was tested in school by a white interviewer who placed objects on a table and said, "Tell me everything you can about this," his response was minimal, consisting mostly of silence and one-word utterances. It appeared that Leon was functioning well below his age level and perhaps had a serious communication disorder or mental retardation. However, on another occasion Leon was interviewed by a black examiner who took him to an apartment in a familiar neighborhood, brought along Leon's best friend and a supply of potato chips, and sat down on the floor with the child. In this situation Leon spoke much more fluently; he had a great deal to say to the adult and to his friend. Labov has also performed a detailed linguistic analysis of the nonstandard English used by many black children and has concluded that traditional classroom tests and tasks have little relevance or accuracy. "There is no reason to believe that any nonstandard vernacular is in itself an obstacle to learning (Labov, 1975, p. 127).

TRY TAKING A CULTURALLY SPECIFIC TEST

Critics have charged that most standardized intelligence and achievement tests are culturally biased. That is, because the tests are developed by and for white, primarily middle-class individuals, the items and scores discriminate against anyone from a different background. To get a feeling for what it might be like to take such a test, try to answer each of the sample items below. If they appear difficult, confusing, foreign, or unanswerable, then you are beginning to understand how test questions can be inexorably entwined with culture.

The first four test items are taken from "People Ain't Dumb—It's Them Tests!" (compiled by the editors of the *Applalachian Review* at West Virginia University) and are based on Appalachian culture. The last four items are taken from The Hana-Butta Test and are based on Hawaiian culture. Correct answers appear at the bottom of the page.

1. Blue tick is
   a. an insect
   b. a food stamp
   c. hound dog
   d. NRA sticker

2. Before it is fit to drink, moonshine must be
   a. aged three months
   b. aged three weeks
   c. aged three days
   d. cooled

3. The most successful method for catching catfish is
   a. gigging
   b. setting a trot line
   c. dynamiting
   d. creating electric shock with two pokers and a car battery

4. A gee-haw-whinny-diddle is a
   a. good time
   b. harness for a horse
   c. toy
   d. type of persimmon

5. If you were at home and someone told you to get "da kine," they would probably mean
   a. a glass of water
   b. a towel
   c. an ash tray
   d. dried fish
   e. any of the above

6. Pakalolo is
   a. salted raw fish and seaweed
   b. whiskey made from ti-root
   c. marijuana
   d. liquor
   e. acid

7. If someone wanted to say dinner was delicious, he would say it was
   a. papa's
   b. kukui
   c. ewa
   d. lola
   e. ono

8. Hana-butta is known statewide as
   a. high butterfat Hana butter
   b. Hana Dairy's margarine
   c. Toto's Snack Bar's famous peanut butter
   d. mucus running from the nose of a person with a bad cold.
   e. a plain ol' peanut butter sandwich

Answers: (1) c; (2) d; (3) c; (4) c; (5) e; (6) c; (7) e; (8) d.

Source: From *Mental Retardation* (2nd ed., p. 124–1215) by J. R. Patton, J. S. Payne, and M. Beirne-Smith, 1986, Columbus, OH: Merrill. Reprinted by permission.

Even though Labov's case study illustrates that one child responded differently to different examiners, it should not be assumed that the race, sex, or age of a teacher or examiner will inevitably affect a child's performance. Brown (1982) reviewed several studies of the effects of examiner race on the performance of culturally diverse children and concluded that there was no general tendency of black and Hispanic students to score higher or lower when tested by white, black, or Hispanic examiners. Characteristics such as the examiner's "ability to evidence a warm, responsive, receptive, but firm style" were found to be more important than race or ethnic group in motivating children to do their best. "This does not preclude the possibility that ethnic or racial variables can influence performance, but it does suggest that to study race alone—without considering other interactional variables—is likely to be futile" (Brown, 1982, p. 165).

Along with an objective recording of behaviors, a child's social and cultural background should be taken into account when performance is assessed. What is normal and acceptable in a child's culture may be regarded as abnormal or unacceptable in school and may result in conflict, mislabeling, or punishment. Gallimore, Boggs, and Jordan (1974) offer the example of several native Hawaiian children who sought help from other children on tests and tasks and seemed to pay little attention to the teacher. This behavior was interpreted as cheating and inattentiveness. Closer obser-

FIGURE 12.1
Checklist of observable student behaviors.

Date of Observation_____	
FIELD-SENSITIVE	FIELD-INDEPENDENT
RELATIONSHIP TO PEERS	
1. Likes to work with others to achieve a common goal. ☐	1. Prefers to work independently. ☐
2. Likes to assist others. ☐	2. Likes to compete and gain individual recognition. ☐
3. Is sensitive to feelings and opinions of others. ☐	3. Task-oriented; is inattentive to social enviornment when working. ☐
PERSONAL RELATIONSHIP TO TEACHER	
1. Openly expresses positive feelings for teacher. ☐	1. Avoids physical contact with teacher. ☐
2. Asks questions about teacher's tastes and personal experiences; seeks to become like teacher. ☐	2. Formal: interactions with teacher are restricted to tasks at hand. ☐

INSTRUCTIONAL RELATIONSHIP TO TEACHER

1. Seeks guidance and demonstration from teacher. ☐

1. Likes to try new tasks without teacher's help. ☐

2. Seeks rewards that strengthen relationship with teacher. ☐

2. Impatient to begin tasks; likes to finish first. ☐

3. Is highly motivated when working individually with teacher. ☐

3. Seeks nonsocial rewards. ☐

THINKING STYLE

1. Functions well when objectives are carefully explained or modeled prior to activity or lesson. ☐

1. Focuses on details and parts of things. ☐

2. Deals well with concepts in humanized or story format. ☐

2. Deals well with math and science concepts. ☐

3. Functions well when curriculum content is made relevant to personal interests and experiences. ☐

3. Likes discovery on trial-and-error learning. ☐

CODE: Never ☐ Seldom ◹ Sometimes ◰ Usually ■

Source: From "Cognitive Styles: Implications for Multiethnic Education" by B. G. Cox and M. Ramirez in *Education in the 80's: Multiethnic Education* (p. 67) by J. A. Banks (Ed.), 1981, Washington, DC: National Education Association. Reprinted by permission.

vation of the children's home and community environments, however, revealed that the Hawaiian children were typically peer-oriented. It was normal for them to share in the responsibility of caring for each other, and they often worked cooperatively on tasks rather than following the directions of an adult.

Cox and Ramirez (1981) report that even though generalizations cannot be made about the learning styles of any group of students, it appears that many black, Hispanic, and other culturally diverse children are more group-oriented, more sensitive to the social environment, and more positively responsive to adult modeling than are white students. Students from certain cultural backgrounds may not learn effectively in highly competitive situations or on nonsocial tasks. They may be uncomfortable with trial-and-error approaches and may not be interested in the fine details of certain concepts and materials. Cox and Ramirez have designed assessment procedures that may be helpful to teachers in determining the particular learning style of a culturally diverse student. Figure 12.1 presents a behavior rating instrument that can be used to evaluate a child's preferences and orientations and then to develop teaching methods and materials that are appropriate.

Nondiscriminatory assessment requires that decisions be based on varied and accurate information. Building rapport with children before testing them; observing their behavior in school, home, and play settings; and consulting with their parents can help teachers and examiners become more aware of cultural differences and reduce the number of students inappropriately placed in special education programs. Paraprofessional personnel or volunteers who are familiar with a child's language and/or cultural background have proven to be valuable assistants in many testing situations (Mattes & Omark, 1984). Figure 12.2 presents a helpful set of questions that can be used in interviewing parents about cultural and environmental influences and the particular experiences the culturally diverse child has had. "Attention to appropriate assessment of minority group children can yield approaches which will lead to the improved assessment of all children" (Jones, 1976, p. 289).

SOME CONCERNS OF SPECIFIC CULTURALLY DIVERSE GROUPS

Elsie J. Smith (1981), a counselor who specializes in working with people of diverse cultural backgrounds, finds it helpful to remember the following saying:

Each individual is—
    like all other people,
    like some other people, and
    like no other person. (p. 180)

We will keep this observation in mind as we consider certain issues that have been of concern to specific cultural groups. It is not our purpose to offer generalizations; each of these cultures in reality consists of many different subcultures, and the degree to which a child inherits a distinct cultural background varies immensely. Instead, we hope to present information that may help teachers and others recognize whether their approaches and interactions with some members of diverse cultural groups are as effective as they can be. Understanding and appreciation of different cultures can go a long way toward avoiding misinterpretations of children's behavior.

Blacks/Afro-Americans

Much has been written about the unique experiences shared by Americans of African descent. Today, black persons constitute the largest ethnic minority group in the United States, about 11.5% of the total population (McDavis, 1980). And the black population of the United States is growing rapidly, at a rate about double that of the white population, mainly because of higher fertility (Schildroth, 1986). Demographic information indicates that poverty and unemployment are facts of life for many black families. Sleeter and Grant (1986), using statistics from the U.S. Department of Commerce, report that the average black family earns only 59% as much as the average white family and that the poverty rate among blacks is more than 35%.

FIGURE 12.2
Guidelines for interviewing parents about cultural and environmental influences.

After talking with community members about the general cultural characteristics of the community, it is still necessary to discover what experiences each child has had. The following set of questions can be used to find out about the direct cultural and environmental experiences of the child so that appropriate educational programs can be planned.

1. What language(s) do the parents speak to each other?
2. What language(s) do the parents speak to the child?
3. What language(s) do the children use with each other?
4. What language does the referred child prefer to use when playing with friends?
5. Who takes care of the child after school? What language is used?
6. Who lives in the home (parents, grandparents, etc.)?
7. How much time does each parent have to interact with the child?
8. With whom does the child play when at home?
9. What television programs are seen in each language?
10. Are stories read to the child? In what language is the reading material written?
11. What language is used in church services, if attended?
12. What does the child do after school and on weekends?
13. What responsibilities does the child have in the home?
14. How is the child expected to act toward parents, teachers, and other adults?
15. In what cultural activities does the family participate?
16. How do the parents expect adults to act toward the child?
17. Are there any specific prohibitions in the everyday interactions between adults and children, for example, do not look adults in the eye when talking to them, do not pat children on the top of the head, do not ask children questions?
18. How long has the family been in this country?
19. How long has the family been in the local community?
20. How much contact does the family have with the homeland? What kind of contact?

Source: From *Speech and Language Assessment for the Bilingual Handicapped* (pp. 111–112) by L. J. Mattes and D. R. Omark, 1984, San Diego: College-Hill. Reprinted by permission.

Cruickshank (1986) describes black children with disabilities as "doubly handicapped . . . a minority within a minority" and notes the unfairness of some widely held attitudes: "Multihandicapped white individuals, such as Helen Keller, are immortalized. However, black cerebral-palsied children have far greater difficulty in receiving equality of service than does the white child similarly handicapped" (p. 18). Johnson (1976) contends that the black exceptional child has certain special characteristics and that educators should proceed beyond discussions of feelings and implement instruction that will help the black exceptional student achieve important goals.

The primary task for the black handicapped child is to master the skills of language, eliminate self-destructive behaviors, and understand that he must become a source of knowledge which will improve his community. To do this, black educators must begin to embrace positively results-oriented techniques such as precision teaching. . . . In the case of exceptional black children the major task is to provide them with the adaptive behaviors which will permit normalization of activities of daily living, the release of latent creativity, and provide a set of technical skills which will permit maximum independence in the community. (p. 170)

E. J. Smith (1981) offers a review of the distinctive cultural and historical perspectives of black Americans, which have sometimes been associated with conflict and misunderstanding in school and other settings. According to Smith, it is the feeling of many blacks that actions speak louder than words, that talk is cheap, and that whites beguile each other with verbal discourse. Much importance is attached to people's nonverbal behavior; blacks may spend much time observing others to see "where they are coming from."

White teachers and counselors generally place a high value on eye contact during interpersonal communication. Many blacks, says Smith, engage in conversation without making eye contact at all times. They may even take part in other activities while still paying attention to a conversation. Smith relates an incident in which a teacher reprimanded a black student for keeping her head down during a swimming lesson; the student insisted she had been paying attention. The teacher then told the student to face her and look her squarely in the eye like the rest of the girls. "So I did," said the student. "The next thing I knew she was telling me to get out of the pool—that she didn't like the way I was looking at her" (p. 155). Communication styles may differ in other ways. Many blacks do not nod their heads or make little "um-hmm" noises during conversation, as whites do, to indicate that they are listening to someone (Hall, 1976). Sensitivity to language and communication practices is important in working with students and parents. However, Smith cautions against trying too hard, noting that blacks often resent white professionals who attempt to use black slang: "Anyone who tries too hard to show you that he understands blacks doesn't understand them at all" (Smith, 1981, p. 169).

The black family in the United States has been the focus of considerable study and interpretation. Norton (1983) describes the black family as a predominantly urban group dependent on the extended family for many support functions and states that "although approximately one-quarter of all black families could be considered in the middle income range, there is an increasing number of black families who are still very poor. The children of these families are growing up in a world that is increasingly separate from most whites, and even from more privileged black children" (p. 192). Smith (1981) contends that black families are basically intact social systems that have served as a source of strength and survival, contrary to the view of the black family as a decaying institution that is the source of many social problems. Smith also challenges the notion that the black family is a matriarchy. Black families with both parents present are similar to white families in their perceptions of power and decision making within the family unit. Many black families include extended relatives who live in or are welcome to drop in at any time; white visitors to the home may have different concepts of privacy and may feel uncomfortable having grandparents, cousins, siblings, and others present when a child's needs are being discussed.

The attitudes of some black parents toward their exceptional children may seem unfamiliar to nonblack professionals. Smith notes that many black parents establish strict standards of behavior in the home, and violations of these rules are often met with physical punishment. White parents may be more inclined to discuss behavior at length with their children and perhaps to use emotional strategies (such as threatening the withdrawal of love) as a form of punishment. Black parents would likely view these strategies as inappropriate. They may also be less inclined than whites to blame or punish themselves or to feel guilty for their children's disabilities or behavior problems. Differences in approach, it should be pointed out, are related to parents' economic and educational levels, as well as to their cultural background.

In one of the few studies to explore racial differences in the perception of exceptionality, Schilit (1977) found that black and white college students held generally similar attitudes toward mental retardation, with two noteworthy exceptions: blacks were "more aware of the inherent dangers that persist in a low socioeconomic environment and what effect they can have on the individual in terms of development" (p. 190), and they held more pessimistic views of the employment potential of people with mental retardation. With respect to the second finding, Schilit conjectured that because the incidence of unemployment is high in the black community as a whole, the black students believed that mentally retarded people would have even more difficulty finding employment. More work needs to be done on the special needs of black exceptional children and on ways of improving cross-cultural communication and parent involvement.

Hispanic Americans

One of the largest and most rapidly growing populations of culturally diverse exceptional children consists of Hispanic-Americans. Although there are many social, cultural, and economic subgroups within this population, culturally relevant methods of instruction and counseling may often be called for.

As in virtually all cultures, the family plays a critical role in the early development and socialization of the Hispanic-American exceptional child. Rivera and Quintana Saylor (1977) offer their view of the traditional Spanish-speaking family.

> First, the family is considered as the most important social unit, and individual interests or aspirations are subordinate to those of the family. Each member has a unique and responsible role with the father being the head and responsible for providing for his family as well as for their behavior in and out of the home. He has a great degree of freedom to practice his *machismo*, which is done in a strict but gentle manner. The mother devotes herself to her husband and children with her personal interests secondary to those. She has the greatest influence in the family but exercises it in subtle ways. The children are treasured and indulged with great amounts of personal and physical affection. They are not without responsibility, however, and this may take precedence over school or personal attainment. When a disabling condition interrupts this system, it may create a serious crisis. (p. 446)

The concept of *machismo* (maleness), referred to in the preceding description, has been the subject of much misinterpretation. Ruiz (1981) cautions against assumptions that Hispanic sex roles are uniform and rigid. Ruiz explains that the term *macho* (male) is used among Hispanics as a flattering term denoting "physical strength, sexual attractiveness, virtue, and potency" (p. 191). It is not meant to imply physical aggressiveness, dominance over women, sexual promiscuity, or excessive use of alcohol. Real masculinity among Hispanics attaches high value to "dignity in conduct, respect for others, love for the family, and affection for children" (Ruiz, 1981, p. 192).

Grossman (1984) describes the Hispanic family as "a fountain of emotional and economic security and support" where children are "brought up to believe that contributing to and sacrificing for the benefit of the group is more important than personal aggrandizement. As a result, they may be highly motivated to do things that have significance for their families, friends, and community. They may prefer to work in groups" (p. 216). Because of their respect for authority, some Hispanic parents "may have difficulty participating in the educational decision-making process as described by P. L. 94–142" (Grossman, 1984, p. 218). They may express agreement with decisions made about their children, even if they disagree with the decisions or do not understand them. Other Hispanic parents may be wary of signing documents such as IEPs or forms necessary for the assessment of their children.

See the Focus feature that follows for a report on one Hispanic child with multiple disabilities.

Castaneda (1976) observes that many Mexican-American children work well on cooperative group projects, where they are not compelled to strive for individual gains. They may be reluctant to ask for a teacher's help; they are accustomed to having family members respond to their nonverbal behavior in a way that avoids the embarrassment of requesting help. In general, children and parents are likely to turn to members of the extended family when help is needed, rather than relying on schools or agencies, which they regard as impersonal. Different value systems may also affect a child's classroom performance. Many non-Hispanic teachers adopt an objective, impartial attitude in school, in the interest of fair and equal treatment of students. However, Hispanic children may take this as a sign of rejection, an indication that the teacher does not care about them. Castaneda (1976) suggests that the teacher of Mexican-American children develop close, personalized relationships with the students and use child-centered, socially reinforcing language, such as "I am proud of you" or "You did that very well."

> The teaching style which is most characteristic in the traditional Mexican American community is *modeling*. The child learns to "do it like the teacher" and wants to become like the teacher. It is important, then, that the teacher relate personal anecdotes and be willing to interact with the child outside the classroom. The most effective rewards are those which result in a closer relationship between the child and the teacher. (p. 188)

Ortiz and Garcia (1986) report that there has been a recent decline in the percentage of Hispanic students who are labeled as mildly mentally retarded or as emotionally disturbed. They note that today "approximately 80% of all handicapped Hispanics are served in two language-related categories: learning disabilities and speech handicapped" (p. 10). This situation raises the importance of distinguishing differences

FROM THE TEACHER'S NOTEBOOK

*Children with disabilities, like all children, have
unique personality traits. They may be endearing,
bizarre, exasperating . . . or "all of the above."
And their behavior may change over a period of
time. Systematic observation is important—but
precise notations of a child's performance on instructional tasks give only a partial picture of
what that student is really like.*

*As a teacher in a residential school for multi-
handicapped children, coauthor Michael Orlansky
kept a notebook. Each day he wrote down brief
notes on the children's behavior. The following
excerpts highlight his observations of one interesting student whose cultural background exerted
a strong influence on his school performance.*

Background. Eduardo is 14 years old. His family
has just emigrated from a Latin American country.
He has never been enrolled in a school program
before. He is extremely small and frail in stature
and has severe vision and hearing impairments, a
heart aliment, slightly deformed fingers and toes,
and a variety of other medical problems. He speaks
only a few words of English but communicates
rather fluently in Spanish. He walks in tiptoe fashion, with his mouth always wide open. He tends to
drool.

September 11. Eduardo seemed happy to be in
our class today. He just wants to talk about volca-
noes and earthquakes, which he seems to be very
interested in.

September 13. Eduardo wants to have my attention exclusively, for the purpose of socializing and
talking in Spanish. He does not initiate communication with the other children but has asked some
questions about them, such as "Will he ever see
again?" and "Where does she live?" He pushes others away roughly if they try to talk to me. He will

need to learn to be a little more tolerant of others.
His efforts to communicate seem almost frantic.

September 15. He has a great fear of losing his
vision. Near the end of the class, he began to cry,
saying, "Miguel, I don't want to be totally blind."
He seems to have gotten the impression that we
will be able to make him see and hear perfectly
well, through miraculous drops that can be put into
his eyes and ears. Otherwise, he seems to be adjusting well enough. He said there is a little girl
with blond hair whom he loves, but he does not
know her name.

September 19. Eduardo is in good spirits. He is
still always talking about earthquakes and volca-
noes. He gets much information about the news
from Spanish radio stations. He said, "I like *blond*
American girls."

September 25. In our lessons I found that Eduardo has a considerable background of knowledge
about Latin American countries. He knows the
names of practically all of the rulers and can discuss such things as climate, economics, and customs. He wants to write a letter to the president
of Venezuela.

September 28. Eduardo is traveling by himself
now. He has been causing some problems in the
cottage by using dirty words in Spanish. Today
four people from his cottage contacted me and said
that something had to be done about this. I talked
to Eduardo. He thought the whole thing was very
funny. He said that another boy had called him a
bad name first.

October 4. Today Eduardo told of an earthquake
that had just occurred in Trenton, New Jersey. He
said it registered 7.5 on the Richter Scale. This
would have meant a major disaster, so I checked it

out and found it was not so. He has also told stories about earthquakes in Philadelphia and Toledo, Ohio. He asks many questions about earthquakes.

October 5. He had a good time at our African dance this afternoon. When John and Larry made a circle around Eduardo and pretended to cook and eat him, he laughed. He said he would like nothing better than to travel around to all the countries in the world and see how people live and dress.

October 9. Eduardo needs to be reminded about grooming and self-care. He's been coming to school with his shirt completely unbuttoned, and he throws his coat down on the floor. This does not go over well at school or in the cottage.

October 13. Eduardo joined our group in a birthday party for Joyce. He wanted to stay with me the whole time and ask unrelated questions, such as how much "magma" (lava?) was in the earth beneath the school building. We are encouraging him to mix with the other children.

October 19. He is using more English. But I think sometimes he gets confused or misinformed. Like this weekend he thought he was going on a camping trip with the Boy Scouts and was all excited.

Actually, he wasn't included on the trip and was very disappointed.

October 23. Eduardo is already counting the days until Thanksgiving vacation. The subject of church came up. He said that on Thanksgiving he would go to church and pray for the Lord to protect him from one of the boys in the cottage. He's been getting into some scraps lately, but I cannot intervene for him all the time. I tell him to take care of himself and to act more responsibly.

October 26. Yesterday afternoon, as they were walking from school together, Eduardo apparently tried to engage in some sexual play with Lilly. Lilly was very upset and fearful. Today I asked Eduardo about what happened. He did not want to talk about it—gazed off into space and tried to change the subject by asking questions, such as "How are you?" "What will we do today?" and the like. Later, we went into a private room and talked "man-to-man," as he says. He wanted to be certain that nobody could hear us. He even asked if the room was bugged, like Watergate. I told Eduardo that he was not being punished but that he had frightened Lilly and that he should not do this sort of thing again (i.e., pulling down girls' pants). He seems to be repentant. He seems to be grasping the idea of *rules*.

Learning new skills . . . making a new friend.

from exceptionalities: assessement procedures should "require evidence that the handi-capping condition exists in the primary language, not only in English. . . . If the discrepancy occurs only in English, it is not a learning disability" (p. 11).

See chapters 4 and 6 for discussion of learning disabilities and communi-cation disorders.

Teachers may find it important to be aware of the nonverbal behaviors of their students and parents from Hispanic backgrounds. The significance of touch provides an illustration. Curt (1984) recalls that when she first came from Puerto Rico to a college in northeastern United States, she was struck by the "strange noncontact, nontouching culture," in which students rarely made physical contact with each other. In contrast, "Latins touch to a degree that is outrageous and threatening and often-times insulting to most Anglos. . . . If two women of the same age and social status meet, there is hugging, kissing and rubbing of upper parts of bodies in some cases. If men of the same age and social status meet, there is beating of backs, a hug maybe, and the firm shaking of hands" (p. 22). Although non-Hispanic teachers will probably not find it feasible to adopt the nonverbal behaviors of another culture, teacher-student and teacher-parent communication may be enhanced by some knowledge of the different significance attached to touch, interpersonal distance, silence, dress, and gestures.

Here are some general suggestions for teachers who work with Hispanic-American exceptional children.

1. Use Spanish in the classroom, including some instruction in Spanish for non-Spanish-speaking students.
2. Provide instruction in English as a second language for children and parents.
3. Introduce children to books, materials, and activities that depict Hispanic people and cultures.
4. Have Spanish-speaking teachers and aides in the school, to facilitate communication with children and parents.
5. Introduce children to Hispanic disabled adults who are leading productive lives.
6. Invite members of the Hispanic community to become involved in planning school-related programs.

American Indians and Other Native Americans

Information about the prevalence of exceptionality among Native American populations is difficult to obtain. Approximately 650,000 of the 1 million American Indians live on or near reservations; the rest are integrated into the general population, mainly in urban areas (Anderson & Ellis, 1980). Many federal, state, tribal, and local agencies provide medical, educational, and social services to Americans of Indian, Eskimo, or other Native descent.

Perhaps to a greater degree than most other cultures, Native Americans often absorb handicapped or disabled children into the family and community without removing them for special services. Non-Native professionals, in fact, often experience difficulty in setting up programs to identify and serve exceptional children on Indian reservations or in Native Alaskan communities (particularly if Native people are not involved in planning and carrying out the programs). Parents may resist having their children removed to be evaluated and educated in distant places.

As Anderson and Ellis (1980) point out, a first step in understanding the Native American's cultural differences is to appreciate the relationship between the individual and the tribe. The "wholeness of the tribe is what gives meaning to the part," they explain. "A flower petal has little beauty by itself but, when it is put together with the other parts of the flower, the whole, which includes the petal, is a thing of great beauty. . . . Indians will judge their worth primarily in terms of whether their behavior serves to better the tribe" (pp. 113–114). The tribe also influences the ways in which many Native Americans view knowledge and accomplishment. Unlike the European or Anglo view that promotes a single individual's understanding and achievements as a learning model, "the tribal form emphasizes knowledge after it works its way through the greatest number of community members" (Parent, 1985, p. 137).

Stewart (1977) illustrates the accepting nature of many Native American families toward a handicapped child by explaining that it is extremely hard to estimate the deaf population among certain Indian groups. Deaf children frequently become shepherds or learn to perform other useful roles in the community; they are not enrolled in schools or classes for the deaf. Among many Native groups it is not considered negative or tragic to have a child born with a disability; "it is assumed the child has the prenatal choice of how he wishes to be born and, if handicapped, is so by choice" (Stewart, 1977, p. 439). Indian languages also show a realistic and unemotional recognition of exceptionality. The Ute Indian term *n'kvat* is translated as "can't hear so can't talk," which Stewart considers much more descriptive than the archaic English term "deaf and dumb." Such attitudes of acceptance, however, may not extend to all exceptional children. Several observers have noted that Natives with obvious physical impairments and children who have seizures are often teased or regarded with alarm by their peers.

Native American students, particularly those from reservations or remote communities, may face special difficulties in making the transition from school to independent and productive adulthood. Kleinfeld (1987) worked in an isolated Alaskan village, where people typically supported themselves through a combination of hunting, casual employment, and government assistance programs. Conditions that led many students to drop out of postsecondary education and training programs included "(1) limited knowledge of the system among students and family members, (2) few models of adults who have blended native and western lifestyles in personally satisfying ways, and (3) great discontinuity between the nurturant world of small, remote villages and the impersonality of a large, modern institution" (p. 553). A special postsecondary counselor program, in which Native students received extensive, personalized assistance in meeting the demands of college and employment, was successful in reducing the dropout rate and improving the students' performance.

The challenges in identifying and serving Native American students who are gifted and talented have been discussed by Sisk (1987). The diversity of this population—encompassing some 490 tribes and 291 different languages—and the varying settings in which Native children are served have been difficult barriers to overcome in developing programs for gifted students. Some educators have found that gifted Native American students tend to have strong skills in observation, visual perception, problem solving, and memory. Activities should emphasize cooperative approaches to problems and de-emphasize competition among peers. "The gifted American Indian will not be dominant but will display independence and curosity in influencing others for the benefit of the group" (Sisk, 1987, p. 234).

Most suggestions for improving the lives of disabled Native Americans focus on broad issues of health, economics, and social development. Richardson (1981) has provided evidence to show that, on the average, the American Indian has a much lower income and shorter life expectancy than other Americans and that there is an extremely high incidence of unemployment, alcoholism, incarceration, and suicide among many Native groups. These problems, of course, merit the attention of the concerned teacher. On a more personal level, however, some advice has been offered for improv-

Contrast this term with the labels discussed in chapter 1.

The identification of gifted children in other culturally diverse groups is also of great concern. Sisk (1987) provides some specific guidelines.

ing interpersonal communication and classroom instruction with Native students and their families (Pepper, 1976; Richardson, 1981).

1. Show children expected behaviors by modeling and having them observe, rather than by verbally instructing them.
2. Don't reward or reprimand a child in front of the class. Quiet, private communication is usually preferred.
3. Develop the child's self-concept with assuring statements, such as "You can do it." Recognize even partial success at a task.
4. Social and academic competition among children may lead to problems; use activities in which children can share and work as teams.
5. Do not overemphasize timed tests and assignments. Many Natives have a flexible attitude toward time and rules.
6. Do not expect direct eye contact. Attention and respect may be conveyed when the Native child avoids eye contact while listening.
7. Display Native pictures or artifacts in your classroom or office; use materials that depict Native people realistically and with dignity.
8. American Indians appreciate a gentle handshake, not overly firm. When greeting people, it is considered polite to offer them something, such as a cup of coffee or a glass of water.
9. Avoid condescending statements and generalizations, such as "I have a good friend who is an Indian" or "Do you Eskimos believe in God?"
10. Acceptance and restatement of a Native person's views are recommended in counseling situations. Emphasize careful listening. Periods of silence are usually acceptable.

Asian Americans

See "Refugee Children from Vietnam: Adjusting to American Schools" on page 467.

Exceptional children of Asian descent constitute a sizable and, in many areas, a growing population. Some regions, notably Hawaii and California, have long-established Asian American communities, and in these and many other states there is a large, recently arrived Asian population. The United States is currently receiving more refugees and immigrants than at any other time in its history, and many of these are from such Asian countries as Cambodia, Korea, Laos, and Vietnam (Scholl, 1986). Relatively few special education programs, however, have been established to address the particular needs of Asian American students.

Wakabayashi (1977) considers Asian Americans "the least acknowledged of the national minorities" in the United States (p. 430) and notes that there are widespread misconceptions of Asian Americans as a monolithic group when, in reality, such cultures as Chinese, Japanese, and Vietnamese are quite different from one another.

Members of certain Asian American populations may be reluctant to seek out special services for disabled children or adults. Sue (1981) notes than Asian parents emphasize their children's obligations to the family unit and abnormal or deviant behaviors are handled within the family as much as possible. This suppression of public acknowledgment of disability probably means that there is a largely invisible population of disabled Asian Americans. In Wakabayashi's (1977) view the traditions and

FOCUS

REFUGEE CHILDREN FROM VIETNAM: ADJUSTING TO AMERICAN SCHOOLS

Tam Thi Dang Wei is a school psychologist who is Vietnamese. Wei points out that many Vietnamese refugee children encounter emotional, social, and educational problems in the United States because of different cultural traditions and expectations. The following incidents illustrate some cross-cultural difficulties that have arisen as Vietnamese students and American schools adjust to each other. Wei provides a brief interpretation of each.

Incident: A Vietnamese girl in the 10th grade in Missouri reportedly refused to go to her gym class. When asked for a valid reason by the gym teacher, she simply said she did not like gym. Only much later did the real reason appear. The girl revealed to a Vietnamese friend that she objected to being seen bare-legged, wearing gym shorts.

Interpretation: Coming from a region of Vietnam where old customs and traditions were still strong and where women, both young and old, were never to be seen bare-legged, this girl confessed to an intense feeling of discomfort when the gym hour occurred. To provide a sense of measure to this interesting case, however, we must add here the case of two Vietnamese high school girls, one in Georgia and the other in Maryland, who were drum majorettes for their respective high school bands. (p. 202)

Incident: An 8-year-old Vietnamese child in an elementary school in Maryland complained of a stomachache every day after his lunch hour. His teacher was mystified because the same food and milk did not make any other child in the class sick. The cause was later identified to be the fresh milk, which was perfectly good but to which the boy's digestive system was not accustomed.

Interpretation: Food habits are different from one culture to the next. Rice is a staple in the Vietnamese diet, whereas bread is a staple in the American diet. Pork is preferred to beef by most Vietnamese; the reverse is true in the United States. Fresh milk is likely to give some Vietnamese an upset stomach. They are used to boiled rather than homogenized milk, and their bodies are said not to produce the type of enzyme necessary to digest fresh milk. (pp. 202–3)

Incident: A teacher thought that his Vietnamese student had an auditory discrimination problem. He found out later that there are sounds in the English language that do not exist in the Vietnamese language. The student simply could not hear them and thus could not pronounce them correctly. Another teacher was surprised to see a Vietnamese child color pictures of eggs brown and cows yellow. The surprise turned into laughter when a Vietnamese friend told the teacher that Vietnamese eggs are brown in color and there are more yellow cows in Vietnam than black or brown cows.

Interpretation: The language problem is still a major handicap for students. It is further complicated by the cultural trait of face saving, which affects the pride and self-esteem of the Vietnamese and causes them frustration and a loss of motivation. It is important that American teachers understand the consequence of failure for these students. (p. 205)

Refugee children are a unique challenge for professionals, not only because they can be misdiagnosed, misclassified, or misunderstood, but also because they may not receive appropriate services when they indeed have handicapping conditions.

Source: Adapted from "The Vietnamese Refugee Child: Understanding Cultural Differences" by T. T. D. Wei in *The Bilingual Exceptional Child* (pp. 197–212) by D. R. Omark and J. G. Erickson (Eds.), 1983, San Diego: College-Hill. Reprinted by permission.

experiences of many Asian Americans endow them with "values and attitudes that are often incongruent with the service delivery vehicles that exist in the public sector" (p. 432). Other observers note that it is more acceptable for Asian Americans to admit to physical problems than to behavioral or psychological difficulties. This tendency may mean that, among Asian Americans, only people with more severe emotional or behavior disorders seek help from schools, clinics, and other programs.

Brower (1983) observes that some Asian students may find it difficult to speak of their own accomplishments, to ask or answer questions in class, or to voluntarily express opinions, lest they appear to be showing off. Also, "personal matters that embarrass or cause hurt or stress are not usually discussed with anyone except family and very close friends" (p. 114). Some Asian students, Brower suggests, may need to be taught about American expectations and values, in order to be more forthright and assertive in educational and employment situations.

"The toughest thing a teacher of Asian students must deal with is the silence; its reasons are complex," observes Fishman (1987, p. 85), who interviewed teachers and students in a largely Asian New York City high school. It may be difficult for a newly arrived student to become accustomed to the typical style of dialogue in American classrooms, in which teachers frequently address students by their first names, ask for their opinions, and seek to recognize individual students for their accomplishments. As one Asian student told Fishman, many of her peers are "afraid of the teacher because we respect the teacher—it's like a god, a mother." Other school procedures can also be inappropriate or disorienting to Asian students, such as changing clothes in front of other students in the gym. "You don't show your body, and then going into gym wearing this little thing and having to go to the bathroom, you've got to come out into the hall. Using knives and forks is confusing, particularly the 'sporks' in the cafeteria, and the foods" (pp. 85–86).

Perhaps because of the tendency of many Asians to deal with exceptionality within the family setting, little has been written about specific approaches that might be employed in the education of disabled or gifted Asian American students. The following perspectives, offered by Jerry Arakawa (1981), an Asian American who is blind, may be helpful for educators to keep in mind as they seek to develop such approaches.

> Being disabled and Asian meant having an additional personality trait that can potentially cause shame to the family. Consequently, the disabled Asian youngster has a less outgoing personality and takes risks less willingly.
>
> In Western culture, individuality is praised. In Asian culture, anything that breaks homogeneity is troubling. And the disabled Asian knows he is different.
>
> The Asian perspective is to minimize the handicap. The emphasis is on adapting and doing as little out of the ordinary as possible. This even means you avoid legal actions against discrimination. To get employment, you tough it out. If buses are inaccessible, you say it doesn't really matter.
>
> Consumerism and advocacy are very hard for a disabled Asian to understand. He or she seeks to avoid underscoring a disability and focusing public attention on it. To do otherwise is discomforting.

In the last few years, attitudes about disability in the Asian community have become more Western. But the basic values remain: Be a high achiever and transcend your disability. Asians want to excel. They want to be the best. (p. 1)

Bilingual Special Education Students

Bilingual, or language minority, children have "been exposed to two languages in natural speaking contexts [and] come from homes where they have made functional use of a language other than that of the dominant culture during interactions with one or more family members" (Mattes & Omark, 1984, p. 2). Some children have handicaps as well as language differences; it is not always easy to distinguish between those children whose learning and communication problems are due to disabilities and those who are solely in need of instruction in English. The high rate of language minority students in special education classes, however, implies that there is a need for tests and referral procedures that will "help teachers to distinguish differences from exceptionalities for language minority students" and to accommodate the differences in the least restrictive educational setting (Teacher Education Division, 1986, p. 25).

In order to rule out the lack of English proficiency as a cause of achievement difficulties, "every language minority child referred to special education should receive a comprehensive language assessment in the native and the English language" (Ortiz & Garcia, 1986, p. 11). It is also advisable to have bilingual teachers or paraprofessionals participate in the assessment process. There is currently a pressing need for bilingual special education teachers with knowledge of "second-language acquisition theories, the possible interactions of cultural differences with handicapping conditions, and other content specific to the education of these children" (Valero-Figueira, 1986, p. 83). The employment and training of bilingual staff members, although critical, is also problematic. The staffing needs of large urban school districts, such as those in New York and Los Angeles, are indeed complex; they may enroll students from as many as 75 different native language backgrounds. And rural districts may have difficulty finding bilingual personnel who speak less-prevalent languages.

Educators disagree about the most effective methods of teaching bilingual students. U.S. Secretary of Education William J. Bennett (1986) has written that some children "come from families who encourage their acquisition of English; some run in peer groups where the native language is a matter of pride. Some arrive speaking languages from which the transition to English is relatively easy; others speak languages whose entire structure is perplexingly different from ours" (p. 62). Bennett maintains that the specific methods to be used in teaching bilingual children should be a local decision but argues strongly that "all American children need to learn to speak, read, and write English as soon as possible" (p. 62). Some professionals and legislators have called for the designation of English as the "exclusive official language of the United States" (Glenn, 1986). Adoption of such a policy would tend to discourage schools from offering instruction in students' native languages.

In contrast to the preceding views, some educators (e.g., Ada, 1986; Cardenas, 1986) maintain that it is a mistake for a bilingual child to make the transition to English too rapidly and that school instruction should be given in both the native

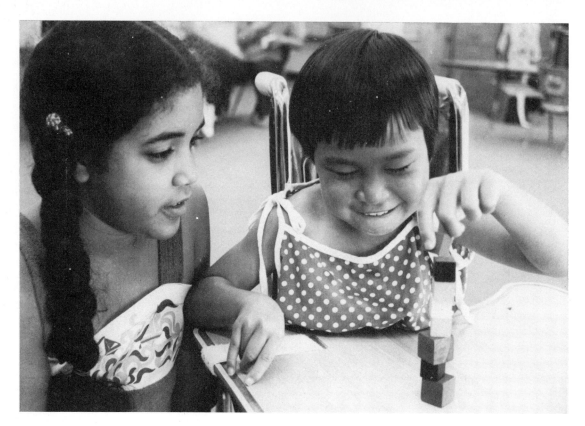

This child's educational program must address her language differences as well as her physical disabilities.

language and in English. "The use of language is imperative to the intellectual development of the child . . . rather than risk premature restriction of native-language usage and communication capability, I recommend continuation of the use of the native language until there is complete assurance of sufficient mastery of the English language" (Cardenas, 1986, p. 361). Although acknowledging that the development of solid cognitive and linguistic skills in a first language is important, Glenn (1986) points out that "the most critical years of language development have already passed before children come to school . . . . we may be perpetuating and compounding the original linguistic confusion by presenting two languages to children who have enough difficulty with one" (p. 655).

Research in bilingual education has not provided clear guidelines to methodology. However, there is general agreement that children acquire English most effectively through actively participating in interactions with teachers, parents, and peers. A child who engages in and talks about interesting experiences will be more likely to develop good English skills than a child who is limited to classroom instruction and teacher correction of errors. Efforts should be made to give bilingual exceptional children a wide variety of opportunities to explore the world through language.

Migrant Students

Migrant students include a group of handicapped children whose needs have been largely unmet because of their families' bilingual-multicultural backgrounds and no-madic life-styles (Salend, Michael, & Taylor, 1984). Migrant students are the sons and daughters of farm workers who typically live in three or four different locations each year; they are usually Hispanic but also include black, white, Asian, and Native American children.

Like other culturally diverse populations, migrant children have educational needs that have been widely neglected until recently, when they became mandated and supported by federal and state legislation (notably P.L. 93–380). Procedures now exist to support the identification of migrant children and to assist them in obtaining a free, appropriate program of public education. The U.S. Department of Education operates a national computerized file of information on migrant children, known as the Migrant Student Record Transfer System, to help schools in the difficult task of maintaining data on students' health, family, and educational performance.

Joyce King-Stoops (1980) has compiled a brief guide for teachers of migrant children. Some of her suggestions may also be applicable to other culturally diverse students with special needs. One strategy that has proven useful has been to employ high school or college students with migrant backgrounds (usually bilingual) as part-time aides in classrooms for younger children. This involvement improves the self-concept of both migrant children and aides, facilitates communication with parents, and encourges some young adults from this culture to consider teaching as a profes-sion. Also, the money earned by the aides is generally greatly needed. King-Stoops emphasizes migrant students' need to experience acceptance and success in school, recommending the use of "short tasks that are appropriate and can be accomplished in a reasonable time" (p. 23).

The development of good language and reading patterns is prerequisite to suc-cess in school and to employment for most students. King-Stoops presents some ac-tivities designed to improve children's listening and speaking skills. Migrant children sometimes speak *pocho*, a mixture of English and Spanish. The teacher should encour-age communication by listening first and then modeling standard speech patterns for the child.

Child: It lunch time. I go *walkando.*
Teacher: It's lunch time. We'll all go walking to lunch now. (King-Stoops, 1980, p. 29)

GUIDELINES FOR TEACHERS OF CULTURALLY DIVERSE EXCEPTIONAL CHILDREN

It would not be possible to offer a comprehensive list of teaching approaches that would apply to all children of diverse cultural backgrounds. In general, it is our view that effective instructional procedures apply to children of all cultural backgrounds. Indeed, when exceptional students have the additional special need of adjusting to a new or different culture or language, it is even more important for the teacher to plan individualized activities, convey expectations clearly, observe and record behavior precisely, and give the child specific, immediate reinforcement in response to performance. Such procedures, coupled with a helpful and friendly attitude on the part of the teacher, can help increase the culturally different exceptional child's motivation and achievement in school.

When developing services to meet the needs of an exceptional child from a culturally diverse background, teachers should obtain as much information as possible about the child, the family, and the cultural group. A useful strategy is to interview parents and others who are familiar with the child and her particular cultural environment. The following questions might be among those asked in an interview:

- ☐ Why have members of the cultural group left their homeland?
- ☐ Why have members of the cultural group settled in the local community?
- ☐ To what extent is poverty experienced by members of the cultural group?
- ☐ What is the typical family size?
- ☐ What roles are assigned to individual family members?
- ☐ What customs, values, and beliefs in the culture have relevance in understanding children's behavior?
- ☐ What are the social functions and leisure activities in which members of the cultural group participate?
- ☐ How do members of the cultural group view the role of an education?
- ☐ How do members of the cultural group view handicapped individuals? (Mattes & Omark, 1984, pp. 43–45)

Information gained from such questions can be used as a basis for determining activities that will be appropriate and reinforcing for a child. The teacher's understanding of a child's behavior in school and of techniques for facilitating communication with parents will also be enhanced.

Although understanding and sensitivity are clearly important, it is also necessary for the teacher of culturally diverse students to use effective instructional practices. Bernick (1986) emphasizes the teaching of basic academic skills in helping students improve their abilities and prospects for employment. After all, "jobs that do not require literacy skills are characterized by unstable hours, low pay, and little opportunity for advancement" (p. 365). Bernick describes five important factors in a successful instructional program for inner-city school dropouts.

- ☐ *A strong assessment component*, with entrance examinations and periodic tests to measure the students' needs and progress.
- ☐ *A focus on basic skills and problem solving*, with instruction that draws heavily on the students' own real-life experiences.
- ☐ *Camaraderie among students and staff members.* A group of students works closely with one primary instructor, rather than rotating among several different instructors.
- ☐ *Computer-assisted instruction*, complementing traditional instruction and allowing each student to proceed at his or her own pace.
- ☐ *Connection to the world of work.* Students need to see that the instruction is leading somewhere, in preparing them for specific jobs or more advanced vocational training. (pp. 366–367)

The teacher of culturally diverse exceptional children should adopt a flexible teaching style, establish a positive climate for learning, and use a variety of approaches to meet individual student needs. With a caring attitude, careful assessment and observation of behavior, and the use of appropriate materials and community resources, the teacher can do a great deal to help exceptional children from different cultural or language backgrounds experience success in school.

SUMMARY

1. Though cultural diversity is a strength of our society, many exceptional students still experience discrimination because of their race, social class, or other differences from the majority. Educators should avoid stereotypes based on race or culture.

2. Special education is becoming increasingly international in scope. Many American educators have learned from their experiences in other countries.

3. About one-third of the children in special education programs are members of culturally diverse groups. In many programs the population of culturally diverse exceptional students is growing.
   a. Students' assessment for placement in special education should be fair; referral should be based on each child's needs rather than on his background.
   b. Schools may need to provide special supportive services for culturally diverse exceptional students.
   c. Special educators should be aware of each child's cultural background in evaluating classroom behaviors.

4. We have chosen to use the term *culturally diverse* to describe exceptional children whose background is different enough to require special methods of assessment, intervention, or counseling.

5. Standardized IQ tests tend to be culturally biased.
   a. They should not be used as the sole criterion for placement in special education.
   b. Translations or adaptations of IQ tests for children from non-English-speaking homes should be used with caution, as they tend to be unreliable and may not reflect the language or dialect used in the home.
   c. Objective, interdisciplinary assessment may help overcome some of the traditional difficulties in assessing culturally diverse children.
   d. Assessment should include observation of the child outside the school. It should consider the child's social and cultural background.

6. Teachers of exceptional black students should be aware of common cultural differences between blacks and whites in communication styles, family relationships, and parental attitudes.

7. Teachers of Hispanic children should keep in mind certain common characteristics that may affect school behavior.
   a. Hispanic familes often place the interests of the family above the interests of the individual person.
   b. Mexican-American children often respond well to close, personalized relationships with their teachers.

c. Classrooms should incorporate the Spanish language and Hispanic culture to facilitate communication with children and their parents.

8. Native Americans tend to absorb handicapped children into the family and community rather than segregating them.
   a. Programs to improve the lives of disabled Native Americans tend to focus on broad issues of health and economic and social development.
   b. Again, teachers should consider common values and behaviors of Native Americans when they interact with the children and their families.

9. Disabled Asian Americans are a sizable, growing population but may be hard to identify because of the culture's attitudes toward disability and achievement. Asian Americans often deal with exceptionality within the family, rather than seeking outside services.

10. Exceptional students from bilingual backgrounds prompt a number of special concerns.
    a. Lack of English proficiency should not be confused with a handicapping condition.
    b. Assessment in the native language is essential.
    c. Some educators believe that bilingual children should learn English as soon as possible, whereas others maintain that they should be taught in the native language until English proficiency is attained.

11. Migrant children, many of whom are from culturally diverse backgrounds, are likely to require special instructional programs.

12. It is recommended that teachers obtain as much information as possible about an exceptional child's cultural and family background. Well-structured instructional approaches that consider each student's individual needs are likely to be effective with culturally diverse students.

FOR MORE INFORMATION

Books

Atkinson, D. R., Morten, G., & Sue, D. W. (1983). *Counseling American minorities* (2nd ed.). Dubuque, IA: William C. Brown.

Baca, L. M., & Cervantes, H. T. (1986). *The bilingual special education interface.* Columbus, OH: Merrill.

Banks, J. A. (1984). *Teaching strategies for ethnic studies* (3rd ed.). Boston: Allyn & Bacon.

Fradd, S. H., & Tikunoff, W. J. (Eds.). (1987). *Bilingual education and bilingual special education: A guide for administrators.* Boston: Little, Brown.

Gollnick, D. M., & Chinn, P. C. (1986). *Multicultural education in a pluralistic society* (2nd ed.). Columbus, OH: Merrill.

Grossman, H. (1984). *Educating Hispanic students: Cultural implications for instruction, classroom management, counseling and assessment.* Springfield, IL: Charles C Thomas.

Kitano, M. K., & Chinn, P. C. (Eds.). (1986). Exceptional Asian children and youth. Reston, VA: Council for Exceptional Children.

Marfo, K., Walker, S., & Charles, B. (Eds.). (1986). *Childhood disability in developing countries: Issues in habilitation and special education.* New York: Praeger.

Mattes, L. J., & Omark, D. R. (1984). *Speech and language assessment for the bilingual handicapped.* San Diego: College-Hill.

Powell, G. J. (Ed.). (1983). *The psychosocial development of minority group children.* New York: Brunner/Mazel.

Tiedt, P. L., & Tiedt, I. M. (1986). *Multicultural teaching: A handbook of activities, information, and resources* (2nd ed.). Boston: Allyn & Bacon.

Willig, A. C., & Greenberg, H. F. (1986). *Bilingualism and learning disabilities: Policy and practice for teachers and administrators.* New York: American Library.

Organization

Council for Exceptional Children, 1920 Association Drive, Reston, VA 22091. Sponsors periodic conferences on the needs of culturally diverse exceptional children. Presents frequent articles on multicultural issues in *Exceptional Children* and *Teaching Exceptional Children.* Makes available annotated bibliographies on bilingual and multicultural exceptional children. Maintains an Office of Minority Concerns and several caucuses of interest to special educators who work with culturally diverse students.

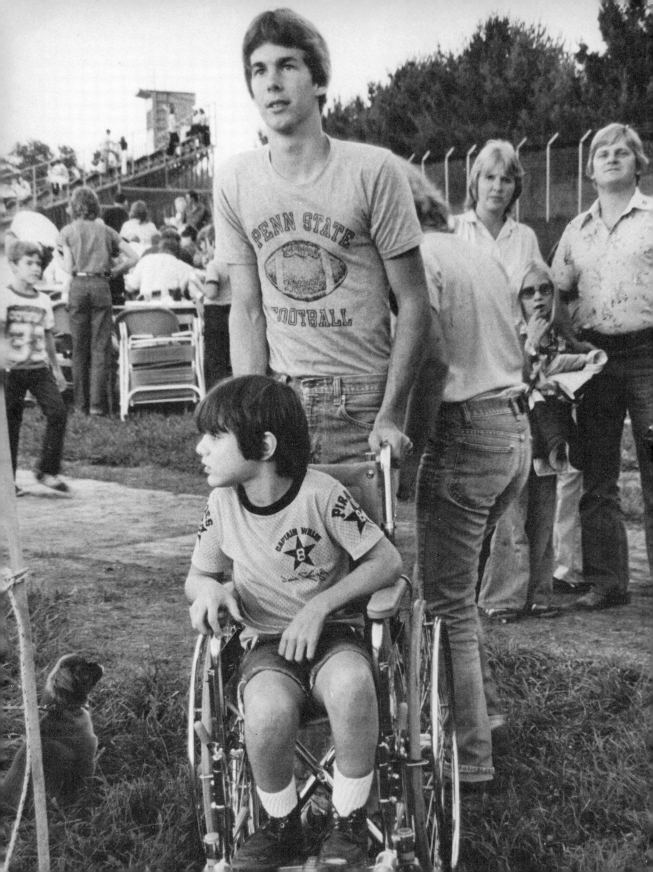

13

WORKING WITH PARENTS AND FAMILIES

A parent is a child's first teacher, the person who is always there giving prompts, encouragement, praise, and corrective feedback. The parent is responsible for helping the young child learn literally hundreds of skills. In many respects no one ever knows as much about a child as a parent does. And nobody else holds as much vested interest in that child. These are safe-enough statements—obviously true for the vast majority of parent-child relationships. Yet only recently has the special education community begun to understand the primary role of parents. Only recently have these fundamental truths been viewed as valuable guidelines for the parent-teacher relationship.

For years parents were viewed by many educators as either troublesome (if they asked many questions or, worse yet, offered suggestions about their child's education) or uncaring (if they did not jump to attention whenever the professional determined that the parent needed something—typically advice from the professional). Parents, too, have often seen professionals as adversaries. But in recent years parent involvement in special education has received a great deal of attention. Parents and teachers are developing better ways to communicate with each other and work together for the common benefit of the exceptional child. In this chapter we will examine the history of the parent-teacher relationship. We will explore some of the reasons that it has not always been so positive in the past and some examples of the progress that has been made. In an attempt to understand a parent's perspective better, we will look at some of the ways a child's handicap can affect the family and the roles and responsibilities of parents and siblings. As we describe some of the techniques and programs that are being developed to improve communication with parents and to involve them in their children's education, you will see that working with parents of exceptional children is certainly among the most important and rewarding skills a teacher can develop.

THE PARENT-TEACHER PARTNERSHIP

Parents and teachers who work actively and effectively with one another comprise a powerful team. Heward, Dardig, and Rossett (1979) have described the benefits of developing a parent-teacher partnership.

A productive parent-professional relationship provides professionals with

☐ Greater understanding of the overall needs of the child and the needs and desires of the parent.
☐ Data for more meaningful selection of target behaviors that are important to the child in her world outside the school.
☐ Access to a wider range of social and activity reinforcers provided by parents.
☐ Increased opportunities to reinforce appropriate behaviors in both school and home settings.
☐ Feedback from parents as to changes in behavior that can be used to improve programs being implemented by professionals and parents.
☐ The ability to comply with legislation mandating continuing parental input to the educational process.

A productive parent-professional relationship provides parents with

☐ Greater understanding of the needs of their child and the objectives of the teacher.
☐ Information on their rights and responsibilities as parents of an exceptional child.
☐ Specific information about their child's school program and how they can become involved.
☐ Specific ways to extend the positive effects of school programming into the home.
☐ Increased skills in helping their child learn functional behaviors that are appropriate for the home environment.
☐ Access to additional important resources (current and future) for their child.

And, of most importance, a productive parent-professional relationship provides the child with

☐ Greater consistency in her two most important environments.
☐ Increased opportunities for learning and growth.
☐ Access to expanded resources and services. (p. 226)

These are all important reasons for establishing a strong parent-teacher relationship. But before we describe some of the ways such a partnership can be developed and maintained, we need to explain some of the reasons that parents and teachers have not always worked well together.

Barriers to Effective Parent-Teacher Interaction

Let's face it—parents and teachers do not always cooperate. They may sometimes even seem to be on two widely different sides, doing battle over what is best for the child. The handicapped child, unfortunately, can never win that battle. He needs to have the people responsible for the two places where he spends most of his life—

A child's first teachers.

home and school—work together to make those environments consistent. Both home and school must be supportive of his job of learning. Some parents and teachers have made assumptions and held attitudes toward one another that have been counter-productive. Parents have complained that professionals are negative, unavailable, or patronizing. Teachers have complained that parents are uninterested, uncooperative, or hostile.

Roos (1980), a special educator who is the father of a mentally retarded child, blames much of the hostility and negative attitudes shown by parents on what he calls professional mishandling. Many professionals hold negative stereotypes and false assumptions about what parents of handicapped children face and need (Donnellan & Mirenda, 1984). These attitudes have often led to poor relationships between parents and professionals.

Sonnenschein (1981) has also described some behaviors of professionals that detract from productive relationships. She examined several attitudes or approaches that, when followed by professionals, create roadblocks to effective partnerships.

☐ *The parent as vulnerable client.* Professionals who see parents only as helpless souls in need of assistance make a grave mistake. Teachers need parents and the things they have to offer as much as parents need teachers.
☐ *Professional distance.* Most professionals in human services develop some degree of professional distance as a means of not getting too involved with a client—

supposedly to maintain objectivity and credibility. But aloofness or coldness in the name of professionalism has hindered and terminated many a parent-teacher relationship. Parents must believe the professional really cares about them.

☐ *The parent as patient.* Some professionals make the faulty assumption that having a handicapped child renders the parent in need of therapy. Roos (1978) writes, "I had suddenly been demoted from the role of a professional to that of the 'parent as patient,' the assumption by some professionals that parents of a retarded child are emotionally maladjusted and are prime candidates for counseling, psychotherapy or tranquilizers" (p. 15).

☐ *The parent as responsible for the child's condition.* Some parents do feel responsible for their child's disability and, with a little encouragement from a professional, can be made to feel completely guilty. A productive parent-professional relationship focuses on remediation of problems, not on a place to lay blame.

☐ *The parent as less intelligent.* Too often information and suggestions provided by parents are given little recognition. Parents are considered too biased, too involved, or not skilled enough to make useful observations. Some professionals do concede that parents have access to needed information but contend that parents are not able to, or should not, make any decisions based on what they know. One study of school personnel found that the majority of the members of IEP planning teams believed that parents are expected to provide information to the planning team but are not expected to participate actively in making decisions about their child's program (Yoshida, Fenton, Kaufman, & Maxwell, 1978).

☐ *The parent as adversary.* Some teachers expect the worst whenever they interact with parents. Even though that attitude can be partially explained by the fact that some teachers have been "burned" by unreasonable parents, it is at best a negative influence on new relationships.

☐ *Tendency to label parents.* Professionals often seem eager to label parents, just as they often do children. If parents disagree with a diagnosis or seek another opinion, they are denying; if they refuse a suggested treatment, they are labeled resistant; and if parents insist that something is wrong with their child despite test evidence to the contrary, they are called anxious. The professional who believes that a parent's perception may be the correct one is rare; yet parents often *do* know best.

To the extent that teachers and other special educators believe and behave in these ways, it is understandable that parents may feel intimidated, confused, or hostile. But the factors working against positive parent-teacher relationships cannot all be attributed to professional mishandling. Some parents are, in fact, difficult to work with or unreasonable.

> The attitudes and behaviors of the parents have also contributed to negative interactions. There is no easy way to tell a mother and father that their child is substantially handicapped. Some parents want to hear the hard truth; others want to be eased into it. Professionals may carefully choose their words with the greatest sensitivity, yet still offend the parents. Sometimes parents are unforgiving and do not realize the difficult position of the professional. They may vent their anger at the professional and discuss the professional's "gross lack of sensitivity" with family and friends. (Turnbull, 1983, p. 19)

There are situations in which parents fight long and hard for services for their child. After the services are found and the child is receiving an appropriate education, the parents continue their intense advocacy until minor issues with professionals become major confrontations. As one mother stated, "For years I have scrapped and fought for services. Now I come on like gangbusters over issues that are really not that important. I don't like what has happened to me. I've ended up to be an aggressive, angry person." This posture leads to unproductive interactions between parents and professionals. (Bronicki & Turnbull, 1987, p. 10)

A purpose in examining some of these causes of parent-teacher friction is not to place blame, but rather to understand better those factors that we can change and improve. Professionals who recognize that some of their own behaviors may decrease the potential for productive relationships with parents are in a better position to change their actions and encourage the benefits that such relationships can provide. One of the first steps is to avoid sweeping generalizations about parents of exceptional children and treat them with respect as individuals. After all, isn't that how teachers want to be treated?

Breaking Down Barriers to Effective Parent-Teacher Interaction

Negative interactions between parents and teachers can be related to a mutual lack of awareness and understanding of each other's roles and responsibilities. During the last decade a number of forces have come together to focus national attention on the importance of a parent-teacher partnership based on mutual respect and participation in decision making (Bronicki & Turnbull, 1987). Although many things have contributed to the increased involvement of parents in the education of their exceptional children, we can view three groups of people as primarily responsible—parents, educators, and legislators.

Parents: Advocates for Changes

The dictionary defines advocate as someone who speaks for or pleads the case of another. Parents of exceptional children have played that role for many years, but in recent history they have done so with impressive effectiveness (Cain, 1976). The first parent group organized for handicapped children was the National Society for Crippled Children, which began in 1921. The National Association for Retarded Children, organized in 1950, and the United Cerebral Palsy Association, organized in 1948, are two national parent organizations that have been largely responsible for making the public aware of their children's needs. The Association for Children and Adults with Learning Disabilities (ACLD) is another group organized by and consisting mostly of parents that has been instrumental in bringing about educational reform. As we saw in chapters 1 and 2, parents were instrumental in bringing about litigation and legislation establishing the rights of handicapped children to education.

In 1980 the National Association for Retarded Children changed its name to the Association for Retarded Citizens.

More than any other group of people, parents themselves have been responsible for their increased involvement in special education. They have formed effective organizations that have been the impetus for much educational reform. As individuals, they are learning more about the educational needs of their children and are seeing more and more the potential benefits of an effective parent-teacher partnership.

Educators: Striving for Greater Impact

Educators have recognized the necessity of expanding the traditional role of the classroom teacher to meet the special needs of handicapped children. This expanded role demands that teaching be viewed as more than delivering the three Rs. Special educators now realize that daily living, social, vocational, and leisure skills are critical to a handicapped student's successful functioning. They now attach a high priority to developing and maintaining the functional skills that will enable a handicapped child or adult to be successful in school, home, work, and community settings.

Because the implementation of this new priority has implications and applications outside the classroom, teachers have begun to look outside the school for assistance and support. Parents are a natural and necessary resource for expanding educational services to the home and community. At the very least, teachers benefit from information provided by parents about their children's success with specific skills outside the classroom.

But parents have proven to be much more than just reporters of behavior change. They can tell what skills their children need to learn and, just as important, which ones their children have already acquired. Parents can work with teachers to provide needed extra practice of skills at home, and even to teach their children new skills. A large and growing body of experimental research shows that parents can enhance the development of their handicapped children by teaching them at home (e.g., Schumaker & Sherman, 1978; Snell & Beckman-Brindley, 1984; Wedel & Fowler, 1984; Wolery, 1979). Research attesting to the positive outcomes of early intervention with handicapped and at-risk preschoolers also supports the increased focus on working cooperatively with parents (e.g., Bailey & Wolery, 1984; Bronfenbrenner, 1974; Smith & Strain, 1984; Tjossem, 1976).

We will examine the effects and methods of early intervention with handicapped children in chapter 14.

In short, educators are giving up the old notions that parents should not be too involved in their children's educational programs or that they should not try to teach their children for fear of doing something wrong. Teachers are realizing that parents are a powerful and necessary ally (Kroth, 1978). Only through an effective parent-teacher partnership can everyone's goals—teacher's, parent's, and child's—be fullfilled.

Legislators: Mandates for Involvement

As we saw in previous chapters, P.L. 94–142 and corresponding state laws mandate parent involvement in the education of handicapped children. The federal law provides statutory guidelines for parent-professional interaction in the provision of a free and appropriate education, referral, testing, placement, and program planning. In addition, the law provides due process procedures if parents believe their child's needs are not being met. Although some educators view P.L. 94–142 as "the parents' law" and are threatened by the new role it specifies for parents, most view it as representing sound educational practice and welcome the increased parent involvement it encourages (Kroth, 1978). As Klein and Schleifer (1980) observe, "The challenge of the 1980s

For a discussion of P.L. 94–142 as it relates to the parent-professional relationship, see Turnbull, Turnbull, Summers, Brotherson, and Benson (1986).

Families react to the presence of a handicapped child in many different ways.

for both parents and professionals will be to find ways to carry out the legislative mandates for collaborative efforts to help children" (p. 3).

In sum, we can attribute special educators' increased interest in working effectively with parents of handicapped children to three related factors:

1. Many parents want to be involved.
2. Research and practice have convinced many educators that their effectiveness can be increased through parental assistance and involvement.
3. The law requires it.

EFFECTS OF A HANDICAPPED CHILD ON PARENTS AND FAMILY

Special educators usually interact with parents of exceptional children for two primary reasons: (1) to collect information and suggestions that can help the teacher do a better job in the classroom and (2) to provide information and assistance to parents for working with their children outside the classroom. The teacher who wants to be both seeker and provider of assistance must be able to communicate effectively with parents. Effective communication requires an understanding of and respect for the responsibilities and challenges faced by parents of exceptional children.

Parental Reactions to a Handicapped Child

A great deal has been written about parents' reactions to the birth of a handicapped child or to the discovery that their child has a learning problem or physical disability. In a review of the literature describing parental responses to the birth of a handicapped child, Blacher (1984) found a consistent theme promoting three stages of adjustment. First, parents are said to experience a period of emotional crisis characterized by shock, denial, and disbelief. This initial reaction is followed by a period of emotional disorganization that includes alternating feelings of anger, guilt, depression, shame, lowered self-esteem, rejection of the child, overprotectiveness, and so on. Finally, it is presumed that parents eventually reach a third stage in which they accept their disabled child.

There is no question that the birth of a handicapped child or the discovery that a child has a disability is an intense and traumatic event (Turnbull & Turnbull, 1985). And there is evidence to show that many parents of handicapped children do experience similar reactions and emotional responses and that most do go through an adjustment process, trying to work their way through their feelings (Eden-Piercy, Blacher, & Eyman, 1986; Featherstone, 1980). But we see two problems with promoting the idea of stages of adjustment. First, it is easy to assume that all parents must pass through a similar sequence of stages and that time is the most important variable in adjustment. In fact, parents react to the arrival of a handicapped child in many different ways (Allen & Affleck, 1985). For some parents years may pass and they are still are not comfortable with their child; others report that having a handicapped child has actually strengthened their life or marriage (Schell, 1981; Weiss & Weiss, 1976). The sequence and time needed for adjustment is different for every parent. The one common thread is that almost all parents can be helped during their adjustment by sensitive and supportive friends and professionals (Schlesinger & Meadow, 1976; Turnbull, 1983).

See Turnbull and Turnbull (1985) for a collection of moving personal stories by parents of handicapped children.

Our second concern with the stages of adjustment is that the stages have a distinct psychiatric flavor, and professionals may mistakenly assume that the parents are maladjusted. Some educators seem to assume that all parents of handicapped children need counseling.

> It may be that many parents do respond in ways that are well-described by the stage model. But it is dangerous to impose this model on all parents. Those who exhibit different response patterns might be inappropriately judged as "deviant." Parents who do not progress as rapidly through the "stages" might be considered slow to adjust. And those who exhibit emotions in a different sequence might be thought of as regressing. (Allen & Affleck, 1985, p. 201)

As Farber (1975) has pointed out, it is a mistake to think of parents of handicapped children as psychological curiosities; they are more like the parents of normal children then they are different. Parenting any child is a tremendous challenge that produces emotional responses and requires adjustment. Parents of handicapped children, like the parents of nonhandicapped children, must sometimes operate under financial, physical, emotional, and marital stress. However, parents of handicapped children must deal with the additional task of securing and relating to the special services needed by their children.

Blackstone (1981), himself the parent of a handicapped child, gives some examples of the ways in which parents of exceptional children are often viewed and treated differently from other parents.

The parent of the normal child skips monthly PTA meetings, and his behavior is considered normal. The parent of the exceptional child skips monthly meetings, and he is said to be uncaring and hard to reach.

A couple with normal children divorce. They are said to be incompatible. The couple with an exceptional child divorce, and it is said that the child ruined the marriage.

The parents of a normal child are told that because their child is having reading difficulties, it would be "nice" if they could work with her at home. The parents of the exceptional child are told that if they do not work with their child, she will not learn! (pp. 29–30)

One way of attempting to understand how a child's disability affects family members is to examine the likely impact of the child's special needs at various ages. Turnbull, Turnbull, Summers, Brotherson, and Benson (1986) have done this by describing the possible issues and concerns faced by parents and nonhandicapped siblings during four life-cycle stages. Table 13.1 provides an outline of their analysis. Results of a study by Wikler (1986) lend support to the concept that parents and siblings face different challenges at different life-cycle stages of the handicapped child. Wikler's study of 60 families found increased levels of family stress at the onset of adolescence and at the onset of adulthood.

TABLE 13.1
Possible issues encountered by parents and siblings at different life-cycle stages of a handicapped individual.

Life Cycle Stage	Parents	Siblings
Early childhood, ages 0–5	Obtaining an accurate diagnosis Informing siblings and relatives Locating services Seeking to find meaning in the exceptionality Clarifying a personal ideology to guide decision making Addressing issues of stigma Identifying positive contributions of exceptionality	Less parental time and energy for sibling needs Feelings of jealousy over less attention Fears associated with misunderstandings of exceptionality
School age, ages 6–12	Establishing routines to carry out family functions Adjusting emotionally to educational implications Clarifying issues of mainstreaming v. special class placement Participating in IEP conferences Locating community resources Arranging for extracurricular activities	Division of responsibility for any physical care needs Oldest female sibling may be at risk Limited family resources for recreation and leisure Informing friends and teachers Possible concern over surpassing younger sibling Issues of mainstreaming into same school Need for basic information on exceptionality

TABLE 13.1 *continued*

Adolescence, ages 13–21	Adjusting emotionally to possible chronicity of exceptionality	Overidentification with sibling
	Identifying issues of emerging sexuality	Greater understanding of differences in people
	Addressing possible peer isolation and rejection	Influence of exceptionality on career choice
	Planning for career/vocational development	Dealing with possible stigma and embarrassment
	Arranging for leisure time activities	Participation in sibling training programs
	Dealing with physical and emotional change of puberty	Opportunity for sibling support groups
	Planning for postsecondary education	
Adulthood, ages 21–	Planning for possible need for guardianship	Possible issues of responsibility for financial support
	Addressing the need for appropriate adult residence	Addressing concerns regarding genetic implications
	Adjusting emotionally to any adult implications of dependency	Introducing new in-laws to exceptionality
	Addressing the need for socialization opportunities outside the family for individual with exceptionality	Need for information on career/living options
		Clarify role of sibling advocacy
	Initiating career choice or vocational program	Possible issues of guardianship

Source: From *Families, Professionals, and Exceptionality: A Special Partnership* (pp. 106–107) by A. P. Turnbull, H. R. Turnbull III, J. A. Summers, M. J. Brotherson, and H. A. Benson, 1986, Columbus, OH: Merrill. Reprinted by permission.

Abuse and Neglect of Handicapped Children

Child abuse and neglect occur with alarming frequency. Each year the National Center on Child Abuse and Neglect receives more than 1 million reports of child abuse and neglect, and it is believed that the true incidence is much higher. When that agency conducted the National Study on the Incidence and Severity of Child Abuse and Neglect (1981), it estimated that only 21% of the suspected cases of child abuse and neglect are reported to protective services agencies. Because the majority of child abuse and neglect cases are never reported, it is impossible to know the true extent of the problem. The estimates vary considerably, but Harrison and Edwards (1983) believe that as many as 20% of all children may be neglected or physically, sexually, or emotionally abused by their parents.

Although the incidence of parental abuse and neglect of children with handicaps is also unknown, Kurtz and Kurtz (1987) state that "a growing body of evidence establishes a convincing connection between child maltreatment and handicapped children" (p. 216). In his review of the research conducted on child abuse, Zirpoli (1987) found that not only were children with handicaps overrepresented in child abuse samples, but they were more likely to be abused for a longer period of time.

Whereas the infant with colic may increase family stress for a limited period, the child with cerebral palsy, or any other long-term or permanent handicap, presents a potential long-term family crisis. As a result, children with handicaps are not only at greater risk for abuse, but for longer periods of time. It is no wonder, then, that children with handicaps are disproportionately represented in child abuse samples. (p. 44)

Is a child's handicapping condition the reason she is abused and neglected, as suggested by some studies (Fontana, 1971; Milner & Wimberley, 1980; Morse, Sahler, & Friedman, 1970)? Or do abuse and neglect produce a handicap in an otherwise normally developing child (Brandwein, 1973; Elmer, 1967, 1977)?

> In many cases, to ask the question of whether children are abused because they are handicapped, or handicapped because they are abused, is something akin to the old question of which came first—the chicken or the egg. We know this much for certain: some children *are* abused because they are handicapped, and some children *are* handicapped because they are abused. (Morgan, 1987, p. 45)

In most instances, however, it would be a mistake to say simply that a child's handicap caused the abuse and neglect. Researchers who have studied child abuse and neglect have come to the conclusion that it has no single cause but is the product of the complex interactions of numerous variables, only one of which concerns the child's characteristics (Kurtz & Kurtz, 1987; Zirpoli, 1987). Just a few of the many factors that have been found to correlate with an increased incidence of child abuse are the parent's own abuse as a child, alcohol or drug dependency, unemployment, poverty, and marital discord. But again, it is important to stress that none of these factors is, in itself, sufficient to cause child abuse. For example, even though it is true that the lower a family's income, the greater the probability that child abuse and neglect will occur, many children from poor families are given loving and nurturing care. Likewise, the great majority of parents of handicapped children provide a loving and nurturing environment.

Readers wishing to learn more about abuse and neglect of children with handicaps should see Kurtz and Kurtz (1987), Morgan (1987), and Zirpoli (1987).

There is a great need for increased awareness of the problem of child abuse and neglect throughout all of society, but especially among professionals who work with children and families. Because teachers see children on a daily basis for most of the year, they are in the best position to identify and report suspected cases of abuse. Yet the National Center on Child Abuse and Neglect (1982) found that only 10% of abuse reports were filed by school personnel. This statistic is especially unfortunate in light of an earlier national survey stating that 49% of abuse reports were made by hospital personnel after the children involved had received serious injuries (Gil, 1970).

All states require teachers and other professionals who frequently come into contact with children to report suspected cases of child abuse and neglect. Indeed, many state laws require any citizen who suspects child abuse and neglect to report it. Failure to do so is usually considered a misdeameanor; and persons who do, in good faith, report suspected cases are immune from any civil or criminal liability. Reports should be filed with the local child welfare department. All educators should become familiar with the child abuse laws in their states and should learn how to recognize indicators of child abuse and neglect.

Information on detecting signs of child abuse and neglect can be obtained from the National Center on Child Abuse and Neglect (address included at the end of the chapter). Anyone can and should report a suspected case of child abuse; reports can be filed anonymously. If you do not know the appropriate local agency to contact, call the toll-free number of the National Child Abuse Hotline: 800–422–4453.

> Educators must be willing to get involved. Unfortunately, they and other professionals are frequently unwilling to file a report even when child abuse is highly sus-

pected. Indeed, it may be very difficult for a person to make a child abuse report even anonymously. However, one must consider the possible consequences of not reporting suspected abuse. (Zirpoli, 1987, p. 46)

The Many Roles of the Exceptional Parent

Parenthood is an awesome responsibility. And parents of handicapped children face even greater responsibility. Educators who are not parents of a handicapped child can never know the 24-hour reality of being an exceptional parent. But they should none-theless try to be aware of the varied and demanding roles such parents must fulfill. Heward, Dardig, and Rossett (1979) have described seven major challenges faced by parents of exceptional children.

1. *Teaching.* Even though all parents are their children's first teachers, most nonhandi-capped children acquire a great many skills without their parents' trying to teach them. This situation often does not exist with handicapped children, who do not acquire many important skills as naturally or as independently as their nonhandi-capped peers (Karnes, Teska, Hodgin, & Badger, 1970; Tjossem, 1976). In addition to systematic teaching techniques, some parents of exceptional children must learn to use, or teach their children to use, special equipment such as hearing aids, braces, wheelchairs, and adapted eating utensils.

2. *Counseling.* All parents are counselors in the sense that they deal with the changing emotions, feelings, and attitudes of their developing children. But in addition to all of the normal joys and pains of helping a child grow up, parents of a handicapped child must deal with the feelings their child has a result of his particular disability. "Will I still be deaf when I grow up?" "I'm not playing outside any more—they always tease me," "Why can't I go swimming like the other kids?" Parents play an important role in determining how the handicapped child comes to feel about him-self. They can help develop an active, outgoing child who confidently tries many new things or a withdrawn child with negative attitudes toward himself and others.

3. *Managing behavior.* Even though all children act out from time to time, the range and severity of maladaptive behaviors of some handicapped children demand more systematic, specialized treatment. Some parents must learn to be behavior thera-pists in order to have a good relationship with their handicapped children (Snell & Beckman-Brindley, 1984).

4. *Parenting nonhandicapped siblings.* In recent years there has been increased rec-ognition that nonhandicapped children are also deeply affected by having a brother or sister with special needs (Beckman-Bell, 1981; Powell & Ogle, 1985). The brothers and sisters of a handicapped child often have concerns related to their sibling's disability: uncertainty regarding the cause of the handicap and its effect on them, uneasiness over the reactions of their friends, a feeling of being left out or of being required to do too much for the handicapped child (Cansler, Martin, & Valand, 1975).

See "One Sister's Story" for the memories and concerns of a woman who grew up with a handicapped brother.

5. *Maintaining the parent-to-parent relationship.* Having a handicapped child often puts certain stresses on the relationship between husband and wife (Featherstone, 1980; Murphy, 1982; Schell, 1981). Those stresses can range from arguing over

whose fault the child's disability is, to disagreeing over what expectations should be made for the child's behavior, to spending so much time, money, and energy on the handicapped child that little is left for one another.

6. *Educating significant others.* Grandparents, aunts and uncles, neighbors, even the school bus driver can all have an important effect on the handicapped child's development. Whereas the parents of a nonhandicapped child can reasonably expect their child to receive certain kinds of treatment from significant others, parents of handicapped children know they cannot simply rely on appropriate interactions. Parents of a handicapped child must try to be sure that, as much as possible, other people interact with their child in a way that facilitates the acquisition and maintenance of adaptive behaviors. Schulz (1978) describes her response to anyone who stares at her Down syndrome son. She looks the person squarely in the eye and says, "You seem interested in my son. Would you like to meet him?" This usually ends the staring and often creates an opportunity to provide information or begin a friendship.

7. *Relating to the school and community.* As we have seen, P.L. 94–142 describes certain rights (and implies certain responsibilities) of parents of handicapped children in regard to their child's education. Although some degree of involvement in the educational process is desirable for all parents, it is a must for exceptional parents. Those parents need to acquire special knowledge (e.g., understanding what

Most educators will never know the 24-hour reality of being the parent of a handicapped child.

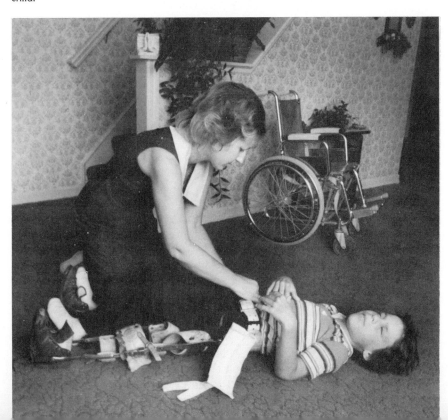

ONE SISTER'S STORY

Siblings for Significant Change (823 United Nations Plaza, New York, NY 10017) is a national organization of people with handicapped brothers and sisters. The organization's director, Gerri Zatlow, dealt with her own need to live a more separate and independent existence by moving out of her mother's apartment in August 1980, at nearly 26 years of age. Now somewhat removed from the situation, her perspectives have altered.

There never was a question of institutionalizing Douglas. From the time we first learned that he was autistic, we resolved to put up a good fight for him . . . not just for his sake, but for ours as well. Doug was clearly an integral part of our family . . . and nothing would change that. We hoped he would respond to a loving environment . . . and he did! Doug grew from a silent little boy into the man of 19 he is today. Handsome and taller than 6 feet, he has a distinct personality and a sense of humor. He has particular likes and dislikes. Similar to the rest of us, there are traits in his nature that are not always pleasant. He can be stubborn and, when crossed, highly argumentative. And—he remains autistic, for the disability does not melt away with each passing year.

The shaping of Douglas has been well worth the battle. He has made phenomenal strides in an excellent public school special education program. However, if the truth be told, a great deal of his progress has been highly attributable to us . . . his family. The process has been an arduous and unrelenting struggle at great emotional expense. The older Doug gets . . . the harder the fight.

As brother and sister we were always close. The public has a distorted view of the autistic child, one of an aloof and cold being. This image may apply to some of the children, but not to all and certainly not to Douglas. My brother was warm, affectionate, and quick to respond to my outward displays of love. He still has an uncanny ability to read my moods, making his own jokes when I am in need of a chuckle or a hug when the time is ripe.

We went everywhere together . . . to movies, restaurants, the park. We took countless walks through the city streets, shopped in supermarkets and made joint efforts to clean up at home. We watched an endless series of Saturday morning cartoons together, long after I had outgrown them. We grew together in our different ways. We spent *too* much time together; I think that was half the problem.

There was no relief from Doug. Day in and day out, his needs had to be tended to regardless of our wants and desires. He always came first. Growing up in a household where only my mother and I were present, the physical responsibility for Douglas was on our shoulders. Much of that burden was mine. Lessening of that responsibility was rare and came in the form of Doug spending a good part of his weekends with my father, and in the summertime when he went to sleep-away camp.

Because Douglas' presence dominated everything, there was no real time for myself. Under these conditions, childhood takes on an uneasy dimension. A sibling is denied the fundamental right of being a child. An opportunity to have friends over did not often materialize because visits were dependent on my brother's moods and behavior. Going out was governed by my mother's need for my assistance in any way. My mother nicknamed me "the other mother" as I took my responsibility with seriousness and maturity in excess of my young years. Unfortunately, the pattern became a way of life.

I am grateful for the 7 years between us in age. Had I been younger, I do not know whether or not I could have coped with my mysterious brother. I do not know whether I would have accepted gracefully the continual sacrifices made to keep Doug home. I am not sure that I could have handled the immense responsibility that I grew so accustomed to.

In addition to the obvious task of physical care, something must be said about the mental effects on us. Throughout my youth, I was cognizant of the fact that Doug's condition was permanent. He would always be vulnerable and need protection, and he was going to live a full life span as a severely handicapped person. I cannot underestimate the impact of that knowledge, especially to a mother. My mother's frequent melancholy was warranted. Frustrated by his condition in the early days, she feared for his future. What compounded the dilemma was that we were very much alone. Some families have assorted relatives to provide respite . . . to take them out for car rides, spend holidays with, or provide emotional support when the going gets rough. Our family is small. My parents are divorced; and although my father was and is as emotionally and financially supportive as he could possibly be, he was not present during moments of household stress and daily crises. Who did we have? Just each other. Still, that is something. Those single parents without benefit of other children to offer help have it even tougher.

It is inevitable that one day I will lose my parents. I will inherit whatever constitutes their estates, be it money or debts, but their most important legacy will be in the form of my autistic brother. As his future guardian, I will acquire and accept the full responsibility for Douglas. As his only sister, I feel that I have already absorbed too much of this burden. I am hoping that long before my parents' demise, Doug's future will be guaranteed. The only alternative to my becoming his perpetual "other mother" is for him to be settled in a group home offering suitable living conditions.

Douglas is not the boy he was 10 years ago. He has gained many skills over the years, all of which make him a superb candidate for a group home. He is totally competent in areas of self-care. One need never remind him to shower, shampoo, or shave. Actually he is rather vain. When his hair gets to an unruly stage, he will request a trip to the "hair stylist." Doug is helpful in the house as he polishes furniture, makes beds, vacuums, sets the table, and cleans the dishes. He also is proficient at doing laundry.

We have not fought this hard for Douglas to be thwarted by a termination of programs. Personally, I have not given so much of myself and my life to Doug only to see his existence end in despair. Nothing can give me back the years of turbulence and prior sublimation that came out of our circumstances. It was all done for Douglas . . . and I will not see my own effort or that of my family wasted. My brother *will* have an option.

Without viable alternatives, many of us will have no choice but to remain the ever constant "keepers" . . . denied the opportunity for an independent life.

a criterion-referenced test is) and learn special skills (e.g., participating effectively in an IEP planning meeting). In addition, parents of handicapped children often have other concerns over and above those expressed by most parents. For example, whereas all parents may be concerned about having adequate playgrounds, exceptional parents may also have to work to make those playgrounds accessible to children who use wheelchairs.

We could correctly say that these seven areas are things *all* parents must deal with. But we think a consideration of the requirements of parenting is useful for at least two reasons. First, it shows that exceptional parents are, in fact, more like other parents than they are different from them. Second, it highlights critical aspects of the job of parenting that can be significantly affected by having a handicapped child. Such an analysis starts us on our way to understanding the responsibilities faced by parents of handicapped children and begins to pinpoint specific areas where teachers and other professionals can provide useful services to parents.

PARENT-TEACHER COMMUNICATION

Regular two-way communication with parents is the foundation of an effective parent-teacher partnership (Kroth, 1985). Without open, honest communication between teacher and parent, many of the positive outcomes listed earlier cannot be achieved. Let's briefly examine the three most-used methods of communication between parents and teachers—conferences, written messages, and the telephone.

Parent-Teacher Conferences

Although parent-teacher conferences are as common to school as recess and homework and have been with us for just about as long, conferences are not always the effective vehicle for communication that they should be. Too often, parent conferences turn out to be stiff, formal affairs, with teachers anxious and parents wondering what bad news they will hear this time. Fortunately, given the increased recognition of the critical role parents play in their child's education and the increased parent participation in the schools as a result of IEP planning meetings, more and more emphasis is being placed on the importance of parent-teacher communication skills. Parents and teachers are learning to talk to one another in more productive ways.

In a face-to-face meeting parents and teachers can exchange information and coordinate their efforts to assist the exceptional child at home and in school. Conferences should not be limited to just the beginning and end of the school year but should be regularly scheduled to maintain a meaningful parent-teacher partnership. More and more educators are viewing the parent-teacher conference as a method for planning and evaluating jointly initiated teaching programs (Heward et al., 1979; Kroth & Simpson, 1977).

Preparing for the Conference

Preparation is the key to effective parent-teacher conferences. Stephens, Blackhurst, and Magliocca (1982) recommend establishing specific objectives for the conference,

The needs and concerns of a handicapped child's brother or sister should not be overlooked.

reviewing the student's cumulative progress, preparing some examples of the student's work along with a graph or chart showing specific performance, and preparing an agenda for the meeting. Figure 13.1 shows an outline that can be used to prepare a parent-teacher conference agenda. Once the conference agenda is planned, the teacher might examine alternative ways of presenting any delicate issues that may have to be discussed, perhaps getting feedback from others on her style and manner of speaking (Roberds-Baxter, 1984).

Turnbull et al. (1986) have devised a form that parents can complete to indicate the types of communication they would prefer to receive from school personnel.

Conducting the Conference

Bennett and Hensen (1977) suggest that teachers should hold parent-teacher conferences in their classrooms because (1) the teacher feels comfortable in familiar sur-

Conference Outline

Date _____   Time _____

Student's Name _____

Parent's Name(s) _____

Teacher's Name _____

Other Staff Present _____

Objectives for Conference:

Student's Strengths:

Area(s) Where Improvement Is Needed:

Questions to Ask Parents:

Parent's Responses/Comments:

Examples of Student's Work/Interactions:

Current Programs and Strategies Used by Teacher:

Suggestions for Parents:

Suggestions from Parents:

Follow-up Activities:
  Parents:

  Teacher:

Date Called for Follow-up and Outcome:

FIGURE 13.1
Parent-teacher conference outline.
Source: From *Working with Parents of Handicapped Children* (p. 233) by W. L. Heward, J. C. Dardig, and A. Rossett, 1979, Columbus, OH: Merrill. Reprinted by permission.

roundings, (2) the teacher has ready access to student files and instructional materials, (3) the classroom itself serves as a reminder to the teacher of things the child has done, and (4) the classroom, with its desks, chairs, and teaching materials, reminds the teacher and parents that the purpose of the conference is their mutual concern for improving the child's education. However, when conducting parent conferences in their classrooms, teachers should not make the mistake of hiding behind their desks, creating a barrier between themselves and the parents, or of seating parents in undersized chairs meant for students. Turnbull et al. (1986) offer guidelines to follow for conferences held in parents' homes.

Stephens and Wolf (1980) recommend a four-step sequence for parent-teacher conferences.

1. *Rapport building.* Establishing mutual trust and the belief that the teacher really cares about the student is important to a good parent-teacher conference. A few minutes should be devoted to relevant small talk. Hochman (1979) suggests beginning with something positive about the child or family ("Teddy's getting along well with his classmates," "Jenny tells me you're moving into a new house") rather than using superficial openings ("Nice weather we're having, isn't it?").

2. *Obtaining information.* Parents can provide teachers with important information for improving instruction. Teachers should use open-ended questions that cannot be answered with a simple yes or no. For example, "Which activities in school has Felix mentioned lately?" is better than "Has Felix told you what we are now doing in school?" The first question encourages the parent to provide more information—the teacher is trying to build conversation, not preside over a question-and-answer session. Throughout the conference the teacher should show genuine interest in listening to the parents' concerns, avoid dominating the conversation, and refrain from using comments that judge, threaten, or function as verbal roadblocks to communication (see Table 13.2).

TABLE 13.2
Communication roadblocks that professionals should avoid in their interactions with parents.

Moralizing:	"You should . . ." "You ought. . ." "It is your responsibility to . . ."
Lecturing:	"I told you . . ." "Do you realize . . ." "One of these days . . ."
Judging/criticizing:	"You're wrong . . ." "One of your problems is . . ." "That was a mistake . . ."
Prying:	"Why?" "How?" "When?" "Who?"
Providing answers prematurely:	"Here's what you do . . ." "I suggest . . ."
Threatening:	"If you do that I'll . . ." "Unless you take my advice . . ."
Ordering:	"You must . . ." "You will . . ." "You have to . . ."
Consoling/excusing:	"You'll be just fine . . ." "You didn't know any better . . ."

TABLE 13.2 *continued*

Diagnosing/analyzing:	"You're just going through the stage of . . ." "You're behaving that way because . . ."
Using sarcasm/cynicism:	"You think you've got it bad . . ." "Life's just a barrel of laughs . . ."
Overusing clichés/phrases:	"You know . . ." "I mean . . ." "That's neat . . ." "Far out . . ."

Source: From *Families, Professionals, and Exceptionality: A Special Partnership* (p. 150) by A. P. Turnbull, H. R. Turnbull III, J. R. Summers, M. J. Brotherson, and H. A. Benson, 1986, Columbus, OH: Merrill.

For detailed descriptions of how to plan and conduct parent conferences, see Kroth (1985), Kroth and Simpson (1977), and Turnbull et al. (1986). Wolf and Stephens (1982) have written a booklet for parents, describing how they might participate more effectively in conferences with teachers.

3. *Providing information.* Parents should be given concrete information about their child in jargon-free language. The teacher should share examples of schoolwork and data on student performance—what has already been learned and what needs to be learned next. When the student's progress has not been as great as was hoped for, parents and teacher should look together for ways to improve it.

4. *Summarizing and follow-up activities.* The conference should end with a summary of what was said. The teacher should review any strategies agreed upon during the conference and indicate the follow-up activities either party will do to help carry out those strategies. Some teachers use carbon paper and make a duplicate copy of their conference notes so that parents will also have a record of what was said or agreed upon.

Written Messages

Even though much can be accomplished in a parent-teacher conference, the amount of time required suggests that conferences should not be the sole means of maintaining parent-teacher communication. In a study conducted with 217 parents of exceptional children, Ammer and Littleton (1983) found that most of the parents (69%) preferred to receive regular information in letters from school rather than through other methods of home-school communication. Some teachers use frequent written messages to communicate with parents. Although the report card that most schools send parents every grading period is a written message, its infrequency and standard format limit its usefulness as a means of communication.

Parents in this same study indicated that their next two most preferred vehicles for receiving information from their children's schools were parent-teacher conferences (51%) and telephone calls from their children's teachers (45%). Home visits were checked by only 19% of the parents, thereby ranking as the least preferred method of establishing or improving home-school communication.

Hochman (1979) regularly sends "happy grams" home with her elementary resource room students (see Figure 13.2). These notes can specify positive things accomplished by students, giving parents an opportunity to praise their children at home and stay abreast of activities in the classroom.

A two-way parent-teacher communication system can be built around a reporting form carried between home and school by the child. The form should be simple to use and read, with space to circle or check responses or write short notes. Such an interactive reporting system can be used on either a daily or a weekly basis, depending on the behaviors involved. Several studies have shown that these two-way communication programs can improve both school and home performance (Dickerson, Spellman, Larsen, & Tyler, 1973; Imber, Imber, & Rothstein, 1979).

Janey had a grrrreat day!

R. Hochman

FIGURE 13.2
A happy gram.

Schumaker, Hovell, and Sherman (1977) used a daily report card system (see Figure 13.3) with three junior high school boys having serious academic and behavior problems. Different teachers marked a card for each boy in each of six different classes. Parents provided privileges (e.g., snacks, television time, staying up an extra half-hour before bed) based on the teachers' ratings of their child's school performance. All three students improved their adherence to classroom rules and their academic performance.

A somewhat similar system is the home-school contract (Heward & Dardig, 1978a). A home-school contract is a **behavioral contract** that specifies parent-delivered rewards contingent on completion of classroom tasks; for example, for each page of the reading workbook completed, the student might earn a quarter to be used to buy a model airplane. Home-school contracts use parent-controlled rewards, build in parent recognition and praise of the child's accomplishments, and involve the teacher and parents together in a positive program to support the child's learning.

The class newsletter is another method some teachers use to increase parent-teacher communication. Even though putting together a class newsletter requires a lot of work, in many cases it is worth the effort. Most teachers have access to a mimeograph, and a one- to three-page monthly newsletter can give parents who don't attend

Although not used for regular or interactive communication with parents, school handbooks and special-purpose handouts describing a program's policies and procedures, personnel, tips, and so on are another means of using written materials to provide information to parents (Kroth, 1985).

FIGURE 13.3
Daily report card.

NAME: ______________________

DATE: ______________________

TEACHER: ______________________

Did the student . . .	YES	NO	
Come on time?			Rules section
Bring supplies?			
Stay in seat?			
Not talk inappropriately?			
Follow directions?			
Raise his hand?			
Not physically disturb others?			
Clean up?			
Pay attention?			
Speak courteously?			
Were you pleased with his performance today?			Teacher satisfaction section
Points on today's classwork			Classwork section
Grade on test assignment			Grades section
Teacher's initials			

Source: From "An Analysis of Daily Report Cards and Parent-Managed Privileges in the Improvement of Adolescents' Classroom Performance" by J. B. Schumaker, M. F. Hovell, and J. A. Sherman, 1977, *Journal of Applied Behavior Analysis, 10,* p. 452.

meetings or open houses information that is too long or detailed to give over the telephone. A newsletter is also an excellent way to recognize those parents who participate in various activities. By making the newsletter a class project, the teacher can include student-written stories and news items and can create an enjoyable learning activity for the entire class.

The Telephone

A brief, pleasant telephone conversation is one of the best ways to maintain communication with parents. Used regularly, telephone calls that focus on positive accomplishments of children let parents and teachers share in the children's success and recognize each other's contributions.

Heron and Axelrod (1976) found that simply telephoning parents and telling them how their children did on a daily word-recognition test resulted in increased parent tutoring of the daily word list and improved scores. Teachers should set aside time on a regular basis so that each child's parent receives a call once every 2 or 3 weeks. Of course, teachers need to find out what times are convenient for parents to receive calls. Keeping a log of the calls helps maintain the schedule and reminds teachers of any necessary follow-up.

Another way teachers can use the telephone is to organize a class telephone "tree." With this system the teacher calls only two or three parents, each of whom calls two or three more, and so on. Telephone trees can be an efficient way to get information to all of the parents associated with a class. And a telephone tree gives parents a way to get actively involved and perhaps to get to know some of the other parents.

Heward and Chapman (1981) used daily recorded telephone messages as a way to increase parent-teacher communication. The teacher of a primary learning disabilities class recorded brief messages on an automatic telephone answering machine. Parents could call 5 nights a week from 5:00 P.M. until 7:00 A.M. the next morning and hear a recorded message like this one:

> Good evening. The children worked very hard today. We are discussing transportation. They enjoyed talking about the airport and all the different kinds of airplanes. The spelling words for tomorrow are *train, t-r-a-i-n; plane, p-l-a-n-e; truck, t-r-u-c-k; automobile, a-u-t-o-m-o-b-i-l-e; and ship, s-h-i-p.* Thank you for calling. (Heward & Chapman, 1981, p. 13)

Figure 13.4 shows the number of telephone calls the teacher received from the parents of the six children in the class each week for the entire school year. The teacher received a total of only five calls for the 32 weeks when the recorded messages were not available (.16 calls per week), compared to 112 calls during the 6 weeks the message system was in operation (18.7 per week). During the nonmessage portions of the study the next day's spelling list was sent home with the children each day, and parents had been requested to help their children with the words. Nonetheless, scores on the daily five-word spelling tests improved for all six students when the recorded messages were available.

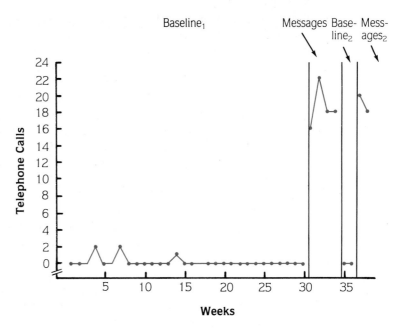

FIGURE 13.4

Graph of telephone calls with and without recorded message.

Source: From "Improving Parent-Teacher Communication Through Recorded Telephone Messages: Systematic Replication in a Special Education Classroom" by W. L. Heward and J. E. Chapman, 1981, *Journal of Special Education Technology, 4,* p. 14. Reprinted by permission.

Teacher-recorded telephone messages can also be used to provide parents with the information and encouragement they need to successfully implement home-based tutoring programs. For an example of how this can be done, see the Focus feature that follows.

There are many ways in which recorded telephone messages can be used to improve parent-teacher communication. Such a system has been used to provide schoolwide and classroom-by-classroom information, good news (such as Citizen of the Month), and suggestions for working with children at home (Minnie, Beane, & Prater, 1987; Test, Cooke, Weiss, Heward, & Heron, 1986). Parent callers can also leave messages for the teacher (e.g., a question or a report on how a home-based instructional program is going), enabling the system to be used for two-way communication.

PARENT INVOLVEMENT

Parents and the Individualized Education Program

As was discussed in chapter 2, an individualized education program (IEP) must be developed for every handicapped child. This requirement of P.L. 94–142 is to ensure that each handicapped child receives educational services suited to his needs. Parents are required to be members of the IEP planning team, although they may waive their right to that membership by signing a document stating that they do not wish to participate.

THE TELEPHONE: AN OVERLOOKED METHOD
OF HOME-SCHOOL COMMUNICATION?

The importance of regular communication between home and school is a topic on which virtually all parents and educators agree. How to manage parent-teacher communication most effectively is the question. A well-conducted conference can accomplish much, but parent-teacher conferences demand a great deal of time from both parties and, realistically, can be held only from time to time. Written notes from the teacher; daily, two-way home-school report card systems; and class newsletters can all be excellent means of communication. Unfortunately, the time required to prepare and reproduce daily notes or a class newsletter, coupled with the uncertainty of student delivery, makes written communications a labor-intensive and unreliable method of parent-teacher communication—at least in terms of communicating with a number of parents on a regular, sustained basis.

Somewhat surprisingly in this burgeoning era of high technology, the telephone—everyday technology that has been with us for decades—has been a relatively unexploited means of parent-teacher communication. Of course, if used in typical fashion, the time required to call and speak individually to the parents of all 15 students enrolled in a resource room program, for example, would place the telephone in the same category as conferences and written messages for regular, sustained communication; a call once a week if you're lucky, but daily communication would most likely be out of the question. Recently, however, teachers have begun to use the telephone in a different way. By recording daily messages on a telephone-answering machine, teachers can provide a great deal of information to parents at relatively little cost. Parents, on the other hand, can call the given number and listen at their convenience, literally 24 hours a day. Parents can also leave messages on the recorder, posing a question, offering a suggestion, and so on.

In addition to information exchange, some studies have begun to explore ways in which teachers can use recorded messages to help parents carry out home-based instruction. One junior high learning disabilities teacher used a telephone-answering machine to manage a summer writing program. Parents of several of her students had indicated their desire to try to help their children maintain or extend some of their academic skills over the summer months. Each day during the 9-week program, the teacher recorded instructions for the session and a story-starter idea. One story starter went like this:

Danger on Shore

You are going up the river in a boat. You feel safe because the unfriendly natives are on the far shore. Suddenly you notice a leak. . . .

Parent and student called together, the student wrote for 10 minutes on that day's topic, and the parent scored the student's writing according to criteria provided by the teacher. The parents rewarded their children for progress and reported the results after the next day's message. Every few days parents mailed the stories to the teacher.

To get an idea of the results of the program, compare the following stories. Story #8 was written by James before his parents started the program to help him write more action words and adjectives. Story #33 was the sixth story written after his parents began to reward adjectives.

8

July 7   James D

First I would go to candy, allways thinking of my self. Later I would go to the meat department. After the meat department I woul go to wine department

---

Aug 12 #33 Talking with a Star   James D

I look up from my salad, thick chocolate milk shake, hot golden crisp french fries, and delicious Big Mac with extra pickles.

I glance through shiney, clear glass and see a small, brown creature with a glowing red chest, short legs, long arms, and a large head with big greenish-blue eyes and a smashed-in nose.

I grab a white napkin and rush up to him. With the tip of his glowing right index finger he writes...

E.T.

Source: Drawn from "A Telephone-Managed, Home-Based Summer Writing Program for LD Adolescents" by M. E. Hasset, C. Engler, N. L. Cooke, D. W. Test, A. B. Weiss, W. L. Heward, and T. E. Heron in *Focus on Behavior Analysis in Education* by W. L. Heward, T. E. Heron, D. S. Hill, and J. Trap-Porter (Eds.), 1984, Columbus, OH: Merrill. Reprinted by permission.

The IEP meeting serves as a communication vehicle between parents and school personnel, and enables them as equal participants, to jointly decide what the child's needs are, what services will be provided to meet those needs, and what the anticipated outcomes will be. (*Federal Register*, 1981, p. 5462)

Clearly, the intent is that parents will play an active decision-making role. According to Turnbull and Turnbull (1982), the belief that parents should share the rights and responsibilities of decision making in regard to their child's educational program is based on two assumptions, which may not be valid in all cases.

1. Parents want to be involved in education decision making and, when given the opportunity, will take advantage of it; and
2. Attending the meeting to plan their child's IEP will enable parents to be decision makers. (p. 116)

However, Turnbull and Turnbull (1982) point out that surveys of what parents say they want from special educators and observations of IEP meetings do not necessarily support these assumptions. In interviews conducted with 32 mothers of handicapped preschool children, Winton and Turnbull (1981) found that, when asked to rank the characteristics of an ideal preschool, the mothers identified parent involvement as the *least* important factor; the factor of greatest import to the mothers was competent, expert teachers. Lusthaus, Lusthaus, and Gibbs (1981) compiled questionnaire results from 98 parents of students enrolled in self-contained classrooms and resource rooms in eight elementary schools in a middle-class, suburban school district. More than half of the parents said they wanted to participate in IEP planning conferences at the level of providing information. The majority were content to let professionals make most decisions. However, when decisions were to be made about what kinds of records should be kept on their children, what medical services were to be provided, or whether their children would be transferred to other schools, more parents wanted to have control over the decisions. Polifka (1981) concluded from a parent survey that parents do want to play an active role in IEP planning.

The research supports a belief we stated earlier: we should not rely on generalizations that we *assume* to be true for all parents of handicapped children. Furthermore, we must view this preliminary research with the understanding that for years most parents have not been asked (and in some instances have not been wanted) to participate in their children's education; then almost overnight they are expected, or even virtually required, to do so. It is not surprising that parents have a variety of feelings about how much their participation is really desired and how much they really can or should contribute.

Studies on what actually happens during IEP meetings are more conclusive. Attendance by parents (mostly mothers) is quite high at IEP conferences, but the level of parental participation is more often passive than active (Goldstein, Strickland, Turnbull, & Curry, 1980; Lynch & Stein, 1982; Scanlon, Arick, & Phelps, 1981). The National Committee for Citizens in Education (1979) surveyed almost 2,300 parents from all over the United States; slightly more than half (52%) of the parents indicated that their children's IEP had been completely written *before* the meeting. Goldstein et al. (1980) observed IEP meetings for mildly handicapped elementary students and found similar results: the average meeting lasted only 36 minutes and consisted mainly of the special education teacher's explaining an already-written IEP to the parent. In another study, observation of 47 IEP conferences revealed the following: (1) in only 6 of the conferences did both mother and father attend, with only mothers attending all others; (2) 28 of the conferences consisted of the special education teacher's explaining an already-completed IEP to the parent(s); (3) approximately one-third of the responses by parents consisted of passive contributions (e.g., head nodding); and (4) the average duration of the meetings was 25 minutes (Vacc, Vallecorsa, Parker, Bonner, Lester, Richardson, & Yates, 1985).

Although these results appear discouraging, they are not necessarily so. Parents are at least being made aware of what special services their children are receiving and why, and passiveness *may* mean satisfaction with the IEPs (Polifka, 1981). Moreover, many parents do take advantage of the IEP meeting to offer significant input into their children's education programs.

> In one recent IEP conference, the mother of a moderately retarded child questioned why her son was being taught to label prehistoric animals verbally. The parent asked the teachers what type of job they expected the child to have as an adult. The teachers replied that they had never really considered job opportunities for the child, since he was only 10. To the teachers, 10 seemed young; to the parents, 10 meant that almost half of his formal education was completed. As the meeting progressed, it was clear that the parents were specifying objectives related to independence as an adult (telling time, reading survival words, sex education) that were different from the more traditional curriculum proposed by the teachers. Through sharing evaluation data, goals for the child, and special problems, all parties involved created a curriculum that met everyone's approval. (Turnbull, 1983, p. 22)

Parents and professionals are working together to increase the level of parent participation in IEP team meetings. The decision-making process developed by Dardig and Heward (1981b) is one technique for recognizing each team member's input. Turnbull, Strickland, and Brantley (1982) describe group training sessions in which parents learn what goes into an IEP and how to participate more actively in its development. One innovative strategy investigated by Goldstein and Turnbull (1982) had school counselors attend the IEP conferences with the parents and serve as advocates by introducing the parents, clarifying jargon, directing questions to parents, verbally praising parents for contributing, and summarizing the decisions made at the meeting. The counselors received no formal training; they were simply given a sheet of instructions outlining their five functions. More contributions were made by parents who were accompanied by a counselor-advocate. Turnbull et al. (1986) offer 45 specific suggestions for steps that school personnel can take before and during the IEP conference to facilitate parent involvement. One of the suggestions is to obtain parents' preferences regarding who will attend the conference, when and where the conference will be held, what special concerns the parents would like addressed at the conference, and so on. Turnbull et al. have also developed a special form for obtaining such preconference information.

Parents as Teachers

All parents are responsible for their children learning many skills. But as we pointed out earlier, most of the things children learn from their parents are not the result of systematic teaching procedures. Instead, children acquire many important skills as a natural result of the everyday interactions between parent and child. For some handicapped children, however, the casual routines of everyday home life may not provide enough practice and feedback to teach them important skills. Many parents have responded by systematically teaching their handicapped children needed self-help and daily living skills or by providing home tutoring sessions to supplement classroom academic instruction.

See Wolery (1979) for an annotated bibliography of research on parents as teachers of their handicapped children.

Educators do not all agree on the role parents should play when it comes to teaching handicapped children. Some professionals give a variety of reasons that parents should not tutor their children: parents do not have the teaching skills required for effective tutoring, home tutoring is likely to end in frustration for both parent and child, most teachers do not have the time necessary to guide and support parents' efforts, and home tutoring may leave the children little rest from instruction (Barsch, 1969; Kronick, 1969; Lerner, 1976). Each of these concerns represents a legitimate problem that can, in fact, occur in individual situations.

The other perspective—that parents *can* effectively serve as teachers for their children—is supported by numerous reports of research studies and parent involvement projects in which parents have successfully taught their children at home. The opinions expressed by the majority of parents who have participated in home-tutoring programs indicate that they considered it a positive experience for both parent and child (Fay, Shapiro, & Trupin, 1978; Sandler & Coren, 1981).

We believe that in most instances in which parents do wish to tutor their children at home, they can and should be helped to do so. When properly conducted, home-based parent teaching strengthens a child's educational program and gives enjoyment to both child and parent. However, it is important for professionals to examine carefully to what extent parent tutoring is appropriate. Not all parents want to teach their children at home or have the time to learn and use the necessary teaching skills (Karnes & Teska, 1980). And professionals must not interpret that situation as an indication that the parents don't care enough about their children (Turnbull & Turnbull, 1982).

There are also other circumstances in which parent tutoring is probably ill advised.

- ☐ if there is parental disagreement over whether or not the child should be tutored
- ☐ if no quiet, non-distracting place is available in the home
- ☐ if tutoring might result in neglect of the needs of other family members
- ☐ if either parent resents the time spent tutoring or feels guilty if tutoring sessions are skipped or cut short
- ☐ if time spent tutoring deprives the child of opportunities to make friends with other children or develop necessary social skills (Maddux & Cummings, 1983, p. 31)

Referring to parents teaching their severely handicapped children at home, Hawkins and Hawkins (1981) write:

> While we are optimistic about training parents to assess, and thus to contribute extensively to the planning of their child's education, we are less optimistic about training parents to carry out those education plans. . . .
>
> On the other hand, training and motivating parents to carry out a *small* number of teaching tasks each day does seem appropriate. These should be tasks that have most of the following characteristics: (1) they are brief, usually requiring no more than three or four minutes each; (2) the ultimate value of them to the parent is obvious (thus self-dressing, but perhaps not block-stacking); (3) they fit the daily routine almost automatically, not requiring a special, noticeable training "session" (thus self-bathing, but not basic communication-board training); (4) they are tasks that cannot be accomplished readily at school alone, either because the opportunities are infrequent or absent (getting up in the morning, toileting), or because training must occur at every opportunity if it is to achieve its objective (mealtime behaviors, walking appropriately with family). (pp. 17–18)

For a review of research documenting the results of using family members in home-based teaching programs with severely handicapped children, see Snell and Beckman-Brindley (1984).

Lovitt (1977) offers four guidelines for parents who do wish to tutor their children at home.

1. *Establish a specific time each day for the tutoring sessions.*
2. *Keep sessions short.* Brief 5- to 10-minute sessions held daily are more likely to be effective than 30- to 40-minute periods, which can produce frustration or be skipped altogether.
3. *Keep responses to the child consistent.* Lovitt (1977) believes it is particularly important for parents to respond to their child's errors in a consistent, matter-of-fact way.

> When Bryan missed a word, I simply wrote it down with little display of emotion. It is extremely important for the teacher-parent to determine what he will do when an error is made. Whatever response is chosen, it must be consistent. Some parents display a crescendo effect toward errors; they ignore the first few, then gradually respond to them with increasing concern. Finally, after a mounting number of errors have been made, panic sets in, and the parent explodes. (p. 175)

By praising the child's successful responses (materials and activities at the child's appropriate instructional level are a must) and providing a consistent, unemotional response to errors (e.g., "Let's read that word again, together"), parents can avoid the frustration and negative results that can occur when home tutoring is mishandled.

4. *Keep a record.* A parent, just like a classroom teacher, can never know the exact effects of his teaching unless a record is kept. A daily record enables both parent and child to see gradual progress that might be missed if subjective opinion is the only basis for evaluation. Most children, disabled or not, do make progress under guided instruction. A record documents that progress, perhaps providing the parent with an opportunity to see the child in a new and positive light.

> Poor parents, they are a beleaguered lot. Although they are criticized if their proge-
> ny do not develop as good citizens, they are generally discouraged from teaching
> them to that end. Nonsense: parents *can* teach their children. It is only necessary
> that they be sane and systematic about their instruction. (Lovitt, 1977, p. 182)

Mercer (1987) offers additional guidelines for parent-tutors. And numerous training manuals and materials have been developed that parents can use directly to teach academic skills (Cassidy & Vukelich, 1978; Cooper & Heron, 1978) and social behaviors (Baker, Brightman, & Hinshaw, 1980; Becker, 1971; Dardig & Heward, 1981a; Patterson, 1979; Smith & Smith, 1976). Information is also available for professionals who wish to help parents implement home-based tutoring programs (Heward et al., 1979; Lillie & Trohanis, 1976).

Parent Education Groups

Education for parenting is not new; Kessler (1966) identifies educational programs for parents dating back to the early 1800s. But as a result of the increased parent involvement in the education of handicapped children, the past decade has witnessed an explosion of programs being offered for and by parents. Parent education groups can serve a variety of purposes—from one-time-only dissemination of information on a new school policy, to make-it-and-take-it workshops in which parents make an instructional material to use at home (e.g., a math facts practice game), to multiple-session programs on participation in IEP planning or child behavior management. Just a few of the many topics addressed by parent education groups are listed in Table 13.3.

For a review of the literature on parent education programs and research, see Dangle and Polster (1984).

There is consistent agreement in the parent education literature on the importance of involving parents in the planning and, whenever possible, the actual conducting of parent groups (Kroth, 1981; Heward et al., 1979; Turnbull et al., 1986). Heward et al. (1979) recommend using both open and closed needs assessment procedures to determine what parents want from a parent program. An open-ended needs assessment consists of questions like these:

1. The best family time for my child is when we _____.
2. I will never forget the time that my child and I _____.
3. When I take my child to the store, I am concerned that he/she will _____.
4. People think my child is unable to _____.
5. I'm worrying about making a decision about my child's _____.
6. Sometimes I think my child will never_____.
7. My child is especially difficult around the house when he/she _____.
8. I give my child a hug when he/she _____.
9. The hardest thing about having a special child is _____.
10. I wish I knew more about _____. (p. 240)

Parents' responses to open-ended questions can provide a tremendous amount of information about what kinds of parent training programs might be needed and appreciated.

A closed needs assessment asks parents to indicate on a list of possibilities those items that they would like to learn more about. For example, with the following topics

TABLE 13.3
Possible topics for parent education groups.

1. Self-help skills (dressing, brushing teeth, etc.)	23. Interpretation of test results
2. Leisure-time activities	24. How to help your mainstreamed child adjust/succeed in the regular class
3. Participation in IEP process	25. Dealing with sibling rivalry
4. Summer reading program	26. Reading to your child at home
5. Teaching your child responsibility and organization	27. Dealing effectively with significant others
6. Interacting with peers	28. Program for grandparents
7. Preparing for the family vacation	29. Fathers-only program
8. Developing and implementing family rules	30. Organizing morning activities
9. Safety in the home	31. Home fire safety and escape
10. Recreation/physical education activities to do at home	32. Helping your handicapped child make friends
11. Gardening with a handicapped child	33. Setting up a parent-run resource room
12. Adapting your home for a wheelchair	34. Organizing a summer odd-job program for children
13. Adapting your home for a blind child	35. Organizing a parent-run respite care exchange system
14. Community resources for parents of handicapped children	36. Acceptance and use of prosthetic equipment
15. Eating/mealtime behaviors	37. Preparing for your child's future
16. Shopping skills	38. Dealing with professionals
17. How to choose/train a baby-sitter	39. Pets for handicapped children: selection and care
18. Making a home study carrel	40. Developing a parent-to-parent support group
19. Cooking skills/activities	
20. Speech activities/games	
21. Home-school communication systems (notes, telephone)	
22. Bicycle safety	

parents might be asked to put one check mark by any item that is something of a problem and two check marks by any area that is of major interest.

___ Bedtime behavior	___ Home chores
___ Eating behavior	___ On-task behavior
___ Interactions with sibling(s)	___ Leisure-time activities
___ Personal cleanliness (dressing, toilet-ing)	___ Employability skills
	___ Interactions with opposite sex
___ Interactions with strangers	___ Making friends
___ Compliance with parental requests	___ Planning for the future
___ Study habits	___ Other

Turnbull et al. (1986) have developed a comprehensive needs assessment device called the Family Information Preference Inventory, which can be used as the basis for planning and individualizing parent education and parent involvement programs. By examining the results of needs assessment questionnaires, parents and professionals together can plan parent education groups that are responsive to the real needs of parents.

How Much Parent Involvement?

It is sometimes all too easy for professionals to get carried away with a concept, especially one like parent involvement with so much promise of positive outcomes. But teachers and everyone else involved with providing special education services to exceptional children should not take a one-sided view of parent involvement. Sometimes the time and energy required for parents to participate in home treatment programs or parent education groups cause stress among family members or guilt if the parents cannot fulfill the teacher's expectations (Doernberg, 1978; Winton & Turnbull, 1981). The time required to provide additional help to a handicapped child may take too much time and attention away from other family members (Kroth, 1981; Turnbull & Turnbull, 1982).

Kroth and his colleagues at the Parent Involvement Center in Albuquerque have developed a model guide for parent involvement. Kroth (1981) describes the Mirror

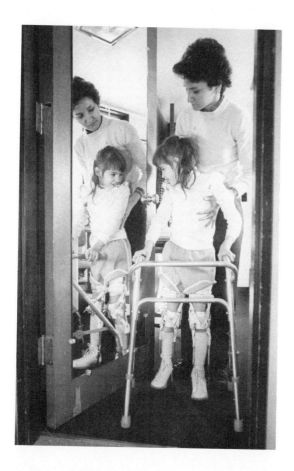

Thanks largely to her parents' involvement, Michelle faces a bright future.

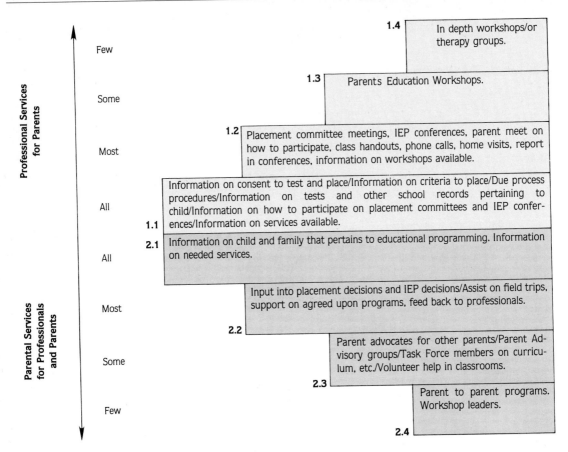

FIGURE 13.5
Mirror model for parent involvement in public schools.
Source: From "Involvement with Parents of Behaviorally Disordered Adolescents" by R. Kroth in *Educating Adolescents with Behavior Disorders* (p. 129) by G. Brown, R. L. McDowell, and J. Smith (Eds.), 1981. Columbus, OH: Merrill. Reprinted by permission.

Cone, Delawyer, and Wolfe (1985) have developed a scale, the Parent/ Family Involvement Index, that can be used to objectively measure the 12 types of parent involvement in the authors' special education program.

Model for Parental Involvement as both a strength and deficit model, recognizing that parents have a great deal to offer as well as a need to receive services from special educators. The model assumes that not all parents need everything that professionals have to offer and that no parents should be expected to provide everything.

The Mirror Model attempts to give parents an equal part in deciding what services they need and what services they might provide to professionals or other parents. The top half of the model, as illustrated in Figure 13.5, assumes that professionals have certain information, knowledge, and skills that should be shared with parents to help them with their children. The bottom half of the model assumes that parents have information, knowledge, and skills that can help professionals be more effective in helping children.

SOME GUIDELINES FOR WORKING EFFECTIVELY WITH PARENTS OF HANDICAPPED CHILDREN

The following suggestions are valuable guidelines for professionals in their interactions with parents.

1. *Don't assume that you know more about the child, her needs, and the ways in which those needs should be met than do the parents.* If you make that assumption, you will often be wrong and, worse, may miss opportunities to get and provide meaningful information.

2. *Speak in plain, everyday language.* Using educationese does not help a professional communicate effectively with parents (or anyone else, for that matter). Lovitt (1982), a strong believer that we must "junk our jargon," gives us this example from a student's official folder.

   > Art shows apraxia due to a vestibular-based deficit. He has laterality, proprioceptive, and sensorimotor dysfunction. Postural ocular deficits are present. He prefers to use right hand but his left hand is more accurate in kinesthesia and proprioception. Nystagmus is depressed during vestibular stimulation. Motor planning activities are difficult for him. (p. 303)

   Wouldn't it be better to state clearly what things Art can do now so that the specific things he needs to learn to do can be identified?

3. *Don't let generalizations about parents of handicapped children guide your efforts.* If you are genuinely interested in what a father or mother feels or needs, ask him or her. Don't assume a parent is in the x, y, or z stage and therefore needs a, b, or c.

4. *Don't be defensive toward or intimidated by parents.* No, you can't really know what it's like to be the parent of a handicapped child unless you are one. But as a trained teacher, you do know a great deal about how to help handicapped children learn; you do it every day, with lots of children. Offer the knowledge and skills you have without apology, and welcome parents' input.

5. *Maintain primary concern for the child.* If you are a child's teacher, you interact with parents in an effort to improve the child's educational program. In that role you are not a marriage counselor or therapist. Offer to refer parents to professionals who are trained and qualified to provide nonspecial-education services if a parent indicates the need.

6. *Help parents strive for realistic optimism.* Handicapped children and their parents benefit little from professionals who are either doom-and-gloom types or who minimize the significance of a disability. Professionals should help parents analyze and prepare for their child's future (Turnbull et al., 1986).

7. *Start with something parents can be successful with.* For many parents, involvement in their child's educational program is a new experience. Don't punish parents who show an interest in helping their child at home by setting them up to fail— by giving them complicated materials, complex instructions, and a heavy schedule of nightly tutoring. Begin with something simple that is likely to be rewarding to the parent.

RESPITE CARE: SUPPORT FOR FAMILIES

"We were really getting worn down. For the first 4 years of Ben's life we averaged 4 hours of sleep a night. We were wearing ourselves out; I have no doubt we would have completely fallen apart." said Ben's mother, Rebecca Arnett. Ben was born with a neurological condition that produces frequent seizures and extreme hyperactivity. "My husband Roger used his vacations for sleeping in. The respite program came along just in time for us.

"It was hard at first. There's an overwhelming guilt that you shouldn't leave your child. We didn't feel like anyone else could understand Ben's problems. But we had to get away. Our church had given us some money with orders to take a vacation. It was the first time Roger and I and our 12-year-old daughter Stacy had really been together since Ben was born. I was upset at first, calling twice a day to see if everything was all right. But it was wonderful, for everybody.

"Cleo Baker, the respite care worker who stayed with Ben that first time and many times since, is something else. She takes him to McDonald's, shopping, all over. When Ben knows she's coming, he runs for his jacket. He loves her. We've had five or six different respite workers stay with Ben during the year we've used the program, and he likes them all.

"Once parents get over that initial period of letting go, they realize that it's OK to have a life of your own apart from your handicapped child. For us it was a real lifesaver."

Nancy Mosure, the director of the respite care program for Franklin County, Ohio, explains: "Respite gives families a chance for a more natural lifestyle. Some of the families we serve have gone years without a real break of any kind. Once they try our program and find that a responsible, trained adult can care for their child, it's like a new lease on life.

"At present we have 20 workers serving about 150 families. Each worker completes a 40-hour training program covering feeding techniques, first aid, use of adaptive equipment, leisure-time activities, and so on. I conduct an initial home visit to explain the program and determine the family's special needs. Our workers can be scheduled for any length of time from 4 hours up to 2 weeks of continuous care. Our respite care is conducted in the family's home or at a new respite facility. A sliding fee scale determines the hourly cost according to income and family size."

Respite care can benefit the handicapped family member as well. Susan Clark told of the time she stayed with Stephanie, a 25-year-old mentally retarded woman, so that her mother, who had not had a vacation since her daughter's birth, could go to Florida. "Stephanie and I went everywhere, to the movies, the county fair, out to eat. She did things she had never done in her life. That week was a vacation for her, too."

Another parent, Jean Williams, describes the program this way: "Our son Tom's autism has meant a lot of restrictions in our family life for the past 25 years, bringing with it many problems and much resentment. At last we have been given a no-strings-attached, low-cost way to loosen some of those restrictions. Funny thing is, our Tom is such a nice guy—it's sure good to be able to get far enough away every so often to be able to see that."

8. *Don't be afraid to say, "I don't know."* Sometimes parents ask educational questions that you can't answer or need services that you can't provide. It's OK to say, "I don't know." The mark of a real professional is knowing when you need help, and parents will think more highly of you.

CONCLUSIONS/FUTURE TRENDS

Special educators and parents will continue to develop better ways of working together for the benefit of handicapped children. In the future more home-based interventions will focus not just on the parent-child relationship but on the interrelationships of all family members. Members of the extended family, such as grandparents, will receive more attention (Harris & Kotsch, 1981), and parent involvement will be viewed more and more as family involvement (Foster, Berger, & McLean, 1981; LeBuffe & LeBuffe, 1982). We are beginning to see parents themselves assume a more active role in running parent involvement programs. In some programs, such as the Regional Intervention Program at George Peabody College, parents are the primary teachers of their handicapped children, training other parents in the teaching techniques and running the program's daily operation (Timm & Rule, 1981).

Professionals and parents are working to develop and provide a wide range of supportive services for families of handicapped children. Programs are being implemented to help parents plan effectively for the future, develop problem-solving skills, and acquire competence in financial planning, coping with stress, locating and using community services, and finding time to relax and enjoy life, to name just a few areas of emphasis. In addition, the development and provision of quality respite care services has become a major issue in many communities. Simply defined, respite care is the temporary care of a disabled individual for the purpose of providing relief to the parent and guardian (Cohen & Warren, 1985). Many parents of severely handicapped children identify the availability of reliable, high-quality respite care as their single most pressing need. Fortunately, because of the efforts of parent advocacy groups and concerned professionals, respite services are becoming more and more available throughout the country.

See page 512 for more about respite care services.

Parents are the most important adults in a child's life. A good teacher should be the next most important adult in a child's life. Working together, parents and teachers can and will make a difference.

SUMMARY

1. Parents of handicapped children and education professionals are developing better ways to work together.
   a. A successful parent-teacher partnership provides benefits for the professional, the parents, and—most important—the child.
   b. Both parent and professionals have contributed to unproductive relationships in the past. The negative attitudes and behaviors of professionals can create roadblocks to effective communication, and some parents are difficult to work with or unreasonable.

    c. Parents and professionals need to understand and be aware of each other's roles and responsibilities.

    d. Actions on the part of parents, concerned educators, and legislators have all helped increase the participation of parents in the special education process.

2. To work with parents effectively, teachers must understand the responsibilities and challenges faced by parents of exceptional children.

    a. All parents need to adjust to the birth of a handicapped child or the discovery that a child is disabled. However, this adjustment process is different for each parent, and educators should not make assumptions about an individual parent's stage of adjustment.

    b. A family member's disability is likely to affect parents and nonhandicapped siblings in different ways during the different stages, or life cycles, of the person's life.

    c. Although the great majority of parents of handicapped children provide loving and nurturing care, studies have found that a disproportionate number of children with handicaps are victims of parental abuse and neglect. Educators have a professional and ethical responsibility to learn how to detect and then to report suspected cases of child abuse and neglect.

    d. Parents face extra responsibilities in raising handicapped children, including teaching and counseling the child, managing behavior, dealing with their other nonhandicapped children and other significant people, maintaining the parent-to-parent relationship, and relating to the school and community.

3. Regular two-way communication is critical to effective parent-teacher partnerships.

    a. At carefully planned conferences parents and teachers can review a child's work, evaluate current programs, and determine strategies for new programs.

    b. Teachers should send frequent written messages home. Possible formats include happy grams, home-school contracts, daily report cards, and class newsletters.

    c. The telephone is another useful tool for regular teacher-parent communication.

4. The extent to which individual parents participate in IEP meetings varies. Involvement ranges from attendance, through which parents at least become aware of what special services their child is receiving, to active participation, through which parents help plan their child's program.

5. Many parents can and should learn to help teach their handicapped child.

6. Parents and professionals should be involved in planning and conducting parent education groups, which can cover a variety of topics.

7. Not all parents can be or need to be fully involved in their children's special education programs. Parents who do not tutor their children or become involved in parent education groups or function as active decision makers at IEP meetings should not be condemned or regarded as uncaring.

8. Professionals should follow certain guidelines in interacting with parents.

    a. Don't assume that you know more about the child, his needs, and the ways in which those needs should be met than do the parents.

    b. Speak in plain, everyday language.

    c. Don't let generalizations about parents of handicapped children guide your efforts.

    d. Don't be defensive toward or intimidated by parents.

    e. Maintain primary concern for the child.

    f. Help parents strive for realistic optimism.

    g. Start with something parents can be successful with.

    h. Don't be afraid to say, "I don't know."

FOR MORE INFORMATION

Journals

The Exceptional Parent. Published six times per year by the Psy-Ed Corporation. Contains articles for parents and professionals on subjects such as improving parent-professional relationships, maintaining family relationships, and managing financial resources.

Books

Chinn, P. C., Winn, J., & Walters, R. H. (1978). *Two-way talking with parents of special children: A process of positive communication.* St. Louis: C. V. Mosby.

Ehly, S. W., Conoley, J. C., & Rosenthal, D. (1985). *Working with parents of exceptional children.* St. Louis: Times Mirror/Mosby College.

Gallagher, J. J., & Vietze, P. (Eds.). (in press). *Families of handicapped persons: Current research, treatment, and policy issues.* Baltimore: Paul H. Brookes.

Kroth, R. (1985). *Communicating with parents of exceptional children* (2nd ed.). Denver: Love.

Seligman, M. (Ed.). (1983). *The family with a handicapped child: Understanding and treatment.* New York: Grune & Stratton.

Stewart, J. C. (1986). *Counseling parents of exceptional children* (2nd ed.). Columbus, OH: Merrill.

Turnbull, A. P., Turnbull, H. R., III, Summers, J. A., Brotherson, M. J., & Benson, H. A. (1986). *Families, professionals, and exceptionality: A special partnership.* Columbus, OH: Merrill.

Turnbull, H. R., III, & Turnbull, A. P. (1985). *Parents speak out: Then & now* (2nd ed.). Columbus, OH: Merrill.

Organizations

Closer Look, 1201 16th Street, NW, Washington, DC 20036.

National Center on Child Abuse and Neglect, U.S. Department of Health and Human Services, P. O. Box 1182, Washington, DC 20013. Offers National Child Abuse Hotline with a toll-free number: 800–422–4453.

National Network of Parent Centers, 9451 Broadway Drive, Bay Harbor, FL 33154.

National Parent CHAIN, 515 W. Giles Lane, Peoria, IL 61614. A volunteer organization to establish a national information and education network for handicapped citizens and their families.

Pacer (Parent Advocacy Coalition for Educational Rights) Center, 4701 Chicago Avenue, South, Minneapolis, MN 55407.

Parents Educational Advocacy Center, 116 W. Jones Street, Raleigh, NC 27611.

PEP (Parents Educating Parents) Project, Georgia Association for Retarded Citizens, 1851 Ram Runway, Suite 104, College Park, GA 30337.

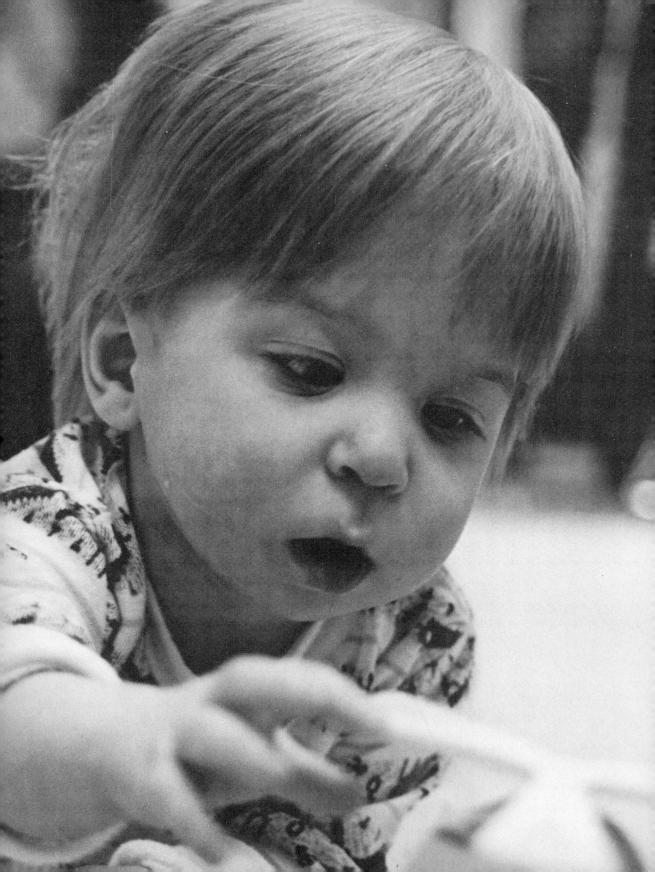

14
EARLY INTERVENTION

M ost normal children experience a phenomenal amount of learning during the critical years from birth to school age. Typical children grow and develop in orderly, predictable ways, learning to move, to play, to communicate, and to be independent. But these are often years of missed opportunity for handicapped children. Normal rates and patterns of child development contrast sharply with the progress experienced by most children with handicaps. Many handicapped preschoolers need carefully planned and implemented instruction to master the basic skills their nonhandicapped peers acquire naturally. Yet not too many years ago professionals often told parents concerned about deficits in their child's development, "Don't worry. Wait and see. She'll probably grow out of it." As a result, the early years became a time when many handicapped children fell further and further behind their nonhandicapped peers.

See chapters 1 and 2 for more on legislation affecting exceptional children.

Only in recent years have special educators become convinced of the need for early identification and intervention. From a virtual absence of educational programs 20 years ago for handicapped children from birth to school-age, early childhood special education has become one of the most prominent and fastest growing components of the entire special education field. Research and development of early intervention services have been aided by federal legislation. The first bill written exclusively for the handicapped preschooler, the Handicapped Children's Early Childhood Assistance Act (P. L. 90–538), was passed in 1968 and continues to provide funding for the development, implementation, and dissemination of diverse and innovative approaches to the education of young handicapped children. In 1972 Head Start (a nationwide program begun in 1965 to provide preschool services to children from low-income families) was required by law to reserve at least 10% of its enrollment capacity for handicapped children. By 1977 13% of all children enrolled in Head Start programs across the country were handicapped—a total of 36,133 children. (Department of Health, Education, and Welfare, 1978); by the 1982–83 school year, that number had risen to almost 55,000 (Finch, 1985).

For a chronology of the development of early childhood education for both nonhandicapped and handicapped children, see Bailey and Wolery (1984).

As discussed previously, the 1975 Education for All Handicapped Children Act (P. L. 94–142) mandated services by 1980 for handicapped children aged 3 to 5, *if* state law or practice already provided education for children in that age group. In the 1980–81 school year only 16 states mandated special education services for the full 3- to 5-year-old range; an additional 22 states required services for handicapped preschoolers at the age of 4 or 5 (U.S. Comptroller General, 1981). To stimulate other states to begin programs for handicapped preschoolers, the law includes a provision called the incentive grant program. Incentive grants provide funds for establishing or improving preschool programs for handicapped children; the grants are distributed on the basis of the number of children who have been identified in the state (Cohen, Semmes, & Guralnick, 1979).

Since 1975 Congress has enacted two bills reauthorizing and amending P. L. 94–142. The first, P. L. 98–199, was passed in 1984 and made funds available to states for the development of comprehensive delivery systems providing special education and related services to all handicapped and at-risk children from birth to the age of 5 years. On October 8, 1986, the Education of the Handicapped Act Amendments of 1986 became law. This law, P. L. 99–457, contained two major provisions concerning the education of handicapped preschoolers. Prior to the passage of this law, Congress estimated that states were serving about 70% of the handicapped children aged 3 to 5 under the voluntary provisions of P. L. 94–142; 31 states and territories did not require special education for at least part of that handicapped population (Koppelman, 1986). Under the incentive grant funding formula for those children, states received approximately $110 for each child served. The 1986 EHA Amendments authorized states to receive $300 for each child served in fiscal year 1987, with funding to increase each succeeding year up to $1,000 for each child served in 1990. P. L. 99–457 also gives states financial incentive to serve more children by providing up to $3,800 for each new handicapped preschooler they enroll. However, by school year 1990–91 all states applying for P. L. 94–142 preschool funds will have to show evidence that they are providing a free, appropriate education to all handicapped children aged 3 to 5 in order to receive any money.

The second major change brought about by the passage of P. L. 99–457 was the provision of incentive grants to states for developing and implementing "statewide, comprehensive, coordinated, multidisciplinary, interagency" services of early intervention for handicapped infants and toddlers (from birth through age 2) and their families. Children with a diagnosed physical or mental condition that places them at risk for a developmental delay are also eligible for services under this program. The legislation requires that the services provided be delivered according to an individualized family services plan (IFSP) developed by an interdisciplinary team that includes the child's parent or parents.

IMPORTANCE OF EARLY INTERVENTION

The earliest and one of the most dramatic demonstrations of the critical importance of early intervention was a classic study by Skeels and Dye (1939). Two "hopeless" baby girls, aged 13 and 16 months, had been transferred from an orphanage to a

Services for infants and preschool children with handicaps are expanding rapidly.

ward of adult women in an institution for the mentally retarded because of lack of room in proper facilities. "The youngsters were pitiful little creatures. They were tearful, had runny noses, and coarse, stringy, and colorless hair; they were emaciated, undersized, and lacked muscle tone or responsiveness. Sad and inactive, the two spent their days rocking and whining" (Skeels, 1966, p. 5). At the time of their transfer, the two children were classified as moderately to severely retarded with IQs estimated at 35 and 46. After 6 months in the ward with the older women, their IQs were measured at 77 and 87, and a few months later both girls had IQs in the mid-90s. Regular intelligence testing like this was not a common procedure; but because of their unusual placement, the children were observed closely.

After learning of the girls' remarkable improvement, Skeels and Dye looked for possible causes. They found that the children had been the recipients of an unusual amount of attention and stimulation. Ward attendants had purchased toys and books for the children, and residents had played and talked with them continuously. Excited by the possibilities, Skeels and Dye convinced the state authorities to permit a most unusual experiment. They selected 11 additional 1- to 2-year-old subjects; all but two of this group were classified as mentally retarded (average IQ of 64) and, by state law at the time, were judged unsuitable for adoption. These experimental children were removed from the nonstimulating orphanage and placed in the one-to-one care of adolescent retarded girls at the institution. Each adolescent "mother" was given training in how to care for her baby—how to hold, feed, talk to, and stimulate the child. No other direct programming or educational experiences were provided for the children.

A contrast group of 12 children under 3 years of age remained in the orphanage, receiving adequate medical and health services but no individual attention. The children in the contrast group had an average IQ of 86 at the beginning of the study; only two were classified as mentally retarded. Two years later the children in both groups were retested. The experimental group showed an average gain of 28 IQ points, enough for 11 of the 13 children to become eligible for adoption and to be placed in good homes. The children in the contrast group had each *lost* an average of 26 IQ points.

More than 25 years later, Skeels located the subjects in the original study. The follow-up results were equally impressive (Skeels, 1966). Of the 13 experimental subjects, 11 had married; the marriages had produced nine children, all of normal intelligence, and only one of the marriages had ended in divorce. The subjects' median level of education was the 12th grade, and four had attended college. All were either employed outside the home or were homemakers, with jobs ranging from professional and business work to domestic service for the two who had not been adopted. Of the original contrast group of 12, four were still institutionalized in 1965. The median level of education for the contrast group was the third grade, and all but one of those who were employed were unskilled laborers.

Although the study by Skeels and Dye (1939) can be questioned because of its lack of tight experimental method, it served as the foundation and catalyst for many subsequent intervention efforts. Skeels (1966) concluded his follow-up study with these words:

> It seems obvious that under present-day conditions there are still countless infants with sound biological constitutions and potentialities for development well within the normal range who will become retarded and noncontributing members of society unless appropriate intervention occurs. It is suggested by the findings of this study and others published in the past 20 years that sufficient knowledge is available to design programs of intervention to counteract the devastating effects of poverty, socio-cultural, and maternal deprivation. . . . The unanswered questions of this study could form the basis for many life-long research projects. If the tragic fate of the twelve contrast group children provokes even a single crucial study that will help prevent such a fate for others, their lives will not have been in vain. (p. 109)

Another research study that highlighted the importance of early intervention was done by Kirk (1958). This study measured the effects of 2 years of preschool training on the social and cognitive development of mentally retarded children (IQs ranging from 40 to 85). Children in the two experimental groups—15 children living in an institution and attending a nursery school and 28 children living at home and also attending a preschool program—showed gains on tests of mental and social development. Children in the two control groups that did not receive the preschool training—12 in an institution and 26 living at home—showed declines in performance. The differences between the groups were maintained over a period of years.

The Milwaukee Project (Garber & Heber, 1973; Heber & Garber, 1971; Strickland, 1971) is another widely cited effort in early intervention. The project was aimed at preventing mental retardation by providing a program of parent education and infant stimulation for children considered to have a high potential for retarded development because of their mothers' levels of intelligence and conditions of poverty. Mothers with IQs of 70 or less and their high-risk infants were chosen subjects for the study. The mothers received training in child care and were taught how to interact with and stimulate their children. Beginning before the age of 6 months, the children also participated in an infant stimulation program conducted by trained teachers. By the age of 3 1/2 the experimental children tested an average of 33 IQ points higher than a control group of children who did not participate in the program.

Hailed as the "Miracle in Milwaukee" by the popular media this study is sometimes offered as proof that a program of maternal education and early infant stimulation can reduce the incidence of cultural-familial mental retardation. However, the Milwaukee Project has also been criticized for its research methods. Page (1972), for example, questions whether bias in sampling and testing was adequately controlled. Nevertheless, according to Garber and Heber, (1973),

> Infant testing difficulties notwithstanding, the present standardized test data, when considered along with performance on learning tasks and language tests, indicate an unquestionably superior present level of cognitive development on the part of the experimental group. Also, the first wave of our children are now in public schools. None have been assigned to classes for the retarded. (p. 114)

We will have to await a follow-up report to see whether the Milwaukee Project children maintain their good start.

Since the 1960s there have been literally hundreds of studies attempting to determine the effects of early intervention on disadvantaged and handicapped children. In a review of reviews, White, Bush, and Casto (1986) found that 94% of a sample of 52 previous reviewers of the early intervention literature concluded that early intervention resulted in substantial immediate benefits for handicapped, at-risk, and disadvantaged children. The immediate benefits included improved cognitive, language, social-emotional, and motor growth and better relationships and functioning with parents and siblings. In an analysis of the long-term effects of early intervention, Lazar and Darlington (1982) pooled the data from 12 follow-up studies of children who had participated in cognitively oriented preschool programs for socioeconomically disadvantaged children. At the time of the follow-up studies, the children who had participated in the preschool programs were in the 3rd to the 12th grades. Fewer of the early intervention children had been placed in special education classes (14% vs. 29%), and fewer had been held back to repeat a school year (26% vs. 37%).

Reviews of the efficacy of early intervention can be found in Bricker (1986); Dunst, Snyder, and Mankinen (1986); and Smith and Strain (1984).

Although the results reported on the long-term efficacy of early intervention are generally positive, numerous methodological problems make it extremely difficult to conduct such research in a scientifically sound manner (Bricker, 1986; Dunst, 1986; Strain & Smith, 1986). Among those problems are the difficulties in selecting meaningful and reliable outcome measures; the wide disparity among handicapped children in the developmental effects of their disabilities; the tremendous variation across early intervention programs in curriculum focus, teaching strategies, length, and intensity of programming; and the ethical concerns of withholding early intervention from some children so that they may be used as a control group for comparison purposes (Bailey & Wolery, 1984).

In a meta-analysis of 74 studies investigating the efficacy of early intervention with handicapped preschoolers, Casto and Mastropieri (1986) concluded that early intervention produces positive effects and that longer, more intensive programs are generally more effective. However, these authors also reported that their analysis did not find support for two conclusions common to the vast majority of previous reviews of the literature. They found no evidence that early intervention programs are more effective when begun at an earlier age as opposed to a later age, and they disagreed with previous reviewers who concluded that greater degrees of parental involvement are associated with greater effectiveness. Casto and Mastropieri's paper has drawn heavy criticism from other experts on early intervention research, who claim the analysis suffers from conceptual and methodological weaknesses (Dunst & Snyder, 1986; Strain & Smith, 1986).

In concluding their critique of the Casto and Mastropieri analysis, Strain and Smith (1986) comment on the large but scientifically questionable body of research that generally indicates positive outcomes of early intervention.

Donnellan (1984) suggests that teachers, policy planners, and other human service providers use the criterion of the "least dangerous assumption" when objective data are not available to indicate clearly which placement, program, or procedure is the best or most appropriate. In these instances decision makers should consider which option will do the least harm to children and their families.

> What do we do then with a data base that is flawed or that offers conflicting results? First, we do not need to apologize for lack of rigor. The methodological weaknesses do not so much reflect poor science or scientists as the reality of field research on complicated questions. The unassailable educational experiment that proves causality once and for all is a myth. Yet, we should not stop trying, with scientific methods, to understand the complexity. . . . Experiments principally designed to determine whether or not early intervention is effective lose their vitality and usefulness. If it looks like a pig, roots, and snorts, it probably is a pig. Similarly, if it looks like we get effects, some weak, some strong, some ambiguous, there probably is a relation between intervention and child outcomes. . . .
>
> Policy and program developers have a professional imperative to proceed using the least dangerous assumption that providing appropriate early intervention services is beneficial to handicapped infants, preschoolers, and their families. (pp. 263–264)

Virtually every special educator today recognizes the importance of early intervention for both handicapped and high-risk children. Most will also agree that the earlier intervention begins, the better. But before intervention can begin, the children must be identified.

IDENTIFICATION AND ASSESSMENT OF HANDICAPPED INFANTS AND PRESCHOOLERS

There is virtual consensus among early childhood experts that the earlier intervention is begun, the better. Child development expert Burton White, who has conducted years of research with nonhandicapped infants and preschoolers in Harvard University's Pre-School Project, believes that the period from 8 months to 3 years is critical to a cognitive and social development. "To begin to look at a child's educational development when he is 2 years of age is already much too late" (White, 1975, p. 4).

If the first years of life are the most important for nonhandicapped children, they are even more critical for the handicapped child, who risks falling even further behind her nonhandicapped age-mates with each passing month.

> These infants at risk for handicapping conditions cannot wait until age 6, or even age 3, before receiving intervention that will help them. If, as we are learning, children as young as 1 or less can make fine discriminations, then that is the age at which programs should begin. (McDaniels, 1977, p. 26)

Smith and Strain (1984) argue that beginning intervention as early as possible in a handicapped child's life is supported by the research literature. Hayden and Pious (1979) contend that some interventions may need to begin at or before birth.

> It is simply never too early to intervene, and . . . from the data base we now have, it seems clear that urgently needed interventions should occur long before a child is born. Once a child has arrived, the work necessarily shifts into amelioration, away from prevention—always a second choice for intervention. . . . Beginning at birth is not too soon. (p. 273)

We know more today than ever before about conditions associated with an increased probability of the birth of a handicapped baby. For example, we know that a history of certain handicaps in a family should make us watch for similar risks to any future children. We know that alcoholism in pregnant women often produces serious physical defects and developmental delays (called **fetal alcohol syndrome**) in their babies (Delaney & Hayden, 1977). We know that malnutrition during pregnancy can produce severe problems, including retardation, in the baby. And we know that

In the United States 3 out of every 100 babies are born with major birth defects.

The earlier intervention is begun, the better.

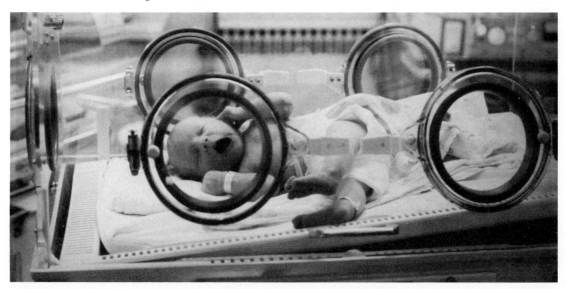

diseases during pregnancy, particularly rubella, can cause serious handicaps in the new-born. Other signs of an at-risk pregnancy include the following:

☐ the birth of a previous child with a chromosomal abnormality
☐ age of the mother over 35 (although women over 35 have only 7% of the babies born, they give birth to more than 33% of all Down syndrome babies)
☐ two or more congenital malformations in the parents
☐ mental retardation in the mother
☐ absence of secondary sex characteristics in the mother
☐ a history of several miscarriages for the mother (Comptroller General, 1977).

With widespread genetic counseling, plus greater public awareness of these conditions as predictors of handicaps, many parents or prospective parents can make better decisions, based on more information, about having a child. Likewise, better prenatal care can reduce the incidence of prematurity and low birth weight, both of which are also associated with an increased frequency of handicaps.

However, even with all these improvements in public awareness, prenatal care, and early education, the possibility of eliminating most handicaps is not likely to be realized in this century (Hayden & Pious, 1979). And so the need for effective early intervention programs will continue to challenge us.

Screening

Beck (1977) believes that only 6.8% of handicapped children can be identified at birth or shortly thereafter. As a general rule, the more severe the handicapping condition, the earlier in life it can be detected. In the delivery room, medical staff can identify certain handicaps, including microcephaly, cleft palate, and other physical deformities, as well as Down syndrome in most instances. Within a few days after birth, the analysis of a newborn's blood and urine can detect metabolic disorders that produce mental retardation if not treated within 4 to 12 weeks. Within the first few weeks other physical characteristics like coma, paralysis, convulsions, or rapidly increasing head size can signal possible handicapping conditions (Parmelee & Michaelis, 1971). Within the first months delays in the development of various critical behaviors can tell a trained observer that an infant is at risk of developing a handicap.

Again, the more pronounced the delay, the easier it is to identify. Some handi-caps, like learning disabilities or mild retardation, do not show up until a child is in school and his performance in academic subjects is clearly behind that of his peers. But even in those cases, if the child is enrolled in a preschool staffed by experienced professionals, it is possible to note learning problems or lags early.

As was discussed in earlier chapters, screening refers to a procedure in which large numbers of children are tested to identify those with a greater likelihood of having a problem. Those children are then referred for more in-depth assessment.

Even though many measures have been developed to screen for high-risk in-fants and children, use of these measures is still far from universal. One national effort is the Early and Periodic Screening, Diagnosis, and Treatment (EPSDT) provision of the Social Security Amendments of 1967. Required since 1972, EPSDT was set up to

THE APGAR SCALE

The Apgar scale is a screening test for newborn infants. Developed in 1952 by Dr. Virginia Apgar, an anesthesiologist, the scale measures the degree of **asphyxia** (oxygen deprivation) an infant experiences during birth. The screening is administered to virtually 100% of the babies born in American hospitals. According to Dr. Frank Bowen, director of neonatology at Children's Hospital in Columbus, Ohio, "Every delivery should have a person whose primary interest is the newborn," and it is this person—nurse, nurse anesthesiologist, or pediatrician— who administers the test.

The test administrator evaluates the infant twice on five physiological measures: heart rate, respiratory effort, response to stimulation, muscle tone, and skin color (see the sample rating form below). On each measure the child is given a score of 0, 1, or 2. The scoring form describes the specific characteristics of each measure so that the results are as objective as possible.

If the newborn receives a low score on the first administration of the test, which is conducted 60 seconds after birth, the delivery room staff takes immediate resuscitation action. The staff's role is to help the infant complete the

APGAR EVALUATION SCALE

			60 sec.	5 min.
Heart rate	Absent	(0)		
	Less than 100	(1)		
	100 to 140	(2)	1	2
Respiratory effort	Apneic	(0)		
	Shallow, irregular	(1)		
	Lusty cry and breathing	(2)	1	1
Response to catheter stimulation	No response	(0)		
	Grimace	(1)		
	Cough or sneeze	(2)	1	2
Muscle tone	Flaccid	(0)		
	Some flexion of extremities	(1)		
	Flexion resisting extension	(2)	1	2
Color	Pale, blue	(0)		
	Body pink, extremities blue	(1)		
	Pink all over	(2)	0	1
	Total		4	8

Signature of Person Rating _____ *Dr. C. E. Merrill* _____

transition to the world outside the mother's body by establishing strong respiration. This first test measures how the baby fared during the birth process.

The scale is given again 5 minutes after birth. At that point a total score of 0 to 3 (out of a possible 10) indicates severe asphyxia; 4 to 6, moderate asphyxia; and 7 to 10, mild asphyxia. "Some stress is assumed on all births," according to Dr. Bowen. The 5-minute score measures how successful any resuscitation efforts were. Again, a low score calls for continuing action to help the infant.

"A 5-minute score of 6 or less deserves fol- low up," says Dr. Bowen, "to determine what is causing the problem and what its long-term con- sequences will be." The Apgar has been shown to identify high-risk infants—those who have a greater-than-normal chance of developing later problems. Research has shown that oxygen depri- vation at birth contributes to neurological impair- ment, and the 5-minute Apgar score correlates well with eventual neurological outcomes.

Although most newborns are evaluated in terms of gestational weight and age and are screened for certain specific disorders, the Apgar scale is at present the only widely used screening test for high-risk infants.

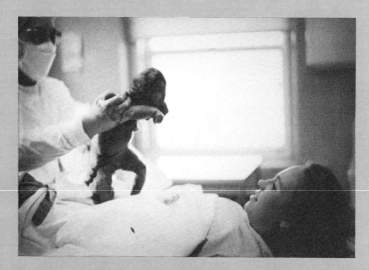

The first Apgar score is obtained when the infant is only one minute old.

identify child health problems and developmental disabilities as early as possible. But EPSDT has drawn criticism, both for failing to reach more of the children it should serve and for failing to provide as much information as it could (Comptroller General, 1977; Warren, 1977). At its best, however, EPSDT is empowered to screen only those children receiving Medicaid; no such program is even recommended by the federal or state governments for other children.

Nonetheless, there are promising developments for the early identification of handicapped and at-risk infants. For example, the SKI*HI Project at Utah State University, in conjunction with the Utah State Health Department, has developed a statewide screening procedure to detect hearing impairment (Finch, 1985). The procedure involves revisions of Utah's birth certificate format to include indicators associated with hearing loss. The project coordinates follow-up home visits to every infant in the state who is discovered to be at risk for hearing loss.

The SKI*HI Project is one of the Handicapped Children's Early Education Projects (HCEEP) funded by the U.S. Department of Education. Other HCEEP projects are described later in this chapter.

One screening procedure that is performed in almost all hospital delivery rooms in the United States is the Apgar scale. It is a quick evaluation of five physiological measures in newborn infants. Another widely practiced screening procedure is the analysis of newborn blood and urine samples to detect the metabolic disorder PKU, which produces mental retardation. And yet, although 48 states had PKU screening programs in 1975, only 8 states routinely screened for six other metabolic disorders that also produce retardation. (Comptroller General, 1977).

The Apgar scale is described on pages 523–24.

One of the most widely used screening instruments for developmental delays is the Denver Developmental Screening Test (DDST) (Frankenburg, Dodds, & Fandal, 1975). The DDST can be administered to children from 1 month to 5 years of age. It assesses 107 skills arranged in four developmental areas: gross motor, language, fine motor-adaptive, and personal-social. Each test item is represented on the scoring form by a bar showing at what ages 25%, 50%, 75%, and 90% of normally developing children can perform that skill (see Figure 14.1). The child is allowed up to three trials per item. A delay is noted when the child cannot perform a skill that 90% of younger children can perform. A child's performance is considered abnormal if two of the developmental areas contain two or more delayed items. The child would then be referred for further detailed assessment of her abilities.

Many other screening measures are available; several are based on the Gesell Developmental Schedules (Gesell et al., 1940; Knobloch & Pasamanick, 1974), which describe normal motor development, adaptive behavior, language, and personal-social behavior in infants and young children. The Bayley Scales of Infant Development (Bayley, 1969), which evaluate an infant's development from 2 to 30 months, are standardized adaptations of the Gesell schedules. The Developmental Screening Inventory (Knobloch, Pasamanick, & Sherard, 1966), also based on the Gesell scales, was designed for pediatricians to use to assess developmental delays in children between 1 and 18 months of age. The Brazelton Neonatal Assessment Scale (Brazelton, 1973) is a more detailed assessment of the newborn.

None of these measures or practices, however, add up to any kind of truly systematic effort to screen all infants. And most state and local screening programs are aimed at older children, especially those about to start school. Identifying high-risk infants and young children most often depends on the experience and concern of the

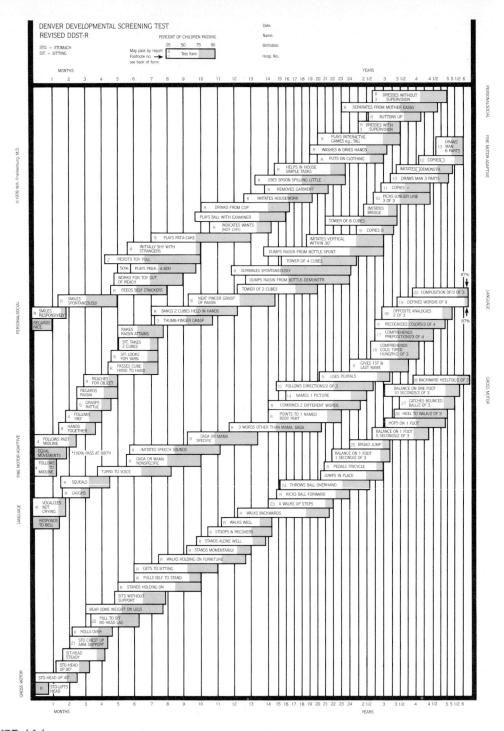

FIGURE 14.1

The Denver Developmental Screening Test.

Source: From *Denver Developmental Screening Test* by W. K. Frankenburg, J. B. Dodds, and A. Fandal, 1975, Denver, CO: LADOCA Project and Publishing Foundation. Reprinted by permission.

adults who deal with them. Chief among those adults are pediatricians and nurses, social workers, day-care staff, preschool teachers, and, most of all, the child's parents. A recent study has shown that mothers' estimates of their preschool children's levels of development correlate highly with those produced by professionals using standardized scales (Gradel, Thompson, & Sheehan, 1981).

Not all children who are screened as high risk will necessarily have handicaps. Some grow up to live normal lives, without any special help. The goal of early screening is to identify a possible or likely handicap before it can take its full toll on the child's future. For those who are identified, screening is only the first step. The next step is a careful and detailed assessment of all of the critical areas of development.

Assessment

McLoughlin and Lewis (1986) state that early childhood assessment should be guided by three questions. First, assessment should determine whether there is a developmental handicap. Second, information gathered during assessment should reveal the nature of the developmental problem. Third, and most important, is the decision as to educational and other services the child needs. Assessment of young children should also be guided by a number of criteria.

☐ Assessments should be conducted in a child's natural environments in a nonthreatening manner (Bailey & Wolery, 1984).

☐ Direct observation of a child's behavior is necessary for an accurate and meaningful determination of the child's abilities. Checklists and rating scales, although sufficient for targeting general areas of strength and weakness, usually do not pinpoint the specific behaviors that define those areas (Halle & Sindelar, 1982).

☐ Assessments should be repeated over time. It is dangerous to decide that a handicap does or does not exist on the basis of one test or observation. The behavior of young children is simply too variable, and the consequences of being wrong too great, to base the decision on one assessment session, no matter how extensive it is (McLoughlin & Lewis, 1986).

☐ A multidisciplinary assessment should be conducted. It is important that the members of a multidisciplinary assessment team cooperate to determine their respective roles before assessment begins (Holm & McCartin, 1978; Orlando, 1981). Rose and Logan (1982) have described the assessment roles usually performed by professionals from the various disciplines concerned with the development of young children (see Table 14.1).

Team members and their roles are discussed in more detail later in this chapter.

> There is some intentional overlapping in the role assignments of team members. This is done in an attempt to eliminate gaps in the assessment process. It also enables the team to consider patterns of behavior in the child and the family. In this way, the team is able to develop the most comprehensive picture of the child and how that child responds to the influences and demands of the environment. (p. 191)

☐ The assessment process should involve parents and family. Information gathered from interviews with parents and observations of parent-child interactions is extremely important in determining meaningful instructional targets. Not only is the

TABLE 14.1

Interdisciplinary team members and role descriptions.

Team Member	Description
Pediatrician	1. Examines previous medical records for information that may explain etiology of developmental delays. 2. Looks into family medical history to determine if genetic or hereditary factors are involved. 3. Coordinates medical care for the child and family.
Clinical nurse	1. Provides assistance in prevention and case finding. 2. Counsels parents on child health, child rearing, and home management of selected problems. 3. Facilitates coordination, planning, and follow-up among the home, educational setting, and health care team.
Pediatric nutritionist	1. Examines conditions that may cause failure to thrive in the child. 2. Informs parents about dietary needs of their child. 3. Develops nutritional plan for the child and family.
Developmental therapist (occupational therapist and/or physical therapist)	1. Assesses gross motor skills, hand functioning, and sensory skills. 2. Develops treatment programs (as needed) that can also be used by parents and educators. 3. OT focuses on deficits in sensory integration. 4. PT emphasizes therapy in gross motor areas.
Developmental psychologist	1. Administers psychological testing in the cognitive and affective domains. 2. Considers differences between test performance and skills demonstrated in other situations. 3. Interprets test results in terms of characteristics and behavior. 4. Helps parents and educators plan programming and management.

information from parents necessary for a complete assessment, but their cooperation and involvement as active partners throughout the assessment process are desired because parents play a critical role in most early intervention programs (Winton, 1986).

☐ The child should be kept motivated during the administration of assessment items, and testing should not continue if the child's attention or performance declines after a period of time. Bailey and Wolery (1984) recommend interspersing desk activities with activities that allow movement and incorporating interesting materials and a gamelike format to maintain the child's interest and performance.

☐ Test items and their administration should be modified if necessary to allow a child with a disability to display his ability. For example, changing the way a test item is presented (perhaps repeating it and using gestural cues) or even partially assisting a child in responding may provide significantly more useful information about the child's current level of functioning than would have been gained by simply marking

TABLE 14.1

continued

Team Member	Description
Early childhood education specialist	1. Helps design assessment strategies that ensure programming goals. 2. Observes and records behavior of the child in a classroom setting. 3. Suggests teaching strategies, curriculum, and behavior management for the child. 4. Works with other team members to develop an individualized education program. 5. Acts as a liasion among the child, parents, and teachers when the child leaves the preschool for another setting.
Communication specialist (speech pathologist and/or audiologist)	1. May assess the amount of information provided by the adults in the child's environment. 2. Determines whether articulation problems may be a function of delayed motor development or neurological impairment. 3. Assesses auditory behaviors, receptive communication behaviors, and expressive communication behaviors. 4. Suggests structuring of classroom environment to foster language development.
Social Worker	1. Visits the family to determine the climate of the home and what feelings the parents and siblings have about one member's handicap. 2. Surveys the expectations and values of the parents to help design an intervention program. 3. Establishes the best process for sharing information and results of assessments between parents and other team members. 4. Helps set up a home program and feedback process between parents and team.

Source: From "Educational and Life/Career Programs for the Mildly Mentally Retarded" by E. Rose and D. R. Logan, 1982, in *Mental Retardation: From Categories to People* by P. T. Cegelka and H. J. Prehm (Eds.), (p. 194). Columbus, OH: Merrill. Reprinted by permission.

a score of zero and proceeding to the next item. Although this suggestion goes against the rules of administering standardized tests, the information acquired about the child's abilities and its usefulness in determining appropriate instructional targets is often more important than any calculation of a test score (McLean & Snyder-McLean, 1978).

A wide variety of assessment devices are available, including both formal, standardized measures and less formal checklists and rating scales based on observations of the child. McGovern and Draper (1978) list more than 45 formal evaluation instruments intended to identify and assess delayed or abnormal progress in intellectual development, auditory perception, or affective and social development. Likewise, Jordan, Hayden, Karnes, and Wood (1977) list a total of 68 standardized tests being used by the nearly 200 model programs funded by HCEEP for young handicapped children.

As more and more intervention programs for young handicapped children are started, the number of informal observation checklists, rating scales, and other assessment devices also grows. Most have been developed by federally funded model programs or by locally sponsored centers for young handicapped children. In general, assessment tools seek to measure a child's development in six key areas.

1. Cognitive development includes such processes as attention, perception, memory, verbal skills, and concept learning, many of which processes are assessed by observing a child's performances in other areas.
2. Motor development includes a child's gross motor skills (like rolling over, crawling, walking, swimming) and fine motor skills (like eye-hand coordination, reaching, touching, grasping).
3. Language development encompasses all of the communication development, including a child's ability to respond nonverbally with gestures, smiles, or actions and the acquisition of spoken language—sounds, words, phrases, sentences, and so on.
4. Self-help skills include skills such as feeding, dressing, and using the toilet without assistance.
5. Play skills include playing with toys, with other children, with games, and in dramatic or fantasy roles.
6. Personal-social skills include child's social responses to adults and to other children, as well as skills in managing her own behaviors when alone.

Generally, these six areas are broken down into specific, observable tasks and sequenced developmentally; that is, in the order in which most children learn them. Sometimes each task is tied to a specific age at which a child should normally be able to perform it. This arrangement allows the observer to note significant delays or gaps, as well as other unusual patterns, in a high-risk child's development.

In addition, several assessment devices have specific sections to test a child's sensory acuity (hearing and sight in particular). And many also try to measure a child's readiness for academic learning, with specific tasks related to early reading and math skills. There are also tests designed to measure a child's readiness for school, such as the Brigance K and 1 Screen for Kindergarten and First Grade (Brigance, 1982) and the Metropolitan Readiness Tests (Nurss & McGauvran, 1976). Readiness tests usually include items assessing a child's prereading and premath skills as well as social-emotional development, gross and fine motor performance, and general cognitive development.

A growing number of early intervention programs are moving away from assessments based entirely on developmental milestones and are incorporating curriculum-based assessment. In a curriculum-based assessment each item relates directly to a skill included in the program's curriculum, thereby providing a direct link between testing, teaching, and progress evaluation.

Of course, the accuracy and usefulness of the assessment information depend not just on the kind of device or method used. The experience and training of the

See Bagnato, Neisworth, and Capone (1986) for a description and rationale of curriculum-based assessment, as well as a review of 21 assessment measures useful for curriculum-based assessment in early childhood special education programs.

observer, the number of observations, the settings in which the child is observed, and the care with which the data are interpreted all affect the reliability of an assessment.

DuBose (1981) has noted the particular difficulty posed by evaluating children with severe handicaps. Because there are so few reliable assessment instruments that can be used with severely impaired children, professionals often need to adapt standardized tests and devise informal assessment tasks. DuBose warns that adaptations must be made and results interpreted with care. The examiner must know why a particular test was given, what it is meant to tap, and what the child's test performances indicate.

As several professionals have noted (Kakalik et al., 1974; Hayden & Edgar, 1977), there are serious dangers if errors are made in screening or assessment. Children who are handicapped but who are not identified may fail to get needed services, and their problems may get worse. On the other hand, children who are not handicapped but who are assessed as such may suffer the stigma of an erroneous label. The identification and assessment of young children with handicaps will continue to be a difficult yet extremely important aspect of special education.

EARLY CHILDHOOD SPECIAL EDUCATION PROGRAMS

Certainly the most notable effort to develop early childhood special education programs is the Handicapped Children's Early Education Program (HCEEP), created through federal legislation in 1968. The purpose of HCEEP is to develop model early intervention programs for handicapped children from birth to age 8. HCEEP, often referred to as the First Chance Network, began with 24 programs funded for a total of $1 million in 1969. By 1984–85 there were 173 different First Chance Network programs throughout all 50 states and in several U.S. territories. A study contracted by the government found that 80% of the 280 demonstration programs funded since 1969 had continued to serve young handicapped children beyond the initial 3-year period of federal support (*Analysis of the Impact of HCEEP*, Littlejon Associates, 1982). That same study revealed a number of other indicators of the program's positive impact.

A model program evaluates the effectiveness of new procedures and techniques (or, as if often the case, a new combination of old techniques) with the hope that, if the model proves effective, it can serve as a basis for developing other similar programs.

☐ More than 30,200 children had been served in continuation projects at no cost to HCEEP.

☐ First Chance Network projects had stimulated a total of 2,157 replications of their services by other agencies and communities.

☐ These replication programs had served 107,850 children.

☐ Of the children who left First Chance Network programs 67% were placed in integrated settings with nonhandicapped children.

☐ The projects had collectively developed more than 3,000 print and audiovisual products on early childhood special education; many of these products have been purchased and distributed by commercial publishers.

By 1985 the U.S. Department of Education considered a total of 22 HCEEP demonstration projects to be nationally validated. These projects have been awarded

Each year the U.S. Department of Education Office of Special Education Programs publishes a directory of all currently funded HCEEP programs. In addition to addresses and the names of contact persons, the directory gives a brief description of each project's purpose, characteristics of the children served, measures of child progress used, type and level of parent involvement, and products developed.

additional funds to help others set up identical programs elsewhere. In general, the First Chance Network and other promising early intervention programs operate on one of three models: a home-based program, a center-based program, or a program that combines home and center as settings for intervention.

Home-Based Programs

As the name suggests, a home-based program depends heavily on the training and cooperation of parents. The parents assume the responsibility of being the primary caregivers and teachers for their handicapped child. Parent training is usually provided by a teacher or trainer who visits the home regularly to guide the parents, act as a consultant, evaluate the success of the intervention, and make regular assessments of the child's progress. In some programs these home visitors (or home teachers or home advisors, as they are often called) are specially trained paraprofessionals. They may visit as frequently as several times a week but probably no less than a few times a month. In some cases they carry the results of their in-home evaluations back to other professionals who make recommendations for changes in the program.

Perhaps the best known home-based program is the nationally validated Portage Project (Shearer & Shearer, 1972). Operated by a consortium of 23 school districts in south-central Wisconsin, the Portage Project has produced its own assessment materials and teaching activities, *The Portage Guide to Early Education*. The basis for the program is 450 behaviors sequenced developmentally and classified into self-help, cognition, socialization, language, and motor skills. A project teacher normally visits the home one day each week, (1) reviewing the child's progress during the previous week, (2) describing activities for the upcoming week, (3) demonstrating to the parent(s) how to carry out the activities with the child, (4) observing the parent and child interacting and offering suggestions and advice as needed, and (5) summarizing where the program stands and indicating what records should be kept during the next week. The Portage Project has now been replicated in hundreds of locations around the country (Shearer & Snider, 1981). A recent review of outcome studies on the Portage Project states that although there are as yet no data available on the project's long-term effects, there is evidence of developmental acceleration in mildly delayed children (Sturmey & Crisp, 1986).

An early intervention program based in the home has several advantages, especially if the home is the handicapped child's own. First of all, the home is the child's natural environment, and parents have been the child's first teachers. In addition, other family members like brothers and sisters and perhaps grandparents have more opportunity to interact with the child, both for instruction and for social contact. These significant others in the child's life can play an important role in the child's growth and development. Also, learning activities and materials conducted in the home are more likely to be natural and appropriate. And it is often true that a parent can spend more time and give more attention to the child than even the most adequately staffed center or school. In addition, parents who are actively involved in helping their child learn and develop clearly have an advantage over parents who feel guilt, frustration, or defeat at their seeming inability to help their handicapped child. (Of course, this does not suggest that parents of a child in a center-based program cannot take an active role in their child's learning and growth). Furthermore, in sparsely populated regions, a home-based program allows a child to live at home while receiving an intensive education, without totally disrupting the family's life.

Home-based programs are not without disadvantages. Because home-based programs place so much responsibility on parents, they are not effective with all families. Not all parents are able or willing to spend the time required to teach their handicapped children, and some who try are not effective teachers. Early childhood special education programs must learn to serve more effectively the large and increasing number of young children who do not reside in the traditional two-parent family—especially the many thousands of children with teenage mothers who are single, uneducated, and poor. Many of these infants and preschoolers are at risk for developmental delays because of the impoverished conditions in which they live. It is unlikely that a parent struggling with the realities of day-to-day survival will be able to meet the added demands of involvement in an early intervention program (Turnbull et al., 1986). In addition, because the parent—usually the mother—is the primary service provider, children in home-based programs may not receive as wide a range of services as they would in a center-based program, where they can be seen by a variety of professionals. Another disadvantage of the home-based program is that the child may not receive sufficient opportunity for social interaction with peers.

Center-Based Programs

In contrast to home-based programs, some early intervention efforts are coordinated and carried out in a special educational setting outside the home. The setting may be part of a hospital complex, a special day-care center, or a preschool. In other cases children may attend a specially designed developmental center or training center that offers a wide range of services for children with varying types and severities of handicaps. In one instance described by Jones (1977), the setting was an outdoor playground specially built on a New York City rooftop. Wherever they are located, these centers offer the combined services of many professionals and paraprofessionals, often from several different fields.

Most center-based programs encourage social interaction, and some try to integrate handicapped children with nonhandicapped children in day-care or preschool classes. In some instances the child attends the center each weekday, sometimes for all or most of the day. In other instances the child may come less frequently, although most centers expect to see each child at least once each week. Sometimes parents are given roles as classroom aides or are encouraged to act as the primary teacher of their child. In a few programs parents may spend time with other professionals or take training while their child is somewhere else in the center. Virtually all of the First Chance programs and most other effective programs for young handicapped children recognize the critical need to involve the parents, and they welcome parents in every aspect of the program.

To get an idea of how some early intervention specialists are using non-handicapped peers to help handicapped pre-schoolers learn social interaction skills, see pages 534–35.

One of the more successful center programs is the Model Preschool Center for Handicapped Children at the University of Washington in Seattle. There, children with a variety of handicaps go to participate in one of several highly specialized programs: an infant learning program, a communication disorders classroom, a preschool where

PEER SOCIAL INITIATIONS: A STRATEGY FOR INFLUENCING THE SOCIAL SKILLS DEVELOPMENT OF HANDICAPPED CHILDREN

In addition to any deficits in cognitive, motor, language, and other developmental areas, young handicapped children typically exhibit problems in social skills. When placed in mainstreamed settings, many handicapped preschoolers interact infrequently and incompetently with other children. Strain and his colleagues (Strain, 1981, in press; Strain & Odom, 1986) have investigated the use of peer social initiations as a means of increasing the social competence of handicapped preschoolers. The procedure involves teaching nonhandicapped peers to direct social overtures to their handicapped classmates. Strain and Odom (1986) recommend that peer intervention agents be taught to make initiations to handicapped children in the form of (1) play opportunities, (2) offers to share, (3) physical assistance, and (4) affection. These initiations are recommended on the basis of naturalistic studies of the social interactions of both nonhandicapped and handicapped preschoolers; the studies showed that such initiations were followed by a positive response more than 50% of the time and that responding to the social bids of others increased a child's social acceptability.

The strategy requires careful arrangement of the classroom environment to encourage increased social interaction. For example, the probability of social interaction can be increased by limiting the number of toys so that children must share in order to participate and by requiring the children to play within a confined area. However, the key feature of the procedure is the careful training of the nonhandicapped peers who are chosen to serve as "confederates." Training sessions usually take between 20 and 25 minutes and incorporate teacher modeling and both teacher and confederate role-playing of the desired social initiation. A sample script of the first training session, in which children learn how to initiate sharing, appears on page 000. Training is followed by daily intervention sessions, in which the teacher arranges an activity for the children that is conducive to social interaction and then provides prompts and verbal reinforcement for the confederate for being a good teacher and for the target handicapped child for being a good player.

Strain and Odom (1986) report that positive results have been documented using the peer initiation intervention with preschool children handicapped by mental retardation, autism, and behavior disorders. The outcomes include an increase in positive social responses by all target children, an increase in social initiations by some target children, an increase in the length of social exchanges by target children, and generalization of social interactions by target children to other integrated preschool settings.

Source: "Peer Social Initiations: Effective Intervention for Social Skills Development of Exceptional Children" by P. S. Strain and S. L. Odom, 1986, *Exceptional Children, 52,* 547. Reprinted by permission.

Session 1: Introduction to System—Share Initiation—Persistence

TEACHER: "Today you are going to learn how to be a good teacher. Sometimes your friends in your class do not know how to play with other children. You are going to learn how to teach them to play. What are you going to do?"

CHILD RESPONSE: "Teach them to play."

TEACHER: "One way you can get your friend to play with you is to share. How do you get your friend to play with you?"

CHILD RESPONSE: "Share."

TEACHER: "Right! You share. When you share, you look at your friend and say, 'Here,' and put a toy in his hand. What do you do?" (Repeat this exercise until the child can repeat these three steps.)

CHILD RESPONSE: "Look at friend and say, 'Here,' and put the toy in his hand."

ADULT MODEL WITH ROLE-PLAYER: "Now, watch me. I am going to share with ____. Tell me if I do it right." (Demonstrate sharing.) "Did I share with ____? What did I do?"

CHILD RESPONSE: "Yea! ____ looked at ____, said 'Here ____' and put a toy in his hand."

ADULT: "Right. I looked at ____ and said, 'Here ____' and put a toy in his hand. Now watch me. See if I share with ____." (Move to the next activity in the classroom. This time provide a negative example of sharing by leaving out the "put in hand" component. Put the toy beside the role-player). "Did I share?" (Correct if necessary and repeat this example if child got it wrong.) "Why not?"

CHILD RESPONSE: "No." "You did not put the toy in ____'s hand."

ADULT: "That's right. I did not put the toy in ____'s hand. When I share, I have to look at ____ and say, 'Here ___' and put the toy in his hand." (Give the child two more positive and two more negative examples of sharing. When the child answers incorrectly about sharing, repeat the example. Vary the negative examples by leaving out different components: looking, saying 'Here,' putting in hand.)

CHILD PRACTICE WITH ADULTS: "Now ____, I want you to get ____ to share with you. What do you do when you share?"

CHILD RESPONSE: Look at ____ and say, 'Here ____,' and put a toy in his hand."

ADULT: "Now, go get ____ to play with you." (For these practice examples, the role-playing adult should be responsive to the child's sharing.) (To the other confederates:) "Did ____ share with ____? What did she/he do?"

CHILD RESPONSE: "Yes/No. Looked at ____ and said, 'Here ____' and put a toy in his hand."

ADULT: (Move to the next activity.) "Now, ____, I want you to share with ____"

Introduce Persistence

TEACHER: "Sometimes when I play with ____, he/she does not want to play back. I have to keep on trying. What do I have to do?"

CHILD RESPONSE: "Keep on trying."

TEACHER: "Right, I have to keep on trying. Watch me. I am going to share with ____. Now I want you to see if I keep on trying." (Role-player will be initially unresponsive.) (Teacher should be persistent until child finally responds.) "Did I get ____ to play with me?" *CHILD:* "Yes." *TEACHER:* "Did he want to play?" *CHILD:* "No." *TEACHER:* "What did I do?" *CHILD:* "Keep on trying." *TEACHER:* "Right, I kept on trying. Watch. See if I can get ____ to play with me this time." (Again, the role-player should be unresponsive at first. Repeat above questions and correct if necessary. Repeat the example until the child responds correctly.)

handicapped children are integrated with normal children, a program for Down syndrome children, and a program for severely handicapped preschoolers. Although all of the programs stress parent involvement, most of the direct instruction with the children takes place at the center. Instruction consists of rigorously applied behavior analysis—careful screening and initial assessment, pinpointing of target behaviors for instruction, precise instructional planning, and daily assessments of progress. Like that in most centers, the curriculum focuses on key areas of development: gross and fine motor, communication, self-help, social behavior, and preacademic skills. Because of its size and its location at a major university, the center's staff is large and can offer the services of many different specialists in teaching, language and communication disorders, psychology, and medicine. By 1985 the Model Preschool's outreach project had assisted 47 other sites in replicating components of the demonstration model (Assael, 1985).

Center-based programs generally offer a number of advantages not easily built into home-based efforts. One important benefit is the opportunity for a team of specialists from different fields—medicine, education, physical and occupational therapy, speech and language pathology, and others—to observe each child and cooperate in intervention and continued assessment. Many centers hold regular meetings (perhaps once a month) at which all those involved with the child sit down to discuss his progress, his response to the strategies used, and new or revised objectives for him. In addition, the opportunity for contact with handicapped and nonhandicapped peers makes center programs especially appealing for some children. And parents involved in center programs no doubt feel some relief at the support they get from professionals working with their child and, in some cases, from other parents with children at the same center.

Disadvantages of a center-based program include the expense of transportation, the cost and maintenance of the center itself, and the probability of less parent involvement than in home-based programs.

Combined Home-Center Programs

Perhaps the most commonly used intervention model is the one that offers both center-based activities and home visitation. Few center programs take children for more than a few hours a day, for up to 5 days a week; but for young handicapped children intervention must be more than a few hours a day. Thus, many programs combine the intensive help of a variety of professionals in a center with the continuous attention and sensitive care of parents at home. This effort to establish intervention that carries over from center to home clearly offers many of the advantages of the two types of programs and negates some of their disadvantages.

A good example of a home-center program is the PEECH (Precise Early Education of Children with Handicaps) Project at the University of Illinois. Designed for children aged 3 or older with mild to moderate handicaps, PEECH combines classroom instruction for up to 10 handicapped and 5 nonhandicapped children. A team approach to intervention and parental involvement includes a classroom teacher and a paraprofessional aide, a psychologist, a speech-language pathologist, and a social worker.

Children spend 2 or 3 hours in class each day with some time in large and small groups and in individualized activites. Parents are included in all stages of the intervention, including policy-making. The project even offers a lending library and toy library for parents to use, as well as a parent newsletter. The ultimate goal of the project is to integrate handicapped youngsters successfully into regular classes whenever possible. In 1985 it was reported that 72 replication sites were using components of the PEECH program (Assael, 1985).

It is probably best to view these choices—home, center, or combined programs—as more alike than different. In fact, they do seem to have more in common than not: carefully sequenced curricula, strong parent involvement, explicit goals and frequent assessment of progress, integration of handicapped and nonhandicapped children whenever possible, and staff teams that consist of specialists in several fields.

CURRICULUM IN EARLY CHILDHOOD SPECIAL EDUCATION PROGRAMS

Most early childhood special education programs employ a developmentally based curriculum (Stramiello, 1978). That is, the typical gains made by nonhandicapped children in sensorimotor development, language, social skills, academic readiness, and so on are used as a basis for sequencing instructional objectives and evaluating child progress. According to Wood and Hurley (1977), developmentally based early intervention programs tend to work with young handicapped children for one of five purposes.

1. *Remediating*, that is, making up for delays or gaps in a child's development, whether in language, motor skills, self-help, or other areas.
2. *Teaching basic processes*, like attention, perception, sensorimotor, language, social skills, and memory.
3. *Teaching developmental tasks*, which are skills in a range of areas (motor, language, self-help, social), in sequences that most closely match the order in which normal children learn them.
4. *Teaching psychological constructs*, like self-concept, creativity, motivation, and cognition, assuming that this training will lead to increased learning later.
5. *Teaching preacademic skills* in prereading, early math, nature studies, art, dance, and so on.

These purposes or approaches are not mutually exclusive, of course. All of them use normal development as a yardstick against which to measure each child's individual needs and progress. In other words, a curriculum may try to give a handicapped child instruction in all the processes or skills that a normal child might develop without specific teaching. Or it might try to measure all of the skills the child has already learned and then teach only those that are missing. But in both instances the ultimate goal is to help the child develop as many of the behaviors of a normal child of the same age as possible.

The developmental curriculum is not the most appropriate for all young children with handicaps. Bailey and Wolery (1984) remind us that the purposes of the early intervention curriculum are to accelerate children's developmental progress and to maximize independent functioning. With some children (e.g., mildly and moderately handicapped children) the primary emphasis is on accelerating developmental progress. With more severely handicapped children, the emphasis is on maximizing independent functioning. (p. 17)

As always, the specific instructional targets for each handicapped child must be individually determined. For more severely handicapped or sensorily impaired preschoolers, the objectives suggested by a developmentally based curriculum may be inappropriate. For these children a functionally based curriculum may be more appropriate, focusing on skills that will enable them to immediately improve their interaction with their environments. For example, Laura is a 5-year-old with multiple handicaps; she is unable to dress herself. Because dressing oneself is a functional skill that increases independent functioning, it would be chosen as an objective for Laura in a functionally based curriculum. Careful assessment would be conducted to determine what specific steps in dressing Laura could not perform, and direct instruction in those steps would follow. By contrast, a curriculum following typical developmental sequences would focus on the developmental prerequisites to getting dressed, such as grasping objects, using various gross- and fine-motor movements, and so on.

Early childhood special educators do not have to choose between a strict developmental or functional approach. Many early intervention programs for handicapped children use a combination of the two approaches, relying on a normal sequence of development as a general guide to the curriculum while using functional considerations in the selection of specific instructional targets for each child. Two areas are important for every early intervention special education program: promoting language development and scheduling activities to be instructionally effective.

Developing Language in Handicapped Preschoolers

A major developmental task of children is to learn the native language of their community. As we mentioned in chapter 6, most children learn to speak and communicate effectively with little or no formal teaching. By the time they enter school, most children have essentially mastered their native tongue. But handicapped children often do not acquire language in the spontaneous, seemingly effortless manner of their nonhandicapped peers (Barney & Landis, 1987). And as handicapped children slip further and further behind their peers, their language deficits make social and academic development even more difficult. Handicapped preschoolers need opportunities and activities directed at language use and development throughout the day.

> The tendency is to schedule a time during the day as "language time." Having done that, we begin to think that the children have been taught language. I don't believe children learn language in this way; language permeates everything we do. (Rieke, quoted in Magliocca, 1980, p. 14)

Eileen Allen and Jane Rieke are two language specialists who, like most of their colleagues, believe that teachers of preschool children must use strategies to help

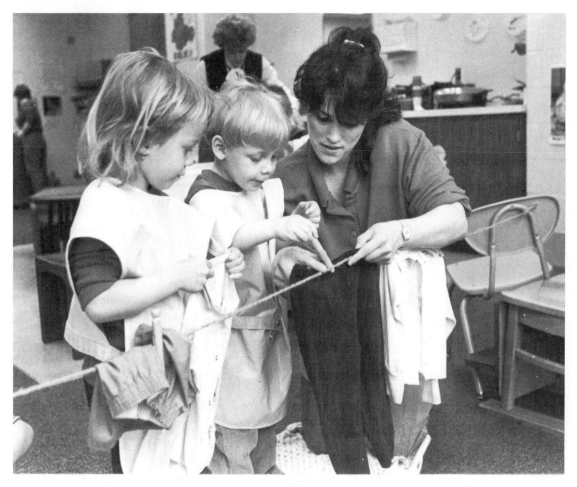

Effective teachers use natural activities to promote the language development of handicapped preschoolers.

children develop language skills all day long, throughout a total program. They also believe that the basic measure of success of a language intervention should be how much the child talks. Research has shown that the more a child talks, the better the child talks (Hart & Risley, 1975; Rieke, Lynch, & Soltman, 1977). Allen (1980a) states that good teachers do three things to ensure that effective intervention is provided for language-delayed children.

1. They arrange the environment in ways demonstrated to be conducive to promoting language: (a) by providing several interesting learning centers (blocks, housekeeping and dramatic play, creative and manipulative materials); (b) by organizing a balance of activities in terms of child-initiated and teacher-structured; and (c) by presenting materials and activities that children enjoy.

2. They manage their own interactions with children so as to maximize effective communication on the part of each language-impaired child, and use every opportunity to teach "on the fly" (White, 1975).
3. They monitor, on a regular basis, the appropriateness of (a) environmental arrangements; (b) their own behavior; and (c) that of the children, in order to validate child progress and thus program effectiveness.   (p. 8)

Two models or approaches teachers can use for systematically encouraging and developing language use throughout the school day are the incidental teaching model (Hart & Risley, 1975) and the communicative interaction model (Rieke et al., 1977). The essential feature of the incidental teaching model is that the child wants something from the teacher—help, approval, information, food, or drink—and the teacher uses such opportunities to promote language use. In other words, whenever the child initiates an interaction with the teacher, the teacher uses that opportunity to get the best possible language from the child. Allen (1980b) offers the following example of an incidental teaching episode described by Hart.

> A four-year-old girl with delayed language stands in front of the teacher with a paint apron in her hand. The teacher says, "What do you need?" (Teacher does *not* anticipate the child's need by putting the apron on the child at the moment.)
>   If the child does not answer, the teacher tells her and gives her a prompt: "It's an apron. Can you say 'apron' ?" If the child says "apron" the teacher ties it while giving descriptive praise, "You said it right. It *is* an apron. I am tying your apron on you." The teacher's last sentence models the next verbal behavior, "Tie my apron," that the teacher will expect once the child has learned to say "apron."
>   If the child does not say "apron," the teacher ties the apron. No further comments are made at this time. The teacher must not coax, nag or pressure the child. If each episode is kept brief and pleasant, the child will contact the teacher frequently. Thus, the teacher will have many opportunities for incidental teaching. If the teacher pressures the child, such incidental learning opportunities will be lost. Some children may learn to avoid the teacher—they will simply do without; other children may learn inappropriate ways, such as whining and crying, to get what they want.

Through repeated interactions of this type, children learn that language is important; it can get them what they want, and teachers listen when they speak and want to hear more about things of interest to them. An important guideline in incidental teaching is to keep interactions brief and pleasant so that there will be many more opportunities. The child should never be interrogated or put on the spot (Allen, 1980a).

In the communicative interaction model the teacher is in the role of facilitator, always seeking to make things happen by saying or doing things that encourage the child to use language. Rieke and her colleagues (1977) recommend that teachers of young children avoid the two-unit, question-and-answer pattern of interaction often typical of adult-child communications. Those interactions do not encourage the child to continue talking and may lead the child to avoid the interrogating adult. Instead, the teacher-facilitator uses a three-unit format for dialogues that may be initiated by either teacher or child.

Child:	Points.
Teacher:	"You want the car? Say 'car'."
Child:	Nods and makes sound approximating "car."
Child:	"Look at my painting."
Teacher:	"You used red, blue and _____?"
Child:	"And green and yellow and some more red."
Child:	"What you doing?"
Teacher:	"Watch me and see if you can tell *me* what I am doing."
Child:	"Play dough—me help?"
Teacher:	(to nonverbal child) "Where did you park your trike?"
Child:	Points to shed.
Teacher:	"In the *shed*; you remembered!"
Teacher:	"What a pretty new dress!"
Child:	"My birthday."
Teacher:	"Your birthday dress! What else did you get for your birthday?"
Teacher:	"You have a new baby at your house! Is it a boy or girl?"
Child:	"Boy."
Teacher:	"A new boy baby! What's his name?" (Allen, 1980a, pp. 9–10)

Both models of assisting children in developing language skills have much in common. Both view the teacher as (1) an astute and systematic observer and recorder of children's language, (2) a sensitive and willing listener, and (3) a systematic responder who helps the child "say it better" through differential feedback (Allen, 1980a).

Developing a Preschool Activity Schedule

Teachers in preschool programs for handicapped children face the challenge of organizing the 2 to 3 hours of the program day into a schedule that meets each child's individual learning needs. The schedule should include both one-to-one and group instruction, provide children with many learning opportunities throughout the day, and allow easy transition from activity to activity. In short, the schedule should provide a framework for maximizing instruction while remaining manageable and flexible. In addition, in integrated programs the manner in which activities are scheduled and organized has considerable effect on the frequency and type of interaction that occurs between handicapped and nonhandicapped children (Burstein, 1986; Strain, 1981) and on the extent to which the mainstreamed handicapped children benefit from instruction (O'Connell, 1986).

Lund and Bos (1981) suggest that teachers begin planning a preschool schedule by determining the basic activities and time blocks. Figure 14.2 shows the components that are common to many preschool programs. The next steps in constructing the schedule are filling in the approximate amount of time to be spent on each activity each day, sequencing the components, scheduling children for individual and group instruction, and assigning staff (teachers, aides, and volunteers).

Recommendations are provided by O'Connell (1986) for structuring the physical arrangement of small-group learning activities in mainstreamed preschool classrooms.

FIGURE 14.2
Considerations in planning a schedule.

Approx. Amount of Time	Components
	Circle—opening exercises that vary in content from day to day or week to week. **Interactive play**—a play area where students interact with peers using teacher-structured materials and activities, e.g., dramatic play centered around a theme, woodworking, kitchen, blockbuilding. **Movement**—gross motor activities in either an indoor or outdoor setting; may also include physical/occupational therapy exercises. **Snack**—fruit juices (natural sugars only), milk, popcorn, dried fruit, granola, etc. **Bathroom**—as scheduled with group or according to individual toileting schedule. **Activity table**—students work at one or several activity tables; activities generally focus on fine motor and preacademic tasks. **Small groups**—students work in small groups on individual and group programs; content of activities varies but usually focuses on communication and preacademic tasks. **Story**—simple picture books, flannel board, hand puppets/finger puppets. **Music**—action songs, finger plays, rhythm band. **Rest/relax**—low lights, mats, listening to soft music, relaxing exercises. **Flex time**—a time when any of the above activities or special experiences (field trips, special guests, etc.) can be planned; activities vary from day to day. **Special needs therapy**—speech/language therapy, occupational therapy, physical therapy, adaptive physical education.

Source: From "Orchestrating the Preschool Classroom: The Daily Schedule" by K. A. Lund and C. S. Bos, 1981. *Teaching Exceptional Children, 14,* p. 121. Copyright by the Council for Exceptional Children. Reprinted by permission.

The physical arrangement of the classroom itself must support the planned activities (see Figure 14.3). Lund and Bos (1981) offer the following suggestions for setting up a preschool classroom:

☐ Place individual work areas and quiet activities together, away from avenues of traffic. This should encourage attending behavior.

☐ Provide a stable area such as an activity table and rug where a variety of group programs can be conducted.

☐ Place the activity table within easy access of storage so that materials can be quickly obtained when working with students.

☐ Place materials used most often close together for accessibility (e.g., clipboard, individual program materials).

☐ Label or color code all storage areas so that aides and volunteers can easily find the needed materials.

☐ Arrange equipment and group areas so that the students can move easily from one activity to another. Picture or color codes can be applied to various work areas.

☐ Provide lockers or cubbies for students so they know where their belongings can be found. Again, add picture cues to help the students identify their lockers.

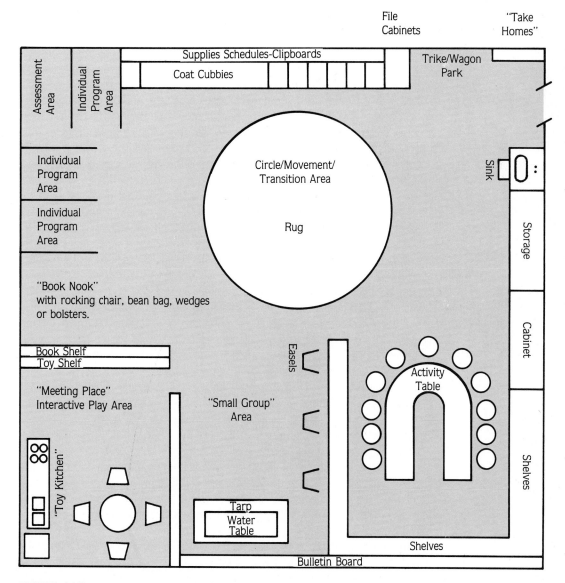

FIGURE 14.3

One arrangement for a preschool classroom.

Source: From "Orchestrating the Preschool Classroom: The Daily Schedule" by K. A. Lund and C. S. Bos, 1981, *Teaching Exceptional Children, 14*, p. 123. Copyright by the Council for Exceptional Children. Reprinted by permission.

WHO CAN HELP?

The success of efforts to prevent handicaps in children and to identify, assess, and intervene with special-needs children as early as possible requires the training and experience of a wide range of professionals. Those discussed here are among the most important.

No other professional has as great an opportunity to prevent certain handicaps as the obstetrician. Because he knows many of the conditions that predict possible handicaps, the obstetrician can examine the family history and recommend genetic counseling if there appears to be a significant risk. Because he sees an expectant mother several times during pregnancy, he can monitor any possible problems that arise, perform or refer her for amniocentesis if necessary, and generally ensure the kind of prenatal care that reduces the risk of problems at birth. In the delivery room the doctor's concern for possible birth trauma can contribute to preventing problems or identifying them early.

In the same way the pediatrician (or perhaps the family doctor) has the chance to see the infant soon after birth and then regularly during the first months of life. Her attention to the Apgar ratings and an immediate postnatal examination of the infant can help prevent problems or identify high-risk infants. Because most moderate to severe handicaps and sensory impairments are recognizable at birth or soon afterward, this doctor's role is critical. In addition, other conditions like parental neglect or abuse may be evident to the attentive physician. For the same reasons, nurses and nurse practitioners can be of enormous help in noting and questioning possible handicaps or conditions in the home that might lead to a handicap.

Other health professionals also contribute to identification, assessment, or treatment of specific problems that can cause handicaps. The ophthalmologist can detect early vision problems, and he or an optometrist can fit a child with corrective lenses. The audiologist can make a careful assessment of a child's hearing so that a hearing aid or other treatment can be prescribed if there is a loss.

In many programs a psychologist assists in the evaluation of a child's social-emotional skills and cognitive development. Psychologists often participate in the initial assessments of a child, frequently giving standardized tests. And staff psychologists often participate in team planning for a child.

Because so large a portion of mild handicaps are based in social and cultural factors, the social worker can be instrumental in helping children receive services. It is often the social worker who is admitted to many homes in low socioeconomic areas, which correlate with higher incidences of mild retardation and learning problems. The case worker can observe young children whose behavior suggests future problems and can refer them for assessment and possible treatment. Later, the social worker may help explain, monitor, or evaluate the progress of a home-based intervention.

Because the acquisition of language is so critical in the development of all children, a speech-language pathologist is an important part of almost every intervention team. Speech and language specialists usually assess every child referred for services, and they participate in the intervention plans for many children. In fact, more than half of the handicapped children enrolled in Head Start programs in 1977 had speech

Both individual and group activities are important for young children with developmental delays.

impairments, and nearly 5% more were deaf or hearing impaired ("HEW," 1978). For all of these children, intervention must include a specialist in language acquisition and speech disorders.

A discussion of cultural-familial, or psychosocial, retardation, occurs in chapter 3.

For children who have physical or multiple handicaps, a physical therapist is important. Physical therapy can help prevent further deterioration of muscles; it can also be applied to teaching a child gross and fine motor coordination. Likewise, the occupational therapist contributes to the intervention program for children with physical, multiple, or other severe impairments. She provides instruction in movement, self-help skills, and the use of adaptive equipment.

For children with mild handicaps, teachers and other staff in regular preschools and day-care centers may be the first to identify certain delays in development or other problems like mild sensory impairments, social-emotional problems, learning difficulties, or language problems. Prompt referral for special education services can often get these children the help they need before they fall significantly behind their peers. As more and more handicapped children are integrated into regular preschools, the role of teachers and paraprofessionals in these settings will become increasingly critical.

The actual delivery of services, whether in a home or center program, most often is the province of the special teacher, regardless of what title that person has. The special teacher must be the most knowledgeable about a child's instructional goals and objectives, the specific strategies and activities that will accomplish them, and the day-to-day progress the child makes. That teacher must be well trained in observing, analyzing, selecting, and sequencing learning tasks so that the child overcomes delays rather than falling further behind. The teacher must be imaginative and willing to try new things but patient enough to give a program a chance once it is begun. Not only must he be able to find what motivates and reinforces a child, but he must also be able to relate to all the other individuals involved in the child's program. In a home-based program the home teacher or visitor must be able to train parents to take the primary responsibility for teaching their own children. Even in center-based programs a large share of the center's parent-training efforts may fall to the special teacher.

Parents—Most Important of All

Of all the people needed to make early intervention work, parents are the most important. Given enough information, parents can help to prevent many risks and causes of handicaps—before pregnancy, before birth, and certainly before a child has gone months or years without help. Given the chance (as recent laws have done), parents can become active in determining their children's educational needs and goals. And given some guidance and training, parents can teach their handicapped children at home and even at school.

See chapter 13 for a detailed discussion of parent involvement.

It is no wonder, then, that the most successful intervention programs for young handicapped children take great care to involve parents. Shearer and Shearer (1977) report that parents involved in early intervention programs for handicapped children have taken roles as members of advisory councils for the programs, consumers who inform others, staff members, primary teachers, recruiters, curriculum developers, counselors, assessment personnel, and evaluators and record keepers.

Parents are the most frequent and constant observers of their children's behavior. They usually know better than anyone else what their children need, and they can help educators set realistic goals. They can report on events in the home that outsiders might never see—for instance, how a child responds to other family members. They can monitor and report on their children's progress at home, beyond the more controlled environment of the center or preschool. In short, they can contribute to their children's programs at every stage—assessment, planning, classroom activities, and evaluation.

Many parents even work in classrooms as teachers, teacher aides, volunteers, or other staff members. Programs like those we examined earlier all contain strong parent involvement. At the Model Preschool Center in Seattle,

> one of the most distinguishing features of this program (for infants) is that parents of enrolled infants are bona fide members of the team. One of the underlying principles is that continuity of care is critical, and that continuity can best be achieved if the parents, who spend so much more time with the infant than do the other team

members, participate in assessment and remediation. (Adams, Beck, Chandler, & Livingston, 1977, p. 304)

At the PEECH Project, a combined home-center program,

> the parent involvement program focuses on helping to provide home assistance to parents and on helping parents to develop a basic understanding of the school and its program. . . . In addition, a weekly workshop is held for the approximately 10 mothers who can attend. Topics during these workshops include reinforcing behaviors at home, selecting safe toys, and parents' responsibilities to the school. (Karnes & Zehrbach, 1977, p. 34)

As we have seen, a number of early intervention programs focus on the home as the best and most natural learning environment and on the parent as the best and most natural teacher for the handicapped child. And as these two statements make clear, even center-based programs rely heavily on parents as teachers who carry the center program into the home. But in our efforts to involve parents, we should heed the warning of Turnbull, Turnbull, Summers, Brotherson, and Benson (1986).

> Early childhood professionals, in their zeal to attain those all-important early developmental gains, should not push parents to the point of burn-out. Early childhood professionals will pass the child on to new programs; their task will be finished when the child reaches school age. But the family will only be beginning a lifetime of responsibility. For early childhood programs, a task equally as important as the achievement of developmental gains is the preparation of families for the long haul. Families must learn to pace themselves, to relax and take time to meet everyone's needs. They must learn that the responsibility of meeting an exceptional child's needs is not a 100-yard dash to be completed in one intensive burst of effort. It is more like a marathon, where slow and steady pacing wins the race (Weyhing, 1983). (p. 93.)

And finally, the authors of the curriculum developed by the Macomb 0–3 Project, an HCEEP early intervention program in Macomb, Illinois, remind us that, when all is said and done, we must not forget that early childhood is supposed to be a fun, happy time for children and for the adults who are fortunate enough to work with them.

> Even though the children for whom this curriculum is intended demonstrate behaviors and conditions that may very well make life difficult for them as well as for their families, please do not forget the importance of play, joy and emotional well-being in interactions with these young children. We as professionals who work with young handicapped children sometimes are so serious about the magnitude of our mission that any element of fun, humor or pleasure is absent in our work with both children and their families.
>
> Part of our mission as professionals in the field of early childhood handicapped education is to possess an art of enjoyment ourselves and to help instill it in the young children and families with whom we work.
>
> Early childhood comes but once in a lifetime. . . Let's make it count! (Hutinger, Marshall, & McCartan, 1983, front matter)

SUMMARY

1. From a virtual absence 20 years ago of education programs for handicapped children from birth to school age, early childhood special education has become one of the most prominent and fastest growing components of the entire special education field.
   a. The first federal legislation written exclusively for the handicapped preschooler was the Handicapped Children's Early Childhood Assistance Act (P.L. 90–538), passed in 1968. This act, still in effect today, provides funding for diverse and innovative approaches to early intervention.
   b. Since 1972 Head Start programs have been required to reserve at least 10% of their enrollment capacity for children with handicaps.
   c. P. L. 99–457, the Education of the Handicapped Act Amendments of 1986, requires by 1991 that states receiving federal funds for special education of preschool children show evidence of serving all 3- to 5-year-old handicapped children. The law also provides monetary incentives to states that serve handicapped and at-risk infants and toddlers from birth to age 2.

2. There are numerous methodological problems in conducting scientifically sound research on the effectiveness (especially long-term) of early intervention with handicapped and at-risk children. Nevertheless, the general conclusion to be drawn from this large body of research is that early intervention does result in positive outcomes for the children who receive it.

3. As much as possible, we should use more genetic counseling, better prenatal care, wider screening for metabolic disorders, and public education to help prevent handicaps.

4. We can use our knowledge to detect certain handicapping conditions during pregnancy, in the delivery room, or soon after birth.
   a. As a rule, the more severe the handicap, the earlier it can be detected.
   b. Good preschool personnel can sometimes note the effects of mild handicaps.

5. In spite of what we know about the advantages of early identification of handicaps, there is no universally used system to screen all infants.
   a. Most newborns do receive an Apgar rating and a screening for certain metabolic disorders.
   b. Other screening tests based on normal child development are widely used only when a concerned adult feels an evaluation is needed.

6. Once a child is identified as being at risk to develop a handicap, the next step is detailed assessment.
   a. This assessment is often conducted by members of an interdisciplinary team.
   b. There are many formal, standardized tests available to assess delayed or abnormal progress in intellectual development, auditory perception, and affective and social development.
   c. There are also a growing number of informal checklists, rating scales, and other assessment devices. Most measure cognitive development, motor development, language development, self-help skills, play skills, and personal-social skills.
   d. Because of the serious effects of failing to identify a child who needs special services or labeling a child handicapped who is not, it is important that the persons doing the assessment be experienced, well trained, and able to interpret the raw data accurately.

e. A growing number of early intervention programs are moving away from assessments based entirely on developmental milestones and are incorporating curriculum-based assessment, in which each item relates directly to a skill included in the program's curriculum—thereby providing a direct link between testing, teaching, and progress evaluation.

7. Most early intervention programs are based on one of three models.
   a. In home-based programs a child's parents act as the primary teachers, with regular training and guidance from a teacher or specially trained paraprofessional who visits the home.
   b. Home-based programs offer the advantages of taking place in a natural environment with appropriate materials, involving family members, and allowing the parents to engage in direct intervention with their child.
   c. In center-based programs a child comes to the center for direct instruction, although the parents are usually involved.
   d. Center programs offer the opportunity for a team of specialists to work with each child and for each child to meet other handicapped and nonhandicapped children.
   e. Many programs offer both home visits and center-based programming, thus combining the advantages of the two models.

8. There are several different approaches to organizing curricula for young children: remediating delays, teaching basic processes, teaching developmental tasks, teaching psychological constructs, and teaching preacademic skills.
   a. All these approaches use normal development as a standard against which to measure each child.
   b. A developmentally based curriculum is not the most appropriate for all children. For more severely handicapped preschoolers a functionally based curriculum is more appropriate, focusing on skills the child can immediately use to improve her interaction and independence in her environment.
   c. Many early intervention programs use a combination of developmental and functional curriculum approaches, relying on a normal sequence of development as a general guide to the curriculum while using functional considerations in the selection of specific instructional targets for each child.
   d. Two important curriculum concerns are promoting language development and scheduling activities to be instructionally effective.

9. A wide range of professionals should be involved in the team that works with young handicapped children.
   a. Obstetricians, pediatricians, and nurses
   b. Other health specialists
   c. Psychologists
   d. Social workers
   e. Speech-language pathologists
   f. Physical and occupational therapists
   g. Teachers and staff in day-care centers and preschools
   h. Special teachers

10. Parents are the most important people in an early intervention program. They can act as advocates, participate in educational planning, observe their children's behavior, help set realistic goals, work in the classroom, and teach their children at home.

FOR MORE INFORMATION

Journals

Day Care and Early Education. Published bimonthly by Human Sciences Press Periodicals. Directed at day-care personnel; focuses on innovative ideas for educating preschool children.

Journal of the Division for Early Childhood. Published by the Division for Early Childhood, Council for Exceptional Children, 1920 Association Drive, Reston, VA 22091.

Topics in Early Childhood Education. Published quarterly by PRO-ED, 5341 Industrial Oaks Boulevard, Austin, TX 78735.

Young Children. Published bimonthly by the National Association for the Education of Young Children. Spotlights current projects, theory, and research in early childhood education as well as practical teaching ideas.

Books

Bailey, D. B., & Wolery, M. (1984). *Teaching infants and preschoolers with handicaps.* Columbus, OH: Merrill.

Cook, R. E., & Armbruster, V. B. (1983). *Adapting early childhood curricula: Suggestions for meeting special needs.* St. Louis: C. V. Mosby.

Guralnick, M. J. (Ed.). (1978). *Early intervention and the integration of handicapped and nonhandicapped children.* Baltimore: University Park Press.

Guralnick, M. J., & Bennett, F. C. (Eds.). (1987). The effectiveness of early intervention for at-risk and handicapped children. New York: Academic Press.

Jordan, J., Hayden, A., Karnes, M., & Wood, M. (Eds.). (1977). *Early education for exceptional children: A handbook of ideas and exemplary practices.* Reston, VA: Council for Exceptional Children.

Lerner, J. W., Mardell-Czudnowski, C., & Goldenberg, D. (1987). *Special education for the early childhood years* (2nd ed.). Englewood Cliffs, NJ: Prentice-Hall.

Neisworth, J. T., & Bagnato, S. J. (1987). *The young exceptional child: Early development and education.* New York: Macmillan.

Peterson, N. L. (1986). *Early intervention for handicapped and at-risk children: An introduction to early childhood-special education.* Denver: Love.

Tjossem, T. D. (Ed.). (1976). *Intervention strategies for high risk infants and young children.* Baltimore: Univesity Park Press.

Organizations

The Division for Early Childhood, Council for Exceptional Children, 1920 Association Drive, Reston, VA 22091.

HCEEP-Funded Early Childhood Research Institutes

Carolina Institute for Research on Early Education of the Handicapped (CIREEH), Frank Porter Graham Child Development Center, University of North Carolina at Chapel Hill, 301 NCNB Plaza, Chapel Hill, NC 27514. Intended to conduct research and develop training materials related to parents and families of moderately and severely handicapped children from birth to 5 years of age.

Early Childhood Research Institute (ECRI), University of Pittsburgh, Western Psychiatric Institute and Clinic, 3811 O'Hara Street, Pittsburgh, PA 15213. Intended to develop procedures for assessing and teaching social and related skills to severely handicapped preschool children so that they can participate successfully in instructional settings with nonhandicapped or less handicapped children.

Early Intervention Research Institute (EIRI), Exceptional Child Center, Utah State University, UMN 68, Logan, UT 84322. Intended to review the findings of previous research on early intervention to determine what is known, what gaps exist, and where future research should focus.

15

ADULTS WITH DISABILITIES

What happens to young adults with disabilities when they leave school and enter the adult community? Do graduates of special education programs find work? Where do they live? How do the social, recreational, and leisure activities of disabled adults compare to the expectations and experiences of most nonhandicapped citizens? How do adults with disabilities rate their quality of life—are they happy? How can the special education programs that children participate in during their school years prepare them for adjustment and successful integration into the adult community? What are the most appropriate and effective programs and services for helping adults with disabilities find and keep meaningful work, locate housing, or use community recreation centers? How can special education interrelate its goals and services with those of other human service agencies, such as vocational education and rehabilitation, residential services, and community recreation programs? Many professionals in special education now view the exploration of and solutions to these questions as the highest priority in their fields.

A number of follow-up studies of graduates of special education programs and some surveys of disabled adults have provided enlightening, if not encouraging, results. The findings on the employment status of recent graduates of secondary special education programs are fairly consistent—about 60% find work after leaving public school (Edgar, 1985), and much of that work is part-time and often at or below minimum wage. As disheartening as these findings are, persons with severe handicaps face a much worse prospect of locating competitive employment (Wehman, Kregel, & Seyfarth, 1985a). Overall, the U.S. Commission on Civil Rights (1983) estimates that between 50% and 75% of all adults with handicaps are unemployed.

Of course, a disability affects more than a person's likelihood of obtaining work. Adults with handicaps face numerous obstacles in day-to-day living that affect where and how they live, how well they can use community resources, and what their opportunities will be for social interaction. Unlike their nonhandicapped peers, a disproportionate number of adults with handicaps continue to live with their parents after graduation, and many report a high degree of social isolation. A survey conducted by

Louis Harris and Associates and reported to the U.S. Congress in 1986 found that 56% of disabled Americans said that their handicaps prevented them from moving about the community, attending cultural or sporting events, and socializing with friends outside their homes.

Findings such as these are helping special educators focus on what has become perhaps the dominant issue in the field today—the transition of young persons with handicaps from school to adult life in the community. Although there are no definitive studies that specify the number of special education students leaving school each year, the number is large and growing. The U.S. Department of Education estimates that between 250,000 and 300,000 young adults with handicaps leave public schools each year (Will, 1986). No longer can special educators be satisfied with evaluation data showing improved performance on school-related tasks. They must work equally hard to ensure that the preparation students receive during their school years plays a direct and positive role in helping them adjust to successful life in the adult community.

In this chapter we will examine three major life areas—employment, residential alternatives, and recreation/leisure opportunities—in which special educators and other human service professionals are working to help adults with disabilities lead productive, self-sufficient, and rewarding lives in the community.

EMPLOYMENT

Work can be defined as using your physical and/or mental energies to accomplish something productive. Our society is based on a work ethic; we place a high value on work and on people who contribute. Besides providing economic support, work offers opportunities for social interaction and a chance to use and enhance skills in a chosen area. Work generates the respect of others, and it can be a source of pride and self-satisfaction (Terkel, 1974).

In spite of the much-heralded accomplishments of some handicapped persons, getting a job represents a major difficulty for the majority of handicapped adults. All young adults face important questions about what to do with their lives—whether to attend college or technical school, whether to work as a bricklayer or an accountant—but for the nonhandicapped the difficulty lies mostly in choosing from a number of options. By contrast, the handicapped adult often has few, if any, options to choose from. Occupational choices are decreased if the handicapped person has limited skills; decreased further in most cases by the nature of the disability; and needlessly decrease, still further by prejudices and misconceptions about handicapped people on the part of many employers. For many handicapped adults, obtaining and holding a job is the major rehabilitation goal.

Section 504 of the Rehabilitation Act forbids job discrimination on the basis of handicap, but the problem remains.

One of the most comprehensive studies of the employment status of young handicapped adults was conducted by Hasazi, Gordon, and Roe (1985); they interviewed 301 young adults who had left secondary special education programs in nine Vermont school districts between 1979 and 1983. The researchers found that only 55% of the former students were employed at the time of the interview, with two-thirds of their jobs being full-time positions. A survey of 234 young adults 4 years

For many adults with disabilities, obtaining and holding a real job is the major goal.

after their leaving secondary special education programs in Colorado found 69% working, with only one-third of those employed on a full-time basis (Mithaug, Horiuchi, & Fanning, 1985). In Virginia parent interviews concerning the employment status and community integration of 300 young adults with mental retardation who had left four public school special education programs revealed an *un*employment rate of 58%, with three-fourths of those employed earning less than $500 per month (Wehman, Kregel, & Seyfarth, 1985b). Analysis of the data for the 117 young adults in the Virginia study with moderate, severe, or profound mental retardation showed that only 25 had jobs (an unemployment rate of 78.6%); of those, 14 had found paid work in the community and 11 were working in sheltered workshops (Wehman, Kregel, & Seyfarth, 1985a). Only 8 of those working earned more than $100 per month.

Although the overall employment rate of 55% found in the Vermont study is discouraging, an even more distressing finding was that only 33% of the female former special education students were employed. This figure compares to a statewide employment rate for females in the same age bracket (20 to 24 years) of 88%.

Competitive Employment

A person who is competitively employed performs work that is valued by an employer, functions in an integrated setting with nonhandicapped co-workers, and earns at or above the federal minimum wage (Rusch, Chadsey-Rusch, & Lagomarcino, 1987). Wehman and Hill (1985) further specify that a person who is truly competitively employed receives no subsidized wages of any kind. Although the unemployment rate of young adults with mild handicaps is much higher than that of the population in general, many graduates of public school special education programs do find paid employment in the community. A study conducted in 15 school districts in the state of Washington followed 827 learning disabled or behaviorally disordered young adults who had graduated from public school special education programs or had left because they were too old to meet eligibility requirements. A total of 634 (or 77%) of these young adults were still employed 1 year after they had left school (Will, 1986). However, only 27% of those working were earning the minimum wage or above. These results and those of the follow-up studies previously reported indicate that opportunities for true competitive employment for adults with handicaps have been very limited in most communities.

Virtually all special educators who have carefully studied the transition of handicapped students from school to adult life believe that only through significant revision of the public school curriculum and improved coordination of school and adult vocational habilitation services can the prospect of competitive employment be enhanced for young adults with disabilities (Bellamy & Horner, 1987; Rusch, Chadsey-Rusch, & Lagomarcino, 1987; Wehman, Kregel, & Barcus, 1985).

Supported Employment

Supported employment provides alternatives for persons with severe disabilities who have historically been unemployed. For adults with mental retardation, the opportunity to earn real wages for real work has been extremely limited in this country. The vast majority of persons with severe handicaps who do obtain work or worklike positions are employed in sheltered workshops or work activity centers, in which the average annual wage in 1979 was $414 (U.S. Department of Labor, 1979). However, this situation is at odds with numerous demonstrations of the employment potential of persons with severe mental retardation who have been provided with systematic training and on-the-job support (Bellamy, Horner, & Inman, 1979; Boles, Bellamy, Horner, & Mank, 1984; Gold, 1972).

Supported employment, or supported work, is a relatively new concept recognizing that many adults with severe disabilities require ongoing, often intensive support in order to obtain, learn, and hold a job. Supported employment is characterized by the performance of real paid work (i.e., work that, if not performed by the employee with disabilities, would have to be performed by a nonhandicapped person who would receive wages for that work) that occurs in regular work sites (often alongside nonhandicapped employees) and requires ongoing support from a supported employment specialist (Will, 1986).

Wehman and Kregel (1985) describe a supported work model that consists of four components: (1) a comprehensive approach to job placement, (2) intensive job-site training and advocacy, (3) ongoing monitoring of client performance, and (4) a systematic approach to long-term job retention and follow-up. The supported employment specialist is the key to making a supported work program effective. The supported employment specialist is a community-based professional who works in a non-profit job placement program, a public vocational or adult services program, or a secondary special education program. Table 15.1 identifies the major activities and responsibilities of a supported employment specialist in each component of the supported work model. Approximately two-thirds of the specialist's time is spent on the job site, orienting the client to the job, training the client in specific job skills, and advocating for the client with employers, supervisors, and nonhandicapped co-workers (Rehder, 1986). The other one-third of the specialist's time is spent in tasks such as working with the client's parents, planning behavioral intervention programs for the client, and training the client in work-related areas such as transportation, money management, and grooming skills.

Although all clients in supported employment continue to receive support and services as needed, the amount of direct on-the-job assistance provided by the sup-

For a thought-provoking examination and debate of the issues concerning whether adults with severe disabilities should be permitted to perform meaningful work without pay in community-based integrated work sites while undergoing extended training, see Brown, Shiraga, et al. (1984) and Bellamy, Rhodes, et al. (1984).

TABLE 15.1

Responsibilities of supported employment specialist during each component of the supported work model proposed by Wehman and Kregel (1985).

Component	Activities
Job placement	Structured efforts at finding jobs for client and matching client strengths to job needs
	Planning of transportation arrangements and/or travel training
	Active involvement with parents on identifying appropriate job for client
	Communication with Social Security Administration
Job site training and advocacy	Trained staff provides behavior skill training aimed at improving client work performance
	Trained staff provides necessary social skill training at job site
	Staff works with employers and coworkers in helping client
Ongoing monitoring	Provides for regular written feedback from employer on client progress
	Utilizes behavioral data related to client work speed, proficiency, need for staff assistance, etc.
	Implements periodic client and parent satisfaction questionnaires
Follow-up and retention	Implements planned effort at reducing staff intervention from job site
	Provides follow-up to employer in form of phone calls and visits to job sites as needed
	Communicates to employer regarding staff accessibility as needed
	Helps client relocate or find new job if necessary

Source: From "A Supported Work Approach to Competitive Employment of Individuals with Moderate and Severe Handicaps" by P. Wehman and J. Kregel, 1985, *Journal of the Association for Persons with Severe Handicaps, 10,* p. 5. Reprinted by permission.

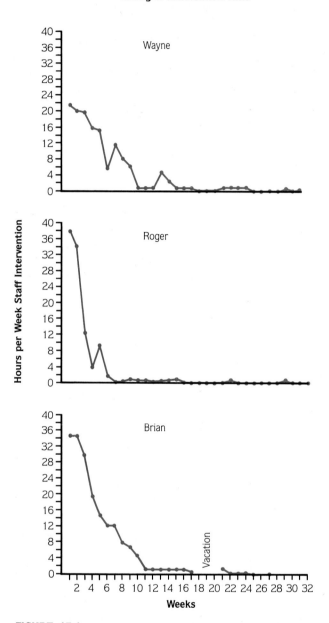

FIGURE 15.1

Number of hours of intervention time spent with three clients in a supported work program.

Source: From "Competitive Employment for Persons with Mental Retardation: A Follow-Up Six Years Later" by P. Wehman, M. Hill, J. W. Hill, V. Brooke, P. Pendleton, and C. Britt, 1985, *Mental Retardation, 23*, p. 278. Reprinted by permission.

ported employment specialist is gradually reduced as the new employee acquires increased competence in completing the job requirements independently (see Figure 15.1).

Wehman, Hill, et al. (1985) describe the employment status of 167 adults who were placed in a total of 252 part- and full-time paid jobs with the supported work model. The clients ranged in age from 18 to 66 years old and had a median IQ score of 49.

> The great majority (86%) were receiving regular financial aid from the government at the time of placement. In fact, 81% earned *under $200 as an annual salary the year prior* to placement which indicates the level of economic independence exhibited by these individuals prior to intervention. A total of 71% lived with their parents or family and 90% lacked skills to use public transportation at the time of their initial placement. (p. 275)

Table 15.2 provides a summary of the employment outcome measures reported by Wehman, Hill, et al. (1985). A total of 252 job placements, most in entry-level minimum wage positions, were made with over 100 different employers, primarily representing service occupations such as cleaning and custodial work in hotels, restaurants, and hospitals. The average length of time employed for all 167 of the persons in the study was 19 months. At the time of the report, 72 clients were still employed.

TABLE 15.2

Summary of key employment outcomes for persons participating in a supported work program.

Numbers Placed (median measured IQ = 49)	
1. Number of clients placed October 1978–December 1984	167
2. Number of clients currently working	72
3. Total number of placements	252
Time Employed	
1. Mean months employed for study population	19 months
2. Mean time employed in first year of labor market (two-thirds of all clients were retained in competitive employment beyond six months)	8.1* months
Monetary Outcomes	
1. Cumulative client wages earned	$1,069,309
2. Cumulative client taxes contributed	$245,941
Costs	
1. Mean staff intervention hours per client	195
2. Mean cost per client	$5,255
3. Mean cost per placement	$3,483

*Mean length of time nonhandicapped coworkers stayed in job in similar or identical industries = five months (based on National Hotel and Restaurant survey of 2300 nonhandicapped workers in food service industry).

Source: "Competitive Employment for Persons with Mental Retardation: A Follow-Up Six Years Later" by P. Wehman, M. Hill, J. W. Hill, V. Brooke, P. Pendleton, and C. Britt, 1985, *Mental Retardation, 23*, p. 275. Reprinted by permission.

See pages 119–20 for a description of how a supported employment program helped one young woman with mental retardation successfully make the transition from school to work.

The authors note that the 8.1 months of employment during their clients' first year on the job compares favorably with the results of a study by the National Hotel and Restaurant Association (1983) that found more than 2,300 nonhandicapped individuals had retained their comparable entry level positions for an average of 5 months. They also point out that the average total cost of $5,255 per client for the supported work program, which resulted in an average of 19 months of paid employment per client, compares favorably with the average annual cost of $4,000 per year for adult day programs (i.e., sheltered workshops and work activity centers). This comparison is especially favorable when one takes into account the total client wages earned and income taxes contributed.

Other models for providing supported employment opportunities for persons with severe handicaps include the work enclave, mobile work crews, the entrepreneurial model, and the structured employment model. In the work enclave a group of persons with handicaps performs work with special training or job supports within a normal business or industry. The work enclave provides a useful alternative to traditional, segregated sheltered employment, offering many of the benefits of integrated employment with nonhandicapped employees as well as the ongoing support necessary for long-term job success.

Rhodes and Valenta (1985) report the preliminary results of a work enclave that resulted in the employment of six persons with severe handicaps. They established a working agreement with Physio Control Corporation of Redmond, Washington, to create a separate production line within the company for the purpose of employing eight persons with severe handicaps. Physio Control employs 900 people in its Redmond facility, where it manufactures biomedical equipment, primarily heart defibrillators. A nonprofit organization called Trillium Employment Services was created to provide the employment training and ongoing support needed by the severely handicapped workers. The work enclave employees have become part of a production line that does subassemblies of defibrillator components, such as chest paddles and wire harnesses. As much as possible, tasks are selected that are of the same type performed by other employees of the company. The work enclave employees are supervised by Physio Control, although legal employment responsibility rests with the support organization (Trillium) until an individual's 3-month productivity averages 65% of the productivity of other Physio Control employees. At that time the individual is hired as a Physio Control employee. Work enclave employees receive wages commensurate with their productivity rates. Training and supervision procedures use a behavioral model, incorporating task analysis and direct instruction of specific job skills as well as arrangement of the physical and social aspects of the work environment to encourage improved work rates (Bellamy, Horner, & Inman, 1979).

Table 15.3 summarizes key data for each of the original eight employees 1 year after the program began. At the end of 1 year, all of the enclave employees were producing at or above 50% of the productivity standard of other Physio employees. Total wages earned by all program employees for the first year were $20,207, including $2,425 paid by the employees in federal income tax. Total public costs for the program were $15,945 for the first year, with the majority of those costs incurred during the first 5 months of the program. With respect to interaction with nonhandicapped employees, Rhodes and Valenta (1985) report:

TABLE 15.3

Key data for eight original employees in an industrial-based work enclave. Summary of first year ending August 6, 1984.

Employee #	Age	Previous Employment Status	Recorded IQ[a]	Months Employed at Physio	Avg. Monthly Wage Prior to Physio	Avg. Monthly Wage at Physio	Total Wages	Current Status
1	31	Work activity center	45	12	$26	$306	$3,670	Trillium employee
2	38	Work activity center	44	.5	$19	NA	$ 130	Terminated (2 weeks)
3	38	Work activity center	43	11	$35	$381	$4,196	Physio employee[b]
4	25	Work activity center	39	4.5	$44	$292	$1,314	Terminated (4 months)
5	26	Work activity center	44	10.5	$110	$306	$3,216	Trillium employee
6	30	Work activity center	37	9.5	$26	$316	$3,004	Trillium employee
7	30	Unemployed (18 months)	33	8.5	-0-	$327	$2,779	Trillium employee[c]
8	22	Unemployed (7 months following graduation)	43	6	-0-	$316	$1,898	Trillium employee
MEAN	30			8	$44[d]	$323	$2,526	

[a]Most recent Wechsler or Stanford-Binet on record
[b]Hired as a Physio employee on June 1, 1984
[c]Hired as a Physio employee on August 27, 1984
[d]Mean based on 6 workers employed by work activity centers prior to entering Physio

Source: From "Industry-Based Supported Employment: An Enclave Approach" by L. Rhodes and L. Valenta, 1985, *Journal of the Association for Persons with Severe Handicaps, 10,* p. 16. Reprinted by permission.

> Managers and supervisors within the assembly area report frequent daily contact between enclave and other employees. These occur within the work environment as well as during breaks and lunch. Contacts are said to be overwhelmingly positive. Social contacts have also occurred through company-sponsored events such as picnics, dinners, and dances, and through privately initiated events between managers and employees. (p. 15)

However, in their conclusion the authors warn that

> for program developers and industrial managers contemplating this alternative, it will be necessary to insure that employees not become segregated from the rest of the working community (much like the "handicapped wing" of a public school). A balance must be attained in providing the structure to support training interven-

tions, to address low productivity, and insure adaptability to changing work demands, without sacrificing the advantages of a normal industrial environment. (p. 18)

The mobile work crew model of supported employment is organized around a small, single-purpose business, such as building or grounds maintenance. A general manager may be responsible for finding and coordinating the work of several small crews of five or six employees, each crew supervised by a supported employment specialist. Mobile work crews are organized as not-for-profit corporations; the extra costs these organizations incur because their employees do not work at full productivity levels are covered by public funds. Such costs are usually less than would be needed

As this new employee's performance improves, his need for direct on-the-job assistance will decrease.

VOCATIONAL TRAINING WITH A FLAVOR

The Country Squire Restaurant in Killingworth, Connecticut, is open for dinner Tuesday through Sunday, in addition to its Monday through Friday Squire lunches. The 25 employees of the Country Squire—the cooks, bakers, waitresses, dishwashers, bartender, cashier—are all adults with handicaps such as mental retardation, autism, and cerebral palsy. Under the supervision of five trainers, they are learning the skills required for various restaurant jobs.

The Country Squire is one of a constellation of small businesses operated by SARAH (the Shoreline Association for Retarded and Handicapped Citizens) in and around Guilford, Connecticut. SARAH's progressive and successful commitment to a nontraditional small-business model for training and em-

ploying persons with disabilities is attracting widespread recognition. Over 100 handicapped adults participate in training and employment programs throughout SARAH's varied businesses—two restaurants, a greenhouse, a landscaping service, and a nine-hole golf course, to name a few. Each of the businesses serves the public and must attract customers and achieve profitability by delivering a high-quality product.

Peter McManus, director of vocational services, indicated that SARAH (which also operates residential and recreational programs) elected not to pursue contracted benchwork, the traditional sheltered employment for handicapped persons. "These are jobs that the private business sector is eliminating through automation. On the other hand, there is an

---

THE CUP & THE BOWL

1. **BAKED ONION GRATINEE** 1.25   1.75

2. **TODAY'S SOUP** . . see blackboard
   Our soups are freshly made daily.

3. **THE SPINACH SALAD** 3.25
   Fresh spinach with garnish of mushrooms, bacon, sliced egg, red oinion and Swiss Cheese. Tossed with a special oil and vinegar dressing. Served with freshly made bread and butter.

4. **THE BURGER** 3.75
   A. With melted Blue Cheese *or*
   B. With sauteed mushrooms
   Hand-pressed chuck steak burger on our own freshly baked English sytle muffin. Served with Squire Fries, lettuce, tomato and a side order of Herb Dressing.

6. **THE QUICHE** . . . . see blackboard
   &
   7. Quiche served with herb green beans, cranberry salad mold on a bed of lettuce with tomato and Herb Dressing.

THE USUAL SANDWICH
   Presented on our own freshly baked pumpernickel and rye bread with Squire Fries and Demi Salad.

8. **HOT PASTRAMI** 2.75

9. **SHAVED HAM & SWISS** . . . 2.95

10. **TUNA SALAD** 2.95

THE UNUSUAL SANDWICH
   Served with Squire Fries and Demi Salad.

11. **CHEESE DREAM** 2.50
   Grilled cheese on whole wheat bread with tomato and herbs.

12. **TURKEY AND HAM MORNAY** 3.75
   Ham, white meat of turkey and fresh broccoli spears arranged on toast. Topped with cheese sauce and broiled till golden.

13. **THE ONLY SQUIRE IN TOWN** 3.65
   Lean hot pastrami, grilled onions, tomatoes, and melted Swiss Cheese layered on pumpernickel & rye bread.

14. **THE BLUE MAX** 3.75
   Ham, turkey, bacon, tomato and Blue Cheese, layered on pumpernickel and rye bread. Topped with Muenster Cheese and broiled until golden.

THE HALF & HALF

15. **SOUP & HALF SANDWICH** 2.50
   A cup of Onion or Today's Soup with ½ of your usual sandwich.

16. **SALAD & HALF SANDWICH** 2.65
   Small Spinach Salad with ½ of your usual sandwich.

THE KIDDIES CORNER
   Served with Squire Fries and Pickles.

(4) **HAMBURG** 1.50

(9) **HAM AND CHEESE** 1.45

(10) **TUNA SALAD** 1.45

(11) **GRILLED CHEESE** 1.25

THE BEVERAGE

A. **COFFEE** 45

B. **HOT TEA** 40

C. **SQUIRE'S ICE TEA** 50

D. **HERB TEA** 45

E. **MILK** 40

F. **SODA** 45
   a. Coke   b. Tab   c. Ginger Ale   d. Orange

THE DESSERT
   See blackboard for selection.

PLEASE ORDER BY
NUMBER OR LETTER.

THANK YOU,

increasing demand for high-quality personal services."

The Country Squire seats up to 72 guests at 25 tables, keeping everyone very busy during the rush hours. The employees smile as they go about their jobs taking orders, slicing meat, removing rolls from the oven, serving food. Waitress Jane Lemley calls it her second home. "I have friends here." For 46-year-old waitress Doris Babcock it's the first job she's ever had. "I love it here." But as much as she loves and respects her employees, restaurant manager Roberta Banks hopes to see them move on to competitive employment. "Many employees now have the skills needed to work in any restaurant or kitchen."

Some people come to the restaurant first out of curiosity, but they return for the food.

to support the work crew employees in activity centers, which provide little or no real work or reimbursement.

The entrepreneurial model provides supported employment for persons with handicaps by establishing a business that takes advantage of existing commercial opportunities within a community. The business hires a small number of individuals with severe disabilities as well as several employees without disabilities. One example of the entrepreneurial model is the Port Townsend Baking Company, a commercial bakery in Port Townsend, Washington.

See pages 563–64 for the description of a Connecticut restaurant based on the entrepreneurial model.

Another form of supported employment is the structured employment model. This model, developed by the Specialized Training Program at the University of Oregon, operates in a small industrial-oriented workshop setting and relies on contract revenues to provide income for employees (Boles, Bellamy, Horner, & Mank, 1984). This model provides intensive training for complex assembly and production contracts. Electronic parts assembly and chain saw assembly are two tasks that have been taught successfully to workers with severe handicaps, who have then been able to earn wages much higher than would have been possible in traditional sheltered workshops. A few nonhandicapped workers may also be employed to integrate the work setting and increase overall productivity.

Sheltered employment

The **sheltered workshop** is the most widely used type of vocational training facility for handicapped adults. In 1966 there were 885 certified sheltered workshops in the United States, serving 47,000 clients. By 1975 those numbers had more than doubled, to 2,766 workshops serving more than 117,000 clients (Victor, 1976). Sheltered workshops serve clients with a wide variety of handicapping conditions—although about half of all clients in sheltered workshops are mentally retarded—and varying degrees of disability. Sheltered workshops can be classified as providing one or more of three types of programs: evaluation and training for competitive employment in the community (commonly referred to as transitional workshops), extended or long-term employment, and work activities.

Many sheltered workshops offer both transitional and extended employment situations within the same building. Transitional workshops continually try to place their clients in competitive employment outside the workshop. Extended employment workshops are operated to provide whatever training and support services are required to enable severely handicapped clients to work productively within the sheltered environment. The Wage and Hour Division of the U.S. Department of Labor requires that clients working in an extended sheltered workshop receive at least 50% of the minimum wage. Clients may be paid an hourly wage or a piecework rate.

All sheltered workshops have at least two elements in common. First, they offer rehabilitation, training, and—in some instances—full employment. Second, in order to provide meaningful work for clients, a sheltered workshop must operate as a business. Sheltered workshops—especially extended workshops that must provide steady, meaningful, paid employment for their clients—generally engage in one of three types of business ventures: contracting, prime manufacturing, or reclamation.

Contracting is the major source of work in most workshops. A contract is an agreement that a sheltered workshop will complete a specified job (e.g., assembling and packaging a company's product) within a specified time for a given price. Most sheltered workshops have one or more professional staff members, called contractors or contract procurement persons, whose sole job is to obtain and negotiate contracts with businesses and industries in the community. Contracts do not come to sheltered workshops as a form of charity or community service. Workshops must bid competitively for each job and therefore must carefully take into account, in addition to whatever wages are paid to workers, the equipment needs, training costs, production rate, overhead, and so on. Successfully operating a sheltered workshop requires good business management.

Prime manufacturing involves the designing, producing, marketing, and shipping of a complete product. The advantage of prime manufacturing over contracting, assuming a successful product is being manufactured, is that the workshops do not have problems with down time when they are between contracts. They can plan their training and labor requirements more directly. Unfortunately, most sheltered workshops are neither staffed nor equipped to handle the more sophisticated business venture of prime manufacturing, although it is hoped that in the future more will be able to do so.

In a salvage or reclamation operation, a workshop purchases or collects salvageable material, performs the salvage or reclamation operation, and then sells the reclaimed product. Salvage and reclamation operations have proven successful for many sheltered workshops because they require a lot of labor, are low in overhead, and usually can continue indefinitely.

Another kind of sheltered work environment, usually not referred to as such, is called a **work activity center.** A work activity center offers programs of activities for clients whose disabilities are so severe as to preclude productive work in most other settings. Rehabilitation and training revolve around concentration and persistence at a task. Intervals of work are often only an hour long, interspersed with other activities—training in social skills, self-help skills, household skills, community skills, and recreation. It is estimated that approximately 100,000 adults with disabilities make use of adult day programs, with about 40,000 being excluded from an opportunity to earn wages (Will, 1986). The remaining 60,000 earn an average of $1.00 per day, or $288 per year.

Sheltered workshops and work activity centers have received increased criticism in recent years. The theoretical purpose of sheltered workshops is to train individuals in specific job-related skills that will enable them to obtain competitive employment. However, few employees of sheltered workshops are ever placed in jobs in the community (only 12% of sheltered workshop employees were placed in community jobs in 1976 according to the U.S. Department of Labor, 1979), and many who are placed do not keep their jobs for long (Brickey, Campbell, & Browning, 1985). Some professionals believe that the poor competitive employment record of sheltered workshop graduates may be more indicative of limitations inherent in sheltered workshops than of the actual employment potential of persons with handicaps. After conducting 9,000 hours of observation in a workshop for adults with mental retardation, Turner (1983) found that "the average individual in workshop society spends less than 50% of his or her time on the lines actually working" (p. 153). Turner found that on-task behavior varied tremendously as a function of the availability of subcontracts and that workers decreased their productivity rates to accommodate times when little subcontracted work was available.

Nisbet and Vincent (1986) compared the behavior of employees with moderate and severe mental retardation in sheltered and community work environments. They found that in sheltered environments inappropriate behavior (e.g., hostility, aggression, inactivity, self-stimulation) was exhibited 8.8 times more frequently than it was in the community work environments.

> In sheltered environments, inactivity accounted for 61% of the inappropriate behavior and in nonsheltered environments, it accounted for 3%. The lack of meaningful work or absence of work altogether due to contract procurement difficulties may, in part, account for the inactivity rather than the inability of the worker with a disability to perform at an acceptable rate over a measurable duration of time. (Nisbet & Vincent, 1986, p. 26)

Brown et al. (1984) are particularly critical of the lack of real work in sheltered workshops and work activity centers.

> Thousands of workers. . . are confined to activity centers and sheltered workshops where they are required to perform "simulated work," "prework," "could be work some day," and "looks like work" year after year. In the process, they are systematically and categorically denied access to the real world of work. (p. 266)

Although the concept of supported work is new and many of its best practices are undoubtedly yet to be discovered, the positive results produced by a variety of supported work models implemented in both urban and rural communities under various economic conditions cause us to wonder along with Wehman, Hill, et al. (1985) about the appropriateness of long-term sheltered employment.

> What this report indicates is that many more persons with mental retardation could be working competitively than currently are employed. . . . Furthermore, our data raise some serious questions about the appropriateness of long-term sheltered workshop employment and work activity center placements for individuals that are labeled mentally retarded who could be benefiting from the economic and social benefits of competitive employment. *Specifically, one might reasonably ask: why should so many persons be placed in adult activity centers and sheltered workshops if they, in fact, can work competitively under appropriate support conditions?* (p. 279)

School-to-Work Transition

During the past few years special educators, parents, and legislators have all focused attention on the problems experienced by young people with handicaps as they move from school to adult life. Results of a 1986 survey of the state educational agencies responsible for the education of handicapped students in all 50 states showed that, out of 35 different topics, vocational training and transition was ranked as the highest priority for in-service training (tied with the least restrictive environment) (McLaughlin, Smith-Davis, & Burke, 1986). The topic of secondary curriculum was tied for fourth. When the same survey was conducted only 4 years before, vocational training had been ranked eighth by the states, and secondary curriculum was not even mentioned. When the parents of 163 high school students with severe handicaps were asked what they perceived to be the most important adult services their children would need after graduation and at 5 years and 10 years thereafter, they ranked a secure vocational placement that offered meaningful work as the first priority for all three points in time (McDonnell, Wilcox, Boles, & Bellamy, 1985).

Congress has also been aware of the difficulties faced by young adults with disabilities. A major section of P.L. 98–199, the Education for Handicapped Children Amendments of 1984, included funds to support a significant effort in improving secondary special education programs and transitional services. Part of the legislation reads as follows:

> The Subcommittee (on the Handicapped) recognizes the overwhelming paucity of effective programming for these handicapped youth, which eventually accounts for unnecessarily large numbers of handicapped adults who become unemployed and therefore dependent on Society. These youth historically have not been adequately prepared for the changes and demands of life after high school. In addition, few, if any, are able to access or appropriately use traditional transitional services. Few services have been designed to assist handicapped young people in their efforts to enter the labor force or attain their goals of becoming self-sufficient adults, and contributing members to our society. (Section 626, P.L. 98–199)

Since the passage of P.L. 98–199, the U.S. Department of Education, Office of Special Education and Rehabilitation Services (OSERS) has made transition from school to work a major priority. OSERS has developed a model of transition services that encompasses three levels of service, each conceptualized as a bridge between the secondary special education curriculum and adult employment (Will, 1985). According to OSERS, the three levels differ in terms of the nature and extent of the services required by the individual with handicaps to make a successful transition from school to work. On the first level are students who require no special transition services. Upon graduation from an appropriate secondary special education curriculum, these young adults, presumably those with mild handicaps, would make use of the generic employment services that are already available to nonhandicapped people in the community (e.g., job placement agencies). Other persons with disabilities would require the time-limited transitional services that are offered by vocational rehabilitation or adult service agencies and are specially designed to help individuals with disabilities gain competitive, independent employment. The third level of transitional services consists of ongoing employment services that are necessary if persons with severe handicaps are to enjoy the benefits of meaningful, paid work. The various models of supported employment examined earlier are examples of ongoing transitional services.

Numerous models for school-to-work transition have been developed (e.g., Freagon et al., 1986; Rusch, Chadsey-Rusch, & Lagomarcino, 1987; Wehman, Kregel, &

A good transition plan must include instruction and practice in community living skills.

Barcus, 1985). All of these models stress the importance of a functional secondary school curriculum that provides work experience in integrated community job sites, systematic coordination between the school and adult service providers, parental involvement and support, and a written individualized transition plan to guide the entire process. Although work-study and vocational training programs for special education students and vocational rehabilitation services for adults with disabilities have existed in every state for a long time, systematic coordination of and communication between schools and community-based adult services have not typically occurred.

The model for school-to-work transition proposed by Wehman, Kregel, and Barcus (1985) involves three stages: the secondary school curriculum, the transition planning process, and placement in meaningful employment (see Figure 15.2). Wehman et al. consider three characteristics critical to good secondary school programs. First, the curriculum must stress functional skills; that is, students must learn vocational skills that they will actually need and use in local employment situations. Second, school-based instruction must be carried out in integrated settings as much as possible (Certo, Haring, & York, 1983). Students with disabilities must be given ample opportunities to learn the interpersonal skills necessary to work effectively with nonhandicapped workers and peers in integrated work sites. Third, community-based instruction should begin as early as about age 12 for students with severe disabilities and must be used for progressively extended periods of time as the student nears graduation. While on work sites in the community, students should receive direct instruction in areas such as specific job skills, ways to increase production rate, and transportation to and from employment sites.

> Students should train and work in the community whenever possible. This is not only to expose them to the community and work expectations, but to expose future employers and coworkers to their potential as reliable employees. (Wehman et al., 1985, p. 29)

Project TIE (Transition Into Employment) at Virginia Commonwealth University is a federally funded program that provides training and assistance to local and state education, vocational rehabilitation, and adult day program services for developing interagency teams to facilitate a smooth school-to-work transition for persons with severe disabilities. The address for Project TIE is included at the end of the chapter.

Three-Stage Vocational Transition Model for Handicapped Youth

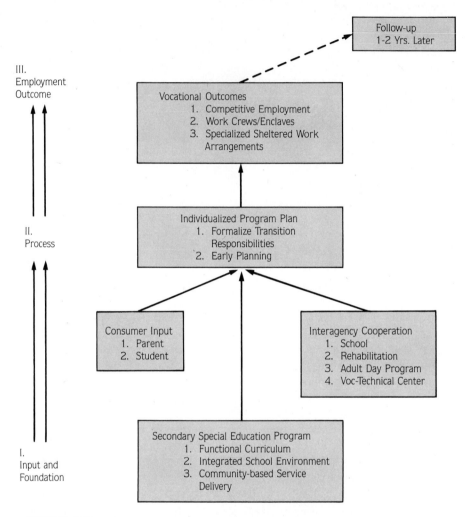

FIGURE 15.2
A three-stage model for helping students with handicaps make a successful transition from school to work.
Source: From "From School to Work: A Vocational Transition Model for Handicapped Students" by P. Wehman, J. Kregel, and J. M. Barcus, 1985, *Exceptional Children, 52,* p. 28. Reprinted by permission.

The development of career awareness and vocational skills should begin in the elementary years for children with severe handicaps. This approach does not require 6-year-old children to be placed on job sites for training. However, appropriate vocational objectives should be selected at each age level (Freagon et al., 1986; Wehman,

1983). For example, elementary students might sample different types of jobs through classroom responsibilities such as watering plants, cleaning chalkboards, or taking messages to the office. Young children with disabilities might also visit community work sites where adults with handicaps are employed. In addition, assessment and teaching of job performance skills can be accomplished with elementary-age special education students through prevocational work samples, which provide practice on skills (e.g., counting, packaging, following directions) and which are related to a variety of potentially available jobs in the community (Scott, Ebbert, & Price, 1986). Middle-school students should begin to spend time at actual community job sites, with an increasing amount of in-school instruction devoted to the development of associated work skills, such as being on time, staying on task, and using interpersonal skills (Egan, Fredericks, & Hendrickson, 1985; Sulzbacher, Haines, Peterson, & Swatman, 1987). Secondary students should spend an increasing amount of time on actual community job sites, with the remaining hours of in-school instruction focusing on the acquisition of functional skills needed in the adult work, domestic, community, and recreational/leisure environments toward which the student is headed (Brown et al., 1979).

Realizing that the actual number of hours spent at a work site will vary according to a student's age and the particular site, Freagon et al. (1986) suggest the following schedule for students with severe disabilities:

☐ Elementary (ages 6–10): 1/2 hour per week on an in-school job, increasing with age
☐ Middle school (ages 11–13): 2 half-days on a community job site
☐ High school (ages 14–18): 2 to 3 full days on a community job site
☐ High school (ages 19–21): as much time as possible on continuing job sites (i.e., the job the young adult will assume after leaving school)

The second stage of this transition model, the development and implementation of an individualized vocational transition plan for every handicapped student, is the key element in the transition process. Input from both student and parents and interagency cooperation are critical to an early planning effort that results in a formalized plan identifying school, community, and home responsibilities.

> Without a written plan specifying the competencies to be acquired by the student and the transition services to be received prior to and following graduation, the other major elements of the transition model will have little impact. The plan should include annual goals and short-term objectives which reflect skills required to function on the job, at home, and in the community. Transition services should also be specified, including referral to appropriate agencies, job placement, and on-the-job follow-up. (Wehman, Kregel, & Barcus, 1985, p. 30)

In addition to being individualized and comprehensive, transition plans must be longitudinal. Wehman, Kregel, and Barcus (1985) recommend that an individual transition plan be written 4 years prior to a student's graduation and that the plan be reviewed and modified as necessary at least once each year until the young adult has adjusted successfully to a postschool vocational placement. During a student's school

FIGURE 15.3
Example of an individualized transition plan.

Student's Name _____ Date of Birth _____ Residence _____ Phone _____

Parent/Guardian _____ Address _____ Phone _____

High School _____ Date of Graduation _____ School year _____ Date of Plan _____

Participants _____

Issues Related to Vocational Transition	Activities	Product	Date of Initiation	Date of Completion	Personnel Involvement
1.0 Job placement	1.1 School staff will meet adult-service agency staff and parents to discuss potential employment options for student and discuss level of follow-up services that could be provided after graduation.	Completed job placement plan: includes vocational interests, times available to work, etc.	September 1	September 1	School staff Adult-service agency follow-up staff Parents Student
	1.2 Student will be placed into competitive employment during the fall semester.	Job analysis survey Vocational service plan	September 8	September 1	School staff Employer Student
	1.3 School staff will provide initial on-the-job training.	Task analysis Individualized program plans, graphs Work performance evaluations Job placement logs	November 1	ongoing	School staff Adult-service agency follow-up staff Employer Student

1.4 School staff will meet with adult-service agency staff and the employer to discuss the transfer of follow-up responsibilities.	Individualized follow-up plan for site: includes time for cooperative programming and gradual fading of school staff involvement	January 15	ongoing	School staff Adult-service agency follow-up staff Employer, student Parent
2.0 Transpor-tation				
2.1 School staff will train student to use the city bus to and from work.	Bus pass Travel training task analysis graph	November 1	November 15	School staff Student
3.0 Income				
3.1 Meet with staff from social security office to discuss how employment will affect student's SSI benefits.	Written letter from Social Security Office outlining the effects on SSI benefits	September 3	September 3	Social Security staff School staff Adult-service agency case manager Parents
4.0 Recreation-leisure				
4.1 Student has time between school and work; has expressed interest in joining fitness center near work.	Membership card	December 1	ongoing	School staff Fitness center staff Student
Student will go to fitness center on Monday, Wednesday, Friday.	Workout schedule	December 1	December 1	Fitness center staff Student

Source: From "Preparing Students for Employment" by F. R. Rusch, J. Chadsey-Rusch, and T. Lagomarcino in *Systematic Instruction of Persons with Severe Handicaps*. (3rd ed.) by M. E. Snell (Ed.), 1987, Columbus, OH: Merrill. Reprinted by permission.

years the transition plan should be part of the IEP. After graduation the transition plan can be a component of the individual written rehabilitation plan if the young adult is served by vocational rehabilitation, or part of an individualized habilitation or service plan if the young adult is served by a community adult services agency (e.g., a county program for people with developmental disabilities). A well-written transition plan ensures that parents are aware of the adult services and employment options available in the community, increases the chances that adult services will be available with few disruptions to the graduating student, and provides school and adult-service personnel with a set of procedures and time lines to follow (Rusch, Chadsey-Rusch, & Lagomarcino, 1987). Figure 15.3 on pages 572–73 shows an example of an individualized transition plan.

The third and final stage of the transition model, multiple employment alternatives, must be available if the school-to-work transition effort is to result in meaningful outcomes for young adults with handicaps. At present many communities provide little in the way of real employment alternatives for adults with disabilities—perhaps a sheltered workshop offering traditional benchwork for persons with mild or moderate disabilities and an adult activity center, often with no opportunity to perform meaningful paid work, for persons with severe disabilities. However, as we saw earlier in this chapter, special educators and vocational habilitation specialists are developing an increasing range of true employment options for adults with disabilities, particularly in the area of competitive and supported employment. As more communities and employers implement these alternative models for employment, a successful and meaningful transition from school to the adult world of work will become reality for young persons with disabilities.

Just as this book went to press, a special issue of the journal Exceptional Children *(edited by Clark and Knowlton, 1987) was published. The entire issue consists of articles discussing models, programs, results, and trends in secondary education and the transition from school to adult life.*

RESIDENTIAL ALTERNATIVES

Where a person lives determines a great deal about how that person lives. Where a person lives influences where he can work, what community services and resources will be available, who his friends will be, what the opportunities for recreation and leisure will be, and, to a great extent, what feelings of self and place in the community will develop. It was not long ago that the total-care institution was the only place you could live if you were severely handicapped and could not live independently or did not live with your family. There were no other options—no such thing as residential alternatives. Today, however, many communities provide a variety of residential options for adults with disabilities. Increased community-based residential services have meant a greater opportunity for adults with more severe disabilities to live in a more normalized setting. We will examine here three different residential alternatives for adults with mental retardation—group homes, foster homes, and semi-independent apartment living—that help to complete the continuum of possible living arrangements between the highly structured and typically segregated public institution and fully independent living. First, however, we will consider the number of persons in the various types of residential settings available to persons with mental retardation and the change in the population of large public institutions.

In 1982 a comprehensive national census was conducted to determine the number of persons with mental retardation and developmental disabilities living in residential facilities in the United States (Hauber, Bruininks, Hill, Lakin, & White, 1984). Table 15.4 shows some of the results of this nationwide survey and compares the 1982 data with the results of a similar census conducted in 1977. The total number of persons with mental retardation who are using the residential services system remained relatively stable from 1977 to 1982 at approximately 250,000 persons, actually declining in proportion to the total U.S. population, which increased by 5.4% during the same period. However, comparison of the number of facilities and the number of persons living in each type of residential facility in 1977 and 1982 reveals a dynamic residential system, particularly in the shift of persons from large public institutions to smaller community-based residences.

The great majority of adults with disabilities needing residential services are those with mental retardation. However, Table 15.4 shows that more than 37,000 persons who were not labeled mentally retarded were living in the residential facilities covered by the 1982 census. These individuals were reported to have other disabilities.

Public Institutions

The largest number of adults with mental retardation in the residential services system is found in public institutions. A national survey by Epple, Jacobson, and Janicki (1985) revealed 247 large, publicly operated residential facilities for persons with mental retardation, averaging 450 residents per facility. Approximately 80% of the residents living in public institutions have severe or profound mental retardation.

Our nation's residential institutions for the mentally retarded and severely disturbed have come under attack both by professionals (e.g., see Blatt, 1976; Blatt & Kaplan, 1966) and by the courts (e.g., *Wyatt* v. *Stickney,* 1972) as being unable to provide the care and educational services needed by their residents. Given the principle of normalization, large residential institutions are inherently inappropriate places in which to place citizens with disabilities, even if all of the institutions were providing humanistic care and good educational programming.

Many families of institutionalized persons with mental retardation, however, do not feel as negative about institutions as do those in the professional community. A survey of the parent or nearest relative of 284 residents living in 40 different institutions found that 88% believed the institution provided the kind of services and care their family members with mental retardation needed (Spreat, Telles, Conroy, Feinstein, & Colombatto, 1985). Further results of this same survey revealed that 87% of those who returned the questionnaire considered the staff at the facility to be "very good." When asked whether they would like their family members transferred out of the institution and into a community-based group home, 60% of the respondents indicated that they were opposed to such a move; only 23% were in favor of such a transfer. When asked under what conditions they would approve the move of their family members to a group home, 58% said they would never approve such a move.

The earlier story on pages 394–95 of the mother of a severely handicapped child and her perspective on public institutions for people with severe disabilities supports this positive view.

However, these results should be interpreted in the context of the respondents' assessment of the ability of the persons with mental retardation to live and work in the community and the respondents' knowledge of community-based residential alternatives. Only half believed their relatives were able to learn more about getting along with others; only 21% believed their relatives could learn to work for pay; 61% considered group homes to be appropriate only for persons with mild mental retar-

TABLE 15.4

Results from two natiowide surveys of residential facilities for persons with mental retardation.

Characteristics	Spec. Foster		Group res. 1–15		Group res. Private 16+		Group res. Public 16+	
	1977	1982	1977	1982	1977	1982	1977	1982
Facility Characteristics								
Number of facilities	5,332	6,587	3,225	6,414	850	886	362	369
Number of residents	15,435	18,252	24,331	43,508	43,336	46,068	167,212	134,943
Mean	2.9	2.8	7.6	6.8	51.6	52.0	464.2	365.7
SD	2.0	1.9	3.2	3.2	60.4	55.7	540.1	383.9
Number of MR residents	14,418	17,147	22,449	42,018	36,998	40,347	154,856	122,971
Operator								
Private/proprietary	100.0%	100.0%	40.0%	27.1%	50.7%	50.2%	.0	.0
Nonprofit	.0	.0	48.2%	63.6%	49.3%	49.8%	.0	.0
Public	.0	.0	11.8%	9.2%	.0	.0	100.0%	100.0%
ICF-MR certified								
Facilities	.0%	.0%	5.0%	18.1%	13.0%	28.3%	62.6%	77.0%
MR beds	.0%	.1%	7.5%	22.1%	22.3%	40.7%	60.2%	86.9%
Avg. per diem per resident	$9.41	$16.15	$16.52	$38.31	$22.78	$45.15	$43.53	$85.84
Movement								
New admissions	22.4%	19.0%	37.2%	25.7%	20.3%	15.7%	5.7%	5.9
Readmissions	2.3%	.9%	2.6%	1.2%	1.3%	1.3%	1.9%	1.9%
Releases	7.0%	7.9%	18.5%	13.4%	13.9%	12.0%	9.2%	11.4%
Deaths	.9%	.9%	.6%	.5%	.8%	.8%	1.5%	1.5%
Est. move due to close	8.7%	8.8%	6.2%	5.8%	2.4%	2.4%	.4%	.5%
Est. net 12 month change	8.2%	2.3%	14.5%	7.3%	4.5%	1.7%	−3.5%	−5.6%
Opened within 4½ years	52.7%	46.7%	71.0%	60.0%	36.1%	19.7%	19.9%	8.8%
Resident characteristics								
Age								
<22	39.0%	37.4%	28.6%	19.8%	44.4%	32.0%	35.8%	22.0%
22–39	24.7%	32.0%	47.9%	53.3%	36.7%	41.8%	41.3%	50.2%
40–62	26.7%	23.1%	21.2%	23.8%	16.3%	22.1%	19.2%	22.9%
63+	9.1%	7.6%	2.2%	3.0%	2.6%	4.1%	3.7%	5.0%
Level of retardation								
Borderline/mild	28.0%	25.9%	34.4%	29.3%	29.0%	26.8%	9.3%	7.0%
Moderate	37.7%	37.7%	41.7%	37.9%	34.9%	29.9%	16.0%	12.9%
Severe	26.5%	26.0%	19.5%	23.2%	23.4%	24.0%	27.9%	24.3%
Profound	7.8%	10.4%	4.4%	9.5%	12.2%	19.3%	46.9%	55.8%
Nonambulatory	7.0%	9.3%	3.5%	5.3%	8.4%	14.4%	23.3%	25.5%
Cannot talk	18.6%	24.9%	11.2%	17.4%	19.7%	24.1%	43.5%	49.1%
Not toilet trained	8.8%	13.1%	4.2%	6.7%	11.6%	16.1%	34.1%	38.0%

	Semi-Independent		Board & Room		Personal Care		Spec. Nursing		Total	
	1977	1982	1977	1982	1977	1982	1977	1982	1977	1982
	236	306	210	185	561	583	249	303	11,025	15,633
	2,356	3,155	2,955	2,559	9,185	7,956	21,103	24,521	285,913	281,042
	10.5	10.3	14.8	13.8	16.4	13.6	86.0	81.1	25.9	18.0
	11.4	8.8	19.6	20.3	24.4	19.8	65.3	61.8	129.8	83.0
	1,993	2,870	1,665	1,264	4,141	4,070	11,275	12,982	247,796	243,669
	15.0%	13.4%	93.5%	94.6%	90.9%	90.4%	76.5%	70.6%	72.4%	62.2%
	75.8%	80.4%	5.5%	4.3%	4.5%	4.8%	18.0%	23.1%	20.2%	31.2%
	9.2%	6.2%	1.0%	1.1%	4.6%	4.8%	5.5%	6.3%	7.3%	6.8%
	1.3%	5.9%	.0	.0	.4%	.5%	21.7%	45.5%	5.2%	11.9%
	1.1%	7.8%	.0	.0	2.8%	2.3%	32.5%	60.2%	43.1%	57.7%
	$16.20	$27.40	$9.60	$15.97	$12.60	$17.05	$25.92	$49.81	$34.23	$61.89
	54.2%	31.9%	30.0%	12.7%	19.8%	14.7%	23.0%	14.4%	13.3%	12.8%
	1.1%	1.0%	3.0%	.9%	3.6%	2.3%	4.7%	2.7%	2.0%	1.0%
	24.8%	18.5%	16.4%	13.0%	10.9%	8.5%	15.5%	8.0%	11.1%	11.5%
	.4%	.3%	.9%	.9%	1.1%	.8%	3.1%	2.3%	1.3%	1.2%
	9.5%	9.4%	7.4%	6.8%	6.7%	5.7%	2.5%	2.6%	2.0%	2.7%
	20.6%	4.9%	8.3%	−7.1%	4.6%	2.0%	6.6%	4.3%	.9%	−.8%
	88.0%	62.5%	38.6%	21.4%	37.9%	27.4%	42.5%	23.4%	55.2%	48.6%
	17.7%	7.7%	10.1%	5.9%	14.7%	10.2%	52.9%	38.2%	36.8%	24.8%
	61.3%	65.4%	33.8%	38.3%	28.6%	31.6%	22.3%	33.6%	39.3%	47.0%
	20.3%	25.5%	42.0%	40.5%	43.4%	41.1%	18.3%	21.8%	19.9%	23.3%
	.7%	1.5%	14.2%	15.3%	13.4%	17.1%	6.6%	6.4%	4.1%	5.0%
	66.1%	61.8%	49.5%	47.1%	30.8%	31.2%	12.8%	9.2%	16.9%	16.8%
	31.1%	32.5%	40.8%	33.6%	40.4%	39.8%	21.6%	16.2%	23.4%	22.8%
	2.7%	5.3%	7.1%	17.6%	18.0%	20.6%	35.9%	26.2%	26.2%	24.0%
	.1%	.4%	2.6%	1.7%	11.1%	8.4%	30.0%	48.5%	33.5%	36.5%
	6.0%	3.7%	1.0%	2.7%	6.0%	5.4%	49.3%	48.3%	18.9%	19.5%
	3.3%	3.7%	6.5%	4.8%	13.0%	16.1%	48.5%	54.0%	34.7%	36.7%
	.8%	.1%	1.0%	3.9%	6.8%	6.5%	45.2%	49.0%	26.1%	26.7%

Source: From "Trends in Residential Services for People Who Are Mentally Retarded: 1977–1982" by B. K. Hill, K. C. Lakin, and R. H. Bruininks, 1984, *Journal of the Association for Persons with Severe Handicaps, 9,* p. 247. Reprinted by permission.

We will consider the re-
sults of one of these
studies later in this chapter.

dation; and only 13% strongly agreed with the statement "I know a lot about group homes and other alternatives to large facilities." Interestingly, several studies have found that the views of parents change dramatically after a family member has been transferred from a large institution to a smaller, community-based residence (Brad-dock & Heller, 1985; Conroy & Bradley, 1985).

Whereas mainstreaming describes putting normalization into effect in school settings, **deinstitutionalization**—the movement of mentally retarded people out of large institutions and into smaller, community-based living environments, such as fos-ter or group homes—further increases the degree of normalization of mentally re-tarded persons who have previously resided in institutions. Deinstitutionalization is more than a philosophy or goal of concerned individuals; it is, and has been, an active movement over the past 20 years. The number of persons with mental retardation living in large, public institutions has decreased from a high of 194,650 in 1967 to 109,827 in 1984 (Braddock, Hemp, & Howes, 1986; Scheerenberger, 1983). From 1977 to 1984 the number of persons residing in institutions for individuals with mental retardation fell by 27%.

In a summary report on the findings of the 1982 residential census, Hill, Lakin, and Bruininks (1984) conclude:

> Public facilities [institutions], which continue to depopulate at a fairly constant rate of 6,000 residents per year, are being replaced by smaller community-based pro-grams that serve individuals with severely/profoundly handicapping conditions. . . . Efforts of this nature [federal and state regulations proposing acceleration of dein-stitutionalization], as well as research and testimony, will undoubtedly continue to develop the perception that appropriate care is community-based care and that such a perception is no less true for people who are severely/profoundly retarded than for those who are mildly retarded or nonretarded. While a formal policy of noninsti-tutionalization may not be imminent, there is considerable longitudinal evidence that through continuing program development efforts of the past few years, that end will be essentially realized by the turn of the century. (p. 249)

Group Homes

Community-based group homes are the fastest growing residential alternative for adults with mental retardation. The number of group homes in the United States nearly doubled from 1977 to 1982, to a total of 6,414 homes serving more than 42,000 persons. Most of the residents released from large institutions find themselves living in group homes. **Group homes** provide family-style living for a group of handi-capped adults, from as few as 3 or 4 to as many as 10 or 15. Most group homes operating today serve adults with mental retardation, although there are some group homes with residents with other handicaps. Group homes vary as to purpose. Some are principally residential and represent a permanent placement for their residents. In this type of group home, educational programming revolves around developing self-care and daily living skills, forming interpersonal relationships, and learning recrea-tional skills and use of leisure time. During the day most residents are outside the group home, employed in the community or in a sheltered workshop.

Other group homes operate more as halfway houses. Their primary function is to prepare the handicapped adult for a more independent living situation, such as a supervised apartment. These transitional group homes typically serve residents who have recently been discharged from institutions, bridging the gap between institutional and community living.

Two key aspects of group homes make them a much more normalized place to live than an institution: their size and their location (Wolfensberger, 1972). Most people grow up in a typical family-sized group, where there is opportunity for personal attention, care, and privacy. Certainly, the 40-beds-to-a-ward, mass-living arrangement common to many institutions cannot be said to be normalized, regardless of the efforts of hardworking, caring staff. By keeping the number of residents in a group home small, there is a greater chance for a familylike atmosphere. Size is also directly related to the neighborhood's ability to assimilate the members of the group home into normal, routine activities within the community, which is a key element of normalization. Indeed, there is some evidence that quality of life is better for persons residing in smaller rather than larger group homes (Rotegard, Hill, & Bruininks, 1983).

See pages 580–81 to find out how two women who spent most of their lives in a large state-run institution feel about living in a group home.

Although research on the effects of the size of group homes has been inconclusive, operators of community residential programs consistently state that residential settings of three or four individuals are much more likely to have their residents integrated into the community (Cooke, 1981). Bronston (1980) offers four arguments favoring small residential settings: (1) the group and the home do not attract undue attention by being larger than a large family; (2) the smaller the number of different individuals in a group home, the more likely the neighborhood will be to absorb them; (3) large groups tend to become self-sufficient, orienting inward and thereby resisting movement outward into the community; and (4) in groups larger than six or eight, house parents and advisors can no longer relate properly to individual group members.

The location and physical characteristics of the group home itself are also vital determinants of its ability to provide a normalized life-style for its residents. A group home must be located within the community, in a residential area, not a commercially zoned district. It must be in an area where residents have convenient access to shopping, schools, churches, public transportation, and recreational facilities. In other words, a group home must be located in a normal residential area where any one of us might live. And it must look like a home, not conspicuously different from any of the other family dwellings on the same street. There definitely should not be a sign out front that reads "Elm Street Group Home for the Retarded."

Janicki and Zigman (1984) studied the location and design characteristics of 386 small group homes in New York state. They found that the homes exhibited a wide variety of styles and configurations, were located in all types of residential neighborhoods, and were in close proximity to commercial and recreational resources (e.g., two-thirds of the residences were within one-fourth of a mile of both a corner store and a bus or subway station). Janicki and Zigman concluded that the homes in their study were "normative, home-like dwellings in terms of their structural aspects, and as such they contribute to the physical integration of the residence program within its

In 1982 the average cost per day for each resident in a large public institution (64-plus residents) for persons with mental retardation was $85.94 (Hauber et al., 1984). By contrast, it cost less than half that amount, $40.29, to support one person living in a small group home (fewer than 6 residents).

JUDY AND KATHY

Judy and Kathy are two of the eight women who live in a group home in Westerville, Ohio. All of the women came there from Columbus Developmental Center (CDC), a large state-run institution for persons with mental retardation. When we visited the group home, Judy and Kathy talked to us about living there.

Judy, where did you live before you came here?
CDC.

Can you tell me what it is like living here compared to CDC? Which do you like better?
I like the group home best. Because you get more privileges. You get more freedom.

What kind of things can you do here that you couldn't do at CDC?
Here you can do a lot of things. Like planting a garden, working on the garden, help to do a lot of things in the house, go to work. And then they give you time to go to work.

Where do you work, Judy?
At Arcraft Workshop [a sheltered workshop].

What do you think about doing housework? Do you like it?
Yes. We get to do chores in the house every day. We get to cook our own food. We don't have to have nobody cook it for you. Each girl has a day to cook.

What do you like to cook best?
Fish, baked potatoes, and sweet potatoes, and then lime punch and lettuce salad.

What would you like to learn to cook?
Macaroni and cheese.

Can you cook it now?
No, Rose [the live-in director of the home] is teaching me.

Have you made any friends since you've come here, Judy?
One of my friends is Kathy, my roommate.

Do you two like to do things together?
Yes. We get to go outside and play, walk around. Talk to each other in our room.

Judy is especially proud of her library card.

Judy, what do you need to learn before you could have your own apartment?
I need to learn how to go shopping by myself. I will have my old man teach me.

Your old man? Do you have a boyfriend?
Yep, Phil.

Phil. Where does he live?
CDC. But he is planning to go out too, out in the community as soon as they find a place for him in a boy's apartment.

Do you ever get to see Phil?
Yep, sure do. He's coming next Tuesday when I get off work, at 3:30.

What are you going to do when he comes?
Cook his best supper for him and my best supper for all the ladies and the caseworkers.

What is his best supper?
Baked potatoes, onion rings, lima beans, meatloaf.

Kathy, how do you like living here?
I like this. This is a nicer home than CDC. We keep our house real nice and neat. And sometimes when I was at CDC, the boys walked in when I was doing something and embarrassed me.

So you have more privacy here?
Yes, it's better.

Your house is beautiful. But here you have to clean it yourself. You don't mind doing the work?
No.

Have you made any friends while you've been here?
Yes, I have. Judy. Judy is my favorite friend here.

What kinds of things do you and Judy do when you have free time?
We go up in our bedroom and talk to each other and also we clean our bedroom every Saturday.

And I help her out when she's sick, and she helps me out when I'm sick.

How about seeing men? Do you have a boyfriend?
Yes, I do. His name is James.

When do you get to see James?
When I go to my boyfriend's house.

How do you get to your boyfriend's house?
Rose drives me.

How did you meet James?
From CDC.

Is he living in a group home now, too?
Yes, on Dennison Road.

Does he like it?
Yes, but he doesn't keep his house clean.

You'll have to tell him about that.
I did.

What did he say?
"I will, honey." Then when I went to his house last week, his house was clean.

What did you say to him?
"Congratulations!"

Tuesday is Kathy's day to clean the yellow bathroom.

neighborhood. If this is true, then it is reasonable to assume that these aspects add to the social integration of their occupants as well" (p. 300).

Wolfensberger and Glenn (1975) have developed a method for assessing the degree to which a service setting meets various criteria of normalization. Called Program Analyses of Service Systems (PASS), the assessment produces a quantitative rating. Pieper and Cappuccilli (1980) have suggested the following set of questions, based on PASS, as a means of determining how appropriate a given residential setting may be. A group home would be considered a normalized setting if all or most of these questions can be answered yes.

☐ Did the residents choose to live in the home?
☐ Is this type of setting usually inhabited by people in the residents' age group?
☐ Do the residents live with others their own age?
☐ Is the home located within a residential neighborhood?
☐ Does the residence look like the other dwellings around it?
☐ Can the number of people living in the residence be reasonably expected to be assimilated into the community?
☐ Are community resources and facilities readily accessible from the residence?
☐ Do the residents have a chance to buy the house?
☐ Do the managers of the place act in an appropriate manner toward the residents?
☐ Are the residents encouraged to do all they can for themselves?
☐ Are the residents encouraged to have personal belongings that are appropriate to their age?
☐ Are residents encouraged to use community resources as much as possible?
☐ Are all the residents' rights acknowledged?
☐ Are the residents being given enough training and assistance to help them grow and develop as individuals?
☐ Would I want to live in the home? Here is the final test. If the residence appears good enough for you to want to live in it, it will probably be an appropriate living arrangement for persons with special needs. We should demand residential arrangements for persons with special needs that are comparable to those inhabited by most nondisabled citizens.

Analysis of real estate data for 525 homes sold around 13 group homes in and around Omaha, Nebraska, showed that group homes did not adversely affect neighborhood property values (Ryan & Coyne, 1985).

New group homes are opening every day all across the country. However, group homes continue to run into obstacles. Communities have been slow to accept group homes into their neighborhoods. Most agencies, service groups, and individuals who have started (or attempted to start) group homes for retarded adults have run into harsh resistance. Convinced that people with mental retardation are dangerous or crazy, that they will have a bad influence on neighborhood children, or that property values will go down if a group home comes into the area, neighborhood associations have too often been effective in keeping group homes from starting.

In 1985 the U.S. Supreme Court unanimously ruled that communities cannot use a discriminatory zoning ordinance to prevent the establishment of group homes for persons with mental retardation in an area already zoned for apartment and other congregate living facilities (*City of Cleburne v. Cleburne Living Center*, 1985). The city of Cleburne, Texas, argued that the nearby presence of a junior high school and the

What's on tonight?

fact that the group home site was located on a 500-year flood plain permitted the city to exclude the group home from that site. The city was also concerned "about the legal responsibility for actions which the mentally retarded might take" and about fire safety, congestion, and the serenity of the neighborhood. In their analysis of the Cleburne decision, the attorneys who prepared a brief on behalf of the group home for the AAMD, CEC, TASH, and four other national disability groups said:

> In each instance, the Supreme Court concluded that the city's purported concerns were a smokescreen for prejudice and unconstitutional discrimination.
>
> Perhaps most significantly, the fears and objections of neighbors were held to be insufficient to support the ordinance because "mere negative attitudes, or fear, unsubstantiated by factors which are properly cognizable in a zoning proceeding, are not permissible bases for treating a home for people with mental retardation differently from" other uses that the law allows. As the Court observed, "Private biases may be outside the reach of the law, but the law cannot, directly or indirectly, give them effect."
>
> [This case] is a useful precedent for arguments that zoning laws cannot be used as a device to discriminate against the housing needs of people who are mentally retarded, and in particular that the fears and irrational prejudices of neighbors who may be opposed to such a group home will not justify its exclusion from the community. (Ellis & Luckasson, 1985, p. 250)

Foster Homes

When a family opens its home to an unrelated person for an extended period of time, the term **foster home** is often used. Although foster homes have been used for years in providing temporary residential services and family care for children (usually wards of the court), more and more families are now beginning to share their homes with handicapped adults. In return for providing room and board for their new family member, foster families receive a modest financial reimbursement.

For the handicapped adult there can be numerous advantages to life in a foster family home. The resident can participate and share in the day-to-day activities of a normal family, receive individual attention from people vitally interested in her continued growth and development, and develop close interpersonal relationships. As part of a family unit, the handicapped adult also has increased opportunities to interact with and be accepted by the community at large.

However, Baker, Seltzer, and Seltzer (1977) warn that, even though adults living in foster homes may be involved regularly with the new family members, they are sometimes discouraged from getting involved with people and activities outside the home, thereby resulting in unnecessary restrictions and isolation.

Apartment Living

Apartment living offers the handicapped adult an even greater opportunity for integration into the community than group homes do. Whereas in a group home the handicapped resident interacts primarily with other handicapped persons, in an apartment-living arrangement (assuming the apartment is in a regular apartment complex), the likelihood of interacting with nonhandicapped persons is increased. Some professionals believe that full integration into the community will be achieved only when all handicapped persons are in private homes or apartments, that even small group homes are too institutional. Bronston (1980) has even suggested that "apartment dwellings could suffice for all our adult service needs, except where acute medical/hospital services were needed to stabilize a person for short-term duration." Three forms of apartment living for handicapped adults are the most common: the apartment cluster, the coresidence apartment, and the maximum-independence apartment.

An apartment cluster consists of a small number of apartments housing handicapped persons and another nearby apartment for a supervisory person or staff. An apartment cluster is an extremely workable arrangement because it allows for a great deal of flexibility in the amount and degree of supervision needed by residents in the various apartments. Whereas some residents might require direct help with such things as shopping, cooking, or even getting dressed, others need only limited assistance or suggestions and prompts. In an apartment cluster some apartments are also occupied by nonhandicapped persons, which facilitates social integration.

A coresidence apartment is shared by a handicapped and a nonhandicapped person. Although this arrangement is sometimes permanent, most coresidence apartments are used as a step toward independent living. The live-in roommates are often unpaid volunteers.

Two to four handicapped adults usually cohabit maximum-independence apartments. These adults have all of the self-care and daily living skills required to take care of themselves and their apartment on a day-to-day basis. A supervisory visit is made once or twice a week to help the residents deal with any special problems they may be having.

Outcomes and Issues in Residential Services

During the early years of the group home movement, many may have thought that small community-based residences were appropriate for more highly skilled persons with mild or moderate levels of mental retardation. Today, however, it is increasingly clear that even those persons labeled severely and profoundly retarded can benefit from the more normalized life offered by community-based residential alternatives. The residential census conducted by Hauber et al. (1984) found that one-third of all individuals residing in group homes in 1982 were persons with severe or profound retardation. Further examination of Table 15.4 shows that even a small percentage of those persons living in semi-independent apartments are people with severe or profound mental retardation. These demographic data support the notion that community-based living for persons with severe disabilities is feasible. But what about the experiences of those persons transferred from large institutions to smaller community residences? Do they find an improved quality of life?

See Williams and Cuvo (1986) for an interesting study evaluating task analytic strategies for teaching apartment upkeep skills (e.g., cleaning the refrigerator, operating the air conditioner/heater) to six adults with severe handicaps.

Given the complexity and variety of community residential programs and the many variables that play a part in determining the quality of life and developmental progress a person experiences, answering these important questions in a definitive, scientific manner is nearly impossible. However, several studies have indicated generally positive outcomes for residents transferred from institutions to group homes. One of the most comprehensive of these studies was reported by Conroy and Bradley (1985), who monitored over a 5-year period the adjustment of 176 persons with mental retardation who were deinstitutionalized from the Pennhurst State School and Hospital in Pennsylvania and placed in community residences. Measures of the adaptive behavior growth of the individuals placed in the community showed gains 10 times greater than that of a matched comparison group remaining in the institution.

For a review of the research literature on the effects of community residential programs on adults with disabilities, see Landesman and Butterfield (in press).

Conroy and Bradley (1985) also conducted interviews with family members and verbal residents prior to and after deinstitutionalization. While still in the institution, the residents described themselves as happy and satisfied with their life in the institution. However, when these same individuals were interviewed again after they had been placed in community-based living arrangements, they said they were happier in the community and did not want to return to the institution. Figure 15.4 shows the tremendous turnaround in attitude toward community placement on the part of the parents and families of these individuals. Conroy and Bradley (1985) summarize the findings of their 5-year study.

> On the average, the people deinstitutionalized under the Pennhurst court order are better off in every way measured. This is an uncommon, but welcome, situation in social science. More often, evaluative results are mixed, and one must balance gains in one area against losses in another. For the people who have moved from Pennhurst to small community residences, results are not mixed. They are conclusive. (p. 322)

It is important to note that of the 176 people deinstitutionalized from Pennhurst and followed-up by Conroy and Bradley (1985), 81% were labeled severely or profoundly mentally retarded.

As encouraging as results such as these are, simply placing a person with disabilities in a small, community-based residence such as a group home does not automatically produce a normalized, adaptive life-style (Landesman & Butterfield, in press). Many problems and challenges are faced by those responsible for planning and imple-

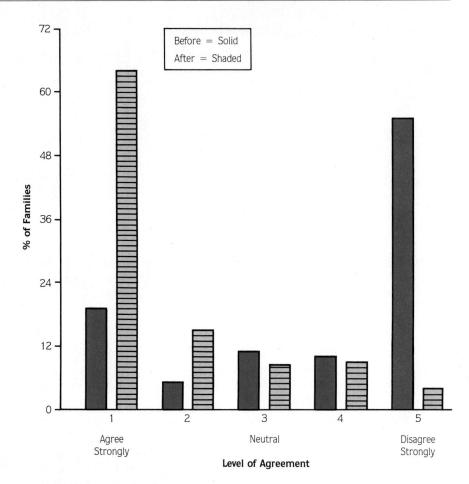

FIGURE 15.4
Attitudes of parents and families regarding transfer of a family member with mental retardation from a state institution to a community-based residential setting—before and after
deinstitutionalization.

Source: From *The Pennhurst Longitudinal Study* (p. 179) by J. W. Conroy and V. J. Bradley, 1985,
Philadelphia: Temple University. Reprinted by permission.

menting community-based residential services for handicapped adults. One kind of
problem has to do with what has been called the relocation syndrome (Cochran, Sran
& Varano, 1977) or transition shock (Coffman & Harris, 1980). The person who has
just left the institution needs support in the community. In the early days of the
deinstitutionalization movement, too many former residents of state institutions were
dumped into the community without having the necessary skills to cope successfully
in their new environment and without easy access to support and follow-up services
to see that the transition was successful. A 1974 statement by the National Association
of Superintendents of Public Residential Facilities of the Mentally Retarded reflects this
concern.

> While the Association advocates without reservation the rights of the retarded to live in the least restrictive environment and to enjoy fully the benefits of a free and open society whenever possible, it does express concern over the manner in which this goal is being realized. First, the quality of community programs and services being offered to the mentally retarded and other developmentally disabled persons in many parts of the country is inadequate. All too often, "community back wards" and "closeting" (being shut up at home) are being substituted for institutional "warehousing." Neither community nor residential back wards or closeting are justified: the rights of the retarded must be respected wherever they reside. (pp. 2–3)

Fortunately, today there are fewer horror stories of institutional residents being released into the community and being victimized or served by the criminal justice system as a result of vagrancy, destitution, or a criminal offense. The major problem is one of providing a flexible system of residential options that truly meets the needs of individuals (Cooke, 1981). Most professionals agree that no one type of residential setting is best for all handicapped adults and that a continuum of options is needed (Bradley, 1978; Fanning, 1975; Seltzer & Seltzer, 1977). But the continuum-of-services approach, with residential options ranging from most restrictive to least restrictive, is not without its problems and critics. The typical continuum of residential options does not guarantee that there will be no gaps between one option and the next, nor does it recognize the possibility that there may be other, perhaps more innovative, alternatives that are appropriate for some individuals (Cooke, 1981). Also, continuum-of-service models usually assume that a person moves into the residential service system at the more restrictive end and must earn his way along (Scheerenberger, 1974). The handicapped person is forced to earn the right to the least restrictive living arrangement.

This is not unlike the continuum of services model of educational placement options, described in chapter 2.

> The underlying philosophy of this model is not at all consistent with civil rights decisions in other areas. The Supreme Court ruled in the 1960s that black people had a right to ride in the front of the bus and to go to their neighborhood schools, rights based simply on their citizenship—not rights they had to earn. But with "developmentally disabled" people we have said you must earn the right to live in an integrated setting. You must behave yourself before we'll ever give you this right. This is clearly a basic form of discrimination. (Hitzing, 1980, p. 84)

Several innovative models for residential services for handicapped adults—based on the belief that residential placements must be adapted to the needs of clients—not vice versa—have been developed in recent years (Apolloni & Cooke, 1981; Hitzing, 1980; Provencal, 1980).

A significant problem faced by planners and administrators of any community-based residential option is securing, training, and keeping competent staff. Direct care staff in residential settings must fill a demanding role, often serving as family member, friend, counselor, and teacher to one individual, all in a day's time. The training received by residential staff members varies considerably from one program to another. The more successful residential service programs place tremendous emphasis on staff training, making it mandatory and ongoing. Most training objectives are practical as opposed to theoretical; they stress first aid, fire safety, nutrition, neighborhood relations, behavior management, instruction in daily living skills, and so on (Cooke, 1981).

Wetzel and Hoschouer (1984) have developed an excellent model of program development and staff training that they call residential teaching communities. One of the central concepts of their model is that everyday activities occurring naturally are the most appropriate and effective opportunities for teaching the daily living and interpersonal skills that residents of community-based programs need to learn. However, as they take advantage of such naturally occurring teaching and learning opportunities, group home staff and other residential service providers must remember that the residence is first and foremost a home, not a school or training center.

RECREATION AND LEISURE

Many of us take our leisure and recreational activities for granted. We are benefiting from a lifetime of learning how to play or how to enjoy a personal hobby or craft. But for many handicapped adults appropriate recreational and leisure-time acitivities do not come easily; in some communities they may not even be available.

Using community recreational resources requires transportation, the physical ability or skills to play the game, and usually other willing and able friends to play with. Often these three variables work effectively to limit the recreational and leisure-time activities available to the handicapped adult. Transportation is not available; her disability does not allow her to swim, bowl, or play tennis; and she has no friends with similar skills and interests and no convenient way to make new friends.

Because of these problems, for adults with disabilities living in community-based residences, the majority of recreational and leisure activities are segregated, handicapped-only outings. To promote community integration, Schleien and Larson (1986) developed and evaluated a successful program for teaching adults with severe mental retardation to make independent use of a community recreation center.

Providing age-appropriate and otherwise normalized recreational and leisure-time activities is an important facet of extending services to handicapped adults. Special educators must realize the importance of including training for recreation and leisure in curricula for handicapped children. Professionals must also realize the increased importance leisure activities hold for unemployed adults with handicaps (Fain, 1986). The range of apparent leisure activities for many adults with disabilities consists of watching great amounts of television, listening to music in the solitude of their rooms, and spending discretionary time socially isolated (Shannon, 1985). Persons with handicaps must be helped to find a self-satisfying life-style, and recreation and enjoyable use of leisure are primary means to that end.

Bigge (1982) describes in detail how numerous games, hobbies, crafts, and projects can be adapted to become enjoyable, worthwhile leisure-time pursuits for handicapped persons. Some of the areas she suggests are raising guinea pigs, music appreciation and study, photography, card games, and nature study. Suggestions have also been made for adapting leisure activities for young adults who are deaf-blind (Hamre-Nietupski, Nietupski, Sandvig, Sandvig, & Ayres, 1984). Some of these authors' recommendations for adapting tasks and materials include using permanent tactile prompts (e.g., attaching fabric to the flipper buttons of a pinball machine), adequately stabilizing materials, enhancing the visual or auditory input provided by the materials (e.g., using large-print, low-vision playing cards), and simplifying the requirements of the task (e.g., raising the front legs on a pinball machine, thereby reducing the speed with which the ball approaches the flippers).

Horseback riding is an outdoor pursuit that is becoming popular with many physically and mentally handicapped persons. Often called therapeutic horsemanship or equine therapy, horseback riding has given many handicapped persons the excitement and thrills of the sport while at the same time improving their gross motor functioning, social skills, and feeling of pride and self-esteem. The National Riding for the Disabled Association, founded in England in 1967 and now associated with groups in many countries, has developed a training program, exercises, and a variety of adaptive equipment to enable persons with just about any kind of disability to ride a horse.

Learning appropriate leisure skills is particularly important for adults with severe handicaps. Most persons with severe handicaps have ample free time but do not use it constructively, often engaging in inappropriate behaviors such as body rocking, hand flapping, or bizarre vocalizations (Wehman & Schleien, 1981). Recently, a number of promising studies have been reported in which leisure skills that are age-appropriate have been taught to moderately and severely retarded adults (Johnson & Bailey, 1977; Nietupski & Svoboda, 1982; Schleien, Kiernan, & Wehman, 1981). Schleien, Wehman, and Kiernan (1981) successfully taught three severely retarded, multihandicapped adults to throw darts, and Hill, Wehman, and Horst (1982) taught a group of severely handicapped young adults to play pinball machines.

Therapeutic Recreation

The National Recreation and Parks Association defines **therapeutic recreation** as

> a process which utilizes recreation services for purposive intervention in some physical, emotional, and/or social behavior to bring about a desired change in that behavior and to promote the growth and development of the individual. . . . Therapeutic recreators, then, are people who use recreation as a medium to assist disabled people to change certain physical, emotional, or social characteristics so they may live their leisure lifestyles as well and independently as possible. Because these individuals are functioning at different and unique levels of ability, therapeutic recreators use recreation in many ways to help them realize their potentials for leisure enjoyment.
>
> Therapeutic recreators are concerned with eliminating or minimizing disability, but further, are concerned with the quality of the person's total existence. This includes not only the physical and emotional self, but the environment in which the individual must live. (p. 1)

Many communities have therapeutic recreation programs. For example, the Division of Therapeutic Recreation of the Cincinnati Recreation Commission offers a full schedule of recreational activities throughout the year for handicapped children and adults. Dancing, bicycling, swimming, softball, tennis, soccer, golf, fishing, camping, and hiking are just some of the activities that are offered for mentally retarded, physically handicapped, autistic, learning disabled, and emotionally disturbed citizens. The program has even begun to teach handicapped children and adults to participate in such high-risk activities as rappelling and canoeing. These efforts have met with great success, as Sam Brown, supervisor of the Division of Therapeutic Recreation, explains: "The increase in pride and self-confidence that a handicapped person experiences after he finds that he too can manage a canoe or get himself safely down the side of a cliff is just tremendous." Brown defines therapeutic recreation as

> recreation that has a secondary benefit. A benefit other than just the fun or recreational aspect—although the fun is extremely important too. The secondary benefit may be increased socialization skills, eye-hand coordination, physical development, or even cognitive or language development. It's planned intervention through recreation, with a definite purpose and goal.

One of the goals of the Cincinnati program is to help handicapped persons move into the recreational mainstream; that is, to participate in integrated activities with nonhandicapped people as much as possible. To help staff evaluate and monitor each participant's progress toward that goal, the Division of Therapeutic Recreation has developed a continuum of five levels.

☐ Level I consists of activities for persons who require a 1:1 or 1:2 staff-to-participant ratio. Mat activities (such as tumbling), music, crafts, and camping are used to help participants increase their sensorimotor and self-help skills.

☐ Level II is a program for people who have basic skills (such as running, throwing, or striking) and are able to begin functioning in a group situation. Team sports such as volleyball and softball are used, but the emphasis is on group interaction rather than on specific rules or skills.

☐ At Level III, teamwork is assumed; the emphasis shifts to learning how to play the game or perform the activity well (e.g., learning to convert spares and to keep score in bowling). Skill improvement is the primary objective in Level III programs.

☐ At Level IV, activities are held in regular community center facilities and are conducted by the regular staff of those facilities instead of by therapeutic recreation specialists. However, the handicapped clients still participate as a segregated group.

☐ Finally, at Level V, handicapped individuals participate in the recreational programs and activities offered by the Cincinnati Recreation Commission for everyone in the community. Staff from the Division of Therapeutic Recreation monitor and follow up on these mainstreaming efforts, working with regular recreation staff somewhat the same way resource room teachers work with regular classroom teachers to help ease the integration of handicapped students into the regular classroom.

COMMUNITY INTEGRATION—AN ELUSIVE GOAL

A continuing problem faced by many adults with disabilities is lack of acceptance as full members of our society, with all of the rights, privileges, and services granted to any citizen. We have made much progress in this regard—witness the litigation and legislation on behalf of handicapped persons that have been discussed throughout this book—but we still have a long way to go. Courts can decree and laws can require, but neither can alter the way individuals feel toward and treat disabled people. Individuals with handicaps often "seem to be in the community but not of it" (Birenbaum,

BONNIE

Bonnie Consolo

Bonnie Consolo is a 44-year-old divorced mother of two teenage boys. She lives in a comfortable split-level house in a midwestern suburb and supports her family with money earned from speaking engagements around the country. Most of the time she drives to those engagements. Bonnie is also currently writing the story of her life, which doesn't sound remarkable until you realize that she was born without arms.

Because of my physical difference, my life is more interesting. I meet more people, possibly because I've been on TV [featured on "60 Minutes" as well as on local programs] and in newspapers. People don't tend to shy away from me. A lot of people consider their lives dull; they're in a rut. My physi-cal difference eliminates the rut for me. Of course people have stared at me for 44½ years and probably will for the rest of my life. It used to bother me but now I realize that it's a normal human reaction to stare at things you're not used to seeing.

Being handicapped doesn't affect me in the community. I feel a lot of pride in my life. God uses my life and everything I do. My just going along, head held high, with a look of pride on my face, helps some people see that there have to be some problems in life to help us to grow. Every time I meet somebody I try to go away a better person. I hope the other person goes away with some kind of better understanding of the relationship, at least, no matter how brief it is.

I am sure, though, that my handicap has a big effect on the men I meet socially. I've been told by a male friend that ever since he met me he's wondered what it would be like to make love to me. This is not an emotional attraction, more a matter of curiosity. I'm sure other men have the same reaction. My personality wouldn't matter. It would take men getting to know me before they could relate to me as a woman. There are a lot of obstacles between men and me; because of the way they've grown up, it would take a bit more for them to relax and see me as a person than it would if I had the same personality but had arms. I suspect they're saying, "What would the guys think? Oh, surely, he could find someone better!" That's a likely first reaction (and possibly their reaction after they do get to know me!).

Even though it seems there are obstacles, I would like to get married again. I've never had the warm, loving relationship I've always wanted, even though I've been married twice. I don't think my handicap affected my first marriage. However, Bill was a paraplegic, so maybe that brought us closer together. My second husband was a person used to getting whatever he wanted. I think he saw me as a means of achieving his goals. He was willing to use my handicap in a way that I, up to that point, wasn't. He pushed for a film to be made of me and got me started on my speaking career. At the time, my younger son was only 3, and I wanted to stay at home and be a wife and mother. Now I'm glad that Frank made me go ahead and do things; I'm not sorry.

When I first had kids. I was worried about what they would think of me, how they would adjust to having a mother who is different. I didn't want them to think of me as anything but Mom, to be embarrassed. So as soon as they were old enough to talk about it, we did. We always laughed and made jokes about it. Now Mark is almost 16 and Matt is 11½. They bring their friends home just like any other teenagers, and we all get along well.

I like what I'm doing now. I have friends all over the country. I feel that if people can cope with me, that's fine. I'm me. There's nothing I can do, or want to do, to change it. In fact, I wouldn't if I could. If people don't like me as I am, that's their problem. I'm happy.

1986). As O'Conner (1983) states, "We should remember there is precious little evidence that, at this point in time, public support of normalization has gone so far that mentally retarded persons would be welcome or even tolerated in most 'nondeviate' social circles" (p. 192).

Most disabled adults believe the biggest barriers to full integration into society are not inaccessible buildings or the actual restrictions imposed by their disabilities, but the differential treatment afforded them by nondisabled people. Just as the terms *racism* and *sexism* indicate prejudiced, discriminatory treatment of racial groups and women, the term *handicapism* has been coined to denote biased reactions toward a person with a disability. Such reactions are based not on any qualities or actual performances of the individual, but on a presumption of what the disabled person must feel or must be like because of the disability. Biklen and Bogdan (1976) define handicapism as

> a theory and set of practices that promote unequal and unjust treatment of people because of apparent or assumed physical or mental disability. It manifests itself in relations between individuals, in social policy and cultural norms, and in the helping professions as well. Handicapism pervades our lives, but the concept of handicapism can also serve as a vital tool by which anyone can scrupulously examine personal and societal behaviors toward disabilities.

Handicapism occurs on personal, professional, and societal levels. Biklen and Bogdan (1976) describe the following examples of handicapism in personal relations.

> First, there is a tendency to presume sadness on the part of the person with a disability. For example, one woman who has a physical disability and who, incidentally smiles a lot, told us of an encounter with a man who said, "It's so good that you can still smile. Lord knows, you don't have much to be happy for."
>
> Second, there is the penchant to pity. You might have heard, "It is a tragedy that it had to happen to her; she had so much going for her." Or people sometimes tell us, "It is so good of you to give up your lives to help the poor souls." Or "My, you must be so patient to work with them. I could never do it."
>
> Third, people without disabilities sometimes focus so intensely on the disability as to make it impossible to recognize that the person with the disability is also simply another person with many of the same emotions, needs, and interests as other people. This attitude is reflected in the perennial questions, "What is it like to be deaf?" "It must be hard to get around in a wheelchair," and "You must really wish you could see sometimes."
>
> Fourth, people with disabilities are often treated as children. Notice for example, that feature films about people with mental retardation and physical handicaps are so frequently titled with first names: "Joey," "Charley," "Larry," and "Walter." We communicate this same message by calling disabled adults by first names when full names and titles would be more appropriate and by talking in a tone reserved for children.
>
> Fifth is avoidance. Having a disability often means being avoided, given the cold shoulder, and stared at from a distance. The phrases "Sorry, I have to go now," "Let's get together sometime [but not now and not any specific time]," and, "I'd like to talk but I have to run" are repeated too consistently for mere coincidence.

Sixth, we all grow up amidst a rampage of handicapist humor. It must take a psychological toll. "Did you hear the one about the moron who threw the clock out the window?" "There was a dwarf with a sawed-off cane. . . ." "Two deaf brothers went into business with each other . . . and a blind man entered the store."

Seventh, people with disabilities frequently find themselves spoken for, as if they were not present or were unable to speak for themselves. In a similar vein, people without disabilities sometimes speak about people with disabilities in front of them, again as if they were objects and not people.

In terms of personal relations, then, if you are labeled "handicapped," handicapism is your biggest burden. It is a no-win situation. You are not simply an ordinary person.

Only when the man or woman with a disability is allowed to be simply an ordinary person—given the opportunity to strive and sometimes succeed and allowed the freedom and dignity to strive and sometimes fail—can normalization become a reality.

SUMMARY

1. Adults with disabilities face numerous obstacles in day-to-day living that affect their ability to obtain and hold a job, their decision on where and how to live, their ability to use community resources, and their opportunities for social interaction.

2. Three statewide follow-up studies of graduates of secondary special education programs reported extremely high rates of unemployment. The majority of the young adults who had found competitive employment were working in part-time, low-paying jobs.

3. Supported employment is a relatively new concept recognizing that many adults with severe handicaps require ongoing support to obtain and hold a job. Supported employment is characterized by the performance of real paid work in regular, integrated work sites; it requires ongoing support from a supported work specialist.

   a. The supported employment specialist is a community-based professional who spends approximately two-thirds of her time on job sites with clients and the remaining time on tasks such as working with parents and training clients in work-related skills (e.g., transportation, money management).

   b. Various models for supported employment include the work enclave, mobile work crews, the entrepreneurial model, and the structured employment model.

4. Many adults with disabilities work in sheltered workshops that provide one, or a combination, of three kinds of programs: training for competitive employment in the community, extended or long-term employment, and work activities.

   a. Approximately 100,000 adults with disabilities attend work activity centers; 40,000 of them do not receive any pay, and the remaining 60,000 earn an average of $288 per year.

   b. Sheltered workshops and work activity centers have received increased criticism in recent years. Although the theoretical purpose of these programs is to prepare individuals for competitive employment in the community, few employees of sheltered workshops are ever placed in jobs in the community.

5. The transition of young adults from school to life in the community has become perhaps the most challenging issue in special education today. Several models for school-to-adult-life transition have been developed. Each stresses the importance of a functional secondary school curriculum that provides work experience in integrated community job sites, systematic coordination between the school and adult service agencies, parental involvement and support, and a written individualized transition plan to guide the entire process.

a. The development of career awareness and vocational skills should begin in the elementary grades for children with severe disabilities. Young children might sample different types of jobs through classroom and in-school responsibilities.

b. Middle school students should begin to spend time (e.g., 2 half-days each week) on actual community job sites, with an increasing amount of in-school instruction devoted to associated work skills, such as being on time, staying on task, and using interpersonal skills.

c. Secondary students should spend an increasing amount of time on actual community job sites, with the remaining hours of in-school instruction focusing on the functional skills needed in the adult work, domestic, community, and recreational/leisure environments toward which the student is headed.

6. Increased community-based residential services have meant greater opportunity for adults with severe disabilities to live in more normalized settings.

a. Deinstitutionalization—the movement of persons with mental retardation out of large public institutions and into smaller, community-based residences such as group homes—has greatly reduced the number of persons residing in institutions. However, there are still approximately 100,000 persons, mostly adults with severe or profound mental retardation, living in large institutions.

b. The number of group homes nearly doubled from 1977 to 1982, to a total of 6,414 homes serving more than 42,000 people.

c. In 1985 the U.S. Supreme Court unanimously ruled that communities cannot use a discriminatory zoning ordinance to prevent the establishment of group homes for persons with mental retardation.

d. Some adults with disabilities reside in foster homes. In a good foster home placement the handicapped adult can participate in the day-to-day activities of family life, receive attention from people interested in his development, and experience close personal relationships.

e. Apartment living offers the handicapped adult an even greater opportunity than group homes afford for integration into the community and interaction with non-handicapped people. There are three common forms of apartment living for adults with disabilities: the apartment cluster, the coresidence apartment, and the maximum-independence apartment.

7. Finding appropriate recreational and leisure-time activities is not easy for handicapped adults. There are too few community resources and recreation training programs.

a. Research has shown that adults with severe disabilities can learn appropriate leisure skills.

b. Many communities are now developing therapeutic recreation programs for children and adults with handicaps.

8. A continuing problem faced by many adults with disabilities is lack of acceptance as full members of society, with all of the rights, privileges, and services granted to any citizen. Handicapism—discriminatory treatment and biased reactions toward a person with a disability—occurs on personal, professional, and societal levels. It must be eliminated before normalization becomes a reality for every man and woman with a disability.

FOR MORE INFORMATION

Journals

Behavioral Residential Treatment. Published quarterly by John Wiley & Sons, Inc., 605 Third Avenue, New York, NY 10158.

Career Development for Exceptional Individuals. Published two times per year by the Division on Career Development, Council for Exceptional Children. Focuses on education and other programs for complete life experiences—including vocational, residential, and leisure activities—for handicapped children and adults.

Books

Apolloni, T., Cappuccilli, J., & Cooke, T. P. (Eds.). (1980). *Achievement in residential services for persons with disabilities: Toward excellence.* Austin, TX: Pro-Ed.

Bellamy, G. T., Horner, R. H., & Inman, D. (1979). *Vocational training of severely retarded adults.* Austin, TX: Pro-Ed.

Bercovici, S. M. (1983). *Barriers to normalization: The restrictive management of retarded persons.* Austin, TX: Pro-Ed.

Brolin, D. E. (1982). *Vocational preparation of persons with handicaps* (2nd ed.). Columbus, OH: Merrill.

Kiernan, W., & Stark, J. (Eds.). (1986). *Pathways to employment for adults with developmental disabilities.* Baltimore: Paul H. Brookes.

Rusch, F. (1986). *Competitive employment.* Baltimore: Paul H. Brookes.

Schalock, R. L. (1983). *Services for the developmentally disabled adult: Development, implementation, and evaluation.* Austin, TX: Pro-Ed.

Wehman, P. (Ed.). (1978). *Recreation programming for developmentally disabled persons.* Baltimore: University Park Press.

Wehman, P. (1981). *Competitive employment: New horizons for severely disabled people.* Baltimore: Paul H. Brookes.

Wetzel, R. J., & Hoschouer, R. L. (1984). *Residential teaching communities: Program development and staff training for developmentally disabled persons.* Glenview, IL: Scott, Foresman.

Organizations

Association on Handicapped Student Service Programs in Post-Secondary Education, P.O. Box 21192, Columbus, OH 43221. A young association devoted to providing accessibility and equal opportunities for disabled college and university students. Includes special interest groups on deafness, learning disabilities, community colleges, and rural institutions.

Division on Career Development, Council for Exceptional Children, 1920 Association Drive, Reston, VA 22091. A relatively new division of CEC that focuses on career and life-style education for handicapped persons.

Rehabilitation Research and Training Center, Virginia Commonwealth Unviersity, 1314 West Main Street, Richmond, VA 23285–0001. Project Transition Into Employment is also part of the RRTC.

POSTSCRIPT

All introductory textbooks contain a great deal of information. In that respect our book is no different from others. But we hope you have gained more than just some basic facts and information about exceptional children and special education. We hope you have examined your own attitudes toward and relationships with handicapped children and adults. We would like to repeat seven of our basic beliefs here.

1. We believe that people with handicaps have a fundamental right to live and participate in settings and programs that are as normalized as possible. And we believe that a defining feature of normalized settings and programs is the integration of handicapped and nonhandicapped participants.
2. We believe that individuals with handicaps have the right to as much independence as we can help them achieve. The ultimate effectiveness of special education should be evaluated in terms of its success in fulfilling that right.
3. We believe that special education must continue to improve its efforts to respond appropriately to all learners with special needs and attributes—the gifted and talented child, the at-risk preschooler, the culturally different exceptional child, the adult with disabilities.
4. We believe that professionals have for too long ignored the needs of parents and families of exceptional children, treating them as patients, clients, or even adversaries instead of partners. And we have failed to recognize parents as their children's first—and in many ways best—teachers. We believe that learning to work effectively with parents is one of the most important skills a special educator can acquire.
5. We believe that the efforts of special educators are most effective when they incorporate the input and services of all of the disciplines in the helping professions. We see our primary responsibility as educators to be the design and implementation of effective instruction for personal, social, vocational, and academic skills.

6. We believe that teachers must demand effectiveness from their instructional approaches. The special educator should not wait patiently for the exceptional child to learn but should modify the instructional program to improve its effectiveness.

7. We believe that exceptional children can succeed in building fuller and more independent lives in the community. We have only begun to discover the ways to improve teaching, increase learning, prevent handicapping conditions, encourage acceptance, and develop technology to compensate for disabilities. We are certain that we have not come as far as we can in helping exceptional individuals to help themselves.

We wrote that we did not necessarily expect you to agree with us, and we still don't. We've restated our views here because we believe that you are now better able to judge these statements in relation to your own beliefs. We will conclude by offering several considerations that will be important in your future role—as a member of the field or a member of the community.

A MEMBER OF THE FIELD

To you, the prospective special educator, we will be most specific, most direct. First, view special education as a *profession* and yourself as a *professional*. View yourself as someone with a set of skills and the knowledge to practice them wisely; you are different from people without your special training.

Second, it is commendable to have a commitment and a desire to help exceptional children. You may be told that you are "wonderful" or "patient" because of this. However, commitment and desire are only a beginning. What exceptional children need more than anything is teachers who are impatient—impatient with lack of progress, impatient with methods, materials, and policies that do not help their students learn and develop.

Finally, teaching exceptional children requires *systematic instruction*. It is demanding work. Prepare yourself for that work in the best way you can. Demand relevant, up-to-date information and hands-on practical experiences from your teacher-education program. Continue your education and training throughout your career. Stay on top of your field.

We do not mean to suggest that special education is a grim, thankless business. Quite the opposite—special education is an exciting, dynamic field that offers a personal satisfaction and feeling of accomplishment unequaled in most areas of endeavor. Welcome aboard!

A MEMBER OF THE COMMUNITY

The degree of success that a handicapped person enjoys in the normal routine of daily life does not depend solely on the handicapped person, or even on the special educator. In large measure, integration of handicapped citizens in contemporary society depends on the attitudes and actions of people who may have little knowledge of or experience with handicapped people. How then do people come to accept a group they do not know?

In effect, society can control who will enter and who will be kept out, much as a gatekeeper lets some visitors pass but refuses others. For a handicapped individual, society's gatekeeper may have been a doctor who urged parents to institutionalize their child or a teacher who resisted having any problem kids in class. It may have been a school psychologist who imposed a label of "trainable mentally retarded" or an employer who wanted nothing to do with hiring handicapped workers. It may have been a social worker, a school board member, a voter. Perhaps saddest of all, it may even have been a parent whose low expectations kept the gate closed.

The way that society views handicapped people influences the way that individual members of the community respond to each handicapped person. The views of society are changing—or are being changed by people who believe that our past principle of exclusion is primitive and unfair. Nowhere can we find a better example of this change than in recent court cases and laws. But everything presented in this book must translate into personal terms for those of you who will not choose careers in special education. Handicapped people *are* different from nonhandicapped people, but they are more *like* nonhandicapped people than unlike them. And the conclusion we hope you have reached is this: every handicapped child and adult must be treated as an individual, not as a member of a category or a labeled group.

IN SUM

Viewing every handicapped individual as a person first and a handicapped person second may be the most important step in integrating that individual into the mainstream of community life. But a change in attitude will not diminish the person's handicap. What it will do is give us a new outlook—more objective and more positive—and will allow us to see a handicap as a set of *special needs*. And viewing handicapped people as individuals with special needs tells us much about how to respond to them—which is the essence of special education.

William Lee Heward grew up in Three Oaks, Michigan. He majored in psychology and sociology as an undergraduate at Western Michigan University and earned his doctorate in special education at the University of Massachusetts.

Bill was a teacher and administrator in an early intervention program for behaviorally handicapped children and their parents. He joined the faculty of the Ohio State University in 1975, and is currently a professor in the Department of Educational Services and Research. His research on the design and analysis of effective methods of instruction for students with learning and behavior handicaps has appeared in many of the field's professional journals, including *Exceptional Children, Mental Retardation, Learning Disability Quarterly, Behavioral Disorders,* and the *Journal of Applied Behavior Analysis.* Bill has co-authored five textbooks, including *Applied Behavior Analysis* (Merrill, 1987), and served as co-editor of *Focus on Behavior Analysis in Education* (Merrill, 1984). He has also written for popular market. His book *Some Are Called Clowns* chronicled his five summers as a pitcher with the Indianapolis Clowns, the last of the "barnstorming" baseball teams.

Bill and his family spent part of 1986 in Portugal and Great Britain where Bill lectured as a Fulbright scholar in special education. In 1985 he received Ohio State's highest honor for teaching, the Alumni Association Distinguished Teaching Award.

Michael Dean Orlansky was born in Philadelphia and raised in New York City. He earned a bachelor's degree from Yale University and a masters degree from Boston College specializing in the education of deaf-blind and multihandicapped children. At the University of Idaho, Mike's Ph.D. dissertation evaluated the effectiveness of two different teaching approaches on the achievement and attitudes of students in an introductory college special education course.

Mike taught children with severe and multiple handicaps for several years at the Perkins School for the Blind in Massachusetts, and at the Washington State School for the Blind. He worked with deaf-blind children and their parents as a regional education specialist in the Northwest. He served in the U.S. Air Force and the U.S. Coast Guard Reserve.

After five years as a professor at the University of Virginia, Mike joined the faculty at Ohio State in 1982, where he is currently an associate professor in the Department of Educational Services and Research. His research has been published in such journals as *Exceptional Children, Child Development, Journal of Hearing and Speech Disorders,* and *Applied Psycholinguistics.* Among Mike's publications are two other books, *Mainstreaming the Visually Impaired Child* and *Voices: Interviews with Handicapped People* (Merrill, 1981), co-authored with Bill Heward. He serves as executive editor of the journal *Education of the Visually Handicapped.*

Mike has given presentations at international special education conferences in Canada, France, and West Germany. He also was recently a Fulbright scholar in special education at the University of Zagreb, Yugoslavia.

REFERENCES

Abt Associates. (1974). *Assessment of selected resources for severely handicapped children and youth* (Vol. 1). Cambridge, MA: Author.

Accreditation Council for Facilities for the Mentally Retarded. (1971). *Standards for residential facilities for the mentally retarded.* Chicago: Joint Commission on Accreditation of Hospitals.

Achenbach, T. M. (1974). *Developmental psychopathology.* New York: Ronald Press.

Ada, A. F. (1986). Creative education for bilingual teachers. *Harvard Educational Review, 56,* 386–394.

Adams, G., Beck, R., Chandler, L., & Livingston, S. S. (1977). The need for adjunctive services in the management of severely and profoundly handicapped individuals: Part II. The infant diagnostic classroom—a community resource. In N. G. Haring & L. J. Brown (Eds.), *Teaching the severely handicapped* (Vol. 2). New York: Grune & Stratton.

Adler, S. (1978). Behavior management: A nutritional approach to the behaviorally disordered and learning disabled child. *Journal of Learning Disabilities, 11,* 651–656.

Aiello, B. (1976, April 25). Up from the basement: A teacher's story. *New York Times,* p. 14.

Alber, M. B. (1974). *Listening: A curriculum guide for teachers of visually impaired students.* Springfield: Illinois Office of Education.

Alberto, P., & Troutman, A. (1982). *Applied behavior analysis for teachers: Influencing student performance.* Columbus, OH: Merrill.

Alberto, P., & Troutman A. P. (1986). *Applied behavior analysis for teachers* (2nd ed.). Columbus, OH: Merrill.

Algozzine, B. (1980). The disturbing child: A matter of opinion. *Behavior Disorders, 5,* 112–115.

Algozzine, B., & Korinek, L. (1985). Where is special education for students with high prevalence handicaps going? *Exceptional Children, 51,* 388–394.

Algozzine, B., & Ysseldyke, J. (1981). Special education services for normal children: Better safe than sorry? *Exceptional Children, 48,* 238–243.

Allen, D. A., & Affleck, G. (1985). Are we stereotyping parents? A postscript to Blacher. *Mental Retardation, 23,* 200–202.

Allen, J. I. (1980). Jogging can modify disruptive behaviors. *Teaching Exceptional Children, 12*(2), 66–70.

Allen, K. E. (1980a). The language impaired child in the preschool: The role of the teacher. *The Directive Teacher, 2*(3), 6–10.

Allen, K. E. (1980b). *Mainstreaming in early childhood education.* Albany, NY: Delmar.

Alley, G., & Deschler, D. (1979). *Teaching the learning disabled adolescent: Strategies and methods.* Denver: Love.

Allsop, J. (1980). Mainstreaming physically handicapped students. *Journal of Research and Development in Education, 13*(4), 37–44.

Alter, M., Gottlieb, B. W., & Gottlieb, J. (1986). Dimensions of assessment of severely and profoundly mentally retarded persons. In P. J. Lazarus & S. S. Strichart (Eds.), *Psychoeducational evaluation of children and adolescents with low-incidence handicaps* (pp. 123–153). Orlando, FL: Grune & Stratton.

Alzate, G. (1978). Analysis of testing problems in Spanish speaking children. In A. H. Fink (Ed.), *International perspectives on future special education.* Reston, VA: Council for Exceptional Children.

American Academy of Ophthalmology. (1985). Health alert. *Journal of Visual Impairment & Blindness, 79,* 234.

American Association for the Study of the Feeble-Minded, 29, 58–70. (1924).

American Council on Science and Health. (1979, May). *Diet and hyperactivity: Is there a relationship?* New York: Author.

603

American Printing House for the Blind. (1985). *Distribution of January, 1985, quota registrations by school, grades, and reading media.* Louisville, KY: Author.

American Psychiatric Association. (1980). *Diagnostic and statistical manual of mental disorders* (3rd ed.). Washington, DC: Author.

American Speech-Language-Hearing Association. (1983). Position paper on social dialects. *ASHA, 25*(9), 23–24.

Ames, L. B. (1977). Learning disabilities: Time to check our roadmaps? *Journal of Learning Disabilities, 10*, 328–330.

Ammer, J. J., & Littleton, B. R. (1983, April). *Parent advocacy: Now more than ever active involvement in education decisions.* Paper presented at the 61st Annual International Convention of the Council for Exceptional Children, Detroit, MI.

Anderson, E. (1985). A. M. Club. In *Teaching: Behavioral Disordered Youth* (Vol. 1, pp. 12–16). Reston, VA: Council for Children with Behavior Disorders.

Anderson, L. E. (Ed.). (1970). *Helping the adolescent with the hidden handicap.* Los Angeles: California Association for Neurologically Handicapped Children.

Anderson, M. J., & Ellis, R. H. (1980). Indian American: The reservation client. In N. A. Vacc & J. P. Wittmer (Eds.), *Let me be me: Special populations and the helping professional* (pp. 107–127). Muncie, IN: Accelerated Development.

Anderson, R. M., Greer, J. G., & Rich, H. L. (1982). An introduction to severely and multiply handicapped persons. In J. G. Greer, R. M. Anderson, & S. J. Odle (Eds.), *Strategies for helping severely and multiply handicapped citizens.* Baltimore: University Park Press.

Anderson-Inman, L. (1986). Bridging the gap: Student-centered strategies for promoting the transfer of learning. *Exceptional Children, 52*, 562–572.

Anthony, D. (1971). *Seeing essential English.* Anaheim, CA: Anaheim School District.

Apolloni, T., & Cooke, T. P. (Eds.). (1981). *California housing resources for persons with special developmental needs.* Unpublished manuscript, California Institute on Human Services at Sonoma State University.

Arakawa, J. (1981). Minority voices: Neither part of a double disabiity is the whole person. *Disabled USA, 4*(8), 1.

Arnold, L. E., Christopher, J., Huestis, R. D., & Smeltzer, D. J. (1978). Megavitamins for minimal brain dysfunction: A placebo controlled study. *Journal of the American Medical Association, 240*, 2642–2643.

Arnold, W. R., & Brungardt, T. M. (1983). *Juvenile misconduct and delinquency.* Boston: Houghton Mifflin.

Assael, D. (Ed.). (1985). *Directory, 1984–85 edition: Handicapped Children's Early Education Program.* Chapel Hill: University of North Carolina, Technical Assistance Development System.

Atkins, C. P., & Cartwright, L. R. (1982). National survey: Preferred language elicitation procedures used in five age categories. *Journal of the American Speech and Hearing Association, 24*, 321–323.

Bachmann, W. (1971). *Influence of selected variables upon economic adaptation of orthopedically handicapped and other health impaired.* Unpublished doctoral dissertation, University of the Pacific.

Baer, D. M. (1981). *How to plan for generalization.* Lawrence, KS: H & H Enterprises.

Baer, D. M. (1984). We already have multiple jeopardy; why try for unending jeopardy? In W. L. Heward, T. E. Heron, D. S. Hill, & J. Trap-Porter (Eds.). *Focus on behavior analysis in education.* Columbus, OH: Merrill.

Baer, D. M., Wolf, M. M., & Risley, T. R. (1968). Some current dimensions of applied behavior analysis. *Journal of Applied Behavior Analysis 1*, 91–97.

Bagnato, S. J., Neisworth, J. T., & Capone, A. (1986). Curriculum-based assessment of the young exceptional child: Rationale and review. *Topics in Early Childhood Special Education, 6*, 97–110.

Bailey, D. B., & Wolery, M. (1984). *Teaching infants and preschoolers with handicaps.* Columbus, OH: Merrill.

Baker, B. L., Brightman, A. J., & Hinshaw, S. P. (1980). *Steps to independence series: Toward independent living.* Champaign, IL: Research Press.

Baker, B. L., Seltzer, G. B., & Seltzer, M. M. (1977). *As close as possible: Community residences for retarded adults.* Boston: Little, Brown.

Baldwin, A. Y. (1978). Curriculum and methods: What is the difference? In A. Y. Baldwin, G. H. Gear, & L. J. Lucita (Eds.), *Educational planning for the gifted: Overcoming cultural, geographic, and socioeconomic barriers.* Reston, VA: Council for Exceptional Children.

Baldwin, A. Y., Gear, G. H., & Lucita, L. J. (Eds.).(1978). *Educational planning for the gifted: Overcoming cultural, geographic, and socioeconomic barriers.* Reston, VA: Council for Exceptional Children.

Balow, I. H., Farr, R., Hogan, T. P., & Prescott, G. A. (1978). Metropolitan Achievement Tests: 1978 Edition. New York: Psychological Corporation.

Banks, J. A. (1977). *Multiethnic education: Practices and promises.* Bloomington, IN: Phi Delta Kappa Educational Foundation.

Bankson, N. W. (1982). The speech and language impaired. In E. L. Meyen (Ed.), *Exceptional children and youth* (2nd ed.). Denver: Love.

Barnett, W. S. (1986). Definition and classification of mental retardation: A reply to Zigler, Balla, and Hodapp. *American Journal of Mental Deficiency, 91*, 111–116.

Barney, L. G., & Landis, C. L. (1987). Development differences in communication. In J. T. Neisworth & S. J. Bagnato, (Eds.), *The young exceptional child: Early development and education* (pp. 262–296). New York: Macmillan.

Baroff, G. S. (1982). Predicting the prevalence of mental retardation in individual catchment areas. *Mental Retardation, 20*, 133–135.

Barr, M. W. (1913). *Mental defectives: Their history, treatment, and training.* Philadelphia: Blakiston.

Barraga, N. C. (1964). *Increased visual behavior in low vision children.* New York: American Foundation for the Blind.

Barraga, N. C. (1970). *Teacher's guide for development of visual learning abilities and utilization of low vision.* Louisvile: American Printing House for the Blind.

Barraga, N. C. (1980). *Source book on low vision.* Louisville: American Printing House for the Blind.

Barraga, N. C. (1983). *Visual handicaps and learning* (rev. ed.). Austin, TX: Exceptional Resources.

Barrera, R. D., & Sulzer-Azaroff, B. (1983). An alternating treatment comparison of oral and total communication training programs with echolalic autistic children. *Journal of Applied Behavior Analysis, 16,* 379–394.

Barsch, R. H. (1969). *The parent-teacher partnership.* Arlington, VA: Council for Exceptional Children.

Barton, L. E., & LaGrow, S. J. (1985). Reduction of stereotypic responding in three visually impaired children. *Education of the Visually Handicapped, 6,* 145–181.

Batshaw, M. L., & Perret, Y. M. (1981). *Children with handicaps: A medical primer.* Baltimore: Paul H. Brookes.

Batshaw, M. L., & Perret, Y. M. (1986). *Children with handicaps: A medical primer* (2nd ed.). Baltimore: Paul H. Brookes.

Bayley, N. (1969). *Bayley's Scales of Infant Development.* New York: Psychological Corporation.

Beatty, L., Madden, R., & Gardner, E. (1966). *Stanford Diagnostic Arithmetic Test.* New York: Harcourt Brace Jovanovich.

Beck, R. (1977). The need for adjunctive services in the management of severely and profoundly handicapped individuals: A view from primary care. In N. G. Haring & L. Brown (Eds.), *Teaching the severely handicapped* (Vol. 2). New York: Grune & Stratton.

Becker, W. C. (1964). Consequences of different kinds of parental discipline. In M. L. Hoffman & L. W. Hoffman (Eds.), *Review of child development research* (Vol. 1). New York: Russell Sage Foundation.

Becker, W. C. (1971). *Parents are teachers.* Champaign, IL: Research Press.

Becker, W. C., & Engelmann, S. E. (1976). *Technical report 1976–1.* Eugene: University of Oregon.

Becker, W. C., Engelmann, S., & Thomas, D. R. (1971). *Teaching: A course in applied psychology.* Chicago: Science Research Associates.

Beckman-Bell, P. (1981). Child-related stress in families of handicapped children. *Topics in Early Childhood Special Education, 1,* 45–53.

Belgrave, F. Z., & Mills, J. (1981). Effect upon desire for social interaction with a physically disabled person of mentioning the disability in different contexts. *Journal of Applied Social Psychology, 11,* 44–57.

Bellamy, G. T. (1985). Transition progress: Comments on Hasazi, Gordon, and Roe. *Exceptional Children, 51,* 474–477.

Bellamy, G. T., & Horner, R. H. (1987). Beyond high school: Residential and employment options after graduation. In M. Snell (Ed.), *Systematic instruction of persons with severe handicaps* (3rd ed., pp. 491–510). Columbus, OH: Merrill.

Bellamy, G. T., Horner, R. H., & Inman, D. (1979). *Vocational training of severely retarded adults.* Baltimore: Paul H. Brookes.

Bellamy, G. T., Rhodes, L. E., Wilcox, B., Albin, J. M., Mank, D. M., Boles, S. M., Horner, R. H., Collins, M., & Turner, J. (1984). Quality and equality in employment services for adults with severe disabilities. *Journal of the Association for Persons with Severe Handicaps, 9,* 270–277.

Bellamy, G. T., & Wilcox, B. (1982). Secondary education for severely handicapped students: Guidelines for quality services. In K. P. Lynch, W. E. Kiernan, & J. A. Stark (Eds.), *Prevocational and vocational education for special needs youth: A blueprint for the 1980s.* Baltimore: Paul H. Brookes.

Bennett, L. M., & Hensen, F. O. (1977). *Keeping in touch with parents: The teacher's best friend.* Hingham, MA: Teaching Resources.

Bennett, R. E., & Ragosta, M. (1984). *A research context for studying admission tests and handicapped populations.* Princeton, NJ: Educational Testing Service.

Bennett, W. J. (1986). *First lessons: A report on elementary education in America.* Washington, DC: U.S. Department of Education.

Bensberg, G. J., & Sigelman, C. K. (1976). Definitions and prevalence. In L. L. Lloyd (Ed.), *Communication assessment and intervention strategies.* Baltimore: University Park Press.

Berg, F. S. (1986). Characteristics of the target population. In F. S. Berg, J. C. Blair, S. H. Viehweg, & A. Wilson-Vlotman, *Educational audiology for the hard of hearing child* (pp. 1–24). Orlando, FL: Grune & Stratton.

Berman, J. L., & Ford, R. (1970). Intelligence quotients and intelligence loss in patients with phenylketonuria and some variant states. *Journal of Pediatrics, 77,* 764–770.

Bernick, M. (1986). Illiteracy and inner-city unemployment. *Phi Delta Kappan, 67*(5), 364–367.

Bernthal, J. E., & Bankson, N. W. (1986). Phonologic disorders: An overview. In J. M. Costello & A. L. Holland (Eds.), *Handbook of speech and language disorders* (pp. 3–24). San Diego: College-Hill.

Bierly, K. (1978). Public Law 94–142: Answers to the questions you're asking. *Instructor, 87*(9), 63–67.

Bigge, J. L. (1982). *Teaching individuals with physical and multiple disabilities.* (2nd ed.). Columbus, OH: Merrill.

Bigge, J. L., & Sirvis, B. (1986). Physical and health impairments. In N. G. Haring & L. McCormick (Eds.), *Exceptional children and youth* (4th ed., pp. 313–354). Columbus, OH: Merrill.

Bijou, S. W. (1966). A functional analysis of retarded development. In N. R. Ellis (Ed.), *International review of research in mental retardation* (Vol. 1). New York: Academic Press.

Bijou, S. W., & Dunitz-Johnson, E. (1981). Interbehavior analysis of developmental disabilities. *Psychological Record, 31*, 305–329.

Biklen, D. (1985). *Achieving the complete school: Strategies for effective mainstreaming.* New York: Teachers College Press.

Biklen, D., & Bogdan, R. (1976). Handicapism in America. *WIN.*

Birenbaum, A. (1986). Symposium overview: Community programs for people with mental retardation. *Mental Retardation, 24*, 145–146.

Bishop, V. E. (1986). Identifying the components of successful mainstreaming. *Journal of Visual Impairment & Blindness, 80*, 939–946.

Bishop, W. (1968). Successful teachers of the gifted. *Exceptional Children, 39*, 317–325.

Blacher, J. (1984). Sequential stages of adjustment to the birth of a child with handicaps: Fact or artifact? *Mental Retardation, 22*, 55–68.

Blackburn, A. C., & Erickson, D. D. (1986). Predictable crises of the gifted student. *Journal of Counseling and Development, 64*, 552–555.

Blackstone, M. (1981). How parents can affect communitization, or, what do you mean I'm a troublemaker? In C. H. Hansen (Ed.), *Severely handicapped persons in the community.* Seattle: University of Washington, PDAS.

Blasch, B. B. (1978). Blindisms: Treatment by punishment and reward in laboratory and natural settings. *Journal of Visual Impairment & Blindness, 72*, 215–230.

Blasco, P. A. (1986). Medical aspects of motor disabilities. In M. J. Hanson & S. R. Harris, *Teaching the young child with motor delays: A guide for parents and professionals* (pp. 11–20). Austin, TX: Pro-Ed.

Blatt, B. (1976). *Revolt of the idiots: A story.* Glen Ridge, NJ: Exceptional Press.

Blatt, B. (1987). *The conquest of mental retardation.* Austin, TX: Pro-Ed.

Blatt, B., & Kaplan, F. (1966). *Christmas in purgatory: A photographic essay on mental retardation.* Boston: Allyn & Bacon.

Bleck, E. E. (1979). Integrating the physically handicapped child. *Journal of School Health, 49*, 141–146.

Bliton, G., & Schroeder, H. J. (1986). *The new future for children with substantial handicaps: The second wave of LRE.* Bloomington: Indiana University Developmental Training Center.

Bloom, B. S. (1985). Generalizations about talent development. In B. S. Bloom (Ed.), *Development of talent in young people* (pp. 507–549). New York: Ballantine Books.

Bloom, B. S. (Ed.). *Taxonomy of educational objectives: Handbook I. Cognitive domain.* New York: David McKay.

Bloom, B. S. (Ed.), (1985). Developing talent in young people. New York: Ballantine Books.

Bloom, L., & Lahey, M. (1978). *Language development and language disorders.* New York: John Wiley.

Bogdan, R. (1986). Exhibiting mentally retarded people for amusement and profit, 1850–1940. *American Journal of Mental Deficiency, 91*, 120–126.

Boles, S. M., Bellamy, G. T., Horner, R. H., & Mank, D. M. (1984). Specialized training program: The structured employment model. In S. C. Paine, G. T. Bellamy, & B. Wilcox (Eds.), *Human services that work: From innovation to standard practice* (pp. 181–208). Baltimore: Paul H. Brookes.

Bonvillian, J. D., & Nelson, K. E. (1976). Sign language acquisition in a mute autistic boy. *Journal of Speech and Hearing Disorders, 41*, 339–347.

Bonvillian, J. D., Orlansky, M. D., & Novack, L. L. (1983). Sign language acquisition and early cognitive and motor development. *Child Development, 54*(6), 1435–1445.

Boone, D. R. (1977). Our profession: Where are we? *Journal of the American Speech and Hearing Association, 19*, 3–6.

Bornstein, H. (1974). Signed English: A manual approach to English language development. *Journal of Speech and Hearing Disorders, 3*, 330–343.

Boshes, B., & Myklebust, H. R. (1964). A neurological and behavioral study of children with learning disorders. *Neurology, 14*, 7–12.

Bostow, D. E., & Bailey, J. (1969). Modification of severe disruptive and aggressive behavior using brief time-out and reinforcement procedures. *Journal of Applied Behavior Analysis, 2*, 31–37.

Bower, E. M. (1969). *Early identification of emotionally handicapped children in school* (2nd ed.). Springfield, IL: Charles C Thomas.

Bower, E. M. (1981). *Early identification of emotionally handicapped children in school* (3rd ed.). Springfield, IL: Charles C Thomas.

Bower, E. M. (1982). Defining emotional disturbance: Public policy and research. *Psychology in the Schools, 19*, 55–60.

Bower, E. M., & Lambert, N. M. (1962). *A process for in-school screening of children with emotional handicaps.* Princeton, NJ: Educational Testing Service.

Braddock, D., & Heller, T. (1985). The closure of mental retardation institutions II: Implications. *Mental Retardation, 23*, 222–229.

Braddock, D., Hemp, R., & Howes, R. (1986). Direct costs of institutional care in the United States. *Mental Retardation, 24*, 9–17.

Bradley, V. (1978). *Deinstitutionalization of developmentally disabled persons: A conceptual analysis and guide.* Baltimore: University Park Press.

Brandwein, H. (1973). The battered child: A definite and significant factor in mental retardation. *Mental Retardation, 11*, 50–51.

Brazelton, T. B. (1973). *Neonatal assessment scale.* Philadelphia: J. B. Lippincott.

Bricker, D. D. (1986). An analysis of early intervention programs: Attendant issues and future directions. In R. J.

Morris & B. Blatt (Eds.), *Special education: Research and trends* (pp. 28–65). New York: Pergamon Press.

Brickey, M. P., Campbell, K. M., & Browning, L. J. (1985). A five-year follow-up of sheltered workshop employees placed in competitive jobs. *Mental Retardation, 23,* 67–73.

Brigance, A. H. (1982). *K & 1 screen for kindergarten and first grade.* N. Billerica, MA: Curriculum Associates.

Brinker, R. P. (1985). Interactions between severely mentally retarded students and other students in integrated and segregated public school settings. *American Journal of Mental Deficiency, 89,* 587–594.

Bronfenbrenner, U. (1974). *A report on longitudinal evaluations of preschool programs: Is early intervention effective?* (Vol. 2). Washington, DC: U.S. Department of Health, Education and Welfare.

Bronicki, G. J., & Turnbull, A. P. (1987). Family-professional interactions. In M. E. Snell (Ed.), *Systematic instruction of persons with severe handicaps* (3rd ed., pp. 9–35). Columbus, OH: Merrill.

Bronston, W. (1980). Matters of design. In T. Apolloni, J. Cappuccilli, & T. P. Cooke (Eds.), *Achievements in residential services for persons with disabilities: Toward excellence.* Baltimore: University Park Press.

Browder, D. M., & Snell, M. E. (1987). Functional academics. In M. E. Snell (Ed.), *Systematic instruction of persons with severe handicaps* (3rd ed., pp. 436–468). Columbus, OH: Merrill.

Brower, I. C. (1983). Counseling Vietnamese. In D. R. Atkinson, G. Morten, & D. W. Sue, *Counseling American minorities* (2nd ed.) (pp. 107-121). Dubuque, IA: William C. Brown.

Brown, B. E. (1982). The influence of postural adjustment of physically handicapped children on teachers' perceptions (Doctoral dissertation, Teachers College of Columbia University, 1981). *Dissertation Abstracts International, 42,* 4393A. (University Microfilms No. 8207305)

Brown, F. (1987). Meaningful assessment of people with severe and profound handicaps. In M. E. Snell (Ed.), *Systematic instruction of persons with severe handicaps* (3rd ed., pp. 39–63). Columbus, OH: Merrill.

Brown, J. R. (1982). Assessment of the culturally different and disadvantaged child. In G. Ulrey & S. J. Rogers (Eds.), *Psychological assessment of handicapped infants and young children* (pp. 163–171). New York: Thieme-Stratton.

Brown, L. (1986). Preface. In R. H. Horner, L. H. Meyer, & H. D. B. Fredericks (Eds.), *Education of learners with severe handicaps: Exemplary service strategies* (pp. xv–xvii). Baltimore: Paul H. Brookes.

Brown, L., Branston-McClean, M. B., Baumgart, D., Vincent, L., Falvey, M., & Shroeder, J. (1979). Using the characteristics of current and subsequent least restrictive environments in the development of curricular content for severely handicapped students. *AAESPH Review, 4,* 407–424.

Brown, L., Shiraga, B., York, J., Kessler, K., Strohm, B., Rogan, P., Sweet, M., Zanella, K., VanDeventer, P., & Loomis, R. (1984). Integrated work opportunities for adults with severe handicaps: The extended training option. *Journal of the Association for Persons with Severe Handicaps, 9,* 262–269.

Brown, L., Shiraga, B., York, J., Kessler, K., Strohm, B., Rogan, P., Sweet, M., Zanella, K., VanDeventer, P., & Loomis, R. (1984). Integrated work opportunities for adults with severe handicaps: The extended training option. *Journal of the Association for Persons with Severe Handicaps, 9,* 262–269.

Brown, N. P. (1982). CAMEO: Computer-assisted management of educational objectives. *Exceptional Children, 49,* 151–153.

Brown, S. C. (1986). Etiological trends, characteristics, and distributions. In A. N. Schildroth & M. A. Karchmer (Eds.), *Deaf children in America* (pp. 33–54). San Diego: College-Hill.

Bruch, C. B. (1975). Assessment of creativity in culturally different children. *The Gifted Child Quarterly, 19,* 164–74.

Bruening, S. E., & Davis, V. J. (1981). Reinforcement effects on the intelligence test performance of institutional retarded adults: Behavioral analysis, directional control, and implications for habilitation. *Applied Research on Mental Retardation, 2,* 307–321.

Bryan, T. H., & Bryan, J. H. (1978). Social interactions of learning disabled children. *Learning Disability Quarterly, 1,* 107–115.

Bryan, W. H., & Jeffrey, D. L. (1982). Education of visually handicapped students in the regular classroom. *Texas Tech Journal of Education, 9,* 125–131.

Bryant, N. D. (1972). Subject variables: Definition, incidence, characteristics, and correlates. In N. D. Bryant & C. E. Kass (Eds.), *Leadership training institute in learning disabilities* (Vol. 1). Washington, DC: Bureau of Education for the Handicapped.

Bull, G. L., & Rushakoff, G. E. (1987). Computers and speech and language disordered individuals. In J. D. Lindsey (Ed.), *Computers and exceptional individuals* (pp. 83–104). Columbus, OH: Merrill.

Bullis, M., & Bull, B. (1986). *Review of research on adolescents and adults with deaf-blindness.* Washington, DC: Catholic University of America, DATA Institute.

Burchard, J. D., & Harig, P. T. (1976). Behavior modification and juvenile delinquency. In H. Leitenberg (Ed.), *Handbook of behavior modification and behavior therapy.* Englewood Cliffs, NJ: Prentice-Hall.

Buros, O. K. (1978). *The eighth mental measurement yearbook.* Highland Park, NJ: Gryphon.

Burstein, N. D. (1986). The effects of classroom organization on mainstreamed preschool children. *Exceptional Children, 52,* 525–534.

Buss, A. H. (1966). *Psychopathology.* New York: John Wlley.

Cain, L. F. (1976). Parent groups: Their role in a better life for the handicapped. *Exceptional Children, 42,* 432–437.

Callahan, C. M. (1979). The gifted and talented woman. In H. H. Passow (Ed.). *The gifted and talented: Their education and development.* Chicago: University of Chicago Press.

Calvert, D. R. (1986). Speech in perspective. In D. M. Luterman (Ed.), *Deafness in perspective* (pp. 167–191). San Diego: College-Hill.

Campbell, P. B. (1979). *Diagnosing the problem: Sex stereotyping in special education.* Newton, MA: Education Development Center.

Campbell, P. H. (1987). Physical management and handling procedures with students with movement dysfunction. In M. E. Snell (Ed.), *Systematic instruction of persons with severe handicaps* (3rd ed., pp. 174–187). Columbus, OH: Merrill.

Campbell, V., Smith, R., & Wool, R. (1982). Adaptive Behavior Scale differences in scores of mentally retarded individuals referred for institutionalization and those never referred. *American Journal of Mental Deficiency, 86,* 425–428.

Cansler, D. P., Martin, G. H., & Valand, M. C. (1975). *Working with families.* Winston-Salem, NC: Kaplan Press.

Cardenas, J. A. (1986). The role of native-language instruction in bilingual education. *Phi Delta Kappan, 67*(5), 359–363.

Carin, A., & Sund, R. B. (1978). *Creative questioning and sensitive listening techniques: A self-concept approach* (2nd ed.). Columbus, OH: Merrill.

Carrow, E. (1974). Carrow Elicited Language Inventory. Austin, TX: Author.

Cartledge, G., & Milburn, J. F. (1986). *Teaching social skills to children: Innovative approaches* (2nd ed.). New York: Pergamon.

Cassidy, J., & Vukelich, C. (1978). Survival reading for parents and kids: A parent education program. *The Reading Teacher, 31,* 638–641.

Castaneda, A. (1976). Cultural democracy and the educational needs of Mexican American children. In R. L. Jones (Ed.), *Mainstreaming and the minority child.* Reston, VA: Council for Exceptional Children.

Casto, G., & Mastropieri, M. A. (1986). The efficacy of early intervention programs: A meta-analysis. *Exceptional Children, 52,* 417–424.

Cavallaro, C. C., & Poulson, C. L. (1985). Teaching language to handicapped children in natural settings. *Education and Treatment of Children, 8,* 1–24.

Cavan, R. S., & Ferdinand, T. N. (1975). *Juvenile delinquency* (3rd ed.). New York: J. B. Lippincott.

Cawley, J. F., & Webster, R. E. (1981). Reading and behavior disorders. In G. Brown, R. L. McDowell, & J. Smith (Eds.), *Educating adolescents with behavior disorders.* Columbus, OH: Merrill.

Center for Residential and Community Services. (1983). *1982 National Survey of Residential Facilities.* Minneapolis: University of Minnesota.

Center on Human Policy. (1986, December). Positive interventions for challenging behavior. *The Association for Persons with Severe Handicaps Newsletter, 12*(12), 44.

Certo, N., Haring, N., & York, R. (1983). *Public school integration of severely handicapped students.* Baltimore: Paul H. Brookes.

Chan, K. S., & Rueda, R. (1979). Poverty and culture in education: Separate but equal. *Exceptional Children, 45,* 421–428.

Chaney, C., & Frodyma, D. A. (1982). A noncategorical program for preschool language development. *TEACHING Exceptional Children, 14,* 152–155.

Chapman, E. K. (1978). *Visually handicapped children and young people.* London: Routledge & Kegan Paul.

Chase, J. B. (1986a). Application of assessment techniques to the totally blind. In P. J. Lazarus & S. S. Strichart (Eds.), *Psychoeducational evaluation of children and adolescents with low-incidence handicaps* (pp. 75–102). Orlando, FL: Grune & Stratton.

Chase, J. B. (1986b). Psychoeducational assessment of visually-impaired learners. In P. J. Lazarus & S. S. Strichart (Eds.), *Psychoeducational evaluation of children and adolescents with low-incidence handicaps* (pp. 41–74). Orlando, FL: Grune & Stratton.

Chelser, B. (1982). ACLD Vocational Committee completes survey on LD adult. *ACLD Newsbriefs, 5,* 20–23.

Childs, R. E. (1981). Perceptions of mainstreaming by regular classroom teachers who teach mainstreamed educable mentally retarded students in the public schools. *Education and Training of the Mentally Retarded, 16,* 225–227.

Chinn, P. C., & Kamp, S. H. (1982). Cultural diversity and exceptionality. In N. G. Haring (Ed.), *Exceptional children and youth* (3rd ed.). Columbus, OH: Merrill.

Chinn, P. C., & McCormick, L. (1986). Cultural diversity and exceptionality. In N. G. Haring & L. McCormick (Eds.), *Exceptional children and youth* (4th ed., pp. 95–117). Columbus, OH: Merrill.

Ciaranello, R. D., Vandenberg, S. R., & Anders, T. F. (1982). Intrinsic and extrinsic determinants of neuronal development: Relation to infantile autism. *Journal of Autism and Developmental Disabilities, 12,* 115–146.

Clark, B. (1983). *Growing up gifted* (2nd ed.). Columbus, OH: Merrill.

Clark, G. M., & Knowlton, H. E. (Eds.). (1987). Special issue: The transition from school to adult life. *Exceptional Children, 53.*

Clarke, B., & Leslie, P. (1980). Environmental alternatives for the hearing handicapped. In J. W. Schifani, R. M. Anderson, & S. J. Odle (Eds.), *Implementing learning in the least restrictive environment: Handicapped children in the mainstream.* Baltimore: University Park Press.

Classification of AAMD from the Committee on Definition and Terminology of CEC-MR. (1979). *Education and Training of the Mentally Retarded, 14,* 74–76.

Clausen. J. A. (1967). Mental deficiency: Development of a concept. *American Journal of Mental Deficiency, 71,* 727–745.

Clausen, J. A. (1972). The continuing problem of defining mental deficiency. *Journal of Special Education, 6,* 97–106.

Clearinghouse for Offender Literacy Programs. (1975). *Literacy: Problems and solutions: A handbook for correctional educators.* Washington, DC: American Bar Association.

Clements, S. D. (1966). *Minimal brain dysfunction in children* (NINDS Monograph No. 3, Public Health Service Bulletin No. 1415). Washington, DC: U.S. Department of Health, Education and Welfare.

Cochran, W. E., Sran, P. K., & Varano, G. A. (1977). The relocation syndrome in mentally retarded individuals. *Mental Retardation, 15,* 10–12.

Coffman, T. L., & Harris, M. C. (1980). Transition shock and adjustments of mentally retarded persons. *Mental Retardation, 18,* 28–32.

Cohen, H. L. (1973). Behavior modification and socially deviant youth. In C. E. Thoresen (Ed.), *Behavior modification in education.* Chicago: University of Chicago Press.

Cohen, S., Semmes, M., & Guralnick, M. J. (1979). Public Law 94–142 and the education of preschool handicapped children. *Exceptional Children, 4,* 279–285.

Cohen, S., & Warren, R. D. (1985). *Respite care: Principles, programs, and policies.* Austin, TX: Pro-Ed.

Cole, E. B., & Paterson, M. M. (1986). Assessment and treatment of phonologic disorders. In J. M. Costello & A. L. Holland (Eds.), *Handbook of speech and language disorders* (pp. 93–127). San Diego: College-Hill.

Comptroller General of the United States. (1977, October 3). *Preventing mental retardation—more can be done.* Report to Congress.

Condon, M. E., York, R., Heal, L. W., & Fortschneider, J. (1986). Acceptance of severely handicapped students by nonhandicapped peers. *Journal of the Association for Persons with Severe Handicaps, 11,* 216–219.

Cone, J. D., Delawyer, D. D., & Wolfe, V. V. (1985). Assessing parent participation: The Parent/Family Involvement Index. *Exceptional Children, 51,* 417–424.

Cone, T. E., Wilson, L. R., Bradley, C. M., & Reese, J. H. (1985). Characteristics of LD students in Iowa: An empirical investigation. *Learning Disability Quarterly, 8,* 211–220.

Congress approves program for preschool handicapped. (1978). *Report on Preschool Education, 22*(10), 10.

Congressional Record, H-12179. (1978, October 10).

Connolly, A., Natchman, W., & Prichett, E. (1973). *Key Math Diagnostic Arithmetic Test.* Circle Pines, MN: American Guidance Service.

Connor, L. E. (1986). Oralism in perspective. In D. M. Luterman (Ed.), *Deafness in perspective* (pp. 116–129). San Diego: College-Hill.

Connors, C. K., Goyette, C., Southwick, D., Lees, J., & Andrulonis, P. (1976). Food additives and hyperkinesis: A controlled double blind study. *Pediatrics, 58,* 154–166.

Conroy, J. W. (1977). Trends in deinstitutionalization of the mentally retarded. *Mental Retardation, 15*(4), 44–66.

Conroy, J. W., & Bradley, V. J. (1985). *The Pennhurst longitudinal study: A report on five years of research and analysis.* Philadelphia: Temple University Developmental Disabilities Center.

Cook, P. S., & Woodhill, J. M. (1976). The Feingold dietary treatment of the hyperkinetic syndrome. *Medical Journal of Australia, 2,* 85–90.

Cooke, N. L., Heron, T. E., & Heward, W. L. (1983). *Peer tutoring: Implementing classwide programs in the primary grades.* Columbus, OH: Special Press.

Cooke, N. L., Heron, T. E., Heward, W. L., & Test, D. W. (1982). Integrating a Down syndrome student into a classwide peer tutoring system. *Mental Retardation, 20,* 22–25.

Cooke, T. P. (1981). Your place or mine? Residential options for people with developmental disabilities. In C. L. Hansen (Ed.), *Severely handicapped persons in the community.* Seattle: University of Washington PDAS.

Cooper, J. O. (1981). *Measuring behavior* (2nd ed.). Columbus, OH: Merrill.

Cooper, J. O. (1987). Measuring and recording behavior. In J. O. Cooper, T. E. Heron, & W. L. Heward, *Applied behavior analysis* (pp. 59–80). Columbus, OH: Merrill.

Cooper, J. O., & Heron, T. E. (1978). Educational materials and strategies for home use. In D. Edge, B. J. Strenecky, & S. I. Mour (Eds.), *Parenting learning-problem children: The professional educator's perspective.* Columbus: Ohio State University, National Center for Educational Materials and Media for the Handicapped.

Cooper, J. O., Heron, T. E., & Heward, W. L. (1987). *Applied behavior analysis.* Columbus, OH: Merrill.

Cooper, J. O., & Johnson, J. (1979). Guidelines for direct and continuous measurement of academic behavior. *The Directive Teacher, 1,* 10–11, 21.

Corbin Sicoli, M. L. (1985). College students with LD: Support systems and programs. *Journal of Reading, Writing, & Learning Disabilities, 1*(4), 59–62.

Cordoni, B. (1982). A directory of college LD services. *Journal of Learning Disabilities, 15,* 529–534.

Corn, A. L. (1986). Low vision and visual efficiency. In G. T. Scholl (Ed.), *Foundations of education for blind and visually handicapped children and youth: Theory and practice* (pp. 99–117). New York: American Foundation for the Blind.

Cornett, R. O. (1974). What is cued speech? *Gallaudet Today, 5,*(2), 3–5.

Cosper, M. R., & Erickson, M. T. (1984). Relationship among observed classroom behavior and three types of teacher ratings. *Behavioral Disorders, 9,* 189–195.

Cott, A. (1972). Megavitamins: The orthomolecular approach to behavioral disorders and learning disabilities. *Academic Therapy, 7,* 245–258.

Coulter, W. A., & Morrow, H. W. (Eds.). (1978). *Adaptive behavior: Concepts and measurements.* New York: Grune & Stratton.

Council for Learning Disabilities. (1986a). Use of discrepancy formulas in the identification of learning disabled individuals. *Learning Disability Quarterly, 9,* 245.

Council for Learning Disabilities. (1986b). Measurement and training of perceptual and perceptual-motor functions. *Learning Disability Quarterly, 9,* 247.

Cox, B. G., & Ramirez, M., III. (1981). Cognitive styles: Implications for multiethnic education. In J. A. Banks (Ed.), *Education in the 80's: Multiethnic education.* Washington, DC: National Education Association.

Cremins, J. J. (1983). *Legal and political issues in special education.* Springfield, IL: Charles C Thomas.

Cruickshank, W. M. (1986). *Disputable decisions in special education.* Ann Arbor: University of Michigan Press.

Culton, G. L. (1986). Speech disorders among college freshmen: A 13-year survey. *Journal of Speech and Hearing Disorders, 51,* 3–7.

Cummins, J. (1986). Psychological assessment of minority students: Out of context, out of focus, out of control? In A. C. Willig & H. F. Greenberg (Eds.), *Bilingualism and learning disabilities: Policy and practice for teachers and administrators* (pp. 3–11). New York: American Library.

Curran, B. E. (1983). *Effects of one-to-one and small-group instruction on incidental learning by moderately/severely handicapped adults.* Unpublished master's thesis. Ohio State University, Columbus.

Curran, J. J., & Algozzine, B. (1980). Ecological disturbance: A test of the matching hypothesis. *Behavioral Disorders, 5,* 159–174.

Currie, W. (1981). Teacher preparation for a pluralistic society. In J. A. Banks (Ed.), *Education in the 80's: Multiethnic education.* Washington, DC: National Education Association.

Curt, C. J. N. (1984). *Non-verbal communication in Puerto Rico* (2nd ed.). Cambridge, MA: Lesley College, Evaluation, Dissemination, and Assessment Center.

Cuvo, A. J., Veitch, V. D., Trace, M. W., & Konke, J. L. (1978). Teaching change computation to the mentally retarded. *Behavior Modification, 2,* 531–548.

Dale, D. M. C. (1984). *Individualised integration: Studies of deaf and partially-hearing children and students in ordinary schools and colleges.* London: Hodder & Stoughton.

D'Angelo, K. (1981). Wordless picture books and the young language-disabled child. *Teaching Exceptional Children, 14,* 34–37.

Dangle, R. F., & Polster, R. A. (Eds.). (1984). *Parent training: Foundations of research and practice.* New York: Guilford.

Dantona, R. (1986). Implications of demographic data for planning of services for deaf-blind children and adults. In D. Ellis (Ed.), *Sensory impairments in mentally handicapped people.* San Diego: College-Hill.

Dardig, J. C., & Heward, W. L. (1981a). *Sign here: A contracting book for children and their parents* (2nd ed.). Bridgewater, NJ: F. Fournies.

Dardig, J. C., & Heward, W. L. (1981b). A systematic procedure for prioritizing IEP goals. *The Directive Teacher, 3,* 6–8.

Davis, H., & Silverman, S. R. (Eds.). (1970). *Hearing and deafness* (3rd ed.). New York: Holt, Rinehart & Winston.

Davis, J. M. (1986). Academic placement in perspective. In D. M. Luterman (Ed.), *Deafness in perspective* (pp. 205–224). San Diego: College-Hill.

DeAvila, E. (1976). Mainstreaming ethnically and linguistically different children: An exercise in paradox or a new approach? In R. I. Jones (Ed.), *Mainstreaming and the minority child.* Reston, VA: Council for Exceptional Children.

Delaney, S., & Hayden, A. (1977). Fetal alcohol syndrome: A review. *AAESPH Review, 2*(3), 164–168.

Delisle, J. (1982). Learning to underachieve. *Roeper Review, 4,* 16–18.

Delpit, L. D. (1986). Dilemmas of a progressive black educator. *Harvard Educational Review, 56,* 379–385.

Delquadri, J., Greenwood, C. R., Whorton, D., Carta, J. J., & Hall, R. V. (1986). Classwide peer tutoring. *Exceptional Children, 52,* 535–542.

Dent, N. E. (1976). Assessing black children for mainstream placement. In R. L. Jones (Ed.), *Mainstreaming and the minority child.* Reston, VA: Council for Exceptional Children.

Denton, D. M. (1972, August 18). *A philosophical foundation for total communication.* Paper presented at the Indiana School for the Deaf, Preschool Parent Conference, Indianapolis.

Deschler, D. D., Lowrey, N., & Alley, G. R. (1979). Programming alternatives for learning disabled adolescents: A nationwide survey. *Academic Therapy, 14*(4).

Deschler, D. D., Schumaker, J. B., & Lenz, B. K. (1984). Academic and cognitive interventions for LD adolescents: Part I. *Journal of Learning Disabilities, 17,* 108–117.

Deschler, D. D., Schumaker, J. B., Lenz, B. K., & Ellis, E. (1984). Academic and cognitive interventions for LD adolescents: Part II. *Journal of Learning Disabilities, 17,* 170–179.

Dickerson, D., Spellman, C. R., Larsen, S. C., & Tyler, L. (1973). Let the cards do the talking: A teacher-parent communication program. *Teaching Exceptional Children, 5,* 170–178.

Divoky, D. (1978). Can diet cure the LD child? *Learning, 3,* 56–57.

Dobelle, W. H. (1977). Current status of research on providing sight to the blind by electrical stimulation of the brain. *Journal of Visual Impairment and Blindness, 71,* 290–297.

Doernberg, N. L. (1978). Some negative effects on family integration of health and educational services for young handicapped children. *Rehabilitation Literature, 39,* 107–110.

Doll, E. A. (1941). The essentials of an inclusive concept of mental deficiency. *American Journal of Mental Deficiency, 46,* 214–219.

Doll, E. A. (1965). Vineland Social Maturity Scale. Circle Pines, MN: American Guidance Service.

Donnellan, A. (1984). The criterion of the least dangerous assumption. *Behavioral Disorders, 9,* 141–150.

Donnellan, A. M., & Mirenda, P. L. (1984). Issues related to professional involvement with families of individuals with autism and other severe handicaps. *Journal of the Association for Persons with Severe Handicaps, 9*, 6–24.

Drabman, R. S., Spitalnik, R., & O'Leary, K. D. (1973). Teaching self-control to disruptive children. *Journal of Abnormal Psychology, 82*, 10–16.

DuBose, R. F. (1981). Assessment of severely impaired young children: Problems and recommendations. *Topics in Early Childhood Special Education, 1*, 9–12.

Dudley-Marling, C. C., & Edmiaston, R. (1985). Social status of learning disabled children and adolescents: A review. *Learning Disability Quarterly, 8*, 189–204.

Duffey, J. D., Salvia, J., Tucker, J., & Ysseldyke, J. (1981). Nonbiased assessment: A need for operationalism. *Exceptional Children, 47*, 427–434.

Dunlap, G., & Koegel, R. L. (1980). Motivating autistic children through stimulus variation. *Journal of Applied Behavior Analysis, 13*, 619–627.

Dunn, L. B. (1965). Peabody Picture Vocabulary Test. Circle Pines, MN: American Guidance Service.

Dunn, L. M. (1968). Special education for the mildly retarded—is much of it justifiable? *Exceptional Children, 35*, 5–24.

Dunn, L. M. (1973). Children with mild general learning disabilities. In L. M. Dunn (Ed.), *Exceptional children in the schools* (2nd ed.). New York: Holt, Rinehart & Winston.

Dunn, L. M., & Markwardt, F. C. (1970). The Peabody Individual Achievement Test. Circle Pines, MN: American Guidance Service.

Dunst, C. J. (1986). Overview of the efficacy of early intervention programs: Methodological and conceptual considerations. In L. Bickman & D. Weatherford (Eds.), *Evaluating early intervention programs for severely handicapped children and their famillies*. Austin, TX: Pro-Ed.

Dunst, C. J., & Snyder, S. W. (1986). A critique of the Utah State University early intervention meta-analysis research. *Exceptional Children, 53*, 269–276.

Dunst, C. J., Snyder, S. W., & Mankinen, M. (1986). Efficacy of early intervention. In M. Wang, H. Walberg, M. Reynolds (Eds.), *Handbook of special education: Research and practice* (Vols. 1–3). Oxford, England: Pergamon Press.

Durand, V. M. (1986). Review of *Strategies for Educating Students with Severe Handicaps*. *Journal of the Association for Persons with Severe Handicaps, 11*, 140–142.

Durrell, D. D. (1955). Durrell Analysis of Reading Difficulty. New York: Harcourt Brace Jovanovich.

Dykes, M. K., & Venn, J. (1983). Using health, physical, and medical data in the classroom. In J. Umbreit (Ed.), *Physical disabilities and health impairments: An introduction* (pp. 259–280). Columbus, OH: Merrill.

Eastman, M. (1978). The Eden express doesn't stop here anymore. *American Pharmacy, 40*, 12–17.

Eden-Piercy, G. V. S., Blacher, J. B., & Eyman, R. K. (1986). Exploring parents' reactions to their young child with severe handicaps. *Mental Retardation, 24*, 285–291.

Edgar, E. (1985). How do special education students fare after they leave school? A response to Hasazi, Gordon, and Roe. *Exceptional Children, 51*, 470–473.

Edgerton, R. B., & Bercovici, S. M. (1976). The cloak of competence: Years later. *American Journal of Mental Deficiency, 80*, 485–497.

Edginton, D. (1976). *The physically handicapped child in your classroom: A handbook for teachers*. Springfield, IL: Charles C Thomas.

Edmonds, C. (1985). Hearing loss with frequent diving: Deaf divers. *Undersea Biomedical Research, 12*, 315–319.

Edwards, P. L. (1986). *Heterogeneous grouping effects on educational service delivery for students with moderate, severe, and profound retardation*. Unpublished manuscript, Kent State University.

Effertz-Tougas, M. (1986, December). Computers offer tool for independent living. *The Association for Persons with Severe Handicaps Newsletter, 12*(12), 3.

Egan, I., Fredericks, H. D., & Hendrickson, K. (1985). Teaching associated work skills to adolescents with severe handicaps. *Education & Treatment of Children, 8*, 239–250.

Egel, A. L. (1981). Reinforcer variation: Implications for motivating developmentally disabled children. *Journal of Applied Behavior Analysis, 14*, 3–12.

Elliott, B. (1979). Look but don't touch: The problems blind children have learning about sexuality. *Disabled USA, 3*(2), 14–17.

Ellis, J. W., & Luckasson, R. A. (1985). Discrimination against people with mental retardation: A comment on the *Cleburne* decision. *Mental Retardation, _* 249–252.

Ellwood, P. (1971). Prescription of wheelchairs. In F. Krussen, F. Kottke, & P. Ellwood, *Handbook of physical medicine and rehabilitation* (2nd ed.). Philadelphia: W. B. Saunders.

Elmer, E. (1967). *Children in jeopardy: A study of abused minors and their families*. Pittsburgh: University of Pittsburgh Press.

Elmer, E. (1977). A follow-up study of traumatized children. *Pediatrics, 59*, 273–279.

Emerick, L. L., & Haynes, W. O. (1986). Diagnosis and evaluation in speech pathology (3rd ed.). Englewood Cliffs, NJ: Prentice-Hall.

Englemann, S. E. (1977). Sequencing cognitive and academic tasks. In R. D. Kneedler & S. G. Tarver (Eds.). *Changing perspectives in special education*. Columbus, OH: Merrill.

Epilepsy Foundation of American. (1974). *Epilepsy school alert*. Washington, DC: Author.

Epple, W. A., Jacobson, J. W., & Janicki, M. P. (1985). Staffing ratios in public institutions for persons with mental retardation in the United States. *Mental Retardation, 23*, 115–124.

Epstein, M. H., Bursuck, W., & Cullinan, D. (1985). Patterns of behavior problems among the learning disabled: II. Boys aged 12–18, girls aged 6–11. *Learning Disability Quarterly, 8*, 123–131.

Epstein, M. H., Cullinan, D., & Lloyd, J. W. (1986). Behavior-problem patterns among the learning disabled: III. Replication across age and sex. *Learning Disability Quarterly, 9,* 43–54.

Epstein, M. H., Cullinan, D., & Rosemier, R. (1983). Patterns of behavior problems among the learning disabled: Boys aged 6–11. *Learning Disability Quarterly, 6,* 305–312.

Epstein, P. B., Detwiler, C. L., & Reitz, A. L. (1985). Describing the clients in programs for behavior disordered children and youth. *Education and Treatment of Children, 8,* 265–273.

Esposito, B. G., & Reed, T. M. (1986). The effects of contact with handicapped persons on young children's attitudes. *Exceptional Children, 54,* 224–229.

Esposito, L., & Campbell, P. H. (1987). Computers and severely and physically handicapped individuals. In J. D. Lindsey (Ed.), *Computers and exceptional individuals* (pp. 105–124). Columbus, OH: Merrill.

Evans, W. H., Evans, S. S., Schmid, R. E., & Pennypacker, H. S. (1985). The effects of exercise on selected classroom behaviors of behaviorally disordered adolescents. *Behavioral Disorders, 11,* 42–51.

Fain, G. S. (1986). Leisure: A moral imperative. *Mental Retardation, 24,* 261–263.

Fanning, J. W. (1975). *A common sense approach to community living arrangements for the mentally retarded.* Springfield, IL: Charles C Thomas.

Farber, B. (1975). Family adaptations to severely mentally retarded children. In M. Begab & S. A. Richardson (Eds.), *The mentally retarded and society: A social science perspective.* Baltimore: University Park Press.

Favell, J. E., Favell, J. E., & McGimsey, J. F. (1978). Relative effectiveness and efficiency of group vs. individual training of severely retarded persons. *American Journal of Mental Deficiency, 83,* 104–109.

Fay, G., Shapiro, S., & Trupin, E. (1978). Should parents teach reading to their children? Further evidence that they should. In D. Edge, B. J. Strenecky, & S. I. Mour (Eds.), *Parenting learning-problem children: The professional educator's perspective.* Columbus: Ohio State University, National Center for Educational Materials and Media for the Handicapped.

Featherstone, H. (1980). *A difference in the family: Living with a disabled child.* New York: Basic Books.

Federal Register. (1977, August 23). Washington, DC: U.S. Government Printing Office.

Federal Register. (1981, January 19). Washington, DC: U.S. Government Printing Office.

Fein, D. J. (1983). The prevalence of speech and language impairments. *ASHA, 25,* 37.

Feingold, B. F. (1975a). Hyperkinesis and learning disabilities linked to artificial food flavors and colors. *American Journal of Nursing, 75,* 797–803.

Feingold, B. F. (1975b) *Why your child is hyperactive.* New York: Random House.

Feingold, B. F. (1976). Hyperkinesis and learning disabilities linked to ingestion of artificial food colors and flavorings. *Journal of Learning Disabilities, 9,* 551–559.

Feldhusen, J., & Sokol, L. (1982). Extra school programming to meet the needs of gifted youth: Super-Saturday. *Gifted Child Quarterly, 26,* 51–56.

Fellows, R. R., Leguire, L. E., Rogers, G. L., & Bremer, D. L. (1986). A theoretical approach to vision stimulation. *Journal of Visual Impairment & Blindness, 80,* 907–909.

Fernald, G. M. (1943). *Remedial techniques in basic school subjects.* New York: McGraw-Hill.

Ferrari, M., & Harris, S. L. (1981). The limits and motivating potential of sensory stimuli as reinforcers for autistic children. *Journal of Applied Behavior Analysis, 14,* 339–343.

Ferrell, K. A. (1984). A second look at sensory aids in early childhood. *Education of the Visually Handicapped, 16,* 83–101.

Ferrell, K. A. (1985). *Reach out and teach.* New York: American Foundation for the Blind.

Ferrell, K. A. (1986). Infancy and early childhood. In G. T. Scholl (Ed.), *Foundations of education for blind and visually handicapped children and youth: Theory and practice* (pp. 119–135). New York: American Foundation for the Blind.

Finch, T. E. (1985). Introduction. In D. Assael (Ed.), *Directory, 1984–85 edition: Handicapped Children's Early Education Program* (pp. ix–xiii). Chapel Hill: University of North Carolina, Technical Assistance Development System.

Fishman, K. D. (1987). American high: At Seward Park, the melting pot still bubbles. *New York, 20*(9), 78–94.

Fiske, E. B. (1976, April 25). Special education is now a matter of civil rights. *New York Times,* p. 14.

Fitzgerald, E. (1929). *Straight language for the deaf.* Washington, DC: Alexander Graham Bell Association for the Deaf.

Flexer, R. W., & Martin, A. S. (1978). Sheltered workshops and vocational training settings. In M. E. Snell (Ed.), *Systematic instruction of the moderately and severely handicapped.* Columbus, OH: Merrill.

Fontana, V. J. (1971). *The maltreated child.* Springfield, IL: Charles C Thomas.

Foster, M., Berger, M., & McLean, M. (1981). Rethinking a good idea: A reassessment of parent involvement. *Topics in Early Childhood Special Education, 1,* 55–65.

Fowler, S. A. (1986). Peer-monitoring and self-monitoring: Alternatives to traditional teacher management. *Exceptional Children, 52,* 573–581.

Fox, L. H. (1977). Sex differences: Implications for program planning for the academically gifted. In J. C. Stanley, W. C. George, & C. H. Solano (Eds.), *The gifted and creative: A fifty-year perspective.* Baltimore: Johns Hopkins.

Frank, A. R. (1973). Breaking down learning tasks: A sequence approach. *Teaching Exceptional Children, 6,* 16–19.

Frankenburg, W. K., Dodds, J., & Fandal, A. (1975). *Denver Developmental Screening Test.* Denver. LADOCA Project.

Frazier, F. M. (1980). Screening and identification of gifted students. In J. B. Jordan & J. A. Grossi (Eds.), *An administrative handbook on developing programs for the gifted and talented.* Reston, VA: Council for Exceptional Children.

Freagon, S. (1982). Present and projected services to meet the needs of severely handicapped children [Keynote address]. In *Proceedings of the National Parent Conference on Children Requiring Extensive Special Education Programming.* Washington, DC: U.S. Department of Education, Special Education Programs.

Freagon, S., Smith, B., Costello, C., Bay, J., Ahlgren C., & Costello, D. (1986). *Procedures and strategies for program development leading to employment of students with moderate and severe handicaps.* DeKalb, IL: Northern Illinois University.

French, R. W., & Jansma, P. (1982). *Special physical education.* Columbus, OH: Merrill.

Friedman, P. R. (1976). *The rights of mentally retarded persons.* New York: Avon.

Friedman, P. R. (1977). Human and legal rights of mentally retarded persons. *International Journal of Mental Health. 6,* 50–72.

Frierson, E. C. (1965). Upper and lower status children: A study of differences. *Exceptional Children, 32,* 83–90.

Frierson, E. C. (1969). The gifted. *Review of Educational Research, 39,* 25–37.

Frostig, M., & Horne, D. (1973). The Frostig program for the development of visual perception (rev. ed.). Chicago: Follett.

Frostig, M., Lefever, D. W., & Whittlesey, J. R. B. (1964). The Marianne Frostig Development Test of Visual Perception. Palo Alto, CA: Consulting Psychology Press.

Furth, H. G. (1973). *Deafness and learning: A psychosocial approach.* Belmont, CA: Wadsworth.

Fusfeld, I. S. (1958). How the deaf communicate: Written language. *American Annals of the Deaf. 103,* 255–263.

Gadow, K. D. (1986). *Children on medication: Volume I. Hyperactivity, learning disabilities, and mental retardation.* San Diego: College-Hill.

Gallagher, J. J. (1975a). Characteristics of gifted children: A research summary. In W. B. Barbe & J. S. Renzulli (Eds.), *Psychology and education of the gifted* (2nd ed.). New York: Irvington.

Gallagher, J. J. (1975b). *Teaching the gifted* (2nd ed.). Boston: Allyn & Bacon.

Gallagher, J. J. (1981). Differential curriculum for the gifted. In A. H. Kramer, D. Bitan, N. Butler-Por, A. Eryatar, & E. Landau (Eds.), *Gifted children: Challenging their potential.* New York: World Council for Gifted and Talented Children.

Gallagher, J. J. (1984). The evolution of special education concepts. In B. Blatt & R. J. Morris (Eds.), *Perspectives in special education: Personal orientations* (pp. 210–232). Glenview, IL: Scott, Foresman.

Gallimore, R., Boggs, J., & Jordan, C. (1974). *Culture, behavior, and education.* Beverly Hills, CA: Sage.

Galton, F. (1936). Genius as inherited. In A. Rothenberg & C. R. Hausman (Eds.), *The creativity question.* Durham, NC: Duke University. (Reprinted from *Hereditary genius: An inquiry into its laws and consequences,* 1869, London: Macmillan.)

Garber, H. C. (1975, May). *Prevention of mental retardation: The Milwaukee Project.* Portland, OR: American Association on Mental Deficiency.

Garber, H., & Heber, R. (1973). *The Milwaukee Project: Early intervention as a technique to prevent mental retardation* [Technical paper]. Storrs: University of Connecticut.

Garcia, R. L. (1981). *Education for cultural pluralism: Global roots stew.* Bloomington, IN: Phil Delta Kappa Educational Foundation.

Gardner, H. (1983). *Frames of mind.* New York: Basic Books.

Garreau, B., Parthelmay, D., Sauvage, D., Leddet, I., & LeLord, G. (1984). A comparison of autistic syndromes with and without associated neurological problems. *Journal of Autism and Developmental Disabilities, 14,* 105–113.

Gast, D. L., & Wolery, M. (1987). Severe maladaptive behaviors. In M. E. Snell (Ed.), *Systematic instruction of persons with severe handicaps* (3rd ed., pp. 300–332). Columbus, OH: Merrill.

Gates, A. T., & McKillop, A. S. (1962). Gates-McKillop Reading Diagnostic Test. New York: Columbia University, Teachers College, Bureau of Publication.

Gaylord-Ross, R. J., Haring, T. G., Breen, C., & Pitts-Conway, V. (1984). The training and generalization of social interaction skills with autistic youth. *Journal of Applied Behavior Analysis, 17,* 229–247.

Gearheart, B. R., & Litton, F. W. (1975). *The trainable retarded: A foundations approach.* St. Louis: C. V. Mosby.

Geers, A. E. (1985). Assessment of hearing impaired children: Determining typical and optimal levels of performance. In F. Powell, T. Finitzo-Hieber, S. Friel-Patti, & D. Henderson (Eds.), *Education of the hearing impaired child* (pp. 57–83). San Diego: College-Hill.

Gelof, M. (1963). Comparisons of systems of classification relating degrees of retardation to measured intelligence. *American Journal of Mental Deficiency. 68,* 297–317.

Gesell, A., & associates. (1940). Gesell Developmental Schedules. 1940 Series. New York: Psychological Corporation.

Gies-Zaborowski, J., & Silverman, F. H. (1986). Documenting the impact of a mild dysarthria on peer perception. *Language, Speech, and Hearing Services in Schools, 17,* 143.

Gil, D. G. (1970). *Violence against children: Physical abuse in the United States.* Cambridge, MA: Harvard University Press.

Gilhool, T. K. (1976). Changing public policies: Roots and forces. *Minnesota Education, 2*(2), 8.

Gillham, B. (Ed.). (1986). *Handicapping conditions in children.* London: Croom Helm.

Glavin, J. P., & Annesley, F. R. (1971). Reading and arithmetic correlates of conduct-problem and withdrawn children. *Journal of Special Education. 5,* 213–219.

Glenn, C. L. (1986). New challenges: A civil rights agenda for the public schools. *Phi Delta Kappan, 67*(9), 653–656.

Glover, J., & Gary, A. L. (1976). Procedures to increase some aspects of creativity. *Journal of Applied Behavior Analysis, 9*, 79–84.

Gluckman, I. B. (1986). Foreword. In T. P. Johnson, *The principal's guide to the educational rights of handicapped students* (pp. v–vi). Reston, VA: National Association of Secondary School Principals.

Goddard, H. H. (1928). *School training of gifted children.* New York: World Book.

Goetz, E. M. (1982). A review of functional analyses of preschool children's creative behaviors. *Education and Treatment of Children, 5*, 157–177.

Goetz, E. M., & Baer, D. M. (1973). Social control of form diversity and the emergence of new forms in children's blockbuilding. *Journal of Applied Behavior Analysis, 6*, 209–218.

Gold, M. W. (1972). Stimulus factors in skill training of the retarded on a complex assembly task: Acquisition, transfer, and retention. *American Journal of Mental Deficiency, 76*, 517–526.

Gold, M. W. (1976). Task analysis of a complex assembly task by the retarded blind. *Exceptional Children, 43*, 73–85.

Gold, M. W. (1980a). An alternative definition of mental retardation. In M. W. Gold (Ed.), *"Did I say that?" Articles and commentary on the Try Another Way System.* Champaign, IL: Research Press.

Gold, M. W. (1980b). *Try another way: Training manual.* Champaign, IL: Research Press.

Golden, G. (1980). Nonstandard therapies in the developmental disabilities. *American Journal of Diseases of Children, 134*, 487–491.

Goldstein, H. (1984). A search for understanding. In B. Blatt & R. J. Morris, *Perspectives in special education: Personal orientations* (pp. 56–100). Glenview, IL: Scott, Foresman.

Goldstein, S., Strickland, B., Turnbull, A. P., & Curry, L. (1980). An observational analysis of the IEP conference. *Exceptional Children, 46*(4), 278–286.

Goldstein, S., & Turnbull, A. P. (1982). The use of two strategies to increase parent participation in the IEP conference. *Exceptional Children, 48*, 360–361.

Gonzales, R. (1980). Mainstreaming your hearing impaired child in 1980: Still an oversimplification. *Journal of Research and Development in Education, 13*(4), 14–21.

Goodenough, F. L., & Harris, D. B. (1963). *The Goodenough-Harris Drawing Test.* New York: Harcourt Brace Jovanovich.

Goodman, L. V. (1976). A bill of rights for the handicapped. *American Education. 12*(6), 6–8.

Gottlieb, J. (1981). Mainstreaming: Fulfilling the promise? *American Journal of Mental Deficiency, 86*, 115–126.

Gottlieb, J., Agard, J. A., Kaufman, M. J., & Semmel, M. I. (1976). Retarded children mainstreamed: Practices as they affect minority group children. In R. L. Jones (Ed.), *Mainstreaming and the minority child.* Reston, VA: Council for Exceptional Children.

Gottlieb, J., & Leyser, Y. (1981). Facilitating the social mainstreaming of retarded children. *Exceptional Education Quarterly, 1*, 57–69.

Gowan, J. C. (1972). *Development of the creative individual.* San Diego: Robert R. Knapp.

Gradel, K., Thompson, M. S., & Sheehan, R. (1981). Parental and professional agreement in early childhood assessment. *Topics in Early Childhood Special Education, 1*, 31–39.

Gray, S. W., Klaus, R. A., Miller, J. O., & Forrester, D. J. (1966). *Before first grade: The early training project for culturally disadvantaged children.* New York: Teachers College Press.

Gray, W. S. (1963). Gray Oral Reading Tests. Indianapolis: Bobbs-Merrill.

Gresham, F. M. (1982). Misguided mainstreaming: The case for social skills training with handicapped children. *Exceptional Children, 48*, 422–433.

Gresham, F. M., & Reschly, D. J. (1986). Social skill deficits and low peer acceptance of mainstreamed learning disabled children. *Learning Disability Quarterly, 9*, 23–32.

Griffing, B. L. (1986). Planning for the future: Programs and services for the blind and visually impaired children. In *Yearbook of the Association for Education and Rehabilitation of the Blind and Visually Impaired* (Vol. 3, pp. 2–11). Alexandria, VA: Association for Education and Rehabilitation of the Blind and Visually Impaired.

Groht, M. A. (1958). *Natural language for deaf children.* Washington, DC: Alexander Graham Bell Association for the Deaf.

Grossman, H. (1984). *Educating Hispanic students: Cultural implications for instruction, classroom management, counseling and assessment.* Springfield, IL: Charles C Thomas.

Grossman, H. J. (Ed.). (1973). *Manual on terminology and classification in mental retardation* (1973 rev.). Washington, DC: American Association on Mental Deficiency.

Grossman, H. J. (Ed.). (1977). *Manual on terminology and classification in mental retardation* (1977 rev.). Washington, DC: American Association on Mental Deficiency.

Grossman, H. J. (Ed). (1983). *Classification in mental retardation.* Washington, DC: American Association on Mental Deficiency.

Grove, N. M. (1982). Conditions resulting in physical disabilities. In J. L. Bigge (Ed.), *Teaching individuals with physical and multiple disabilities* (2nd ed.). Columbus, OH: Merrill.

Guess, D., Benson, H. A., & Siegel-Causey, E. (1985). Concepts and issues related to choice-making and autonomy among persons with severe disabilities. *Journal of the Association for Persons with Severe Handicaps, 10*, 79–86.

Guess, P. D., & Mulligan, M. (1982). The severely and profoundly handicapped. In E. L. Meyen (Ed.), *Exceptional children and youth: An introduction* (2nd ed.). Denver: Love.

Guilford, J. P. (1956). The structure of intellect. *Psychological Bulletin, 53*(4), 276–293.

Guilford, J. P. (1959). Traits of creativity. In H. H. Anderson (Ed.), *Creativity and its cultivation.* New York: Harper & Brothers.

Gurcsick, B. (1981). Justifying your program with a diagnostic-prescriptive approach. *Gifted Child Today, 19,* 12–13.

Gustason, G., Pfetzing, D., & Zawolkow, E. (1980). *Signing exact English.* Los Alamitos, CA: Modern Signs Press.

Hagen, E. (1980). *Identification of the gifted.* New York: Teachers College Press.

Hagerty, G. J., & Abramson, M. (1987). Impediments for implementing national policy change for mildly handicapped students. *Exceptional Children, 53,* 315–323.

Hall, A., Scholl, G. T., & Swallow, R. M. (1986). Psychoeducational assessment. In G. T. Scholl (Ed.), *Foundations of education for blind and visually handicapped children and youth: Theory and practice* (pp. 187–214). New York: American Foundation for the Blind.

Hall, E. T. (1976). How cultures collide. *Psychology Today, 10*(2), 66–74, 97.

Hallahan, D. P., & Cruickshank, W. M. (1973). *Psychoeducational foundations of learning disabilities.* Englewood Cliffs, NJ: Prentice-Hall.

Hallahan, D. P., & Kauffman, J. M. (1976). *Introduction to learning disabilities: A psychoeducational approach.* Englewood Cliffs, NJ: Prentice-Hall.

Hallahan, D. P., & Kauffman, J. M. (1977). Labels, categories, behaviors: ED, LD, and EMR reconsidered. *Journal of Special Education, 11,* 139–149.

Hallahan, D. P., & Kauffman, J. M. (1978). *Exceptional children: Introduction to special education.* Englewood Cliffs, NJ: Prentice-Hall.

Halle, J. W., & Sindelar, P. T. (1982). Behavioral observation methodologies for early childhood education. *Topics in Early Childhood Special Education, 2,* 43–54.

Ham, R.. (1986). Techniques of stuttering therapy. Englewood Cliffs, NJ: Prentice-Hall.

Hammer, E. K. (1978, December 13). *Issues in assessment.* Paper presented at the National Conference on Innovation in Education for Deaf-Blind Children and Youth, Alexandria, Virginia.

Hammill, D. D. (1976). Defining learning disabilities for programmatic purposes. *Academic Therapy, 12,* 29–37.

Hammill, D. D. (1980). The field of learning disabilities: A futuristic perspective. *Learning Disability Quarterly, 3,* 2–9.

Hammill, D. D., Goodman, L., & Wiederholt, J. T. (1974). Visual-motor processes: Can we train them? *Reading Teacher, 27,* 469–478.

Hammill, D. D., & Larsen, S. (1974). The effectiveness of psycholinguistic training. *Exceptional Children, 41,* 5–15.

Hammill, D. D., & Larsen, S. (1978). The effectiveness of psycholinguistic training: A reaffirmation of position. *Exceptional Children, 44,* 402–417.

Hammill, D. D., Leigh, J. E., McNutt, G., & Larsen, S. C. (1981). A new definition of learning disabilities. *Learning Disability Quarterly, 4,* 336–342.

Hamre-Nietupski, S., Nietupski, J., Sandvig, R., Sandvig, M. B., & Ayres, B. (1984). Leisure skills instruction in a community residential setting with young adults who are deaf/

blind severely handicapped. *Journal of the Association for Persons with Severe Handicaps, 9,* 49–54.

Haring, N. G. (1978). The severely handicapped. In N. G. Haring (Ed.), *Behavior of exceptional children* (2nd ed.). Columbus, OH: Merrill.

Haring, N. G., Bateman, B., & Carnine, D. (1977). Direct instruction—DISTAR. In N. G. Haring & B. Bateman (Eds.), *Teaching the learning disabled child.* Englewood Cliffs, NJ: Prentice-Hall.

Haring, N. G., Lovitt, T. C., Eaton, M. D., & Hansen, C. L. (1978). *The fourth R: Research in the classroom.* Columbus, OH: Merrill.

Haring, N. G., & Smith, J. (1978). The profoundly handicapped. In N. G. Haring (Ed.), *Behavior of exceptional children* (2nd ed.). Columbus, OH: Merrill.

Harris, G., & Kotsch, L. S. (1981). Extended families and young handicapped children. *Topics in Early Childhood Special Education, 1,* 29–35.

Harris, W. J., & Schutz, P. N. B. (1986). *The special education resource program: Rationale and Implementation.* Columbus, OH: Merrill.

Harrison, R., & Edwards, J. (1983). *Child abuse.* Portland, OR: Ednick.

Hart, B., & Risley, T. R. (1975). Incidental teaching of language in the preschool. *Journal of Applied Behavior Analysis, 8,* 411–420.

Hasazi, S. B., Gordon, L. R., & Roe, C. A. (1985). Factors associated with the employment status of handicapped youth exiting high school from 1979 to 1983. *Exceptional Children, 51,* 455–469.

Hasselbring, T., & Hamlet, C. (1983). *Aimstar: A computer software program.* Portland, OR: ASIEO Education.

Hatlen, P. H. (1976, Winter). Priorities in education programs for visually handicapped children and youth. *Division for the Visually Handicapped Newsletter,* 8–11.

Hatlen, P. H. (1978, Fall). The role of the teacher of the visually impaired: A self-definition. *Division for the Visually Handicapped Newsletter,* 5.

Hatten, J. T., & Hatten, P. W. (1975). *Natural language.* Tucson: Communication Skill Builders.

Hauber, F. A., Bruininks, R. H., Hill, B. K., Lakin, K. C., & White, C. C. (1984). *National census of residential facilities: Fiscal year 1982.* Minneapolis: University of Minnesota, Center for Residential and Community Services.

Hawkins, R. P. (1984). What is "meaningful" behavior change in a severely/profoundly retarded learner? The view of a behavior analytic parent. In W. L. Heward, T. E. Heron, D. S. Hill, & J. Trap-Porter (Eds.), *Focus on behavior analysis in education.* Columbus, OH: Merrill.

Hawkins, R. P., & Hawkins, K. K. (1981). Parental observations on the education of severely retarded children: Can it be done in the classroom? *Analysis and Intervention in Development Disabilities, 1,* 13–22.

Haycock, G. S. (1933). *The teaching of speech.* Stoke-on-Trent, England: Hill & Ainsworth.

Hayden, A. H., & Edgar, E. B. (1977). Identification, screening, and assessment. In J. B. Jordan, A. H. Hayden, M. B. Karnes, & M. M. Woods (Eds.), *Early childhood education for exceptional children: A handbook of ideas and exemplary practices.* Reston, VA: Council for Exceptional Children.

Hayden, A. H., & Edgar, E. (1978). Developing individualized education programs for young handicapped children. *Teaching Exceptional Children, 10,* 67–70.

Hayden, A., Morris, K., & Bailey, D. (1977). *The effects of early education.* Seattle: University of Washington, Model Preschool Center for Handicapped Children.

Hayden, A. H., & Pious C. G. (1979). The case for early intervention. In R. York & E. Edgar (Eds.), *Teaching the severely handicapped* (Vol. 4). Seattle: American Association for the Education of the Severely/Profoundly Handicapped.

Haywood, H. C. (1979). What happened to mild and moderate mental retardation? *American Journal of Mental Deficiency, 83,* 427–431.

Heber, R. F. (1961). A manual on terminology and classification in mental retardation (rev. ed.). *Monograph Supplement American Journal of Mental Deficiency, 64.*

Heber, R. F., & Garber, H. (1971). An experiment in prevention of cultural-familial mental retardation. In D. A. Primrose (Ed.), *Proceedings of the Second Congress of the International Association for the Scientific Study of Mental Deficiency.* Warsaw: Polish Medical Publishers.

Hechinger, F. M. (1976, April 25). Bringing the handicapped into the mainstream. *New York Times,* 15.

Hegde, M. N. (1986). Treatment of fluency disorders: State of the art. In J. M. Costello & A. L. Holland (Eds.), *Handbook of speech and language disorders* (pp. 505–538). San Diego: College-Hill.

Heim, K. M., et al. (1980). Juvenile detention: Another boundary issue for physicians. *Pediatrics, 66,* 239–245.

Heinze, T. (1986). Communication skills. In G. T. Scholl (Ed.), *Foundations of education for blind and visually handicapped children and youth: Theory and practice* (pp. 301–314). New York: American Foundation for the Blind.

Hemming, H., Lavender, T., & Pill, R. (1981). Quality of life of mentally retarded adults transferred from large institutions to new small units. *American Journal of Mental Deficiency, 86,* 157–169.

Henderson, J. (1986). *Making regular schools special.* New York: Schocken.

Heron, T. E. (1978). Maintaining the mainstreamed child in the regular classroom: The decision-making process. *Journal of Learning Disabilities, 11,* 210–216.

Heron, T. E., & Axelrod, S. (1976). Effectiveness of feedback to mothers concerning their children's word-recognition performance. *Reading Improvement, 13,* 74–81.

Heron, T. E., & Harris, K. C. (1982). *The educational consultant: Helping professionals, parents, and mainstreamed students.* Boston: Allyn & Bacon.

Heron, T. E., & Harris, K. C. (1987). *The educational consultant: Helping professionals, parents, and mainstreamed students.* Austin, TX: Pro-Ed.

Heron, T. E., & Skinner, M. E. (1981). Criteria for defining the regular classroom as the least restrictive environment for LD students. *Learning Disability Quarterly, 4,* 115–121.

Heston, L. L. (1970). The genetics of schizophrenic and schizoid disease. *Science, 167,* 249–256.

HEW reports 13 percent of Head Start children are handicapped. (1978). *Report on Preschool Education,* 10.

Heward, W. L. (1978). Visual Response System: A mediated resource room for children with learning problems. *Journal of Special Education Technology, 2,* 40–46.

Heward, W. L. (1979). Teaching students to control their own behavior: A critical skill. *Exceptional Teacher, 1,* 3–5, 11.

Heward, W. L. (1987a). Self-management. In J. O. Cooper, T. E. Heron, & W. L. Heward, *Applied behavior analysis* (pp. 515–549). Columbus, OH: Merrill.

Heward, W. L. (1987b). Promoting the generality of behavior change. In J. O. Cooper, T. E. Heron, & W. L. Heward, *Applied behavior analysis* (pp. 552–583). Columbus, OH: Merrill.

Heward, W. L., & Chapman, J. E. (1981). Improving parent-teacher communication through recorded telephone messages: Systematic replication in a special education classroom. *Journal of Special Education Technology, 4,* 11–19.

Heward, W. L., & Dardig, J. C. (1978a). Improving the parent-teacher relationship through contingency contracting. In D. Edge, B. J. Strenecky, & S. I. Mour (Eds.), *Parenting learning-problem children: The professional educator's perspective.* Columbus: Ohio State University, National Center for Educational Materials and Media for the Handicapped.

Heward, W. L., Dardig, J. C., & Rossett, A. (1979). *Working with parents of handicapped children,* Columbus, OH: Merrill.

Heward, W. L., Eachus, H. T., & Christopher, J. (1974). *Establishment of talking in an elective mute.* Unpublished manuscript, University of Massachusetts.

Heward, W. L., Heron, T. E., & Cooke, N. L. (1982). Tutor huddle: Key element in a classwide peer tutoring system. *Elementary School Journal, 83,* 115–123.

Heward, W. L., Heron, T. E., Hill, D. S., & Trap-Porter J. (Eds.). (1984). *Focus on behavior analysis in education.* Columbus, OH: Merrill.

Hewett, F. M. (1964). A hierarchy of educational tasks for children with learning disorders. *Exceptional Children, 31,* 207–214.

Hewett, F. M. (1968). *The emotionally disturbed child in the classroom.* Boston: Allyn & Bacon.

Hewett, F. M., & Forness, S. R. (1977). *Education of exceptional learners* (2nd ed.). Boston: Allyn & Bacon.

Hewett, F. M., & Taylor, F. D. (1980). *The emotionally disturbed child in the classroom: The ochestration of success.* Boston: Allyn & Bacon.

Hieronymous, A. N., & Lindquist, E. F. (1978). Iowa Tests of Basic Skills. Boston: Houghton Mifflin.

Hill, B. K., Lakin, K. C., & Bruininks, R. H. (1984). Trends in residential services for people who are mentally retarded: 1977–1982. *Journal of the Association for Persons with Severe Handicaps, 9,* 243–250.

Hill, E. W., & Jacobson, W. H. (1985). Controversial issues in orientation and mobility: Then and now. *Education of the Visually Handicapped, 17,* 59–70.

Hill, J. W., Wehman, P., & Horst G. (1982). Toward generalization of appropriate leisure and social behavior in severely handicapped youth: Pinball machine use. *Journal of the Association for the Severely Handicapped. 6*(4), 38–44.

Hilliard, A. G., III. (1975). The strengths and weaknesses of cognitive tests for young children. In J. D. Andrews (Ed.), *One child indivisible.* Washington, DC: National Association for the Education of Young Children.

Hingtgen, J. N., & Bryson, C. Q. (1972). Recent developments in the study of early childhood psychoses: Infantile autism, childhood schizophrenia, and related disorders. *Schizophrenia Bulletin* (No. 5), 8–54.

Hirschberg, G., Lewis, C., & Thomas, D. (1964). *Rehabilitation.* Philadelphia: Lippincott.

Hitzing, W. (1980). ENCOR and beyond. In T. Apolloni, J. Cappuccilli, & T. P. Cooke (Eds.), *Achievements in residential services for persons with disabilities: Total excellence.* Baltimore: University Park Press.

Hobbs, N. (1966). Helping the disturbed child: Psychological and ecological strategies. *American Psychologist, 21,* 1105–1115.

Hobbs, N. (1975). *The futures of children.* San Francisco: Jossey-Bass.

Hobbs, N. (Ed.). (1976a). *Issues in the classification of children* (Vol. 1). San Francisco: Jossey-Bass.

Hobbs, N. (Ed.). (1976b). *Issues in the classification of children* (Vol. 2). San Francisco: Jossey-Bass.

Hobbs, N. (1982). *The troubled and troubling child.* San Francisco: Jossey-Bass.

Hochman, R. (1979). Communicating with parents about the classroom. *Exceptional Teacher, 1*(3), 6–7.

Hoemann, H. W., & Briga, J. I. (1981). Hearing impairments. In J. M. Kauffman & D. P. Hallahan (Eds.), *Handbook of special education.* Englewood Cliffs, NJ: Prentice-Hall.

Hofmeister, A. M., & Friedman, S. G. (1986). The application of technology to the education of persons with severe handicaps. In R. H. Horner, L. H. Meyer, & H. D. B. Fredericks (Eds.), *Education of learners with severe handicaps: Exemplary service strategies* (pp. 351–367). Baltimore: Paul H. Brookes.

Holland, A. L., & Reinmuth, O. M. (1982). Aphasia in adults. In G. H. Shames & E. H. Wiig (Eds.), *Human communication disorders: An introduction.* Columbus, OH: Merrill.

Hollingworth, L. S. (1975). *Children above 180 IQ: Stanford-Binet: Origin and development* (reprint ed.). New York: Arno Press.

Holm, V., & McCartin, R. (1978). Interdisciplinary child development team: Team issues and training in interdisciplinaries. In K. E. Allen, V. A. Holm, & R. I. Schiefelbusch (Eds.), *Early Intervention: A team approach.* Baltimore: University Park Press.

Hops, H., Beickel, S., & Walker, H. M. (1976). *CLASS (Contingencies for Learning Academic and Social Skills): Manual for consultants.* Eugene: University of Oregon, Center at Oregon for Research in Behavioral Education of the Handicapped.

Horner, J. (1986). Moderate aphasia. In J. M. Costello & A. L. Holland (Eds.), *Handbook of speech and language disorders* (pp. 891–915). San Diego: College-Hill.

Horner, R. H., McDonnell, J. J., & Bellamy, G. T. (1986). Teaching generalized skills: General case instruction in simulation and community settings. In R. H. Horner, L. H. Meyer, & H. D. B. Fredericks (Eds.), *Education of learners with severe handicaps: Exemplary service strategies* (pp. 289–314). Baltimore: Paul H. Brookes.

Horst, G., Wehman, P., Hill, J. W., & Bailey, C. (1981). Developing age-appropriate leisure skills in severely handicapped adolescents. *Teaching Exceptional Children, 14,* 11–16.

Howell, K. (1983). *Inside special education.* Columbus, OH: Merrill.

Howell, K. W., Kaplan, J. S., & O'Connell, C. Y. (1979). *Evaluating exceptional children: A task analysis approach.* Columbus, OH: Merrill.

Howell, K., & Morehead, M. K. (1987). *Curriculum based evaluation in special and remedial education.* Columbus, OH: Merrill.

Hubbell, R. (1985). Language and linguistics. In P. Skinner & R. Shelton (Eds.), *Speech, language, and hearing: Normal processes and disorders* (2nd ed.). New York: Wiley.

Huberty, T. J., Koller, J. R., & Ten Brink, T. D. (1980). Adaptive behavior in the definition of mental retardation. *Exceptional Children, 46,* 256–261.

Huebner, K. M. (1986). Social skills. In G. T. Scholl (Ed.), *Foundations for education for blind and visually handicapped children and youth: Theory and practice* (pp. 341–362). New York: American Foundation for the Blind.

Hull, F. M., Mielke, P. W., Willeford, J. A., & Timmons, R. J. (1976). *National speech and hearing survey* (Final report; Project No. 50978; Grant No. OE–32–15–0050–5010 [607]). Washington, DC: U.S. Department of Health, Education, and Welfare.

Hunsucker, P. F., Nelson, R. O., & Clark, R. P. (1986). Standardization and evaluation of the Classroom Adaptive Behavior Checklist for school use. *Exceptional Children, 53,* 69–71.

Huntze, S. L. (1985). A position paper of the Council for Children with Behavioral Disorders. *Behavioral Disorders, 10,* 167–174.

Hutinger, P. L., Marshall, S., & McCarten, K. (1983). *Core curriculum: Macomb 0–3 regional project* (3rd ed.). Macomb: Western Illinois University.

Imber, S. C., Imber, R. B., & Rothstein, C. (1979). Modifying independent work habits: An effective parent-teacher communication program. *Exceptional Children, 46,* 218–221.

Ireland, W. W. (1900). *The mental affections of children: Idiocy, imbecility, and insanity.* Philadelphia: Blakiston.

Irving Independent School District v. Tatro, 104 S. Ct. 3371, 82 L.Ed. 2d 664 (1984).

Iscoe, I., & Payne, S. (1972). Development of a revised scale for the functional classification of exceptional children. In E. P. Trapp & P. Himelstein (Eds.), *Readings on the exceptional child.* New York: Appleton-Century-Crofts.

Itard, J. M. G. (1962). [*The wild boy of Aveyron.*] (G. Humphrey & M. Humphrey, Eds. and Trans.). New York: Appleton-Century-Crofts. (Originally published 1894)

Janicki, M. P., & Zigman, W. B. (1984). Physical and environmental design characteristics of community residences. *Mental Retardation, 22,* 294–301.

Jastak, J. F., & Jastak, S. R. (1965). The Wide Range Achievement Test (rev. ed.). Wilmington, DE: Guidance Associates.

Jastak, J. F., & Wilkinson, G. S. (1984). The Wide Range Achievement Test—Revised. Wilmington, DE: Jastak Associates.

Jellinek, M. (1986). Foreword. In J. Henderson, *Making regular schools special* (pp. ix–xvii). New York: Schocken.

Jenkins, J. R., Speltz, M. L., & Odom, S. L. (1985). Integrating normal and handicapped preschoolers: Effects on child development and social interaction. *Exceptional Children, 52,* 7–17.

Johnson, D., & Myklebust, H. (1967). *Learning disabilities: Educational principles and practices.* New York: Grune & Stratton.

Johnson, J. L. (1976). Mainstreaming black children. In R. L. Jones (Ed.), *Mainstreaming and the minority child.* Reston VA: Council for Exceptional Children.

Johnson, M., & Bailey, J. (1977). The modification of leisure behavior in a halfway house for retarded women. *Journal of Applied Behavior Analysis, 10,* 273–282.

Johnson, T. P. (1986). *The principal's guide to the educational rights of handicapped students.* Reston, VA: National Association of Secondary School Principals.

Johnson, T. S. (1986). Voice Disorders: The measurement of clinical progress. In J. M. Costello & A. L. Holland (Eds.), *Handbook of speech and language disorders* (pp. 477–502). San Diego: College-Hill.

Joiner, L. M., & Sabatino, D. A. (1981). A policy study of P. L. 94-142. *Exceptional Children, 46,* 24–32.

Jonas, G. (1976). *Stuttering: The disorder of many theories.* New York: Farrar, Straus & Giroux.

Jones, M. H. (1977). Physical facilities and environments. In J. B. Jordan, A. H. Hayden, M. B. Karnes, & M. M. Woods (Eds.), *Early childhood education for exceptional children: A handbook of ideas and exemplary practices.* Reston, VA: Council for Exceptional Children.

Jones, M. H. (1983). Cerebral palsy. In J. Umbreit (Ed.), *Physical disabilities and health impairments: An introduction* (pp. 41–58). Columbus, OH: Merrill.

Jones, R. L. (Ed.). (1976). *Mainstreaming and the minority child.* Reston, VA: Council for Exceptional Children.

Jordan, J. B., Hayden, A. H., Karnes, M. B., & Wood, M. M. (Eds.). (1977). *Early childhood education for exceptional children: A handbook of ideas and exemplary practices.* Reston, VA: Council for Exceptional Children.

Journal of Applied Behavior Analysis. (1968–1983). Lawrence, KS: Society for the Experimental Analysis of Behavior.

Justen, J. E. (1976). Who are the severely handicapped? A problem in definition. *AAESPH Review, 1*(2), 1–12.

Kaiser-Kupfer, M. I., & Morris, J. (1985). Advances in human genetics: The long range impact on blindness and the visually impaired. *Yearbook of the Association for Education and Rehabilitation of the Blind and Visually Impaired* (Vol. 2, pp. 46–49). Alexandria, VA: Association for Education and Rehabilitation of the Blind and Visually Impaired.

Kakalik, J. S., Brewer, G. D., Dougharty, L. A., Fleischauer, P. D., Genesky, S. M., & Wallen, L. M. (1974). *Improving services to handicapped children.* Santa Monica, CA: Rand Corporation.

Kamp, S. H., & Chinn, P. C. (1982). *A multiethnic curriculum for special education students.* Reston, VA: Council for Exceptional Children.

Kampfe, C. M. (1984). Mainstreaming: Some practical suggestions for teachers and administrators. In R. H. Hull & K. I. Dilka (Eds.), *The hearing-impaired child in school* (pp. 99–112). Orlando, FL: Grune & Stratton.

Karnes, M. B., Shwedel, A. M., & Williams, M. (1983). Combining instructional models for young gifted children. *Teaching Exceptional Children, 15,* 128–135.

Karnes, M. B., & Teska, J. A. (1980). Toward successful parent involvement in programs for handicapped children. In J. J. Gallagher (Ed.), *New directions for exceptional children: Parents and families of handicapped children* (Vol. 4, pp. 85–109). San Francisco: Jossey-Bass.

Karnes, M. B., Teska, J. A., Hodgins, A. S., & Badger, E. D. (1970). Educational intervention at home by mothers of disadvantaged infants. *Child Development, 41,* 925–935.

Karnes, M. B., & Zehrback, R. R. (1977). Alternative modes for delivering services to young handicapped children. In J. B. Jordan, A. H. Hayden, M. B. Karnes, & M. M. Wood (Eds.), *Early childhood education for exceptional children: A handbook of ideas and exemplary practices.* Reston, VA: Council for Exceptional Children.

Kasari, C., & Filler, J. W. (1981). Using inflatables with severely motorically involved infants and preschoolers. *TEACHING Exceptional Children, 14*(1), 22–26.

Kass, C. R. (1970). Final report, Advanced Institute for Leadership Personnel in Learning Disabilities. Washington, DC: U.S. Office of Education, Bureau of Education for the Handicapped.

Katz, L., Mathis, S. L., & Merrill, E. C. (1978). *The deaf child in the public schools* (2nd ed.). Danville, IL: Interstate Printers & Publishers.

Kauffman, J. M. (1977). *Characteristics of children's behavior disorders.* Columbus, OH: Merrill.

Kauffman, J. M. (1980). Where special education for disturbed children is going: A personal view. *Exceptional Children, 48,* 522–527.

Kauffman, J. M. (1981a). *Characteristics of children's behavior disorders* (2nd ed.). Columbus, OH: Merrill.

Kauffman, J. M. (Ed.). (1981b). Special issue: Are all children educable? *Analysis and Intervention in Developmental Disabilities, 1*(1).

Kauffman, J. M. (1985a). *Characteristics of children's behavior disorders* (3rd ed.). Columbus, OH: Merrill.

Kauffman, J. M. (1985b). An interview with James M. Kauffman. *Directive Teacher, 7*(1), 12–14.

Kauffman, J. M. (1986). Educating children with behavior disorders. In R. J. Morris & B. Blatt (Eds.), *Special education: Research and trends* (pp. 249–271). New York: Pergamon.

Kauffman, J. M., & Hallahan, D. P. (Eds.). (1976). *Teaching children with learning disabilities: Personal perspectives.* Columbus, OH: Merrill.

Kauffman, J. M., & Krouse, J. (1981). The cult of educability: Searching for the substance of things hoped for; the evidence of things not seen. *Analysis and Intervention in Developmental Disabilities, 1*(1), 53–61.

Kaufman, A., & Kaufman, N. (1983). *Kaufman Assessment Battery for Children, interpretive manual.* Circle Pines, MN: American Guidance Service.

Kavale, K. (1981). Functions of the Illinois Test of Psycholinguistic Abilities (ITPA): Are they trainable? *Exceptional Children, 47,* 496–510.

Kavale, K., & Mattison, P. D. (1983). "One jumped off the balance beam": Meta-analysis of perceptual-motor training. *Journal of Learning Disabilities, 16,* 165–173.

Keating, D. P. (1980). Four faces of creativity: The continuing plight of the intellectually underserved. *Gifted Child Quarterly, 24,* 56–61.

Keller, W. D., & Bundy, R. S. (1980). Effects of unilateral hearing loss upon educational achievement. *Child Care, Health & Development, 6,* 93–100.

Kelly, D. J., & Rice, M. L. (1986). A strategy for language assessment of young children: A combination of two approaches. *Language, Speech, and Hearing Services in Schools, 17,* 83–94.

Kelly, R. R. (1987). Computers and sensory impaired individuals. In J. D. Lindsey (Ed.), *Computers and exceptional individuals* (pp. 125–146). Columbus, OH: Merrill.

Kelly, T. J., Bullock, L. M., & Dykes, M. K. (1977). Behavioral disorders: Teachers' perceptions. *Exceptional Children, 43,* 316–318.

Kenney, K. W., & Prather, E. M. (1986). Articulation development in preschool children: Consistency of productions. *Journal of Speech and Hearing Research, 29,* 29–36.

Keogh, B. K., & Margolis, J. (1976). Learn to labor and to wait: Attentional problems of children with learning disorders. *Journal of Learning Disabilities, 9,* 276–286.

Kephart, N. C. (1971). *The slow learner in the classroom* (2nd ed.). Columbus, OH: Merrill.

Kern, L., Koegel, R. L., & Dunlap, G. (1984). The influence of vigorous versus mild exercise on autistic stereotyped behaviors. *Journal of Autism and Developmental Disabilities, 14,* 57–67.

Kerr, B. (1985). Smart girls, gifted women: Special guidance concerns. *Roeper Review,* 30–33.

Kerr, M. M., & Nelson, C. M. (1983). *Strategies for managing behavior problems in the classroom.* Columbus, OH: Merrill.

Kershner, J., Hawks, W., & Grekin, R. (1977). *Megavitamins and learning disorders: A controlled double-blind experiment.* Unpublished manuscript, Ontario Institute for Studies in Education.

Kessler, J. W. (1966). *Psychopathology of childhood.* Englewood Cliffs, NJ: Prentice-Hall.

Khatena, J. (1976). Major directions in creativity research. *Gifted Child Quarterly, 20*(3), 336–349.

Kidd, J. W. (1979). An open letter to the Committee on Technology and Classification of AAMD from the Committee on Definition and Terminology of CEC-MR. *Education and Training of the Mentally Retarded, 14,* 74–76.

King-Stoops, J. (1980). *Migrant education: Teaching the wandering ones.* Bloomington, IN: Phi Delta Kappa Educational Foundation.

Kirchner, C. (1985). *Data on blindness and visual impairment in the United States.* New York: American Foundation for the Blind.

Kirk, S. A. (1958). *Early education of the mentally retarded: An experimental study.* Urbana: University of Illinois.

Kirk, S. A. (1963). Behavioral diagnosis and remediation of learning disabilities. In *Proceedings of the Conference on Exploration into the Problems of the Perceptually Handicapped Child.* Chicago: Perceptually Handicapped Children.

Kirk, S. A. (1978a). Foreword. In D. F. Moores, *Educating the deaf: Psychology, principles, and practices.* Boston: Houghton Mifflin.

Kirk, S. A. (1978b). An interview with Samuel Kirk. *Academic Therapy, 13,* 617–620.

Kirk, S. A. (1981). Foreword to the first edition. In D. F. Moores, *Educating the deaf: Psychology, principles and practices* (2nd ed.). Boston: Houghton Mifflin.

Kirk, S. A., & Elkins, J. (1975). Characteristics of children enrolled in the child service demonstration centers. *Journal of Learning Disabilities, 8,* 630–637.

Kirk, S. A., McCarthy, J. J., & Kirk, W. D. (1968). Illinois Test of Psycholinguistic Abilities (rev. ed.). Urbana: University of Illinois Press.

Klein, S. D., & Schleifer, M. J. (1980). The challenge for the 1980s: Parent-professional collaboration. *The Exceptional Parent, 10*(1), 2–3.

Kleinberg, S. B. (1982). *Educating the chronically ill child.* Rockville, MD: Aspen.

Kleinfeld, J. (1987). Guiding minority students into adulthood. *Phi Delta Kappan, 68*(7), 553–554.

Klima, E., & Bellugi, U. (1979). *The signs of language.* Cambridge, MA: Harvard University Press.

Klinghammer, H. D. (1964). Social perception of the deaf and of the blind by their voices and their speech. In *Report of the proceedings of the International Congress on the Education of the Deaf and of the 41st meeting of the Convention of American Instructors of the Deaf.* Washington, DC: U.S. Government Printing Office.

Kluwin, T. N. (1985). Profiling the deaf student who is a problem in the classroom. *Adolescence, 20,* 863–875.

Knitzer, J. (1982). *Unclaimed children: The failure of public responsibility to children and adolescents in need of mental health services.* Washington, DC: Children's Defense Fund.

Knobloch, H., & Pasamanick, B. (1974). *Gesell's and Amatruda's developmental diagnosis: The evaluation and management of normal and abnormal neuropsychotic development in infancy and early childhood.* Hagerstown, MD: Harper & Row.

Knobloch, H., Pasamanick, B., & Sherard, E. S., Jr. (1966). Developmental Screening Inventory. New York: Psychological Corporation.

Knoblock, P. (1982). *Teaching and mainstreaming autistic children.* Denver: Love.

Koestler, F. (1976). *The unseen minority: A social history of blindness in the United States.* New York: David McKay.

Kokaska, C. J., & Skolnik, J. (1986). Employment suggestions from LD adults. *Academic Therapy, 21,* 573–577.

Kolstoe, O. P. (1972). *Mental retardation: An educational viewpoint.* New York: Holt, Rinehart & Winston.

Kolstoe, O. P., & Frey, R. (1965). *A high school work-study program for mentally subnormal students.* Carbondale: Southern Illinois Press.

Koppelman, J. (Ed.). (1986). Reagan signs bill expanding services to handicapped preschoolers. *Report to Preschool Programs, 18*(21), 3–4.

Korabek, C. A., & Cuvo, A. J. (1986). Children with spina bifida: Educational implications of their medical characteristics. *Education and Treatment of Children, 9,* 142–152.

Krim, M. (1969). Scientific research and mental retardation. *President's Committee on Mental Retardation Message* (No. 16). Washington, DC: U.S. Government Printing Office.

Kronick, D. (1969). *They too can succeed: A practical guide for parents of learning-disabled children.* San Rafael, CA: Academic Therapy.

Kroth, R. L. (1978). Parents: Powerful and necessary allies. *Teaching Exceptional Children, 10,* 88–90.

Kroth, R. L. (1981). Involvement with parents of behaviorally disordered adolescents. In G. Brown, R. L. McDowell, & J. Smith (Eds.), *Educating adolescents with behavior disorders.* Columbus. OH: Merrill.

Kroth, R. L. (1985). *Communicating with parents of exceptional children* (2nd ed.). Denver: Love.

Kroth, R. L., & Simpson, R. (1977). *Parent conferences as a teaching strategy.* Denver: Love.

Kugel, R. B., & Wolfensberger, W. (Eds.). (1969). *Changing patterns in residential services for the mentally retarded.* Washington, DC: Superintendent of Documents.

Kuhlman, F. (1924). Mental deficiency, feeble-mindedness, and defective delinquency. *American Association for the Study of the Feeble-Minded, 29,* 58–70.

Kurtz, G., & Kurtz, P. D. (1987). Child abuse and neglect. In J. T. Neisworth & S. J. Bagnato, *The young exceptional child: Early development and education* (pp. 206–229). New York: Macmillan.

Labov, W. (1975). The logic of nonstandard English. In P. Stoller (Ed.), *Black American English: Its background and its usage in the schools and in literature.* New York: Dell.

Lambert, N., Windmiller, M., Cole, L., & Figueroa, R. (1975). AAMD Adaptive Behavior Scale, Public School Version (1974 rev.). Washington, DC: American Association on Mental Deficiency.

Lancaster, J. (1806). *Improvement in education.* London: Collins & Perkins.

Landesman, S., & Butterfield, E. C. (in press). Normalization and deinstitutionalization of mentally retarded individuals: Controversy and facts. *American Psychologist.*

Larsen, L. A. (1976). Deinstitutionalization. In M. A. Thomas (Ed.), *Hey, don't forget about me! Education's investment in the severely, profoundly, and multiple handicapped.* Reston, VA: Council for Exceptional Children.

Larsen, S. C. (1978). Learning disabilities and the professional educator. *Learning Disability Quarterly, 1,* 5–12.

LaVigna, G. W., & Donnellan, A. M. (1987). Alternatives to punishment: Solving behavior problems with non-aversive strategies. Los Angeles: Institute for Applied Behavior Analysis.

LaVor, M. L. (1976). Federal legislation for exceptional persons: A history. In F. J. Weintraub, A. Abeson, J. Ballard, & M. L. LaVor (Eds.), *Public policy and education of exceptional children.* Reston, VA: Council for Exceptional Children.

Lazar, D., & Darlington, R. (1979, October). *Lasting effects after preschool: A report by the central staff of the consortium for longitudinal studies.* (DHEW Publication No. [OHDS] 80–30179). Washington, DC: U.S. Department of Health, Education, and Welfare.

Lazar, I., & Darlington, R. (1982). Lasting effects of early education: A report from the consortium for longitudinal studies. *Monographs of the Society for Research in Child Development, 47*(2 & 3, Serial No. 195).

LeBuffe, L. A., & LeBuffe, J. R. (1982). The learning vacation: A formula for parent education. *Teaching Exceptional Children. 14,* 182–195.

Leff, R. B. (1975). *How to use the telephone.* Paoli, PA: Instructo Corporation.

Leonard, L. B. (1982). Early language development and language disorders. In G. H. Shames & E. H. Wiig (Eds.), *Human communication disorders: An introduction.* Columbus, OH: Merrill.

Leonard, L. B. (1986). Conversational replies of children with specific language impairments. *Journal of Speech and Hearing Research, 29,* 114–119.

Leone, P., Lovitt, T. C., & Hansen, C. (1981). A descriptive follow-up study of learning disabled boys. *Learning Disability Quarterly, 4,* 152–162.

Lerner, J. (1976). *Children with learning disabilities* (2nd ed.). Boston: Houghton Mifflin.

Levine, M. N. (1986). Psychoeducational evaluation of children and adolescents with cerebral palsy. In P. J. Lazarus & S. S. Strichart (Eds.), *Psychoeducational evaluation of children and adolescents with low-incidence handicaps* (pp. 267–284). Orlando, FL: Grune & Stratton.

Levitt, E. E. (1957). The results of psychotherapy with children: An evaluation. *Journal of Consulting Psychology, 21,* 189–196.

Levitt, E. E. (1963). Psychotherapy with children: A further evaluation. *Behavior Research and Therapy, 1,* 45–51.

Levitt, H. (1985). Technology and the education of the hearing impaired. In F. Powell, T. Finitzo-Hieber, S. Friel-Patti, & D. Henderson (Eds.), *Education of the hearing impaired child* (pp. 119–129). San Diego: College-Hill.

Lewis, R. B., & Doorlag, D. H. (1987). *Teaching special students in the mainstream* (2nd ed.). Columbus, OH: Merrill.

Liebergott, J., Favors, A., von Hippel, C. S., & Needleman, H. L. (1978). *Mainstreaming preschoolers: Children with speech and language impairments.* (Stock no. 017–092–00033–2). Washington DC: U.S. Government Printing Office.

Lieberman, L. M. (1985). Special education and regular education: A merger made in heaven? *Exceptional Children, 51,* 513–516.

Lillie, D. L., and Trohanis, P. L. (Eds.). (1976). *Teaching parents to teach.* New York: Walker.

Lilly, M. S. (1986). The relationship between general and specific education: A new face on an old issue. *Counterpoint, 6*(1), 10.

Lindfors, J. W. (1987). *Children's language and learning* (2nd ed.). Englewood Cliffs, NJ: Prentice-Hall.

Lindman, F. T., & McIntyre, J. M. (1961). *The mentally disabled and the law.* Chicago: University of Chicago Press.

Linebaugh, C. W. (1986). Mild aphasia. In J. M. Costello & A. L. Holland (Eds.), *Handbook of speech and language disorders* (pp. 871–889). San Diego: College-Hill.

Ling, D. (Ed.). (1984). *Early intervention for hearing-impaired children: Total communication options.* San Diego: College-Hill.

Lingwell, J. (1982, July 15). Remarks quoted in M. Kelly, Parent's Almanac: Early Stutterers. *Washington Post,* p. D5.

Livingston-White, D., Utter, C., & Woodard, Q. E. (1985). Follow-up study of visually impaired students of the Michigan School for the Blind. *Journal of Visual Impairment & Blindness, 79,* 150–153.

Lotter, V. (1966). Epidemiology of autistic conditions in young children—Part 1: Prevalence. *Social Psychiatry, 1*(3), 124–137.

Lovaas, O. I. (1982, September). *An Overview of the Young Autism Project.* Paper presented at the annual convention of the American Psychological Association, Washington, DC.

Lovaas, O. I., Koegel, R. L., Simmons, J. Q., & Long, J. S. (1973). Some generalization and follow-up measures on autistic children in behavior therapy. *Journal of Applied Behavior Analysis, 6,* 131–166.

Lovaas, O. I., & Newsom, C. D. (1976). Behavior modification with psychotic children. In H. Leitenberg (Ed.), *Handbook of behavior modification and behavior therapy.* Englewood Cliffs, NJ: Prentice-Hall.

Lovitt, T. C. (1975a). Applied behavior analysis and learning disabilities—Part I: Characteristics of ABA, general recommendations and suggestions for practitioners. *Journal of Learning Disabilities, 8,* 432–443.

Lovitt, T. C. (1975b). Applied behavior analysis and learning disabilities—Part II: Specific research recommendations and suggestions for practitioners. *Journal of Learning Disabilities, 8,* 504–518.

Lovitt, T. C. (1977). *In spite of my resistance . . . I've learned from children.* Columbus, OH: Merrill.

Lovitt, T. C. (1978). The learning disabled. In N. G. Haring (Ed.), *Behavior of exceptional children* (2nd ed.). Columbus, OH: Merrill.

Lovitt, T. C. (1982). *Because of my persistence . . . I've learned from children.* Columbus, OH: Merrill.

Lovitt, T. C. (1984). *Tactics of teaching.* Columbus, OH: Merrill.

Lowell, E. L., & Pollack, D. B. (1974). Remedial practices with the hearing impaired. In S. Dickson (Ed.), *Communication disorders: Remedial principles and practices.* Glenview, IL: Scott, Foresman.

Lowenfeld, B. (Ed.). (1973). *The visually handicapped child in school.* New York: John Day.

Lowenthal, B. (1981). Effect of small-group instruction on language-delayed preschoolers. *Exceptional Children, 48,* 178–179.

Ludlow, B. L., & Sobsey, R. (1984). *The school's role in educating severely handicapped students.* Bloomington, IN: Phi Delta Kappa Educational Foundation.

Lund, K. A., & Bos, C. S. (1981). Orchestrating the preschool classroom: The daily schedule. *TEACHING Exceptional Children, 14,* 120–125.

Lund, K. A., Foster, G. E., & McCall-Perez, F. C. (1978). The effectiveness of psycholinguistic training: A reevaluation. *Exceptional Children, 44,* 310–319.

Lusthaus, C. S., Lusthaus, E. W., & Gibbs, H. (1981). Parents' role in the decision process. *Exceptional Children, 48,* 256–257.

Luterman, D. M. (Ed.). (1986). *Deafness in perspective.* San Diego: College-Hill.

Lynas, W. (1986). *Integrating the handicapped into ordinary schools: A study of hearing-impaired pupils.* London: Croom Helm.

Lynch, E. W., & Stein, R. (1982). Perspectives on parent participation in special education. *Exceptional Education Quarterly, 3*(2), 56–63.

MacCarthy, A., & Connell, J. (1984). Audiological screening and assessment. In G. Lindsay (Ed.), *Screening for children with special needs* (pp. 63–85). London: Croom Helm.

MacDonald, L., & Barton, L. E. (1986). Measuring severity of behavior: A revision of Part II of the Adaptive Behavior Scale. *American Journal of Mental Deficiency, 90,* 418–424.

MacFadyen, J. T. (1986). Educated monkeys help the disabled to help themselves. *Smithsonian, 17*(7), 125–133.

MacMillan, D. L. (1982). *Mental retardation in school and society* (2nd ed.). Boston: Little, Brown.

Maddux, C. D., & Cummings, R. E. (1983). Parental home tutoring: Aids and cautions. *The Exceptional Parent, 13*(4), 30–33.

Madle, R. A. (1978). Alternative residential placements. In J. T. Neisworth & R. M. Smith (Eds.), *Retardation: Issues, assessment, and intervention.* New York: McGraw-Hill.

Maestas y Moores, J., & Moores, D. F. (1980). Language training with the young deaf child. In D. Bricker (Ed.), *Early language intervention with handicapped children.* San Francisco: Jossey-Bass.

Mager, R. F. (1972). *Goal Analysis,* Belmont, CA: Fearon.

Magliocca, L. A. (1980). Interview with Jane Rieke. *The Directive Teacher, 2*(3), 14.

Maker, C. J. (1977). *Providing programs for the gifted handicapped.* Reston, VA: Council for Exceptional Children.

Maker, C. J. (1982). *Teaching models in education of the gifted.* Rockville, MD: Aspen.

Maker, C. J. (Ed.). (1986). *Critical issues in gifted education: Defensible programs for the gifted.* Rockville, MD: Aspen.

Malone, C. (Ed.). (1978). Disadvantaged and gifted handicapped. *Gifted Child Quarterly, 22.*

Mansdorf, I. J. (1977). Rapid token training of an institution ward using modeling. *Mental Retardation, 15*(4), 37–39.

Mansour, S. L. (1985). 1985 ASHA demographic update. *ASHA, 27*(7), 55.

Marbach, W. D. (1982, July 12). Building the bionic man. *Newsweek,* pp. 78–79.

Marfo, K. (1986). Confronting childhood disability in the developing countries. In K. Marfo, S. Walker, & B. Charles (Eds.), *Childhood disability in developing countries: Issues in habilitation and special education* (pp. 3–26). New York: Praeger.

Marland, S. P. (1971). *Education of the gifted and talented.* Washington, DC: U.S. Office of Education.

Marland, S. (1972). *Education of the gifted and talented* (Report to Congress). Washington, DC: U.S. Government Printing Office.

Marsh, G. E., Gearheart, C. K., & Gearheart, B. R. (1978). *The learning disabled adolescent: Program alternatives in the secondary school.* St. Louis: C. V. Mosby.

Marshall, A. E., & Heward, W. L. (1979). Teaching self-management to incarcerated youth. *Behavioral Disorders, 4,* 215–226.

Martin, B. (1975). Parent-child relations. In F. D. Horowitz (Ed.), *Review of child development research* (Vol. 4). Chicago: University of Chicago Press.

Martin, R. R., & Lindamood, L. P. (1986). Stuttering and spontaneous recovery: Implications for the speech-language pathologist. *Language, Speech, and Hearing Services in Schools, 17,* 207–218.

Mattes, L. J., & Omark, D. R. (1984). *Speech and language assessment for the bilingual handicapped.* San Diego: College-Hill.

Matthews, J. (1982). The professions of speech-language pathology and audiology. In G. H. Shames & E. H. Wiig (Eds.), *Human communication disorders: An introduction.* Columbus, OH: Merrill.

Mayhall, W., & Jenkins. J. (1977). Scheduling daily or less-than-daily instruction: Implications for resource programs. *Journal of Learning Disabilities. 10,* 150–163.

Mayo, L. W. (1962). *A proposed program for national action to combat mental retardation.* Report of the President's Committee on Mental Retardation. Washington, DC: U.S. Government Printing Office.

McCormick, L., & Schiefelbush, R. L. (1984). *Early language intervention: An introduction.* Columbus, OH: Merrill.

McDaniels, G. (1977). Successful programs for young handicapped children. *Educational Horizons, 56*(1), 26–27, 30–33.

McDavis, R. J. (1980). The black client. In N. A. Vacc & J. P. Wittmer (Eds.), *Let me be me: Special populations and the helping professional* (pp. 151–174). Muncie, IN: Accelerated Development.

McDonnell, J. J., Wilcox, B., Boles, S. M., & Bellamy, G. T. (1985). Transition issues facing youth with severe disabilities: Parent's perspective. *Journal of the Association for Persons with Severe Handicaps, 10,* 61–65.

McGovern, J. E., & Draper, D. (1978). Identification, assessment, and intervention. In N. H. Fallen with J. E. McGovern (Eds.), *Young children with special needs.* Columbus, OH: Merrill.

McIntire, J. C. (1985). The future role of residential schools for visually impaired students. *Journal of Visual Impairment & Blindness, 79,* 161–164.

McKinney, J. D. (1985). The search for subtypes of specific learning disability. *Annual Progress in Child Psychiatry & Child Development,* 542–559.

McLaughlin, M. J., Smith-Davis, J., & Burke, P. J. (1986). *Personnel to educate the handicapped in America: A status report.* College Park, MD: University of Maryland, Institute for the Study of Exceptional Children and Youth.

McLean, J. E., & Snyder-McLean, L. K. (1978). *A transactional approach to early language training.* Columbus, OH: Merrill.

McLoughlin, J. A., & Kelly, D. (1982). Issues facing the resource teacher. *Learning Disability Quarterly, 5,* 58–64.

McLoughlin, J. A., & Lewis, R. B. (1986). *Assessing special students* (2nd ed.). Columbus, OH: Merrill.

McLoughlin, J. A., & Netick, A. (1983). Defining learning disabilities: A new and cooperative direction. *Journal of Learning Disabilities, 16,* 21–23.

McNutt, G. & Heller, G. (1978). Services for the learning disabled adolescent: A survey. *Learning Disability Quarterly, 1,* 101–103.

Meadow, K. P. (1980). *Deafness and child development.* Berkeley: University of California Press.

Meadow-Orlans, K. P. (1985). Social and psychological effects of hearing loss in adulthood: A literature review. In H. Orlans (Ed.), *Adjustment to adult hearing loss* (pp. 35–57). San Diego: College-Hill.

Meehl, P. (1969). Schizotoxia, schizotypy, schizophrenia. In A. Buss (Ed.), *Theories of schizophrenia.* New York: Atherton.

Meeker, M. N. (1969). *The structure of intellect: Its interpretation and uses.* Columbus, OH: Merrill.

Mendelsohn, S. R., & Jennings, K. D. (1986). Characteristics of emotionally disturbed children referred for special education assessment. *Child Psychiatry & Human Development, 16,* 154–170.

Menolascino, F. J., & Eyde, D. R. (1979). Biophysical bases of autism. *Behavioral Disorders, 5,* 41–47.

Menolascino, F. L. (1977). *Challenges in mental retardation: Progressive ideology and sources.* New York: Human Services Press.

Mercer, C. D. (1987). *Students with learning disabilities* (3rd ed.). Columbus, OH: Merrill.

Mercer, C. D., Hughes, C., & Mercer, A. R. (1985). Learning disabilities definitions used by state education departments. *Learning Disability Quarterly, 8,* 45–55.

Mercer, J. R. (1973a). *Labelling the mentally retarded.* Berkeley: University of California Press.

Mercer, J. R. (1973b). The myth of 3% prevalence. In R. K. Eymon, C. E. Meyers, & G. Tarjon (Eds.), *Sociobehavioral studies in mental retardation* [Monographs of the American Association on Mental Deficiency, No. 1].

Mercer, J. R. (1981). Testing and assessment practices in multiethnic education. In J. A. Banks (Ed.), *Education in the 80's: Multiethnic education.* Washington, DC: National Education Association.

Mesinger, J. F. (1985). Commentary on "A rationale for the merger of special and regular education" or, is it now time for the lamb to lie down with the lion? *Exceptional Children, 51,* 510–512.

Meyen, E. L. (Ed.). (1978). *Exceptional children and youth: An introduction.* Denver: Love.

Meyer, L. H., & Evans, I. M. (1986). Modification of excess behavior: An adaptive and functional approach for educational and community contexts. In R. H. Horner, L. H. Meyer, & H. D. B. Fredericks (Eds.), *Education of learners with severe handicaps: Exemplary service strategies* (pp. 315–350). Baltimore: Paul H. Brookes.

Meyerson, L., Kerr, N., & Michael, J. L. (1967). Behavior modification in rehabilitation. In S. W. Bijou & D. M. Baer (Eds.), *Child development: Readings in experimental analysis.* New York: Appleton-Century-Crofts.

Miller, D. (1979). *Ophthalmology: The essentials.* Boston: Houghton Mifflin.

Miller, J., & Allaire, J. (1987). Augmentative communication. In M. E. Snell (Ed.), *Systematic instruction of persons with severe handicaps* (3rd ed., pp. 273–297). Columbus, OH: Merrill.

Miller, W. H. (1985). The role of residential schools for the blind in educating visually impaired students. *Journal of Visual Impairment & Blindness, 79,* 160.

Milner, J. S., & Wimberley, R. C. (1980). Prediction and explanation of child abuse. *Journal of Clinical Psychology, 36,* 875–884.

Minner, S., Beane, A., & Prater, G. (1987). Try telephone answering machines. *Teaching Exceptional Children, 19,* 62–63.

Minskoff, E. (1975). Research on psycholinguistic training: Critique and guidelines. *Exceptional Children, 42,* 136–144.

Mitchell, B. (1982). An update on the state of gifted/talented education in the U.S. *Phi Delta Kappan, 64,* 357–358.

Mitchell, P. B. (Ed.). (1981). *A policymaker's guide to issues in gifted and talented education.* Washington, DC: National Association of State Boards of Education.

Mithaug, D. E., & Hagmeier, L. D. (1978). The development of procedures to assess prevocational competencies of severely handicapped young adults. *AAESPH Review, 3,* 94–115.

Mithaug, D. E., Horiuchi, C. N., & Fanning, P. N. (1985). A report on the Colorado statewide follow-up survey of special education students. *Exceptional Children, 51,* 397–404.

Montgomery, P. A., & Van Fleet, D. (1978). Evaluation of behavioral and academic change through the Re-Ed process. *Behavioral Disorders, 3,* 136–146.

Moon, M. S., & Bunker, L. (1987). Recreation and motor skills programming. In M. E. Snell (Ed.), *Systematic instruction of persons with severe handicaps* (3rd ed., pp. 214–244). Columbus, OH: Merrill.

Moore, P. (1982). Voice disorders. In G. H. Shames & E. H. Wiig (Eds.), *Human communication disorders: An introduction.* Columbus, OH: Merrill.

Moores, D. F. (1985). Educational programs and services for hearing impaired children: Issues and options. In F. Powell, T. Finitzo-Hieber, S. Friel-Patti, & D. Henderson (Eds.), *Education of the hearing impaired child* (pp. 3–20). San Diego: College-Hill.

Moores, D. F. (1987). *Educating the deaf: Psychology, principles and practices* (3rd ed.). Boston: Houghton Mifflin.

Moores, D. F., & Kluwin, T. N. (1986). Issues in school placement. In A. N. Schildroth & M. A. Karchmer (Eds.), *Deaf children in America* (pp. 105–123). San Diego: College-Hill.

Moores, D. F., & Maestas y Moores, J. (1981). Special adaptations necessitated by hearing impairments. In J. M. Kauffman & D. P. Hallahan (Eds.), *Handbook of special education.* Englewood Cliffs, NJ: Prentice-Hall.

Morgan, S. R. (1987). *Abuse and neglect of handicapped children*. San Diego: College-Hill.

Morse, C. W., Sahler, O. Z., & Friedman, S. B. (1970). A three-year follow-up study of abused and neglected children. *American Journal of Diseases of Children, 120*, 439–446.

Morse, W. C. (1975). The education of socially maladjusted and emotionally disturbed children. In W. M. Cruickshank & G. O. Johnson (Eds.), *Education of exceptional children and youth* (3rd ed.). Englewood Cliffs, NJ: Prentice-Hall.

Morse, W. C. (1976). Worksheet on life-space interviewing for teachers. In N. Long, W. Morse, & R. Newman (Eds.), *Conflict in the classroom*. Belmont, CA: Wadsworth.

Morse, W. C., Cutler, R. L., & Fink, A. H. (1964). *Public school classes for the emotionally handicapped: A research analysis*. Washington, DC: Council for Exceptional Children.

Morsink, C. V., Thomas, C. C., & Smith-Davis, J. (in press). Noncategorical special education programs: Process and outcomes. In M. C. Wang, M. C. Reynolds, & H. J. Walberg (Eds.), *The handbook of special education: Research and practice*. Oxford, England: Pergamon.

Mow, S. (1973). How do you dance without music? In D. Watson (Ed.), *Readings on deafness*. New York: New York University School of Education, Deafness Research and Training Center.

Moyer, J. R., & Dardig, J. C. (1978). Practical task analysis for special educators. *Teaching Exceptional Children*. 1–16.

Mullins, J. B. (1979). *A teacher's guide to management of physically handicapped students*. Springfield, IL: Charles C Thomas.

Murphy, A. (1986). Issues in special-education law. In J. Henderson, *Making regular schools special* (pp. 86–92). New York: Schocken.

Murphy, A. T. (1982). The family with a handicapped child: A review of the literature. *Developmental and Behavioral Pediatrics. 3*(2), 73–82.

Murray, C. A. (1976). *The link between learning disabilities and juvenile delinquency: Current theory and knowledge*. Washington, DC: American Institute for Research.

Myers, P. I., & Hammill, D. D. (1976). *Methods for learning disorders* (2nd ed.). New York: John Wiley.

Myers, P. I., & Hammill, D. D. (1982). *Learning disabilities: Basic concepts, assessment practices, and instructional strategies*. Austin, TX: Pro-Ed.

Naisbitt, J. (1982). *Megatrends: Ten new directions transforming our lives*. New York: Warner Books.

Napierkowski, H. (1981). The role of language in the intellectual development of the deaf child. *TEACHING Exceptional Children. 14*, 106–109.

National Association for Retarded Citizens. (1976). *Educating the twenty-four hour retarded child*. Arlington, TX: Author.

National Association for Superintendents of Public Residential Facilities for the Mentally Retarded. (1974). *Contemporary issues in residential programming*. Washington, DC: President's Committee on Mental Retardation.

National Association of State Directors of Special Education. (1986). *Severely handicapped youth exiting public education: Issues and concerns*. Washington, DC: Author.

National Center for Health Statistics. (1975). *Prevalence of selected impairments: United States—1971*. (Publication No. [HRA] 75–1526). Washington, DC: Department of Health, Education and Welfare.

National Center for Health Statistics. (1981). *Prevalence of selected impairments: United States—1977*. (Publication No. [PHS] 82–1562). Washington, DC: Department of Health, Education and Welfare.

National Center on Child Abuse and Neglect. (1982). *Profile of child abuse and neglect*. Washington, DC: U.S. Department of Health and Human Services.

National Commission on Space. (1986). *Pioneering the space frontier*. New York: Bantam Books.

National Committee for Citizens in Education. (1979). Unpublished manuscript serving as basis for congressional testimony.

National Hotel and Restaurant Association. (1983). Personal communication with Dr. Philip Nelen, Washington, DC.

National Joint Committee on Learning Disabilities. (1981). *Learning disabilities: Issues on definition*. Unpublished manuscript.

National Society for Autistic Children. (1977, September). A short definition of autism. *Newsletter*.

National study on the incidence and severity of child abuse and neglect (DHHS Publication 81–30325). (1981). Washington, DC: U.S. Department of Health and Human Services, National Center of Child Abuse and Neglect.

Navarre, J. (1983). How the teacher of the gifted can use the S.O.I. *Gifted Child Today, 26*, 17–18.

Neisworth, J. T., & Smith, R. M. (Eds.). (1978). *Retardation: Issues, assessment, and intervention*. New York: McGraw-Hill.

Nelson, C. M. (1971). Techniques for screening conduct-disturbed children. *Exceptional Children, 37*, 501–507.

Nelson, C. M., & Polsgrove, L. (1984). Behavior analysis in special education: White rabbit or white elephant? *Remedial and Special Education, 5*(4), 6–17.

Nelson, K. B., & Ellenberg, J.H. (1986). Antecedents of cerebral palsy: Multivariate analysis of risk. *New England Journal of Medicine, 315*, 81–86.

Newman, P. L., Creaghead, N. A., & Secord, W. A. (1985). *Assessment and remediation of articulatory and phonological disorders*. Columbus, OH: Merrill.

Nietupski, J., & Svoboda, R. (1982). Teaching a cooperative leisure skill to severely handicapped adults. *Education and Training of the Mentally Retarded, 17*, 38–43.

Nihira, K., Foster, R., Shellhaas, M., & Leland, H. (1974). AAMD Adaptive Behavior Scale (1974 rev.). Washington, DC: American Association of Mental Deficiency.

Nisbet, J., & Vincent, L. (1986). The differences in inappropriate behavior and instructional interactions in sheltered and nonsheltered work environments. *Journal of the Association for Persons with Severe Handicaps, 11,* 19–27.

Noonan, M. J., Brown, F., Mulligan, M., & Rettig, M. A. (1982). Educability of severely handicapped persons: Both sides of the issue. *Journal of the Association for the Severely Handicapped, 7*(1), 3–12.

Norman, C. A., & Zigmond, N. (1980). Characteristics of children labeled and served as learning disabled in school systems affiliated with Child Service Demonstration centers. *Journal of Learning Disabilities, 13,* 542–547.

Norris, C. (Ed.). (1975). *Letters from deaf students.* Eureka, CA: Alinda Press.

Northcott, W. H., & Erickson, L. C. (1977). *The UNISTAPS Project.* St. Paul: Minnesota Department of Education.

Northern, J. L., & Lemme, M. (1982). Hearing and auditory disorders. In G. H. Shames & E. H. Wiig (Eds.), *Human communication disorders: An introduction.* Columbus, OH: Merrill.

Norton, D. G. (1983). Black family life patterns, the development of self and cognitive development of black children. In G. J. Powell (Ed.), *The psychosocial development of minority group children* (pp. 181–193). New York: Brunner/Mazel.

Nurss, J. R., & McGauvran, M. E. (1976). *Metropolitan Readiness Test.* Cleveland: Psychological Corporation.

Oakland, T. (1980). An evaluation of the ABIE, pluristic norms, and estimated learning potential. *Journal of School Psychology, 18,* 3–11.

O'Brien, J. (1971). How we detect mental retardation before birth. *Medical Times, 99,* 103.

O'Connell, J. C. (1986). Managing small group instruction in an integrated preschool setting. *Teaching Exceptional Children, 18,* 166–171.

O'Conner, G. (1983). Presidential address 1983: Social support of mentally retarded persons. *Mental Retardation, 21,* 187–196.

Ohanian, S. (1987). Notes on Japan from an American schoolteacher. *Phi Delta Kappan, 68*(5), 360–367.

O'Leary, S. G., & Dubey, D. R. (1979). Applications of self-control procedures by children: A review. *Journal of Applied Behavior Analysis, 12,* 449–465.

Oliver, L. I. (1974). *Behavior patterns in school and youth 12–17 years* (National Health Survey, Series 11, No. 139, U.S. Department of Health, Education and Welfare). Washington, DC: U.S. Government Printing Office.

Olson, J., Algozzine, B., & Schmid, R. E. (1980). Mild, moderate, and severe EH: An empty distinction? *Behavioral Disorders, 5,* 96–101.

Orelove, F. P. (1982a). Acquisition of incidental learning in moderately and severely handicapped adults. *Education and Training of the Mentally Retarded, 17,* 131–136.

Orelove, F. P. (1982b). *Educating all handicapped persons: How can we get there from here?* Paper presented at the Conference on Behavior Analysis in Education, Ohio State University, Columbus.

Orelove, F. P. (1984). The educability debate: A review and a look ahead. In W. L. Heward, T. E. Heron, D. S. Hill, & J. Trap-Porter (Eds.), *Focus on behavior analysis in education* (pp. 271–281). Columbus, OH: Merrill.

Orlando, C. (1981). Multidisciplinary team approaches in the assessment of handicapped preschool children. *Topics in Early Childhood Special Education, 1,* 23–30.

Orlansky, J. Z. (1979). *Mainstreaming the hearing impaired child: An educational alternative.* Ann Arbor, MI: University Microfilms International. (Catalog No. AU00322)

Orlansky, M. D. (1986a). The importance of communication for planning transitional programs for persons who are deaf-blind. In *Yearbook of the Association for Education and Rehabilitation of the Blind and Visually Impaired* (Vol. 3, pp. 35–40). Washington, DC: Association for Education and Rehabilitation of the Blind and Visually Impaired.

Orlansky, M. D. (1986b). Multiply handicapped. In J. V. Van Cleve (Ed.), *Gallaudet encyclopedia of deaf people and deafness* (Vol. 2, pp. 335–357). New York: McGraw-Hill.

Orlansky, M. D., & Bonvillian, J. D. (1985). Sign language acquisition: Language development in children of deaf parents and implications for other populations. *Merrill-Palmer Quarterly, 31,* 127–143.

Orlansky, M. D., & Heward, W. L. (1981). *Voices: Interviews with handicapped people.* Columbus, OH: Merrill.

Ortiz, A. A., & Garcia, S. B. (1986). Characteristics of limited English proficient Hispanic students served in programs for the learning disabled: Implications for policy and practice. *Counterpoint, 7*(1), 10–11.

Osguthorpe, R. T., & Scruggs, T. E. (1986). Special education students as tutors: A review and analysis. *Remedial and Special Education, 7*(4), 15–26.

Page, E. B. (1972). Miracle in Milwaukee: Raising the IQ. *Educational Researcher, 15,* 8–16.

Pancsofar, E., & Blackwell, R. (1986). *A user's guide to community entry for the severely handicapped.* Albany: State University of New York Press.

Parent, E. A. (1985). Review of *Between sacred mountains: Stories and lessons from the land. Harvard Educational Review. 55,* 134–137.

Parette, H. P., & Hourcade, J. J. (1986). Management strategies for orthopedically handicapped students. *Teaching Exceptional Children, 18*(4), 282–286.

Parmelee, A. H., & Michaelis, R. (1971). Neurological examination of the newborn. In J. Hellmuth (Ed.), *Exceptional infant* (Vol. 2). New York: Brunner/Mazel.

Patrick, J. L., & Reschly, D. L. (1982). Relationship of state educational criteria and demographic variables to school-system prevalence of mental retardation. *American Journal of Mental Deficiency, 86,* 351–360.

Patterson, G. R. (1979). *Living with children: New methods for parents and teachers* (rev. ed.). Champaign, IL: Research Press.

Patterson, G. R. (1980). Mothers: The unacknowledged victims. *Monographs of the Society for Research in Child Development, 45* (5, Serial No. 186).

Patterson, G. R., Cobb, J. A., & Ray, R. S. (1972). Direct intervention in the classroom: A set of procedures for the aggressive child. In F. W. Clark, D. R. Evans, & L. A. Hammerlynch (Eds.), *Implementing behavioral programs in schools and clinics.* Champaign, IL: Research Press.

Patterson, G. R., Reid, J. B., Jones, R. R., & Conger, R. E. (1975). *A social learning approach to family intervention: Vol. 1. Families with aggressive children.* Eugene, OR: Castalia.

Patton, J. R. (1986). A historical overview. In J. R. Patton, J. S. Payne, & M. Beirne-Smith, *Mental retardation* (2nd ed.). Columbus, OH: Merrill.

Payne, J. S., & Patton, J. R. (1981). *Mental retardation.* Columbus, OH: Merrill.

Payne, J. S., Patton, J. R., & Patton, F. E. (1986). Adaptive behavior. In J. R. Patton, J. S. Payne, & M. Beirne-Smith, *Mental Retardation* (2nd ed.). Columbus, OH: Merrill.

Peck, C. A., & Semmel, M. I. (1982). Identifying the least restrictive environment (LRE) for children with severe handicaps: Toward an empirical analysis. *Journal of the Association for the Severely Handicapped, 7*(1), 56–63.

Peizer, E. (1975). Wheelchairs. In *Atlas of orthotics.* St. Louis: C. V. Mosby.

Pepper, F. C. (1976). Teaching the American Indian child in mainstream settings. In R. L. Jones (Ed.). *Mainstreaming and the minority child.* Reston, VA: Council for Exceptional Children.

Perkins, W. H. (1977). *Speech pathology.* St. Louis: C. V. Mosby.

Perlmutter, B. F., & Parus, M. V. (1983). Identifying children with learning disabilities: A comparison of diagnostic procedures across school districts. *Learning Disability Quarterly, 6,* 321–328.

Pfeiffer, S. I. (1982). The superiority of team decision making. *Exceptional Children, 49,* 68–69.

Pieper, B., & Cappuccilli, J. (1980). Beyond the family and the institution: The sanctity of liberty. In T. Apolloni, J. Cappuccilli, and T. P. Cooke (Eds.), *Achievements in residential services for persons with disabilities: Toward excellence.* Baltimore: University Park Press.

Pieper, E. (1983). *The teacher and the child with spina bifida* (2nd ed.). Rockville, MD: Spina Bifida Association of America.

Polifka, J. C. (1981). Compliance with Public Law 94–142 and consumer satisfaction. *Exceptional Children, 48,* 250–253.

Polloway, E. A. (1984). The integration of mildly retarded students in the schools: A historical review. *Remedial and Special Education, 5*(4), 18–28.

Polloway, E. A., Cronin, M. E., & Patton, J. R. (1986). The efficacy of group versus one-to-one instruction: A review. *Remedial and Special Education, 7*(1), 22–30.

Powell, T. H., & Ogle, P. A. (1985). *Brothers and sisters: A special part of exceptional families.* Baltimore: Paul H. Brookes.

Prasse, D. P. (1986). Litigation and special education: An introduction. *Exceptional Children, 52,* 311–312.

Pratt, M. W., Luszcz, M. A., & Brown, M. E. (1980). Measuring dimensions of the quality of care in small community residences. *American Journal of Mental Deficiency, 85,* 188–194.

President's Committee on Mental Retardation. (1969). *The six-hour retarded child.* Washington, DC: U.S. Department of Health, Education and Welfare.

Pressey, S. L. (1955). Concerning the nature and nurture of genius. *Scientific Monthly, 80,* 123–129.

Pressey, S. L. (1962). Educational acceleration: Occasional procedure or major issue? *Personnel and Guidance Journal, 12*–17.

Prinz, P. M., & Nelson, K. E. (1985). "Alligator eats cookie": Acquisition of writing and reading skills by deaf children using the microcomputer. *Applied Psycholinguistics, 6,* 283–306.

Prinz, P. M., & Prinz, E. A. (1979). Simultaneous acquisition of ASL and spoken English in a hearing child of a deaf mother and hearing father. *Sign Language Studies, 25,* 283–296.

Provencal, G. (1980). The Macomb-Oakland regional center. In T. Apolloni, J. Cappucilli, & T. P. Cooke (Eds.), *Achievements in residential services for persons with disabilities: Toward excellence.* Baltimore: University Park Press.

Putnam, J. W., & Bruininks, R. H. (1986). Future directions in deinstitutionalization and education: A Delphi investigation. *Exceptional Children, 53,* 55–62.

Quay, H. C. (1968). The faces of educational exceptionality: Conceptual framework for assessment, grouping, and instruction. *Exceptional Children, 35,* 25–31.

Quay, H. C. (1972). Patterns of aggression, withdrawal and immaturity. In H. C. Quay & J. S. Werry (Eds.), *Psychopathological disorders of childhood.* New York: John Wiley.

Quay, H. C. (1975). Classification in the treatment of delinquency and antisocial behavior. In N. Hobbs (Eds.), *Issues in the classification of children* (Vol. 1). San Francisco: Jossey-Bass.

Quay, H. C. (1979). Classification. In H. C. Quay & J. S. Werry (Eds.), *Psychopathological disorders of children* (2nd ed.). New York: Wiley.

Quigley, S. P., & Paul, P. V. (1984). ASL and ESL? *Topics in Early Childhood Special Education, 3*(4), 17–26.

Quigley, S. P., & Paul, P. V. (1986). A perspective on academic achievement. In D. M. Luterman (Ed.), *Deafness in perspective* (pp. 55–86). San Diego: College-Hill.

Rauth, M. (1980). *A guide to understanding the Education for All Handicapped Children Act (P.L. 94–142).* Washington, DC: American Federation of Teachers, AFL-CIO.

Raver, S. (1984). Modification of head droop during conversation in a 3-year-old visually impaired child: A case study. *Journal of Visual Impairment & Blindness, 78,* 307–310.

Rawlings, B. W., & King, S. J. (1986). Postsecondary educational opportunities for deaf students. In A. N. Schildroth & M. A. Karchmer (Eds.), *Deaf children in America* (pp. 231–257). San Diego: College-Hill.

Reagan, T. (1985). The deaf as a linguistic minority: Educational considerations. *Harvard Educational Review, 55,* 265–277.

Reed, V. A. (1986). *An introduction to children with language disorders.* New York: Macmillan.

Reger, R. (1974). What does "mainstreaming" mean? *Journal of Learning Disabilities, 7,* 513–515.

Rehder, K. V. (Ed.). (1986). *Rehabilitation Research and Training Center Newsletter, 3*(3). Richmond: Virginia Commonwealth University.

Reichle, J., & Keogh, W. J. (1986). Communication instruction for learners with severe handicaps: Some unresolved issues. In R. H. Horner, L. H. Meyer, & H. D. B. Fredericks (Eds.), *Education of learners with severe handicaps: Exemplary service strategies* (pp. 189–219). Baltimore: Paul H. Brookes.

Reid, D. H., & Favell, J. (1984). Group instruction with persons who have severe disabilities: A critical review. *Journal of the Association for Persons with Severe Handicaps, 9,* 167–177.

Reis, S. M., & Cellerino, M. (1983). Guiding gifted students through independent study. *Teaching Exceptional Children, 15,* 136–139.

Renfrew, C. E. (1972). *Speech disorders in children.* Oxford, England: Pergamon Press.

Renzulli, J. S. (1977). *The enrichment triad model: A guide for developing defensible programs for the gifted and talented.* Weathersfield, CT: Creative Learning Press.

Renzulli, J. S. (1978). What makes giftedness?: Reexamining a definition. *Phi Delta Kappan, 61,* 180–184.

Renzulli, J. S. (1982). What makes a problem real: Stalking the illusive meaning of qualitative differences in gifted education. *Gifted Child Quarterly, 26,* 147–156.

Renzulli, J. S. (1986). *Systems and models for developing programs for the gifted and talented.* Mansfield Center, CT: Creative Learning Press.

Renzulli, J. S., Reis, S. M., & Smith, L. H. (1981). *The revolving door identification model.* Mansfield Center, CT: Creative Learning Press.

Renzulli, J. S., & Smith, L. (1979). *A guidebook for developing individualized educational programs (IEP) for gifted and talented students.* Mansfield Center, CT: Creative Learning Press.

Repp, A. C., & Barton, L. E. (1980). Naturalistic observations of institutionalized retarded persons: A comparison of licensure decisions and behavioral observations. *Journal of Applied Behavior Analysis, 13,* 333–341.

Reynolds, M. C. (1978). Staying out of jail. *Teaching Exceptional Children, 10,* 60–62.

Reynolds, M. C., & Birch, J. W. (1982). *Teaching exceptional children in all America's schools* (2nd ed.). Reston, VA: Council for Exceptional Children.

Reynolds, M. C., Wang, M. C., & Walberg, H. J. (1987). The necessary restructuring of special and regular education. *Exceptional Children, 53,* 391–398.

Rhodes, L. E., & Valenta, L. (1985). Industry-based supported employment: An enclave approach. *Journal of the Association for Persons with Severe Handicaps, 10,* 12–20.

Rhodes, W. C., & Head, S. (Eds.). (1974). *A study of child variance: Vol 3. Service delivery systems.* Ann Arbor: University of Michigan.

Rhodes, W. C., & Tracy, M. L. (Eds.). (1972a). *A study of child variance: Vol 1. Theories.* Ann Arbor: University of Michigan.

Rhodes, W. C., & Tracy, M. L. (Eds.). (1972b). *A study of child variance: Vol 2. Interventions.* Ann Arbor: University of Michigan.

Rhyne, J. M. (1982). Comprehension of synthetic speech by blind children. *Journal of Visual Impairment & Blindness, 76,* 313–316.

Rich, H. L., Beck, M. A., & Coleman, T. W., Jr. (1982). Behavior management: The psychoeducational model. In R. L. McDowell, G. W. Adamson, & F. H. Wood (Eds.), *Teaching emotionally disturbed children* (pp. 131–166). Boston: Little, Brown.

Richardson, E. H. (1981). Cultural and historical perspectives in counseling American Indians. In D. W. Sue, *Counseling the culturally different: Theory and practice.* New York: John Wiley.

Richardson, S. A. (1978). Careers of mentally retarded young persons: Services, jobs, and interpersonal relations. *American Journal of Mental Deficiency, 82,* 349–358.

Richmond, V. P., & McCroskey, J. C. (1985). *Communication: Apprehension, avoidance, and effectiveness.* Scottsdale, AZ: Gorsuch Scarisbrick.

Rickert, E. S., Alvino, J. J., & McDonnell, R. C. (1985). Identification of gifted students: An update. *Roeper Review, 8,* 68–72.

Rieke, J. A., Lynch, L. L., & Soltman, S. F. (1977). *Teaching strategies for language development.* New York: Grune & Stratton.

Ries, P. (1986). Characteristics of hearing impaired youth in the general population and of students in special educational programs for the hearing impaired. In A. N. Schildroth & M. A. Karchmer (Eds.), *Deaf children in America* (pp. 1–31). San Diego: College-Hill.

Rimland, B. (1964). *Infantile autism.* New York: Appleton-Century-Crofts.

Rimland, B. (1971). The differentiation of childhood psychoses: An analysis for checklists for 2,218 psychotic children. *Journal of Autism and Childhood Schizophrenia, 1,* 161–174.

Rincover, A., Cook, R., Peoples, A., & Packard, D. (1979). Sensory extinction and sensory reinforcement principles for programming multiple adaptive behavior change. *Journal of Applied Behavior Analysis, 12,* 221–233.

Ritvo, E. R., Ritvo, E. C., & Brothers, A. M. (1982). Genetic and immunohematologic factors in autism. *Journal of Autism and Developmental Disabilities, 12,* 109–114.

Rivera, O. A., & Quintana Saylor, L. (1977). Unique problems of handicapped individuals with Spanish surnames. In *The*

White House Conference on Handicapped Individuals (Vol. 1). Washington DC: U.S. Government Printing Office.

Robbins, L. (1966). *Deviant children grown up.* Baltimore: Williams & Wilkins.

Roberds-Baxter, S. (1984). The parent connection: Enhancing the affective component of parent conferences. *Teaching Exceptional Children, 17* (1), 55–58.

Roberts, F. K. (1986). Education for the visually handicapped: A social and educational history. In G. T. Scholl (Ed.), *Foundations of education for blind and visually handicapped children and youth: Theory and practice* (pp. 1–18). New York: American Foundation for the Blind.

Robins, L. N. (1979). Follow-up studies. In H. C. Quay & J. S. Werry (Eds.), *Psychopathological disorders of childhood* (2nd ed.). New York: John Wiley.

Robinson, D. (1982). The IEP: Meaningful individualized education in Utah. *Phi Delta Kappan, 64,* 205–206.

Robinson, N. M., & Robinson, H. B. (1976). *The mentally retarded child: A psychological approach* (2nd ed.). New York: McGraw-Hill.

Rooney, T. E. (1982). Signing vs. speech: What's a parent to do? *SEE What's Happening, 1*(1), 6–8.

Roos, P. (1978). Parents of mentally retarded children—misunderstood and mistreated. In A. P. Turnbull & H. R. Turnbull (Eds.), *Parents speak out: Views from the other side of the two-way mirror.* Columbus, OH: Merrill.

Roos, P. (1980). The handling and mishandling of parents of mentally retarded persons. In F. Menolascino (Ed.), *Bridging the gap.* New York: John Wiley.

Rorschach, H. (1942). *Rorschach psychodiagnostic plates.* New York: Psychological Corporation.

Rose, E., & Logan, D. R. (1982). Educational and life/career programs for the mildly mentally retarded. In P. T. Cegelka & H. J. Prehm (Eds.), *Mental retardation: From categories to people.* Columbus, OH: Merrill.

Rose, T. L. (1978). The functional relationship between artificial food colors and hyperactivity. *Journal of Applied Behavior Analysis, 11,* 439–446.

Rosen, C. D., & Gerring, J. P. (1986). *Head trauma: Educational reintegration.* San Diego: College-Hill.

Rosenbaum, M. S., & Drabman, R. S. (1979). Self-control training in the classroom: A review and critique. *Journal of Applied Behavior Analysis, 12,* 467–485.

Ross A. O., (1974). *Psychological disorders of children.* New York: McGraw-Hill.

Ross, M. (1981). Review, overview, and other educational considerations. In M. Ross & L. W. Nober (Eds.), *Educating hard of hearing children.* Reston, VA: Council for Exceptional Children.

Ross, M. (1986). A perspective on amplification: Then and now. In D. M. Luterman (Ed.), *Deafness in perspective* (pp. 35–53). San Diego: College-Hill.

Rotegard, L. L., Hill, B. K., & Bruininks, R. H. (1983). Environmental characteristics of residential facilities for mentally retarded persons in the United States. *American Journal of Mental Deficiency, 88,* 49–56.

Rothman, E. P. (1977). *Troubled teachers.* New York: David McKay.

Rubin, R. A., & Balow, B. (1971). Learning and behavior disorders: A longitudinal study. *Exceptional Children, 38,* 293–299.

Rubin, R. A., & Balow, B. E. (1978). Prevalence of teacher identified behavior problems: A longitudinal study. *Exceptional Children, 45,* 102–111.

Ruconich, R. (1984). Evaluating microcomputer access technology for use by visually impaired students. *Education of the Visually Handicapped, 15,* 119–125.

Ruiz, R. A. (1981). Cultural and historical perspectives in counseling Hispanics. In D. W. Sue, *Counseling the culturally different: Theory and practice.* New York: John Wiley.

Rules for the education of handicapped children. (1982). Columbus: Ohio Department of Education.

Rusch, F. R., Chadsey-Rusch, J., & Lagomarcino, T. (1987). Preparing students for employment. In M. E. Snell (Ed.), *Systematic instruction of persons with severe handicaps* (3rd ed., pp. 471–490). Columbus, OH: Merrill.

Rusch, F. R., & Mithaug, D. E. (1980). *Vocational training for mentally retarded adults: A behavior analytic approach.* Champaign, IL: Research Press.

Russo, D. C., & Koegel, R. L. (1977). A method for integrating an autistic child in a normal public-school classroom. *Journal of Applied Behavior Analysis, 10,* 579–590.

Rutherford, R. B., Nelson, C. M., & Wolford, B. I. (1985). Special education in the most restrictive environment: Correctional/special education. *Journal of Special Education, 19,* 59–71.

Rutter, M. (1965). Medical aspects of the education of psychotic (autistic) children. In P. T. B. Western (Ed.), *Some approaches to teaching autistic children.* Oxford, England: Pergamon Press.

Rutter, M. (1976). *Helping troubled children.* New York: Plenum.

Ryan, C. S., & Coyne, A. (1985). Effects of group homes on neighborhood property values. *Mental Retardation, 23,* 241–245.

Sabornie, E. J., & Kauffman, J. M. (1986). Social acceptance of learning disabled adolescents. *Learning Disability Quarterly, 9,* 55–60.

Sacco, P. R. (1986). The elephant revisited. *Hearsay: Journal of the Ohio Speech and Hearing Association, 1,* 80–83.

Sacks, O. (1986, March 27). Mysteries of the deaf. *New York Review of Books, 33* (5).

Sailor, W., & Haring, N. G. (1977). Some current directions in education of the severely/multiply handicapped. *AAESPH Review, 2,* 67–87.

Salend, S. J., Michael, R. J., & Taylor, M. (1984). Competencies necessary for instructing migrant handicapped students. *Exceptional Children, 51,* 50–55.

Salvia, J. (1978). Perspectives on the nature of retardation. In J. T. Neisworth & R. M. Smith (Eds.), *Retardation: Issues, assessment, and intervention.* New York: McGraw-Hill.

Salvia, J., & Ysseldyke, J. E. (1985). *Assessment in remedial and special education* (3rd ed.). Boston: Houghton Mifflin.

Sameroff, A. J., & Chandler, M. J. (1975). Reproductive risk and the continuum of caretaking casualty. In F. D. Horowitz (Ed.), *Review of child development research* (Vol. 4). Chicago: University of Chicago Press.

Samuda, R. J. (1976). Problems and issues in assessment of minority group children. In R. L. Jones (Ed.), *Mainstreaming and the minority child*. Reston, VA: Council for Exceptional Children.

Samuels, S. J. & Miller, N. L. (1985). Failure to find attention differences between learning disabled and normal children on classroom and laboratory tasks. *Exceptional Children, 51,* 358–375.

Sandler, A., & Coren, A. (1981). Integrated instruction at home and school: Parents' perspective. *Education and Training of the Mentally Retarded, 16*(3), 183–187.

Sansone, J., & Zigmond, N. (1986). Evaluating mainstreaming through an analysis of students' schedules. *Exceptional Children, 52,* 452–458.

Sapon-Shevin, M. (1978). Another look at mainstreaming: Exceptionality, normality and the nature of difference. *Phi Delta Kappan, 60,* 119–121.

Sapon-Shevin, M. (1987). The national education reports and special education: Implications for students. *Exceptional Children, 53,* 300–306.

Sass-Lehrer, M. (1986). Competencies for effective teaching of hearing impaired students. *Exceptional Children, 53,* 230–234.

Sattler, J. M. (1982). *Assessment of children's intelligence and special abilities* (2nd ed.). Boston: Allyn & Bacon.

Scanlon, C. A., Arick, J., & Phelps, N. (1981). Participation in the development of the IEP: Parents' perspective. *Exceptional Children, 47,* 373–374.

Schalock, R. L., Harper, R. S., & Carver, G. (1981). Independent living placement: Five years later. *American Journal of Mental Deficiency, 86,* 170–177.

Scharr, K. (1976, February). Community core ordered for D.C. mental patients. *APA Monitor, 7*(2), 1.

Scheerenberger, R. C. (1974). A model for deinstitutionalization. *Mental Retardation, 12,* 3–7.

Scheerenberger, R. C. (1982). Treatment from ancient times to the present. In P. T. Cegelka & H. J. Prehm (Eds.), *Mental Retardation: From categories to people*. Columbus, OH: Merrill.

Scheerenberger, R. C. (1983a). *A history of mental retardation: A quarter century of promise*. Baltimore: Paul H. Brookes.

Sheerenberger, R. C. (1983b). *Public residential services for the mentally retarded*. Madison, WI: National Association of Superintendents of Public Residential Facilities for the Mentally Retarded.

Schell, G. C. (1981). The young handicapped child: A family perspective. *Topics in Early Childhood Special Education, 1,* 21–27.

Schiefelbusch, R. L., & McCormick, L. (1981). Language and speech disorders. In J. M. Kauffman & D. P. Hallahan (Eds.), *Handbook of special education*. Englewood Cliffs, NJ: Prentice-Hall.

Schildroth, A. N. (1986). Residential schools for deaf students: A decade in review. In A. N. Schildroth & M. A. Karchmer (Eds.), *Deaf children in America* (pp. 83–104). San Diego: College-Hill.

Schilit, J. (1977). Black versus white perception of mental retardation. *Exceptional Children, 44,* 189–190.

Schleichkorn, J. (1983). *Coping with cerebral palsy: Questions parents often ask*. Austin, TX: Pro-Ed.

Schleien, S. J., Kiernan, J., & Wehman P. (1981). Evaluation of an age-appropriate leisure skills program for moderately retarded adults. *Education and Training of the Mentally Retarded, 16,* 13–19.

Schleien, S. J., & Larson, A. (1986). Adult leisure education for the independent use of a community recreation center. *Journal of the Association for Persons with Severe Handicaps, 11,* 39–44.

Schleien, S. J., Wehman, P., & Kiernan, J. (1981). Teaching leisure skills to severely handicapped adults: An age-appropriate darts game. *Journal of Applied Behavior Analysis, 14,* 513–519.

Schlesinger, H. S. (1985). Deafness, mental health, and language. In F. Powell, T. Finitzo-Hieber, S. Friel-Patti, & D. Henderson (Eds.), *Education of the hearing impaired child* (pp. 103–116). San Diego: College-Hill.

Schlesinger, H. S., & Meadow, K. P. (1976). Emotional support for parents. In D. L. Lillie & P. L. Trohanis (Eds.), *Teaching parents to teach*. New York: Walker.

Schmid, R. E. (1979). Historical perspective. In C. D. Mercer, *Children and adolescents with learning disabilities*. Columbus, OH: Merrill.

Scholl, G. T. (Ed.). (1986a). *Foundations of education for blind and visually handicapped children and youth: Theory and practice*. New York: American Foundation for the Blind.

Scholl, G. T. (1986b). Multicultural considerations. In G. T. Scholl (Ed.), *Foundations of education for blind and visually handicapped children and youth* (pp. 165–182). New York: American Foundation for the blind.

Scholl, G. T. (1987). Appropriate education for visually handicapped students. *Teaching Exceptional Children, 19* (2), 33–36.

Schultz, E., Salvia, J., & Feinn, J. (1974). Prevalence of behavioral symptoms in rural elementary school children. *Journal of Abnormal Psychology, 1,* 17–24.

Schulz, J. B. (1978). The parent-professional conflict. In A. P. Turnbull & H. R. Turnbull (Eds.), *Parents speak out: Views from the other side of the two-way mirror*. Columbus, OH: Merrill.

Schumaker, J. B., Deschler, D. D., Alley, G. R., & Warner, M. M. (1983). Toward the development of an intervention model for learning disabled adolescents. In J. K. Torgeson & B. Y. L. Wong (Eds.), *Learning disabilities: Some new perspectives*. New York: Academic Press.

Schumaker, J. B., Hovell, M. F., & Sherman, J. A. (1977). An analysis of daily report cards and parent-managed privileges in the improvement of adolescents' classroom performance. *Journal of Applied Behavior Analysis, 10,* 449–464.

Schumaker, J. B., & Sherman, J. A. (1978). Parent as intervention agent: From birth onward. In R. L. Schiefelbusch (Ed.), *Language intervention strategies* (pp. 237–315). Baltimore: University Park Press.

Scott, M. L., Ebbert, A., & Price, D. (1986). Assessing and teaching employability skills with prevocational work samples. *The Directive Teacher, 8*(1), 3–5.

Scranton, T., & Downs, M. (1975). Elementary and secondary learning disabilities programs in the U.S.: A survey. *Journal of Learning Disabilities, 8,* 394–399.

Seagoe, M. V. (1974). Some characteristics of gifted children. In R. A. Martinson (Ed.), *The identification of the gifted and talented.* Ventura, CA: Office of the Ventura County Superintendent of Schools.

Sears, P. S. (1979). The Terman genetic studies of genius, 1922–1972. In A. H. Passow (Ed.), *The gifted and the talented: Their education and development* (pp. 75–96). Chicago: University of Chicago Press.

Sears, R. R. (1977). Sources of life satisfaction of the Terman gifted men. *American Psychologist, 32*(2), 119–128.

Secord, W. (1981). *Test of Minimal Articulation Competence.* Columbus, OH: Merrill.

Seltzer, M. M., & Seltzer, G. B. (1977). Community living: Accommodations and vocations. In P. Mittler (Ed.), *Research to practice in mental retardation* (Vol 1). Baltimore: University Park Press.

Semel, E. M., & Wiig, E. H. (1980). *Clinical evaluation of language functions.* Columbus, OH: Merrill.

Shannon, G. (1985). *Characteristics influencing current recreational patterns of persons with mental retardation.* Unpublished doctoral dissertation, Brandeis University.

Shearer, D. E., & Snider, R. S. (1981). On providing a practical approach to the early education of children. *Child Behavior Therapy, 3,* 78–80.

Shearer, M. S., & Shearer, D. E. (1972). The Portage project: A model for early childhood education. *Exceptional Children, 39,* 210–217.

Shearer, M. S., & Shearer, D. E. (1977). Parent involvement. In J. B. Jordan, A. H. Hayden, M. B. Karnes, & M. M. Wood (Eds.), *Early childhood education for exceptional children: A handbook of ideas and exemplary practices.* Reston, VA: Council for Exceptional Children.

Sheppard, L., & Smith, M. L. (1981, February). *Evaluation of the identification of perceptual-communicative disorders in Colorado: Final report.* Boulder, CO: Laboratory of Educational Research.

Shevin, M., & Klein, N. K. (1984). The importance of choice-making skills for students with severe disabilities. *Journal of the Association for Persons with Severe Handicaps, 9,* 159–166.

Shewan, C. M. (1986). Characteristics of clinical services provided by ASHA members. *ASHA, 28*(1), 29.

Shivers, J. S., & Fait, H. F. (1985). *Special recreational services: Therapeutic and adapted.* Philadelphia: Lea & Febiger.

Silberberg, N. E., & Silberberg, M. C. (1974). *Who speaks for the child?* Springfield, IL: Charles C Thomas.

Silverman, L. K. (1986). What happens to the gifted girls? In C. J. Maker (Ed.), *Critical issues in gifted education: Defensible programs for the gifted.* Rockville, MD: Aspen.

Simpkins, K. E. (1987). What do teachers of visually handicapped students think about P.L. 94–142?: Part I. *Division for the Visually Handicapped Quarterly, 31*(2), 18–22.

Simpson, R. L. (1981). Screening and assessment strategies for behaviorally disordered adolescents. In G. Brown, R. L. McDowell, & J. Smith (Eds.), *Educating adolescents with behavior disorders.* Columbus, OH: Merrill.

Sirvis, B. (1982). The physically disabled. In E. L. Meyen (Ed.), *Exceptional children and youth: An introduction* (2nd ed.). Denver: Love.

Sisk, D. A. (1978). Education of the gifted and talented: A national perspective. *Journal for the Education of the Gifted, 1,* 5–24.

Sisk, D. (1984, October). *A national survey of gifted programs.* Presentation to the National Business Consortium for Gifted and Talented, Washington, DC.

Sisk, D. (1987). *Creative teaching of the gifted.* New York: McGraw-Hill.

Skeels, H. M. (1966). Adult status of children with contrasting early life experiences. *Monographs of the Society for Research in Child Development, 31* (No. 3).

Skeels, H. M., & Dye, H. B. (1939). A study of the effects of differential stimulation on mentally retarded children. *Convention Proceedings American Association on Mental Deficiency, 44,* 114–136.

Sleeter, C. E. (1986). Learning disabilities: The social construction of a special education category. *Exceptional Children, 53,* 46–54.

Sleeter, C. E., & Grant, C. A. (1986). Success for all students. *Phi Delta Kappan, 68*(4), 297–299.

Slingerland, B. H. (1971). *A multi-sensory approach to language arts for specific language disability children: A guide for primary teachers.* Cambridge, MA: Educators Publishing Service.

Smith, B. J., & Strain, P. S. (1984). *The argument for early intervention.* Reston, VA: ERIC Information Service Digest, ERIC Clearinghouse on Handicapped and Gifted Children.

Smith, D. D., & Robinson, S. (1986). Educating the learning disabled. In R. J. Morris & B. Blatt (Eds.), *Special education: Research and trends* (pp. 222–248). New York: Pergamon Press.

Smith, E. J. (1981). Cultural and historical perspectives in counseling blacks. In D. W. Sue, *Counseling the culturally different: Theory and practice.* New York: John Wiley.

Smith, J. M., & Smith, D. E. (1976). *Child management: A program for parents and teachers.* Champaign, IL: Research Press.

Smith, O. S. (1984). Severely and profoundly physically handicapped students. In P. J. Valletutti & B. M. Sims-Tucker (Eds.), *Severely and profoundly handicapped students: Their nature and needs* (pp. 85–152). Baltimore: Paul H. Brookes.

Smith, R. M. (1971). *An introduction to mental retardation*. New York: McGraw-Hill.

Smith, R. M., & Neisworth, J. T. (1975). *The exceptional child: A functional approach*. New York: McGraw-Hill.

Smith, R. M., Neisworth, J. T., & Hunt, F. M. (1983). *The exceptional child: A functional approach* (2nd ed.). New York: McGraw-Hill.

Smithdas, R. (1981). Psychological aspects of deaf-blindness. In S. R. Walsh & R. Holzberg (Eds.), *Understanding and educating the deaf-blind/severely and profoundly handicapped: An international perspective*. Springfield, IL: Charles C Thomas.

Snell, M. E. (Ed.). (1978). *Systematic instruction of the moderately and severely handicapped*. Columbus, OH: Merrill.

Snell, M. E. (Ed.). (1987). *Systematic instruction of persons with severe handicaps*. (3rd ed.). Columbus, OH: Merrill.

Snell, M. E., & Beckman-Brindley, S. (1984). Family involvement in intervention with children having severe handicaps. *Journal of the Association for Persons with Severe Handicaps, 9*, 213–230.

Snell, M. E., & Renzaglia, A. M. (1982). Moderate, severe, and profound handicaps. In N. G. Haring (Ed.), *Exceptional children and youth* (3rd ed.). Columbus, OH: Merrill.

Snell, M. E., & Renzaglia, A. M. (1986). Moderate, severe, and profound handicaps. In N. G. Haring & L. McCormick (Eds.), *Exceptional children and youth* (4th ed., pp. 271–310). Columbus, OH: Merrill.

Sonnenschein, P. (1981). Parents and professionals: An uneasy relationship. *TEACHING Exceptional Children, 14*, 62–65.

Sontag, E., Sailor, W., & Smith, J. (1977). The severely/profoundly handicapped: Who are they? Where are we? *Journal of Special Education, 11*(1), 5–11.

Sowell, V., Packer, R., Poplin, M., & Larsen, S. (1979). The effects of psycholinguistic training on improving psycholinguistic skills. *Learning Disability Quarterly, 2*, 69–77.

Spache, G. D. (1963). *Diagnostic Reading Scales*. Monterey: California Test Bureau.

Sparrow, S. S., Balla, D. A., & Cicchetti, D. V. (1984). *Vineland Adaptive Behavior Scales*. Circle Pines, MN: American Guidance Service.

Spenciner, L. J. (1972). Differences between blind and partially sighted children in rejection by sighted peers in integrated classrooms, grades 2–8. In B. W. Tuckman (Ed.), *Conducting educational research*. New York: Harcourt Brace Jovanovich.

Spindler, G. D. (1974). *Education and cultural process*. New York: Holt, Rinehart & Winston.

Spradlin, J. E., & Spradlin, R. R. (1976). Developing necessary skills for entry into classroom teaching arrangements. In N. G. Haring & R. L. Schiefelbusch (Eds.), *Teaching special children*. New York: McGraw-Hill.

Spreat, S., Telles, J. T., Conroy, J. W., Feinstein, C., & Colombatto, J. J. (1985). *Attitudes toward deinstitutionalization: A national survey of families of institutionalized mentally retarded persons* [Occasional paper of the NASPRFMR]. Philadelphia: Temple University.

Spring, C., & Sandoval, J. (1976). Food additives and hyperkinesis: A critical evaluation of the evidence. *Journal of Learning Disabilities, 9*, 560–569.

Stainback, S., & Stainback, W. (1985). *Integration of students with severe handicaps into regular schools*. Reston, VA: Council for Exceptional Children.

Stainback, W., & Stainback, S. (1984). A rationale for the merger of special and regular education. *Exceptional Children, 51*, 102–111.

Stainback, W., Stainback, S., Raschke, D., & Anderson, R. J. (1981). Three methods of encouraging interactions between severely retarded and nonhandicapped students. *Education and Training of the Mentally Retarded, 16*, 188–192.

Stanley, J. C., Keating, D. P., & Fox, L. H. (1974). *Mathematical talent: Discovery, description, and development*. Baltimore: Johns Hopkins.

Stephens, T. M. (1977). *Teaching skills to children with learning and behavior disorders*. Columbus, OH: Merrill.

Stephens, T. M. (1978). *Social skills in the classroom*. Columbus, OH: Cedars Press.

Stephens, T. M. (1982). *CRC: Criterion-Referenced Curriculum*. Columbus, OH: Merrill.

Stephens, T. M., Blackhurst, A. E., & Magliocca, L. A. (1982). *Teaching mainstreamed students*. New York: John Wiley.

Stephens, T. M., & Wolf, J. S. (1978). The gifted child. In N. G. Haring (Ed.), *Behavior of exceptional children: An introduction to special education* (2nd ed.). Columbus, OH: Merrill.

Stephens, T. M., & Wolf, J. S. (1980). *Effective skills in parent/teacher conferencing*. Columbus: Ohio State University, National Center for Educational Materials and Media for the Handicapped.

Sternberg, R. J. (1979). The nature of mental abilities. *American Psychologist, 34*, 214–230.

Sternberg, R. J. (1987). Critical thinking: Its nature, measurement, and improvement. In J. B. Baron & R. J. Sternberg, *Teaching thinking skills: Theory and practice*. New York: W. H. Freeman.

Sternberg, R. J., & Davidson, J. E. (1985). Cognitive development in the gifted and talented. In F. D. Horowitz & M. O'Brien (Eds.), *The gifted and talented: Developmental perspectives* (pp. 37–74). Washington, DC: American Psychological Association.

Stewart, J. L. (1977). Unique problems of handicapped Native Americans. In *The White House Conference on Handicapped Individuals* (Vol. 1). Washington, DC: U.S. Government Printing Office.

Stocker, C. S. (1973). *Listening for the visually impaired: A teaching manual*. Springfield, IL: Charles C Thomas.

Storm, R. H., & Willis, J. H. (1978). Small-group training as an alternative to individual programs for profoundly retarded persons. *American Journal of Mental Deficiency, 83,* 283–288.

Stowell, L. J., & Terry, C. (1977). Mainstreaming: Present shock. *Illinois Libraries, 59,* 475–477.

Strain, P. S. (1981). Peer-mediated treatment of exceptional children's social withdrawal. *Exceptional Education Quarterly, 1,* 83–95.

Strain, P. S. (in press). Programmatic research on peer-mediated interventions. In B. H. Schneider, J. E. Ledingham, & K. H. Rubin (Eds.), *Research strategies in children's social skill training.* Baltimore: Paul H. Brookes.

Strain, P. S., Guralnick, M. J., & Walker, H. M. (Eds.). (1986). *Children's social behavior: Development, assessment, and modification.* Orlando, FL: Academic Press.

Strain, P. S., & Odom, S. L. (1986). Peer social initiations: Effective intervention for social skills development of exceptional children. *Exceptional Children, 52,* 543–551.

Strain, P. S., & Smith, B. J. (1986). A counter-interpretation of early intervention effects: A response to Casto and Mastropieri. *Exceptional Children, 53,* 260–265.

Stramiello, A. (1978). *A descriptive study of selected features of handicapped children's early education programs.* Greeley: University of Northern Colorado.

Strichart, S. S., & Lazarus, P. J. (1986). Low-incidence assessment: Influences and issues. In P. J. Lazarus & S. S. Strichart (Eds.), *Psychoeducational evaluation of children and adolescents with low-incidence handicaps* (pp. 1–15). Orlando, FL: Grune & Stratton.

Strickland, S. P. (1971). Can slum children learn? *American Education, 7*(6), 3–7.

Sturmey, P., & Crisp, A. G. (1986). Portage guide to early education: A review of research. *Educational Psychology, 6*(2), 139–157.

Sue, D. W. (1981). *Counseling the culturally different: Theory and practice.* New York: John Wiley.

Sulzbacher, S., Haines, R., Peterson, S. L., & Swatman, F. M. (1987). Encourage appropriate coffee break behavior. *Teaching Exceptional Children, 19*(2), 8–12.

Sulzer-Azaroff, B., & Mayer, G. R. (1977). *Applying behavior analysis procedures with children and youth.* New York: Holt, Rinehart & Winston.

Sulzer-Azaroff, B., & Mayer, G. R. (1986). *Achieving educational excellence.* New York: Holt, Rinehart & Winston.

Suran, B. G., & Rizzo, J. V. (1979). *Special children: An integrative approach.* Glenview, IL: Scott, Foresman.

Swack, M. J. (1969). Therapeutic role of the teacher of physically handicapped children. *Exceptional Children, 35,* 371–374.

Swallow, R. M. (1978, May). *Cognitive development.* Paper presented at the North American Conference on Visually Handicapped Infants and Preschool Children, Minneapolis.

Swallow, R. M., & Conner, A. (1982). Aural reading. In S. S. Mangold (Ed.), *A teacher's guide to the special educational needs of blind and visually handicapped children* (pp. 119–135). New York: American Foundation for the Blind.

Swassing, R. (1978). The fourth R for the gifted and talented. *Ohio Media Spectrum, 30*(3), 59–61.

Swassing, R. (1984). The multiple component alternative. *Gifted Child Today, 33,* 10–11.

Tarjan, G., Wright, S. W., Eyman, R. K., & Keeran, C. V. (1973). Natural history of mental retardation: Some aspects of epidemiology. *American Journal of Mental Deficiency, 77,* 396–379.

Tawney, J. W. (1977). New considerations for the severely and profoundly handicapped. In R. D. Kneedler & S. G. Tarver (Eds.), *Changing perspectives in special education.* Columbus, OH: Merrill.

Tawney, J. W., & Smith, J. (1981). An analysis of the forum: Issues in education of the severely and profoundly retarded. *Exceptional Children, 48,* 5–18.

Taylor, S. J., Biklen, D., & Searl, S. J. (1986). *Preparing for life: A manual for parents on least restrictive environment.* Boston: Federation for Children with Special Needs.

Teacher Education Division. (1986). *The national inquiry into the future of education for students with special needs.* Reston, VA: Council for Exceptional Children.

Templin, M. C. (1957). Templin Speech Sound Discrimination Test. In M. C. Templin, *Certain language skills in children.* Minneapolis: University of Minnesota Press.

Templin, M. C., & Darley, F. L. (1969). *The Templin-Darley Test of Articulation* (2nd ed.). Iowa City: University of Iowa, Bureau of Educational Research and Service, Division of Extension and University Services.

Terkel, S. (1974). *Working: People talk about what they do all day and how they feel about what they do.* New York: Pantheon.

Terman, L. M. (1916). *The measurement of intelligence.* Boston: Houghton Mifflin.

Terman, L. M. (1925). *The mental and physical traits of a thousand gifted children.* Stanford, CA: Stanford University Press.

Terman, L. M., & Merrill, M. A. (1973). Stanford-Binet Intelligence Scale: Manual for the third revision, Form L-M. Boston: Houghton Mifflin.

Test, D. W., Cooke, N. L., Weiss, A. B., Heward, W. L., & Heron, T. E. (1986). A home-school communication system for special education. *The Pointer, 30,* 4–7.

Test, D. W., & Heward, W. L. (1983). Teaching road signs and traffic laws to learning disabled students. *Learning Disability Quarterly, 6,* 80–83.

Thomas, A., Chess, S., & Birch, H. G. (1968). *Temperament and behavior disorders in children.* New York: New York University Press.

Thomas, D. R., Becker, W. C., & Armstrong, M. (1968). Production and elimination of disruptive classroom behavior by systematically varying teachers' behavior. *Journal of Applied Behavior Analysis, 1,* 35–45.

Thomas, G., & Jackson, G. (1986). The whole-school approach to integration. *British Journal of Special Education, 13*(1), 27–29.

Thomas, S. B. (1985). *Legal issues in special education.* Topeka, KS: National Organization on Legal Problems in Education.

Thompson, K. (1984). The speech therapist and language disorders. In G. Lindsay (Ed.), *Screening for children with special needs: Multidisciplinary approaches* (pp. 86–97). London: Croom Helm.

Thurman, D. (1978). Mainstreaming and the visually impaired: A report from Atlantic Canada. *Education of the Visually Handicapped, 10,* 35–37.

Timm, M. D., & Rule, S. (1981). RIP: A cost-effective parent-implemented program for handicapped children. *Early Childhood Development and Care, 7,* 147–163.

Tjossem, T. D. (Ed.). (1976). *Intervention strategies for high risk infants and young children.* Baltimore: University Park Press.

Todd, J. H. (1986). Resources, media, and technology. In G. T. Scholl (Ed.), *Foundations of education for blind and visually handicapped children and youth: Theory and practice* (pp. 285–296). New York: American Foundation for the Blind.

Tomes, L., & Sanger, D. D. (1986). Attitudes of interdisciplinary team members toward speech-language services in public schools. *Language, Speech, and Hearing Services in Schools, 17,* 230–240.

Tomlinson-Keasey, C., Brawley, R., & Peterson, B. (1986). An analysis of an interactive videodisc system for teaching, language skills to deaf students. *Exceptional Child, 33* (1), 49–55.

Tooze, D. (1981). *Independence training for visually handicapped children.* Baltimore: University Park Press.

Torrance, E. P. (1977). *Discovery and nurturance of giftedness in the culturally different.* Reston, VA: Council for Exceptional Children.

Tredgold, A. F. (1937). *A textbook on mental deficiency.* Baltimore: Wood.

Tucker, J. A. (1985). Curriculum-based assessment: An introduction. *Exceptional Children, 52,* 199–204.

Turnbull, A., & Bronicki, G. J. B. (1986). Changing second graders' attitudes toward people with mental retardation: Using kid power. *Mental Retardation, 24,* 44–45.

Turnbull, A. P. (1983). Parent-professional interactions. In M. E. Snell (Ed.), *Systematic instruction of the moderately and severely handicapped* (2nd ed.). Columbus, OH: Merrill.

Turnbull, A. P., Strickland, B., & Brantley, J. C. (1982). *Developing and implementing individualized education programs* (2nd ed.). Columbus, OH: Merrill.

Turnbull, A. P., & Turnbull, H. R. (1982). Parent involvement in the education of handicapped children: A critique. *Mental Retardation, 20,* 115–122.

Turnbull, A. P., Turnbull, H. R., Summers, J. A., Brotherson, M. J., & Benson, H. A. (1986). *Families, professionals, and exceptionality: A special partnership.* Columbus, OH: Merrill.

Turnbull, H. R. (1986a). Appropriate education and Rowley. *Exceptional Children, 52,* 347–352.

Turnbull, H. R. (1986b). *Free appropriate public education: The law and children with disabilities.* Denver: Love.

Turnbull, H. R., & Turnbull, A. P. (1985). *Parents speak out: Then & now.* Columbus, OH: Merrill.

Turner, J. (1983). Workshop society: Ethnographic observations in a work setting for retarded adults. In K. Kernan, M. Begab, & R. Edgerton (Eds.), *Environments and behavior: The adaptation of mentally retarded persons* (pp. 147–171). Austin, TX: Pro-Ed.

Tuttle, D. W. (1984). *Self-esteem and adjusting with blindness: The process of responding to life's demands.* Springfield, IL: Charles C Thomas.

Ulicny, G. R., Thompson, S. K., Favell, J. E., & Thompson, M. S. (1985). The active assessment of educability: A case study. *Journal of the Association for Persons with Severe Handicaps, 10,* 111–114.

Ulrey, G. (1982). Assessment considerations with language impaired children. In G. Ulrey & S. J. Rogers (Eds.), *Psychological assessment of handicapped infants and young children* (pp. 123–134). New York: Thieme-Stratton.

U.S. Commission on Civil Rights (1983, September). *Accommodating the spectrum of individual abilities* [Clearinghouse Publication 81]. Washington, DC: U.S. Government Printing Office.

U.S. Comptroller General. (1981, September 30). *Disparities still exist in who gets special education.* Report to the chairman, Subcommittee on Select Education, Committee on Education and Labor, House of Representatives of the United States.

U.S. Department of Education. (1982). Sources for statistics on disability. In *Programs for the Handicapped,* No. 4, 9–13.

U.S. Department of Education. (1985). *Seventh annual report to Congress on the implementation of the Education of the Handicapped Act.* Washington, DC: Author.

U.S. Department of Education. (1986). *Eighth annual report to Congress on the implementation of the Education of the Handicapped Act.* Washington, DC: Author.

U.S. Department of Justice, Federal Bureau of Investigation. (1981). *Uniform Crime Reports for the United States, 1981.* Washington, DC: Author.

U.S. Department of Labor. (1979). *Study of handicapped clients in sheltered workshops (Vol. 2).* Washington, DC: Author.

Vacc, N. A., Vallecorsa, A. L., Parker, A., Bonner, S., Lester, C., Richardson, S., & Yates, C. (1985). Parents' and educators' participation in IEP conferences. *Education & Treatment of Children, 8,* 153–162.

Valcante, G. (1986). Educational implications of current research on the syndrome of autism. *Behavioral Disorders, 11,* 131–139.

Valero-Figueira, E. (1986). Bilingual special education personnel preparation: An integrated model. *Teacher Education and Special Education, 9,* 82–88.

van den Pol, R. A., Iwata, B. A., Ivancic, M. T., Page T. J., Neef, N. A., & Whitely, F. P. (1981). Teaching the handicapped to eat in public places: Acquisition, generalization, and maintenance of restaurant skills. *Journal of Applied Behavior Analysis, 14,* 61–69.

van Dijk, J. (1983). *Rubella handicapped children: The effects of bi-lateral cataract and/or hearing impairment on behaviour and learning.* Lisse, Netherlands: Swets & Zeitlinger.

Van Houten, R. (1979). Social validation: The evolution of standards of competency for target behaviors. *Journal of Applied Behavior Analysis, 12,* 581–591.

Van Riper, C. (1972). *Speech correction: Principles and methods* (5th ed.). Englewood Cliffs, NJ: Prentice-Hall.

Van Riper, C., & Emerick L. L. (1984). *Speech correction: An introduction to speech pathology.* Englewood Cliffs, NJ: Prentice-Hall.

Van Tassel-Baska, J. (1983). The teacher as counselor for the gifted. *TEACHING Exceptional Children, 15,* 144–150.

Van Tassel-Baska, J. (1986). Acceleration. In C. J. Maker (Ed.), *Critical issues in gifted education: Defensible programs for the gifted.* Rockville, MD: Aspen.

Vargas, J. G., & Moxley, R. A. (1979). Teaching for thinking and creativity: The radical behaviorist's view. In A. E. Lawson (Ed.), *The psychology of teaching for thinking and creativity, 1980 AETS Yearbook.* Columbus: Ohio State University.

Venn, J., Morganstern, L., & Dykes, M. K. (1979). Checklists for evaluating the fit and function of orthoses, prostheses, and wheelchairs in the classroom. *TEACHING Exceptional Children, 11,* 51–56.

Verhaaren, P. R., & Connor, F. P. (1981). Physical disabilities. In J. M. Kauffman & D. P. Hallahan (Eds.), *Handbook of special education.* Englewood Cliffs, NJ: Prentice-Hall.

Victor, J. (1976, April). Some selected findings from the Greenleigh Associates study of sheltered workshops. In *The Auburn conference on the Greenleigh study of sheltered workshops.* Auburn, AL: Auburn University, Rehabilitation Services Education Department.

Vitello, S. J. (1986). The *Tatro* case: Who gets what and why. *Exceptional Children, 52,* 353–356.

Vorrath, H. H., & Brendtro, L. K. (1974). *Positive peer culture.* Chicago: Aldine.

Wahler, R. G., & Dumas, J. E. (1986). "A chip off the old block": Some interpersonal characteristics of coercive children across generations. In P. S. Strain, M. J. Guralnick, & H. M. Walker (Eds.), *Children's social behavior: Development, assessment, and modification* (pp. 49–91). Orlando, FL: Academic Press.

Wakabayashi, R. (1977). Unique problems of handicapped Asian Americans. In *The White House Conference on Handicapped Individuals* (Vol. 1). Washington, DC: U.S. Government Printing Office.

Walker, H. M. (1979). *The acting-out child: Coping with classroom disruption.* Boston: Allyn & Bacon.

Walker, H. M., & Buckley, N. K. (1973). Teacher attention to appropriate and inappropriate classroom behavior: An individual case study. *Focus on Exceptional Children, 5,* 5–11.

Walker, H. M., & Hops, H. (1976). Use of normative peer data as a standard for evaluating classroom treatment effects. *Journal of Applied Behavior Analysis, 9,* 159–168.

Walker, L. A. (1986). *A loss for words: The story of deafness in a family.* New York: Harper & Row.

Wallace, G., & McLoughlin, J. A. (1979). *Learning disabilities: Concepts and characteristics* (2nd ed.). Columbus, OH: Merrill.

Wang, M. C., & Reynolds, M. C. (1985). Avoiding the "Catch 22" in special education reform. *Exceptional Children, 51,* 497–502.

Ward, M. E. (1979). Children with visual impairments. In M. S. Lilly (Ed.), *Children with exceptional needs: A survey of special education.* New York: Holt, Rinehart & Winston.

Ward, M. E. (1986). The visual system. In G. T. Scholl (Ed.), *Foundations of education for blind and visually handicapped children and youth: Theory and practice* (pp. 35–64). New York: American Foundation for the Blind.

Warger, C. L., Aldinger, L. E., & Okun, K. A. (1983). *Mainstreaming in the secondary school: The role of the regular teacher.* Bloomington, IN: Phi Delta Kappa Educational Foundation.

Warren, J. (1977). Early and periodic screening, diagnosis, and treatment. *Educational Researcher,* 14–15, 20.

Warren, S. A. (1986). Education in institutions. In M. S. Crissey & M. Rosen (Eds.), *Institutions for the mentally retarded: A changing role in changing times* (pp. 63–78). Austin, TX: Pro-Ed.

Webster, A., & Ellwood, J. (1985). *The hearing-impaired child in the ordinary school.* London: Croom Helm.

Wechsler, D. (1974). *Manual for the Wechsler Intelligence Scale for Children—Revised.* New York: Psychological Corporation.

Wedel, J. W., & Fowler, S. A. (1984). "Read me a story, Mom": A home-tutoring program to teach prereading skills to language-delayed children. *Behavior Modification, 8,* 245–266.

Wehman, P. (1983). Toward the employability of severely handicapped children and youth. *Teaching Exceptional Children, 15,* 220–225.

Wehman, P., & Hill, J. W. (Eds.). (1985). *Competitive employment for persons with mental retardation.* Richmond: Virginia Commonwealth University. Rehabilitation Research and Training Center.

Wehman, P., Hill, M., Brooke, V., Pendleton, P., & Britt, C. (1985). Competitive employment for persons with mental retardation: A follow-up six years later. *Mental Retardation, 23,* 274–281.

Wehman, P., Hill, M., Goodall, P., Cleveland, P., Brooke, V., & Pentecost, J. H. (1982). Job placement and follow-up of moderately and severely handicapped individuals after three years. *Journal of the Association for the Severely Handicapped, 7*(2), 5–16.

Wehman, P., & Kregel, J. (1985). A supported work approach to competitive employment of individuals with moderate and severe handicaps. *Journal of the Association for Persons with Severe Handicaps, 10,* 3–11.

Wehman, P., Kregel, J., & Barcus, J. M. (1985). From school to work: A vocational transition model for handicapped students. *Exceptional Children, 52,* 25–37.

Wehman, P., Kregel, J., & Seyfarth, J. (1985a). Transition from school to work for individuals with severe handicaps: A follow-up study. *Journal for the Association for Persons with Severe Handicaps, 10,* 132–136.

Wehman, P., Kregel, J., & Seyfarth, J. (1985b). Employment outlook for young adults with mental retardation. *Rehabilitation Counseling Bulletin, 5,* 343–354.

Wehman, P., Renzaglia, A. M., & Bates, P. (1985). *Functional living skills for moderately and severely handicapped individuals.* Austin, TX: Pro-Ed.

Wehman, P., & Schleien, S. J. (1981). *Lesiure programs for handicapped persons: Adaptations, techniques, and curriculum.* Baltimore: University Park Press.

Weintraub, F. J. (1986). *Goals for the future of special education.* Reston, VA: Council for Exceptional Children.

Weintraub, F. J., & Abeson, A. (1974). New education policies for the handicapped: The quiet revolution. *Phi Delta Kappan, 55,* 526–529, 569.

Weiss, A., Cooke, N. L., Grossman, M. A., Ryno-Vrabel, M., & Hassett, M. E. (1983). *Home-school communication: Setting up a telephone-managed program.* Columbus, OH: Special Press.

Weiss, C. E., & Lillywhite, H. S. (1976). *Communicative disorders: A handbook for prevention and early intervention.* St. Louis: C. V. Mosby.

Weiss, H. G., & Weiss, M. S. (1976). *Home is a learning place: A parent's guide to learning disabilities.* Boston: Little, Brown.

Wepman, J. M. (1958). *Wepman Auditory Discrimination Test.* Chicago: Language Research Associates.

Werry, J., & Quay, H. C. (1971). The prevalence of behavior symptoms in younger elementary school children. *American Journal of Orthopsychiatry, 41,* 136–143.

Wetzel, R. J., & Hoschouer, R. L. (1984). *Residential teaching communities.* Glenview, IL: Scott, Foresman.

Weyhing, M. C. (1983). Parental reactions to handicapped children and familial adjustments to routines of care. In J. A. Mulik & S. M. Pueschell (Eds.), *Parent-professional partnerships in developmental disabilities* (pp. 125–138). Cambridge, MA: Ware Press.

Whelan, R. J. (1981). Prologue. In G. Brown, R. L. McDowell, & J. Smith (Eds.), *Educating adolescents with behavior disorders.* Columbus, OH: Merrill.

White, B. L. (1975). *The first three years of life.* Englewood Cliffs, NJ: Prentice-Hall.

White, K. R., Bush, D., & Casto, G. (1986). Let the past be prologue: Learning from previous reviews of early intervention efficacy research. *Journal of Special Education, 19*(4), 417–428.

White, O. R. (1986). Precision teaching—precision learning. *Exceptional Children, 52,* 522–534.

White, O. R., & Haring, N. G. (1980). *Exceptional teaching* (2nd ed.). Columbus, OH: Merrill.

White, W. J. (1985). Perspectives on the education and training of learning disabled adults. *Learning Disability Quarterly, 8,* 231–236.

Whitmore, J. R. (1980). *Giftedness, conflict, and underachievement.* Boston: Allyn & Bacon.

Whitmore, J. R., & Maker, C. J. (1985). Intellectual giftedness in disabled persons. Rockville, MD: Aspen.

Wiederholt, J. L. (1974a). Historical perspectives on the education of the learning disabled. In L. Mann & D. Sabatino (Eds.), *The second review of special education.* Philadelphia: JSE Press.

Wiederholt, J. L. (1974b). Planning resource rooms for the mildly handicapped. *Focus on Exceptional Children, 6,* 1–10.

Wiederholt, J. L., Hammill, D. D., & Brown, V. (1978). *The resource teacher: A guide to effective practice.* Boston: Allyn & Bacon.

Wikler, L. D. (1986). Periodic stresses of families of older mentally retarded children: An exploratory study. *American Journal of Mental Deficiency, 90,* 703–706.

Will, M. (1985). Bridges from school to working life: OSERS programming for the transition of youth with disabilities. *Rehabilitation World, 9,* 4–7.

Will, M. C. (1986a). Educating children with learning problems: A shared responsibility. *Exceptional Children, 52,* 411–415.

Will, M. (1986b). *Eighth annual report to Congress on the implementation of the Education of the Handicapped Act.* Washington, DC: U.S. Department of Education, Office of Special Education and Rehabilitation Services.

Williams, F. E. (1970). *Classroom ideas for encouraging thinking and feeling.* Buffalo. NY: D.O.K.

Williams, G. E., & Cuvo, A. J. (1986). Training apartment upkeep skills to rehabilitation clients: A comparison of task analytic strategies. *Journal of Applied Behavior Analysis, 19,* 39–51.

Williams, J. (1977). The impact and implication of litigation. In G. Markel (Ed.), *Proceedings of the University of Michigan Institute on the Impact and Implications of State and Federal Legislation Affecting Handicapped Individuals.* Ann Arbor: University of Michigan, School of Education.

Williamson, G. G. (1978). The individualized education program: An interdisciplinary endeavor. In B. Sirvis, J. W. Baken, & G. G. Williamson (Eds.), *Unique aspects of the IEP for the physically handicapped, homebound, and hospitalized.* Reston, VA: Council for Exceptional Children.

Willig, A. C., & Greenberg, H. F. (1986). *Bilingualism and learning disabilities: Policy and practice for teachers and administrators.* New York: American Library.

Willoughby, D. M. (1980). *A resource guide for parents and educators of blind children.* Baltimore: National Federation of the Blind.

Winer, M. (1978). A course on resources for the newly blind. *Journal of Visual Impairment & Blindness. 72,* 331–315.

Winitz, H. (1977). Articulation disorders: From prescription to description. *Journal of Speech and Hearing Disorders. 42,* 143–147.

Winkler, B., Armstrong, K., Moehlis, J., Nietupski, J., & Whalen-Carrell, B. (1982). Ad guide preparation and delivery for severly handicapped students. *Teaching Exceptional Children, 15*, 29–33.

Winton, P. (1986). Effective strategies for involving families in intervention efforts. *Focus on Exceptional Children, 19*(2), 1–12.

Winton, P., & Turnbull, A. P. (1981). Parent involvement as viewed by parents of preschool handicapped children. *Topics in Early Childhood Special Education, 1*, 11–19.

Witty, P. A. (1930). A study of one hundred gifted children. University of Kansas, *Bulletin of Education, 2*(7).

Witty, P. A. (1940). Contributions to the IQ controversy from the study of superior deviates. *School and Society, 51*, 503–508.

Witty, P. A. (1962). A decade of progress in the study of the gifted and creative pupil. In W. B. Barbe & T. M. Stephens (Eds.), *Attention to the gifted a decade later.* Columbus: Ohio Department of Education.

Witty, P. A., & Jenkins, M. D. (1934). The educational achievement of a group of gifted Negro children. *Journal of Educational Psychology, 25*, 585–597.

Wolery, M. (1979). *Parents as teachers of their handicapped children: An annotated bibliography.* Seattle: WESTAR.

Wolf, J. S., & Stephens, T. M. (1982). *Effective skills in parent/teacher conferencing: The parents' perspective.* Columbus: Ohio State University, National Center for Educational Materials and Media for the Handicapped.

Wolf, M. M. (1978). Social validity: The case for subjective measurement, or how applied behavior analysis is finding its heart. *Journal of Applied Behavior Analysis, 11*, 203–214.

Wolfe, D., & Rawlings, B. W. (1986). *Hearing impaired students in postsecondary education.* Washington, DC: National Clearinghouse on Postsecondary Education for Handicapped Individuals.

Wolfensberger, W. (1969). The origin and nature of our institutional models. In R. B. Kugel & W. Wolfensberger (Eds.), *Changing patterns in residential services for the mentally retarded.* Washington, DC: President's Committee on Mental Retardation.

Wolfensberger, W. (1972). *Normalization: The principle of normalization in human services.* Toronto, Canada: National Institute on Mental Retardation.

Wolfensberger, W. (1976). The origin and nature of our institutional models. In R. B. Kugel & A. Shearer (Eds.), *Changing patterns in residential services for the mentally retarded.* Washington, DC: President's Committee on Mental Retardation.

Wolfensberger, W., & Glenn, L. (1975). *Program analysis of service systems.* Toronto, Canada: National Institute on Mental Retardation.

Wolff, A. B. & Harkins, J. E. (1986). Multihandicapped students. In A. N. Schildroth & M. A. Karchmer (Eds.), *Deaf Children in America* (pp. 55–81). San Diego: College-Hill.

Wolk, S., & Schildroth, A. N. (1986). Deaf children and speech intelligibility: A national study. In A. N. Schildroth & M. A. Karchmer (Eds.), *Deaf children in America* (pp. 139–159). San Diego: College-Hill.

Wood, F. H. (1985). Issues in the identification and placement of behaviorially disordered students. *Behavioral Disorders, 10*, 219–228.

Wood, F. H., & Zabel, R. H. (1978). Making sense of reports on the incidence of behavior disorders/emotional disturbance in school-aged populations. *Psychology in the Schools, 15*, (pp. 45–51). Minneapolis: University of Minnesota.

Wood, M. M., & Hurley, O. L. (1977). Curriculum and instruction. In J. B. Jordan, A. H. Hayden, M. B. Karnes, & M. M. Wood (Eds.), *Early childhood education for exceptional children: A handbook of ideas and exemplary practices.* Reston, VA: Council for Exceptional Children.

Woodcock, R. (1974). *Woodcock Reading Mastery Tests.* Circle Pines, MN: American Guidance Services.

Wyatt v. Stickney, 344 F. Supp. 387, 344 F. Supp. 373 (M.D. Ala. 1972), 334 F. Supp. 1341, 325 F. Supp. 781 (M.D. Ala. 1971), aff'd sub nom. Wyatt v. Aderholt, 503 F. 2d 1305 (5th Cir. 1974).

Yates, J. R. (1986, May). Paper presented at the Symposium on the Future of Special Education. Reston, VA: Council for Exceptional Children.

Yoshida, R., Fenton, K., Kaufman, M. J., & Maxwell, J. P. (1978). Parental involvement in the special education pupil planning process: The school's perspective. *Exceptional Children, 44*, 531–533.

Ysseldyke, J., Algozzine, B., Richey, L., & Graden, J. (1982). Declaring students eligible for learning disability services: Why bother with the data? *Learning Disability Quarterly, 5*, 37–44.

Ysseldyke, J. E., & Salvia, J. (1974). Diagnostic-prescriptive teaching: Two models. *Exceptional Children, 41*, 181–186.

Ysseldyke, J. E., Thurlow, M., Graden, J., Wesson, C., Algozzine, B., & Deno, S. (1983). Generalizations from five years of research on assessment and decision making: The University of Minnesota Institute. *Exceptional Education Quarterly, 4*(1), 75–93.

Yurt, R. W., & Pruitt, B. A. (1983). Burns. In J. Umbreit (Ed.), *Physical disabilities and health impairments: An introduction* (pp. 175–184). Columbus, OH: Merrill.

Zacharkow, D. (1984). *Wheelchair posture and pressure sores.* Springfield, IL: Charles C Thomas.

Zakariasen, H. (1979). Is there a child with epilepsy in the classroom? *Education Unlimited, 1*, 14–16.

Zettel, J. J. (1979). Gifted and talented education over half a decade of change. *Journal for the Education of the Gifted, 3*, 14–37.

Zigler, E., Balla, D., & Hodapp, R. (1984). On the definition and classification of mental retardation. *American Journal of Mental Deficiency, 89*, 215–230.

Zigmond, N., & Miller, S. E. (1986). Assessment for instructional planning. *Exceptional Children, 52*, 501–509.

Zirkel, P. A., & Stevens, P. L. (1986). Commentary: The law concerning public education for the gifted. *West's Education Law Reporter, 34*, 353–367.

Zirpoli, T. J. (1987). Child abuse and children with handicaps. *Remedial and Special Education, 7*(2), 39–48.

GLOSSARY

acceleration An educational approach that provides a child with learning experiences usually given to older children; most often used with gifted and talented children.

accommodation The adjustment of the eye for seeing at different distances. Accomplished by muscles that change the shape of the lens to bring an image into clear focus on the retina.

adaptive device Any piece of equipment designed to improve the function of a body part. Examples include standing tables and special spoons that can be used by people with weak hands or poor muscle control.

adventitious handicap A handicap that develops at any time after birth, from disease, trauma, or any other cause; most frequently used with sensory or physical impairments. Contrasts with *congenital* handicap.

advocate Anyone who pleads the cause of a handicapped person or group of handicapped people, especially in legal or administrative proceedings or public forums.

albinism A congenital condition marked by deficiency in, or total lack of, pigmentation. People with albinism have pale skin; white hair, eyebrows, and eyelashes; and eyes with pink or pale blue pupils.

amblyopia Dimness of sight without apparent change in the eye's structures; can lead to blindness in the affected eye if not corrected.

amniocentesis The insertion of a hollow needle through the abdomen into the uterus of a pregnant woman. Used to obtain amniotic fluid in order to determine the presence of genetic and chromosomal abnormalities. The sex of the fetus can also be determined.

anoxia A lack of oxygen severe enough to cause tissue damage; can cause permanent brain damage and mental retardation.

aphasia Loss of speech functions; often, but not always, refers to inability to speak because of brain lesions.

applied behavior analysis "The science in which procedures derived from the principles of behavior are systematically applied to improve socially significant behavior to a meaningful degree and to demonstrate experimentally that the procedures employed were responsible for the improvement in behavior" (Cooper, Heron, & Heward, 1987, p. 14).

aqueous humor Fluid that occupies the space between the lens and the cornea of the eye.

articulation The production of distinct language sounds by the vocal organs.

asphyxia A lack of oxygen usually caused by interruption of respiration; can cause unconsciousness and/or brain damage.

astigmatism A defect of vision usually caused by irregularities in the cornea; results in blurred vision and difficulties in focusing. Can usually be corrected by lenses.

ataxia Poor sense of balance and body position and lack of coordination of the voluntary muscles; characteristic of one type of cerebral palsy.

athetosis A type of cerebral palsy characterized by large, irregular, uncontrollable twisting motions. The muscles may be tense and rigid or loose and flaccid. Often accompanied by difficulty with oral language.

at risk A term used to refer to children who are not currently identified as handicapped or disabled but who are considered to have a greater-than-usual chance of developing a handicap. Physicians use the terms *at risk* or *high risk* to refer to pregnancies with a greater-than-normal probability of producing a baby with handicaps.

audiogram A graph of the faintest level of sound a person can hear at least 50% of the time at each of several frequencies, including the entire frequency range of normal speech.

audiology The science of hearing.

audiometer   A device that generates sounds at specific frequencies and intensities; used to examine hearing.

auditory training   A program that works on listening skills to teach hearing impaired persons to make as much use as possible of their residual hearing.

autistic   Displaying a severe behavior disorder usually characterized by extreme withdrawal and lack of language and communication skills. Lack of affect, self-stimulation, self-abuse, and aggressive behavior are also common in autistic children.

baseline   A measure of the level or amount of behavior prior to implementation of an instructional procedure that is to be evaluated. Baseline data are used as an objective measure against which to compare and evaluate the results obtained during instruction.

behavior modification   The systematic application of procedures derived from the principles of behavior (e.g., reinforcement) in order to achieve desired changes in behavior.

behavioral contract   An agreement between two parties in which one agrees to complete a specified task (e.g., a child agrees to complete a homework assignment by the next morning) and in return the other party agrees to provide a specific reward (e.g., the teacher allows the child to have 10 minutes of free time) upon completion of the task.

binocular vision   Vision using both eyes working together to perceive a single image.

blind, legally   See *legally blind*.

braille   A system of writing letters, numbers, and other language symbols with a combination of six raised dots. Blind persons can be taught to read the dots with their fingertips.

cataract   A reduction or loss of vision that occurs when the crystalline lens of the eye becomes cloudy or opaque.

catheter   A tube inserted into a body to permit injections or withdrawal of fluids or to keep a passageway open; often refers to a tube inserted into the bladder to remove urine from a person who does not have effective bladder control.

cerebral palsy   Motor impairment caused by brain damage, which is usually inflicted during the prenatal period or during the birth process. Can involve a wide variety of symptoms (see *ataxia*, *athetosis*, *rigidity*, *spasticity*, and *tremor*) and range from mild to severe. Neither curable nor progressive.

cleft palate   A congenital split in the palate that results in an excessive nasal quality of the voice. Can often be repaired by surgery or dental appliance.

communication   The process by which individuals interact with, transmit, and receive messages by any means, including sounds, symbols, and gestures.

conduct disorder   A group of behavior disorders including disobedience, disruptiveness, fighting, and tantrums, as identified by Quay (1975).

conductive hearing loss   Hearing loss caused by obstructions in the outer or middle ear or malformations that interfere with the conduction of sound waves to the inner ear. Can often be corrected surgically or medically.

congenital   Any condition that is present at birth. Contrasts with *adventitious* handicap.

continuum of services   The range of different placement and instructional options that a school district can use to serve handicapped children. Typically depicted as a pyramid, ranging from the least restrictive placement (regular classroom) at the bottom to the most restrictive placement (institution or hospital) at the top.

cornea   The transparent part of the eyeball that admits light to the interior.

Cri-du-chat syndrome   A chromosomal abnormality resulting from deletion of material from the fifth pair of chromosomes. It usually results in severe retardation. Its name is French for "cat cry," named for the high-pitched crying of the child due to a related larynx dysfunction.

cultural-familial mental retardation   Any case of mental retardation for which an organic cause cannot be found; suggests that retardation can be caused by a poor social and cultural environment

curriculum-based assessment   Evaluation of a student's progress in terms of his performance on the skills that comprise the curriculum of the local school.

cystic fibrosis   An inherited disorder that causes a dysfunction of the pancreas, mucus, salivary, and sweat glands. Cystic fibrosis causes severe, long-term respiratory difficulties. No cure is currently available.

deafness   Inability to use hearing to understand speech, even with a hearing aid.

decibel (dB)   The unit used to describe the relative intensity of sound on a scale beginning at zero. Zero dB refers to the faintest sound a person with normal hearing can detect.

deinstitutionalization   The entire social movement to transfer handicapped persons, especially persons with mental retardation, from large institutions to smaller, community-based residences and work settings.

diabetes   See *juvenile diabetes mellitus*.

diabetic retinopathy   Type of vision impairment caused by hemorrhages on the retina and other disorders of blood circulation in people with diabetes.

dialect   A variety within a specific language; can involve variation in pronunciation, word choice, word order, and inflected forms.

differential reinforcement of other behavior (DRO)   A behavior modification technique in which any behavior except the targeted maladaptive response is reinforced; results in a reduction of the inappropriate behavior.

diplegia   Paralysis that affects either both arms or both legs.

disability   Refers to the reduced function or loss of a particular body part or organ.

Down syndrome   A chromosomal anomaly that often causes moderate to severe mental retardation, along with certain physical characteristics such as a large tongue, heart problems, poor muscle tone, and a broad, flat bridge of the nose. Formerly called *mongolism*, it occurs in all racial groups.

due process   Set of legal steps and proceedings carried out according to established rules and principles; designed to protect an individual's constitutional and legal rights.

duration (of behavior)   Measure of how long a person engages in a given activity.

dyslexia   A disturbance in the ability to read or learn to read.

echolalia   The repetition of what other people say as if echoing them; characteristic of some children with delayed development, severe behavior disorders, and communication disorders.

electroencephalograph (EEG)   Device that detects and records brain wave patterns.

enrichment   Educational approach that provides a child with extra learning experiences that the standard curriculum would not normally include. Most often used with gifted and talented children.

epilepsy   Convulsive disorder that causes sudden seizures (see *grand mal seizure*, *psychomotor seizure*, and *petit mal seizure*); can usually be controlled with medication, although the drugs may have undesirable side effects; may be temporary or lifelong.

equal protection   Legal concept included in the 14th Amendment to the U.S. Constitution, stipulating that no state may deny any person equality or liberty because of that person's classification according to race, nationality, or religion. Several major court cases leading to the passage of P.L. 94–142 found that handicapped children were not provided equal protection if they were denied access to an appropriate education solely because they were handicapped.

etiology   The cause(s) of an abnormal condition or disease. Includes genetic, physiological, and environmental or psychological factors.

evoked-response audiometry   A method of testing hearing by measuring the electrical activity generated by the auditory nerve in response to auditory stimulation. Often used to measure the hearing of infants and children considered difficult to test.

exceptional children   Children whose performance deviates from the norm, either below or above, to the extent that special educational programming is needed.

extinction   A behavior modification procedure in which reinforcement for a previously reinforced behavior is withheld. For example, a teacher may ignore a child's disruptive behavior instead of scolding. If the actual reinforcers that are maintaining the behavior are identified and withheld, the behavior will gradually decrease in rate until it no longer, or seldom, occurs.

fetal alcohol syndrome   A condition sometimes found in the infants of alcoholic mothers; can involve low birth weight, severe retardation, and cardiac, limb, and other physical defects.

field of vision   The expanse of space visible with both eyes looking straight ahead; measured in degrees; 180° is considered normal.

fluency   The rate and smoothness with which a movement is made. In communication, the rate and ease of speech; the most common speech fluency disorder is stuttering.

foster home   A living arrangement in which a family shares its home with a person who is not a relative. Long used with children who for some reason cannot live with their parents temporarily, foster homes are now being used with disabled adults as well.

generalization   Performing a behavior under conditions other than those under which the behavior was originally learned. *Stimulus generalization* occurs when a person performs a behavior in the presence of relevant stimuli (people, settings, instructional materials) other than those that were present originally. For instance, stimulus generalization occurs when a child who has learned to label baseballs and beach balls as "ball" identifies a basketball as "ball." *Response generalization* occurs when a person performs relevant behaviors that were never directly trained but are similar to the original trained behavior. For example, a child may be taught to say, "Hello, how are you?" and "Hi, nice to see you," as greetings. If the child combines the two to say, "Hi, how are you?" response generalization has taken place.

genetic counseling   A discussion between a specially trained medical counselor and persons who are considering having a child, about the chances of having a handicapped child, based on the prospective parents' genetic backgrounds.

glaucoma   An eye disease characterized by abnormally high pressure inside the eyeball. If left untreated, it can cause total blindness, but if detected early most cases can be arrested.

grand mal seizure   The most severe type of epileptic seizure, in which the individual has violent convulsions, loses consciousness, and becomes rigid.

group home   A residential arrangement for handicapped adults, especially persons with mental retardation, in which several residents live together in a house with non-handicapped supervisors. The residents usually have outside jobs.

handicap   The problems a person with a disability or behavioral characteristic considered unusual by society encounters when interacting with the environment.

handicapism   Prejudice or discrimination based solely on a person's disabilty, without regard for individual characteristics.

hard of hearing   Describes hearing loss that makes it difficult, although not impossible, to comprehend speech through the sense of hearing alone.

hearing impaired   Describes anyone who has a hearing loss significant enough to require special education, training, and/or adaptations; includes both deaf and hard-of-hearing conditions.

hemiplegia   Paralysis of both the arm and the leg on the same side of the body.

hemophilia   An inherited deficiency in blood-clotting ability, which can cause serious internal bleeding.

hertz (Hz)   A unit of sound frequency equal to one cycle per second; used to measure pitch.

hydrocephalus   A condition present at birth or developing soon afterward; involves an enlarged head caused by cerebral spinal fluid accumulating in the cranial cavity; often causes brain damage and severe retardation. Sometimes treated successfully with a *shunt*.

hyperactive   Describes excessive motor activity or restlessness.

hyperopia   Farsightedness; condition in which the image comes to a focus behind the retina instead of on it, causing difficulty in seeing near objects.

immaturity   Group of behavior disorders, including short attention span, extreme passivity, daydreaming, preference for younger playmates, and clumsiness, as identified by Quay (1975).

impairment   Often used as a synonym for disability, although the term refers technically to diseased or defective tissue.

incidence   The percentage of people who, at some time in their lives, will be identified as having a specific condition. Sometimes reported as the number of births per 1,000 with a given condition.

individualized education program (IEP)   Written document required by P.L. 94–142 for every handicapped child; includes statements of present performance, annual goals, short-term instructional objectives, specific educational services needed, relevant dates, regular education program participation, and evaluation procedures; must be signed by parents as well as educational personnel.

individualized family services plan (IFSP)   A requirement of P.L. 99–457, Education of the Handicapped Act Amendments of 1986, for the coordination of early intervention services for handcapped infants and toddlers. Similar to the IEP that is required for all school-age handicapped children.

inflection   Change in pitch or loudness of the voice to indicate mood or emphasis.

in-service training   Any educational program designed to provide practicing professionals (such as teachers, administrators, physical therapists) with additional knowledge and skills.

interdisciplinary team   Group of professionals from different disciplines (e.g., education, psychology, speech and language, medicine) who work together to plan and implement a handicapped child's individualized education program (IEP).

interindividual differences   Differences between two or more people in one skill or set of skills.

intervention   All the efforts made on behalf of handicapped children and adults; may be preventive, remedial, or compensatory.

intraindividual differences   Differences within one individual on two or more measures of performance.

iris   The opaque, colored portion of the eye that contracts and expands to change the size of the pupil.

juvenile diabetes mellitus   A children's disease characterized by inadequate secretion or use of insulin and the resulting excessive sugar in the blood and urine. Managed with diet and/or medication but can be difficult to control. Can cause coma and, eventually, death if left untreated or treated improperly. Can also lead to visual impairments and limb amputation. Not curable at the present time.

language   A system of vocal symbols (sounds) that give a group of people who understand the language a way to communicate. Nonverbal languages, such as American sign language, use movements and physical symbols instead of sounds.

least restrictive environment   The educational setting in which a handicapped child can succeed and which is most like the regular classroom.

legally blind   Visual acuity of 20/200 or less in the better eye after the best possible correction with glasses or contact lenses, or vision restricted to a field of 20 degrees or less. Acuity of 20/200 means the eye can see clearly at 20 feet what the normal eye can see at 200 feet.

lens   The clear part of the eye that focuses rays of light on the retina.

longitudinal study   A research study that follows one subject or group of subjects over an extended period of time, usually several years.

low prevalence disability   A disability that occurs relatively infrequently in the general population; in particular, used to refer to vision and hearing impairments, severe mental retardation, severe behavior disorders such as autism, and multiple handicaps.

low vision   Vision so limited that special educational services are required; nonetheless, permits learning through the visual channel.

macular degeneration   A deterioration of the central part of the retina, which causes difficulty in seeing details clearly.

magnitude (of behavior)   The force with which a response is emitted.

mainstreaming   The return to the regular classroom, for all or part of the school day, of handicapped children previously educated exclusively in segregated (self-contained) settings.

meningitis   An inflammation of the membranes covering the brain and spinal cord; can cause problems with sight and hearing and/or mental retardation.

meningocele   Type of spina bifida in which the covering of the spinal cord protrudes through an opening in the vertebrae, but the cord itself and the nerve roots are enclosed.

mental retardation   "Significantly subaverage general intellectual functioning existing concurrently with deficits in adaptive behavior and manifested during the developmental period" (Grossman, 1973, p. 5).

microcephalus   A condition characterized by an abnormally small skull with resulting brain damage and mental retardation.

minimal brain dysfunction   A once-popular term used to describe the learning disabilty of children with no actual (clinical) evidence of brain damage.

mobility   The ability to move safely and efficiently from one point to another.

model program   A program that implements and evaluates new procedures or techniques in order to serve as a basis for development of other similar programs.

monoplegia   Paralysis affecting one limb.

morpheme   The smallest element of a language that carries meaning.

multifactored testing   Assessment and evaluation of a handicapped child with a variety of test instruments and observation procedures. Required by P.L. 94–142 when assessment is for educational placement of a child who is to receive special education services. Helps prevent the possiblity of misdiagnosing and misplacing a student as the result of considering only one test score.

muscular dystrohpy   A group of diseases that gradually weaken muscle tissue, usually becoming evident by the age of 4 or 5.

myelomeningocele   A protrusion on the back of a child with spina bifida, consisting of a sac of nerve tissue bulging through a cleft in the spine.

myopia   Nearsightedness; results when light is focused on a point in front of the retina, resulting in a blurred image for distant objects.

neurologic impairment   Any physical disability caused by damage to the central nervous system (brain, spinal cord, ganglia, and nerves).

normal curve   A mathematically derived curve depicting the probability or distribution of a given variable (such as a physical trait or test score) in the general population. Indicates that approximately 68.26% of the population will fall within one standard deviation above and below the mean; approximately 27.18% will fall between one and two standard deviations either above or below the mean; and less than 3% will achieve more extreme scores of more than two standard deviations in either direction.

normalization   The principle of allowing each handicapped person's life to be as normal as possible in all aspects, including residence, schooling, work, recreational activities, and overall independence. Similarities between handicapped and nonhandicapped people of the same age are emphasized.

nystagmus   A rapid, involuntary, rhythmic movement of the eyes that may cause difficulty in reading or fixating on an object.

occupational therapist   A professional who programs and/or delivers instructional activities and materials to help handicapped children and adults learn to participate in useful activities.

ocular motility   The eye's ability to move.

operant audiometry   Method of measuring hearing by conditioning the subject to make an observable response to sound. For example, a child may be taught to drop a block into a box each time she hears a tone from the audiometer. Once this response is conditioned, the volume and pitch of the tone can be gradually decreased. When the child no longer drops the block into the box, the audiologist knows the child cannot hear the tone. This procedure is used to test the hearing of nonverbal children and adults.

optic nerve   The nerve that carries impulses from the eye to the brain.

oral   An approach to education of deaf children that stresses learning to speak as the essential element of integration into the hearing world.

orientation   The ability to establish one's position in relation to the environment.

orthopedic impairment   Any disability caused by disorders to the musculoskeletal system.

osteogenesis imperfecta   A hereditary condition in which the bones do not grow normally and break easily; sometimes called brittle bones.

otitis media   An infection or inflammation of the middle ear that can cause a conductive hearing loss.

overcorrection   A behavior modification procedure in which the learner must make restitution for, or repair, the effects of his undesirable behavior and then leave the environment in even better shape. Used to decrease the rate of undesirable behaviors.

paraplegia   Paralysis of the lower part of the body, including both legs; usually results from injury to or disease of the spinal cord.

paraprofessionals (in education)   Trained classroom aides who assist teachers; may include parents.

perceptual handicap A term formerly used to describe some conditions now included under *learning disability*; usually referred to problems with no known physical cause.

perinatal Occurring at or immediately after birth.

peripheral vision Vision at the outer limits of the field of vision.

personality disorder A group of behavior disorders, including social withdrawal, anxiety, depression, feelings of inferiority, guilt, shyness, and unhappiness, as identified by Quay (1975).

petit mal seizure A type of epileptic seizure in which the individual loses consciousness, usually for less than half a minute; can occur very frequently in some children.

phenylketonuria (PKU) An inherited metabolic disease that can cause severe retardation; can now be detected at birth and the detrimental effects prevented with a special diet.

phonemes The smallest unit of sound that can be identified in a spoken language. There are 36 phonemes, or sound families, in the English language.

photophobia Extreme sensitivity of the eyes to light; occurs most notably in albino children.

physical therapist A professional trained to help people with disabilities develop and maintain muscular and orthopedic capability and make correct and useful movement.

positive reinforcement Presentation of a stimulus or event after a behavior has been emitted and has the effect of increasing the occurrence of that behavior in the future.

postlingual Occurring after the development of language; usually used to classify hearing losses that begin after a person has learned to speak.

postnatal Occurring after birth.

precision teaching An approach to instruction that pinpoints the behaviors to be changed; measures the initial frequency of those behaviors; sets an aim, or goal, for the child's improvement; uses direct, daily measurements to monitor progress made under an instructional program; graphs results of those measurements; and changes the program if progress is not adequate.

prelingual Describes a hearing impairment that develops before a child has acquired speech and language.

prenatal Occurring before birth.

prevalence The number of people who have a certain condition at any given time.

projective tests Psychological tests that require a person to respond to a standardized task or set of stimuli (e.g., draw a picture or interpret an ink blot); responses are thought to be a projection of the test-taker's personality and are scored according to the given test's scoring manual to produce a personality profile.

prosthesis Any device used to replace a missing or impaired body part.

psychomotor seizure A type of epileptic seizure in which an individual goes through a period of inappropriate activity but is not aware of that activity.

psychosocial disadvantage Category of causation for mental retardation that requires evidence of subnormal intellectual functioning in at least one parent and one or more siblings (when there are siblings). Typically associated with impoverished environments involving poor housing, inadequate diets, and inadequate medical care. The term is used, often synonymously with *cultural-familial retardation*, when no organic cause can be identified.

psychotic Describes a severe behavior disorder.

pupil The circular hole in the center of the iris of the eye, which contracts and expands to let light pass through.

quadriplegia Paralysis of all four limbs.

rate (of behavior) A measure of how often a particular action is performed; usually reported as the average number of responses per minute.

refraction The bending or deflection of light rays from a straight path as they pass from one medium (e.g., air) into another (e.g., the eye). Used by eye specialists in assessing and correcting vision.

rehabilitation A social service program designed to teach a newly handicapped person basic skills needed for independence.

reinforcement See *positive reinforcement*.

remediation An educational program designed to teach a person to overcome a handicap through training and education.

residual hearing The remaining hearing, however slight, of a hearing impaired person.

resource room Classroom in which certain students spend part of the school day and receive individualized special education services.

retina A sheet of nerve tissue at the back of the eye on which an image is focused.

retinitis pigmentosa An eye disease in which the retina gradually degenerates and atrophies, causing the field of vision to become progressively more narrow.

retinopathy of prematurity A condition characterized by an abnormally dense growth of blood vessels and scar tissue in the eye, often causing visual field loss and retinal detachment. Usually caused by high levels of oxygen administered to premature infants in incubators. Also called *retrolental fibroplasia* (*RLF*).

retrolental fibroplasia (RLF) See *retinopathy of prematurity*.

rigidity A type of cerebral palsy characterized by increased muscle tone, minimal muscle elasticity, and little or no stretch reflex.

rubella German measles; when contracted by a woman during the first trimester of pregnancy, may cause visual impairments, hearing impairments, mental retardation, and/or other birth defects in the child.

schizophrenic Describes a severe behavior disorder characterized by loss of contact with one's surroundings and inappropriate affect and actions.

screening A procedure in which groups of children are examined and/or tested in an effort to identify high-risk children; identified children are then referred for more intensive examination and assessment.

self-contained class A special classroom, usually located within a regular public school building, that includes only exceptional children.

semantics The study of meaning in language.

sensorineural hearing loss A hearing loss caused by damage to the auditory nerve or the inner ear.

sheltered workshop A structured work environment where persons with disabilities receive employment training and perform work for pay. May provide transitional services for some individuals (i.e., short-term training for competitive employment in the community) and permanent work settings for others.

shunt Tube inserted in the body to divert fluid from one body part to another; often implanted in people with hydrocephalus to remove extra cerebrospinal fluid from the head and send it directly into the heart or intestines.

social validity A desirable characteristic of the objectives, procedures, and results of instruction, indicating their appropriateness for the learner. For example, the goal of riding a bus independently would have social validity for learners residing in most cities, but not for those in small towns or rural areas.

socialized aggression A group of behavior disorders, including truancy, gang membership, theft, and delinquency, as identified by Quay (1975).

spasticity A type of cerebral palsy characterized by tense, contracted muscles.

special education The individually planned and systematically monitored arrangement of physical settings, special equipment and materials, teaching procedures, and other interventions designed to help learners with special needs achieve the greatest possible personal self-sufficiency and success in school and community.

speech A system of using breath and muscles to create specific sounds for communicating.

spina bifida A congenital malformation of the spine in which the vertebrae that normally protect the spine do not develop fully; may involve loss of sensation and severe muscle weakness in the lower part of the body.

spina bifida occulta A type of spina bifida that usually does not cause serious disability. Although the vertebrae do not close, there is no protrusion of the spinal cord and membranes.

standard deviation A unit used to measure the amount by which a particular score varies from the mean of all scores in the norm sample.

stereotype An overgeneralized or inaccurate attitude held toward all members of a particular group, on the basis of a common characteristic such as age, sex, race, or disability.

stereotypic (stereotyped) behavior Repetitive nonfunctional movements (e.g., hand flapping, rocking), characteristic of autism and other severe handicaps.

stimulus control A condition in which a behavior is emitted more often in the presence of a particular stimulus than it is in the absence of that stimulus.

strabismus A condition in which one eye cannot attain binocular vision with the other eye because of imbalanced muscles.

stuttering A complex disorder of fluency of speech, affecting the smooth flow of words; may involve repetition of sounds or words, prolonged sounds, facial grimaces, muscle tension, and other physical behaviors.

supported employment An approach to helping persons with disabilities find, learn, and maintain paid employment at regular work sites in the community. A supported employment specialist assists the handicapped worker perform the job, gradually reducing the amount of on-the-job assistance as the employee's work performance improves over time.

syntax The system of rules governing the meaningful arrangement of words in a language.

therapeutic recreation A process that utilizes recreation services for purposive intervention in some physical, emotional, and/or social behavior to bring about a desired change in that behavior and to promote the growth and development of the individual.

time-out A behavior management technique that involves removing the opportunity for reinforcement for a specific period of time following an inappropriate behavior; results in a reduction of the inappropriate behavior.

token economy System of reinforcing various behaviors by delivering tokens (e.g., stars, points, poker chips) when specified behaviors are emitted. Tokens are accumulated and turned in for the individual's choice of items on a "menu" of backup reinforcers (e.g., a sticker, hall monitor for a day).

topography (of behavior) The physical shape or form of a response.

total communication An approach to education of deaf students that combines oral speech, sign language, and fingerspelling.

tremor A type of cerebral palsy characterized by regular, strong, uncontrolled movements. May cause less overall difficulty in movement than other types of cerebral palsy.

triplegia Paralysis of any three limbs; relatively rare.

Turner's syndrome A sex chromosomal disorder in females, resulting from an absence of one of the X chromosomes. Although not usually a cause of mental retardation, it is often associated with learning problems. It also causes lack of secondary sex characteristics, sterility, and short stature.

Usher's syndrome An inherited combination of visual and hearing impairments. Usually, the person is born with a profound hearing loss and loses vision gradually in adulthood because of retinitis pigmentosa, which affects the visual field.

visual acuity   The ability to clearly distinguish forms or discriminate details at a specified distance.

visual efficiency   An inclusive term used to describe how effectively a person uses his vision. Includes such factors as control of eye movements, near and distant visual acuity, and speed and quality of visual processing.

vitreous humor   The jellylike fluid that fills most of the interior of the eyeball.

vocational rehabilitation   A program designed to help adults with disabilities obtain and hold employment.

work activity center   A sheltered work and activity program for severely disabled persons; teaches concentration and persistence, along with basic life skills, for little or no pay.

NAME INDEX

SUBJECT INDEX